reviews of Beyond

" *A global awakening to the treacherous lies that have kept mankind enslaved and ignorant for millennia is now well underway. The quislings engaged in the coverup of corruption, scandal and subversion are shoveling sand against the tide. Thanks, in no small measure, to modern day prophet Brad Olsen, their time and that of our odious overlords are at an end. Congratulations dear reader. By cracking open* Beyond Esoteric: Escaping Prison Planet, *you have joined in this glorious restoration.*" **–Richard Syrett, Broadcaster, guest-host Coast to Coast AM**

" *This kind of brilliant work is what is needed more than anything in the World right now, to open up our eyes to what is really going on. Only deep research and material like this can give us greater awareness, help us to navigate these times with greater discernment and wisdom and help us to take our power back. If we don't understand what we are up against, then we won't be making choices based in clarity or true knowledge and this is what we as humans need in this critical time, where waking up can no longer be delayed. I highly recommend people read this. It is one of the greatest guide books out there that you will get!*" **–Laura Eisenhower, Author, Astrologer and International Speaker**

" *'Whoever controls the narrative controls the world.' This is the powerful idea driving Brad Olsen's masterful exposé of the deceptive narratives of Earth's hidden controllers. He systematically lays out the complicity of the mass media in hiding the truth about ruthless population control mechanisms; the historic suppression of free energy; efforts to create an Orwellian New World Order; the existence of extraterrestrial life; and much more. In* Beyond Esoteric, *Brad provides wise counsel on how to navigate a path through the hidden controllers' thicket of lies to reach a higher understanding and emancipation.*" **–Michael Salla, Ph.D. Author of** *Rise of the Red Dragon*

" *There are countless guides available today about strange mysteries and secret symbols, but few authors look beyond the surface of these subjects for greater meaning. In these information packed pages, Brad Olsen reveals a stunning guide to our Universe and a unified field theory of metaphysics. This is the result of his extensive research into the dark and mysterious world of the occult; leaving no stone unturned in his never-ending pursuit of hidden mysteries. Most importantly, this book proves that our ancestors possessed lost ancient technologies and that the sciences of today were once the esoteric knowledge of yesterday.*" **–Jonny Enoch, Esoteric Researcher, and Host on Gaia TV**

more reviews of **Beyond Esoteric**

" *A worldwide explorer makes a journey down the rabbit hole connecting the dots and leading us to the undeniable and inspiring conclusion, it's all in our hands. The Future of Humanity is at stake and we hold the keys. Beyond Esoteric educates and enlightens."* –**Kerry Cassidy, Project Camelot, author of *REBEL GENE: Secret Space and the Future of Humanity***

" *As a truth seeker for decades, traveling the world to explore the mysteries of all time, Brad has dedicated his life to revealing that which lies beyond the veil of secrecy. In his third book of the* Esoteric Series, *Brad holds nothing back! He blows the lid off of the 3D matrix where the deception, delusion and disinformation of a deep, dark agenda have misled humanity for far too long. Gnosis will set us free from the 'Prison Planet' so together we can create a New Earth where truth, sovereignty, equality and unity prevail. Brad's book,* Beyond Esoteric, *gives you the power of knowledge and the freedom from entrapment so you can transcend the matrix!"* –**Suzanne Ross, Creator of *SciSpi.TV*, Author of the *Up! Trilogy* and host of *Transcend the Matrix* on TFR**

" *Brad Olsen's* Esoteric Series *ends with 'esoteric tourism' at its best with* Beyond Esoteric, *a cultural exploration into expanded consciousness, quantum mechanics, inter-dimensional awareness of the visible and the invisible, and much more. A compendium of the best in conspiracy research, you will find interesting anecdotes on the New World Order and all the various Illuminati groups that have generated it, some plausible, others outlandish, but all a part of today's struggle to achieve a greater awareness in order to free ourselves from this prison planet."* –**Leo Lyon Zagami, Author of the *Confessions of an Illuminati* series**

" Beyond Esoteric *is a portal into the coveted knowledge of everything you ever wanted to know about how the world is controlled and by whom, but didn't know where to look. Think,* Cliff Notes, *for world domination! Brad Olsen takes us on a journey into the lesser-known workings of globalization and control, explaining the mechanisms of implementation that we all unknowingly participate in. Control the public narrative and the people will compliantly follow. Within these pages is found the who's who of neofascism, tracing its financial, political, and ideological roots from Europe to America, continuing at full throttle to the New World Order agendas of today. Chapter after chapter, the depth and complexities of the organizations, structures and methodologies used to control humankind are revealed. Where we come from and more importantly, where we are heading as a country, culture, people and planet is the revelation of this, Brad Olsen's, finest work."* –**Sid Goldberg, two-time Emmy Award winning Director**

Beyond Esoteric

Escaping Prison Planet

by BRAD OLSEN

CONSORTIUM OF COLLECTIVE CONSCIOUSNESS PUBLISHING

www.CCCPublishing.com • www.BradOlsen.com • www.EsotericSeries.com

Beyond Esoteric: Escaping Prison Planet

1ˢᵗ edition
Esoteric Series :: Volume III

Copyright © 2021 by Bradford C. Olsen
Published by the Consortium of Collective Consciousness Publishing™

As is common in a historic and reference book such as this, much of the information included on these pages has been collected from diverse sources. When possible, the information has been checked and double-checked. Almost every topic has at least three data points, that is, three different sources that report the same information. Even with special effort to be accurate and thorough, the author and publisher cannot vouch for each and every reference. The author and publisher assume no responsibility or liability for any outcome, loss, arrest, or injury that occurs as a result of information or advice contained in this book. As with the purchase of goods or services, *caveat emptor* is the prevailing responsibility of the purchaser, and the same is true for the student of the esoteric.

Library of Congress Cataloging-in-Publication Data:

Olsen, Bradford C.
    BEYOND ESOTERIC: ESCAPING PRISON PLANET / Bradford C. Olsen
        p. cm.
    Includes index
    print ISBN 978-1888729740 (Pbk.)
    ebook ISBN 978-1888729757 (all formats)

1. Spirituality—Guidebooks. 2. Metaphysics—Esoteric. I. Title
    Library of Congress Catalog Card Number: 2015930354

Printed in the United States of America.

10 9 8 7 6 5 4

The Dating System used in this text is based upon the modern method of using Before Current Era (BCE) instead of Before Christ (B.C.), and Current Era (CE) rather than "In the year of the Lord" *anno Domini* (A.D.). Those unfamiliar with this dating system should take note that 1 B.C. is the same as 1 BCE and everything then counts backward just the same. Similarly, 1 A.D. is 1 CE with all the years counting forward to the present, or Current Era.

To assist in universal understanding, all measurements of length, distance, area, weight, size, and volume are listed in the metric system.

also by Brad Olsen

2018
Modern Esoteric:
Beyond our Senses

2016
Future Esoteric:
The Unseen Realms

2008
Sacred Places North America:
108 Destinations

2007
Sacred Places Europe:
108 Destinations

2004
Sacred Places Around the World:
108 Destinations

2001
World Stompers:
A Global Travel Manifesto

1999
In Search of Adventure:
A Wild Travel Anthology

1997
Extreme Adventures Northern California

1997
Extreme Adventures Hawaii

BEYOND ESOTERIC:

ESCAPING PRISON PLANET

FRONT MATTER:

AUTHOR'S KARMA STATEMENT 11
INTRODUCTION 19

BACK MATTER:

CONCLUSION................................449
ACKNOWLEDGEMENTS 463
INDEX 464

NEO·FASCISM:

The herd, the mob, the unwashed masses are considered farm animals and are seldom, if ever, allowed to know the truth by their keepers. They believe, they graze and they bleat; they live and die by what they are told.

DIMENSIONS:

THE NEW FASCISM 37

THE OCCULT AND FASCISM 55

WORLD CONTROL 71

VATICAN NAZIS 91

AMERICAN NAZIS 107

MK-ULTRA 131

BIG BROTHER 147

GEOENGINEERING 167

EMBARGO:

It's not about the lights in the sky, it's about the lies on the ground. History, because it is written by academics beholden to their sponsors, never ever tells the full truth, let alone how our planet has been acquainted with ultraterrestrials for millennia.

DIMENSIONS:

THE TRUTH EMBARGO 189

SUPPRESSED HUMAN ORIGINS 207

ALTERNATIVE 1, 2, 3 225

MEET THE NEW BOSS 247

BEING AWARE OF PREDATORY SPECIES 267

ET IS ALREADY HOME 287

TRANSHUMANIST AGENDA 305

ÜBERMIND:

All frequency emanates from one sacred divine source of consciousness. We live in an age where we are hypnotized by our own ignorance, and controlled by an invisible master. To break from the false matrix, we must first free our minds.

DIMENSIONS:

TECHNOLOGY LEAP. 325

BRAINS OF THE FUTURE. 343

COSMIC AWARENESS. 359

EXOTIC METALS 375

CRYSTALS 391

ACHIEVING ÜBERMIND 403

THE BIOTERRAIN 415

MORGELLON NANOBOTS 431

AUTHOR'S KARMA STATEMENT

"The dumbing down of America is most evident in the slow decay of substantive content in the enormously influential media, the 30-second sound bites (now down to 10 seconds or less), the lowest common denominator programming, credulous presentations on pseudoscience and superstition, but especially a kind of celebration of ignorance. As I write, the number one video cassette rental in America is the movie *Dumb and Dumber*. *Beavis and Butthead* remains popular (and influential) with young TV viewers. The plain lesson is that study and learning—not just of science, but of anything—are avoidable, even undesirable." –Carl Sagan
(1995) The Demon-Haunted World: Science as a Candle in the Dark

THE late scientific author, Carl Sagan, chided the mainstream media in 1995 for their role in social engineering and the potential damage it would cause. The media has for the last century (since the advent of radio) been the greatest influence on our collective society. Ivory-towered media executives, with support of the alphabet agencies and their "4 a.m. talking points," can direct our national intellect and steer the narrative by what stories they tell and which they omit. They are the captains of our mutual rational and emotional destiny, and Sagan's comment condemns their unfortunately fruitful efforts to turn young minds away from reason and towards stupidity. This was almost three decades ago, and the effect has since been exacerbated by an order of magnitude. Now we've experienced reality TV and a reality show president, and the actual measured "dumbing down of America" is taking place. The last thing the elite wants is an informed, empowered public mobilizing any grassroots movement to oppose government tyranny.[1]

Despite the dumbing down of America, we're also experiencing a major shift in both physical and spiritual vibrations. It's difficult to understand what will happen to our physical bodies, but ancient scriptures, pagan and monotheistical legends, mystery schools and secret fraternal orders have all given indications of what this experience will be like. Similarly, I have long understood that these same people behind the "mysteries" were hiding a lot of truth from humanity. They were using their knowledge and resources to ensure the survival of the bloodline families and the Orders, rather than guiding humanity to a positive future.

For this final book in the *Esoteric Series*, many of the subjects I cover do not come from long-standing esoteric traditions, but are new to the human experience: From the changing human body and mind through transhumanism, to the truth embargo on our true origins as a species and the blackout on anything related to extraterrestrials. Of course, fascism has been around for a long, long time, but it relates to the other forbidden subjects contained in this book, and gives us an insight into the dilemma we find ourselves in today. These are subjects *beyond* the scope of normal *esoteric* studies, hence the title, and the *escape from prison planet* we find the human race encountering at this time of our greatest transformation.

Once the truth comes out, this will be the Shift of the Ages, the transcendental ascension of monumental changes to humanity. Those unprepared for this transition will likely not be able to cope with the rapid changes in the psyche. The only way to prepare for what is to come is what we have sought after our entire lives. The simple truth. Not the embargo on truth about extraterrestrial visitations to Earth, government corruption, commercial scams, religious scandals or anything external, but the truth within ourselves, within our psyches, within our shadow or spiritual selves.[2]

Unfortunately, most of us are still unaware of any kind of shift or predatory forces that seek to keep us enslaved. Most people are so embedded in the current system that they will fight to protect it, even though it serves to defeat us all. People have been hypnotized into believing that the artificial world they live in is real. They see anyone that wants to expose the truth as the enemy. Anytime someone speaks the truth, they are immediately slandered as a crazy conspiracy theory nut job. So, because most people believe in the illusion, they gladly protect it, and condemn others who speak of any form of "alternative narrative." They fight and die to uphold the very prison in which they exist. What's more, when their earnings are depleted for food and shelter, their labors are no longer viewed as an opportunity for economic advancement, but rather as an act of self-preservation. In the real world, that's called slavery, and people simply don't have the time to explore these subjects in depth.

THE UNIVERSE IS ALIVE

There is a singular mega-identity that formed all that we see, including ourselves. We are ultimately holograms of a far greater intelligence that created the universe. Separation is an illusion created for the purpose of the Creator knowing Itself. Consciousness interconnects all things. If we do not perceive ourselves as truly being one with everything and everyone, we are still living in "the illusion." It can take many, many lifetimes, through multiple dimensional levels or "densities," to fully shake off the amnesia and remember who and what we really are.

1   Hagopian, Joachim, "The Dumbing Down of America—By Design" *Global Research*, January 30, 2018.
2   Hitchens, Christopher. *God is Not Great: How Religion Poisons Everything.* Hachette Book Group, New York, NY, 2007.

The universe is providing each of us with a form of insight that can help us see the control matrix well enough to withdraw consent. This gives us the internal strength to stand on our own and the courage to walk a path alone without someone there to protect us, guide us, or just plain agree with our opinions.

We stumble about in ignorance, fear and pain, all of which is ultimately caused by our lack of understanding of our true selves. All we need to conquer in life is merely ourselves. If you want to understand what your true inner fears are, analyze your ambitions *and* your inhibitions. Know Thyself.

When you fear loss, fear death, fear war, fear terrorism or fear change, you're giving others the ability to control you based on those fears. When you fight against poverty or against racism, when you fight for relationships or for freedom, you are attempting to express outwardly that which has been placed before you to conquer inwardly. These societal problems are mirrors of our fears. This is why it's important to love and only love. Love those who stand with you but especially those who stand against you. Don't look at your fears as a threat. Rather, when fear arises, reinterpret it. Understand that this material world is only a physical manifestation of either the love or fear in your consciousness emanating outward into the world.

ENTERING A NEW ERA

Inner knowing, or *noetics*, is as essential to our daily lives as technology, if not more so. The Institute of Noetic Sciences (IONS) is dedicated to researching the realms of internal wisdom in an effort to liberate humanity from restricting beliefs and behaviors. More than 40 years of consciousness research at IONS suggests that cultivating an open-hearted curiosity is the potent antidote to constricting fears, contentions and regrets. When we are free from thoughts, emotions and reactions that breed negativity, we are empowered to enact positive change within our own lives, our communities and the larger world. But first we need to break free from the shackles of illusion.

The false narratives being constantly woven and promulgated by the oligarchy (i.e. the handful of powerful plutocrat-owned corporate conglomerates which control the U.S. media) are actually the weakest point in its armor. A concerted effort to weaken public trust in its narratives has the potential to bring the entire thing crashing down when people see through "fake news." The beginning of an awakening is happening. Never before have we witnessed such a widespread and concerted grassroots assault on the lies and manipulations of the deep state's propaganda machine. Never before has the deep state's grip on public consciousness been this tenuous. Since whoever controls the consensus narrative controls all power in the most powerful nation on earth, this is a very exciting time to be alive. Just tell yourself: "Truth has (now) arrived, and Falsehood perished: for Falsehood is (by its nature) bound to perish."[3]

This unprecedented escalation in the grassroots alternative media war upon the establishment propaganda machine may be the most significant event happening in the world right now, because whoever controls the narrative controls the world. The real currency which drives humanity isn't gold, isn't money, isn't plutocratic fiats, isn't the petrodollar, isn't even military strength—it is the narrative. We are now witnessing the U.S. power establishment begin to completely lose control of the public narrative for the first time in history, and with it, brutal blatant forms of censorship. Apparently, it is possible to shoot the messenger.

For the very first time, a crucial percentage of the population began telling their own stories about what was happening in America, instead of the scripted stories the talking

3   Booker, Christopher, *The Seven Basic Plots: Why We Tell Stories.* Continuum International Publishing Group Ltd. 2005.

heads on TV were told to tell. The term *deep state* became a household phrase when people began considering alternative narratives about what was happening with Russia and Syria. People read unauthorized emails and shared unauthorized ideas about their content, advancing unauthorized narratives which ultimately resulted in the unexpected election of a relatively unauthorized president. It also prompted conversations about UFO disclosure, secret space programs, exotic propulsion discussed by mainstream physicists, and giant leaps in human consciousness.

The fundamental reality is that we live in a universe where action is a natural consequence of thought. All actions result from thoughts of desired change. We often attribute the change to the actions. But the reality is that the change in our thoughts is the true origin of the change in our experienced manifestations, since the actions would never have occurred had the thoughts not changed first. When change does not occur, it is because we continue to think the same thoughts of frustration and the impossibility of change. If we want change, then we must change our thoughts, and nothing does this more effectively than the introduction of new information. What we are taught about history in American schools is not history, but a fairy tale. Better stated, it is propaganda designed to hoodwink an unsuspecting society about its true heritage and the treasonous acts and sabotage that were conceived in order to bring about a New World Order.

FAILED WORLD ORDER

What is this plan for a New World Order? In a nutshell, it goes like this. The Dark Agenda of the secret planners of the New World Order is to reduce the world's population to a "sustainable" level "in perpetual balance with nature" by means of ruthless population control, an agenda via population and reproduction control, and a mass culling of the population through various "soft kill" operations. Those include abortion upon request, toxic adulteration of fluoridated water and GMO food supplies, release of weaponized human-made viruses, human-made pandemics, mass forced vaccination campaigns and a planned Third World War. The same group of people who have been involved in HIV/AIDS research to develop an HIV immunization, a vaccine which has never come to market, are the same group of people now working with the U.S. Government to distribute a COVID vaccine.[4]

When the "strategy of tension" has most of us in a desperate situation, the Dark Agenda will impose itself in the form of a global feudal-fascist state. The drastically reduced world population will be introduced to a World Government, World Religion, World Army, World Central Bank, World Currency and be mandatory vaccinated and micro-chipped. In short, first kill 90% of the world's population, and then enslave the hapless survivors to be ruled by an unelected elite. In an Orwellian dystopian scenario, those who oppose Big Brother will have their resources cut off, or be poisoned by their microchip.

But the time is up for this failed and murderous system. The Old World Order is fading, and those who "see with new eyes" are emerging as the future. If you want peace on Earth, if you want justice for the innocent, if you want an end to corruption, consider the contents of this book with an open mind. It is now possible to identify the who, what, where and how a small control group has taken control of the institutions of the West, and by extension, most of the world. But their time has come to an end and we must begin a "truth and reconciliation" period to reclaim the garden which is planet Earth from the police state globalists. It is becoming clear that multinational corporations have subverted our traditional constitutional government in order

4   Shilhavy, Brian, "Dr. Fauci and the NIH's History in Experimenting on Foster Children and Using Aborted Fetal Tissue to Develop an HIV Vaccine" *Medical Kidnap*, https://medicalkidnap.com/2020/06/25/dr-fauci-and-the-nihs-history-in-experimenting-on-foster-children-and-using-aborted-fetal-tissue-to-develop-an-hiv-vaccine/

to protect the knowledge they have acquired from extraterrestrial technology in a "Truth Embargo." Such technology includes fiber optics, lasers and integrated circuit chips, and will include many other advanced technological breakthroughs including anti-gravity and free energy. Indeed, the mass media is complicit and self-censoring so we are not being given the vital information we need to make informed decisions in life. The black budget spending and how the multinationals have managed to maintain their UFO whitewash for so long has been covered in my previous two books (*Future Esoteric: The Unseen Realms*, 2016, and *Modern Esoteric: Beyond Our Senses*, 2018), but new information is provided in this volume.

Humanity now has the ability to network and share information at a wildly unprecedented rate. With that ability has come the potential for that power to move into the hands of the people—as the public begins telling its own stories on a widespread, mainstream scale. Don't ever let anyone tell you you're not doing something hugely important by using your online presence to undermine and attack these outlets at every opportunity; indeed, at this point in history, it may be the most important thing that any one human being can do.

FLIPPING THE SCRIPT

I am reminded on a daily basis how much I detest the neo-fascist deception that comes out of our government and is megaphoned by the controlled mass media. We have the technology to do incredible good. We can reverse droughts, defend against all of our enemy's weapons (making war obsolete) and we can even reverse the aging process. Yes, the super elite on this planet has decided to withhold most technological advances from the people so that we can continue to play out the old worn-out game of one side going to war with the other, keeping the people divided and ignorant. It is all about control, manipulation and degrading the human race—and I am sick of it. I understand why whistle-blowers do what they do because they get so disgusted that they cannot take it anymore. I had to remind myself that placing any kind of faith in this banker-hijacked government is naïve at best. The elite are not going to relinquish control and allow humankind to become what we were intended to become. Therefore, the "über-mind" technology is going to continue to be withheld, or rolled out when it has a "soft kill" application, and human suffering will continue as it has for some time. Most people probably don't think too much about this, but are you aware of just how much of your income is being used to fuel the military industrial complex? Conveniently omitted from the corporate-owned and state-run media organizations is the fact that for over a decade over 50 percent of our tax dollars are spent just on the military. Fortunately, the six U.S. military branches are loyal to the President, and honor their constitutional oaths. Whoever controls the funding controls the "science" and alleged truthful reporting on statistics.[5]

Cognitive dissonance is the mental result of this nefarious assault on the mind. We then try to resolve the dissonance by creating a host of illusions and defense mechanisms in order to protect a fragile, fearful mind from falling apart. People will only see what they are mentally capable of processing. Often the most analytically intelligent people will blot out their inner wisdom and common sense in favor of contrived explanations that are more comfortable. They can't grasp the bigger picture because they are so absorbed in separating and categorizing reality that they fail to see what is most obvious, partly because it doesn't fit into their ego-centric, self-dominated world view. Their self-assured arrogance can stunt the growth of the rest of us by not suspecting those truly in control. In short, we need to develop healthy skepticism toward those truly in control in order to begin to recognize the myriad of agendas in operation.

5   Lindorff, Dave, "Your Tax Dollars at War: More Than 53% of Your Tax Payment Goes to the Military" *Common Dream*, https://www.commondreams.org/views/2010/04/13/your-tax-dollars-war-more-53-your-tax-payment-goes-military

ASCENSION IS UPON US

Despite most people feeling powerless to affect any kind of meaningful change, we actually do have the power to influence global events. Starting in our own minds, we can begin to manifest an Event. By visualizing change, we are actually creating the Event according to exact principles for manifestation. If you look at human history, change is always made by a group of a few individuals who know they are awake and aware. Awake and aware individuals, even one, can change the world. One person with a vision is enough to change the world. One Gandhi was enough. One Tesla was enough. And more people sharing that vision makes the change even more likely.

This ascension period leading up to the Event will be difficult for some and easy for others who are capable of visualizing change. That is to say, that anyone with a negative, dark or heavy density will not be able to cloak or hide in the elevated frequencies of the Fifth Dimension Reality (5D). Brutal truths are going to be revealed. It's as if the oxygen we breathe will no longer support their dark intentions and operations. A collapse of epic proportions of the established institutions is upon us as we move *beyond* the esoteric. Speaking of oxygen, all bacterial pathogens, viruses, and parasites are anaerobic and thrive in the absence of oxygen. In fact, they are poisoned by oxygen. Even cancer cells perish with abundant oxygen. Similar to cutting a disease off with oxygen, dark or heavy densities will no longer be able to hide in this elevated frequency. It seems to have been happening with a prolonged "soft disclosure" but is unfolding rapidly these days.

Some words of ascension from my friend Laura Eisenhower:

> Our bodies are going through a lot. Going from Carbon based to Crystalline and into Higher Earth energies, is an incredible transition and transformation. Laughing a lot is important. Detoxing and trusting yourself more. Spirit holds dominion over physical matter. We are coming out of a mind-control that threw us into a lot of survival and compromise. We are the advanced Technology here and we are powerful. Stay strong in your Sovereign awareness and know you can manifest anything!

LOVE-ATTRACTION PHENOMENA

Truly the duality in our world needs some context. You can go into a pitch-black room full of evil, full of darkness and light a little candle and instantly that darkness flees—but you cannot do the opposite. You can't go into a well-lit room full of truth, wisdom, righteousness, joy, health and harmony with the universal power and try with any amount of darkness and go into that well-lit room and have any effect whatsoever. This is the nature of the Earth Dilemma we face today. However, with only a few flickers of light in the darkness, there still is a shift toward getting brighter every day. The greatest lesson to remember is that we're on the winning side—and we will win in the end.

Always remember your reality affects you and only you. When you see your fears for what they are and master your emotions, then and only then will you truly be free. As you are reading these words, understand that it is not a fight to be fought, it is not a war to be waged, no gun rights have to be exercised, and not a finger has to be lifted to win this epic struggle. Most people wonder how one person can possibly make a difference. They ask if all this is so simple, and all this information is available, why hasn't someone else conquered their fears and changed the world for all of us? This is the most difficult and beautiful conundrum to our lives. Your reality affects you and only you. Your curiosity has led you to this genre of information to serve a very specific purpose in your life. I am honored to be in service to all and release the contents of this book. Writing and composing the *Esoteric Series* has been a labor of love for the last decade of my life. In humble gratitude I offer this information.

Self-betterment needs to be a top priority for us all. Always strive to be the best person you can possibly be. In order to be on the right side of history during this monumental change, it is very important to follow these "Personal Codes of Ethics."[6]

1. *Be honest: The more honest you are, the more trustworthy you become.*
2. *Have integrity: The better of a person you are, the better an image you present.*
3. *Be responsible: You must be responsible in life so that others can rely on you.*
4. *Tell the truth: The value of truth is immeasurable, because without it, the world would just be filled with lies.*
5. *Give credit where credit is due: Failing to credit people for their ideas/works, is considered stealing and we are cheating them of their hard work.*
6. *Be courteous: Every act of kindness makes a difference in the life of someone.*
7. *Have respect: One of the most important things is to treat other as you wish to be treated.*
8. *Trust and be Trustworthy: Trust is the building block of relationships we create in our lives.*
9. *Be harmonious: To live together and get along with everyone is a "delicacy" that we all long for.*
10. *Don't change who you are to please others: It's not worth becoming a completely different person simply to make other people happy because by doing so, you may be making yourself unhappy.*

Also, let's never lose our sense of humor as we collectively experience this transformational period in human history. This excerpt from Monty Python's film, *The Meaning of Life,* offers some perspective:

CHAIRMAN: *...Which brings us once again to the urgent realization of just how much there is still left to own. Item six on the agenda: the meaning of life. Now, uh, Harry, you've had some thoughts on this.*

HARRY: *That's right. Yeah, I've had a team working on this over the past few weeks, and, uh, what we've come up with can be reduced to two fundamental concepts. One: people are not wearing enough hats. Two: matter is energy. In the universe, there are many energy fields which we cannot normally perceive. Some energies have a spiritual source which act upon a person's soul. However, this soul does not exist ab initio, as orthodox Christianity teaches. It has to be brought into existence by a process of guided self-observation. However, this is rarely achieved, owing to man's unique ability to be distracted from spiritual matters by everyday trivia.*

BERT: *What was that about hats, again?*

As always, take the information discussed in this book and research it for yourself, and arrive at your own conclusions. Anyone telling you what the truth is, or claiming they have the answer, is likely leading you astray for one reason or another. In this new era of intense censorship, we live at a time when owning the narrative by those who wish to control our thought is being challenged for the first time in human history. Stay vigilant.

~ Brad Olsen
Santa Cruz, CA

November, 2021 (4th printing update)

6   Shay, Maura, "Personal Codes of Ethics" *PaperDue:* **https://www.paperdue.com/essay/personal-code-of-ethics-thesis-28429.com**

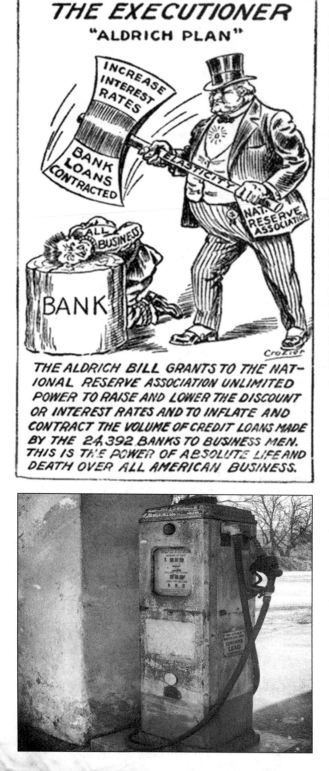

This vintage cartoon shows how there was a widespread understanding, in the early 20th Century, of the danger we faced if we allowed private bankers to seize control of our financial system, and they did. The Federal Reserve System was originally called the National Reserve System, and was presented in 1911 and 1912 via the Aldrich Plan. The idea was to outsource the control of the U.S. financial system to a private consortium of international bankers. Americans then essentially rent their money from these bankers – and pay them for the honor of using it in the form of interest. As billionaires, the trust and collateral of these bankers is supposedly superior to any "reserve" within the U.S. government itself.

In the late 1880s, trade journals in the electrical sciences were predicting free electricity and free energy in the near future. Incredible discoveries about the nature of electricity were becoming common place. Nikola Tesla was demonstrating "wireless lighting" and other wonders associated with high frequency currents. But there is no money in "free" applications, and the profitable gas, oil, and coal became the dominant energy sources for over a century.

Beyond Esoteric
INTRODUCTION

"The conscious and intelligent manipulation of the organized habits and opinions of the masses is an important element in democratic society. Those who manipulate this unseen mechanism of society constitute an invisible government which is the true ruling power of our country. ... We are governed, our minds are molded, our tastes formed, our ideas suggested, largely by men we have never heard of." –Edward Bernays, Propaganda

WHAT was true to Bernays a century ago is true now. It only takes a rudimentary understanding of human psychology to manipulate someone. Bernays was recruited by the U.S. government to study the science of modern propaganda in 1917. This science has been in research and development for over a century. Don't underestimate its power. The mind control techniques of Edward Bernays are now being seen as pervasive and far-reaching, as he was a key figure of the 20th century ruling elite, which continues to act as a secret society. In his 1928 book, *Propaganda*, Bernays justified their existence by stating: "We need an invisible government. The conscious and intelligent manipulation of the habits and opinions of the masses is an important element of democracy. Public opinion can be regulated through technology. Movies are the greatest unconscious carrier of the propaganda tool. It's a great distribution of ideas and opinions, films can standardize the habits and opinions of a nation. The Elites who manipulate public opinion are the invisible government which is the true ruling power of the country."[1]

1   Bernays, Edward, *Propaganda*. Originally published in 1928.

There have been many types of secret societies, along with occult and esoteric religious influences. Over the millennia, some were created for sinister purposes, yet others out of religions to further a certain agenda. Some were created with good intentions, and some today have well-meaning people in them doing good. Bernays also tipped us off that "propaganda is the executive arm of the invisible government," meaning the Nightly News is merely the shaping of mass perception according to the owners of the media. Governed either by or on behalf of the people who fleece us, we cannot be surprised to discover that all public services are being re-engineered for the benefit of private capital. Masters of propaganda agree, from its inventor, Jewish public relations expert Edward Bernays, to the Nazi Minister of Propaganda, Joseph Goebbels, that a lie can be turned into truth by constant repetition. The bigger the lie, the "more pure" it is, the more complete the success in turning it into "The Truth." "Less pure" lies partly based in fact or half-truths open themselves to factual challenge.

Bernays' trailblazing marketing campaigns profoundly changed the functioning of American society. The "King of Spin" basically created "consumerism" by creating a culture wherein Americans bought for pleasure instead of buying for survival. For this reason, he was considered by *Life* magazine to be in the Top 100 most influential Americans of the 20th century. Touted as the father of public relations, he even sold water fluoridation to Americans. Furthermore, Bernays, as a nephew of Sigmund Freud, applied his uncle's ideas on psychological persuasion for the benefit of industry and government propaganda.

Of the many myths that befog the modern political mind, none is so corrupting of understanding or so incongruent with historical fact as the notion that the wealthy and the powerful do not conspire. Of course they do. They conspire continually, habitually, effectively, diabolically and on a scale that boggles the imagination. To deny this conspiracy fact is to deny both overwhelming empirical evidence and elementary reason. And they know we are a species ruled by cycles, patterns, and perception. Once the behavior is understood, we can be manipulated under the will and intention of a sophisticated "fake news" media campaign. We are told we are individuals, but treated as cattle. We are the herd on the quest of convenience and luxury. We consume like locusts, under the guise of ego and "you only live once." This is linear thinking at its worst, namely, the idea that we are born, and die, so take what you can while you're here, and indulge every warped desire, because you are never going to be able to have this life again; that resources are for this life alone, with none left for the next. We forget we are a part of nature, and just as nature "dies" each winter, only to be "born again" in the spring, so are we. It's a cycle we should apply to ourselves. We can wake up from this grand illusion, or we can remain asleep. The choice is each of ours, and ours alone.[2]

INTO THE AGE OF TRANSPARENCY

For the first time in history we are able to peek into every aspect of the secret ruling elite. Call it palace intrigue. Apart from the public relations spectacle of royal weddings, there are certain plans that need to be exposed and stopped for the sake of all life on the planet. There is a stark possibility that the human race itself could break off into two transhumanist branches of both evolution and de-evolution. Basically, everything we love and hold dear on planet Earth is in jeopardy. It is past time humanity had the ultimate "100th Monkey" wake-up call. But first, it has come time for us all to stop being controlled by these elites and their mainstream media lies. Until we stop listening to mainstream media, we can never be truly free.

In a world driven mad by the Western elite's "strategy of tension," it would seem they have succeeded in getting a majority of people addicted to fear, and use those in fear to fight

2   Ouspensky, P.D., *In Search of the Miraculous: The Definitive Exploration of G. I. Gurdjieff's Mystical Thought and Universal View*. Harvest Books.

and protect their way of thinking. George Orwell predicted that "the farther a society drifts from the truth, the more it despises those who speak it." These status quo protectors of society will object if you advance the story or bring a new perspective to some of these "out there" conspiracy theories, especially if they might include extraterrestrials. They will call you gullible, or accuse you of being "asleep." Of course, angry people need "fear porn" to hold onto, because it makes their reality more "real." Many people are going around pointing fingers at others, calling them "sheep," and the whole time claiming that they themselves are awake. Of course, the accusers are the ones who are sleeping, refusing to think outside the box, unable to understand the nature of propaganda, and are disconnected from rational thought. A wise goal for each of us is to apply critical thinking to any problem, by being objective about any information we run across, and applying the scientific method. We need to be fearless detectives and objective researchers, that is, allow the evidence to direct us and always base our conclusions on facts, no matter how weird the potential outcome may seem. In a sense, we are all still in a control system designed to let us believe we are awake. Yet, for those who embrace love as a solution, it is easy to see how others are still inside the matrix being controlled by fear, fighting for the machine. The classic Morpheus quote from *The Matrix* fits perfectly:

> *The Matrix is a system, Neo. That system is our enemy. But when you're inside, you look around, what do you see? Businessmen, teachers, lawyers, carpenters. The very minds of the people we are trying to save. But until we do, these people are still a part of that system and that makes them our enemy. You have to understand, most of these people are not ready to be unplugged. And many of them are so inured, so hopelessly dependent on the system, that they will fight to protect it.*

OUR RIGGED AND FAKE WORLD

It can be argued that every important institution in America has been sold out, corrupted and politically rigged to favor Big Government and Big Business. "America is a lost country," explains Paul Craig Roberts. "The total corruption of every public and the private institution is complete. Nothing remains but tyranny. And lies. Endless lies." Medicine, science, elections, the media, health care, money, education, search engine results and social media—we are living in a fabricated fairy tale.[3]

CNN, Reuters and the Associated Press are all now shameless promoters of every big lie across every sector of society, from experimental vaccines and GMOs to elections and politics. The federal government itself is incapable of doing anything other than lying, and it has totally corrupted the entire realm of science by pulling the strings of funding via the *National Institutes of Health* (NIH) and the *National Science Foundation* (NSF).

The Federal Drug Administration (FDA) is entirely corrupt, as is the US Department of Agriculture (USDA). Both function now as little more than marketing propaganda pushers for Big Pharma and Big Biotech. Similarly, Google, YouTube, Facebook and Twitter are all rigged, too, censoring the voices they don't want anyone to hear while highlighting the establishment lies they wish to promote.

Every branch of government is weaponized against the people and used as an assault tool against political enemies who threaten the status quo. All the usual suspects in the alphabet soup of government agencies are implicated: IRS, FDA, FTC, DEA, EPA, USDA, CIA, NSA, and isn't it interesting that the Internet's biggest search engine, Google, named their parent corporation "Alphabet"? Similarly, every branch of medicine is hijacked by globalist agendas to make sure medicine never makes anyone healthier, more alert or more cognitively capable of thinking for themselves. The Center for Disease Control (CDC) has been caught in more than one scandal show-

3   Guliani, Lisa, "The United States Isn't a Country—It's a Corporation!" https://www.serendipity.li/jsmill/us_corporation.htm

ing manipulated results that go against what they announce to the world. The United States has higher vaccination rates than any other country. The USA also has very high infant mortality rates. American children experience epidemic levels of chronic diseases including autism, attention deficit disorder, learning disabilities, autoimmune disorders, asthma, epilepsy and allergies. If vaccinations were so effective in improving the health of children, why do the statistics not bear this out? In fact, the opposite has been shown to be the case.[4]

"The Elephant in the Room" is an important, serious and obvious topic, which everyone is aware of, but which nobody wants to discuss, as such discussion is considered to be uncomfortable. It would cause cognitive dissonance, which is the psychological distress felt when a person is presented with a truth that contradicts a previously deeply-held belief. That the government health agencies may be working against our best interests is a good example of inducing cognitive dissonance. Everyone assumes government health agencies are working to ensure better health for its citizens. Another example is the often-referred to "climate change." While indeed mountain glaciers are melting around the world, and CO2 emissions are largely blamed, it is rare to hear a voice in the wilderness who will proclaim geoengineering as the real culprit.

AN ESOTERIC PERSPECTIVE

Yet, not everything esoteric or occult is from the dark side. Fundamentalist Christians often label everything termed esoteric as Satanic, but that is a very narrow view. Certain esoteric views are actually a remnant of our ancestors' ancient wisdom. Some societies began as fully-fledged esoteric orders, but became watered down with time, lacking people with sufficient inner awakening to participate in them, similar to the way Freemasonry (or even the Illuminati) were once of a pure nature. The Illuminati were once the enlightened ones, and Freemasonry claimed to "make good men better men." As sure as day turns into night, these institutions became infiltrated by dark forces. People motivated by greed and power took control these organizations at the highest levels, and took advantage of their secretive nature. The original good intentions of Freemasonry and the Illuminati were hijacked to fulfill sinister purposes.

The Chinese sage, Lao Tzu, once said that "symbols rule the world, not rules or laws." Symbols communicate at a deeper level than words, because symbols are decoded by the right, intuitive brain, whereas words are decoded by the left, logical brain. Symbols are able to penetrate more deeply into our subconscious, which is why the elite are so obsessed with their occult corporate and governmental logos of red crosses, rising suns, all-seeing eyes, pyramids, 666, the rings of Saturn, hexagrams and inverted pentagrams. Words attempt to rule the world, but they can never be as powerful as symbols.

As we examine the esoteric subjects in this book from a different perspective, it is necessary to know what we are up against. There is good and evil on Earth, or a distinct duality that exists, however we care to word it. We would be naïve to think otherwise. Bottom line: there are good guys and bad guys not only here, but across the universe as well. Both are allowed to present their messages to us. The future we experience is the result of the choices we make. Thus, the best way to defeat the dark forces is to understand their *modus operandi*. For starters, there have always been levels of secrecy in many areas of life, especially in some areas of government and the military, for example. Yet, citizens assume the government and military are working for their benefit and these institutions are rarely seen as functioning as their invisible masters. Yet, esoteric societies have used secrecy out of necessity for their own protection for ages; but now, the age of secrecy is over, and these esoteric subjects can be codified and understood.

• •
4   Adams, Mike, "Everything is Rigged." **https://www.naturalnews.com/054857_rigged_elections_fake_media_fairy_tales.html**

THE MANY WAYS TO DIRTY A CONVERSATION

An appeal to ridicule (also called appeal to mockery, *ab absurdo*, or the horse laugh) describes an informal fallacy which presents an opponent's argument as absurd, ridiculous, or in any way humorous, attempting to make of it a foregone conclusion that the argument lacks any substance which would merit consideration.

An appeal to ridicule is often found in the form of comparing a nuanced circumstance or argument to a laughably commonplace occurrence or some other irrelevancy on the basis of comedic timing, wordplay, or making an opponent and their argument the object of a joke. This is a rhetorical tactic that mocks an opponent's argument or viewpoint, attempting to inspire an emotional reaction in the audience and to highlight any counter-intuitive aspects of that nuanced argument, making it appear foolish and contrary to common sense.

The practice of quoting out of context (sometimes referred to as "contextomy" and quote mining), is an informal fallacy and a type of false attribution in which a passage is removed from its surrounding matter in such a way as to distort its intended meaning. Contextomies are stereotypically intentional, but may also occur accidentally if someone misinterprets the meaning and omits something essential to clarifying it, thinking it non-essential. Short sound bites are used successfully on "low information voters." As a straw man argument, which is frequently found in politics, it involves quoting an opponent out of context in order to misrepresent their position (typically to make it seem more simplistic or extreme) in order to make it easier to refute. Sooner or later we wake up to the sheer scale of the manipulation in our lives, and what we find ain't pretty.

"The Emperor Has No Clothes" is an expression that is often used to describe a situation in which people, afraid of being an outlier, are afraid to speak up about something obvious that their eyes or logic are telling them to be true—even if everybody around them is afraid to say anything. The expression comes from a fairy tale by Hans Christian Anderson entitled *The Emperor's New Clothes*.

WHEN IS ENOUGH ENOUGH?

We are not protected from negativity any more than our collective free will decides. When we act in selfish, manipulative, controlling or violent ways, that in turn allows elite controllers to do the same things to us on a larger scale. There comes a time when we need to crystallize all that's being plainly revealed into a very clear picture that brings personal action and a conscious response. The global engineers are enacting a full spectrum attack on humanity, not just to subdue, control and transform the world's populations, but to reduce it by slowly maiming and killing it off in a dark depopulation agenda.

The common awareness of these programs extends to such arenas as geoengineering and electromagnetic warfare, radiation contamination and a full-on global fracking agenda, full spectrum geopolitical hegemony, invasive medical and pharmaceutical fascism, and the tightening economic vice grip on people's supply lines and their very survival.

We are up against elite planning organizations with seemingly unlimited resources. Many are operating openly with benign names such as the Rand Corporation, the Stanford Institute, the Rockefeller Foundation, the Carnegie Institute, the Red Cross, the Council on Foreign Relations, the Institute for the Advancement of the Sciences, the Ford Foundation, the Trilateral Commission, the Jesuit Society of Jesus and many more. But most Americans cannot see the forest for the trees and have no suspicions about such organizations. After all, like the "Patriot Act," they must be looking out for our collective good. It is pointless to get angry learning these facts. Humanity as a collective has created these problems. Some of them have built up from thousands of years of karmic patterns.

"If You See Something, Say Something" is an official Department of Homeland Security slogan, post-9/11, to get citizens to notify authorities if they hear or see something suspicious. In this neo-Fascist doublespeak, it is really the perpetrators of the biggest crimes who try to pass off their dastardly deeds onto patsies, or any other perceived enemy.

CONSPIRACIES AND MOTIVES

The CIA was the creator of the phrase, "conspiracy theory." They invented the term and put it into wide circulation to smear and defame people questioning the JFK assassination. The CIA's campaign to popularize the phrase "conspiracy theory" and make conspiracy beliefs a target of ridicule and hostility must be credited, unfortunately, with being one of the most successful propaganda initiatives of all time, which lasts to this day.

In other words, people who use the terms "conspiracy theory" and "conspiracy theorist" as an insult should recognize they are doing so as the result of a well-documented, undisputed, historically-real conspiracy by the CIA to cover-up the JFK assassination. That campaign, by the way, was completely illegal, and the CIA officers involved were criminals. Consequently, the government since JFK should be considered illegitimate. By definition, any government following a *coup d'état* is illegitimate. The CIA, according to their charter, is barred from all domestic activities, yet it routinely breaks the law to conduct domestic operations ranging from propaganda to assassinations.

As we examine large sections of history that need revisioning, including the myriad number of paranormal mysteries, and why there appears to be a grand cover-up of many things that will collectively advance the human race, we must examine these issues with the eye of a detective. No real conspiracy holds water unless there is a believable motive behind it. Conspiracies of human activities in the recent past—for example, the assassination of both Kennedy brothers, or the belief that 9/11 was an inside job, may not be fully resolved until we tap into the complete and true historical record. The comprehensive record of the past is said to be contained in the ancient Akashic Records, or can be accessed by very advanced stargate technology such as the "Yellow Cube" which can access an uncritical and completely accurate account of every event in history. Until that day we should always be rethinking history, assuming there are covered-up motives, and keep our minds open to alternative viewpoints. After all, history is usually written by the winners of any conflict.

Indeed, "future conspiracies" are still in the process of playing out, and can still be changed by us. The future is nothing but a series of probabilities. As we shall see later, there is always a need for a manufactured enemy of the United States, and the future timeline is not set. In the second half of the 20th Century we saw the communist threat and the ensuing Cold War. In the early part of the 21st Century we have the fabricated War on Terror. Next up, according to Carol Rosin (who learned about it from Wernher von Braun) is a planned false flag alien invasion of Earth using advanced holographic technology. As we shall see, great forces of money and power are behind the non-disclosure of UFO technology, as well as the suppression of free energy, space travel, the Akashic Records, advanced human abilities, and so much more. It is easier to keep a populous ignorant and in a constant state of fear than if they had free access to information and were enlightened. And what if there had been an alien agenda here on Earth, not for merely decades, but for centuries or millennia? According to former Naval Intelligence officer and UFO researcher William Cooper, "It was learned (by the secret government) that aliens had been and were then manipulating masses of people through secret societies, witchcraft, magic, the occult, and religion." When the truth is far stranger than fiction, in the view of a secret government, there was no other choice than to keep the whole matter under the maximum level of top secrecy.

Fast forward to today. Everything is upside down in the modern world that we can call the "big lie." Why are the world's most profitable businesses Big Oil, finance, chemicals, war, pharmaceuticals, "illegal" drugs, human slavery and prostitution? Why do "democratic" governments need to rule their people with oppressive, police-state tactics? Why do these "democracies" poison the food, the water, the air and the land? Why do they tax and regulate their people into slavery? It is simple to understand when you put these questions into human terms. We know how people occupy niches in our own circles of influence, and what motivates them. In a way, we all have to try and maximize our opportunities within a given set of circumstances—the reality of which is that some can be depended upon to lie, cheat and/or steal their way into success within the current operating framework. The system is set up that way.

MEDIA MADNESS

To focus on a large aspect of the "big lie," consider how we can be utterly manipulated by the media. Walter Lippmann's book, *Public Opinion*, published in 1922, detailed a study in which he and Edward Bernays were involved while in London during the First World War. Ostensibly the study literally painted pictures inside people's heads, which were cunningly and deliberately designed by expert craftsmen to mislead not only individuals, but entire societies. This kind of marketing has since become a highly refined science. When the mainstream media was hijacked and became a tool of Madison Avenue advertising firms, as suggested and enabled by Edward Bernays himself, it became a tool used for mind control of the masses and to advance an evil agenda to corrupt and enslave the masses. Mass media is the most powerful tool used by the ruling class to manipulate the public. It shapes and molds opinions and attitudes and defines what is normal and acceptable. There are many indications that our press lies to us in whatever ways are necessary to support the ruling elite, because. the press, in fact, is the instrument of the ruling elite.

On December 8, 2016, the government created a veritable and suspicious "Ministry of Truth" when then-president Barack Obama quietly signed the "Countering Disinformation and Propaganda Act" into law. Long before "fake news" became a major media topic, the U.S. government was already planning its legally-backed crackdown on anything it would eventually label "fake news."

When the "Countering Disinformation and Propaganda Act" passed in the Senate, it was quietly inserted inside the 2017 National Defense Authorization Act (NDAA) Conference Report. And now, the Countering Disinformation and Propaganda Act is law, seen as part of national defense. It would seem Congress is aligning with the philosophy of Hitler's propaganda minister Joseph Goebbels: "If you tell a lie big enough and keep repeating it, people will eventually come to believe it." Since creating fake news is now legal, it can be parroted across all networks, and hammered into our heads until the repetition makes us believe it is true. Now the real threat to the fake narrative is the alternative media, in which laws against our freedom of speech are currently underway.

Here is an excerpt of a statement issued by the generously-funded Senators Rob Portman (R-Ohio) and Chris Murphy (D-Conn) on the signing into law of a bill that further chips away at press liberties in the USA. It further sets the stage for future witch hunts and website shutdowns, purely as a result of an accusation that any one media outlet or site is considered as a source of "disinformation and propaganda." This is sufficient cause to merit shut down by the government. "The use of propaganda to undermine democracy has hit a new low. But now we are finally in a position to confront this threat head-on and get out the truth. By building up independent, objective journalism in places like Eastern Europe, we can start to fight back by exposing these fake narratives and empowering local communities to protect themselves," said Murphy. "I'm proud that our bill was signed into law, and I look forward to working with Senator Portman to make sure these tools and new resources are effectively used to get out the truth."

UNWORKABLE PROPAGANDA

Just the fact that the realistic, awakened and aware perspective of seeing these realities for what they are has been portrayed as "conspiratorial" puts the control issue way over the top, not just in an Orwellian incredulity, but exactly where the dark forces want it placed in the mass mind. In plain reality of course, it's a very real conspiracy, and they're clearly executing a stated agenda, one we're fully aware of, and which has the potential to depopulate many unaware people. Naturally they have to decry anything that opposes their agenda, and here is where the battle lines are drawn. Every "news item" that's reported from any official source is deliberately distorted to the point of insanity, turning many facts on their heads while attacking anyone who might offer something truly constructive to the world. Meanwhile, the CIA has had operatives in every large media organization since the 1950s under "Operation Mockingbird," (in part, the brainchild of Nazi immigrants to America in the late 1940s.)

The media manipulation has reached new heights, through language sorcery and meme repetition, as the Bernays-inspired "Mad Men" have been known to have been extremely successful. Most people never even stop to question anything sounding like an "authority," hence the worship of men in white coats with strings of degrees after their names, "talking heads," and other institutions like these which sound the least bit credible. The problem is that the media is controlled by corporations that are controlled by the super-rich who have an interest in keeping the public in a trance, as well as ignorant, anxious, fearful, highly suggestible and vulnerable to control and manipulation. The nation is experiencing the effects of a scientifically-induced nervous breakdown. Psychological warfare and economic warfare are both being used against an unsuspecting public.

Almost hourly we're reading of new exposés regarding critical health issues, from the disastrous effects of vaccines and pharmaceutical drugs to the cover up of what is actually in our adulterated and genetically-modified food as well as in our drinking water and the very air we breathe. Yet the free exchange of ideas is the only way to make progress, and that itself is being limited thanks to the "Countering Disinformation and Propaganda Act." Laws that restrict free speech are a crime against us all and a roadblock to progress. Today the mainstream media has been "weaponized" against America, and currently poses a very real risk to your liberties, health and safety.[5]

Preston James, writing for *Veterans Today,* exposes the treachery of captured operations:

> *We now know for certain that the deep state has been using the U.S. Government and its secret factions in various agencies like DHS, FEMA, NSA, the FBI, the CIA, and foreign groups like the Mossad, DVD and other subcontractors, to repeatedly engineer and stage Gladio-style false flag attacks. These false flag terror attacks cannot be effectively deployed unless the Mainstream Media, Intel and Law Enforcement are tightly controlled. Any breakdown could mean the whole system becomes exposed. In order for the public to be effectively bamboozled into believing the government's fake lie narratives in the Major Mass Media that always accompany their false flag attacks, that fascist government must have gained control over the existing Mainstream Media, Intel and Law Enforcement. And these fake lie narratives come from the deep state, ruled over by the cabal of hugely influential, and vastly rich and powerful individuals.*

5   James, Preston, "Is the Pentagon functioning as part of a RICO crime Syndicate?" *Veterans Today:* **https://www.veteranstodayarchives. com/2015/11/13/is-the-pentagon-functioning-as-part-of-a-rico-crime-syndicate/**

THE USA CORPORATE DICTATORSHIP

Nearly every American is unaware that the United States Corporation came about just after the Civil War. The "USA" as a constitutional republic's last year was 1870. The Act of 1871 was passed by a corrupt Congress, creating a separate form of government for Washington D.C., essentially turning it into a corporation, outside the jurisdiction of the Constitution of the USA. It was decided that employees would be called "citizens." So, when you say in court or on paper that you are a citizen of the United States, you are not a free American, but an employee of USA, Inc.

Corporations dictate every aspect of life in America, including the food we eat, the water we drink the air we breathe, our exposure to toxins, to stress, the energy we use and our healthcare choices. It also affects our sovereignty as free citizens. On June 5, 1933, Congress passed House Joint Resolution HJR-192 in order to suspend the gold standard and abrogate the gold clause in the U.S. national constitution. Since then, no one in America has been able to lawfully pay a debt. HJR-192 also made all citizens private corporations to be used as collateral for international loans. Consent was manufactured so the government can access the International Monetary Fund through your exemption account, created at your birth and backed by the bond attached to your birth certificate.

Because we seem to have a myriad of offerings from corporations that can sometimes benefit us does not mean we are a free people. It means we are given a set number of choices determined by specific corporations. Did you know that your birth certificate is a contract with a corporation masquerading as a government? This legal identity is called a "Strawman," whilst your flesh and blood identity is called a "Freeman." For most ordinary people, our work schedules (again dictated by corporations) determine the amount of free time we are allowed. This is the measured time we must use to pursue other interests outside of work. In America, this time is purposely extremely limited. It is all we are given to cultivate relationships with family and friends, raise our children, and enjoy entertainment and relaxation. It's just enough to recharge us for our real purpose in life, which is to serve the Corporations.

How Did George Orwell's Worst Nightmare Come to Be?

In 1948, there was a sensible law passed so that our government couldn't use domestic propaganda against its own citizens. This was essentially overturned in May 2012, just seven months before Sandy Hook, when a Texas Republican introduced an act called HR 5736 Smith-Mundt Modernization Act of 2012, which was an amendment to the 1948 bill, making it *legal* for the government to disseminate its own propaganda in America using the press, publications, the radio, motion-picture films, the Internet and social media, while also giving themselves the right to put any propaganda they want directly into the archives, no questions asked. Which means these lies in time will officially become history in an Orwellian "Ministry of Propaganda." We all know we've been already receiving propaganda through films and the mainstream media for decades, so the question arises as to what level they intend to take it with this bill. This bill died in the Senate, but was brought up again and passed as an amendment in the 2012 National Defense Authorization Act (NDAA) found on pages 326-328. As stated on *MaxKeiser.com*, "it is the same exact bill except one word is left out. The article goes on to mention that Section B expressly allows the use of propaganda domestically, as long as there is some possibility that at least one non-US citizen will eventually receive the given communication. This is why we see so many false flag operations, and this is why false flags will continue—they made it legal just before Sandy Hook."

When someone mentions "The New World Order," it conjures up thoughts of conspiracy involving the Illuminati, the Freemasons, Skull and Bones, old privileged family wealth and royal lineage. Beneath that, remember the already bought-and-paid-for world leaders and the secret agenda. If we were to drill down to the real cause, there are 10 key dates that Americans can point to in terms of pinpointing when America began to crumble:

1. In 1870, Rockefeller's Standard Oil set into motion the creation of the American corporatocracy in which corporations, not citizens, run the federal government of the United States. The Act of 1871 was passed by a corrupt Congress and signed into law by the alcoholic president Ulysses S. Grant. Not only was the USA restructured as a corporation, but a separate form of government applied to the city-state of Washington D.C. This essentially created the corporate military wing of the "Empire of Three Cities," along with the City of London controlling the finances, and the Vatican City overseeing spirituality.

2. The year 1913 is an important year, not just because it marked the year income tax was introduced, but that the banksters totally gained control over our economy through the passage of the Federal Reserve Act. This culminated in the bankers removing America from the gold standard in 1971, and marked the ushering in of controlling America through debt management.

3. Just as World War II was coming to a close, in 1944, the Bretton Woods Agreement Conference essentially saw the United States totally surrendering its sovereignty to the Rothschild/Rockefeller banking empires by forcing the nations of the world to accept the dictates of the centralized banking system.

4. In 1947, the CIA and the National Security Council became operational and marked the birth of the national police state surveillance grid. The CIA, an outgrowth of the World War II spy organization called the Office of Strategic Services (OSS), became a permanent structure in the American landscape. Today, the CIA is a private corporation which operates as a prostitute for global banking interests, as it does not represent the United States. The CIA has been termed the "enforcement arm" of the Council on Foreign Relations. Incidentally, 1947 is also the year of the Roswell crash and President Truman's creation of Majestic 12. This year marks the beginning of the false narrative pertaining to everything surrounding UFO and ET issues. It also marks the year that Operation Highjump was prematurely aborted after Admiral Byrd was faced with an enemy in Antarctica, that could "fly pole to pole, at incredible speeds."

5. In 1948, the creation of the United Nations was heralded as a way to end world conflicts. Problem is, it was built on land donated by the Rockefeller family. This marked the beginning of the end of the political sovereignty of the United States. Many researchers believe when the gun confiscation troops come house-to-house, they will be UN blue-helmeted troops operating under the authority of the UN Small Arms Treaty, which John Kerry unconstitutionally signed into law without the required approval of the Senate. Certainly, the creation of the International Council for Local Environmental Initiatives (ICLEI) and Agenda 21 has UN origins, and this cancer upon America has its roots in the United Nations.

6. The 1960 election was primarily determined by the images on television as the underdog, the charismatic JFK, defeated the favorite, Richard Nixon. Since that time, many Americans have been conditioned to ignore the encroachment of tyranny because of television and the subsequent propagandizing of this medium of communication. Richard Nixon famously quipped, "Americans won't believe anything until they see it on TV."

7. In 1968, the United States crossed an important threshold, as it became a nation that imported more than it exported. In this year, Congress allowed corporations, with impunity, to relocate overseas for reasons of cheap labor and monopolistic price-fixing. This trend continued through the free trade agreements until, a half century later, we have a mere 14% left of what was once our proud American manufacturing base. Nixon taking the dollar off the gold standard three years later would greatly decrease the value of the dollar by making it strictly a fiat currency.

8. *On September 11, 2001, the national police state surveillance grid reached maturity. This false flag event created, under the guise of national security, the American Stasi: The Department of Homeland Security. It also created the Patriot Act, in which every communication that we engage in is monitored, but only for our own protection of course. This event also gave new over-reaching powers to airport security, with the creation of the Transportation Security Administration (TSA). It also gave rise to the prominence of the Federal Emergency Management Agency (FEMA) to control every resource, every asset and even our freedom.*

9. *In 2008, this nation elected Barack Obama to the presidency despite serious questions regarding his true nationality, his stunning lack of political experience and his decided lack of devotion to the Constitutional ideals emanating from the days of his "community activism." Even his signature "Affordable Care Act" is anything but, and was quite clearly introduced for the benefit of the insurance and medical corporations.*

10. *On New Year's Eve 2011, when few people were paying attention, the United States blew apart the Constitution when Congress passed the National Defense Authorization Act (NDAA) and Obama signed it into law. The NDAA obliterated all civil liberties because this marked the day that our government became the brown shirt Gestapo, the East German Stasi and the KGB all rolled into one organization. Any government that can imprison and indefinitely detain its citizens without due process of law is an unmasked dictatorship which has genocidal intentions waiting in the wings. We were also assured that average citizens were not being spied on by James Clapper of the NSA, and whistleblower Edward Snowden proved later we were being lied to all along.*[6]

THE UFO QUESTION

Some may dismiss this book for even contemplating any truth to the UFO enigma, but that comes from a place of innocent ignorance. It is easy to dismiss something without properly investigating the subject for oneself, and the thought of an idea like this still remaining in the category of a "fringe" topic is unsettling. The masses continue to ignore a tremendous amount of evidence that points to the fact that we are not alone, and that we've actually been visited…over a long period of time.

The problem with the UFO phenomenon as it stands today is there are so many unanswered questions. So many different types of craft. So many different types of beings that people swear (upon pain of total public humiliation) contacted them. So many abductions and cattle mutilations. It is logical to conclude that someone must know what is going on. And not just a part of it (the many isolated personal accounts) but the "big picture," and that includes a multitude of dimensions replete with many different intelligences. UFO researcher Trevor James and others have said, "a working knowledge of occult science is indispensable to UFO investigations."

What if the reason the UFO/ET information is forbidden is because zero-point energy and anti-gravity technologies were reverse-engineered from downed extraterrestrial craft, dating back to the Roswell crash landings in July, 1947? After all, why would any-

6   Hodges, Dave, "12 Dates Which Led to the Destruction of America" *My Daily Informer:* https://www.mydailyinformer.com/12-dates-which-led-to-the-destruction-of-america/

one deny a non-polluting free energy source that can do so much good for the world? In a word: Power—of which money is only a symbol.

What if the unrelenting might of the "military industrial complex" President Eisenhower warned us about in his 1960 closing address was already involved in something much, much bigger? Something that includes backward-engineered technology "that can take ET home," as suggested by Skunk Works boss Ben Rich? Or, according to Herman Oberth, one of the founding fathers of rocketry and astronautics, "flying saucers are real and...they are space ships from another solar system. I think that they possibly are manned by intelligent observers who are members of a race that may have been investigating our Earth for centuries."

What if a breakaway civilization started building settlements on other satellites—including the moon, Mars, certain asteroids and other moons as well? What if one or several Secret Space Programs began mining for raw materials in our solar system—finding everything they would ever need—and set up a vast industrial operation off-planet?

What if the first being that was allegedly captured and interrogated in the Roswell crash was only one of a variety of intelligent civilizations our "government" began trading with? Dr. Pierre Guerin, a scientist with the French National Council for Scientific Research stated that "(UFO) behavior is more akin to magic than to physics as we know it." Adding also that, "the modern UFOnauts and demons of past days are probably identical."

A NEW DAWN

And what would happen when the embargo on truth ends and we have an awakened mass human population? What about a race who can finally ally with positive ETs? Indeed, we will quickly learn we live in a multiverse, and we as the human race ourselves, are a hybridized species. We will learn there are at least 40 different humanoid extraterrestrial groups that have tinkered around with our DNA—and for many thousands of years. We will discover we have a much broader spectrum of emotions than most other human species out there. It is both our single greatest weakness and our most powerful strength—that is, once we learn how to harness its power for the positive.[7]

A select few people currently have access to technology beyond our wildest dreams. One of the technologies we are directly aware of will desalinate ocean water, generate free energy and produce any element in the Periodic Table as a by-product. This technology already has the quiet support of one of the most prestigious universities in the country.

In 1901, Nikola Tesla figured out how to tap into the zero-point energy field—a discovery that would have made power plants obsolete. J. P. Morgan didn't like the idea of free energy, having just invested heavily in the copper wire that was required in electrical wiring. So, the industrialist got his cronies in Washington D.C. to stop Tesla and had them confiscate all his work. Since then, no patents have been issued on any inventions or energy systems that threaten to replace the status quo (*Who Killed the Electric Car?* indeed). A century later, our growth has stagnated, our vehicles are still saddled with gasoline-dependent internal combustion engines, glaciers around the world are melting, cancer runs rampant from our needless exposure to the rising amount of toxins being pumped every day into our environment, and 80% of the world's population lives in abject poverty.

Many skeptics ask "why don't ETs just show themselves?" The extraterrestrials, positive or negative, are simply not allowed to make a big showing. They cannot spontaneously decide to drop in and make an appearance on *The Tonight Show*. The Prime Directive (an alleged law of the universe) is not just a theme you hear about on *Star Trek*, but it is an absolute law in the universe that all beings, positive and

7   Sheldrake, Rupert, *Dogs That Know When Their Owners Are Coming Home.* Broadway Books, 2011.

negative, must follow. The higher-level beings cannot simply reveal themselves to us. There must be a calling, where a sufficient number of people request their help, before intervention can occur.

Part of that calling is that the people of the world are waking up to the massive amount of control and manipulation we have been subjected to over the decades. Mike Adams "The Health Ranger" produced an informative list on *Natural News* of how the world we live in is fake and the system is rigged. His list "What exactly is rigged?" is as follows:

- *The entire mainstream media*
- *Google search engine and Google News*
- *Facebook and Twitter*
- *The DNC and the RNC (both 100% rigged by globalists)*
- *Every federal agency (EPA, FDA, etc.)*
- *The entire justice system (makes a total farce of real justice)*
- *Interest rates and the value of the money supply (central banksters)*
- *Academia (all public universities)*
- *EPA's "safe" limits on pesticides (all rigged by Big Biotech)*
- *Food and food labeling (all run by corrupt food companies)*
- *Public education (rigged into Common Core anti-knowledge idiocy)*
- *Banking and finance (all controlled by globalists)*
- *Government economics figures and statistics*
- *Medicine and pharmaceuticals (rigged to maximize profits)*
- *Big Science (totally rigged by government agenda pushers)*
- *The music industry (most top singers can't sing at all)*
- *Weapons manufacturers and war corporations*
- *The illegal drug trade (it's run by the government)*
- *Political elections (all 100% rigged at the federal level)*
- *Political polls (now rigged by Reuters, too)*
- *The health insurance industry (rigged by Obamacare)*
- *College admissions (legally discriminates against Whites and Asians)*
- *9/11 and domestic terrorism (all rigged "official stories")*
- *Oil and energy industries*
- *The rule of law (rigged in favor of the rich and powerful)*
- *Infectious disease and the CDC (a constant stream of lies)*
- *Hollywood (all run by globalists)*
- *Climate change science (all a grand science hoax)*
- *Press release services (they only allow official narratives)*
- *History (what you are taught is mostly a lie)*
- *Government grants (only given out to those who further the agenda)*
- *Government bids (only awarded to those who kick back funds to corrupt officials)*
- *Consciousness and free will (we are all taught consciousness doesn't exist)*
- *Ethnobotany (medicinal and spiritual use of healing plants)*
- *Life on other planets (the obvious truth is kept from us all)*
- *The origin of the universe (the official narrative is a laughable fairy tale)*

THE REAL PHILOSOPHER'S STONE?

Is there a secret substance known to the ancient world that can regenerate the body, unlock psychic powers and allow us to access higher states of consciousness? Taken in the right amount, over a long period of time, monatomic gold (monatomic meaning consisting of one atom in the molecule) can assist humans to live to 120 years or longer, become psychic, stimulate the third eye, and much more. It will also link the right and left hemispheres of the brain. When that happens, you are able to use your entire brain, it will give you an enhanced ability to manifest, and most importantly it has energy which will unravel your DNA and make repairs to any faults. It will also make you more psychic.

Alchemy is a science that has its roots in antiquity. References to the "Philosopher's Stone," the "Elixir of Life," and "Manna" all refer to a substance known and valued for its ability to turn base metals into precious ones, such as gold and silver. Alchemy can generally be defined as an ancient art form that sought purification of the soul and immortality, called the Philosopher's Stone in the West. This desire for transformation worked in parallel with the transmutation of chemical elements, where gold symbolized perfection. Alchemists were the first to make medicines and pharmaceuticals, and they endeavored to understand the material basis of the world. Although the alchemists practiced actual chemistry and medicine, the big prize was attempting to turn lead into gold, which symbolized a spiritual transmutation equivalent to an awakened consciousness present in all forms, and was also believed to be the consciousness that created the universe.

The monatomic family of metals does not react with any other elements. They produce the least amount of electrical resistance. Gold and silver are used in computer boards, and offer far less resistance than copper. Less resistance to electrons flowing means more conductivity. Interestingly, there is no way to destroy gold except for aqua regia, a highly corrosive mixture of acids. It is a combination of one part nitric acid and three parts hydrochloric acid. Only this will dissolve gold. It was so named aqua regia because it can dissolve the royal metals, or noble metals, such gold and platinum. However, ruthenium, tantalum, iridium, osmium, titanium, rhodium and a few other metals are capable of withstanding aqua regia's corrosive properties. New discoveries in exotic metals and crystals, as well as very old knowledge of their usage, are discussed in the chapters in the ÜberMind Section.

WHAT CAN YOU DO?

Stop playing their game. Take back your power. Stop paying interest rates that enrich the already bloated banking system. Stop paying bills you don't really owe. Debt elimination! Attempt to stop using their fiat currencies. Experiment with barter, or investing in cryptocurrencies or precious metals. There are ways if you open your mind and look for the gaps in their fences that keep the sheeple in their pasture. Are you chattel or a real person? You are the one who makes that choice using your free will.

Be aware of what is going on within mass media and know the intention is to shape perceptions. Like discovering the magician's trick, when you are informed you will not be lured into the new propaganda lies. The ones who stand apart and have quality and values are the ones who are going to have a profitable future. Don't let the herd mentality force you, don't let your desire for acceptance lead you into acting a way you would not normally act. We are created as individuals to stand out, not fit in, success can be defined as your ability to stay true to yourself.

David Icke recognizes it is up to us to wake up and enforce change. He writes:

> What is the hidden agenda behind current world events involving Syria, Russia, China, Iran, the USA and NATO countries? Could this be what I (David Icke) predicted many years ago? The perfect storm which will provide the opportunity to usher in the New World Order? It is obvious that our world is undergoing major changes with the threat of world war, an impending financial collapse, the rapid deterioration of individual and community ethics and the dehumanization of entire societies. We live in a time where humanity is being asked to choose between apathy or taking responsibility for the world that we have helped create.

The worldwide Internet has become the new Gutenberg press and despite the numerous misinformation sites, the truth is still being advanced and can spread like wildfire across the country instantly. Truth resonates and once out, its massive dissemination all over the world and diffusion among the masses cannot be stopped.

And from these introductory beginnings we are set to go "Beyond Esoteric" in our survey of the brave new world we are confronted with. The goal would be how we can get out of the current mess we find ourselves in. There is hope for humanity and our world, and this is "the escape from Prison Planet"—venturing to go where no person has gone before, understanding the transhumanist trap we face, and using the latest technology in a way that can improve our lives, not making us slaves to a New World Order neo-fascist dystopia that would make George Orwell roll over in his grave. In order to fight tyranny, we must be armed with knowledge. We must open ourselves to our greatest human potential. Once we know the difference between the lies we are being spoon-fed and the proper use of our free will, this world will change, inexorably for the better, one person at a time.

The 34th President of the United States, Dwight D. Eisenhower, warned us about the unwarranted power and impending dangers of the "Military-Industrial Complex" in his 1961 farewell address. And though the U.S. military now occupies more than 140 countries and has saturated the sea with ships, the skies with bombers and the land with troops, the full extent of Eisenhower's warning lies beneath the surface of things, tied up in projects that many military personnel are not even aware of. The implications of bringing black budget projects into the light are so vast and so profound that the Military-Industrial Complex has expended every possible effort to keep these projects secret—the very notion of their existence scorned by the talking-head skeptics, marginalizing the conversation into the territory of "conspiracy theory."

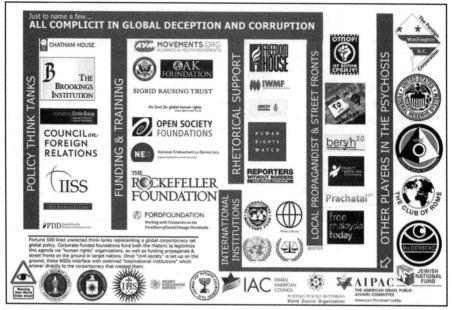

Corporate logos are full of occult symbology. These are the deep state operations of the cabal.

The building in the picture is Palazzo Braschi in Rome, the headquarters of the Fascist Party Federation. The menacing "Big Brother" portrait is Benito Mussolini, one of the most notorious fascist dictators in history. Mussolini's headquarters during WW II was designed to strike fear in the minds of Italians, so they would not question the authority of the State.

During the dawn of Ufology in the United States, unidentified flying objects made themselves known to the leaders of the free world, buzzing over the White House, the Capitol building, and the Pentagon. Seemingly, the unknown objects were defying the very governmental agencies sworn to protect the United States from foreign powers. Washington National Airport and Andrews Air Force Base picked up a number of UFOs on their radar screens on July 19, 1952, over the nation's most sensitive buildings. Most UFO researchers today do not think these craft were extraterrestrial, but back-engineered German craft that remained as a "third power" after WW II. The overflight of D.C. was a show of power and forced the U.S. government into a treaty where the German factions were given access to government and corporate resources to help them build their bases and ships in our Solar System and beyond.

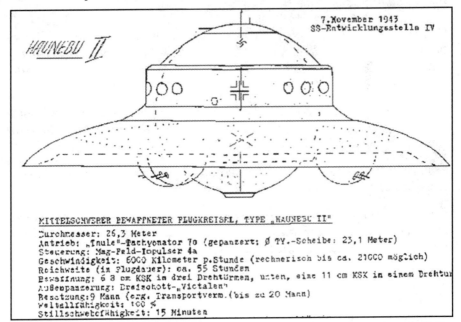

The Nazis were working on several *Flugscheiben* or "flight disc" designs during the early 1940s. The most notorious of these designs was the fabled V7, also called the haunebu craft, which was likely the first Earth-made spaceship of the Modern Age to take a man to the Moon.

NEO·FASCISM

The herd, the mob, the unwashed masses are considered farm animals and are seldom, if ever, allowed to know the truth by their keepers. They believe, they graze and they bleat; they live and die by what they are told.

"So do not be afraid of them, for there is nothing concealed that will not be disclosed, or hidden that will not be made known." –Matthew 10:26

"The liberty of a democracy is not safe if the people tolerate the growth of private power to a point where it comes stronger than their democratic state itself. That, in its essence, is fascism—ownership of government by an individual, by a group." –President Franklin D. Roosevelt

"The objective of war is not to fight and die for your country, it's to make the other bastard die for his country!" –General George Patton

"The easiest way to gain control of a population is to carry out acts of terror. (The public) will clamor for such laws if their personal security is threatened." –Soviet Dictator Josef Stalin

"Voice or no voice, the people can always be brought to the bidding of the leaders. That is easy. All you have to do is tell them they are being attacked and denounce the pacifists for lack of patriotism, and exposing the country to greater danger." –Nazi Leader Hermann Göring

"I never would have agreed to the formation of the Central Intelligence Agency back in forty-seven, if I had known it would become the American Gestapo." –Former President Harry S. Truman in (1961)

"You may choose to look the other way, but you can never say again that you did not know." –William Wilberforce (1791)

"The basic tool for manipulation of reality is the manipulation of words. If you can control the meaning of words, you can control the people who must use the words." –Author Philip K. Dick

"The secret to wealth, fame, and fortune is to know something that no one else knows." –Billionaire Aristotle Onassis

"To preserve our independence, we must not let our rulers load us with perpetual debt. We must make our election between economy and liberty, or profusion and servitude." –Thomas Jefferson

THE NEW FASCISM

"What we euphemistically call free market capitalism is merely fascism in civilian garb. Corporate oligarchs and government are one and the same, thus the ever prevalent 'revolving door' between the ruling and business elite and the progressive exclusion of the average citizen from meaningful civic involvement. Also, the proliferation of propaganda and fear mongering designed to foster the bigotry, hatred, and insecurity of the more ignorant and insular segments of society serves to keep the people focused on collective negative traits of their cohorts rather than those who systematically work to drain the wealth of the economy for their own purposes." –Bernard Martin

TO fully grasp the situation we face as citizens of the USA, we must understand how we got to this point. We also need to define our terms. To begin, the Italian dictator Benito Mussolini is credited with creating the word "fascism." He defined it as "the merger of government and the corporation." He also said a more accurate word would be "corporatism." In our school textbooks we were told the USA was involved in WW II to defeat fascism. In that age, it was government politicians taking over corporations. In the new, or "neo-fascist" model of today, it is the corporation heads who control those top people in government. The continuity of the corporate Federal U.S. government, and hence the continued domination of the military-industrial, petro-pharma complex is in place exclusively to enable the corporate, banker-elite to maintain power. We've witnessed the financial rape of this country by the banksters and their co-

conspirators in the government, who have failed to prosecute a single case against any of the "Too Big to Fail" swindle, despite outright theft of trillions of dollars.

By using Mussolini's definition ("the merger of government and the corporation"), can we claim that the United States is anything but fascist? The term fascism was applied to the way the Nazis and Hitler operated, as well as to the way communists and Stalin operated. What the term fascist ultimately really means is corporatism, ultra-militarism and authoritarianism combined, with an expansionist foreign policy. And that's us—what one can see the USA has become. However, if you look up the definition of "fascism" in any American Dictionary after 2009, both online and in "mainstream" Dictionaries, you will find all have changed to omit any usage of the word "corporatism." Now they flip the definition to say it is "fundamentally opposed to democracy and liberalism," or "right wing ideology." The "Ministry of Thought" strikes again!

The truth is, neo-fascism doesn't look like a podium-pounding demagogue. It looks more like a shadow government that can read our emails and texts at any time, that can pinpoint any person's position 24/7 using GPS, that propagandizes us legally, and tosses in the occasional false flag to keep us in a constant state of fear and submission. Indeed, the term fascism has changed (and even morphed into its opposite) since the WW II era. When speaking about the left wing, Winston Churchill was quoted as saying "the fascists of the future will call themselves anti-fascists." Isn't that what we see demonstrated with the ANTIFA (Anti-Fascist) groups protesting in Europe and America?

Sinclair Lewis once opined that if fascism ever comes to America, it will be wrapped in the flag and carrying a cross. A fascist is a totalitarian who supports an all-powerful and centralized state that can do no wrong—precisely because it is the government. Fascism views political violence, war, and imperialism as a means to achieve national rejuvenation. It asserts that stronger nations have the right to expand their territory by displacing weaker nations.[1]

Oligarchy means rule by the few. Plutocracy is rule by the wealthy. Corporatocracy is a society governed or controlled by corporations. We have all three in the USA. The new fascism is the corporate takeover and control of the United States Government, thereby subverting the Constitution and most of our rights. The concept of a U.S. Government today is fraudulent, since we are not citizens of that "corporation." If the U.S. Government is conducting this type of activity, they are in violation of the laws if the United States of America and should be criminally prosecuted. In essence, we're violating our citizens' rights to protect these criminal individuals who violate this very basic tenet of American Law. Many believe the Deep State—defined as "military, intelligence and government officials who try to secretly manipulate government policy"—is working behind the facade of the constitutional U.S. government. President Donald Trump says it has taken control of the central government.

THE RISE OF ANTIFA

The domestic terrorist group ANTIFA is supposed to be opposed to fascism, but in reality, they are *anti*-Free Assembly and *anti*-First Amendment freedom of speech. The group has staged numerous violent riots that have caused millions of dollars-worth of property damage. In June, 2017, the Department of Homeland Security (DHS) in New Jersey officially listed ANTIFA as a domestic terrorist organization after they launched a rash of violent attacks targeting supporters of Donald Trump.

The New Jersey DHS described the situation as:

••••••••••••••••••••••••••••••••••••

1   Fetzer, James Henry, "Americans threatened by own 'fascistic' government: Scholar." *Press TV*

Self-described Antifa groups have been established across the United States and in several major cities, including New York, Philadelphia, Chicago, and San Francisco. A majority of New Jersey-based anarchist groups are affiliated with the Antifa movement and are opposed to 'fascism,' racism, and law enforcement. Antifa groups coordinate regionally and have participated in protests in New York City and Philadelphia. There are three loosely organized chapters in New Jersey, known as the North Jersey Antifa, the South Jersey Antifa, and the Hub City Antifa New Brunswick (Middlesex County).

"Antifa" is short for anti-fascists. The term is used to define a broad group of people whose political beliefs lean toward the left—often the far left—but do not conform with the Democratic Party platform. The group doesn't have an official leader or headquarters, although groups in certain states hold regular meetings. Some employ radical or militant tactics to get their message across. In America, they focus more on fighting far-right and white supremacist ideology directly than on encouraging pro-left policy.

In reality, billionaire George Soros has been known to fund groups such as "Black Lives Matter," and other protests, riots, domestic terrorists and a violent left. The Soros-backed Democrat group known as ANTIFA is leading what many are calling "the resistance." Well-organized protests feature alarmist rhetoric and have a proclivity to devolve into anarchic violence. Rioters smashed storefront windows, assaulted innocent bystanders and torched vehicles all in the name of opposing Trump. Such antics harken back to a quote of then-California governor Ronald Reagan during a 1975 interview with *60 Minutes*, when he said, "If fascism ever comes to America, it will come in the name of liberalism."

CORPORATIONS OUT OF CONTROL

The biggest issue the citizens of the USA, indeed all people of the planet, will have to deal with sooner rather than later is the question of how to regulate large transnational corporations. Because they operate across borders, they constantly seek loopholes and migrate to places where corrupt officials let them get away with murder, pollution, tax-evasion and other crimes. When corporations take over the government, it is known as neofascism. In other words, if the nations of the world do not do something about this situation ASAP, we will end up with a fascist New World Order.[2]

There are common themes that generally surface when one speaks of fascist-style states. All fascist regimes have an assertive ultra-nationalism that frequently feeds off a sense of victimhood. This need to assert a frequently mythical notion of national power and greatness (often through war or imperial expansion) generally produces a militarization of society as well as a rewriting of history to support the new agenda. Fascist governments frequently evolve into police states to suppress dissent and maintain the regime.

And herein lies the problem. The Act of 1871 created two constitutions and made the United States a corporation. We're fascists now because the definition of fascism is when corporations take over the government, and the citizens are beholden to their government. Our Democrats and Republicans are all bought off by the corporations. The entire U.S. government is a huge system based on the illusion of democracy.

THE CROWN REPUBLIC

To have the Declaration of Independence recognized internationally, Middle Templar King George III agreed (in the Treaty of Paris of 1783) to establish the legal Crown entity of the incorporated United States, referred to internally as the Crown Temple States (Colonies). States spelled with a capital letter 'S,' denotes a

2   Icke, David, *The Biggest Secret: The Book That Will Change the World.* London, UK, 1999.

legal entity of the Crown. At least five Templar Bar Attorneys, under solemn oath to the Crown, signed the American Declaration of Independence. This means that both parties were agents of the Crown. There is no lawful effect when a party signs as both the first and second parties. The Declaration was simply an internal memo circulating among private members of the Crown. The original 13 colonies were actually called companies. We sing patriotic songs like "the Star-Spangled Banner" but a banner is a corporate advertisement, not a flag.

Another ruse used to hoodwink natural persons is by enfranchisement. Those cards in your wallet bearing your name spelled in all capital letters means that you have been enfranchised and have the status of a corporation. These invisible contracts include, birth certificates, citizenship records, employment agreements, driver's licenses and bank accounts. It is perhaps helpful to note here that contracts do not now, nor have they ever had to be stated in writing in order to be enforceable by American judges. If it is written down, it is merely a written statement of the contract. The Crown views our participation in these contracts of commercial equity as being voluntary and that any gain accrued is taxable, as the gain wouldn't have been possible were it not for the Crown.

As the United States of America corporation, it has shareholders and directors. The USA is, and always has been, a huge corporation ruled from abroad. Its initial name was the Virginia Company and it is owned by the British Crown and the Vatican, who receive their yearly share of the profits. According to David Icke in *The Biggest Secret*:

> *The lands of the Virginia Company were granted to the colonies under a Deed of Trust (on lease) and therefore they could not claim ownership of the land. ...The monarch, through his Council for the Colonies, insisted that members of the colonies impose the Christian religion on all the people, including the Native Americans. ... The criminal courts on the lands of the Virginia Company were to be operated under Admiralty Law, the law of the sea, and the civil courts under common law, the law of the land. ...Now, get this. All of the above still applies today!*

THE DAY THE REPUBLIC DIED

When Congress passed the "Act of 1871" on February 21, 1871, it created a separate corporate government for the District of Columbia. This treasonous act allowed the District of Columbia to operate as a corporation outside the original Constitution of the USA and outside of the best interests of American citizens. The District of Columbia is one of the Empire of Three Cities, which also include the private inner City of London for finance, and the Vatican City for spiritual control. Thus, the United States of America is a corporate fiction—the USA has been incorporated since 1871—and the so-called "government" has no jurisdiction outside of Washington D.C. Yet, the country has been occupied financially by the triumvirate of the Bank of England/the Rothschild family/and the Vatican.

When the Forty-First Congress passed the Act of 1871, titled "An Act to Provide a Government for the District of Columbia," to provide a separate form of government for the District of Columbia (a ten-mile square parcel of land, as specified in the Acts of the Forty-first Congress, Section 34, Session III, chapters 61 and 62), it actually had no constitutional authority to do so. Yet, the District of Columbia would essentially become the military force of the world.

The Act of 1871, which took place under the weak presidency of Ulysses S. Grant, was a strategic move by foreign interests, essentially international bankers, who were intent upon gaining a stranglehold on the coffers and neck of America. Since then, the UNITED STATES OF AMERICA CORPORATION has been based out of Washington D.C.—an extra-territorial enclave inside the Republic of the United States of America.

But what was the motive for this move by foreign interests? An answer lies in looking at the circumstances of those days. The Act of 1871 was passed at a vulnerable time in America. Our nation was essentially bankrupt—weakened, fractured at the seams and financially depleted in the aftermath of the Civil War. The Civil War itself was nothing more than a calculated "front" for some rather fancy footwork by corporate backroom players. The Congress realized our country was in dire financial straits, so they cut a deal with the international bankers.

It is important to remember that banks do not lend us money just out of the goodness of their hearts. There has to be some sort of collateral or some strings attached which puts you and me (the borrower) into a subservient position. The conniving international bankers were not about to lend our floundering nation any money without some serious stipulations. So, they devised a brilliant way of getting their foot in the door of the United States. This was a prize they had coveted for some time, but had been unable to grasp, thanks to our Founding Fathers, who despised them and held them in check; thus, the Act of 1871 was passed.

When you hear some individuals say that the Constitution is null and void, this is an over-simplification, but with some kernels of truth. Consider how our government has been transformed over time, from a municipal or service-oriented entity to a corporate or profit-oriented entity. We are being ruled by a "de facto," or unlawful, form of government, which can be seen as the corporate body of the death-mongers—The Controllers. With the passage of the Act of 1871, a series of subtle and overt deceptions were set in motion—all in conjunction and collusion with the Congress, which knowingly and deliberately sold "We the People" down the river.

THE DAY AMERICA BECAME A CORPORATION

You may reference the UNITED STATES CODE (note the capitalization, indicating the corporation, not the Republic), Title 28, Part 6, Chapter 176, Subchapter (A), in section 3002 in definition (15). This states unequivocally that the UNITED STATES is a federal corporation. Realize, too, that the corporation is not a separate and distinct entity from the government. It *is* the government. This is extremely important. Thus, "We the People" are considered corporate commercial inventory. It can be referred to as the "corporate empire of the UNITED STATES," which operates under Roman Civil Law outside of the Constitution.

In summary, this Act formed the corporation known as THE UNITED STATES, in all caps, indicating the corporation, not the Republic. With the "Act of 1871," our Constitution was defaced in the sense that the title was block-capitalized and the word "for" was changed to the word "of" in the title. The original Constitution drafted by the Founding Fathers was written with this wording: "The Constitution *for* (emphasis mine) the United States of America."

When the original Constitution was suspended, the United States became defined as a "Federal Corporation" as per legal code 28 U.S.C. § 3002. The de facto (corporate) Constitution reads: The Constitution OF the UNITED STATES of America. This makes all lawyers and judges as "officers of the court," who therefore work for the very system that has been stealing from and misrepresenting this nation for over 150 years. That would be an automatic "conflict of interest" on their part because they are "officers of the court." Secondly, all courts work for the "state," which in turn, works for the "corporate government." Remember, the government is a "corporation," and therefore falls under the rules and laws of the Uniform Commercial Code (UCC).

With the Legislative Act of February 21, 1871, Congress chartered a Federal Company entitled "United States," aka "US Inc." and "USA Inc." Shockingly, this means that Congress, under no Constitutional authority to do so, created a separate form of government for the District of Columbia, which is a ten mile square parcel of land, originally built on reclaimed swamp land. This is our "legislative democracy." Consequently, parents unknowingly have been registering their newborn children as property—"a thing" which is "domiciled" or controlled by the law of a private corporation, not the *de jure* Republic formed by the Declaration of Independence and the Constitution. Since the United States is in fact a corporation, what is the main purpose of any corporation? To manage an endeavor in order to achieve profits, of course! Over the last century war has proven to be the most profitable business in which to be engaged. Today, more than ever before, we have a perpetual war against an enemy we cannot find, and there is no one country the "terrorist" enemy calls home.

Benefits came with this new citizenship (membership in the corporation), but with the benefits came duties and responsibilities totally regulated by the legislature for the District of Columbia (corporation). If you and your children are property identified on a birth certificate, domiciled in Washington, D.C., one of your duties may be to go and fight in a profit-making enterprise (war) for the corporation (United States, Inc.) of which you are a member. The new class of citizen was given the right to vote in the "democracy" in 1870 by way of the 15th Amendment. All that is required is an application to vote.

THE UNITED STATES EXISTS IN TWO FORMS

How was the Constitution usurped by the corporations? First, we have to understand the professional Congressional plutocrats in *WashedUp Deceit* don't give a care about the US(A), but instead are invested and profiting from war and the Mega-Corp(se). They need to be challenged in court! America is now a corporate plutocracy. This nation is "We the Corporation," and we have two Constitutions. The original "We the People" Constitution has been dormant since 1871.

> *1. The original United States that was in operation until 1860; a collection of sovereign Republics in the union. Under the original Constitution, the States controlled the Federal Government; the Federal Government did not control the States and had very little authority.*

> *2. The original United States has been usurped by a separate and different UNITED STATES formed in 1871, which only controls the District of Columbia and its territories, and which is actually a corporation (the UNITED STATES CORPORATION) that acts as our current government. The United States Corporation operates under Corporate/Commercial/Public Law rather than Common/Private Law.*

The original Constitution was never removed; it has simply lain dormant since 1871. This fact was made clear by Supreme Court Justice Marshall Harlan (Downes v. Bidwell, 182, U.S. 244 1901) by giving the following dissenting opinion: "Two national governments exist; one to be maintained under the Constitution, with all its restrictions; the other to be maintained by Congress outside and Independently of that Instrument."

ADMIRALITY JURISDICTION

The power that controls America is based in Britain and Europe because that is where the power is located that owns the United States Corporation. By the way, if you think it is strange that a court on dry land could be administered under Maritime Law, look at US Code, Title 18 B 7. It says that Admiralty Jurisdiction is applicable in the following locations: (1) the high seas; (2) any American ship; (3) any lands reserved or acquired for the use of the United States, and under the exclusive or concurrent jurisdiction thereof, or any place purchased or otherwise acquired by the United States by consent of the legislature of the state.

All this is founded on Roman law because the Illuminati have been playing this same game throughout the centuries, wherever they have gone. The major politicians know that this is how things are and so do the government administrators, judges, lawyers and insider "journalists."[3]

Jordan Maxwell, in his 1990 slideshow presentation on *Hidden Symbols*, had this to say: "If you notice on the bottom of your birth certificate it says Department of Commerce. It is a property of the Department of Commerce because you are nothing more than a piece of commercial material. That's why if you're out of work you don't go to the unemployment office, you go to the Office of Human Resources, because you're just a human resource."

After all, Maxwell reminds us, the Judge sits on the bench for the bank. Banks are on both sides of a river. A river bank directs the flow of the current-sea—the currency, the cash flow. The current-sea is "deposited" from bank to bank down the river. We're just "consumers" to advertise to, just "human resources" to be used up like batteries, and they are the "social engineers," molding us "useless eaters" into wage slavery.

YOUR BIRTH CERTIFICATE BOND IS WORTH BILLIONS

When you are born, your parents register you with the government as a CORPORATION by receiving and signing a birth certificate. Your birth certificate was monetized and converted into a UNITED STATES Government Bond shortly after your birth by your mother. Your net worth became unlimited, that is, worth billions of dollars. This is, of course, without yours, nor your mother's or father's knowledge or complicity. It is automatic, with no explanation given.

In a few years after birth, your Corporation will receive a taxpayer ID# called a social security number. This is so you can be used as collateral for the government to acquire debt. That's right, you and your labor, time, and energy is what backs up the National debt. You are stock. This all came about when the UNITED STATES covertly declared bankruptcy in 1933, and under the bankruptcy the Straw Man law became known.

The USA Incorporated is nothing more than a foreign invading criminal banking/military occupying hostile enemy. The BLM, IRS, FBI, TSA, DHS, FEMA, CIA, and other alphabet agencies are all invading enemies of *We the People*, and our 50-state landmass. The Republic is dead, and now we are just fodder for the Corporation.

You must be made aware that the members of Congress do NOT work for you and me. Rather, they work for the Corporate entity known as THE UNITED STATES. This is why we can't get them to do anything on our behalf or answer to us—as in the case with the illegal income tax—among many other things. Contrary to popular belief, our Congressional representatives are not our civil servants. They do not work for us. They are the servants of the corporate government and carry out its bidding.

The corporate government of the UNITED STATES has no jurisdiction or authority in any state of the Republic beyond the District of Columbia. You are presumed to know the law. They know you don't know the law, or your history for that matter, because this information has not been taught to you. No concerted effort has been made to inform you. As a Sovereign, you are entitled to full disclosure of the facts. As a slave, you are entitled to nothing other than what the corporation decides to "give" you—at a price. Therefore, always be wary of accepting so-called "benefits" from the corporation of THE UNITED STATES.

3 Maxwell, Jordan, *Matrix of Power: Secrets of World Control*. Book Tree, 2014.

SOLD US DOWN THE RIVER

In the finer print, it can be found that decapitation by guillotine (ICD 9 E 978 Legal Execution) is listed as a legal form of execution within the "Affordable Care Act." It comes in through the World Health Organization (WHO) as an agency of the United Nations (UN) and shouldn't be in any U.S. law.[4] The UN and the WHO are both controlled by the Western global elite, having set them up after WW II as a cleverly disguised method of continuing Nazi power. This is easily understood simply by knowing that the Rockefellers had a half interest in the Nazi corporation IG Farben, the pharmaceutical and chemical conglomerate that financed Hitler and operated the concentration camps. The Rockefellers now bankroll and control the WHO along with the very same pharmaceutical companies that ran the experiments at Auschwitz.

Former President Obama's National Defense Resources Preparedness Executive Order of March 16, 2013, does to the country as a whole what the 2012 National Defense Authorization Act did to the Constitution in particular—completely eviscerates any due process or judicial oversight for any action by the Government deemed to be in the interest of "national security." Like the NDAA, this overreaching Executive Order puts the government completely above the law, which, in a democracy, is never supposed to happen. The United States is essentially now under martial law without the exigencies of a national emergency.

According to six of our former presidents, one vice-president, and a myriad of other high profile political leaders, an invisible government that is "incredibly evil in intent" has been in control of the U.S. government "ever since the days of Andrew Jackson," that is, since at least 1835, the last year the USA had no debt and was beholden to no private central bank. Many of our most revered American statesmen, including George Washington, Thomas Jefferson, John Calhoun, Theodore Roosevelt, Woodrow Wilson, Franklin D. Roosevelt, John F. Kennedy and Daniel Inouye warned about an invisible government. John Francis Hylan, Mayor of New York City in 1922 said, "It operates under cover of a self-created screen [and] seizes our executive officers, legislative bodies, schools, courts, newspapers and every agency created for the public protection." As a result President Woodrow Wilson said, "we have come to be one of the worst ruled, one of the most completely controlled and dominated, governments in the civilized world— no longer a government by free opinion, no longer a government by conviction and the vote of the majority, but a government by the opinion and the duress of small groups of dominant men. Congress committed treason against the People, who were considered Sovereign under the Declaration of Independence and the organic Constitution."

THE DAY AMERICA LOST CONTROL
OF THE MONEY SYSTEM

It was in 1910 that House of Rothschild agent Jacob Schiff decided that the time had come for his seizure of our money system. His chief lieutenants in that seizure were Colonel Edward Mandell House whose entire career was that of chief executive and courier for Schiff, Bernard Barouk, and Herbert Lehman. In the fall of that year, they assembled in a secret conclave at the Jekyll Island Hunt Club, owned by J.P. Morgan at Jekyll Island, Georgia. Among those present were J.P. Morgan, John D. Rockefeller, Colonel House, Senator Nelson Aldrich, Schiff, Stillman and Vanderlip of the New York National City Bank, W. and J. Seligman, Eugene Myer, Bernard Baruch, Herbert Lehman and Paul Warburg—in short, all of the international bankers in America. A week later they emerged with what they called the Federal Reserve System. Senator Aldrich was tasked to railroad it through Congress, but they held

· ·
4   Here is the UN/WHO coding for Obamacare that include decapitation and other references that are bizarre. ICD 9 E 978 "Legal Execution."
https://www.truthandaction.org/obamacare-codes-legalized-executions-beheading-loss-privacy/

that railroading in abeyance for one chief reason. They would first have to plant their man, an obedient tool, in the White House to sign the Federal Reserve Act into law. They knew that even if the Senate would pass that act unanimously, the pro-antitrust President Taft would promptly veto it. So, they waited.

In 1912, their man, Woodrow Wilson, was elected to the presidency. Shortly after Wilson was inaugurated, Senator Aldrich railroaded the Federal Reserve Act through both houses of Congress and Wilson promptly signed it and the Federal Reserve Act became law. That heinous act of treason was committed on December 23, 1913, two days before Christmas when all the members of Congress, except for several carefully picked Representatives and three equally carefully picked Senators, were away from Washington. How treasonous was that act? Our founding fathers knew full well the corrupting power of money. They knew that whoever had that power held the destiny of our nation in his hands. Therefore, they carefully guarded this power when they set forth in the Constitution that Congress alone, the elected representatives of the people, would have the power. The Constitutional language on this point is brief, concise, and specific, stated in Article I, Section 8, Paragraph 5, defining the duties and powers of Congress "to coin money, regulate the value thereof, and of foreign coin, and the standard of weights and measures." But on that tragic, unforgettable day of infamy, December 23, 1913, the men who were sent to Washington to safeguard our interests, the Representatives and Senators and Woodrow Wilson, delivered the destiny of our nation into the hands of two aliens from Eastern Europe, Jacob Schiff and Paul Warburg. Warburg was a very recent immigrant who came here on orders from Rothschild for the express purpose of blueprinting that tragic Federal Reserve Act.[5]

JFK TRIED TO BREAK-UP THE CENTRAL BANK

Even before he was President, John F. Kennedy understood the predatory nature of private central banking. He understood why Andrew Jackson fought so hard to end the Second Bank of the United States. His father, Joseph Kennedy, was quoted as saying in the July 26th, 1936, issue of *The New York Times*: "Fifty men have run America, and that's a high figure." As President, JFK wrote and signed Executive Order 11110 which ordered the U.S. Treasury to issue a new public currency, the "United States Note." There were $5 and $2 notes just making it into circulation when he was assassinated in Dallas. These notes are highly-valued collector's items now, with a characteristic fringe of red ink, and with the omission of the name "Federal Reserve Note."

Kennedy was working with President Sukarno of Indonesia who was at that time the signatory for the Global Collateral Accounts. These were intended to be used for humanitarian purposes, but were subverted at the time of the Bretton Woods agreement at the end of WW II. The intention of Kennedy and Sukarno was to end the reign of the globalist privately-owned central banking system—which is the main reason that JFK was killed. Sukarno, for his part, remained under house arrest for the rest of his life.

The misperception was preserved, and even today the vast majority of the American people think that the Federal Reserve System is a United States Government-owned agency. That is positively false. All of the stock of the federal reserve banks is owned by the member banks and the heads of the member banks are all members of the hierarchy of the great Illuminati conspiracy known today as the Council on Foreign Relations.

THE UNITED STATES OF AMERICA, INC.

This private foreign-owned and off-shore corporation circa 1783, 1871, and re-incorporated again in 1925, that is owned and controlled by the international Rothschild

5 Mullins, Eustace, *The Secrets of the Federal Reserve*. Bridger House Publishers Inc., 1991.

bankster cartel, Crown Corp., and Vatican Incorporated, undertook an unlawful and covert bankruptcy of our nation in 1933 by FDR and the traitors in Congress.

What we can see now is that there is no lawful government—only a private foreign-owned off-shore corporation. Our nation is no longer under the Constitution of 1776, nor are the courts. We now suffer under the International Uniform Commercial Code (UCC), which does not recognize the rights granted to every citizen under the Constitution. Under the UCC, citizens have "granted privileges" that the corrupt system can change at any time without notice. Under the UCC, you are presumed guilty as an enemy of the corporate-state. Under the UCC, you are assumed to be owned as commercial property by the USA Inc. as a debt-slave to the international banksters.

"We the People," without our knowledge or contractual agreement, were collateralized and monetized as commercial property and soul-less corporate fictions to cover all debts incurred by this de facto fraudulent USA Inc., in 1933, which is still under the British Crown ownership and Virginia Trust Holding Company since 1606.

Under the private business charter for USA Inc., it clearly states that USA Inc., has no lawful authority, jurisdiction or lawful interstate nexus within the 50-state geographical landmass. This is clearly stated in the Washington D.C. Reorganization Act., which is also a private foreign-owned off-shore corporation. The horrible ugly truth is finally beginning to be exposed. It has been hidden from We the People since the inception of our so-called Constitutional Republic, ratified in 1789.

THE DEATH OF DEMOCRACY

In 1887, Alexander Tyler, a Scottish history professor at the University of Edinburgh, had this to say about the fall of the Athenian democracy some 2,200 years prior:

> *A democracy is always temporary in nature; it simply cannot exist as a permanent form of government. A democracy will continue to exist up until the time that voters discover that they can vote themselves generous gifts from the public treasury. From that moment on, the majority always votes for the candidates who promise the most benefits from the public treasury, with the result that every democracy will finally collapse over loose fiscal policy, (which is) always followed by a dictatorship.* [6]

Alexander Tyler continues:

> *The average age of the world's greatest civilizations from the beginning of history, has been about 200 years. During those 200 years, these nations always progressed through the following sequence: From bondage to spiritual faith; From spiritual faith to great courage; From courage to liberty; From liberty to abundance; From abundance to complacency; From complacency to apathy; From apathy to dependence; From dependence back into bondage.*

The illegal 2005 Supreme Court decision of Citizens United made it possible for the Israeli-American Sheldon Adelson organized crime magnate now operating out of Macao, China, to essentially buy control of both Houses of Congress in the 2008 election. This brought Congress under control of this International Crime Syndicate which specializes in human trafficking and narcotics, according to *Veterans Today* editor, Gordon Duff. Adelson stands accused of profiting off of prostitutes in his Macao casinos and taking huge billion-dollar profits. He could then can buy up the U.S. Congress, similar to past elections, all thanks to some notably deeply-compromised and owned U.S. Supreme Court Justices who passed the horrendous judgment that "Corporations have the same rights as citizens."

....

6   *World Truth.TV,* "The Top of the Pyramid: The Rothschilds, The British Crown and the Vatican Rule The World." **https://worldtruth.tv/the-top-of-the-pyramid-the-rothschilds-the-british-crown-and-the-vatican-rule-the-world/**

MONOPOLY MONEY

The U.S. dollar is a fiat currency, as is the UK's pound sterling, the euro and almost every other major currency. With no gold reserve to back them up, their value hinges on the people's belief that they hold worth. It is simply made up. So how does money get made? A private, for profit central bank prints it and lends it to the government (or other banks) at an interest rate. So, the Central Bank prints $100 and gives it to the government on the basis that it returns $101. You may have already spotted the first flaw in this process. The additional $1 can only ever come from the Central Bank. There is never enough money. The second issue is that all money then becomes debt. A brilliant scam, to be sure.

Wall Street and the City of London have run up phantom paper debts of more than ten times the annual earnings of the entire planet. It is a system designed to spectacularly crash at its end point. Not only can the Bankers (or governments) never pay it back, the combined earning power of the earth could not pay it back in less than ten years even if every last cent of our productive power went solely to pay off this debt. It is mathematically certain that someday it will come crashing down.

Fascist ideology consistently invokes a strong national currency and the primacy of the state. Leaders such as Benito Mussolini in Italy and Adolf Hitler in Germany embodied the state and claimed indisputable power. It advocates a mixed economy, with the principal goal of achieving autonomy to secure national self-sufficiency and independence through protectionist and interventionist economic policies.

Fascist movements emphasize a belligerent, virulent form of nationalism (chauvinism) and a distrust of foreigners (xenophobia), the latter closely linked to the ethnocentrism of many fascist movements. The typical fascist state also embraces militarism, a belief in the rigors and virtues of military life as an individual and national ideal, meaning much of public life was organized along military lines and an emphasis put on uniforms, parades, and monumental architecture.[7]

THE "SLOW KILL"

How many toxins can one take before death comes prematurely? Government agencies were set up to prevent us from harm, but have been bought out by the corporations they were designed to regulate. Our lives as Americans are directly threatened by the following corrupt and fraudulent agencies:

1. *The FDA is really the Fraud and Death Administration, which does not regulate sunscreen, yet skin is the largest organ of your body and absorbs chemicals such as BPA, parabens, triclosan, and fluoride.*

2. *The USDA is slowly killing you too by legalizing GMOs, Aspartame, Roundup, and pesticide residues on our food.*

3. *The Department of Defense is poisoning you with aluminum, barium, strontium and other toxins sprayed by airliners to combat "Solar Radiation Management." But really what it's for is weather manipulation.*

4. *The Department of Energy is slowly killing us with nuclear radiation from Three Mile Island (as with Chernobyl and Fukushima) from faulty General Electric reactors. The DoE has had free energy technology locked up for over a century and will not allow its release.*

5. *The FCC is killing you with 5G (Fifth Generation radiation), which is microwave radiation from cell phones, smart meters and WiFi routers. France and*

7   *World Future Fund:* http://www.worldfuturefund.org/wffmaster/Reading/Germany/mussolini.htm

Russia have outlawed WiFi in schools. Other European countries are soon to follow. Meanwhile in this country, the FCC refuses to test WiFi which delivers an even more lethal dose of radiation.

6. *The Department of Education is moving towards mandating vaccines which include mercury, aluminum, formaldehyde, squalene, SV40 and other live simian viruses.*

7. *The National Education Association (funded by the Rockefellers) gave large sums of money to colleges and inserted their own board members. Shortly thereafter, allopathic drugs became the focus of medical schools, not foods or herbs.*

AGENDA 21

In another example of government agency over-reach, "Agenda 21" was established in 1992 at the United Nations Conference on Environment and Development in Rio de Janeiro, Brazil. The conference was hosted by Maurice Strong, a Canadian oil and business billionaire and long-time front man for the Rothschilds and Rockefellers. Strong has been a leader of their exploit-the-environment-to-scam-the-people program which is now in full flow. Strong is a member of the Club of Rome, the corrupt environmental Hidden Hand in the Round Table network that includes the Bilderberg Group, the Trilateral Commission and the Council on Foreign Relations.

The central points of Agenda 21 were to demand and plot the central global control of all land; all private property; all water sources and distribution; all other resources which includes people in its definition; all energy supplies and distribution and all food production and distribution. Agenda 21 is called "the agenda for the 21st century," and that agenda most certainly refers to global fascism/communism. The goals have since been updated in "Agenda 2030."

This is a summary of what Agenda 21, in the name of sustainable development and biodiversity, is seeking to impose. This includes an end to national sovereignty and state planning and management of all land resources, ecosystems, deserts, forests, mountains, oceans and fresh water; agriculture; rural development; biotechnology; and ensuring "equity." It also calls for the State to "define the role" of business and financial resources, such as the abolition of private property because it's not "sustainable."

Reading between the lines, there is also a call for "restructuring" the family unit, suggesting children be raised by the State. There will be major restrictions on movement of travel and creation of "human settlement zones." There will be mass resettlement as people are forced to vacate land where they currently live. People will be told what their job will be. There will also be a dumbing down of education, which is currently being achieved. And lastly, a mass global depopulation, in pursuit of all the above. Researcher Julian Websdale describes it further:

> *This horrific plan is being coordinated through the United Nations, the stalking horse for world dictatorship, via a non-governmental network once called the International Council of Local Environmental Initiatives (ICLEI), and now known as Local Governments for Sustainability although still using the shortened name ICLEI. The United Nations is now opening "embassies" around the world called "UN Houses" under the guise of raising awareness of UN activities, but not the activities that people really need to know about. They have opened one in Hunter Square, Edinburgh, Scotland, for example.*

> *Local Governments for Sustainability (ICLEI) and other organizations are integrating the plan into every village, town, city and region and it is already*

becoming widespread across the world. The organizational infrastructure of Agenda 21 is already at fantastic proportions, and involves government agencies, non-governmental organizations (NGOs), think-tanks, trusts, foundations, "training" (mind control) operations and "initiatives" which have been building the infrastructure for what they call "the post-industrial, post-democratic" society—all while the public go about their daily business, oblivious of the prison being built all around them by the hour.[8]

THE FORBIDDEN LANDS

The United Nations Wildlands Project is a plan to rewild over 50% of America and make it off limits to humans. The concept of forbidden zones is nothing new. Agenda 21 has a similar concept laid out to protect the planet from the people. For those unfamiliar with the United Nations Agenda 21 "sustainable development" plan, writer and anti-Agenda 21 activist Rosa Koire describes it as this:

In a nutshell, the plan calls for governments to take control of all land use and not leave any of the decision making in the hands of private property owners. It is assumed that people are not good stewards of their land and the government will do a better job if they are in control. Individual rights in general are to give way to the needs of communities as determined by the governing body. Another program, called the Wildlands Project, spells out how most of the land is to be set aside for non-humans.

The Wildlands Project came out of the United Nations Convention on Biological Diversity the year before Agenda 21 was adopted at the 1992 U.N. Rio Summit. Chapter 15 of the initial Agenda 21 document from the 1992 Rio Summit is titled "Conservation of Biological Diversity" and begins like this:

The objectives and activities in this chapter of Agenda 21 are intended to improve the conservation of biological diversity and the sustainable use of biological resources, as well as to support the Convention on Biological Diversity. "Sustainability" is one of the key buzzwords Agenda 21 uses to justify this huge takeover and consolidation, not just of populations, but of power. The description for The World in 2050 *starts with this:*

The world's population is exploding, wild species are vanishing, our environment is degrading, and the costs of resources from oil to water are going nowhere but up. So, what kind of world are we leaving for our children and grandchildren?

Curiously (or tellingly), the year before Agenda 21 was being adopted, the Club of Rome published *The First Global Revolution*, stating:

In searching for a new enemy to unite us, we came up with the idea that pollution, the threat of global warming, water shortages, famine and the like, would fit the bill. In their totality and in their interactions these phenomena do constitute a common threat which demands the solidarity of all peoples. ...All these dangers are caused by human intervention and it is only through changed attitudes and behavior that they can be overcome. The real enemy, then, is humanity itself.

It is interesting that the year 2050 is the same year as the Rockefeller Foundation-funded, Agenda 21-based America 2050, the plan to double population in 11 dense, tightly controlled urban mega-regions across the USA.[9]

• •

8 Websdale, Julian, "Agenda 21: The Plan for a Global Fascist Dictatorship." **http://wakeup-world.com/2014/08/05/agenda-21-the-plan-for-a-global-fascist-dictatorship/**

9 Dykes, Aaron & Melissa, Truthstream Media Future Earth Agenda 21s *Forbidden Zones*.

STEPPING OUT OF THE MATRIX

Orwell once told us, "in a time of universal deceit, telling the truth is a revolutionary act." It's also true that in an age of corporate globalism enforced by the American Empire, lies and deception are precisely how the power elite gets what it wants. It is how that elite controls us for its enrichment. It's bad enough that we pay these people to be lied to, that we pay them to destroy entire nations in our name. It's even worse that so many of us are even now not awake to that fact. In the movie *The Matrix*, Morpheus states:

> *Have you ever had a dream, Neo, that you were so sure was real? What if you were unable to wake from that dream? How would you know the difference between the dream world and the real world?*

We have consistently been called "conspiracy theorists" throughout the COVID event by government bureaucrats and the media. But, we were were right about almost everything, and the mainstream media has been wrong about almost everything. Either that, or they have been knowingly lying about almost everything. In the neo-fascist world they've even made it *legal* to propagandize the people with fake news. In the USA, this was done in 2013 by stripping away the last of the "truth in media" laws when the Smith-Mundt Act was "reformed," fully allowing the CIA to disseminate propaganda. The CIA's long term effort to completely control the news media with Operation Mockingbird had shifted into overdrive.

But as bad as things are, they can improve. Look around. You will see signs of it everywhere. People who are waking up. People who realize that their newspapers and TV news are lying to them. People who know their governments do not have their best intersts in mind. It is our job to strip away the illusions we have been fed, and to begin the arduous but rewarding task of telling truth to power.

On June 4, 1963, President John F. Kennedy signed Executive Order 11110, authorizing the U.S. Treasury to issue paper currency that could be redeemed for silver held by the treasury. As a result, this U.S. currency was printed in denominations of $2 and $5 and inscribed with the words "United States Note" instead of "Federal Reserve Note."

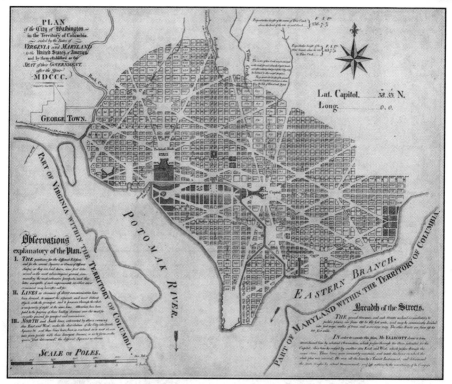

This 1792 map (published by Hill) entitled "Plan of the City of Washington" shows the street layout of the city in its early development. You can see the U.S. capital and the "President's House." This is when the plan of the "City of Washington, in the Territory of Columbia" was to be ceded, but at the time this map was made, it was still a part of the states of Virginia and Maryland.

Kennedy's order was intended to wean the Federal Reserve System away from printing money, beginning a smooth transition toward returning the printing press to the hands of the American government.

SOCIAL SECURITY NUMBER FACTS

1.) AREA NUMBER

The "AREA NUMBER" is the first 3 digits, assigned by geographical region. Prior to 1973, cards were issued in Social Security offices around the country and the area number represented the office code where the card was issued. This DID NOT necessarily have to be in the area where the applicant lived, since a person could apply for their card in any Social Security office.

Since 1973, when the SSA began assigning SSN's and issuing cards centrally from "BALTIMORE", the area number ASSIGNED has been based on the ZIP CODE in the mailing address provided on the application for the ORIGINAL Social Security card. The applicant's mailing address does NOT have to be the same as their place of residence. Thus, the area number DOES NOT necessarily represent the state of residence of the applicant regardless of whether the card was issued prior to, or after, 1973.

2.) Group Number

The middle 2 digits are the GROUP NUMBER. The group numbers range from 01 to 99. However, they are not assigned in consecutive order. For administrative reasons, group numbers are issued in the following order:

1.) Odd numbers from 01 through 09
2.) Even numbers from 10 through 98
3.) Even numbers from 02 through 08
4.) Odd numbers from 11 through 99

As an example, group numbers 98 is issued before 11

The slow but very real progression into fascism as charted by the Lego police officer. Perception of a new reality takes time, often many years, but then a new generation comes to believe this is the way it has always been.

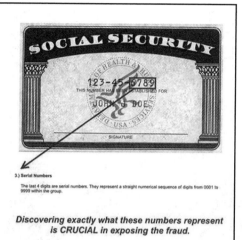

3.) Serial Numbers

The last 4 digits are serial numbers. They represent a straight numerical sequence of digits from 0001 to 9999 within the group.

Discovering exactly what these numbers represent is CRUCIAL in exposing the fraud.

Up to and including 1913, the United States added numerous private laws to its books that facilitated the increase of subjects and property for the United States Corporation. The 14th Amendment provided for a new class of citizens: "United States citizens," which had not formerly been recognized. Until the 14th Amendment in 1868, there were no persons born or naturalized in the United States. They had all been born or naturalized in one of the several states. Up until that point in time, there was only state citizenship. After the Civil War, a new class of citizenship was recognized, and was the beginning of the "democracy" (not the *de jure* republic) sited in the District of Columbia. The American people in the republic located in the several states could choose to benefit (receive a benefit) as one of these new United States citizens *by choice* (kind of). This initial nexus for this new citizenship started with the birth certificate under the provisions of the Sheppard-Towner Maternity and Infancy Protection Act of 1921. This act required that all children born be registered by way of a certificate of live birth, in exchange for which they would receive back a birth certificate describing the property. The specific provisions of the act required that the statement of domicile of the property described on the birth certificate would be Washington, D.C. This Act was ruled unconstitutional in 1922; yet it continued in force until 1929 when it was repealed. Now it is most important to note that the provisions for birth registration as contained in the Sheppard-Towner Maternity and Infancy Protection Act were dropped virtually unchanged into the body of the Social Security Act of 1935. It is also equally important to note that most people readily interchange residency and domicile believing they are one and the same. They are not. Residency is where are you are currently living and domicile is superior in that it is where you ultimately intend to return and is the venue of law by which you declare to be bound. Domicile gets really interesting when you learn the United States is a British corporation established by the Act of 1871 wherein: Effectively and legally, the United States is a Corporation and its judiciary operates under Emergency International Maritime Law (hence the gold fringe around the flag in the forum as our public notice).

Did you know that when you are born in the USA, your parents register you with the government AS A CORPORATION by receiving and signing a birth certificate? In a few years, you as a Corporation will receive a taxpayer ID# called a Social Security number. This is so you can be used as COLLATERAL for the government to acquire debt. You heard that right, YOU and your labor, time and energy is what backs up the National Debt. You are a stock.

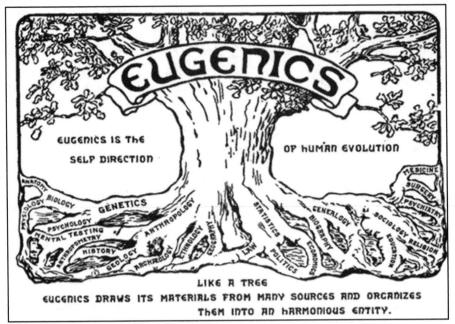

In 1948 Julian Huxley, brother of author Aldous Huxley, argued at the United Nations that we can no longer support eugenics, because Hitler made it unacceptable. However, he stated, we can use conservation to the same effect. At the end of World War II, where they were openly exposing Nazi ideals covered up as so-called ecological necessity.

It is very important to understand that eugenics is not only just about population reduction. It is ultimately about controlling which characteristics are expressed in human society by breeding certain desired characteristics into the gene pool and breeding undesired characteristics out of the gene pool. Survival of the selected.

THE OCCULT
AND FASCISM

"The underlying, primary psychic reality is so inconceivably complex that it can be grasped only at the farthest reach of intuition, and then but very dimly. That is why it needs symbols." –Carl Jung

A "global elite" have always existed, whether it be the aristocracy in ancient Greece and Rome, the church in the Middle Ages and beyond, or the "deep state" politics of today. Perhaps the elite bloodline families have indeed continued to preserve their stranglehold over the human race, flooding us with misinformation, controlling our perception of the world, and dictating what type of life we should desire. We are like robots, encouraged to fit the mold and do the same things. There is a complete control over the human race, and to think that Black Magic could be used to control the masses is disturbing.

The occult is employed in a new kind of fascism today among some of the elite globalists, who completely control almost every aspect of our lives, from health and finance to politics and education. There are politicians and other public figures who are involved in these types of things, for various reasons, but they rank low in the hierarchy. Research indicates that occult ceremonies and rituals at the upper levels go far beyond what anyone can imagine. In the most basic terms, occult simply means "hidden."

Why is it so hard to believe that occult practices are a real tool for control? Perhaps because our understanding of the limits of reality is controlled by the very same people accused of these practices. As Manly P. Hall writes in his epic book, *The Secret Teachings of All Ages,* "The masses, deprived of their birthright of understanding and groveling in ignorance, eventually became the abject slaves of the spiritual impostors. Superstition universally prevailed and the black magicians completely dominated national affairs, with the result that humanity still suffers from the sophistries of the priestcrafts of Atlantis and Egypt."[1] Manly P. Hall also noted in *The Lion's Roar*: "When the human race learns the language of symbolism, a great veil will fall from the eyes of men." This "ceremonial magic" is essentially the use of rituals and techniques to invoke and control "spirits," or lifeforms, that could be existing within other dimensions or worlds. For example, according to Manly P. Hall:

> *A magician, enveloped in sanctified vestments and carrying a wand inscribed with hieroglyphic figures, could by the power vested in certain words and symbols control the invisible inhabitants of the elements and of the astral world. While the elaborate ceremonial magic of antiquity was not necessarily evil, there arose from its perversion several false schools of sorcery, or black magic.*

OCCULT FASCISM COMES TO THE USA

Are we being mentally conditioned to accept our servitude? Have occult practices contributed to the elite controllers having a wider concentration of power over our minds? False flag terror events have become mainstay in Europe and the USA, and are performed to achieve a specific agenda. The philosopher and author, Gavin Nascimento, who has been censored on social media platforms, made this observation: "The illiterate of the 21st century will not be those who cannot read or write, but those who cannot unlearn the many lies that they have been conditioned to believe, and seek out the hidden knowledge that they have been conditioned to reject."

In the dualistic world in which we live, there are two types of occult rituals. White magic deals with the noble and morally pure, and cannot be used to accomplish selfish ends. Ego, greed, and personal desire have no place in white magic. Black magic, on the other hand, uses inverted symbolism, and uses pure symbols with noble meanings and perverts them for an opposite advantage. Inverted symbolism seems to be the way to invoke spirits for malevolent purposes. Among the information uncovered by Wikileaks was an invitation to Clinton campaign chairman, John Podesta, to attend a "Spirit Cooking Dinner." This was a dark sacrament practiced by Aleister Crowley in which a "Cake of Light," that included honey, oil, menstrual blood and sperm, would be baked and eaten.[2]

Looking into various subjects, from MK-Ultra and other forms of mind control to the information coming out from whistleblowers and cabal insiders, the use of ceremonial magic for perverse reasons by the elite is really not that far-fetched. Although scary to contemplate, it does happen. Those whom we consider our leaders, those in positions of great power, those behind the global corporatocracy we see today and the propaganda we're all subject to, could all be guided by "spirits" from places we have yet to learn about. And as a result, the massive manipulation of humanity could be guided by these "demonic" entities.[3] In the Modern Era, Western occult practices originated in European nations, and in turn, these practices made their way "across the pond" to afflict the USA. And while a multitude of examples of its use date back millennia, the following are some classic cases of Western occultism being employed in the last few centuries, and note how it still affects us to this day.

JOHN DEE AND HIS CRYSTAL BALL

The reign of Elizabeth I of England (who was the daughter of Henry VIII and Ann Boleyn) was an era of open borders and open minds. It became known as the Elizabethan era. The period is famous for the flourishing of English drama, led by playwrights such as William Shakespeare and Christopher Marlowe, and for the seafar-

••••••••••••••••••••••••••••••••

1   Hall, Manly P. *The Secret Teachings of All Ages*. Philosophical Research Society. 2008.

2   Walia, Arjun, "How some of the world's elite use black magic rituals to conjure up entities for more power." *Collective Evolution.com*; November 1, 2017.

3   DuQuette, Lon Milo, *The Key to Solomon's Key*. 2nd ed. CCC Publishing, 2010.

ing prowess of English adventurers such as Sir Francis Drake. The court of Elizabeth I retained Sir Francis Bacon as her legal counsel, and John Dee as an astrologer advisor. John Dee was a mathematician, astronomer and philosopher, and was the first to introduce "spy craft" and occult sciences to the Crown. Dee was an ardent promoter of mathematics and a respected astronomer, as well as a leading expert in navigation, having trained many of those who would conduct England's voyages of discovery.

John Dee was also the quintessential sorcerer. Using crystals and mirrors, Dee was allegedly able to communicate with various spirit guides, who (in 1597) famously instructed him in to urge Elizabeth I to restrain from a naval response when the Spanish armada was beginning to surround England for invasion. Just before a major landing was to occur, an unusually strong storm descended and scattered most of the armada. The storm forced Spain into a hasty retreat, never to attempt invasion again.

Along with his efforts advising Elizabeth I, Dee immersed himself in the worlds of sorcery, astrology and Hermetic philosophy. He devoted much time and effort in the last 30 years of his life to attempting to commune with angels in order to learn the universal language of creation.[4] John Dee is considered (more or less) the father of Western espionage. Both the British MI5 and MI6, as well as the CIA, looked to his original communications with other-worldly entities which could intercede on behalf of their "clients," as a psychic-level advantage over adversaries.

In the century following the Age of Enlightenment, just as the West began to colonize the East through trade and conquest, the Eastern occult practices quietly began to invade the West, first through the stories of sailors and merchants, then through authors and philosophers. The superior communications of the West enabled a speedy transmission of ideas. The 19th century German philosopher, Arthur Schopenhauer, is among the East's first messengers, but its most active propagandist was another extraordinary personage, Madame Blavatsky.

THEOSOPHY

Helena Petrovna Blavatsky was born in the Ukraine in 1831. After various wanderings and adventures, including marriage, she landed in New York in 1873. There she proclaimed an interest in, and knowledge of, Eastern esoteric doctrines. In New York she met Colonel Henry Steel Olcott, and with his assistance founded the Theosophical Society two years later. Its avowed aim was the study of "hidden wisdom," thought to be an unfashionable pursuit even back then; yet it still survives today. In 1878, Madame Blavatsky and Colonel Olcott sailed to India, where the Theosophical Society met with unexpected success. After some years of acclaim, and then a series of scandals involving allegations that Blavatsky's boasted mediumistic powers were fraudulent, she returned to Europe, where she died in 1891.

After her death, the Theosophical Society fell into the hands of Anna Kingsford and Edward Maitland and continued to flourish. Then treachery intervened and public ridicule was the result. Annie Besant and C. W. Leadbeater produced a bogus World Messiah, Krishnamurti, who eventually publicly repudiated the role thrust upon him. This brought Theosophy into a richly deserved ridicule from which it never fully recovered, though even today it has a considerable following.

The Theosophical Society was, and is, of little consequence in itself. It is significant only insofar as it transmitted on a very large scale the doctrines contained in Madame Blavatsky's astonishing books, *Isis Unveiled* (1877) and *The Secret Doctrine* (1888). Madame Blavatsky went so far as to claim that the composition of her books was assisted by clairvoyance, and that obscure works and quotations had suddenly appeared in obe-

4 Zagami, Leo Lyon, *Confessions of an Illuminati, Volume I: The Whole Truth About the Illuminati and the New World Order.* 2nd ed. CCC Publishing, 2019.

dience to her needs and desires. She claimed that she was familiar with "the oldest book in the world," the incalculably ancient text of Tibetan origin, *Stanzas of Dzyan*, which formed the basis for *The Secret Doctrine*. She also maintained that the Hidden or Invisible Masters were in regular communication with her personally.

The fact remains that Madame Blavatsky's writings had influence far beyond that which is usually assigned to them. They challenged Christianity, which Blavatsky loathed, and she proclaimed in its stead a Westernized Hinduism, with its attractive doctrines of reincarnation and karma. Her writings led people to seek alternatives to the Christian religion, and to suspect the existence of non-material occult forces as mysterious and intangible as electricity, thus preparing the way in the popular mind for future scientific investigation.

Although Theosophy taught that the use of ceremonial magic to aid evolution was dangerous and to be eschewed, it also was to have a renaissance, aided partly by an increasing acceptance of theosophical doctrines. The Eastern esoteric tradition began to pervade the West at roughly the same time that the West's own slumbering esoteric tradition began to awaken. The West's esoteric tradition was an amalgam of lore drawn from the magic of Egypt and Chaldea, the Hebrew Qabalah, the Tarot, Rosicrucianism, Freemasonry, and the works of medieval magicians, wizards and alchemists.[5]

NIETZSCHE'S SUPERMAN

The philosopher Friedrich Nietzsche (1844-1900) is most famous for his view that the existence of most people is so pitiful an affair that one could define existence as suffering, creating an "existential nihilism" that life has no intrinsic meaning or value. But looking further into his ideas, he also affirmed that for those with "eyes to see," existence was joy. He maintained that one could enjoy the actual physical experience of will power, and one who did so permanently would be the next stage in humankind's evolution, the *Übermensch*, or "Superman."

In his books *Thus Spake Zarathustra, Beyond Good and Evil, Twilight of the Idols, The Will to Power* and other works of genius, Nietzsche reduced the edifices of previous philosophers to rubble. He despised mediocrity, equality, democracy and pacifism. He exalted ecstasy, elites, Supermen and struggle. He prophesied the advent of the Superman and of a master race of Supermen, but, contrary to popular opinion, he despised Germans as conforming maniacs and despaired of their evolutionary possibilities. Nevertheless, Adolf Hitler seized upon Nietzsche's *Übermensch* concept of the Germanic people, holding them up as the master race.

Nietzsche concentrated his attack upon the values which his world held to be absolute, and famously declared that there was no such thing as good or evil, but all values are relative in the eye of the beholder. Beyond limitations like good and evil is the will—that people must overcome themselves, their values and limitations, and identify with their free will. Then the individual will achieve the goal, which is to be the Superman.

Whereas Nietzsche taught that the Superman is the imminent next stage in human evolution, Blavatsky announced that Supermen already existed, that they were the Hidden Masters who inhabited Central Asia, and that they could be contacted telepathically by those who had been initiated into their mysteries. Whereas the chemists and physicists taught that there was little more to learn about a universe of matter, Blavatsky insisted that there was much more to learn about a universe of spirit, which could act upon the former. And whereas biologists taught that man evolved from the apes, Blavatsky proclaimed that there have been four root races prior to our own, which included the ancient civilizations of lost Lemuria and Atlantis; that evolution has been assisted by divine kings from the stars, that the Aryans are the purest of the fifth root race, and, more

5   Pauwels, L. & Bergier, J., *The Dawn of Magic*, Granada Publishing Ltd; Panther, London, 1964.

sinisterly, that the Jews are a degenerate link between the fourth and fifth root races, and hence are sub-human, a proposition with which Adolf Hitler concurred.

Hitler took from Nietzsche concepts of evolution, the Will to Power, and the Superman, but forgot Nietzsche's insistence that the Superman overcomes not others, but himself. It should not be surprising that Hitler was also part of this occult renaissance. For his reading told him that by a one-pointed concentration of the will, whether by turning inward (yoga) or outward (magic), he could attain a mystic vision of the universe, become the Superman and fulfill his every desire.

Adolf Hitler thought that the only true species of humans, the species with potential for human evolution, were the Aryan people. He followed Blavatsky in believing that the Aryans had originated through a mutation in the latter days of Atlantis. Shortly before the catastrophic floods which submerged that fabulous civilization, Manu, the last of the Atlantean Supermen, had led the Aryans across Europe and Asia to the Gobi Desert, and thence to the mountains of Tibet. The descendants of these Aryans subsequently colonized the world and created civilization anew, but were poisoned by the creed of Judeo-Christianity and by race-pollution, and, furthermore, lost their magical faculties, which it became the task of the Führer to reawaken.

Not all the Aryans had allowed their faculties to atrophy, however, as some had stayed in Tibet and their descendants had retained the ancient wisdom. These were the present-day Hidden Masters and Unknown Supermen, who preserved the occult secrets of Initiation. It is through this distortion of the works of Blavatsky and Nietzsche that Hitler could become the most infamous fascist dictator the world has ever known, and enlist a gullible German people into the atrocities of World War II.

IN SEARCH OF VRIL

In the early 1900s, there were a variety of secret/occult societies in Germany, the main ones being the Bavarian Illuminati, the Freemasons, the Rosicrucians, the Thule Society and the Vril Society. Each of these five societies, although all based in secrecy and mysticism, had its particular role and function. Of these five, two were especially noted for their occult connections—the Vril Society and its purely German offshoot, the Thule Society.

The first society was formed in 1917. Located in Munich, it was a melting pot of many orders. In 1921, Hitler was engaged as an orator and, inspired by the beliefs of the Thule Society, his plan for a thousand-year Reich was born. The Vril Society, formed in 1919, was an offshoot of the Thule Society. This group included mediums and experts on ancient philosophies and scripts, particularly those of the Sumerians and Babylonians. There were also two scientists who were well versed in alternative energies. It was their aim to communicate with luminaries from the past and even to travel in time.

The Vril emblem was the "Black Sun"—a secret philosophy thousands of years old, which provided the foundation on which the occult practitioners of the Third Reich would later build. The Black Sun symbol can be found in many Babylonian and Assyrian places of worship. It stood for the godhead's inner light in the form of a cross.

The Vril Force or Vril Energy was said to be derived from the Black Sun, a big ball of "Prima Materia" which supposedly exists in the center of the Earth, giving light to the *Vril-ya* and putting out radiation in the form of Vril. The Vril Society believed that Aryans were the actual biological ancestors of the Black Sun.

With important information supposedly channeled from the extraterrestrials, the Vril society eventually built the Vril Machine, which was a saucer-shaped machine that was an interdimensional or time travel machine. This craft was called the *Jenseitsflugmas-*

chine or "Other World Flight Machine." The Thule and Vril societies used their members in the German business community to raise funds for the construction of this machine under the code letters J-F-M. By 1922, parts for the machine began arriving independently from various industrial sources paid in full by the Thule and Vril.[6]

VRIL SOCIETY

The Luminous Lodge, or Vril Society was founded in 1917 when four people interested in the occult met in a cafe in Vienna, Austria. There was one woman and three men. The woman was an avowed "spiritual medium." They met under a veil of mystery and secrecy. They discussed secret revelations, the coming of the new age, the Spear of Destiny, the magical violet black stone, and making contact with ancient ancestors living underground or those from distant worlds. Their source of power was the *Schwarze Sonne* or "Black Sun," an infinite beam of light which, though invisible to the human eye, exists in anti-matter. The Vril named themselves after the ancient Sumerian word *Vri-Il*, meaning "God-like."

The next year, a group of Vril psychic channelers, mostly women who let their hair grow long, began meeting regularly over the border in an old Bavarian hunting lodge near Berchtesgaden, Germany. The psychic women were known as the *Vrilerinnen* and were headed by Maria Orsich. The Society allegedly taught concentration exercises designed to awaken the forces of Vril, and their main goal was to achieve *raumflug* or "spaceflight" to reach Aldebaran, a star system from which the psychic channelers had received communications. To achieve the building aspects of the craft, the Vril Society joined the *Thule Gesellschaft* to fund an ambitious program involving an inter-dimensional flight machine based on psychic revelations from the Aldebaran ET channel sessions. These psychic mediums eventually aided the Nazis in the development of several versions of anti-gravity flying discs. The smaller discs, named the "Vril discs" because of their use of this mysterious energy source, are given an origin as inventions of the Vril Society, a subset of the Thule Society. Three counter-rotating magnetic fields, one on top of the other, would supply the lift.

The Vril emblem became the Black Sun, said to represent secret philosophies over a thousand years old, and provided the esoteric foundation on which the occult practitioners of the Third Reich would later be built. The leading advocate of the Vril Society was Karl Haushofer, one of Germany's foremost experts on the Far East. Early members of the Vril Society are said to have included Adolf Hitler, Alfred Rosenberg, Rudolf Hess, Heinrich Himmler, Hermann Göring, and Hitler's personal physician, Dr. Theodor Morell. These were among the original members of the Thule Society, after they joined Vril in 1919. One year later, Thulist Dr. Krohn helped to create the Nazi flag, an emblem that linked Eastern and Western occultism.

In common with the vast majority of occultists, Heinrich Himmler accepted the theory of reincarnation. At a speech made in Dachau in 1936, he informed high-ranking SS officers that they had all met before, in previous lives, and that after their present lives ended, they would meet again. Himmler thought that he himself was the reincarnation of a ninth-century personality, King Heinrich the Fowler, whom he also claimed as a distant ancestor. He revered the memory of the first of the Saxon kings, who had defeated a Polish invasion from the east, and he referred to his tomb in Quedlinburg Cathedral as "a sacred spot" to which "we Germans make pilgrimage."

THULE SOCIETY

The *Thule Gesellschaft*, or "Thule Society" taught a system of personal empowerment based upon a joining between *völkisch* occultism, and the teachings of Arab

6   Swartz, Tim R., *Admiral Byrd's Secret Journey Beyond the Poles.* Global Communications, 2007.

mystics picked up in the Middle East and North Africa. At the time, Karl Haushofer introduced the group to the wisdom of Gurdjieff, derived from Sufi mystics and Tibetan lamas, as well as the Zen mysticism of the Japanese Green Dragon Society. These teachings stressed the existence of certain centers of power, or chakras, in the human body which correspond to the endocrine glands of Western science. In most human beings, these chakras are dormant, but they can be activated by yoga exercises to bring the practitioner some rather unusual powers, most notably that of being able to impose one's will upon others. The student is usually taught to resist this temptation, but Haushofer had little interest in ethics.

Concurrently, the psychics of the Vril Society allegedly channeled high technology blueprints from advanced beings, after which the Thule Society was created to implement the designs. They went on to build something called the Vril Machine. It allegedly was a saucer-shaped interdimensional time travel machine. A German writer, John von Helsing, describes the discovery of a crashed saucer in the Black Forest in 1936 and says that this technology was taken and combined with the information the Vril Society had received through channeling and was made into a further project called the Haunebu. With Hitler in power in 1933, both Thule and Vril Societies allegedly received official state backing for continued disc development programs aimed at both spaceflight and possibly a war machine. After 1941, Adolph Hitler officially forbade secret societies, so both Thule and Vril became documented under the SS E-IV unit.

The dye was cast to begin classifying state secrets. In the spring of 1934, Berlin's police chief banned all forms of fortune telling. There followed a confiscation of occult books throughout Germany, and many booksellers of the esoteric were "persuaded" to sell something else. Freemasonry was exposed, and even Rudolf von Sebottendorff, founder of the *Thule Gesellschaft*, discovered to his astonishment that he was now *persona non grata*. His book, *Bevor Hitler Kam*, and his lectures, both of which revealed the occult origins of Nazism and the influence of the Thulists, led to his arrest and imprisonment. Soon all Sebottendorf's writings were suppressed and the Thule Group was dissolved. Even a former membership in the group and in the German Order was made a disqualification for holding office. Sebottendorff was eventually released only on condition that he leave the Reich and promise to keep silent about the Nazis' occult connections.

The Gestapo was unleashed upon the few remaining astrologers, mystics and occultists outside the SS (*Schutzstaffel*, meaning "Protection Squadron"), who, it was thought, might have influenced Deputy *Führer* Rudolf Hess's May, 10th 1941, solo flight to Scotland. One of those soon arrested was Karl Haushofer. Although he was eventually released, this demonstrates Haushofer's lack of personal influence on the Führer by 1941. Hitler no longer had any time for men with independent minds, so the Professor was of no more use to him. He lived on, encouraging from the sidelines the movement he had played so significant a part in spawning. Its ultimate failure would break him.[7] On the night of 10-11, March 1946, Karl Haushofer committed suicide when he drank arsenic with his wife, who would then hang herself.

In the waning days of the war, Hitler was quoted as cryptically saying "in this war there does not exist victors or vanquished, only the dead and living, but the last battalion will be a German battalion." It should be noted that after the conclusion of World War II, the SS did not surrender, nor did the Third Reich disband. SS officers would go on to escape through the various "rat lines;" some were recruited to work for the Soviets, the UK, and the "Project Paperclip" scientists and officers in the USA. They were still loyal to their *völkisch* origins, and would go on to become the *Dritte Macht* or "Third Power," establishing a Fourth Reich, which has implications that continue to this day.

•••••••••••••••••••••••••••••••
7   Spence, Lewis, *The Occult Causes of the Present War*. London, 1940.

SS AHNENERBE

The stamp of the Grand Master's obsession with the esoteric was revealed even more plainly in one of the major departments of the SS, the *Ahnenerbe*, or Ancestral Heritage Department. This had its origins in an occult society founded in 1933 by Friedrich Hielscher. In 1935, as *Reichsführer* of the SS, Himmler made the *Ahnenerbe* an official organization. It was secretive and attached to the *Schutzstaffel*, under the direction of Hermann Wirth, the author of the *Uralinda Chronicle*. Himmler considered Wirth to be an expert on Aryan prehistory. A friend of Karl Haushofer, Wirth was an occultist whose cranky obsessions caused even Himmler to question the wisdom of the appointment. But under his leadership, the *Ahnenerbe* recruited every expert on occultism whom it considered useful from the debris of the magical Orders which the Nazis had banned.

In 1939, the *Ahnenerbe* was turned into a full department of the SS, and Wirth was eventually replaced by SS Colonel Wolfram Sievers, a black-bearded occultist, who was eventually tried at Nuremberg and sentenced to death by hanging. Under Sievers's direction, the *Ahnenerbe* organization grew swiftly until it numbered 50 branches. Extraordinarily enough, Germany spent more money on the researches of the *Ahnenerbe* than the USA did on its first atomic bomb project. What exactly did the *Ahnenerbe* do? Authors Pauwels and Bergier in *The Morning of the Magicians* have revealed the bizarre truth:

> *These researches ranged from strictly scientific activities to the practice of occultism, and from vivisection practised on prisoners to espionage on behalf of the secret societies. Negotiations were entered into with Skorzeny with a view to stealing the Holy Grail, and Himmler created a special section for the collection of information "in the sphere of the supernatural.*

When the German troops were evacuating Naples, Italy, in the waning days of WW II, Himmler gave repeated orders that they should not forget to take away with them the enormous tombstone of the last Hohenstaufen Emperor. In 1943, after the fall of Mussolini, the Reichsführer summoned the six greatest experts in Germany on occultism to a villa in the outskirts of Berlin to discover the place where the Duce was being held as prisoner. Meetings of the General Staff began with yoga concentration exercises. Mussolini's position was discovered, and a daring raid led by Otto Skorzeny extracted the prisoner, and for a short while Mussolini was free, but would be captured again and executed.

When German bombers failed to damage Oxford, England, the *Ahnenerbe* immediately investigated what they believed to be the magically-protective powers of the city's cathedral bells. Himmler displayed an intense and earnest interest in all of these activities. Of still greater importance to him were the activities of the *Ahnenerbe*'s "Institute of scientific research for national defense," which performed medical experiments on living human beings which were based upon the craziest occult speculations. Experiments included: high altitude simulation tests, the pressure of which caused victims to go mad before dying in acute agony; freezing experiments, in which men and women were frozen alive, after which various methods of reviving them were sometimes put to the test; vivisection without anesthetics; the sterilization of Jews by irradiating their testicles and ovaries with X-rays; and the amassing of a large collection of Jewish skulls and skeletons for study.

Friedrich Hielscher has rightly been described as "one of the most mysterious figures of the twentieth century," for he may have influenced the SS on a scale far greater than is usually ascribed to him. Unfortunately, much more research is required before we can ascertain the precise importance of Hielscher, though there is no doubt that he was indeed the spiritual mentor of SS Colonel Sievers, head of the *Ahnenerbe*. When Sievers was tried at Nuremberg, Hielscher gave evidence on his behalf, making intentionally absurd racial and political statements. He asked if he could accompany Sievers to the gallows, and this favor was granted, without anyone realizing Hielscher's true motive. Within the confines of the condemned cell, the two magicians proceeded to intone the prayers of their secret cult. Sievers, who had shown no sign of remorse during the trial, then went peacefully to his death, while his teacher returned to permanent obscurity.[8]

DIVINATION

The Thule Society, which insisted on measuring the skulls of prospective candidates to ensure they were of Aryan origin, also attached great importance to the study of runes. They were also fascinated with the sagas of the Teutonic tribes, along with *Völkisch* occultism. It was within the confines of the expanding ranks of the *Schutzstaffel* that Nazism found its most concentrated and essential expression, for this Order fulfilled almost every one of the ideals which obsessed Adolf Hitler.

The man responsible for implementing Hitler's dreams was the most sinister figure of the Third Reich after Hitler himself, Heinrich Himmler, Reichsführer SS, who, like Hitler, united in his personality that curious combination of the banal and the demonic which we have noticed in other leading Nazis. A perfect bureaucrat, devoid of all traces of emotion, Himmler's grand passion was nevertheless, the occult.

Heinrich Himmler relied for his advancement upon an unquestioning loyalty to Hitler, an uncritical devotion to Nazism, and unexciting but thoroughly conscientious bureaucratic skills. A chicken farmer by profession, his polite but stern manner reminded observers of an elementary schoolteacher. Although he had joined the Nazis in 1923, they paid little attention to the dutiful little nonentity. Eventually, Hitler found him a job in 1929, as Commander of a very small organization known as the SS. This started as the bodyguard unit of the Nazi elite, and subordinate to the *Sturmabteilung* (SA) literally Storm Detachment, the Nazi Party's original paramilitary, but distrusted by Hitler. The SS would become something different. Only Himmler seems to have regarded his task as something other than a backwater for a devoted subordinate.

One of the first tasks of the SS was to eliminate other occult groups in Germany. A long list of prohibited societies was compiled, including the Theosophical Society, all groups derived from Rudolf Steiner or the Golden Dawn, Aleister Crowley's O.T.O., and even the Order of New Templars, whose leader, Lanz von Liebenfels, was forbidden to write for their publication. To be a magician became as dangerous as being a Jew.[9]

There were many reasons for this occult purge, which reveals Hitler's considerable concern with esoteric matters rather than (as some allege) his lack of interest. Firstly, no totalitarian regime can tolerate secret societies. Secondly, as leader of a European nation, Hitler wanted to demonstrate the respectability of Nazism, and could not permit rumors about his magical preoccupations which would damage both his national and his international prestige. Thirdly, as an occultist himself, he appreciated the danger of allowing other magicians to work independently of his control. Fourthly, he insisted that magic was only for the secret society within the Nazi party, and hence could be practiced only by an Order with a total commitment to him and to his desires, the SS or *Schutzstaffel*.

Hitler's policy was to make the occult world serve him as totally as did every other German institution. This meant an end to *völkisch* occultism, and its replacement by a faith which to Hitler was entirely clear and truthful for those with eyes to see. This he enunciated in no uncertain terms at the Reich Party Congress of 1938:

8 Kolko, Gabriel, *The Triumph of Conservatism*. Kolko. MacMillan and Company New York. 1963.

9 Marrs, Jim, *Rule by Secrecy: The Hidden History that Connects the Trilateral Commission, the Freemasons and the Great Pyramids*. HarperCollins Publishers. New York. 2000.

At the pinnacle of our programme stands not mysterious premonition, but clear knowledge and hence open avowal. But woe if the movement or the state, through the insinuation of obscure mystical elements, should give unclear orders. And it is enough if this lack of clarity is contained merely in words. There is already a danger if orders are given for the setting up of so-called cult-places, because this alone will give birth to the necessity subsequently to devise so-called cult games and cult rituals. Our cult is exclusively cultivation of that which is natural and hence willed by God.

OCCULT PRACTICES LOST THE WAR

Upon consolidating the Thule and Vril Societies, Heinrich Himmler had employed the worthiest members and subjects into the meteorological section of the SS *Ahnenerbe* department. These psychics confidently declared that the Russian winter of 1941-1942 would be relatively mild. Hitler believed them, and hence saw no need for his soldiers to be provided with winter clothing. The results of this decision were disastrous for Germany, and the tide of the war turned. The first snow fell in early October.

By early November, temperatures had fallen below zero. Lubricating oil froze and jammed the German guns. German synthetic fuel separated into two component parts. Dressed in light summer uniforms, lacking warm headgear, winter boots, protective clothing, or goggles to prevent snow blindness, thousands of soldiers dropped from frostbite or died of exposure while performing their natural functions. In December the temperature dropped to minus forty degrees Centigrade, and the Red Army launched an all-out counter-attack against the stalled advances of the *Wehrmacht*. Obsessed by the desire to capture Moscow, Hitler forbade retreat, and ignored the conditions in which his troops were fighting; but Moscow remained in Russian hands, and the Red Army steadily pushed back the German troops. When General Heinz Guderian insisted upon the necessity for a tactical retreat, Hitler retorted: "As to the cold, I will see to that. Attack." Whatever he thought, whatever he desired, his Armies could not hold out against the Russians, and suffered before Moscow their first defeat of the war. Thus did a mystical theory lead, by spring 1942, to 1,168,000 German casualties, excluding the sick.

Hitler came to believe completely in his own infallibility. Previously, the Führer's decisions, though prompted by his intuition and predictive powers, had been based upon calculations, albeit those of a gambler. Now he adopted the view that whatever he did was right, simply because he did it, and no one dared check, criticize or question his insistence upon his own omnipotence. Previously, he had used facts, albeit in an extraordinary way; but now he simply refused to accept the existence of facts that displeased him. An occultist would say that he fell victim to the occupational disease of black magicians—that is, total megalomania coupled with an inability to recognize the realities around him.

Even this did not put a stop to the attempts of the Nazis to make military use of esoteric doctrines. It was also in 1942 that a new occult fad captured the minds of Germany's masters, that is, radiesthesia, or the use of pendulums. This was employed by the fervently pro-Nazi German Navy when the British began to destroy increasing numbers of U-boats. A Pendulum Institute, under a Captain Hans Roeder, was established within the confines of Berlin's Naval Research Institute. Month after month, clairvoyants and psychics sat with their pendulums swinging over charts of the Atlantic, endeavoring by this method to divine the whereabouts of British convoys. The results eventually proved unimpressive, and yet another group of occultists experienced the concentration camp.

Part of these failures is a result of the SS being structured like a religious order, rather than a political organization. In order to join in the first place, one had to satisfy stringent racial requirements, which demanded Nordic blood, and to pass a rigorous physical examination. Ideally, thought Himmler, all important posts should be filled by men with pure Nordic blood, and he even hoped that within 120 years, the entire German race would be of this type. After all, it was from this stock that the Superman would be bred, as Lanz von Liebenfels had long ago foreseen. If the candidate passed, he then had to undergo a lengthy period of testing and training, rather like a potential Jesuit candidate. Part of this training was in the mystical significance of runes. He would only be allowed to assume the black SS uniform (though without the collar patches) on the anniversary of Hitler's 1923 putsch which first followed his acceptance. He then received a provisional SS identity card on the next anniversary of Hitler's appointment as Chancellor.

WEWELSBURG CASTLE

On the anniversary of Hitler's birthday, Himmler took part in a neo-pagan ceremony in which he swore "obedience unto death" to Adolf Hitler. This entitled him to a full SS identity card and to collar patches on his uniform, but still not to full membership. Next, on the ensuing 1st of October, came an examination in a catechism which contained the fundamentals of SS religious and political doctrines, part of which stated, "We believe in God, we believe in Germany which He created in His world and in the *Führer*, Adolf Hitler, whom He has sent us." After a period of service in both the Labor Corps and the Army, the successful candidate (Himmler) was at long last initiated into the Order, and received the coveted SS dagger in commemoration.

The vast majority of the Order's inner rites were performed in the Renaissance castle of Wewelsburg in Westphalia. Himmler reportedly imagined the castle as a focus for the rebirth of the Knights of the Round Table and appointed twelve SS officers as his followers, who would gather at various rooms throughout the castle and perform unknown rites. This castle was the nerve center of the Black Order, where its most sacred and secret rites were performed by its greatest initiates. For the broad mass of SS men, there was a compulsory pagan religion based upon these rites which was derived from the occultism of List and Liebenfels.

By 1941, the SS had virtually become an independent state within the Third Reich. SS men were not subject to any jurisdiction other than their own courts: they were forbidden to converse with non-initiates unless circumstances made this essential: and when criticized at meetings, they would simply walk out. "A veil of secrecy descended over the activities of the SS," writes Heinz Höhne. "No one, not even a member of the party or a SA man, was allowed to know what the SS was doing; Himmler's Order began to withdraw into a twilight of mystery."

TIBETAN NAZIS

The Nazis certainly took an extraordinary interest in Tibet. As soon as funds were available, the *Ahnenerbe* mounted a series of expeditions to that distant land, which followed one after another in rapid succession until 1943. They sent out teams of archaeologists and explorers in an attempt to establish a Germanic cultural and racial origin. They were also keenly interested in acquiring ancient texts, archaeological artifacts, and in studying esoteric Tibetan human powers. Another goal of tracing the roots of the Aryan race to Central Asia was to establish a link with the mythical land of Agartha and Shambhala, supposedly underground kingdoms of hidden occult power usually centered in and associated with Tibet.[10]

In Tibet, acting on orders from SS Colonel Wolfram Sievers, Dr. Scheffer was in contact with a number of lamas in various monasteries, and he brought back with him to Munich, for scientific examination, some "Aryan" horses and "Aryan" bees, whose honey had special qualities. Another fascination with the Tibetans was their attainment of super-human abilities. The most important of these abilities was harnessing the chakra

10 Stevens, Henry, *Dark Star: Unresolved Post-War Nazi Mysteries.* Adventures Unlimited. Kempton, IL. 2011.

centers according to the systems Karl Haushofer was teaching—which was that which corresponds to the pineal gland between and behind the eyebrows. When activated, it confers enhanced human powers and magical vision.

Nor was this interest one-sided. Tibetan monks were recruited to make their way to the SS strongholds in Germany. Some colonies of Tibetan lamas settled in Munich and Berlin as early as 1926. One of them, known as "the man with the green gloves," was said to "possess the keys to the kingdom of Agartha." He had predictive powers, for he forecasted successfully the number of Nazi deputies elected to the Reichstag. It is said that Hitler consulted him regularly. And when the Soviet army took Berlin in 1945, they found to their astonishment many dozens of Tibetan corpses in German army uniforms. Some were found dead by ritual suicide, placed around in a circle, deep within the Berlin bunkers. The bodies were recognized as Tibetan by a Mongolian soldier fighting for Soviets at the end of the war.

EUGENICS AND WORLD CONTROL

After World War II and the subsequent occupation of Germany, Allied military commanders were stunned to discover the penetrating depth of the Nazi regime's state secrets. The world's best intelligence organization was not the least of these revelations. Also discovered were massive and meticulous research files on secret societies, eugenics and other scientific pursuits that boggled the imagination of the Allied command. Even more spectacular was an entire web of underground rocket and flying saucer factories with accompanying technology that still defies ordinary beliefs. A missing U-boat fleet possessing the most advanced submarine technology in the world left many wondering if the Nazis had escaped with yet more secrets, or even with Hitler himself. Behind all of these mysteries was an even deeper element: a secret order known to initiates as the Order of the Black Sun, an organization so feared that it is now illegal to even print their symbols and insignia in modern German society.

Some things never change. As during the Third Reich, several vaccines were made at the vaccine production facilities of IDT Biologika, where they remain today. IDT Biologika has coincidently already created and patented a combined rabies/ebola vaccine.[11] This facility is on the island of Riems, which was once the Nazi biological warfare research institute, the "Reichsforschungsanstalt Insel Riems," under the direct command of SS leader and eugenicist Heinrich Himmler. During the Third Reich, doctors and public health officials implemented utilitarianism in its most extreme form to justify conducting horrific scientific experiments on people. After World War II, the Nuremberg Tribunal justices presiding over The Nazi Doctors Trial declared utilitarianism to be a pseudo-ethic. They issued the Nuremberg Code outlining the "informed consent principle," which is supposed to guide research on humans and the future ethical practice standards of medicine.

But the desire for a global fascist ruling government did not end with the collapse of the Axis powers. The ideology simply moved elsewhere. As we'll learn in the next chapter, the globalists today are headquartered in London and centered on the Rothschild-dominated Bank of England, MI6, and the secretive Round Table society, which spawned the Royal Institute of International Affairs and the Council of 300. The American branches include the Council on Foreign Relations, the CIA and the Rockefeller Foundation, which all ensure the American people continue to finance and enforce the one-world tyranny. The Bush family has owed its prominence to this cabal ever since Grandfather Prescott Bush helped arrange financing for Nazi Germany.

•••
11 Vaccine production facilities of IDT BIOLOGIKA: https://idt-biologika.com/

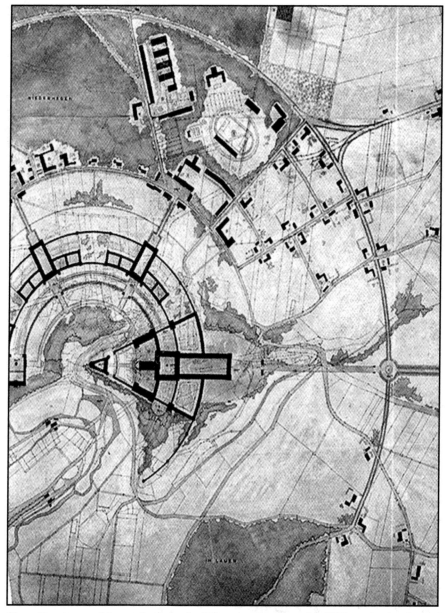

Above is a picture of the castle as the tip of the spear, based on this SS blueprint for plans of the outlying area around Wewelsburg. The small triangle in the center of the circle, forming the tip of the "spear," is Wewelsburg Castle. Himmler used the Wewelsburg castle to promote the SS and various mystical philosophies. The castle was known as the tip of the spear in reference to the Spear of Longinus, also called the Spear of Destiny, which is the supposed spear that pierced Christ's side. There has been much debate about George Soros being a junior officer of this inner circle and taking the Spear of Destiny when the SS was disbanded. It has been suggested that Soros is using the sacred artifact to promote the neo-fascist "New World Order."

This letter from Albert Pike was originally on display at the British Museum's Library, and was mysteriously taken down in the 1970s and never seen again. It predicts "the Third World War must be fomented by taking advantage of the differences caused by the 'agentur' of the 'Illuminati' between the political Zionists and the leaders of Islamic World. The war must be conducted in such a way that Islam (the Moslem Arabic World) and political Zionism (the State of Israel) mutually destroy each other. Meanwhile, the other nations, once more divided on this issue will be constrained to fight to the point of complete physical, moral, spiritual and economical exhaustion. We shall unleash the Nihilists and the Atheists, and we shall provoke a formidable social cataclysm which in all its horror will show clearly to the nations the effect of absolute atheism, origin of savagery and of the most bloody turmoil. Then everywhere, the citizens, obliged to defend themselves against the world minority of revolutionaries, will exterminate those destroyers of civilization, and the multitude, disillusioned with Christianity, whose deistic spirits will from that moment be without compass or direction, anxious for an ideal, but without knowing where to render its adoration, will receive the true light through the universal manifestation of the pure doctrine of Lucifer, brought finally out in the public view. This manifestation will result from the general reactionary movement which will follow the destruction of Christianity and Atheism, both conquered and exterminated at the same time."

The *Schwarze Sonne* ("Black Sun") symbol was a central image of the Vril Society, and can be seen on the floor of Wewelsburg Castle's North Tower in the former SS Generals' Hall. Interestingly, the Black Sun symbol can also be found in many ancient Babylonian and Assyrian places of worship. The Black Sun depicted the godhead's inner light in the form of a round cross, and includes shapes of the Nazi swastika. It also has similarities with the German Knight's Cross.

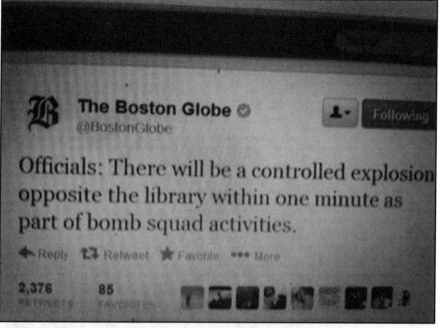

Whenever the cabal-controlled government / Mainstream Media complex's false-narratives about their false flag terror attacks start being rejected by a growing portion of the populace, this means that the neo-fascist regime behind such attacks is being seriously challenged.

In 1935, *Reichsführer* Heinrich Himmler founded the *H Sonderkommando*—H standing for *Hexe*, the German word for witch—to collate as much material as possible on sorcery, the occult and the supernatural. The bulk of the collection was called the "Witches Library" and concentrated on witches and their persecution in medieval Germany. The books were intended to be stored at Wewelsburg Castle in western Germany, the "Black Camelot" of Nazism, where Himmler created a court of SS "knights" modelled on the legend of King Arthur and the Knights of the Round Table.

False flag terror and a wide variety of crimes against humanity are violations of the U.S. Constitution, International Law, the laws of many other nations, and include murder, mass-murder, promotion of pedophilia and satanism, targeting of dissidents and numerous types of crimes that compromise human integrity.

It is also known beyond any shadow of a doubt that crisis actors have been hired in advance for many of these false flag events. Advertising for these individuals has been recovered and faces of various crisis actors matched showing that the same actors occasionally have been used more than once. It is also known for a fact that many of these crisis events have had DHS/FEMA live-shooter drills scheduled for that same day or immediately before.

WORLD CONTROL

"Capitalism is the extraordinary belief that the nastiest men with the nastiest motives will somehow work for the benefit of everyone." –John Maynard Keynes

WHETHER we like it or not, everyone is now being confronted with evidence that the world is being controlled by powerful, occult-driven and extremely negative forces operating behind the scenes. Secret organizations such as the Bilderberg Group, Illuminati, Skull and Bones, Bohemian Grove, the Club of Rome and others appear to form an interlocking web of control that is worldwide in scope and is systematically eliminating all social safety nets.

But how did it come to this, and how do they do it? The real core of this group's power lies in the control of the money system—through the Federal Reserve banking families and their international equivalent, the Bank for International Settlements (BIS). The general public holds the vague idea that the World Bank (WB) and the International Monetary Fund (IMF) are forces for good, helping developing nations with loans and other assistance to improve their economies. But the truth is that the World Bank and the IMF are the prime causes of increased poverty and suffering around the globe. Indeed, all the biggest banks are in bed together. The Fed, BIS, IMF and World Bank are all implicated in a vast conspiracy to lie to the public and create artificial investor confidence that benefits no one but themselves.

The ultimate battleground has become the United States. Our citizens have inalienable rights granted to them, a strong constitution, a loyal military, and the right to bear arms. But it can be argued that all the most important government agencies have been taken over by a financial terrorism network. This network has blackmailed or bought off leaders of both the Republican and Democratic parties, and have established a dominant role in all three branches of government and throughout the mainstream media. They have complete control of the economy, the stock market, the U.S. Treasury, the Federal Reserve, the World Bank, the IMF and the global banking system. Once the economic concept of "vertical integration" can be understood (which is when the same entities generate money from a variety of industries), it's then apparent that the same cabal owns Big Industry, Big Agriculture, Big Finance, Big Media and Big Government. This is an organized criminal operation—an imperial fascist movement that is determined to destroy our very way of life. Clearly, a war has already been launched against us.

Above all else, those who govern seek to control what the masses accept as true, and there is nothing that they will not do in order to achieve this goal, since such control is the sole source of their power. Specifically, to control all the major media outlets is the central reason why they are able to control the public narrative. The naive belief that those who govern would not brazenly manipulate knowledge simply for their own benefit is the single most important belief that supports this continued fascist reign. This belief always leads to confusion, despair, and relentless cynicism from within the ranks of those who are controlled. Once this belief is abandoned, however, free will returns absolutely, and great change is inevitable.

CAPITALISM FAILED

For decades, the wealthiest 20 countries led by the U.S. have gotten exponentially wealthier at the expense of the poorest 175 nations, who in turn have gotten even poorer.[1] That has been the result of the elite of the Western Hemisphere's brain child called the "New World Order," a movement led mainly by self-appointed global governments like the International Monetary Fund (IMF) and the World Trade Organization (WTO). The Federal Reserve is also privately-owned and an unelected group of bankers are the real movers and shakers in the USA.

The Federal Reserve (Fed) was created by a corrupt Congress in 1913, and was given the previously-assigned Congressional responsibility of money creation. Ever since, the buying power of the dollar has declined in value by over 95%. The Fed does this by inflation or expansion of the money supply. This acts as a hidden tax that requires you to pay more dollars for every product and service to recoup that loss in purchasing power due to inflation. In addition to this, the Federal Reserve artificially sets interest rates, funds the bailouts and wars, and can rig economic winners and losers.

Capitalism is in crisis. The international financial meltdown is closing in. America is under attack, not from terrorists, but from within. A New World Order has been established and is determined to bring about a one-world government and a one- world religious system in which everyone will be required to accept a RFID (radio frequency identification) bio-chip in a cash-less society. The ultimate goal is to literally and arbitrarily create their own world government, and put it in place.

The two old tricks that dug it out of past crises—war and shopping—simply will not work anymore. The proletariat, as Karl Marx saw it, has been under continuous assault. Factories have shut down, jobs have disappeared, trade unions have been disbanded. The citizens making up the proletariat have, over the years, been pitted against each other in every possible way. The top 400 richest people own more wealth now than the bottom 185 million Americans taken together. That is a medieval structure, with those at the top of the hierarchy calling the shots, and rarely called into

••••••••••••••••••••••••••••••
1   Roy, Arundhati, *Capitalism: A Ghost Story.* Corbis Magazine (from Outlook), 3/26/2012: **https://www.outlookindia.com/magazine/story/** **capitalism-a-ghost-story/280234**

account for their crimes. You might not see the strings on our puppet politicians, but they're there. This is not a "conspiracy theory." The proof is absolutely irrefutable— and is so widely available that everyone is talking about it now. Free market capitalism has collapsed and has now become a rigged global market.

Since the financial collapse of 2008, followed by the 2020-2022 crash from COVID-19, Americans have lost an unprecedented amount of national wealth. Trillions upon trillions of our tax dollars have been looted by Wall Street, by endless wars, by enormous subsidies for the most profitable global corporations, and by tax cuts for the richest one percent of the population. Never before, in the history of civilization, has a nation been so thoroughly and systematically fleeced. This is all the result of a coordinated economic attack by a global banking cartel against 99% of the U.S. population. Until we can become politically intelligent enough to see this as the reality and root cause of our current crisis, we will not be able to overcome it. Our living standards will continue to decline and we all will be sentenced to a slow death in a neo-feudal system built on debt slavery.

MASTERS AND COMMANDERS

In 1992, former British intelligence agent, Dr. John Coleman, first published *Conspirators Hierarchy: The Story of the Committee of 300*. It has since been revised in several editions. With laudable scholarship and meticulous research, Dr. Coleman identifies the players and carefully details the New World Order agenda of worldwide domination and control. In a real-life *Hunger Games* scenario, Dr. Coleman accurately summarizes the intent and purpose of the global elite who direct the Committee of 300 as follows:

> A One World Government and one-unit monetary system, under permanent non-elected hereditary oligarchists who self-select from among their numbers in the form of a feudal system as it was in the Middle Ages. In this One World entity, population will be limited by restrictions on the number of children per family, diseases, wars, famines, until one billion people who are useful to the ruling class, in areas which will be strictly and clearly defined, remain as the total world population.
>
> There will be no middle class, only rulers and the servants. All laws will be uniform under a legal system of world courts practicing the same unified code of laws, backed up by a One World Government police force and a One World unified military to enforce laws in all former countries where no national boundaries shall exist. The system will be on the basis of a welfare state; those who are obedient and subservient to the One World Government will be rewarded with the means to live; those who are rebellious will simply be starved to death or be declared outlaws, thus a target for anyone who wishes to kill them. Privately owned firearms or weapons of any kind will be prohibited.[2]

During World War II, every country on both sides of the conflict was financed by the very same private bankers who lent out every dollar these countries used to finance their war effort—at interest! In the ensuing years, ordinary people on both sides endured incredible hardships. World War II cost over 50 million lives, and when it was over each country that participated was left with a huge debt to the banks. Who benefited? John D. Rockefeller stayed home and he profited over 200 million dollars.

For international bankers, there is nothing more profitable than war. And when it is taken into account that these same international bankers now control all major media outlets, advertise to all oil cartels and arms dealers, finance all the main political parties, and control all world currencies, is it any wonder the world stays in a state of constant conflict and war?

••

2   Coleman, John, *Conspirators Hierarchy: The Story of the Committee of 300 (4th edition).* page 161, WIR, 1997.

THE BRITISH ROYALS AND THE ROUND TABLE

To understand the problem, we'll have to get to know a few of the players. Firstly, there are two operant Crowns in England, with one obviously being Queen Elizabeth II. Although extremely wealthy, the Queen functions largely in a ceremonial capacity and serves to deflect attention away from the other Crown, who issues her marching orders through their control of the English Parliament. This other Crown is comprised of a committee of 12 banks headed by the Bank of England (controlled by the House of Rothschild). They rule the financial world from the 717-acre, independent sovereign state known as The City of London. The City (Financial District) is not a political part of London, England or the United Kingdom. It is similar to Vatican City which does not have the same laws as Rome or Italy, and to Washington D.C. acting as an independent city-state within the USA. This triumvirate of three is called the Empire of Three Cities, and, shockingly, their shadowy leaders have effectively ruled the Western Hemisphere for over a century.

Secret organizations such as the Bilderberg Group, Skull and Bones, the Bohemian Grove, the Club of Rome and others appear to form an interlocking web of control that is worldwide in scope, and works in tandem to systematically eliminate all social safety nets. The origins of groups of today were the progeny of the Round Table, who all were illuminated Freemasons, those inner-circle Masons who have been tied to the Illuminati for close to three centuries.

According to Dr. John Coleman's book, *Conspirators Hierarchy*, the Rothschilds exert political control through the secretive Business Roundtable, which they created in 1909 with the help of South African international industrialist Cecil Rhodes and Lord Alfred Milner. Cecil Rhodes was a Rothschild protégé who founded the Standard Chartered Bank, as well as the infamous Round Table secret society. As one of the original globalists, Cecil Rhodes was planning for future generations. At the time of his death in 1902, his last will and testament was implemented through the establishment of the Royal Institute for International Affairs in London. Its sister globalist think tank in the USA is the Council on Foreign Relations (CFR). Rhodes' last will aspired, "to establish a trust, to and for the establishment and promotion and development of a secret society, the true aim and object whereof shall be the extension of British rule throughout the world...and the ultimate recovery of the United States of America as an integral part of the British Empire."

To this end, Cecil Rhodes put forward his own vision of an expanded British Empire at the end of the 19th century that would be achieved by the formation of a secret society, which he named the Round Table. Cecil Rhodes is best known for the Rhodes Scholarship, which is granted by Oxford University. Also of some renown, the oil industry propagandist Cambridge Energy Research Associates operates out of the Rhodes-supported Cambridge University. Rhodes' secret society was formed with the following objectives: the furtherance of the British Empire by the bringing of the entire uncivilized world under British rule; the recovery of the United States; and making the Anglo-Saxon race but one Empire. In an era when "the sun never sets on the British Empire," Cecil Rhodes' dream was not only probable, it was possible.

By Rhodes' dictates, this secret society would have "its members in every part of the British Empire," including in the schools and universities, as well as to select new members in the Colonial legislatures. He also envisaged this secret society owning "portions of the press, for the press rules the mind of the people." For the puppet masters who seek absolute control of political individuals and institutions, there are methods of control beyond lobbying, bribery and threats of violence. Part of the *modus operandi* appears to be the systematic "honey traps" that compromise politicians with drugs, sex and even child sexual abuse. Once such behaviors are established, they are used as blackmail to control politicians with threats of disclosure of their scandal if they do not follow the hidden agenda.[3] Such was the case with Jeffrey Epstein and his "Orgy Island."

In pursuing this course, Rhodes was in many respects one of the first true modern heirs to Adam Weishaupt, founder of the Bavarian Illuminati, who also espoused these principles. A professor of law at the University of Ingolstadt and a former Jesuit priest, Weishaupt created the Illuminati in 1776 to achieve his radical, utopian goal of transforming society. He envisaged a world devoid of "princes and nations," in which the human race would "become one family." The descendent secret organizations today know no national boundaries, are above the laws of all countries as entities which control every aspect of politics, religion, commerce and industry; banking, insurance, mining, the drug trade and the petroleum industry—a group answerable to no one but its members. Cecil Rhodes's colonizing globalist technique of using secret societies to advance business interests would blossom in the 20th century. The New World Order would follow the methodology of the British godfather, Cecil Rhodes, and Protocols of Zionist godfather Theodor Herzl, plus American kingpins David Rockefeller and Zbigniew Brzezinski, calling their elite apparatus the Council for Foreign Relations and the Trilateral Commission.

SYNARCHIST RULE BY SECRECY

Synarchism is a term used to define a new concept of political alliances by an international cabal of financiers and industrialists based on fascist principles and rule by a secret elite. The word synarchy describes a shadow government, a form of government where political power effectively rests with those operating a "deep state," in contrast to an "oligarchy" where the elite is known by the public. These secretive controllers were early financial supporters of Hitler and the Nazi Party. The key period of the growth of synarchism followed on the heels of the Russian Revolution and led to the rise of the Pan European Movement (PEM) in 1922. The PEM was embraced by powerful forces inside Germany—including the wealthy banker Max Warburg, who financed the movement. Warburg was a director of IG Farben, the cartel that helped elevate Adolf Hitler to power. The rise of Nazi Germany was the first overt attempt at One World Government.

Webster's definition for *synarchy* is limited entirely to "joint rule or sovereignty." Although Germany lost World War II, these secretive power brokers did not go away and are now commonly known as the deep state. Many would say they've only gotten stronger. Now their final objective is control over a post-industrial society. These are the people who are the masterminds behind the establishment of a New World Order.

Today the American form of "democracy" has little to do with genuine democratic representation, but rather more closely resembles a revolving fascist dictatorship beholden to the interests of a wealthy elite and big business. The Italian P2 (Propaganda Due) secret society was a "textbook example" of an attempt to establish a synarchy, as it united politicians, the Catholic Church, and the Mafia-controlled drug economy.

In the United States, one such secret society worthy of note is Yale University's Order of Skull and Bones. Entry into the order involves elaborate ritual and is accompanied by a change of name. No longer is the neophyte known by his family name, but assumes the identity of a knight. Bonesmen include George W. Bush, his father George Bush Senior, Senator John Kerry, and many other globalists.[4]

The Problem...

To recap, we have seen the Bavarian Illuminati coming out of Germany in the 18th centu-

3   Zagami, Leo Lyon, *Confessions of an Illuminati, Volume II: The Time of Revelation and Tribulation Leading up to 2020.* CCC Publishing, 2016.

4   Stiglitz, Joseph, *The Price of Inequality.* W.W. Norton & Co, 2012.

ry, the Round Table secret society coming out of the United Kingdom in the 19th century, and the actualization of synarchy in the 20th century. All are controlled by a few select individuals who wield tremendous power, also known as the heads of the 13 bloodline families. Their secret names may have changed after Illuminati, generations have passed, but their world control agenda has only gotten stronger in this modern age.

For the sake of simplicity let's refer to these unelected rulers as the "cabal," who are the global elite and consist of those with tremendous amounts of both wealth and power in our world. Like any group, the cabal has both individuals and factions with specific agendas. All are extraordinarily wealthy, well-connected, and own the most important corporations. Members of the global elite generally do all they can to keep their existence and their activities secret, knowing that if people find out about them and their immense power, they will demand change. Even with the means for change we think we possess; it's now widely recognized that most election vote-tabulating technologies have been compromised and are manipulated to help yield the results desired by the cabal.

False flag incidents allow the cabal to respond in whatever way they intended to act in the first place, a concept author David Icke calls "order out of chaos," or "problem-reaction-solution." He writes that there are few, if any, public events that are not engineered, or at least strategically used by the cabal:

> You want to introduce something you know the people won't like. So you first create a problem, a rising crime rate, more violence, a terrorist bomb. You make sure someone else is blamed for this problem. So you create a "patsy," as they call them in America, a Timothy McVeigh or a Lee Harvey Oswald. This brings us to stage two, the reaction from the people, such as, "This can't go on; what are they going to do about it?" This allows them to then openly offer the solution to the problems they have created.

The Reaction…

The cabal are masters at cleverly engaging the population in their mass psychological operations, and making us seem to desire our own servitude. Their psy-ops are designed to make us agreeable to their covert agendas, which are hidden in plain sight. Henry Kissinger, in an address to the Bilderberg meeting at Evian, France on May 21st, 1992 stated: "The one thing every man fears is the unknown. When presented with this scenario, individual rights will be willingly relinquished for the guarantee of their well-being granted to them by the world government." Sheep to slaughter.

The cabal is quite good at instigating and executing false flag operations to achieve specific goals. Good examples are 9/11 to inject the U.S. Armed Forces into Middle Eastern conflicts; Sandy Hook and Parkland, FL for gun control; Boston Bombing to test martial law. The end goal is a one-world government. When a government or other entity secretly pretends to be its own enemy and launches an attack against itself, this is called a false flag operation. This is done to fool unsuspecting people into believing that there is a greater threat than actually exists, and to manipulate the public into supporting war agendas. It is through use of the highly-organized military and intelligence services that the cabal, working together with key allies in government and the media, are able to carry out major false flag operations. The problem for the cabal is they have been overused, and now people are waking up to the faux-reality deception. Their false flag operations don't work any longer.

The complexity of an operation like this is staggering—as this cabal effectively controls the mainstream media to influence what stories run, plus they use murder, torture, blackmail and bribery to ensure their plans are never exposed. In our society, corporations and their sponsors have deep pockets that can hire an "expert" to stand up in a suit and tie or laboratory jacket and say anything the cabal orders. In this case they are very well-organized, and have seized power very effectively—particularly in the U.S., U.K., Germany, France and Italy—namely the G5 nations, as well as the United Nations at several crucial levels. It should be noted that the United Nations is the corporate and royal elite's New World Order. It proposes a "New Global Ethic" of Earth worship, a return to the mercantile system for trade, and political rule by an aristocratic oligarchy. An honest look at the UN provides many compelling reasons why the USA should withdraw from any future funding or empowerment.[5]

The Solution...

A plutonomy is the science of production and distribution of wealth, and in this model the media still publishes what the market wants. But the problem is while we are the so-called consumers of media, we are not a customer any more than a cow in a feedlot is the master of its own diet. We get what we're given. Former CIA Director William Colby once said, "The CIA owns everyone of any significance in the major media." Clearly, the Western media is a Ministry of Propaganda for Washington. The mainstream media keeps us uninformed and misinformed about many of the most important issues of our day while including just enough entertainment and accurate but unimportant information to keep us coming back for more.

As people become outraged and frightened by the latest false flag attacks, they demand a solution to the problem. Often this has a police or military reaction. It's a very good technique for boosting the Arms Industry. But do we really need weapons to fight wars? Or do we need wars to create a market for weapons? After all, the economies of Europe, U.S. and Israel depend hugely on their weapons industry. It's the one thing they haven't outsourced to China yet. Fifty-three cents of every U.S. tax dollar goes for the military and war. Peace cannot be achieved in a system where there are people who make profits on war.

Starvation and disease are epidemic in much of the world, and even in the modern countries there is widespread poverty and economic hardship. Many of the big problems of our time are related to unbridled pursuit of profits without regard for human rights or the environment. What if a man has an apartment stacked to the ceiling with magazines? We'd call him nuts. Similarly, if a woman had a trailer home full of cats, we'd call her crazy. But when people pathologically hoard so much wealth that they impoverish an entire nation, we put them on the cover of *Fortune* magazine and they are presented as role models.

CITY OF LONDON

In a classic "problem, reaction, solution" formula, the needed enemies for needed wars can be created if the secret planners have the technological help of a nation that has hundreds of years practice in creating its own enemies. This nation is the City of London, a separate nation state like the Vatican, located within England. There is a reason England has been referred to as "Perfidious Albion" for centuries, referring to its diplomatic sleights, duplicity, and treachery by monarchs or governments of the UK (or England prior to 1707) in their pursuit of self-interest. They have been known for their ability to institute chaos inside nations they want to control by their usual well-developed strategy of "Divide and Conquer." According to Preston James of *Veterans Today*, they are experts at creating long term provocations between different nations that have competing economic interests. They do this in order to later establish a beachhead from which to control the removal of natural resources and accrued wealth.

The starkest example is the Opium Wars, where England forcibly brought opiate addiction to China as a covert act of war in order to recover all the silver and gold paid to

5   Wilcock, David, "The real power brokers of world control, and their house of cards ready to fall." **https://divinecosmos.com/davids-blog/1043-massarrests/**

import tea, silk, and spices from China. China was a net exporter, and had large trade surpluses with most Western countries. The Boxer Rebellion ultimately led to two short wars, thus compromising China's sovereignty and economic power for almost a century. Within a decade after the end of the Second Opium War, China's share of global GDP had fallen by half. What we are now seeing is the "controlled implosion" of the Western oligarchical financial system of tyranny. Let's examine some of the other secret power brokers of the modern age who seek to enslave humanity, starting with the Club of Rome.

CLUB OF ROME

This secretive think tank, now based in Winterthur, Switzerland, stimulated considerable public attention in 1972 with the first report to the Club of Rome. This report was called *The Limits to Growth*. It stated: "If the present growth trends in world population, industrialization, pollution, food production, and resource depletion continue unchanged, the limits to growth on the planet will be reached sometime within the next one hundred years." The report went on to predict "the human ecological footprint cannot continue to grow." This infamous report was a Malthusian blueprint on how the human population needed to be reduced in order to prevent an ecological collapse, which in itself was merely a disguised version of the abhorrent eugenicist ideas that were circulating in the early part of the 20th century and eventually died out with Hitler. The widely discredited population bomb paranoia of the 70's and 80's was gradually replaced by the climate change fearmongering that we see the organization pushing today, which again is merely another regurgitation of the eugenics-obsessed policies of the elite.[6]

The work of the Club is strengthened and amplified by the activities of the National Associations in over 30 countries worldwide. The Club of Rome currently consists of approximately 100 individual members, over 30 national and regional associations, the International Centre in Winterthur, a European Support Centre in Vienna and the Club of Rome Foundation. This foundation provides the opportunity for major individual donors to be involved by participating in the development and dissemination of the Club's projects and messages. Prominent members of the Club of Rome include Al Gore and Maurice Strong, both of whom are intimately involved with privately-owned carbon trading groups like the Chicago Climate Exchange.

AMERICAN POLICY GROUPS

In 1903, the Banker's Trust was set up by the heads of eight bloodline families. As a precursor to the Fed, it acted as a "bankers' bank" by holding the reserves of other banks and trust companies and loaning them money when they needed additional reserves due to unexpected withdrawals. Benjamin Strong, of the Banker's Trust, went on to become the first Governor of the New York Federal Reserve Bank. The 1913 creation of the Federal Reserve fused the power of the eight families to the military and diplomatic might of the U.S. government. If their overseas loans went unpaid, the oligarchs could now deploy the U.S. Marines to collect on debts. Morgan, Chase and Citibank formed an international lending syndicate.

By the 1920s, the expansion of U.S. capitalism had begun to look outwards, mainly for raw materials and overseas markets. Foundations began to formulate the concept of global corporate governance. In 1924, the Rockefeller and Carnegie foundations jointly created what is today the most powerful foreign policy pressure group in the world—the Council on Foreign Relations, which later came to be funded by the Ford Foundation as well. The CFR was also co-created by the Sovereign Military Order of Malta (SMOM) after their creation of the Royal Institute of International Affairs in

----

6   Maher, Suzanne, "The Club of Rome and Their Eugenics Agenda." http://byebyebluesky.com/the-club-of-rome-and-their-eugenics-agenda/

1919. All eleven of the World Bank's presidents since 1946 have been members of the CFR. These bankers have presented themselves as missionaries of the poor, by loaning capital (at interest) to the developing world. In reality, they are vulture capitalists. These powerful entities control the 1871 corporation known as the United States. Both are arms of the SMOM via their inner cores within "The City" known as Pilgrim Society, Order of the Garter, and Committee of 300.

Over the years, the CFR's membership has included 22 U.S. Secretaries of State. There were five CFR members in the 1943 steering committee that planned the United Nations, and an $8.5 million grant from John D. Rockefeller bought the land on which the UN's New York headquarters stands. The CFR was instrumental in creating the United Nations. Interestingly, the SMOM has "permanent observer status" within the United Nations. By 1993, according to an editorial by Richard Harwood on the October 30th op-ed page of the *Washington Post*, that power apparently has been consolidated: "That the CFR has been in control of the foreign policy of the United States for some time should now be beyond question."

By 1947, the newly created CIA was supported by and began working closely with the CFR. At this point there becomes a big question of accountability. According to John Stockwell, a former CIA official and whistleblowing author, "It is the function of the CIA to keep the world unstable, and to propagandize and teach the American people to hate, so we will let the Establishment spend any amount of money on arms." Clearly the CFR is the Establishment. Filmmaker Anthony Hilder always maintained that the "CIA was the enforcement arm of the CFR." With the CFR having control of the CIA, they are able to direct the narrative of world events, sometimes of their own making. For example, the CIA originally introduced the term "conspiracy theory" to deflect those who denied the findings of the Warren Commission that Oswald acted alone in killing JFK. Still today, esoteric researchers bristle at being labeled "conspiracy theorists." But what if there are "shills" undermining and steering the debate? Another question asks if there are secret agents on the government payroll tasked with infiltrating and undermining activist groups. A quote from "Countering Criticism of the Warren Commission Report," a 1967 CIA dispatch, explains how to disarm conspiracy theorists: "Our ploy should point out, as applicable, that the critics are (I) wedded to theories adopted before the evidence was in, (II) politically interested, (III) financially interested, (IV) hasty and inaccurate in their research, or (V) infatuated with their own theories."

The Aspen Institute is another international club of local elites, businessmen, bureaucrats, politicians, and policymakers with franchises in several countries, including India. Many key scientists, politicians, and industrialists are members of the CFR, the Trilateral Commission and the Aspen Institute. The Koch brothers have contributed vast sums of money to the Aspen Institute, and have the naming rights on some buildings and programs. David Koch has a mansion just outside of Aspen, Colorado. Along with his older brother Charles, their coal-mining operation (called Koch Industries) is scattered around several huge areas in western Colorado and elsewhere. You could call it a conflict of interest when David Koch sponsors the PBS science show called *Nova*, or makes large donations to the Aspen Institute, and those same funded institutions are meant to toe the line according to the Koch brothers' version of "science."

The transnational equivalent of the CFR is the Trilateral Commission, set up in 1973 by David Rockefeller, as well as the former U.S. National Security Advisor Zbigniew Brzezinski, the Chase-Manhattan Bank, and some other private eminences. Brzezinski was a founding member of the Afghan Mujahideen, the forefathers of the Taliban. The purpose of the Trilateralists is to create an enduring bond of friendship and cooperation between the elites of North America, Europe and Japan.

It has now extended its tentacles to become a wider influential commission, including new members from China and India.

TOO BIG TO FAIL BANKSTERS

The mission of the power elites was to integrate central banking into the system, eliminate the gold standard, gain cheap credit and thereby earn money from inflation. Although J.P. Morgan and John D. Rockefeller were originally financial adversaries, they had a common mission called ultimate power; therefore, they created a merger. In 1896, J.P. Morgan and John D. Rockefeller merged their banking enterprises, eventually to become JPMorgan Chase & Co, which allowed them to expand their empires with the aid of government. Both powerful men knew that through the government enforcing their cartel's best interests, they would have the greatest advantage. They had a marketing campaign to sell the idea to the public, recognizing that inflation from loans would finance their businesses. Their idea was to regulate the Federal Reserve System, because with the gold standard, there was no way that they could manipulate the interest rate; ergo no interest rate, meaning no money for their initiatives.

The international and central banking systems are, at their core, designed to concentrate wealth in the hands of the very few and enslave the rest of us with the burden of ever-increasing interest payments on debt. This is debt which would never have accrued if countries were allowed to operate with sovereignty. According to *The Times* editor Sir William Rees-Mogg, "The value of paper money is precisely the value of a politician's promise, as high or low as you put that; the value of gold, on the other hand, is protected by the inability of politicians to manufacture it."

At the 1944 Bretton Woods Conference, the World Bank and IMF decided that the U.S. dollar should be the reserve currency of the world, and that in order to enhance the penetration of global capital, it would be necessary to universalize and standardize business practices in an open marketplace. The U.S. dollar became the global reserve currency, as per the Bretton Woods Agreement, and the U.S. dollar is a Federal Reserve Note.

The financial catastrophe of 2008 has made the public increasingly mistrustful of the Fed and its covert activities. A poll conducted by *Bloomberg* in 2010 showed that the majority of Americans believed that the Fed should be severely reigned in or abolished.[7] In a separate survey conducted by *Rasmussen* in 2010, 80 percent of Americans believed that the Fed should be thoroughly audited. During the recent economic crisis, it has poured trillions of dollars into the economy with no oversight, has made secret agreements with foreign banks and governments, and has refused to tell Congress who is getting the money or to give the details of what deals are being made. But this is changing.

END THE FED

The Federal Reserve Act of 1913 was passed by Congress on December 23rd just before the Christmas break, and on the same day signed into law by President Woodrow Wilson. The main purpose was supposedly to mitigate bank runs after financial panics, but now it is known that these financial crises were created by the very same people who created the Central Bank! Also, according to Article I, Section 8, of the U.S. Constitution, the U.S. Congress is the only institution that has the authority to "coin Money, regulate the Value thereof, and of foreign Coin, and fix the Standard of Weights and Measures." So why is the Federal Reserve still in operation, especially after the Federal Reserve system was originally chartered for only 20 years? These people always find a way around. Congress rechartered the Federal Reserve Banks into perpetuity with the McFadden Act of 1927, so there is currently no "expiration date" or repeal date for the Federal Reserve.

....
7   Zumbrun, Joshua, "More Than Half of U.S. Wants Fed Curbed or Abolished." https://www.bloomberg.com/news/articles/2010-12-09/more-than-half-of-americans-want-fed-reined-in-or-abolished

It is not federal and it has no reserves. It is not backed by anything of value. The entire economy is based on the shuffling of IOU notes, which only exists because of our belief that it is real. It is because we have allowed a private banking consortium to take over the money supply that the national debt exists, a debt that can never be repaid.

Never count on the Federal Reserve to fix any problems. They are the problem! In the same year in which the Federal Reserve Bank was born, the U.S. banking scion, J. Pierpont Morgan, died, and the Rockefeller Foundation was formed. The House of Morgan had presided over American finance from the corner of Wall Street and Broad, acting as a quasi-U.S. central bank since 1838, when George Peabody founded it in London.

For over a century running, there have been so many more questions than answers. Such as how the U.S. national debt could be more than 5,000 times larger than it was when the Federal Reserve was created in 1913. Why were the Federal Reserve *and* the personal income tax both pushed through Congress in the same year? Why does the Federal Reserve argue in court that it is "not an agency" of the federal government? Why do all 187 nations that belong to the IMF have a central bank? Since its inception in 1913, the Federal Reserve has helped to devalue our dollar by over 97%.

INTERNAL RACKET SCAM

American citizens might be under the impression that the Internal Revenue Service (IRS) is a branch of the government that collects taxes from working citizens in order to fund the government. But such an impression would be wrong. Similar to the Federal Reserve, the IRS is owned by private entities, some even residing outside our country. In reality, the operation is merely a collection agency for the Federal Reserve. Both the Federal Reserve and the IRS were founded in 1913, and both have been pseudo-governmental agencies for over a century. The Federal Reserve is a private bank based out of Europe and owned by various entities, including the Rothschilds and Warburgs. The Fed lends our government money, while our tax money is collected by the IRS and sent directly to the Federal Reserve banking system.

Looked at another way, the U.S. Government is financed in much the same way people might finance their homes. The politicians spend so much money that there is no way that the taxes collected would be enough to pay for all their activities, so they have to borrow money from the banking cartels, and in turn tell the banking cartels that they will collect the money to service the loans from the citizens. Unfortunately, all of the tax money collected by the IRS goes only to interest payments against the enormous national debt, which keeps climbing and we keep paying. Illegal as it is, they have the bigger guns.

Of course, we all know that if we don't pay our taxes the IRS has the "right" to garnish our wages, freeze our bank accounts, and seize our assets. This is because our government sold us out to the banking cartels as collateral many years ago, simply ignoring the American Revolution principle of "no taxation without representation." Illegal scams like this have come and gone throughout the ages. Just before we won our independence from Great Britain, we were subjects that were required to pay exorbitant taxes to the monarchy. We were not represented, and this led to the Boston Tea Party, and the rest is history. When we begin to really understand how the system actually operates, we begin to see how these enterprises operate much like organized crime. The government is the enforcement division, the IRS is the collection division, and the big banks are for money laundering.

ILLUMINATI BY ANY OTHER NAME

The cabal's world control represents a re-occurring problem that never goes away. Also called the Illuminati, the alliance of Rothschild finance and European aristocracy is secretly coordinated by a Luciferian dogma hidden within the uppermost levels of Freemasonry. There is an old saying in journalism that when you can't make sense of a story, follow the money. If we follow the money of the Bank of International Settlements, we'll find it is owned by the Federal Reserve, Bank of England, Bank of Italy, Bank of Canada, Swiss National Bank, Nederlandsche Bank, Bundesbank and the Bank of France. Historian Carroll Quigley wrote in his epic book, *Tragedy and Hope,* that the BIS was part of a plan, "to create a world system of financial control in private hands able to dominate the political system of each country and the economy of the world as a whole. ...to be controlled in a feudalistic fashion by the central banks of the world acting in concert by secret agreements."

The U.S. government had a historical distrust of the BIS, lobbying unsuccessfully for its demise at the 1944 post-WWII Bretton Woods Conference. In fact, the Eight Families' power was exacerbated, with the Bretton Woods creation of the IMF and the World Bank. The U.S. Federal Reserve only took shares in the BIS in September, 1994. The BIS holds at least 10% of monetary reserves for at least 80 of the world's central banks, the IMF and other multilateral institutions. It serves as a financial agent for international agreements, collects information on the global economy and serves as lender of last resort to prevent global financial collapse. The BIS promotes an agenda of monopoly capitalist fascism. Many researchers assert that the BIS is at the nadir of global drug money laundering. The cabal has a finger in every pie that is profitable.

To further understand who controls these operations, we can learn details from a comprehensive 2011 Swiss report SFI studying 1,318 "core" companies. They were found to own a controlling interest in other corporations that, in total, are earning 20 percent of all the money there is to make in the world. This fact alone reveals that there is an astonishing monopoly at play in the world. Any interconnected matrix of control like this should be subject to vast, sweeping anti-trust legislation. Profits add up to an additional 60% of global revenues. The 80% majority includes pharmaceutical companies, clothing manufacturers, agriculture providers, gadget-makers, mining consortiums, telecommunications companies, defense contractors, food manufacturers and the media complex. The remaining 20% of "hold-outs" are probably in foreign nations who somehow managed to resist this vast banking cabal. When the SFI team further untangled the web of ownership, it found much of ownership tracked back to a "super-entity" of 147 even more tightly knit companies—all of their ownership was held by other members of the super-entity—that controlled 40% of the total wealth in the world. The banks found to be most influential include: Barclays; Goldman Sachs; JPMorgan Chase; Vanguard Group; UBS; Deutsche Bank; Bank of New York Melon; Morgan Stanley; Bank of America; and Société Générale. According to the SFI study, a large portion of control, "flows to a small tightly-knit core of financial institutions." The researchers described the core as an economic "super-entity," that should raise important red flag issues for policymakers and researchers. Of course, the implications are enormous for all citizens around the world.

BANKRUPTING THE WORLD

The upper level of the cabal pyramid is a tightly compartmentalized need-to-know basis structure including planning committees, of which the public has little or no knowledge of their existence or influence. Of course, it was created that way for maximum security. The sheer magnitude and complex web of deceit surrounding the individuals and organizations involved in this conspiracy is mind boggling, even for the most astute among us. Most people react with disbelief and skepticism towards the topic of planned bankruptcy of all citizens, unaware that they have been conditioned to react with skepticism by media and institutional influences.

According to a former insider at the World Bank, ex-Senior Counsel Karen Hudes, the World Bank has more or less directed the economic policies of the Developing World by coercing and cracking open the markets of country after country for global financial domination. It is no coincidence that BIS is headquartered in Switzerland, a favorite hiding place for the wealth of the global aristocracy and headquarters for the P2 Italian Freemason's Alpina Lodge and Nazi International. Other institutions which the bloodline families control include the World Economic Forum, the International Monetary Conference and the World Trade Organization.[8]

The United States is developing into a desperate, almost Third World society defined by a hardening caste system driven by the insatiable greed of its wealthiest citizens. We are now approaching the level of inequality that marks dysfunctional societies. It is a club that we distinctly do not want to join, such as Bangladesh, Haiti, Burundi, and the Philippines. Such dramatic inequalities are the byproduct of a bubble-strewn economy beholden to a deregulated and all-powerful financial industry, all too often dictating government policies through its lobbying and money politics.

All our institutions are slowly shutting down, but in our society, there's one whose doors are always wide open, and increasingly so, and that is the prison system. One has to wonder, if all the countries in the world are in debt, where did all the money go? Who are we in so much debt to?

With the government acting as the enforcement division of the IRS and the Federal Reserve, what we have now is the "Department of Homeland Security" to do the dirty work. The central bankers know they have to establish a fascist state in order to ensure their "debt" gets paid. They are also the ones behind 9/11 and the whole "war on terror" ruse, which are pretexts to establish a police state. All countries are "indebted" to the same clique, so the Deep State plans to merge them into a thinly-disguised totalitarian one world government. Until the general population recognizes the real enemy, society is at war against itself—and it's all by design.

PSYCHOPATHS RUN WALL STREET

A psychopath is a person with a mental disorder characterized primarily by a lack of empathy and remorse, shallow emotions, egocentricity, heartlessness, and deceptiveness towards others. Heartlessness is related to an inability to experience important social emotions, like love or remorse. Psychopaths, who clearly lack empathy, are at a disadvantage—or so the thinking goes. However, empathy requires taking other people's feelings into consideration, walking in their shoes, so to speak. Walking requires energy. Luckily for psychopaths, no "walking" is required, unless it involves walking over other people to get what they want. Empathy is built on a foundation of emotions. Although vital for binding and meaningful relationships, emotions often cloud judgment. In the extreme, emotions can actually impede one's ability to think in a critical manner.

The CFA Institute, an investment and financial analysis organization, reports in *CFA Magazine* that one out of every 10 Wall Street employees is a clinical psychopath. That makes psychopathy 10 times more prevalent among New York's financial elite than among us common folk, for which the accepted statistic is a more palatable one in 100. Psychopaths "generally lack empathy and interest in what other people feel or think," according to the study. "At the same time, they display an abundance of charm, charisma, intelligence, credentials, an unparalleled capacity for…manipulation, and a drive for thrill seeking." That Wall Street should harbor more than its share of psychopaths, then, will come as no shock to those frustrated by the entitlement and greed of the one percent. The study also shows how easily psychopaths can pass for normal; blending into our lives as co-workers, friends and even romantic partners.

The sociopaths who run Wall Street and other massive corporations are only concerned about profit and rarely about people. By the nature of being a sociopath, they are con-

8   Newman, Alex, "World Bank Insider Blows Whistle on Corruption, Federal Reserve." https://thenewamerican.com/world-bank-insider-blows-whistle-on-corruption-federal-reserve/

tinually planning how to make sure their evil plans always work out. On the other hand, your average non-evil person has no plan at all about stopping evil or making sure "goodness" prevails. We just stumble through life thinking everyone should treat each other right and maybe go off and play some frisbee golf. But that does not change the fact that sociopaths do not have a conscience, which leaves the door open for all sorts of unfathomable actions to take place. And make no mistake, sociopaths know how to climb the corporate ladder par excellence. They occupy most of the really top positions in government and the nefarious world of finance.[9]

Is it any wonder that we still use 19th century energy technology? The Federation of American Scientists released a report stating that there have been over 5,000 patents that have been classified for "national security." Any patent that gets above 70% efficiency in converting energy is automatically classified by the U.S. Patent Office. What that means is that if anybody invents something that could challenge oil as the dominant energy source, the world will never see it. This is another regressive policy, thanks to the massive lobby power of Big Oil and the psychopathic Rockefeller dynasty.

MONEY IS THE ROOT OF ALL EVIL

Markets are not provided by nature. They are constructed—by laws, rules, and institutions. All of these have moral bases of one sort or another. Hence, all markets are moral, according to *someone's* sense of morality. The only question is, whose morality? The people with the most money are the ones least able to imagine a world without it. Their opinions currently shape the world. The poor can earn redemption only by suffering and thus, supposedly, getting an incentive to do better.

Many people are duped into believing that their taxes go towards building infrastructure, such as roads and schools, and without taxes the country would fall apart. In fact, the money is borrowed by the private banks and we are taxed in order to pay back the interest on the loans. Every person living in the Western world, who has a job, is required to give up about one quarter of their wages as income tax. And that money goes directly into the pockets of the individuals who run the world banking system. It is one big privately-run scam.

Consolidation of the global monetary system is leading us to the New World Order with the objective of a single currency and total control. Moves towards globalization of the world marketplace via organizations such as NAFTA and the WTO are further implementing the NWO agenda, as are moves to institute a one-world currency, ferment riots and revolutions, and remove citizens basic rights, not just in the USA, but around the globe. The banking empire and their use of money as a control mechanism over the people is a planetary cancer. It must be addressed as such and ultimately eliminated. The Golden Rule is not "He who owns the gold makes the rules."

Historically, American democracy is premised on the moral principle that citizens care about each other and that a robust public debate is the way to make the citizens more responsible for themselves and each other. After all, who is the market economy for? All of us. Equally. But with the sway of conservative morality, we are moving toward a 1 percent economy—for the bankers, the wealthy investors, and the super-rich like the six members of the family that owns Walmart and has accumulated more wealth than the bottom 30% of Americans combined. Six people! We can't stand idly by and watch an imaginary money system cause real death and destruction of the world and its inhabitants.

Money is fiction, but knowledge is power, so the more we learn about those who wish to impose a new fascism for world control, the better we'll be positioned to counter their evil agenda.

• •
9   Lefferts, Daniel, "5 Ways to Spot The Psychopath In Your Life": https://www.huffpost.com/entry/psychology-book_n_1315990#s747885 &title=Inhumane_or_simply

Author and political activist George Bernard Shaw, a member of the Fabian Society and proponent of eugenics, insisted that "the only fundamental and possible socialism is the socialization of the selective breeding of man."

A 1927 news headline documents when America was sold to five billionaire families who make claim to "Controlling society." By 1927, the deal was done, preceded by the Act of 1871, then the Federal Reserve Act in 1913. After control of the money system, the mass manipulation of America began. WW I, The Great Depression as an intermission and reset, then WW II. The bankers made ungodly hoards of cash and the countries involved went into massive debt to the bankers who loaned at interest all the countries money. The Rothschilds, DuPonts, Rockefellers, Morgans and Warburg family dynasties continue to steer the agenda of the USA and the Western world.

Hegelian Dialectic

Agenda
Centralization of power

Thesis
Manufactured terrorist threat

Anti-Thesis
Repressive police state

Synthesis
Removal of freedoms, transfer of power from the many to the few

With every secret agenda, there is a desired outcome. The Hegelian Dialectic has been studied by the elites and put into operation for over a century. To understand this tool for manipulation is to understand every hidden agenda and false flag in this modern age. It is also known as "Problem-Reaction-Solution."

Ever since the Knights Templar were betrayed by the Ashkenazi moneylenders in 1307, Jews were banned from entering Masonic lodges. It was not until 1782 that Adam Weishaupt and his Jewish "illuminati" associates were allowed to enter Masonic lodges again, and systematically took over the highest rankings of Freemasonry. Pictured is the "Freemasons Hall" of Great Queen Street in Covent Garden, London, England.

Leading Masonic authorities in the 18th and 19th centuries held a distinctively Christian interpretation of Freemasonry. Such leaders as Rev. James Anderson, William J. Hughan, William Hutchinson, Rev. George Oliver, and others had a Christian view of their Craft. Hutchinson, in particular, noted that Jesus Christ was the example for the Master Mason. He stated, "The Master Mason represents a man under the Christian doctrine saved from the grave of iniquity and raised to the faith of salvation. As the great testimonial that we are risen from the state of corruption, we bear the emblem of the Holy Trinity as the insignia of our vows and of the origin of the Master's order."

Only the most hated prisoners got "Hung, Drawn & Quartered." This barbaric form of execution was reserved for enemies of the crown, who had usually been convicted of treason. The condemned would be hung until half dead, then taken down and quartered alive. After that, their members and bowels would be cut out of their bodies and thrown into a nearby pit of fire, and the prisoner would be kept alive as long as possible to watch. The "quarters" of the body, were then, "hung" in various prescribed locations, as a deterrent to any other citizens of the realm, who might dare to be "treasonous" to the monarchy. The fact they formerly were publicly able to get away with this shows that, historically, "Members of the Royal bloodline" were absolutely cruel and evil.

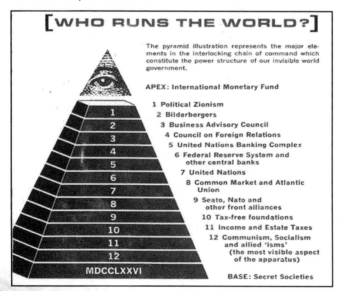

A study by the Swiss Federal Institute of Technology in Zurich has found that a mere 147 corporations control the world—orchestrating events and controlling governments. The analysis, which looked at the relationships between 43,000 trans-national corporations, identified only a tiny handful of mega-corporations, mostly banks, which held a disproportionate amount of power over world events.

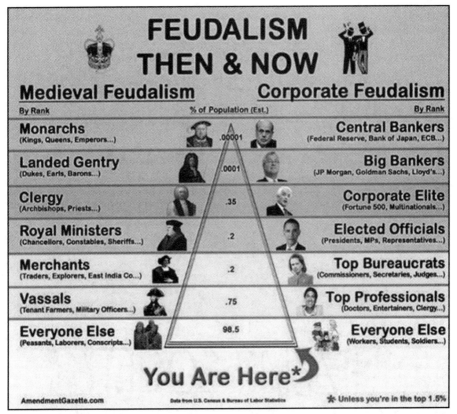

FEUDALISM THEN & NOW

Medieval Feudalism (By Rank)	% of Population (Est.)	Corporate Feudalism (By Rank)
Monarchs (Kings, Queens, Emperors...)	.00001	**Central Bankers** (Federal Reserve, Bank of Japan, ECB...)
Landed Gentry (Dukes, Earls, Barons...)	.0001	**Big Bankers** (JP Morgan, Goldman Sachs, Lloyd's...)
Clergy (Archbishops, Priests...)	.35	**Corporate Elite** (Fortune 500, Multinationals...)
Royal Ministers (Chancellors, Constables, Sheriffs...)	.2	**Elected Officials** (Presidents, MPs, Representatives...)
Merchants (Traders, Explorers, East India Co...)	.2	**Top Bureaucrats** (Commissioners, Secretaries, Judges...)
Vassals (Tenant Farmers, Military Officers...)	.75	**Top Professionals** (Doctors, Entertainers, Clergy...)
Everyone Else (Peasants, Laborers, Conscripts...)	98.5	**Everyone Else** (Workers, Students, Soldiers...)

You Are Here*

AmendmentGazette.com — Data from U.S. Census & Bureau of Labor Statistics — *Unless you're in the top 1.5%

All of today's think tanks originate from the Committee of 300, and include the Round Table started by Cecil Rhodes, plus the later-formed organizations seen on this chart. The Committee of 300 now call themselves "World Government Founders for the New World Order." Queen Elizabeth II is the head of the Committee of 300, which is modeled after the British East India Company's Council of 300, founded by the British aristocracy in 1727.

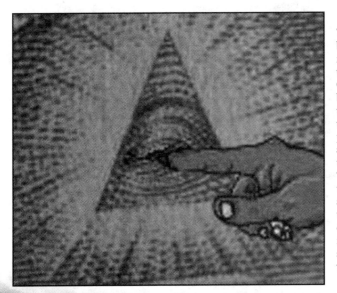

The USA is, and always has been, a huge corporation ruled from abroad. Its initial name was the Virginia Company and it is owned by the British Crown and the Vatican, who receive their yearly share of the profits. The U.S. presidents are appointed CEO's and their allegiance is to the "board of directors," not to the American citizens. We are seen as employees of the company and voting is designed as a distraction meant to offer us the illusion that we have a say in who controls us.

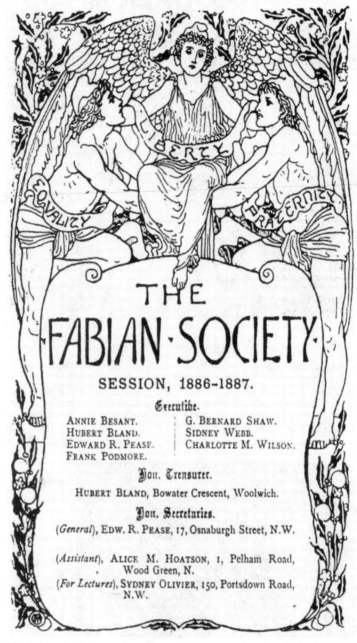

The Fabian Society was heavily promoting eugenics already in the 1800s. Eugenics is a racist ideology invented by Edward Bulwer Lytton, Francis Galton and his cousin Charles Darwin. Eugenics is a racist and faux-scientific ideology designed to damage the Working Class and create a brain drain in Africa and India.

VATICAN NAZIS

"The Jesuits are a military organization, not a religious
order. Their chief is a general of an army, not the
mere father abbot of a monastery. And the aim of
this organization is power—power in its most despotic
exercise—absolute power, universal power, power
to control the world by the volition of a single man.
Jesuitism is the most absolute of despotisms, and at the
same time the greatest and most enormous of abuses."
–Napoleon Bonaparte

HOW did everything go so terribly wrong with the largest religious institution on the planet? Considering that most Catholic parishioners are honest and moralistic people who follow the teachings of Jesus Christ, the Church should represent a force for good—from top to bottom. But it's the top of the hierarchy that is most troubling. There needs to be transparency all the way to the top, particularly the actions of the inner population living within Vatican City. Most especially curious about the pecking order is a seated Jesuit pope for the first time in history. What is the Jesuit Order, and why was it banned from a dozen countries just over 200 years ago? How did the upper echelon of the Catholic Church become so opposite to what they claim to represent? In a few words: spiritual thought control and financial power. Just as money is the root of all evil, it is also the primary cause of the seven deadly sins: gluttony, greed, envy, pride, lust, wrath and sloth. Everything has become inverted.

The hypocrisy is thick when looking at the words and actions from those at the very top. How can a filthy-rich institution preach spiritual values of poverty and chastity while cardinals, bishops and priests have covered up crimes of sexual abuse? Why has the church fought and resisted the compensation claims of their sexually, emotionally and spiritually-traumatized victims? Over the past five decades, more than 1,500 priests and bishops have been identified globally in the sexual assault of tens of thousands of boys and girls in their trusting congregations and orphanages.

In terms of neofascism, Vatican City is the perfect political prototype for a corporate entity. It answers to nobody. It pays taxes to nobody. Its bishops and priests have diplomatic immunity all over the world. It even has its own embassies. It owns more real estate than any other entity on the planet. It was never about God, Jesus or Christianity; it is about power and control and fashion "statements." The Vatican has major shareholding in most top corporations—Lockheed Martin and Bank of America being just two examples.[1]

Vatican City has only a thousand residents, and most of them live very private lives. Most members of the cabal are also members in the highest ranks of numerous secretive and occult societies, which in many cases extend straight back into the bloodlines of the ancient world. Consider how the pharaohs of Egypt were considered living gods. When the power of the Mediterranean world moved to Rome, the Caesars were considered living gods. Now we have the pope in Vatican City whom millions of Catholics worldwide believe has a direct connection with god. All roads lead to Rome.

A NAZI AND VATICAN CONCORDAT

The Nazi rise to power was official when Paul von Hindenburg appointed Adolf Hitler chancellor on January 30, 1933. Half a year later a Concordat was signed on July 20, 1933, in Vatican City between representatives of the German Reich and of the Holy See. The *Reichskonkordat* was ratified, and for all intents and purposes, is still in effect today. The exchange of instruments of ratification took place in Vatican City on September 10th, 1933 when the Concordat and the Final Protocol came into force pursuant to Article 34 of the Reich Concordat. The fact that the *Reichskonkordat* continues to apply in international law has the consequence that the resulting obligations on both sides are to be met by the contracting parties.

At the end of hostilities in World War II, the country of Germany surrendered the three fighting divisions to the Allies. The Third Reich never surrendered. The German "Nazi" Third Reich was only defeated militarily in 1945, not politically. The European aristocracy in Catholic countries and German nationalists with their ties to the Vatican never ended. It lives on today under the guise of the United Nations, the World Health Organization, the World Bank and the European Union (occupied Europe) and militarily with a new name, called NATO. The *Reichskonkordat* of 1933 that created the Vatican and the German Nazi Third Reich war treaty alliance by Article 123 (2) Basic Law remains still in force. It states:

> *Article 123 (2) Basic Law does not mean that Länder legislations are constitutionally bound by the schooling provisions of the Reich Concordat and therefore cannot make any contrary laws. Article 123 (2) Basic Law instead implies as regards the schooling provisions of the Reich Concordat only that they shall as long as they were still in force before entry into force of the Basic Law continue to apply although deriving from a treaty not concluded by the Länder, now solely entitled to decide in this area.*[2]

VATICAN NAZI RAT LINES

Before and after WW II, the Vatican authority recognized the *Reichskonkordat* by fully supporting Hitler and his Nazi regime. Some high-ranking Nazis were allowed shelter in Catholic monasteries, disguised as monks, including Martin Bormann, reportedly at Montserrat, Spain. The Vatican was also complicit in organizing and helping

1   Logan, Gordon, "One World Pecking Order" https://tapnewswire.com/2011/10/one-world-pecking-order/

2   The *Reichskonkordat* of 1933 that created the Vatican German Nazi Third Reich war treaty alliance is by Article 123 (2) Basic Law still in force today: https://law.utexas.edu/transnational/foreign-law-translations/german/case.php?id=597#top

operate the so-called "rat lines," those escape routes for former Nazi officers to leave Europe for Latin American and other countries, replete with new identities. This network, called *die Spinne* (German for "the Spider"), was a post-World War II organization, largely designed by Bormann, to help certain Nazi war criminals escape justice.[3] The so-called *Kameradenwerk* was a relief organization for Nazi criminals that helped fugitives escape, and had maintained close political, social, and business ties with the Vatican. Researcher Christopher Everard writes:

> Several Popes have supported Nazism. Not only that, but the Vatican supplied "Escape Funds" for former Nazi officers who fled to South America and Africa after the war. These Nazi war criminals were given Knights of Malta passports. The Knights of Malta are a micro-nation with United Nations status, and are the smallest nation on earth—they have no land—just plush offices close to the Vatican. You have to be a Catholic to be a "citizen"—and it is these Knights of Malta who colluded with the Vatican to assist Nazis to escape. But if that wasn't bad enough, we can see a similarity between the Bavarian-British Royals who financed Hitler, such as Prince Carl Eduard Saxe-Coburg and the Von Hessen clan—and the Knights of Malta; they all support the idea of a One Nation EU Superstate. They all supported Hitler. (Descendants of) these people are still in control to this day.

Monsignor Giovanni Battista Montini was an OSS operative in Southeast Asia at the end of World War II. He was later appointed Pope Paul VI from 1963 until his death in 1978. After the war, he used the welfare organization of the Catholic Charities (called *Caritas International*) to provide refugee travel documents, aiding in their escape to fascist-friendly countries, including Spain, Syria and various South American countries. The Knights of Malta, the Red Cross and other Vatican-based aid agencies also participated in establishing the rat lines, including assistance in assuming new identities and financial support.[4]

Which other Nazis did the Vatican rat line network help to escape at the end of WW II? The list reads like a Who's Who of serial killers. Most researchers claim the following people were given sanctuary by the Vatican and Knights of Malta diplomatic services and helped them evade justice. One of the most notorious was Klaus Barbie, the cruel Gestapo officer known as the "Butcher of Lyons," who lived out the rest of his life behind a sawmill in Bolivia. There was Franz Stangl, Commandant of the notorious Treblinka extermination camp, who was arrested in Brazil in 1967, and died in prison awaiting trial. Gustav Wagner was Commandant of Sorbibor extermination camp and died an old man in São Paulo, Brazil, completely escaping justice. Alois Brunner, a brutal official in the Jewish deportation program lived out his natural life and died in Syria in 2010. One of the most famous Nazis to escape was Adolf Eichmann, a chief architect of the Holocaust, who was captured and secretly whisked off to Israel, where he was tried and executed in 1960. Dr. Josef Mengele, the "White Angel" of Auschwitz concentration camp, completely escaped justice under a new identity. Then there was the Deputy *Führer* Martin Bormann, tried at Nuremberg *in absentia* and sentenced to death, which is strange because he supposedly died in Berlin in the waning days of the war. Yet Bormann kept popping up all around Argentina and elsewhere in South America during the 1950s.[5]

JESUITS INFILTRATE THESOPHY

After Madame Blavatsky died in 1891, the Theosophical movement she founded less than a decade earlier was said to have several thousand adepts. Such an opportunity for a controlled opposition platform must have been very tempting to a secretive religious

3 Rauschning, Hermann, *Germany's Revolution of Destruction*. London, 1939.
4 Shirer, William, *The Rise and Fall of the Third Reich* (Secker & Warburg Ltd, London 1964).
5 Ravenscroft, Trevor, *The Spear of Destiny*. Transworld Publishers Ltd; Corgi, London 1972.

order. Post-mortem, there was a covert Jesuit takeover of the organization which positioned Theosophy as the heart of the pseudo-spirituality movement of the New World Order. Theosophy became a key component in the advent of the One World Religion concept.

Esoteric investigative reporter Leo Lyon Zagami outlines in his book, *The Invisible Master*, a detailed account of a malevolent ET presence called the "Secret Chiefs." These entities have historically been associated with Jesuit leaders, the Nazi elite, and the founder of Theosophy:

> *Certainly, it is hard to believe that these Invisible Masters could be involved not only with the benevolent side of humanity but also with the wicked, as in the case of Nazism and Himmler, who also admired the figure of Blavatsky and her studies. When German race theorists incorporated Blavatsky's narrative, it was within a larger program of asserting German superiority, but there was also in it the hidden hand of the Invisible Masters. In 1888, Blavatsky published her* magnum opus, *the two-volume set* The Secret Doctrine. *In this work, she outlines a new vision of humanity's evolution, one that places the Aryans at the top of a racial hierarchy. She claimed these revelations came from occult sources, meaning her Secret Chiefs, and she went on informing of various German occult organizations of the Illuminati network which, in turn, would later lay the foundation for the racial theories of Nazism.*

> *The creation of a temple for communication by the SS elite (Wewelsberg), with the Secret Chiefs, considered the true Invisible Masters of esoteric Nazism, shows the ambivalence of the values of these entities from a typical human perspective. Often we have a limited understanding of their intervention in human affairs because we view it from their immortal perspective, not tied to our space-time reality. If we want to think like a Secret Chief or an Invisible Master, we have to have, first of all, a good idea of infinity. ...and then proceed as Jesus did, but also Gautama Buddha, the historical Buddha. That is why Esoteric Nazism had a very strong bond with Tibetan Buddhism, and with a few Buddhist sects who work in this direction in the hope of overcoming the impositions of our present understanding of the space-time continuum, so that we may have an otherwise inaccessible vision for common mortals.*[6]

Jesuit priest Malachi Martin, who served in Rome, broke ranks and declared that a private enthronement of Satan in the Vatican took place in 1963. According to Eric Gajewski, a traditional Catholic and founder of the TradCatKnight website and YouTube channel: "There's no question that Lucifer was enthroned at the Vatican. These Luciferians hide behind the collar and they have a plan to usher in this Luciferian New Age. ...there is a battle between Lucifer/Satan [versus] God and the [traditional] Catholic Church."

MALEVOLENT SPIRITUAL WORLD

The works of multiple scholars, from Plato to Manly P. Hall, and further down the line, suggest it is essentially the use of rituals and techniques which actually invoke and control "spirits" or lifeforms that could be existing within other dimensions or worlds. For example, according to Hall:

> *A magician, enveloped in sanctified vestments and carrying a wand inscribed with hieroglyphic figures, could by the power vested in certain words and symbols control the invisible inhabitants of the elements and of the astral world. While the elaborate ceremonial magic of antiquity was not necessarily evil, there arose from its perversion several false schools of sorcery, or black magic. ...By means of the secret processes of ceremonial magic it is possible to contact these invisible creatures and gain their help in some human undertaking. Good spirits willingly lend their as-*

6   Zagami, Leo Lyon, *The Invisible Master: Secret Chiefs, Unknown Superiors, and the Puppet Masters Who Pull the Strings of Occult Power from the Alien World*. CCC Publishing, 2018.

sistance to any worthy enterprise, but evil spirits serve only those who live to pervert and destroy. ...The most dangerous form of black magic is the scientific perversion of occult power for the gratification of personal desire.

The Vatican claims to be following the word of "God," but multiple insiders have come forth speaking about the predominant practice of Satanism within the Vatican. In Hall's book, he provides many examples of how ceremonial magic, sorcery, and more were all practiced, and are a driving force among some very powerful people. He goes into the how's, what's and why's, but that which used to be pure, according to Hall, was taken and perverted by the world's elite, who, according to Hall and many others, still practice "black magic" to this very day. A distinction must be made between black magic and white magic. Basically, black magic is the process of using entities to accomplish a goal through ceremonial magic. White magic is mostly used for personal empowerment and is generally harmless.[7]

VATICAN ASTRONOMERS

The Vatican has been leasing time on or actually purchasing many of the world's observatories with powerful telescopes. In addition, the Vatican has built its own state of the art high-powered stereo telescope called L.U.C.I.F.E.R., which stands for "Large Binocular Telescope Near-infrared Utility with Camera and Integral Field Unit for Extragalactic Research." It is a chilled instrument attached to a telescope in Arizona. And yes, it's named for the Devil, whose name itself means "morning star" (and which) happens to be right next to the Vatican Observatory on Mt. Graham in Tucson.

Obviously, the Vatican is deeply invested in watching the skies and waiting for the appearance of some major event that they believe will change human beliefs, culture and society forever. They even give the year 2022 as an arrival date. Vatican insiders believe this coming event will shift humankind from the ordinary mundane everyday life concerns to a new esoteric mindset, quite foreign to most.

The Vatican is awaiting the appearance of their true Messiah, Lucifer, who will be an extraterrestrial that will come to Earth to take over and rule from the Catholic Church in a new "Third" Temple built in Jerusalem. Moves are already underway to acquire and demolish the Al-Aqsa Mosque on Temple Mount. The Catholic Church has obtained secret agreements, with all parties involved, to administer Jerusalem as an open, international territory, ushering in their long-anticipated One World Religion.

The final prophecy of the Mary apparition of Fatima in 1917 has never been revealed to the public. It relates to the imposter pope that will usher in a socialistic one-world religion. The final message of Fatima is: "In the end, my immaculate heart will triumph." This suggests the New World Order will ultimately fail, but there will be a spiritual warfare battle first.[8]

THE JESUITS

Historically, the Jesuit "Society of Jesus" mission was established in 1540 and organized as a military order to eliminate Protestant Christianity throughout the world. Later, it set its sights on the United States as being the last frontier to be conquered. The Jesuits' self-proclaimed mission is to educate and assist the underprivileged in society. To that end, they are actively engaged in evangelization and apostolic ministry in 112 nations. Some researchers think that's the cover story, when actually they worship Lucifer (not Satan) and practice the most sadistic forms of human sacrifice, homosexuality, pedophilia, black magic, and murder. Members of the Society of Jesus have been implicated in the Catholic Church child sexual abuse scandal.

....
7   Mullins, Eustace, *The World Order: Our Secret Rulers: A Study in the Hegemony of Parasitism.* Omnia Veritas Ltd, 1985.
8   Moore, George, *Confessions of a Young Man* (Penguin Books Ltd, London 1939).

To maintain their image, the Jesuits employ (and finance) the services of multiple al-phabet agencies in the USA, including the NSA, DHS, FEMA, OSS, ONI, FBI, CIA, DIA, DEA, the Pentagon, the Department of Defense, NASA, the Federal Reserve, the Internal Revenue Service, the Congress, and other Federal agencies as deemed neces-sary. According to Preston James of *Veterans Today*, foreign military and intelligence agencies have historically been under Jesuit control, and they include the German SS, Deutsche *Verteidigungs Dienst* (underground Abwehr/DVD), the British MI5 and MI6, the Israeli Mossad, NATO, Interpol, the KGB, the Chilean DINA, and even the United Nations, to name the largest. There are other NGOs. Assassinations are carried out by the aforementioned intelligence agencies and their Mafia partners in the drug and gam-bling trades, often with collateral assistance from the Knights of Malta, the Freemasons, the Knights of Columbus, and the Italian secret society P2 (Propaganda Due).[9]

The Society of Jesus proclaims it is in "service" to the Vatican and to humankind by "assist-ing the downtrodden through education." The Jesuits are the Catholic religious order with the second highest number of Catholic schools which they run. These are 168 tertiary institutions in 40 countries and 324 secondary schools in 55 countries. Only the "Broth-ers of the Christian Schools" have more, with over 560 Lasallian educational institutions. One school with primarily Jesuit influence is Stonyhurst College in Lancashire, England, known as a "Catholic" institution that boasts of its association with the Society of Jesus.

George H. Walker, business partner with the Bush family, was a self-proclaimed Episcopalian who "spent part of his education in England at Stonyhurst College," according to his *Wikipedia* biography. This ties in to the Jesuits, because Prescott Bush was married in 1921 to Dorothy Walker at Kennebunkport, Maine. George H. Walker eventually became the president of the W.A. Harriman & Co. invest-ment firm and assisted Averell Harriman in acquiring the Hamburg-Amerika Line. This shipping company, with the aid of the highly-corrupt New York bank, almost single-handedly was responsible for the infiltration of Nazis into the U.S.—both before and after the war. Today, it is obvious that total cooperation was secured by gaining complete control of the New York Port Authority, the Immigration and Naturalization Service, and key posts and persons all the way to the top in the U.S. government. With the level of "protection" afforded the Hamburg-Amerika Line, money could be shipped to the UBC (New York-based Union Banking Corporation) and Brown Brothers Harriman, ultimately to be laundered and then returned to Hitler in Germany. But the Nazis were not the sole beneficiaries of the loot. The Nazis were the pawns for a far more sinister authority—the Vatican, the Jesuit Order and the "Black Pope."[10]

THE BLACK POPE

Further investigation reveals that Pope Francis is covertly controlled by the Superior General of the Society of Jesus, Peter Hans Kolvenbach, also known as the Black Pope. The administrative offices where Jesuit business is conducted (called the General Curia) is located in "Rome," but more specifically, within the Vatican. Following the dictates of Ignatius Loyola's "25 Sessions" and the leadership of the Superior General, the ultimate goal of the General Curia is to "destroy and rebuild the Temple of Solomon, reestablishing the seat of the Pope in Israel."

The Jesuits are a covert continuation of a diabolical Babylonian ritual sacrifice and as-sassination cult that morphed and rebranded itself into the Knights Templar at the time of the Crusades, and then rebranded into the Jesuits under the masquerade of the "So-ciety of Jesus." Their agenda is nothing less than world domination.

9   Fagan, Myron, *CFR Completely Unmasked as Illuminati in U.S.* Cinema Educational Guild, 1966.
10 Goodson, Stephen Mitford: *A History of Central Banking and the Enslavement of Mankind*; Black House Publishing, 2014.

The Society employs a variety of ruthless tactics to accomplish its long-term goal of a New World Order, including a One World Religion, that pays homage to their Black Pope. One method is carrying out political assassinations of world leaders who refuse to comply with its demands. These assassinations in the U.S. have included presidents (Abraham Lincoln and JFK), cabinet members, congressmen, senators, diplomats, journalists, scientists and religious and business leaders.[11]

THE DIRTY BUSINESS

The Vatican City was established in 1929 by the Lateran Treaty, signed by Cardinal Secretary of State Pietro Gasparri, on behalf of the Holy See. The word "See" is thus often applied to the area over which the bishop exercises authority. The Holy See is the Episcopal Jurisdiction of the Catholic Church in Rome, in which its bishop is commonly known as the pope. Such a rigid hierarchy is an easy way for the planners of the New World Order to exert their control. The Holy See as a "legal person" bears many similarities with the British Crown, or the Citizens United ruling in the USA. Under the Vatican model, the pope legally has complete and utter control over every single person on the planet. Is it any wonder the pope has endorsed the New World Order?

The "Unholy Trinity" consists of financial power based in the City of London, the spiritual control exerted from the City of Vatican, plus the City of Columbia, otherwise known as a district located at the heart of Washington D.C., where the largest military force in the world is centered. These are each independent states within states which compose "The Empire of Three Cities." The first controls the world economy through the central banks, the second is religious control over the Earth, and the third is military control over the planet. Together they make the very unholy trinity which forms the Egyptian pyramid "All-Seeing Eye" that we can see on the back of the privately-owned Federal Reserve note, used as the American dollar, to maintain the colony in debt and under the Queen.[12]

Money is the main tool that counts for everything these days. The fact that the Rothschilds are the richest family on the planet and also of the Jewish faith has led to misplaced hate. It is unacceptable to blame all Jews for the acts of the Rothschild family. Similarly, we cannot hold all Catholics responsible for the actions of the Black Pope, or condemn all Muslims for the atrocities committed by suicide bombers in the name of Islam. The power elite of the Jewish faith use their religion to fend off attacks against them. Any effort made to expose them is described as a hate crime against all Jews. Almost all investigations of international bankers wind up with the investigators being attacked as anti-Semitic. This has made the subject of wealthy Jews taboo for fear of being labeled anti-Semitic. International finance and banking are not primarily "Jewish," although the Bank of England has been controlled by the Rothschild family since the early 1800s. Many of the most powerful banking interests in the world are run by "Gentiles." One of the most powerful forces in international banking is the Knights of Malta, a Roman Catholic military order controlled by the Jesuit Superior General.

In an example of "talking to power," Gordon Logan examines the "One World Pecking Order" on the TAP Blog, a forum used by independent writers:

> I once knew an MI6 officer who was a killer on occasion, and a lot of other things. He was also a Catholic, and I even drove him to confession once. He was also a member of Opus Dei. I also found evidence that he was a Freemason. He was a big fan of the Freemason Ratzinger. So, he was a real-life Dan Brown character, with a bit of Le Carre mixed in.

11 Nietzsche, F., *Thus Spake Zarathustra*. New York, 1937.

12 Henderson, Dean, *The Federal Reserve Cartel: The Eight Families*: June 01, 2011, **https://www.globalresearch.ca/the-federal-reserve-cartel-the-eight-families/25080**

What was interesting was his view of the hierarchy of power. He was circumspect when talking about the power of bankers—he considered that a rather dangerous subject since the conspiracy was still under wraps in those days. He was also circumspect about Jews, especially those he had to work with. In fact, at one point he was ordered to patch up his relations with them. I made a point of getting on well with everybody, so he asked me to help him! He didn't say anything about Jesuits, though he was quite aware of the pecking order of power.

I must say I find it difficult to believe that Jesuits wield power that is at all comparable to that of the top Zionist bankers like Lloyd Blankfein, who says he "does God's work." Then of course there is the obvious cover-up of the colossal Rothschild wealth, which itself conceals colossal political power with its concomitant secrecy in places like the U.S. Treasury, where every last cent of the huge, coerced and odious federal debt is collateralized by America's huge resources and of course the resources of many other countries, thanks to the World Bank and the IMF.

Anybody who believes that the Rothschilds somehow "missed out" in America is wrong. The owners of the Fed are in the Rothschild pocket and have been for over a century. Even the mighty J.P. Morgan turned out to be a Rothschild pawn, when his will was read. Without Rothschild, Israel and the Jews would be nothing. "We have nothing to lose but our chains," as their house charlatan, Marx, once said.

By "connecting the dots" it is apparent that Goldman Sachs is one of the main Federal Reserve banking conglomerates. So is JP Morgan Chase, including a financial set-up that was allegedly used to process more than a billion euros for the Vatican bank. Italian investigators suspect that it was also used to launder funds from dubious sources. The lower-level employees probably would never know this, but the higher-ups at JP Morgan are directly aware that an attack against Goldman Sachs is a direct attack against JP Morgan, the Federal Reserve, and the Illuminati. Many "truth" researchers have concluded that the Vatican has been penetrated at the highest levels by the Illuminati, most especially by the members of the P2 Freemason Lodge of Rome.[13]

KNIGHTS OF MALTA AND P2

Brexit aside, there is a gaping hole at the center of the EU Superstate, and that is Switzerland which is not a member; neither is Vatican City, nor is the sovereign Knights of Malta. In fact, Andorra, Liechtenstein, Monaco and San Marino are micronations in Europe which have all refused to join the EU Superstate structure. Despite this, their economies are booming and have not required any "bail outs," probably due to the fact that they operate low taxation governments.

Cardinal Spellman was a religious leader of the Knights of Malta based out of New York City. He was a protégé of Cardinal Pacelli, Pope Pius XII, who is often accused of collaboration with the Nazis. Spellman is responsible for introducing Ngo Dinh Diem to Allen Dulles, and then proposing his presidency of South Vietnam to President Kennedy. When Diem resisted the introduction of American troops into Vietnam, Dulles told General Westmoreland to go ahead anyway, and our CIA helped to kill Diem.

P2 was always more than just your "average" Masonic lodge. It had members who were Italy's leading industrialists. Cumulatively, their business interests dominated manufacturing business in Italy, Monaco, France and Germany. P2 was headed publicly by Licio Gelli—also known as the "Puppet Master."

For all intent and purposes, P2 was the "interface" between the Bavarian-British Nazi financiers, such as Prince Carl Eduard Saxe-Coburg and the Von Hessen clan—and the

13 Sampson, Anthony, *The Money Lenders: The People and Politics of the World Banking Crisis.* Penguin Books. New York. 1981.

Knights of Malta communist-fascist factions which supported the ideals of a One Nation EU Superstate. It is interesting to note that the Knights of Malta—although it is a "nation" based in Rome—is officially not part of the E.U. Superstate.[14]

VATICAN BANKERS

Banco Ambrosiano was an Italian bank which collapsed in 1982 with the suspicious death of banker Roberto Calvi, or "God's Banker," who was found hanging under Blackfriars bridge in London. His high-profile death had all the hallmarks of a Masonic assassination. Roberto Calvi had close ties and multiple friendships linked to the P2 Masonic lodge. Calvi had just transferred a vast amount of cash from Banco Ambrosiano to the P2 Masonic organization, bankrupting his bank in the process. It is interesting to note that the major shareholder in Banco Ambrosiano was the Vatican itself. It appears there was in-fighting between the Vatican and Masonic factions, or it may have been a money-laundering operation, clearing the accounts of Banco Ambrosiano of money that had tracer-lines leading to criminal activity. Subsequently, the bank collapsed. And, as any detective knows, when a bank collapses, its files and archives often disappear into a "black hole." Perhaps that was the main intention—to "sanitize" the trail of money held in Banco Ambrosiano's accounts and silence the messenger?

The Vatican is located within the epicenter of a vast, interlocking global corporate cabal. This does not mean the Vatican itself is evil, nor are most of the people working there—but they have a very serious money laundering problem. JP Morgan Chase closed the Vatican bank's account in March, 2012, along with an Italian branch of the U.S. banking giant because of concerns about a lack of transparency at the Holy See's financial institution, Italian newspapers reported. The closure move by JP Morgan Chase, which was also reported by two leading general newspapers—*Corriere della Sera* and *La Stampa*—was a further blow to the Vatican's Institute for Works of Religion (IOR) bank. This bank's image has been tarnished by a string of scandals, including accusations of money laundering and fraud. The IOR is regarded as something akin to a trust company for clandestine monetary transactions that is not only used by the Church, but allegedly also by the mafia as well as corrupt politicians and companies. The bank's exotic status of belonging to a religious monarchy in a sovereign state the size of a city park has shielded it from investigations and unpleasant external monitoring. The public image of the bank has also been harmed by the so-called "Vatileaks" scandal, in which highly sensitive documents, including letters to Pope Benedict, were published in the Italian media. The Vatican has tried to put behind it scandals that have included accusations of money laundering and fraud. Many whistleblowers claim that the Vatican is the "spiritual head" of the Illuminati.[15]

THE VAMPIRE OCTOPUS

The Institute for the Works of Religion, commonly known as the Vatican Bank, had supplied banking services to escaping former Nazis, and has been complicit in other crimes. The Vatican Bank was headed from 2009 to 2012 by Ettore Gotti Tedeschi, and like many Vatican Bank bosses before him, he has been questioned over irregularities and scandals. When Mr. Tedeschi was placed under investigation in 2010, the Vatican said it was "perplexed and astonished," and expressed full confidence in Mr. Tedeschi. As part of the inquiry, Italian tax police seized 23 million euros that the Vatican Bank had tried to transfer from a small Italian bank called Credito Artigianato. In a separate case, Tedeschi's home in Piacenza, Italy, was raided in 2012, along with his two work offices in Milan.

Essentially, nearly every country in the world is run by a shadow government, which owes its loyalty to the New World Order controlled by a 13-member Illuminati Council. The

14 Allem Gary, *The Rockefeller File*. '76 Press. Seal Beach, CA. 1977.
15 Editors of Executive Intelligence Review, *Dope Inc.: The Book That Drove Kissinger Crazy*. Washington, DC. 1992.

New World Order is a long-term plan for the elite of the Western World to control all the people of Earth. The Ring of Power are the super-rich families who wish to control us all through the current financial system, military might, as well as religious control. The wealthiest organization on the planet is also a religious order called the Catholic Church.

An "octopus" of privately-held corporations now span the world. Under the fraudulent TPP and the TTIP agreements, corporations will become satellite states or "micro-nations" much like the Vatican has become, with their own closed secret law courts, their own diplomatic immunity and their tax-free status. They will now have the same rights and powers as governments. They will be able to sue governments for loss of income due to wage labor laws, health laws, and environmental laws—in fact, any government regulation that they see as a hindrance to their profitability.

The Black Nobility, the Jesuits, the Illuminati and the Zionist Bankers will change like chameleons; in fact, they already have. They are now the CEOs of these corporations and have successfully removed themselves from nation-state status and the thrones on which they once sat, and distanced themselves from the altars at which they once served as priests and from the central banks which they once controlled. Pope Francis is reported to be a Freemason; not a true pope but an imposter pope, and there have been others before him. Pope Francis once made the curious comment: "Communists make the best Christians."

RENT-BOY VATICAN SEX RINGS

In July, 2013, *The Times of London* reported that Don Patrizio Poggi, a parish priest in Rome who served five years for sexually abusing teenage boys, had filed a complaint with Italian police, alleging the existence of a Vatican "rent-boy" ring. According to the newspaper, Poggi claims that a former officer of the Carabinieri, Italy's military police, served as the pimp:

> *The former Carabinieri police officer pulled up outside a bar known as Twink—slang for a gay youth—next to Rome's central station. He was driving a Fiat Panda marked "Emergency Blood" so he could easily park. There, he picked up Romanian immigrant "rent-boys," some underage, for gay encounters with Catholic priests around Rome.*

While Poggi's accusation sounds like a deeply-twisted and morally-depraved dark thriller, the *Times* says his allegations "gained some credibility from the fact that he was accompanied by Monsignor Luca Lorusso, an adviser to the Papal Nuncio to Italy, who is himself a confidante of Pope Francis." Cardinal Agostino Vallini, head of the Catholic Vicariate of Rome, dismissed Poggi's accusations as slander, "motivated perhaps by a spirit of revenge or personal resentment." However, Poggi maintains that he came forward to report an abuse of power: "The hiring of the boys by the three took place essentially by using their desperation and the lack of means of support that characterized their social condition," he charged.

The emerging picture is the Catholic Church in Rome operating as a secret gay cabal, but the accusations only get worse. The *Times of London*'s account does not include other claims by Poggi published elsewhere regarding "selling consecrated hosts for Satanic rites." Such a Vatican-wide "rent-boy" ring seemed more plausible, but the Satanic rite claim only continues to widen.

A SICK OCCULT RELIGION

Priests in Catholic churches all around the world have been accused of sex scandals, including those within the Vatican. Some claim the Vatican has paid over four billion dollars since 1950 to settle sexual abuse claims. Far too often these stories involve priests taking advantage of their positions of authority and trust in order to sexually abuse those under their care, often children.

Poggi also accused the former Carabinieri of selling consecrated hosts for Satanic rites. He also reportedly presented documentary and photographic evidence to police in the company of two senior Vatican clergymen, who vouched for his credibility. Leo Lyon Zagami has written a series of books based on Illuminati insider testimony, including human sacrifices at the Vatican in a small chapel called San Lorenzo in Piscibus, and the Ninth Circle Satanic cult run out of the Vatican and other Catholic properties.[16] There is a tie-in with the global elite, and the merging of Vatican occult beliefs. As David Wilcock writes:

> Unfortunately, these top Deep State people have a very, very sick occult religion that includes pedophilia and Satanic-type practices, such as animal and human sacrifice. Strangely, their religious tradition requires them to "hide it out in the open" and tell us what they are doing, such as in thinly-disguised fiction. They feel that if they openly show us what they are doing (in films and staged events), and we still fall for it, then we deserve to be enslaved.

The Q posts have stated that "symbolism will be their downfall." More and more people are waking up to the brutal reality of pedophilia and Satanic-type practices at the highest levels. Sexual abuse scandals within the Vatican have been made public, and the Pope has been forced to comment on it many times. Whether he is personally involved or not is unknown, as there may very well be good forces within the Vatican as well, and perhaps conflicts among those who are part of the various orders. Pope Francis recently compared sexual child abuse to a "Satanic mass," which was an interesting correlation.

THE VATICAN IN PERSPECTIVE

The Catholic Church is the biggest global financial power, wealth accumulator, and property owner in existence, possessing more material wealth than any bank, corporation, giant trust or government anywhere on the globe. The Vatican authority rules over approximately two billion of the world's seven billion people. The colossal wealth of the Vatican includes enormous investments with the Rothschilds in Britain, France, and the USA, with Big Oil energy companies like Shell and weapons corporations like General Electric. The Vatican reserve of solid gold bullion, worth many billions, is stored with the Rothschild-controlled Bank of England and the U.S. Federal Reserve Bank.

So how did the Vatican accumulate all that wealth over the millennium? One method was to put a price-tag on sin. Many bishops and popes actively marketed guilt, sin, and fear for profit, by selling indulgences. Worshippers were encouraged to pre-pay for sins they hadn't yet committed and get pardoned ahead of time. Those who didn't pay-up risked eternal damnation. Another method was to get wealthy land owners to hand-over their land/fortune to the church on their death bed, in exchange for a blessing which would supposedly enable them to go directly to heaven. And of course, priests were not allowed to marry, and this would prevent the transfer of any wealth or property onto their family. It all stayed with the Church.

While 2/3 of the world's residents earn less than $2 a day and 1/5 of the world's population is underfed or starving to death, the Vatican hoards the world's wealth and profits from it on the stock market. At the same time, it preaches about giving. This has to change.

• •

16 Zagami, Leo Lyon, *Confessions of an Illuminati, Volume III: Espionage, Templars and Satanism in the Shadows of the Vatican.* CCC Publishing, 2017.

Pope Pius XII was nicknamed "Hitler's Pope." Before his election to the papacy, he served as secretary of the Department of Extraordinary Ecclesiastical Affairs, papal nuncio to Germany, and Cardinal Secretary of State, in which capacity he worked to conclude treaties with European and Latin American nations, most notably the *Reichskonkordat* with Nazi Germany.

The Jesuits were founded just before the Council of Trent (1545–1563) and the ensuing Counter-Reformation that would introduce reforms within the Catholic Church, and so counter the Protestant Reformation throughout Catholic Europe. The Jesuits also supported the Nazis, as they are seen giving the salute during the war.

Ein Erzbischof segnet das Hakenkreuzbanner

One of the most popular destinations for the Nazi officers was Argentina. In a fascinating photo we see "An Archbishop Blesses the Swastika Banner." The subcaption reads: "Before the Cathedral of Buenos Aires, Archbishop Dr. Luis Copello blesses the swastika flag of the German pilgrim group, who had gone to the Eucharistic Congress in Argentina. This ceremony was attended by the German Ambassador and the Argentine Foreign Minister." The photograph was published in the Nazis' foremost newspaper, *Der Stürmer*, in July 1935 (no. 29), when Hitler was preparing to decree the swastika banner the national flag of Germany.

JOSEPH GREINER

STARB
HIER
AM
2·1·36
DEN
FIEBERTOD
IM
DIENSTE
DEUTSCHER
FORSCHUNGS
ARBEIT
—
DEUTSCHE
AMAZONAS
JARY
EXPEDITION
1935-37

Remnants of Catholic Nazis are found all over South America, including in the Amazon region, as pictured here. Axis Italian dictator Benito Mussolini was also a Catholic, and famously said "fascism is the merger of the state and corporate power."

The more we do to you, the less you seem to believe we are doing it.

- Joseph Mengele

Josef Mengele was a German SS officer and physician stationed at the Auschwitz concentration camp, where he conducted genetic research on human subjects. His subsequent experiments focused primarily on twins, with little regard for the health or safety of the victims. Mengele sailed to Argentina in July, 1949, assisted by the "Rat Line" network. He drowned in 1979 after suffering a stroke while swimming off the Brazilian coast, and was buried under a false name. Mengele's remains were disinterred and positively identified by forensic examination in 1985.

What is the purpose of placing a chemtrails tanker plane spraying over the planet on this Vatican coin? Hidden in plain sight?

One of the stages used by Pope Francis during his Brazilian tour in July, 2013. It would seem there is an occult meaning in the reptilian eyes peering from behind.

Hitler's bunker in Berlin, where he supposedly committed suicide in 1945. According to another account, he escaped war-ravaged Germany with Martin Bormann and others before the end of the war. High ranking Nazis lived out the rest of their lives in fascist-controlled Argentina and other Latin American countries.

Wieluń, Poland, just after German Luftwaffe bombing on the 1st of September, 1939. Not only did this bombing provide a spark for World War II, but it is generally believed to be the first terrorist bombing in history. The Luftwaffe started bombing Wieluń at 4:40 a.m., five minutes before the shelling of *Westerplatte*, which has traditionally been considered the beginning of World War II. It killed an estimated 1,300 civilians, injured hundreds more and destroyed 90% of the town center. There were no military targets of any importance in the area. The casualty rate was more than twice as high as Guernica, Spain, another civilian-targeted city.

The unusual fires in California that burned trees from the inside, melted car engines but left plastic bins nearby unburned, and "vaporized" select properties but not others were caused by Directed Energy Weapons (DEWs) mounted on unmanned drones. These fires were started each year from 2018 to 2021 and were employed as a strategy of tension, a false flag terror method to inflict fear and push a political agenda, as was revealed in the Operation Gladio trials. The Agenda 2030 plan is to depoulate California, and allow globalists to acquire property for pennies on the dollar.

AMERICAN NAZIS

"The people can always be brought to the bidding of the leaders. That is easy. All you have to do is tell them they are being attacked and denounce the pacifists for lack of patriotism and exposing the country to danger. It works the same way in any country." –Hermann Göring, statement given at the 1946 Nuremberg trials

WHEN the words "fascist government" are mentioned, two of the biggest players from the Axis Powers come to mind—Mussolini's Italy and Nazi Germany. The USA went to war to fight these fascist regimes at a great cost in lives and capital. So how did the USA not only get infected by a new form of fascism, but became the beacon for a corporate dictatorship less than a century later?

During World War II, the Nazi effort was to unite all of Europe through war, and ultimately the rest of the world, but it failed miserably. When it was clear Germany was going to lose the war, key Nazi officers and rich industrialists met in Strasbourg on August 10th, 1944, to discuss post-war survival strategies in what would become the Fourth Reich. After the war, these fleeing Nazis, financed with vast war spoils, traded in their SS uniforms for business suits, escaped to Argentina and other sympathetic countries, and continued their worldwide fascist vision. Others were brought over to the USA under Operation Paperclip, but it is believed their loyalty to the Reich never ended. American Nazis also include those re-established in South America and Antarctica.[1]

After the war ended, those who believed in the fascist dream decided that another approach would be necessary. Instead of war, a united Europe dominated by Germany would be achieved through international treaties and diplomacy. In 1957, the European Economic Community was established, and it began with just six countries: Belgium,

1   Cooper, Harry, *Hitler in Argentina*, The Hitler Escape Trilogy, 2014.

France, Italy, Luxembourg, the Netherlands, and West Germany. Since that time, it has expanded to 28 nations and has become known as the "European Union." Still today, the "criminal government of billionaires" run powerful multinational corporations, who in turn dictate policy to England and the EU Superstate. The USA, because of its size, would also fall ill to the neo-fascist infection—in its new incarnation of Big Business dominating top government positions.

AMERICAN NAZIS AND BILDERBERGERS

The Bilderbergs first met in 1954 in a Dutch hotel of the same name, and one of the founders of the group was Prince Bernhard of the Netherlands. Not only was he a key establishing member, but Prince Bernhard actually served as the organization's chairman until 1976. Although little known, Prince Bernhard actually belonged to the Nazi Party and was a ranking SS officer at one time. The following is from an article that appeared in the *Telegraph* newspaper entitled, "Bernhard, a Secret History," which has revealed that the prince was a member of the German Nazi party until 1934, three years before he married Princess Juliana, the future queen of the Netherlands. The article goes on to explain how Bernhard was instrumental in bringing together the looted wealth of the Nazis, and incorporated fascism into the political realm of the Bilderberg Group.[2]

Indeed, the concept of a common currency for the European Union, now called the euro, was conceived and developed by the Bilderberg Group. This organization has always been at the forefront of European unity, but few people have any idea where this shadow organization came from that created an EU Superstate.

Annejet van der Zijl, a Dutch historian, has found membership documents in Berlin's Humboldt University that prove Prince Bernhard, who studied there, had joined *Deutsche Studentenschaft*, a National Socialist student fraternity, as well as the Nazi NSDAP and its paramilitary wing, the *Sturmabteilung*. Perhaps sensing he was on the wrong side of history, he left all Nazi-affiliated groups upon leaving the university in December of 1934, when he went to work for the German chemical giant, IG Farben. And Prince Bernhard's association with IG Farben also links him to the Nazis. The following comes from a book entitled *The Nazi Hydra in America* by Glen Yeadon:

> *The Bilderberg group, founded by Prince Bernhard of the Netherlands, held its first meeting in 1954. The prince, a former officer in the SS, had worked in IG Farben's notorious NW7 group, which served as spies for the Third Reich. Bernhard belonged to the Dutch branch of the Knights Templar. In 1954, he was appointed to govern the Dutch order. John Foster Dulles was one of the most helpful Americans in setting up the Bilderberg Group. Incidentally, in 1954 Dulles testified in favor of a bill designed to return vested enemy assets, such as GAF, to their previous owners.*

As the quote above illustrates, John Foster Dulles was instrumental in helping the Bilderberg Group get established. His brother, Allen Dulles, was responsible for orchestrating Operation Paperclip, which enabled large numbers of Nazi scientists and spy chiefs (among others) to come into the United States and start working for the U.S. government in various capacities. Allen Dulles was so passionate about this program that it continued even when two presidents tried to shut it down. It was Allen Dulles' CIA Operation Paperclip that assimilated Nazi scientists into the American establishment by obscuring their histories and preventing efforts to bring their true stories to light. The project was led by officers in the United States Army. Although the program officially ended in September 1947, those officers and others carried out a conspiracy until the mid-1950s (that bypassed both law and presidential directive) to keep Opera-

2   Snyder, Michael "Bilderberg: Started by a Nazi, still with the same agenda." Blacklisted News: http://www.911forum.org.uk/board/view-topic.php?p=170200#170200

tion Paperclip going. Neither Presidents Truman nor Eisenhower were informed that their instructions were ignored. President Kennedy fired Allen Dulles as Director of the CIA, and wanted to "splinter the CIA in a thousand pieces and scatter it to the winds." In a classic fox guarding the hen house scenario, Allen Dulles would come back to serve on the Warren Commission, investigating the assassination of JFK.

Of course, nobody associated with the Bilderberg Group would ever use the word "Nazi" or the phrase "working for the Deep State" to describe themselves. That term has become so associated with evil that nobody wants anything to do with it. But the values and the principles of the Nazis endure in organizations such as the Bilderberg Group, where actions speak louder than words. The ultimate goal, of course, is a One World Government that dominates the entire planet. Let us hope and pray that they are never able to achieve that. Humanity is in a race between waking up and rejecting this system, or many generations of subservient rule under an oppressive corporatocracy.

NATIONAL SECURITY STATE

What is commonly called the "National Security State" came into existence following World War II. Its official beginning was the National Security Act of 1947, by which President Truman organized the Joint Chiefs of Staff (JCS) under an appointed Chairman, and established the National Security Council (NSC) to advise him. Eisenhower would later create the position of National Security Adviser to preside over the National Security Council and report directly to the President. The founding texts of this Cold War apparatus are characterized by an alarmist exaggeration of the ambitions and power of the Soviet military, largely provoked by Paperclip Nazi Reinhard Gehlen, playing each side against the other. The United States justified its right to intervene in the internal affairs of any country, near or far, according to the idea that if it leaned slightly to the left, it could trigger a "domino effect" and cause the collapse of an entire region under communist influence. This "Truman Doctrine" of 1947 was what led the USA into the Vietnam conflict. The NSC-68 report dated April 7th 1950, asserted that the Kremlin posed a threat capable of the "destruction not only of this Republic but of civilization itself." Its main author, Paul Nitze, considered a preemptive nuclear attack against the USSR desirable, but impractical, "unless it is demonstrably in the nature of a counter-attack to a blow which is on its way or about to be delivered." For "the idea of 'preventive' war—in the sense of a military attack not provoked by a military attack upon us or our allies—is generally unacceptable to Americans." This report thus raises an issue quite different from that of deterrence, the official justification of the atomic arsenal: how to strike first, strong enough to crush the striking power of the enemy, while maintaining an air of self-defense.[3]

The 1947 National Security Act also gave birth to the CIA (the Central Intelligence Agency), officially to centralize Intelligence for use by the President. However, its budget has largely been devoted (since 1952) to its Directorate of Plans, which has as its specialty, "covert operations," defined by the directive NSC-10/2 as any activities "which are conducted or sponsored by this Government against hostile foreign states or groups or in support of friendly foreign states or groups, but which are so planned and executed that any U.S. Government responsibility for them is not evident to unauthorized persons and that if uncovered the U.S. Government can plausibly disclaim any responsibility for them." Designed theoretically to absolve the President of all illegal actions in case of public disclosure, the principle of "plausible deniability" gives the CIA almost complete autonomy. In fact, it relieves the agency of the need to reveal its operations to the President, while still allowing for Presidential protection in the event of failure. George Kennan, who prepared the document NSC-10/2, would later call it "the greatest mistake I ever made."

3   James, Preston, "The Third Hijacking of America?" https://www.veteranstoday.com/2017/12/26/the-third-hijacking-of-america/

On three continents, the CIA, directed by Allen Dulles, overthrew democratically elected governments and replaced them with dictatorships under U.S. tutelage. Its first major success was in the Middle East, with the 1953 coup against the Iranian Prime Minister Mohammad Mossadegh, who intended to nationalize the Anglo-Iranian Oil Company (AOIC), renamed British Petroleum in 1954. The CIA then flew the Shah of Iran Mohammad Pahlavi into Tehran, and proceeded to train his dreaded secret police, the SAVAK. Around the same time, in Latin America, the CIA oversaw the coup against the elected president of Guatemala, Jacobo Arbenz, by a military junta responsible for more than 200,000 civilian deaths from 1954 to 1996. By his plan to redistribute a portion of land to 100,000 poor farmers, Arbenz threatened the interests of the multinational United Fruit Company, the giant banana corporation that held more than 90% of the land. There is a dirty laundry list of other CIA-supported overthrows of democratically elected governments in South American countries and elsewhere. A CIA manual entitled *A Study of Assassination*, written in 1953 and declassified in 1997, contains detailed instructions on the various methods of murder by weapons, bombs or simulated accidents. In some cases, it is recommended that assassins be "clandestine agents or members of criminal organizations."[4]

And while the National Security State and the CIA are not even a century old, the individuals behind the movement of establishing fascist governments have been at it for a very long time. The Deep State is believed to be a clandestine network entrenched inside the government, bureaucracies, intelligence agencies, and other governmental entities. "We see the government of God over the world is hidden," Francis Bacon wrote in 1605, describing the deepest of deep states: (the lord's reign over us), which Bacon thought a good model for earthly rule. "Obscure and invisible" was how Bacon thought government worked best, that is, according to the French concept of *laissez faire* "hands off" government.

ENTER PROJECT PAPERCLIP

In an attempt to allow German scientists to help in postwar efforts, Truman agreed in September, 1946, to authorize "Project Paperclip," a program to bring Nazi German scientists to America. The plan was originally intended to debrief them and send them back to Germany. However, when the U.S. realized the extent of their knowledge and expertise, plans changed. In the government's employment of former Nazis, American agents worked very closely with those people who were part of a regime that was characterized by fascism, violence against its own people, domestic surveillance, and other similarly undemocratic attributes. Until Donald Trump took them on, the CIA "deep state" was essentially an alternative network of power that ran the country, no matter who was in the White House. Given their role in financing the Third Reich, it should be no surprise that the shadow government transferred the best and brightest Nazis operating in Europe away from the Nuremberg trials, and into America to continue their work in developing more efficient weapons and technology for military applications.

Under Operation Paperclip, the Joint Intelligence Objectives Agency (JIOA) employed many of the scientists, intelligence officers, the MK-Ultra *Mind Kontrolle* psychiatric researchers, and rocket engineers affiliated with the applied military development for the Nazi party, including a division of scientists working on remote control technology. The role of the newly-formed CIA from the Office of Strategic Services (OSS), was, in part, to preserve the SS networks for postwar anticommunist activities, while on the U.S. payroll. The former German operatives were "scrubbed and bleached" of their dark past, as they were allowed to work for the United States government unbeknownst to the vast majority of public at the time.

4   Putney, Alexander, R. *Veil of Invisibility*. Human Resonance, 2009. **The Promise Revealed.**

What history books don't tell us is that JFK and Khrushchev were intent on developing a joint space program following the dangerous Cuban Missile Crisis. These early negotiations were another nail in JFK's coffin, as the Military Industrial Complex (MIC) and their Paperclip Nazi's wanted to keep them separate. The reason for this was to maximize funding through a fictional "space race," and keep up the guise that the true threat was the "commies," not the ongoing Nazi fascist Fourth Reich, which was infiltrating America with CIA and U.S. fascist "bankster" help. They were purposely put into positions of power in MIC Corporations, at NASA, and within the Justice and State Department. It is interesting to note a similar infiltration was tried in the USSR, but was much less successful; however, the use of ex-Nazi's in their space program kept the conduit of information and sabotage and the hidden Reich agenda working on both sides of that *faux* space race. Meanwhile, trillions of dollars were diverted on both sides of the race and used to bolster a fascist agenda by using the veil of national security to hide their treasonous actions and intentions.

THE FOURTH REICH IN AMERICA

We can now learn how this new form of fascism came to take hold in the United States. It started in earnest when former Third Reich Nazis came to the USA, not just Wernher von Braun and his team of rocket scientists, but top military officers, Eastern Block spies, and sadistic mind control psychiatrists as well. The justification was to help win a possible war against the Soviets or other foreign enemies. But that was not its true goal. The main purpose was to destroy America from within—by creating a Fourth Reich, or New World Order in America slowly, beginning in the year 1945. The Nazi enemy has been living right underneath the noses of the American public for over 70 years without anyone suspecting a thing. Of course, many of the original Nazis are dead, but the ideology lives on. As we've read, the ultra-secret Bilderberg Group has had Nazi connections from the very beginning, and it continues to advance the neo-fascist agenda to this very day. The following are just a few examples of the Fourth Reich in America:

Just like the Nazis, *they advocate for highly-centralized national governments that are heavily socialized, with a national police force such as our current Homeland Security. This runs against the Posse Comitatus Act, which limits the powers of the Federal government in using federal military personnel to enforce domestic policies within the United States.*

Just like the Nazis, *the cabal is deeply committed to globalization. The Nazis sought to establish their empire through war, while the cabal seeks to do it through diplomacy, negotiation and intelligence.*

Just like the Nazis, *they believe in strict gun control for the general population, centralized government-controlled education and the removal of organized religion (especially Christianity) from public life. And just like the Nazis, they are deeply committed to eugenics and population control. These days, they use language that is more "politically correct," but most of them are absolutely convinced that the number one problem in our world today is overpopulation, and they're determined to do something about it with a variety of "slow kill" programs.*

Just like the Nazis, *they believe that they are the elite of the world, they scorn other races, and they believe in using military power to advance their cause when necessary. And they have employed the Deep State, which is a clandestine network entrenched inside the government, bureaucracy, intelligence agencies, and other governmental entities. Powerful bureaucrats with access to government secrets and trusted media friends certainly do try to influence top government officials from the shadows.*

Similar to the brutal East German Stasi, the new secret state seeks to spy on everyone and control us through the Internet. William Binney, the former Technology Director of the NSA said, "Germany is a post-fascist state, and they know it. USA is a pre-fascist state, and does *not* know it." What we're seeing is the totalitarian police state being created to enforce the new global banker's government agenda.

"The world needs to understand, Americans confront a threat from their own government," said Dr. James Henry Fetzer, a former editor at *Veterans Today* and a retired professor in Madison, Wisconsin. "The Department of Homeland Security was modeled after the East German Stasi that was widely recognized to be the most effective secret police in world history."

"There's an attempt going on here in the United States to militarize the police, many of whom are being trained in Israel to turn them into regarding American citizens as the enemy, just as the Israelis treat Palestinians as the enemy." Fetzer argued that many acts of gun violence such as the Sandy Hook school shooting in Newtown, Connecticut, are "fabricated, fake, contrived events" staged by the U.S. Government to ban Americans from bearing firearms. "They would love to take away our weapons because it's only a hundred million plus armed Americans that stand between Homeland Security and imposition of a fascistic military state in the USA," Fetzer concluded.

A DEPOPULATION AGENDA

Since the covert infiltration and fascist overthrow, we have to ask ourselves: what does America even stand for anymore? We have seen many alarming declines. Elimination of popular democracy. Rigged elections. Restricted civil rights. Growing hypocrisy. Growing police brutality. False flag operations. Poisonous GMO foods. Destruction of the environment. An alarming decline in bees. Bank bailouts with citizen's money. Seizure of personal assets. Unemployment. Growing poverty. Growing military expenditures. Pollution. Deregulation. No corporate financial liability. Indemnification for the elite for their financial crimes. Legalized fraud. Media propaganda. Gutted social services. No savings. No house. No retirement. No hope. No future. Nobody with much to pursue happiness with, except the 1%?

The cabal has been very creative in coming up with a multitude of different ways to try to kill the majority of people on Earth. All of these disasters, the chemtrails, fluoride added to water, NDAA, Monsanto Protection Act, killing the bees, fracking, "accidental" oil spills, wars, economic collapses, cancers put into inoculations, mandatory vaccines, Agenda 21, 5G untested rollout, are strong indications that Earth has already been invaded by malevolent "service-to-self " ETs which hate the human race. Monsanto, IG Farben, many pharma-chemical companies such as Bayer are part of Agenda 21, the depopulation agenda of the "Fallen Angels," that is, the Draco/Annunaki and other service-to-self ETs, who don't like humans, yet who live among us and operate through corrupt humans.

Because Western governments have been taken over by these service-to-self ETs, who see the planet as grossly overpopulated as outlined on the Georgia Guidestones, and who enforce Agenda 21, what we have is depopulation, and a dumbed down, compliant "sheeple." This is also the reason for the chemtrails, fluoride, and most vaccines. They are afraid of humanity waking up and our DNA activating. Drug makers (Big Pharma) simply don't make money on healthy people. They literally bank on the diseases we contract through a polluted life, and this perpetuates their business in the drug-manufacturing industry.

NAZIS IN THE HOMELAND

In 1936, William Dodd, the U.S. Ambassador to Germany, wrote a letter to President Franklin D. Roosevelt in which he stated:

A clique of U.S. industrialists is hell-bent to bring a fascist state to supplant our democratic government and is working closely with the fascist regime in Germany and Italy. I have had plenty of opportunity in my post in Berlin to witness how close some of our American ruling families are to the Nazi regime. ... A prominent executive of one of the largest corporations, told me point blank that he would be ready to take definite action to bring fascism into America if President Roosevelt continued his progressive policies. Certain American industrialists had a great deal to do with bringing fascist regimes into being in both Germany and Italy. They extended aid to help Fascism occupy the seat of power, and they are helping to keep it there. Propagandists for fascist groups try to dismiss the fascist scare. We should be aware of the symptoms. When industrialists ignore laws designed for social and economic progress they will seek recourse to a fascist state when the institutions of our government compel them to comply with the provisions.

The Germans, or the Reich in this case, kept the best projects and technology for themselves. It was moved to Argentina and a few other places. The gold was spread around and backed developments such as the international banking that became the world bank and the IMF. The Russians, the British and the U.S. all had reasons, manifold reasons, to never let the public know what was going on.

The proven record of Prescott Bush's involvement in financing the Nazi war machine dovetails with the fact that he was part of a criminal cabal that actively sought to impose a fascist coup in America. Prescott did not succeed but many would argue that two generations down the line the mission has all but been accomplished. Think about it: How could it be that Prescott Bush's Nazi war profits were silently returned to him? How could Bush escape his treason charges and later win the political office of Senator of Connecticut in 1954? How could his son and his grandson both become U.S. Presidents despite such massive treason on public record?

HITLER SURVIVED WORLD WAR II

We all know the story that on April 30, 1945, Adolf Hitler committed suicide in his underground bunker. His body was later discovered and identified by the Soviets before being rushed back to Russia. Is it really possible that the Soviets have been lying all this time, and that history has purposely been rewritten? With the Soviet occupation of Germany, Hitler's supposed remains were quickly hidden and sent off to Russia, never to be seen from again. That is until 2009, when an archeologist from Connecticut State, Nicholas Bellatoni was allowed to perform DNA testing on one of the skull fragments recovered.

What he discovered set off a reaction through the intelligence and scholarly communities. Not only did the DNA not match any recorded samples thought to be Hitler's, they were of a female, and did not match Eva Braun's familiar DNA either. So, the question is, what did the Soviets discover in the bunker, and where is Hitler? There is evidence that the most hated man in history escaped war torn Germany in the waning days of the war and lived a bucolic and peaceful life in the beautiful foothills of the Andes Mountains in various safe houses, including the Inalco House in a high security compound near San Carlos de Bariloche, Argentina.[5]

Newly declassified FBI documents in 2014 provide evidence that the U.S. government

5   CIA declassified memo shows Hitler alive in 1950s in South America: **https://www.documentcloud.org/documents/3988205-HITLER-ADOLF-0003.html#document/p2**

knew full well that Hitler was alive, and was freely moving around different South American fascist countries long after World War II ended. What's more, the American intelligence community also knew. The FBI documents determine that not only were Hitler and Eva Braun's suicides faked, the infamous pair also had help from the director of the OSS himself, Allen Dulles.

It seemed unbelievable until the release of the FBI documents on their site called "The Vault," which determine the fascist Peron government of Argentina not only welcomed the former German dictator, but also aided in his hiding. The unnamed informant in the now declassified documents gave detailed directions to the villages that Hitler and his party had passed through, plus credible physical details concerning Hitler, such as his suffering from ulcers and asthma. This evidence and much more is masterfully presented in the three seasons of History Channel's hit show *Hunting Hitler*.

THE GEHLEN ORGANIZATION

The Central Intelligence Agency finally confirmed in 2000 that a high-ranking Nazi general placed his anti-Soviet spy ring at the disposal of the United States during the early days of the Cold War. The National Archives reported in a release dated from September, 2000, that the CIA had filed an affidavit in U.S. District Court, that reads in part:

> ...*acknowledging an intelligence relationship with German General Reinhard Gehlen that it has kept secret for 50 years. ...The CIA's announcement marks the first acknowledgement by that agency that it had any relationship with Gehlen and opens the way for declassification of records about the relationship.*

Gehlen was Hitler's senior intelligence officer on the Eastern Front during the war and transferred his expertise and contacts to the U.S. as World War II reached its climax. The Gehlen network of agents in Europe—including many with Nazi backgrounds who were bailed out of prisoner-of-war camps by U.S. intelligence officers— was known as the Gehlen Organization and received millions of dollars in funding from the U.S. until 1956. After the war, at the request of U.S. occupation forces in Europe, he set up the "Gehlen Organization," a counter-espionage network that supplied the Pentagon and the CIA with the bulk of their intelligence on the Soviet Union and Eastern Europe. The organization, which employed thousands of people, many of them former Nazis, was the forerunner of West Germany's secret service, the Federal Intelligence Service called *Bundesnachrichtendienst* (BND). It was formally recognized in 1956, and Gehlen headed it until he retired in 1968.[6]

His vast knowledge of the Soviet Union, its leaders, its intelligence, and extensive spy network would be of great value to the Allies. To achieve that end, Gehlen had all of his files put onto microfilm and then led the leaders of his unit toward the Alps where, in the earth beneath a hut near Lake Spitzing in Upper Bavaria, he and his men buried fifty large steel boxes, the archives of their intelligence unit. Gehlen and his men then sought out a contingent of American troops and surrendered to them. A deal was quickly struck to bring the men and microfilm over to the USA.

The Gehlen Organization, as it became known, was funded with $7 million and first operated in the Soviet zone of Eastern Germany. Gehlen's own headquarters at Pullach evaluated the information culled from tens of thousands of willing spies. Who were these armies of the night that flocked to Gehlen's banner? They came from the tattered ranks of German prisoners-of-war who were released over a period of several years following World War II. Gehlen's men interviewed each and every one of these men, writing out details of their service experiences. Those who had been moles or who had turned propa-

6   Gehlen Org declassification, and FBI documents prove Hitler survived in Argentina after WW II: **https://vault.fbi.gov/adolf-hitler/adolf-hitler-part-01-of-04/view/**

gandists for the Soviets were eliminated. Those who had special knowledge of the Russian military and civilians and who proved loyal to the West were enlisted as agents.

Other agents, thousands of them, were already in place. These were Gehlen's "sleeper" agents in Russia, Poland, the Baltic states, in Romania, Bulgaria, Hungary, Albania, Czechoslovakia and, especially, in East Germany. Gehlen's service operated under the auspices of the U.S. until the establishment of the Federal Republic of Germany, when Gehlen's organization was absorbed into the West German government. His bureau was known as the "Org" to its members, but officially it was called the Federal Intelligence Service, and, in 1956, the BND. Gehlen's operations were chiefly directed against the East German Ministry of State and Security, the Communist political police *Staatssicherheitsdienst* (SSD), The Nazis' Gehlen Organization and Nazi Otto Skorzeny's ODESSA worked together after the war. In Martin Lee's book *The Beast Reawakens* (2000), he reveals that former U.S. intelligence officer, William Corson, disclosed that "Gehlen's Organization was designed to protect the ODESSA Nazis."

Throughout the 1950s and 1960s, Gehlen expanded his organization until he became the most powerful man in Europe, according to the National Archives. His agents operated in the U.S., England, France, and in the Middle East, working with both the Egyptian secret service and Israel's Mossad. His organization is largely regarded as stoking the paranoia between NATO and the Soviets, thus exacerbating the Cold War. All the while Gehlen's loyalties remained with former Nazi German nationalists and the largely invisible third power, the Fourth Reich. He retired in 1968, replaced by one of his old subordinates, Lieutenant General Gerhard Wessel. Eleven years later, Reinhard Gehlen died of natural causes. He is remembered today as the "spymaster's spymaster," one of the greatest intelligence chiefs in history.

THE MONEY-MAN MARTIN BORMANN

Martin Bormann, having risen to a position of great power in the Nazi Party by 1933, established and administered the "Adolf Hitler Endowment Fund of German Industry," supported by "donations" from successful German entrepreneurs. Bormann also managed all of Hitler's business affairs and personal finances after gaining a reputation as an assassin and intimidator of trade union organizers. He became one of the most powerful leaders of the Third Reich. By the end of 1944, Bormann was virtually Hitler's deputy and his closest collaborator, showing an uncanny ability to exploit Hitler's weaknesses and personal peculiarities in order to increase his own power. He took detailed notes on everything Hitler said. Always in attendance with the *Führer*, he took care of tiresome administrative details and skillfully steered Hitler into approval of his own schemes. By the waning months of the war, Bormann acquired the inside track for displacing dangerous rivals like Göring, Goebbels, Speer and even Himmler, whose access to the *Führer* he controlled himself. Bormann exploited his position of trust to build a wall against reality, in which Hitler could indulge his fantasies and in which more sensible, conciliatory proposals from other members of the Party were screened from him. Bormann reduced everything to simple, administrative formulae that freed Hitler from the burdens of paper work. He drew up Hitler's appointments calendar and decided whom he should see and not see. Hitler rewarded such trusted assistants as Bormann, whom he once called "my most loyal Party comrade." He was made executive head of the *Volkssturm*, the "people's storm" of the German civilian population, organized just as the Allies stood poised to invade the Reich.

The year 1943 marked a turning point in the war. The Axis was in retreat and it was clear that the Allies were advancing toward a clear victory. Realizing this, Bormann planned *Aktion Feuerland* (Tierra del Fuego) with the intention of negotiating favorable conditions with the West for surrender. Secretly he was planning the escape of Hitler and the evacuation of Nazi treasures to the Southern Hemisphere. This included countless looted works of art accumulated from years of plunder in the occupied countries. In addition, Bormann offered sensitive information about advanced Nazi secret weapons and the location of researchers and technicians for the United States to recruit. Furthermore, he was offering the surrender of millions of Wehrmacht soldiers who still fought in Italy.

At this point virtually the secret ruler of Germany, Bormann did not cease his Machiavellian bureaucratic intrigues against his rivals. As a result of his machinations, Hitler dismissed Göring who ended up at the Nuremberg Trials, and Himmler's influence was severely curtailed when he attempted to become *Führer* himself. It was the indispensable Bormann, the most mysterious and sinister figure in the Third Reich, who signed Hitler's political testament and who acted as the witness to his marriage to Eva Braun.

Doubts have persisted that Bormann died in the concluding days of the fall of Berlin and the end of World War II in Europe. Numerous sightings of Bormann had been reported in Europe, beginning in 1946, when his presence in a North Italian and Spanish monastery was announced. In the same year, his wife Gerda (a rabid Nazi and daughter of Supreme Party Judge, Walter Buch) died of cancer in South Tyrol, though his ten children survived the war. It was then alleged that Bormann had escaped like other Nazis along the Rat Lines to Switzerland, then to Rome via South America. Rumored to have settled in Argentina where he was living secretly as a millionaire, allegedly spotted in Brazil and also in Chile, Bormann's whereabouts proved as elusive as the anonymity in which he first rose to power. Having been sentenced to death *in absentia* at Nuremberg on October 1, 1946, he was formally pronounced dead by a West German court in April, 1973, but his precise fate remains unknown, according to the National Archives. But in reality, according to English radio host and researcher Tony Gosling, Martin Bormann, Hitler's top deputy, started 750 companies after the war, bolstering the power of the Fourth Reich. Gosling continues:

> Bormann's organization controlled Germany's big business, and via its investments controlled much of the rest of the world's economy. It was the repository for the stolen wealth of Europe, estimated by British intelligence to have been more than $180 billion by the end of 1943. Bormann had been banking under his own name from his office in Germany in Deutsche Bank of Buenos Aires since 1941; that he held one joint account with Argentinean dictator Juan Peron; and on August 4, 5 and 14, 1967, he had written checks on demand accounts in National City Bank (Overseas Division) of New York, The Chase Manhattan Bank, and Manufacturer's Hanover Trust Co., all cleared through Deutsche Bank of Buenos Aires.

In 1944, Hearst newspapers reporter Burnet Hershey described the Nazis' escape route via Spain. Bormann failed to divest himself of more than a dozen enemy nation business relationships that he managed on behalf Fritz Thyssen and Prescott Bush, until as late as 1951. The records also show that George H. W. Bush and the Averell Harriman's conducted business after World War II with related concerns, doing business in or moving assets into Switzerland, Panama, Argentina and Brazil—all critical outposts for the flight of Nazi capital after Germany's surrender in 1945.[7]

Martin Bormann's success in spreading the Nazis' assets around the world was heralded at the Nuremberg Trials by Hermann Schmitz, head of I.G. Farben and a director of the Bank for International Settlements (BIS). Farben's N.W.7 division was, of course, close to Himmler's SS and the Gestapo. Incidentally, Prince Bernhard of the Netherlands, who formed the Bilderberg Group in 1954, was a Nazi SS officer who also worked for N.W.7. At Nuremberg, Schmitz testified:

7   *The New Hampshire Gazette*, November 7, 2003.

We can continue. We have an operational plan. However, I don't believe our board members will be detained long. Nor will I. But we must go through a procedure of investigation before release, so I have been told by our N.W.7 people who have excellent contacts in Washington.

Continuing after Operation Paperclip, the CIA's Operation Bloodstone brought Nazis to the USA and was originally approved on June 10, 1948, by the State-War-Navy Coordinating Committee. One of the original sponsors of Operation Bloodstone was Robert Lovett of the War Department, who was also a member of the Council on Foreign Relations (CFR). According to Christopher Simpson in his book, *Blowback* (1988), one month after Operation Bloodstone was approved, it was expanded to cover covert operations, including sabotage and assassinations. John D. Rockefeller III was a senior Navy staff member of the State-War-Navy Coordinating Committee, which approved Operation Bloodstone.

THE ROCKEFELLERS

The elder William Rockefeller, father to the first billionaire John D., was a shameful secret his wealthy sons tried to keep hidden. The elder Rockefeller was a literal snake oil salesman and con artist who sold "cancer cures" to women door-to-door. He had a reputation for being a "devil." He married Eliza, John D. Rockefeller's mother, and later had two children by his mistress/maid. Then he left his family and took off for parts unknown, marrying a woman 25 years his junior while still married to Eliza. To round off his infamous career, he was also indicted for rape. Joseph Pulitzer offered an $8,000 reward for information about this Rockefeller patriarch and his checkered past, which uncovered some clues Rockefeller's sons had kept under wraps.

If it weren't for wars, the Rockefellers might not be what they are today. During the Civil War, the young entrepreneur, John D. Rockefeller, sold grain, hay, and meats to the Union army at inflated prices. He invested the money in Samuel Andrews' oil refinery, which was the start of Standard Oil. During World War II, the Rockefeller family profited from both the Allies (who used Standard Oil products) and the Axis Powers, who also used Standard Oil products. John D. Rockefeller used his oil wealth to acquire Equitable Trust, which had acquired several large banks and corporations by the 1920s. The Great Depression helped consolidate Rockefeller's power. His Chase Bank merged with Kuhn Loeb's Manhattan Bank to form Chase Manhattan, cementing a long-time family relationship. The Kuhn-Loeb's had financed—along with Rothschilds—Rockefeller's quest to become king of the oil patch. National City Bank of Cleveland provided John D. with the money needed to embark upon his monopolization of the U.S. oil industry. The bank was identified in Congressional hearings as being one of three Rothschild-owned banks in the U.S. during the 1870s, when Rockefeller first incorporated as Standard Oil of Ohio.

Various Rockefellers have funded, founded or led the following policy-creating institutions:

The Council on Foreign Relations—David, David Jr., Nelson, John D. III, John D. IV (Jay), Peggy Dulany, Rockefeller Foundation, Rockefeller Brothers Fund.
The Trilateral Commission—David, Rockefeller Brothers Fund.
The Bilderberg Group—David, John D. IV.
The Asia Society—John D. III, John D. IV, Charles, David.
The Population Council—John D. III.
The Council of the Americas—David.
The Group of Thirty—The Rockefeller Foundation.
The World Economic Forum—David.
The Brookings Institution—Junior.

*The Peterson Institute (Formerly the Institute for International Economics)—
    David, Monica.*
The International Executive Service Corps—David.
The Institute for Pacific Relations—Junior.
The League of Nations—Junior.
*The United Nations—Junior, John D. III, Nelson, David, Peggy Dulany,
    Rockefeller Brothers Fund.*
The United Nations Association—David, Monica.

Richard Rockefeller died in a plane crash on Friday the 13th, in June, 2014. He was head of *Médecins Sans Frontières*, a group that has pledged to vaccinate all children under five years of age in the world. Given the huge amount of misinformed Malthusian propaganda emitting from Rockefeller think tanks about the need to reduce the world's population, it is hard to believe that Richard wanted to vaccinate all those children which would have helped to increase the world population.

The Rockefellers were instrumental in forming the depopulation-oriented Club of Rome at their family estate in Bellagio, Italy. Their Pocantico Hills estate gave birth to the Trilateral Commission. The family is a major funder of the eugenics movement which inspired Hitler, and furthermore, of human cloning and the current DNA obsession in US scientific circles.

John D. Rockefeller Jr. headed the Population Council until his death. His namesake son, John "Jay" Rockefeller IV, was a Senator from West Virginia. Brother Winthrop Rockefeller was Lieutenant Governor of Arkansas and remains the most powerful man in that state. In an October 1975 interview with *Playboy* magazine, Vice-President Nelson Rockefeller—who was also Governor of New York—articulated his family's patronizing worldview, "I am a great believer in planning—economic, social, political, military, total world planning."

But of all the Rockefeller brothers, it is Trilateral Commission (TC) founder and Chase Manhattan Chairman, David, who has spearheaded the family's fascist agenda on a global scale. He defended the Shah of Iran, the South African apartheid regime and the Chilean Pinochet junta. He was the biggest financier of the Council on Foreign Relations (CFR), the Trilateral Commission (TC) and (during the Vietnam War), the Committee for an Effective and Durable Peace in Asia—a contract bonanza for those who made their living off of the conflict.

Companies under Rockefeller control include Exxon Mobil, Chevron Texaco, BP Amoco, Marathon Oil, Freeport-McMoRan, Quaker Oats, ASARCO, United, Delta, Northwest, ITT, International Harvester, Xerox, Boeing, Westinghouse, Hewlett-Packard, Honeywell, International Paper, Pfizer, Motorola, Monsanto, Union Carbide and General Foods.

The Rockefeller Foundation has close financial ties to both Ford and Carnegie Foundations. Other family philanthropic endeavors include the Rockefeller Brothers Fund, the Rockefeller Institute for Medical Research, the General Education Board, Rockefeller University and the University of Chicago—which churns out a steady stream of far-right economists as apologists for international capital, including Milton Friedman.

The Federal Reserve Board families have presided over the introduction of sperm-killing chemicals into household products such as shampoo, soap and tooth-paste and cancer-causing chemicals into our daily foods. They have also turned the U.S. medical establishment into a bunch of goons who poison cancer patients with radiation and chemicals. They have also dumbed down the education system and hijacked the political system.[8]

••

8   Solomon, Steven, *The Confidence Game: How Un-Elected Central Bankers are Governing the Changed World Economy*. Simon & Schuster. New York. 1995.

THE BUSH CRIME FAMILY

George H.W. Bush's father, the late U.S. Senator Prescott Sheldon Bush, was a director and shareholder of companies that profited from their involvement with the financial backers of Nazi Germany. The *Guardian* newspaper and others has obtained confirmation from newly-discovered files in the U.S. National Archives that Prescott Bush was a high-ranking director at Union Banking Corporation, and was a financial architect of Nazism. In 1942, Prescott Bush was slapped with the "Trading with the Enemy" act and shut down, but immediately after the war the assets were returned and all charges dropped.[9]

It had been discovered that the Nazis were laundering stolen money from Europe through the UBC (Union Banking Corporation) and sending it back to Adolf Hitler through Fritz Thyssen, the Warburgs, I.G. Farben and others. Arms and oil shipments intended to assist the Nazi cause and enrich the likes of Prescott Bush's father, Samuel P. Bush, and the Rockefeller family were halted in 1942, though dividends were ultimately paid to the perpetrators after World War II. Prescott Sheldon Bush received $1.5 million, the value of one share of the UBC stock he owned. The total assets of UBC were estimated to be worth more than $4 billion at the time. To avoid further embarrassment to the Wall Street traitors who should have been tried for treason, the National Archives "burned" the associated records "in order to save space," temporarily salvaging the reputation of Samuel P. Bush. The destruction of these documents did little to erase other government records that showed an affinity of this "family" to conduct business with the Nazis. There is some evidence that his son, George H.W. Bush, was really German-born George Scherff, and changed his last name when he was placed in the Bush foster family to be groomed for his rise to power.[10]

Prescott's son, George H.W. "Poppy" Bush is one of the few Americans who could never recall where he was, or what he was doing, when JFK was assassinated. As a matter of fact, for over 20 years, he could not recall any details at all. Perhaps this selective amnesia is because there are photos of him standing in front of the Texas School Book Depository Building during the assassination. He was 39 years old at the time and chairman of the Harris County (Houston) Republican Party and an outspoken critic of JFK. But on 21 November 1963, Poppy Bush was staying at the Sheraton Hotel in downtown Dallas and spoke that very evening to the American Association of Oil Drilling Contractors. Sometime later, he was reportedly at "the ratification meeting" at the home of Clint Murchison, Sr., receiving last minute instructions and toasting JFK's murder the night before it happened.

George H.W. Bush has a long dirty laundry list of involvement with CIA covert operations and top governmental positions. Having controlled the Deep State as the CIA director (1976-77), then CFR director (1977-79) leading up to his vice presidency (1981-1989), then as the first out-of-the-closet New World Order president (1989 to 1993), and then even continuing the behind the scenes influence (under Bill Clinton) and then under his son, George W. Bush. It is revealed that Bush senior had employed the youngest Arkansas governor (Clinton) as his cocaine dealer out of the USA from rural Mena, Arkansas, throughout Bill's crime-filled dozen-year run as state governor.

During Bush's Iran-Contra era, Bill Clinton laundered over a billion dollars a year in CIA drug money through his little airport. Profits from the "war on drugs" catapulted the rise of both the Bush and Clinton crime families as they busily paid off and appointed enough court judges, federal and state attorneys, state police and FBI officials,

9   "How Bush's grandfather helped Hitler's rise to power" https://www.theguardian.com/world/2004/sep/25/usa.secondworldwar
10 Orion, Eric, "The Hitler / Bush Connection" 2003.

to effectively keep at bay all their scandals of countless murders, serial rapes and child sex-trafficking investigations, while financing their lucrative, off-the-books, CIA black budget. The Bush crime cabal has been in power controlling the CIA for over a half century, but it has always been subservient to its big boss, called the Khazarian Mafia, also known as the Rothschild World Zionist private fiat currency Central "Banksters," and their right hand, the International Zionist Crime Syndicate.

George H.W. Bush's son, the younger George W. Bush, was not elected, but put into office by his brother Jeb's rigging of the Florida vote, and then the Supreme Court, for some unknown reason, supported the man who lost the popular vote. Within a year in office, George W. Bush witnessed the largest attack on U.S. soil, which allowed him to install the Patriot Act, eerily similar to Hitler's Enabling Act, and the Homeland Security Act, which created a standing army in the USA, an act specifically forbidden under the Constitution. From there, he put out directives and signed an agreement with the WHO, which arranged for the end of U.S. sovereignty, and opened the door for a takeover by UN troops and the WHO when the time was right. Those are three efforts at political coups, one in each generation— the first one failed, the second one assassinated a president and replaced him with someone who opened up a full-blown war on Vietnam as desired by elements of the U.S. military, and the third coup depends upon a "pandemic" emergency laid out in advance, as seen with COVID-19.

Quarantining and mandatory vaccination rest upon two intersecting orders signed by George W. Bush in 2007, with neither voted on by Congress. "The Shrub" signed a Presidential Directive on May 9, 2007, which gives the White House unprecedented dictatorial power over the government and the country by bypassing the U.S. Congress and obliterating the separation of powers. The directive also places the Secretary of Homeland Security in charge of domestic "security," similar to the Gestapo secret police of Nazi Germany.

Also in 2007, Bush put into force International Health Regulations which stipulate that in the event of the declaration of a global pandemic emergency, the UN and the WHO will take control of the country, along with DHS and FEMA. In Europe, the WHO and NATO would take control. These regulations raise the issue regarding separation of powers, as the authority to enter into any international treaty is solely held to the federal government and expressly prohibited to the states.

Between the two orders, neither voted on by Congress, the mere declaration by the WHO of a "pandemic emergency," if the president also declares such an emergency, triggers two things: first, the end of Constitutional government in the U.S. with control of the country ceded to the President ruling alone (with support from DHS), and second, for two foreign entities (the WHO and UN troops), to enter the USA, and side by side, with a now massively-armed DHS and FEMA, take control of the country.

John Ellis "Jeb" Bush was born on February 11, 1953, but did not attend Yale or join Skull and Bones like his father and older brother. He became an American businessman and politician, who served as the 43rd Governor of Florida from 1999 to 2007. He is the second son of former President George H.W. Bush and former First Lady Barbara Bush, and the younger brother of former President George W. Bush. When Jeb Bush ran unsuccessfully for president in 2016, he had amassed more Super-PAC anonymous-donor money than any other candidate in history. This should be a hint about his family's monumental secret connections. Like all members of the Bush Crime Family, Jeb Bush is well aware if his family's dubious past, and their hidden history.[11]

11 Wilcock, David, "Secret Space Program Revealed: Two New Radio Shows, Transcript!" *Divine Cosmos.com*, June 14, 2015.

BARBARA CROWLEY-BUSH

Few people understand that one of the most notorious individuals in British history may have contributed to the lineage of two U.S. Presidents. Pauline Pierce, the mother of Barbara Bush, was known to frequent the bedrooms of the rich and famous. Pauline was reportedly working as Aleister Crowley's assistant in 1924, when he was attempting to reach the highest degree of the *Ordo Templi Orientis* (O.T.O.) through the practices of sexual debauchery. It has been reported that Pauline and Aleister were in France together around September and October of 1924. Upon returning to America and her boyfriend here, Pauline gave birth to Barbara Pierce on June 8th, 1925. Barbara Pierce married George H. W. Bush, who eventually became the 41st President, who had their first son on July 6, 1946, who became the 43rd President of the United States.

Nine months after the ritual "sexcapades" with "The Great Beast 666," Aleister Crowley, Pauline Pierce gave birth to Barbara Pierce, who became Barbara Bush. The infamous practitioner of "sex magick," whose motto was "Do What Thou Wilt," came to know a great many remarkable people in the early 20th century, including the maternal grandmother of George W. Bush. But who was Barbara's father? The chronology indicates that it could have been Crowley, but it could just as easily have been Marvin Pierce. The truth regarding Crowlean sexual rituals is disclosed only to the highest initiates of the O.T.O. (*Ordo Templi Orientis*) in a document misleadingly titled "Emblems and Modes of Use."[12]

Is Aleister Crowley the father of Barbara Bush? Even she may have never known for certain. Indeed, there is no way to verify if she had ever been told, and if so, would certainly never admit it. However, many have noticed the personal resemblance—and this similarity is not just physical. Many will recall the former First Lady's callous remark in the aftermath of the Katrina disaster, calling the refugees being housed in the Houston Astrodome "underprivileged anyway, so this is working very well for them." Aleister Crowley had a similar reaction to the loss of life which occurred during the ascent of Kangchenjunga Mountain in India, an expedition Crowley commanded, and brashly commented, "this is precisely the sort of thing with which I have no sympathy whatsoever."

WHY JFK WAS REALLY KILLED

There are rumors that President John F. Kennedy was tired of working with CIA spy chiefs before his death. It is certain that JFK was considering pulling out of Vietnam and a détente with the Soviets, a move decried by war hawks throughout the Beltway. The CIA may have feared that Kennedy would break up their organization altogether. Is it possible that the CIA—or rogue elements within the spy agency—were so worried about losing their jobs they ordered the hit? In his capacity as a CIA asset, George H.W. Bush can be seen in pictures overlooking Dealey Plaza on that fateful day in Dallas. The famous Zapruder film of the murder shows the limousine driver, Secret Service Agent William Greer, turning around and shooting JFK in the head with a handgun. Most people pointed to shots fired by a gunman on the grassy knoll, while other shots came from a manhole below the underpass and the Book Repository Building. It was a very well-coordinated hit, with guilt quickly deflected to the patsy, Lee Harvey Oswald, then glossed over with the fraudulent Warren Commission. Is it possible, even likely, that Poppy (George H.W.) had a hand in the JFK assassination and subsequent cover-up every step of the way?

It's no doubt JFK had made a lot of powerful enemies. Consider these facts: his stance against organized crime and use of his brother Bobby as Attorney General against them; his refusal to go recklessly into WW III, a full scale nuclear war with the Soviets over the Cuban Missile Crisis, coupled with his last minute refusal to be drawn into a CIA invasion of Cuba; his commitment to a withdrawal from Vietnam;

12 Zagami, Leo Lyon, *Confessions of an Illuminati, Volume I: The Whole Truth About the Illuminati and the New World Order.* 2nd ed. CCC Publishing, 2019.

his planning to drop LBJ as Vice-President in the next election; and his printing of real U.S. Treasury Dollars, which was an attempt to ease out the City of London's private Federal Reserve System and their phony fiat currency debt-notes (used by Americans at pernicious accruing interest). Together, these efforts illegally sealed his fate at Dealey Plaza on November 22, 1963.

The American *Coup d'état* on November 22, 1963, ushered in the full Fourth Reich fascism, spear-headed by the CIA and their City of London supported drug-trafficking satanic pedophile Cabal. JFK's assassination was a Secret Shadow Government (SSG) *Coup d'état*, designed to serve as a public example of what the SSG will do to anyone in the presidency or a high government position who goes outside their allowed parameters. The assassination of JFK transformed the U.S. into a fascist state, which technically remains an illegitimate government to this day.

J. EDGAR HOOVER

J. Edgar Hoover had to guard his legacy. When it comes to other individuals who may have had means, motive and an opportunity to kill JFK, there are few better contenders than FBI Director J. Edgar Hoover. Hoover may have felt that the Kennedy brothers were jeopardizing his anti-communist crusade by refocusing government priorities on the Mafia. Hoover may also have feared that he'd be removed from power due to his controversial and epic history. If true, few would have been better placed to organize a hit—and nobody would be better placed to cover it up afterwards.

It is Hoover who helped establish the FBI, and without whose help the Nazi criminals could never have entered the USA. He worked in Interpol with founder Reinhard Heydrich, SS head of Nazi police from 1940 to 1942, and his successor, SS officer Ernst Kaltenbrunner, later hanged at Nuremberg. Hoover's career involved extensive mob connections, and his death has yet to be fully investigated. Hoover was a gutless, anti-American, Nazi sympathizer. He was a known homosexual and transvestite, thus considered by many a moral degenerate, whereas his actual crimes involved pedophilia and being a Nazi sympathizer. He wore dresses and liked to be called "Mary." Hoover fired all of the good FBI personnel and hired all white, Christian fascists, some of whom were anti-American, homosexual Nazi-sympathizers just like himself! They were known as Hoover's G-Men or "Gay Men."

HENRY KISSINGER

The "godfather" of the Bilderberg Group is the former U.S. Secretary of State, Henry Kissinger. He has attended their gatherings almost every year, even as an elder statesman in his nineties. This is a man that is so committed to globalization that he even wrote a book entitled *World Order*. But what hardly anyone knows is that he actually discussed overthrowing the West German government with a group of "disgruntled Nazis" back in the 1970s, according to a German academic who has unearthed damning evidence.

As we've learned, the Vatican and the Red Cross helped Nazis escape to freedom and establish new identities in South American countries. Henry Kissinger worked with General Lucius Clay at Oberammergau, and then with key stateside Army Intelligence and CIA units responsible for bringing in the Nazi spies under Project Paperclip. Kissinger, who came from Germany to join U.S. Army Intelligence during World War II, had as his "mentor" the mysterious Fritz Kraemer. Kraemer's 30-year silent career in the Pentagon was in the plans division, including the prepping of Alexander Haig. His silent career in the Pentagon may also have concealed his real identity as Fritz Kraemer, prisoner #33 in the dockets at Dachau, the special Lieutenant to Hitler. Mr. Kissinger still relies on his advice, and did so while Secretary of State.

In a series of remarkable admissions by former Nixon-era Secretary of State, Henry Kissinger, he reveals the current situation in the world forum of geopolitics and economics.

> The United States is baiting China and Russia, and the final nail in the coffin will be Iran, which is, of course, the main target of Israel. We have allowed China to increase their military strength and Russia to recover from Sovietization, to give them a false sense of bravado, this will create an altogether faster demise for them. We're like the sharp shooter daring the mob to pick up the gun, and when they try, it's bang bang. The coming war will be so severe that only one superpower can win, and that's us, folks. This is why the EU is in such a hurry to form a complete superstate because they know what is coming, and to survive, Europe will have to be one whole cohesive state. Their urgency tells me that they know full well that the big showdown is upon us. 'O how I have dreamed of this delightful moment. ...Control oil and you control nations; control food and you control the people. ...If you are an ordinary person, then you can prepare yourself for war by moving to the countryside and building a farm, but you must take guns with you, as the hordes of starving will be roaming. Also, even though the elite will have their safe havens and specialist shelters, they must be just as careful during the war as the ordinary civilians, because their shelters can still be compromised. We told the military that we would have to take over seven Middle Eastern countries for their resources and they have nearly completed their job. We all know what I think of the military, but I have to say they have obeyed orders superfluously this time. It is just that last stepping stone, i.e. Iran which will really tip the balance. How long can China and Russia stand by and watch America clean up? The great Russian bear and Chinese sickle will be roused from their slumber and this is when Israel will have to fight with all its might and weapons to kill as many Arabs as it can. Hopefully if all goes well, half the Middle East will be Israeli. Our young have been trained well for the last decade or so on combat console games, it was interesting to see the new Call of Duty Modern Warfare 3 game, which mirrors exactly what is to come in the near future with its predictive programming. Our young, in the U.S. and West, are prepared because they have been programmed to be good soldiers, cannon fodder, and when they will be ordered to go out into the streets and fight those crazy Chins and Russkies, they will obey their orders. Out of the ashes we shall build a new society, there will only be one superpower left, and that one will be the global government that wins. Don't forget, the United States, has the best weapons, we have stuff that no other nation has, and we will introduce those weapons to the world when the time is right.[13]

Kissinger likely had a part in the Watergate crimes; Southeast Asia mass murders (Vietnam, Cambodia, Laos); installing Chilean mass murdering dictator Pinochet; Operation Condor's mass killings in South America, and more recently served as Serbia's Ex-Dictator Slobodan Milosevic's Advisor. He consistently advocated going to war against Iran. It was interesting when President George W. Bush nominated Kissinger as chairman of the September 11 investigating commission. It's like picking a bank robber to investigate a fraud scandal. He later declined this job under enormous protests.

JAMES CLAPPER

Ultimately, known globalist James A. Clapper controlled all intelligence in the USA, yet has demonstrated himself to be an enemy of America. After gaining the highest security clearances in government, Clapper then worked for GeoEye, was on the board of three government contractors, worked for Detica (British military intelligence), BAE Systems, SRA International and Booz Allen Hamilton.

In an example of the new generation of American Nazis, James Clapper had the following agencies under his control: Central Intelligence Agency, National Security Agency, Department of Homeland Security, Federal Bureau of Investigation, Department of State, Department of the Treasury, Defense Intelligence Agency, Air Force Intelligence, Army Intelligence, Marine Corps Intelligence, Navy Intelligence, Coast Guard Intelligence, Department of Energy, National Reconnaissance Office, Drug Enforcement Administration, and the National Geospatial-Intelligence Agency.

He ordered the Office of the Director of National Intelligence to place all the collected intelligence from these 17 agencies under his control. And remember that the CIA has the all-powerful "international security" clearance which gave Clapper a higher security position that any of the other agencies listed, and higher than our elected officials including the President.

Clapper was called to the Congress and under oath swore that the NSA did not spy on Americans in any fashion. He perjured himself repeatedly with the lie that no surveillance was going on at all on any American. This was, of course, found to be false. In fact, the NSA spies on every American and even has a file for every person in America extracted principally from the Internet, Google, Facebook (all social media), every PC, phones, and bank accounts among other sources. Snowden's "leaks" have become the bane of the NSA, who had to admit they certainly do spy on Americans, because Obama expanded the NDAA to include Americans as warfare combatants.

Centralization of power with just a few people usually goes wrong and, in this case, it has gone very wrong. Clapper is not interested in accurate intelligence; he is simply a 4 a.m. talking points propaganda machine like the Nazi Bureau of Information. Clapper wants us to believe anything that he says, without any proof, simply based upon the fact that "17 intelligence agencies" all agree with him. Essentially, any statements from James Clapper speaks as well for the other "16 intelligence agencies," even if there is no evidence, and even if no other agency was asked its opinion.

There was a time when thousands of American Nazis rallied at Madison Square Garden in New York City. American Nazis and Nazi Sympathizers like the Skinheads have been around since the 1930s, and curiously hailed George Washington as the "first fascist."

Only 19 high-ranking Nazi officers were convicted in the Nuremberg Trials. The rest escaped along the "rat lines," and some went on to create NASA, the CIA and the Federal Republic of Germany. The Nuremberg trials of former Nazi doctors established "Informed Consent." A corrupt government violates that with mandatory vaccinations that we have to get in order to go to work, travel and purchase food. As Henry Kissinger said to control the people you control the food. Then all of us should grow Victory Gardens like in WW II until we can overthrow this treasonous domestic enemy.

American soldiers discover Édouard Manet's "In the Conservatory" painting hidden in Germany's Merkers salt mines in 1945, along with large amounts of Nazi gold, and many other stolen works of art. Martin Bormann helped with the evacuation of the Nazi treasure to the Southern Hemisphere, accumulated from years of plunder in the occupied countries, and including countless looted works of art. Many still have never been recovered.

According to Otto Skorzeny from an excerpt in the book, *The Hitler / Bush Connection*, pictured here is the Scherff family and a few friends (circa 1938). Holding "Mother" Scherff's hand at left is Martin Bormann. In front is Reinhardt Gehlen. In back is Josef Mengele and to his right is Skorzeny as a young man. At center right (in the German navy uniform) is George H. Scherff, Jr. and his father George H. Scherff, Sr. Bormann became Hitler's second in command. Reinhardt Gehlen was a chief SS officer and assassin who was smuggled out of Germany under Operation Paperclip. Skorzeny was Hitler's bodyguard and SS spy/assassin who came to the U.S. after the war under Project Paperclip. Skorzeny and George H.W. Bush were instrumental in merging Nazi SS intelligence with the OSI to form the CIA with "Wild Bill" Donovan and Allen Dulles. These individuals were also part of CIA mind control experiments such as MK-Ultra. SS officer and physician Josef Mengele, the notoriously sadistic "Angel of Death" of Auschwitz, escaped Germany to South America after the war. George H. Scherff, Jr., became the 41st President of the United States as George H.W. Bush.

Future presidents Bill Clinton and George Bush with Governor George Wallace at a BBQ in 1983. One of the businesses attributed to the CIA by many researchers is drug and gun smuggling. A private researcher named Stew Webb claims to have found "the smoking gun" linking President Bill Clinton to the CIA as a long-term and "deep cover" operative. The ties were obvious in the 1980s when the agency used an airstrip in western Arkansas as part of a money laundering and drugs for money scam, which continued through the many Clinton appointments. The small airport at Mena, Arkansas, has long been known as a trans-shipment landing strip used by the CIA.

Three days before his 19th birthday, George H.W. Bush became the youngest aviator in the U.S. Navy. However, new research suggests U.S. Navy Pilot George H.W. Bush was really a spy for Nazi Germany. It is alleged that George Herbert Walker Bush murdered his two crew members by deliberately sabotaging his Grumman TBF Avenger in order to deliver the advanced gun system to the Nazis, who were waiting with a U-Boat to collect the downed plane.

George W. Bush plays a little dirty rugby for Yale in 1966. Prescott, George H.W. and George W. were all members of the Skull and Bones secret society known for practicing strange occult rituals such as mock human sacrifices. The two ex-presidents were known to attend Bohemian Grove, where members of high society perform strange occult rituals such as mock human sacrifices in front of a large owl idol.

Hitler &
Grandpa Bush

George W. Bush's grandfather, the late U.S. Senator Prescott Bush, seen here with Adolf Hitler, was a director and shareholder of companies that profited from their involvement with the financial backers of Nazi Germany. Prescott Bush had assets seized under the "Trading with the Enemy Act" for funding Nazis.

The Kennedy family leaves the funeral of John F. Kennedy in 1963. President George H.W. Bush said in confidence to a reporter in June, 1992, "If the American people ever find out what we have done, they will chase us down the streets and lynch us."

Aleister Crowley   Barbara Bush

Aleister Crowley was the infamous practitioner of "sex magick," whose motto was "Do What Thou Wilt," and he was very promiscuous. Nine months after the ritual sexcapades with "The Great Beast 666" Crowley, Pauline Pierce gave birth to Barbara Pierce, who became Barbara Bush. The resemblance is uncanny.

The Rockefellers earned big money, thanks to one of Standard Oil's largest stock-holders: I.G. Farben, a German chemical industry conglomerate that manufactured Zyklon B, the cyanide-based pesticide used in Nazi camps. Who runs the World Health Organization? The main funders of the WHO are the Rockefellers and Bill Gates. The Rockefellers had half interest in I.G. Farben, the Germany pharmaceutical and chemical consortium that funded Hitler.

MK-ULTRA

"The ultimate tyranny in a society is not control by
martial law. It is control by the psychological manipulation
of consciousness through which reality is defined so
that those who exist within it do not even realize that
they are in prison. They do not even realize that there is
something outside of where they exist."
–Barbara Marciniak, The Pleiadeans

GOVERNMENT is nothing more than a way to control people. We don't have these mass shootings because Americans are crazy, or because we have the right to bear arms. We have these mass shootings because we have a Deep State that wants Americans to be disarmed. Lone nuts don't commit these military style attacks alone. Rogue intelligence agencies are involved. Since WW II, American intelligence services have been involved in mind control and Satanic Ritual Abuse (SRA), and work on creating the perfect Manchurian Candidate. Visual stimuli and "triggers" are reinforced throughout our popular media. In 2013, TV star Roseanne Barr said "MK-Ultra mind control rules in Hollywood."

After World War II, the climate of worldwide conflict changed and the dawn of the Cold War altered the direction of military strategy. The United States saw a need to establish an agency to conduct worldwide intelligence-gathering operations and to engage in espionage and counter-terrorism. During the war, the Office of Strategic Services (OSS) occupied this role. After the war, the National Security Act of 1947 officially established the Central Intelligence Agency (CIA) with the intent to expand these operations and create a formal authority to oversee covert activities worldwide. The Nazi Intelligence unit was offered to the CIA, from which many sinister projects later stemmed, including MK-Ultra, Operation Midnight Climax, Artichoke, and Monarch. Project MK-Ultra was the code name for a covert mind control and chemical interrogation research program, run by the

Office of Scientific Intelligence. The etymology of "MK" stands for *Mind Kontrolle*. The obvious translation of the German word "Kontrolle" into English is "control."

These covert sinister projects were formally authorized under Allen Dulles in 1953, as a direct result of Nazi scientists' influence on U.S. Intelligence through Project Paperclip. The projects involved the use of "many methodologies to manipulate individual mental states and alter brain function, including the surreptitious administration of drugs and other chemicals, sensory deprivation, isolation, verbal and sexual abuse," in order to induce a state of trauma-based mind control in their victims. It wasn't until the Church Committee Congressional hearings in 1975 that many of the CIA's activities in the MK-Ultra programs would come to light.

In the months following World War II, American and German submarines and cargo ships were used to transport their illegal Nazi cargo and billions of dollars of stolen European money to America. The SS Nazis were smuggled into our country through the North Atlantic Ocean, and landed offshore of Montauk, New York. As the American submarines arrived at night off the Long Island coast, the OSS was waiting to pick them up on locally-owned commercial fishing boats. The Nazis were then given fisherman's clothes to wear and taken to Camp Hero near Montauk, NY. The Nazis were given a hero's welcome when they arrived, and have been treated like royalty ever since by the entire U.S./Nazi Government, especially the OSS, CIA, OSI and the FBI. Unfortunately, these are not simply different countries and religions, but rather psychopaths perpetuating wars and causing enormous devastation. TV was developed as a military mass mind-control weapon and first tested in Nazi Germany in 1936 to broadcast the Olympics.

MK-Ultra was created in Nazi Germany before the war, largely based on Carl Jung's "collective unconscious" research in *The Red Book*, and then moved to the U.S. under Operation Paperclip. A host of German doctors, procured from the post-war Nazi talent pool, were an invaluable asset toward the development of MK-Ultra. About half of the Paperclip personnel were rocket scientists working in aviation and aerospace, while the other half, the more secretive group, joined the CIA in the intelligence division, and this included sadistic mind control Nazi psychologists.

In affiliation with the CIA, these sadistic scientists developed "PDH" (Pain/Drugs/Hypnosis) technology to fracture subjects' personalities into specialized, compartmentalized human "robots" for purposes of assassination and retaining classified information, but not breaking under interrogation. This evil technology has also been used in drug transport, sex slavery, super soldiers and other missions requiring the utmost in endurance, information secrecy, containment and deniability. The United Nations and the World Health Organization were set up right after World War II, posing as peace and health organizations but in fact were covert means to continue the Nazi regime of total global control and genocide. This became the infamous "New World Order," promoted by both Adolf Hitler and George H.W. Bush himself. It is important to know who created the CIA, what their nefarious activities are, and how they can be countered in their program of mass deception. As poet Walter Scott noted in the early 19th century, "Oh what a tangled web we weave, when first we practice to deceive."

MIND CONTROL

Sometimes referred to as the CIA's mind control program, MK-Ultra was the code name given to an illegal program of experiments on human subjects, designed and undertaken by the United States Central Intelligence Agency, the CIA. Experiments on humans were intended to identify and develop drugs and procedures to be used in interrogations and torture, in order to weaken the individual and force confessions through mind control.

Organized through the Scientific Intelligence Division of the CIA, the project coordinated with the Special Operations Division of the U.S. Army's Chemical Corps. The program began in the early 1950s, was officially sanctioned in 1953, but was reduced in scope in 1964. The program was further curtailed in 1967 and officially halted in 1973... or so they say. Some researchers believe certain programs are still in operation today.

The program was known to have engaged in many illegal activities. In particular, it used unwitting U.S. and Canadian citizens as its test subjects which led to controversy regarding its legitimacy. MK-Ultra used numerous methodologies to manipulate people's mental states and alter brain function, including the administration of drugs, especially LSD and other chemicals. Also used were hypnosis, sensory deprivation, isolation, verbal and sexual abuse, as well as various forms of torture.

One of the first missions tasked of the new agency was to study behavioral engineering and mind control. Various programs uncovered at the Church Committee Congressional hearings said it began in the early 1950s, continuing at least through the late 1960s, using U.S. citizens as unwitting test subjects. Project MK-Ultra was brought first to wide public attention in 1975 by Congress and by the Rockefeller Commission. Investigative efforts were hampered by the fact that CIA Director Richard Helms ordered all MK-Ultra files destroyed in 1973. Although the CIA insisted that MK-Ultra-type experiments were abandoned, CIA veteran Victor Marchetti has stated in various interviews that the agency routinely conducts disinformation campaigns and that CIA mind control research has continued unabated.[1]

It first started when the CIA decided to expand its efforts in the area of behavior modification with the advent of Project Blue Bird, approved by then-director and known Nazi sympathizer Allen Dulles in 1950. Its objectives were to first discover a means of conditioning personnel to prevent unauthorized extraction of information from them by known means. Then investigate the possibility of control of an individual by application of special interrogation techniques, followed by an investigation of memory enhancement. Lastly, it was used to establish defensive means for preventing hostile control of agency personnel upon being captured and interrogated.

In August 1951, Project Blue Bird was renamed Project Artichoke, which evaluated offensive uses of interrogation techniques, including hypnosis and drugs. The program ceased in 1956. Three years prior to the halt of Project Artichoke, Project MK-Ultra came into existence on April 13, 1953, along the lines proposed by Richard Helms, Deputy Director of Central Intelligence (DDCI), with the rationale of establishing a "special funding mechanism of extreme sensitivity."

MK-Ultra called for numerous mind control experiments to be conducted on a variety of patients. Secrecy was key, because the paranoia of being infiltrated by a Cold War spy meant all operations would be segmented from each other to prevent any one person from understanding the full scope of the project. To maintain secrecy and avoid bias in results, researchers would either not tell the patients they were being given drugs, or the patients would be lied to and experimented on without their consent. Over 44 different American colleges and universities were used in Project MK-Ultra. In addition, numerous hospitals, prisons, and pharmaceutical companies were paid by CIA front companies to conduct various experiments without raising suspicion. In total, over 80 separate research entities were paid through various CIA subprograms to conduct the experiments, and most of the researchers had no idea why they were running the experiments or for whom they were working. Operations for MK-Ultra were so secretive, even the agents running the CIA front companies were alleged to have not known anything beyond their own operations.

1 Lupan, Carmen: https://nanobrainimplant.com/2013/07/14/mind-control-remote-neural-monitoring-daniel-estulin-and-magnus-olsson-on-russia-today/

Finding thousands of willing test subjects for such a massive program, while maintaining secrecy, would be difficult. Officials determined the best way to conduct experimentation without raising public suspicion or tipping off the enemy was to not tell anybody—even the subjects. Subjects the least likely to "put up a fight" were chosen. Nursing homes, prisons, and mental hospitals were popular sources for test subjects. Sometimes prostitutes were employed to lure unsuspecting men to a "flop house" where they were given various drugs, both knowingly and unknowingly, and tested on how suggestable they would become. LSD would also be administered to doctors, military personnel, CIA agents, and members of the general public—in most cases without their knowledge.

The CIA would later admit the tests made little scientific sense since, among other reasons, the agents doing the monitoring of MK-Ultra were not qualified scientific observers. Dr. Sidney Gottlieb, one leading researcher responsible for MK-Ultra, has said little on the record about the program other than admitting at his retirement in 1972 that the results were "useless." A follow-up report from the U.S. General Accounting Office in 1984 would reveal that between 1940 and 1974, the CIA exposed thousands of human test subjects to hazardous substances. Of course, with no remaining program documents and few witnesses willing to talk, most expect the true numbers to be much higher.[2]

JOSEF MENGELE

Josef Mengele, the infamous "Angel of Death," was known for the killing of thousands of those imprisoned at Auschwitz, for performing sadistic biological experiments upon the prisoners in the death camps, and for having a penchant for "studying" twins. Having studied biology at the University of Munich, then working as a research assistant at Frankfurt University Institute for Hereditary Biology and Racial Hygiene, Mengele joined the *Sturmabteilung*, or "Stormtroopers," a paramilitary organization for the Nazi Party.

Josef Mengele was arguably one of the evilest men in history. He was a German SS officer and a physician in the Nazi concentration camp at Auschwitz. In 1940, he was placed in the reserve medical corps, after which he served with the 5th SS Panzergrenadier Division Wiking on the Eastern Front. In 1942, he was wounded at the Soviet front and was pronounced medically unfit for combat. He was then promoted to the rank of *SS-Hauptsturmführer* (Captain) for saving the lives of three German soldiers. In May 1943, Mengele replaced another doctor who had fallen ill at the Nazi concentration camp at Birkenau. On 24, May 1943, he became medical officer of Auschwitz-Birkenau's *Zigeunerfamilienlager*—the "Gypsy Family Camp." Mengele used Auschwitz as an opportunity to continue his research on heredity, using inmates for human experimentation. He initially gained notoriety for being one of the SS physicians who supervised the selection of arriving transports of prisoners, to determine whom he'd use as subjects for medical experiments and who were to become forced laborers. But he is far more infamous for performing human experiments on camp inmates, including children, for which Mengele was labeled the "Angel of Death."

The conventional wisdom says Mengele survived the war and, after a period of living incognito in Germany, fled to South America. There he evaded capture for the rest of his life, despite being hunted as a Nazi war criminal. Survivors of MK-Ultra said Nazi Auschwitz doctor Josef Mengele not only relocated with a new identity under Project Paperclip, but traveled all over the United States directing MK-Ultra experiments, especially on American children. There are hundreds if not thousands of survivors who testify they endured trauma-based mind control under the supervision of Dr. Josef Mengele.[3]

• •
2   James, Preston: https://catyoung.weebly.com/home/preston-james-fooling-american-masses-with-false-flag-terror-no-longer-easy
3   Posner, Gerald, Ware, John. "Mengele: The Complete Story" http://amzn.to/16m2vTC

THE INFAMOUS DULLES BROTHERS

The MK-Ultra Project, a hideous "mind control program" was developed by the CIA during Allen Dulles' reign as director. Its protocols dosed unsuspecting people with LSD, pushed the limits of sleep deprivation, and engaged in other deeply unethical experiments. The program has been exposed, bit by bit, over decades, thanks to lawsuits and persistent investigative reporting. An "American Nazi" to the tee, Allen Dulles masterminded the creation of the CIA, assisted former Nazis to relocate in America, covered up the assassination of JFK from his Warren Commission position, and struck a deal with the Muslim Brotherhood to create mind-controlled assassins. Brother John Foster Dulles presided over the phony Goldman Sachs trusts before the 1929 stock market crash and helped his brother overthrow governments in Iran and Guatemala. Both were Skull and Bones, Council on Foreign Relations (CFR) insiders and 33rd Degree Masons. Avery Dulles is the son of John Foster Dulles, then Secretary of State, and a nephew to Allen Dulles, then CIA director. Avery worked with Martin Bormann to help his escape to freedom in Argentina, and worked as an advisor at Georgetown University. He also is a member of the Knights of Malta. The Dulles and Rockefeller families are cousins.

Allen Dulles was the chief architect of U.S.-Nazi business and spy networks. He worked closely with his brother, John Foster Dulles, as lawyer and international finance specialist for Sullivan & Cromwell, a Wall Street law firm from 1927 to 1941. While there, he worked with top Nazi industrialists and played a pivotal role in promoting U.S.-Nazi corporate relations. Allen worked with Prescott Bush, who ran Union Banking Corporation for the Nazis. Allen was legal counsel for Standard Oil and the Nazis' I.G. Farben, co-owned by the Rockefellers. Other U.S. millionaires allied to the Nazis were: William Randolph Hearst Sr., Andrew Mellon, Irene DuPont, Henry Ford and J.P. Morgan. Morgan, DuPont and others were even involved in a fascist plot to overthrow the U.S. government in 1934, but were never prosecuted.

President Roosevelt, realizing Dulles was a traitor, had his New York "Office of Coordinator of Information" wiretapped from 1941-42. Some Dulles-linked firms, such as Bush's Union Bank, were then seized under the Trading with the Enemy Act. Roosevelt's plan to charge Dulles with treason failed when Dulles was warned in 1944 and covered his tracks. By the end of the year, in November 1944, the U.S. Senate Military Affairs Committee's Subcommittee on War Mobilization issued a report on Cartels and National Security that indicated the Nazis "are already deploying their economic reserves throughout the world." Roosevelt's plan to reverse course died with him in 1945, and the Dulles Brothers only became more powerful.[4]

When the war concluded, Dulles negotiated the agreement with General Reinhard Gehlen in 1945 to establish a Nazi spy network within the OSS. Dulles helped in the development of the CIA in 1947, became its deputy director in 1951, and its director from 1953 until being fired by JFK in 1961. He oversaw numerous covert operations, such as election rigging in Italy (1948), coups in Iran (1953) and Guatemala (1954), and many other notorious operations. After the Union Banking Corporation returned from liquidation, Prescott Bush and George Herbert Walker received $1.5 million in 1951. Dulles was fired by President Kennedy after the failed invasion of Cuba at the Bay of Pigs, and as a member of the Warren Commission, he promoted the theory that a "lone gunman" assassinated John F. Kennedy in 1963.

THE CIA WAS A NAZI CREATION

The original CIA started many years ago when the OSS, the original CIA, acquired the gold and assets of the countries involved in World War II. The gold

4   Davis, Randy "Nazis in the Attic." http://emperors-clothes.com/articles/randy/swas2.htm

of Germany and Japan that had been amassed and stolen from many other countries during the war and ended up in the hands of the CIA, but this couldn't be openly admitted. The CIA was not about to give back the largest pile of gold ever amassed. This gold was outside of the U.S. and was being held in secure Philippine caves and private Swiss banks. Had it been brought back into America and added to the U.S. Treasury, it could have destabilized the dollar and world currencies.

The CIA overrides all other intelligence agencies because it can always pull the "international security" card from its sleeve and trump the lesser agencies which only have the lower priority "national security." Presidential executive orders can be top secret and can be kept from agencies not responsible for their enforcement. So, if the president conducts "international" top-secret business, he can exclude U.S. intelligence agencies from this top secret intel, because they only have lower national security clearance. Essentially, the president of the United States currently conducts "international" warfare without the U.S. Congress, Supreme Court, or U.S. citizens even knowing those wars exist. The president can also wage all types of war secretly within U.S. borders, because Obama changed the National Defense Authorization Act, with Congressional approval, to give him those powers. Other extraordinary presidential powers have been consolidated through numerous executive orders since the Obama presidency.

The president now holds more power than ever and these powers are unconstitutional, illegal, and unethical. If you read the executive orders that are made available on the National Registry, you will see that Obama had conducted secret warfare on foreign countries and individuals both outside of and inside America. It is scary enough to know that under the auspices of "national security," the president can seize all assets in America under these new powers. But scarier than this is that the CIA can still trump the president under the auspices of "international security." The CIA has positioned itself to be a higher authority than Congress, the President, or We the People and can act in secrecy in all of its affairs.[5]

THE CIA IS OUT OF CONTROL

Isn't it ironic that John F. Kennedy, 35th President of the USA, assassinated on November 23, 1963, stated: "If the United States ever experiences an attempt at a coup to overthrow the government, it will come from the CIA. The agency represents a tremendous power and total unaccountability to anyone."

Remember Chile's 9/11? The CIA has been fond of assassinating Latin American leaders who stand up to multinational corporations and central banks who try to exploit their country's people and resources. They later founded the School of the Americas, which trained death squads that would kill presidents and establish fascist dictatorships. The School of the Americas is still alive and active.

The CIA's black budget is almost equal to UK's entire Defense Budget. Historically, the CIA is a covert extension of the UK's MI6 after World War II to re-annex the USA, (as is Pakistan's ISI), to work outside British accountability for the United Monarchical colonial advantage against a democratic free world! In reference to the U.S. Intelligence Community, CIA Director William Colby said:

> Socially as well as professionally, they cliqued together, forming a sealed fraternity. They ate together at their own special favorite restaurants; they partied almost only among themselves; their families drifted to each other, so that their defense did not always have to be up. In this way they increasingly separated themselves from the ordinary world, and developed a rather skewed view of the world. Their own dedicated double life became the proper norm, and they looked down on the rest of the citizenry.

5   Icke, David, *Children of the Matrix*. Bridge of Love. Scottsdale, AZ. 2000.

Some of the most notorious SS Nazis were brought to America (in addition to Operation Paperclip) through a secret underground network known as the Odessa or *Die Spinne* "The Spider." Most of Hitler's SS of the Third Reich merged with the OSS to create the CIA and to become the Fourth Reich in America. They had help once they arrived in America from the Assistant Secretary of War and ardent Nazi-sympathizer, John J. McCloy and the Dulles Brother Nazis. The CIA was created to lie to the American Public. It was created to hide its beloved Nazis, to keep hidden non-polluting, non-oil burning, free energy and Tesla Technology from the American public and the rest of the world. It worked with its Nazis to create a Fourth Reich or New World Order in America. It was not created to protect or help American Citizens, but to serve its neofascist regime. Can you name one good thing that the CIA has ever done for America? The American CIA and FBI agencies consider themselves to be above the law and do not respond to or acknowledge Freedom of Information Act requests.

CIA SHENANIGANS

It is a known fact that the CIA has been involved in the international drug trade, hence the nickname "Cocaine Import Agency." Control of the opium/heroin trade is another reason for taking out the competition in developing nations. This is a trillion dollar industry. Often, weapons are supplied to poorer, cash-strapped nations in exchange for drugs like opium/heroin or cocaine, and the covert American government agents ship the drugs across Asia, Europe and Central America for resale.[6]

The CIA neofascists also used their stolen World War II loot to help fund neo-Nazi fundamentalist, conservative, right-wing, anti-freedom groups like Operation Rescue, The Brotherhood of Aryan Nations hate group, the KKK and Republican president-appointed Supreme Court Justices such as Scalia, Thomas and Souter. These were the same anti-freedom Supreme Court Justices who unjustly and illegally refused Al Gore's request for a re-count. That was a sad day for American Democracy. Many of the CIA's New World Order fascists became consultants for Government Affiliated Companies such as the S.A.I.C. (Science Application International Corporations). S.A.I.C. is really CIA spelled backwards.

Most of the major corporations in the world which accidentally discovered accounting irregularities that "mistakenly" caused CEO's to make millions of dollars while workers and shareholders lost millions of dollars had the CIA's SS New World Order Nazis as consultants. These included companies such as W.R. Grace Co., Enron, World Com, Tyco, all S.A.I.C.-supported companies like NASA, Telcordia Technologies, Lucent Technology, every airline company, Bayer, Merck, American Home Products and most other major pharmaceutical companies. The CIA's New World Order SS Nazis have been conspiring with the CEO's of the largest companies in the world to create the troubled depression-like economy we have today. Is it any wonder that it just happened? No, it was carefully planned.

In September, 2019, Stephen Kinzer's new book, entitled *Poisoner in Chief: Sidney Gottlieb and the CIA Search for Mind Control,* was released. It detailed how directors of the CIA mind control program, MK-Ultra, used the laboratories at Fort Detrick, Maryland, as a key base of operations. Although the laboratory destroyed most of its records in 1973, some of its secrets have been revealed in declassified documents, as well as through interviews and as a result of Congressional investigations. Together, these sources reveal Fort Detrick's central role in MK-Ultra and in the manufacture of poisons intended to kill foreign leaders. In 1970, President Richard Nixon ordered all government agencies to destroy their supplies of biological toxins. Army scientists complied. Gottlieb hesitated. He had spent years assembling this deadly pharmacopeia and did not want to destroy it. After meeting with CIA Director Richard Helms, he reluctantly agreed that he had no choice.

6   CIA drugs-for-weapons trade: **https://www.youtube.com/watch?v=5b6kf5PIzX4&ab_channel=bondageprincess**

Ever wonder why we never see all the footage of the shooting crime of a "lone nut," who is usually a mind-controlled patsy? It's because the security video reels of the "shooters" won't match the mass media narrative of the event, so the public never sees the complete footage. The first thing the Feds do when they swoop onto a mass shooting scene is confiscate all security video footage from the inside and out of the location. They also confiscate any footage from surrounding stores or ATMs just to be sure they have it all. Then, it's always only one mass shooter, the "lone shooter," even after early reports usually have survivors and witnesses talking about multiple shooters. That is how we can tell when a violent event is a staged false flag event. Usually, real people still die, but it doesn't go down the way it's told for days and weeks after by MSM, and nobody ever sees or can access the security surveillance footage.

MANCHURIAN CANDIDATE

The term "Manchurian Candidate" derives from a 1959 novel by Richard Condon titled *The Manchurian Candidate*. Condon portrays a platoon of American soldiers during the Korean War who were sent to Manchuria (a region in northeast China), where they were detained, brainwashed, given alter personalities and programmed to assassinate key individuals in an attempt to overthrow the U.S. government. As a result, the term Manchurian Candidate now signifies a person who has had his or her personality split into "alters," who can commit murder or other acts without any conscious knowledge of what they've done. Their "alter-ego" did the killing, and when they return to their normal consciousness, they cannot remember what they've done. Such a system of creating alters was of utmost importance to MK-Ultra programmers.

The CIA has declassified over 18,000 pages of documents on extensive mind-control programs carried out since the early 1950s. These documents prove that the government developed a Manchurian Candidate program which was quite real. Through the Freedom of Information Act, these documents can be acquired directly from the U.S. government. There are extensive quotes on the creation of Manchurian Candidates from the most revealing of these documents.

Below is a sample of just two of these declassified documents and one scientific article depicting the Manchurian Candidate program. These documents and quotes show that the riveting concepts from the book and film, *The Manchurian Candidate,* are more fact than fiction. First, two declassified CIA documents describe the experimental creation of alter personalities in two 19-year-old girls and an experiment on creating unsuspecting assassins:

> *These subjects have clearly demonstrated that they can pass from a fully awake state to a deep hypnotic state by telephone, by receiving written matter, or by the use of code, signal, or words, and that control of those hypnotized can be passed from one individual to another without great difficulty. It has also been shown by experimentation with these girls that they can act as unwilling couriers for information purposes.*

> *Miss [deleted] was instructed (having previously expressed a fear of firearms) that she would use every method at her disposal to awaken miss [deleted] (now in a deep hypnotic sleep). Failing this, she would pick up a pistol and fire it at Miss [deleted]. She was instructed that her rage would be so great that she would not hesitate to "kill" [deleted]. Miss [deleted] carried out these suggestions including firing the (unloaded) gun at [deleted], and then proceeded to fall into a deep sleep. After proper suggestions were made, both were awakened. Miss [deleted] expressed absolute denial that the foregoing sequence had happened.[7]*

---

7   Declassified CIA document dated Jan. 7, 1953 describes creating alters (CIA Mori ID 190684). A second document dated Feb. 10, 1954 describes an experiment on creating unsuspecting assassins (CIA Mori ID 190691).

In a 1971 *Science Digest* article, Dr. G.H. Estabrooks states:

> *By the 1920s clinical hypnotists learned to split certain individuals into multiple personalities like Jekyll-Hyde's. During World War II, I worked this technique with a Marine lieutenant I'll call Jones. I split his personality into Jones A and Jones B. Jones A, once a "normal" working Marine, became entirely different. He talked communist doctrine and meant it. He was welcomed enthusiastically by communist cells, and was deliberately given a dishonorable discharge. Jones B was the deeper personality, knew all the thoughts of Jones A, and was "imprinted" to say nothing during conscious phases. All I had to do was hypnotize him, get in touch with Jones B, and I had a pipeline straight into the Communist camp.*[8]

These are just a few of the many disturbing experiments which reveal severe abuse of power on unsuspecting citizens for over 60 years to date. The development of a sophisticated Manchurian Candidate program is clearly defined in the 18,000 pages of released documents—and these are only the tip of the iceberg. The CIA still refuses to release many thousands of pages. And millions of pages of secret documents on the program were destroyed by the order of CIA Director Richard Helms in 1973, when he was tipped off that there was going to be a Congressional investigation into the CIA's mind control activities.

In another example of a film imitating reality, according to Benjamin Fulford reporting in August, 2019, he discovered from the Russians, NSA, and other sources that German Chancellor Angela Merkel, former UK Prime Minister Theresa May, and other leaders were genetically-created daughters of Adolf Hitler. We now find out that former U.S. President Barack Obama's mother was also a Hitler daughter. It turns out that the movie, *The Boys from Brazil,* was based on true fact, except that it was girls, not boys.

PROJECT MONARCH

Project Monarch derives its name from the monarch butterfly, not from royalty. When a person is undergoing trauma induced by electroshock, a feeling of light-headedness is evidenced as if one is floating or fluttering like a butterfly. There is also a symbolic representation pertaining to the transformation or metamorphosis of this beautiful insect from a caterpillar to a cocoon (dormancy, inactivity), to a butterfly (beautiful new creation) which will return to its point of origin. Such is the migratory pattern that makes this species unique. Occultic symbolism also gives additional insight into the true meaning of the word, psyche. It is the word for both "soul" and "butterfly," coming from the belief that human souls become butterflies while searching for a new reincarnation.

Due to the severe trauma induced through electroshock, sexual abuse and other methods, the mind splits off from the core into alternate personalities. Formerly referred to as Multiple Personality Disorder, it is presently recognized as Dissociative Identity Disorder and is the basis for Monarch programming. Further conditioning of the victim's mind is enhanced through hypnotism, double-bind coercion, pleasure-pain reversals, and food, water, sleep and sensory deprivation, along with various drugs which alter certain cerebral functions. The next stage is to embed and compress detailed commands or messages within the specified alter personality. This is achieved through the use of hi-tech headsets, in conjunction with computer-driven generators, which emit inaudible sound waves or harmonics that affect the RNA covering of neuron pathways to the subconscious and unconscious mind.

Cathy O'Brien was an unwilling victim of Project Monarch, including being forced into prostitution with those in the upper echelons of world politics. Other forced covert

8 Drudgaard, Lars, "History of RFID-chips, Directed Energy Weapons." ICAACT interview **https://icaact.org/audio-icaact-radio.html#.XWFwOJNKhyB**

assignments were as a "drug mule" and courier, and being involved with the country music industry's relationship with illegal CIA activities. As a child, she was first sexually abused by her father as well as by a network of child pornographers. She claims she was forced by the CIA to participate in the government mind-control program called Project Monarch, which is a subsection of MK-Ultra. Under hypnosis, she was able to recall memories of sexual abuse—of both herself and her daughter—by international pedophile rings, drug barons, and Satanists, who allegedly used a form of "trauma-based mind control programming" to make her a sex slave, and used her to blackmail prominent individuals. The Jeffrey Epstein case exposing underaged sex slaves on Orgy Island corroborates the claims of O'Brien. Project Monarch caused her to develop a multiple personality disorder, but only during alternate personality episodes. She was able to have near total recall with her "alters." What's interesting on Wikipedia is a page called "Cathy O'Brien (conspiracy theorist)," yet no page devoted to Project Monarch.[9]

Originally designed as a program to be used for interrogation purposes, the MK-Ultra program followed many of the guidelines listed in the declassified Kubark Interrogation Manual, which lists a method of interrogation known as the "Alice in Wonderland" method. The method involves a confusion technique to detach the interviewee from reality.[10]

Countless self-proclaimed victims of these horrific trauma-based mind control experiments attest to the use of Disney films for their programming, especially child victims. Films like Wizard of Oz and Alice in Wonderland were reportedly a staple in mind-control programming, as the imagery optimized the traumatized victim's ability to dissociate and accept programming instructions. A passage from the declassified Kubark Interrogation Manual states:

> Because such candidates were and are selected young, before the ego has fully formed, children's stories were favorite modelling texts, such as The Wizard of Oz and Alice in Wonderland. Hence the connection with the entire Disney empire's involvement in such programming.

MK-ULTRA ENHANCED BY TECHNOLOGY

Very few people are aware of the actual link between neuroscience, cybernetics, artificial intelligence, neuro-chips, transhumanism, the science of cyborgs, robotics, somatic surveillance, behavior control, the thought police and human enhancement. They all go hand in hand, and never in our history before has this issue been as important to understand as it is now. More on these subjects will be covered in the Über-Mind Section of this book.

The main reason for concern is that this new technology, that really began to be developed only in the early 1950s but is by now very advanced, remains completely unregulated and the public is unaware of the implications. There is also a complete amnesia about its early development, as radio host Lars Drudgaard mentioned in a 2012 interview. The CIA funded experiments on people without consent through leading universities and by hiring prominent neuroscientists of that time. These experiments (since the 1950s) have been brutal, destroying every aspect of a person's life, while hiding behind curtains of National Security and secrecy, but also behind psychiatry diagnoses which are highly subjective. Lee Harvey Oswald, Sirhan Sirhan, Charles Manson, John Hinckley Jr., Mark Chapman, David Koresh, Timothy McVeigh and John Salvi are some notable names of infamy, strongly suspected of being subject to MK-Ultra trauma-based mind-control programming.[11]

9   Estabrooks, Dr. G.H. Science Digest, April 1971, pp. 44-50.
10   Wikipedia: "Cathy O'Brien (conspiracy theorist)" https://en.wikipedia.org/wiki/Cathy_O%27Brien_(conspiracy_theorist)#Project_Monarch
11   The Sharp Edge/ Corey's Digs. "Keys to The Magic Kingdom" https://www.coreysdigs.com/trafficking/exposing-the-keys-to-disneys-operations-and-agenda

The attorney for assassin Sirhan Sirhan asserts that his client was under the influence of hypnosis from the MK-Ultra program when he shot Robert Kennedy in 1968. To this day, Sirhan Sirhan can recall nothing of the actual shooting by his "alter." Several researchers have proposed that Jonestown in Guyana was actually one of the test sites for MK-Ultra, and that it was no coincidence that outspoken CIA-critic Congressman Leo Ryan was assassinated on his visit. The list goes on and on, including the Colorado "Batman" shooter and other "lone nuts" who go on shooting rampages. The end result is more losses of our freedoms. These all appear to be results of the "Problem-Reaction-Solution" strategy. It's highly unlikely the CIA has terminated all experimental psychotherapy and drug-testing programs. The ever-changing climate of war suggests that this type of experimentation isn't going away anytime soon. Thus, the need to root out all of the remaining fascist public servants in America, and to break up the CIA into splinters as JFK suggested nearly 60 years ago.

Another reason why dealing with the mind-implant issue is important is the fact that both the USA and the EU pour billions of dollars and euros into brain research every year. This brain research is very focused on not only understanding the brain, but is also concerned with merging human beings and machines. This can involve the following: using neuro-implants to correct behavior and enhance intelligence; use of A.I. and the "Internet of things;" plus create robots and other machines that think and make autonomous intelligent decisions just as humans do.

Transhumanist advocate Ray Kurzweil, whose predictions about future technological developments have been correct at least until now, claims that by the mid-2030s, implant-technology will have advanced so far that A.I. will surpass human intelligence and humanity will be completely transformed by the change. We cannot know right now whether his prediction is right or wrong, but we should at least have the right to decide on the kind of future we want.

RFID CHIP CONTROL OF THE MASSES

As far back as 2004, Applied Digital and Digital Angel Corporation announced that VeriChip, the world's first implantable radio frequency identification (RFID) microchip for human use, had been cleared by the U.S. Food and Drug Administration for medical uses in the USA. The VeriChip Health Information Micro Transponder System consists of an implantable RFID micro transponder, an inserter, a proprietary hand-held scanner and a secure database containing the patient-approved healthcare information. We will be sold on the fact that we all need them because they will contain our personal medical history, our currency, and all of our access keys and passwords. Life will be so much easier and safer after being implanted; we will be told. It will be an idea so good that it will be made mandatory.

About the size of a grain of rice, the VeriChip is a subdermal radio frequency microchip that is inserted under the skin in a brief out-patient procedure. While the VeriChip cannot be seen by the human eye, each chip contains a unique 16-digit verification number that is captured by briefly passing a scanner over the insertion site. The captured 16-digit number links to the database via encrypted Internet access. The previously-stored information is then conveyed via the Internet to the registered requesting healthcare provider, for example.

Demented visions (such as this) of a world ruled by an Anglo-American federation represents one of the first attempts in the 20th century by a power-elite Cabal to bypass democracy. This is in order to achieve its goal of overriding national sovereignty, and establishing a supra-national form of governance. This is occurring in America right now. The fascist American police state is forming by following these ten easy steps: **1.** Invoke a terrifying internal and external enemy (War on Terror); **2.** Create a gulag (FEMA camps and Guantanamo Bay); **3.** Develop a thug caste (Homeland Security); **4.** Set up an internal surveillance system (CIA, NSA, RFID chips, etc.); **5.** Harass citizens' groups (moles); **6.** Engage in arbitrary detention and interrogation (catch and release); **7.** Target key individuals (blackmail and control those in charge); **8.** Control the press (mainstream media consolidation); **9.** Dissent equals treason (you are either with us or against us); **10.** Suspend the rule of law (Patriot Act, NDAA, etc.). According to author Ian Williams Goddard, "A society whose citizens refuse to see and investigate the facts, who refuse to believe that their government and their media will routinely lie to them and fabricate a reality contrary to verifiable facts, is a society that chooses and deserves the police state dictatorship it's going to get." After all, the laws of karma dictate that we ultimately get what we deserve.

Until RFID chips are used for mass population control, psychiatric drugs are also employed. "The drug industry buys the professors first, then chiefs of departments, then the other chief physicians and so on. They don't buy junior doctors," said Dr. Peter Gøtzsche. Big Pharma drugs kill around 200,000 Americans every year—half of them die while doing what their doctors advised or prescribed. Sadly, the side effects and medical errors combine to cause the third leading cause of death in America. Ask your doctor if taking their advice is right for you.

THEY CONTROL ALL TOP POLITICIANS

In the last century, almost every U.S. President, Vice-President, Congressman and Senator after Teddy Roosevelt, except for the Kennedy brothers and Donald Trump, have gone along with the illegal Bush Plan for a New World Order. In America, upwards of 95% of all Congressional delegates have been compromised or blackmailed in some way. Prescott Bush allegedly laundered vast amounts of wealth and exerted his political influence to create the American OSS, with young George Herbert Walker Bush as its up and coming leader. Since it is a Congressionally- established fact that Prescott Bush was in business with the Nazis during World War II, we can safely say that the Bush/Nazi connection existed, and that connection was still alive through U.S. presidents George H.W. Bush and George W. Bush.

There is some evidence that Nikola Tesla was murdered by intelligence agents on January 6, 1943, who stole his greatest inventions such as the anti-gravity flying disks, invisibility technology, and a "Death Ray," along with earthquake and weather modification machines. Around this time, and well before the end of World War II, Admiral Wilhelm Canaris, head of the Nazi *Abwehr* "Defense Intelligence," decided to regroup as a Third Power. It had been determined that Germany would "lose" the war and the organization was forced to move "underground." Their long-range plans, described in the "Madrid Circular," a document discovered after the war, were to covertly infiltrate the United States and eventually take over the country, in part by using mass mind control, thus establishing a "1000-year Reich" without ever firing a shot. The *Abwehr* has since become the *Deutsche Verteidigungs Dienst*, or "German Defense Agency (DVD)." The agency's motto is: *Für uns, ist der Krieg niemals vorbei*, or "For us, the war is never over."[12]

THE DAWN OF SUPER-FASCISM

At first the Secret Shadow Government was a regular fascist government just like Nazi Germany. This was a union between the state and the corporation with the state directing the corporations, defense contractors, and private industry. Then the large corporations, especially the aerospace and arms contractors, stacked the government and used it to serve their exclusive needs. This is best described as super-

12 Orion, Eric, "The Hitler / Bush Connection" 2003.

fascism where the corporation and state merge, but the corporation controls the state and uses it for its own corporate interests.

In the decades following World War II, the Cabal became more and more independent and dominant over the official Intel agencies and the Pentagon. This was due to its transformation into black, deep-black and beyond-black un-acknowledged programs, which were related to joint projects in conjunction with cooperating extraterrestrials to backward-engineer anti-gravity crafts for humans' defense use. Of course, this was all protected under the strictest of all secrecy classifications: "Cosmic Top Secret." Soon the deep-black and beyond-black secret unacknowledged defense contractor programs became so dominant that they began calling all the shots inside the visible Federal DC government, albeit in deep secret from the American people and most members of Congress. As author Preston James describes:

> This type of fascism where the state and the corporation merge but the corporation controls the state, stacks it with its choices and uses it for its own corporate welfare and funding like pigs at the D.C. taxpayer trough, is best called super-fascism. In this super-fascist system that evolved under MJ-12's control, the CIA, Mossad, FBI and other alphabets became tools, deniable cutouts to do the dirty work of the deep-black and beyond-black Secret Shadow Government elements.

The American Central Intelligence Agency and their "privatized" adjuncts, such as private security firm Wackenhut, have long engaged in overthrowing foreign governments, assassinating popular U.S. leaders and officials, and causing fake foreign and domestic "emergencies" and coups. Why is it hard then to believe they would not also orchestrate, on a vast scale, the overthrowing of the American Central Government, to favor, for example, the British—itching to return us to a puppet-colony status? Some contend we may see the American Constitution overthrown by such means, and the nation run by martial law with our rights suspended. This would be as a way of dealing with an expected U.S. financial collapse and new Great Depression. Researcher David Icke has said for decades that there would come a time when all the back-room planning of the globalists will have to be executed out in the open. We are now seeing the roll-out of a One World Currency, a One World Religion, and a One World Government.

The CIA was publicly exposed for using illegal MK-Ultra practices in Congressional hearings in the 1970s, but there is no indication that they've stopped or anything has changed. It has been further revealed that the CIA is the "central node" controlling defense and intelligence contractors. At the highest levels, the CIA is a control system and the enforcement arm for what we have been calling the Cabal. It should be obvious, therefore, to conclude that MK-Ultra and other similar practices are routinely being used on their employees, as well as the general population. Their mass mind control operations have never ended.

The *fasces* is the symbol of fascism. The symbol is a bound bundle of wood rods surrounding an axe. In ancient Rome, the *fasces* symbolized a magistrate's power and jurisdiction. The image became the symbol of Mussolini's government. Fascist movements share commitments to create a "proletarian nation" that wields the power of corporatism, a system that later came to be called "state capitalism," with a government under a charismatic leader.

The corrupt fascist corporatism in America is apparent in the Supreme Court decision called "Citizens United," which grants corporations the same rights as citizens: "The U.S. Supreme Court decision... means the nation has entered a post-constitutional era. It means that extraordinary rendition of U.S. citizens on U.S. soil by our government is legal. It means that the courts, like the legislative and executive branches of government, exclusively serve corporate power—one of the core definitions of fascism. It means that the internal mechanisms of state are so corrupted and subservient to corporate power that there is no hope of reform or protection for citizens under our most basic constitutional rights. It means that the consent of the governed—a poll by OpenCongress.com showed that this provision had a 98 percent disapproval rating—is a cruel joke. And it means that if we do not rapidly build militant (*Washington's Blog* believes in non-violence) mass movements to overthrow corporate tyranny, including breaking the back of the two-party duopoly that is the mask of corporate power, we will lose our liberty. ...In declining to hear the case Hedges v. Obama and declining to review the NDAA, the Supreme Court has turned its back on precedent, dating back to the Civil War era, that holds that the military cannot police the streets of America," said attorney Carl Mayer, who along with Bruce Afran devoted countless unpaid hours to the suit. Chris Hedges goes on to say, "This is a major blow to civil liberties. It gives the green light to the military to detain people without trial or counsel in military installations, including secret installations abroad. There is little left of judicial review of presidential action during wartime."

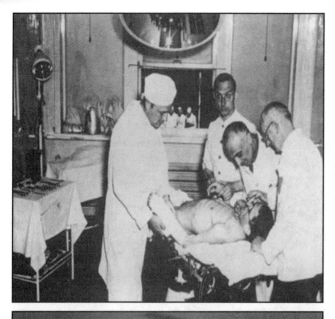

MK-Ultra is a sadistic CIA project that involves satanic ritual abuse. Victims are drugged, hypnotized, traumatized, given electric-shock and other treatments to rewire their brains. These mind-controlled zombies have been used as spies, assassins, sex-slaves, and even as celebrities. Through MK-Ultra, CIA handlers have created Manchurian Candidates willing to act on command, even against their own conscience. Through Project Paperclip, Nazi medical facilities were relocated to the USA to continue conducting their "research."

"The war is not meant to be won, it is meant to be continuous. Hierarchical society is only possible on the basis of poverty and ignorance...
The war is waged by the ruling group against its own subjects and its object is not the victory over either Eurasia or East Asia, but to keep the very structure of society intact."
-George Orwell, 1949, from "1984"

George Orwell predicted the police state coming to America. He also foresaw the notion of a perpetual enemy, and false flag operations used to sway public opinion in a desired way.

Psychological operations, or psyops, are CIA programs meant to work on the mass population. Psyops are a version of trauma-based mind control on a group level, in which the programming is violent and shocking, reverting people to the basic fear emotion, that is known to override the rational mind. MK-Ultra utilized experts in how the mind works and knew how to effectively influence what they wished others to believe. Through TV, social media, by blackmailing and subliminal advertising, psyops are designed for "setting people up" to have specific emotional responses.

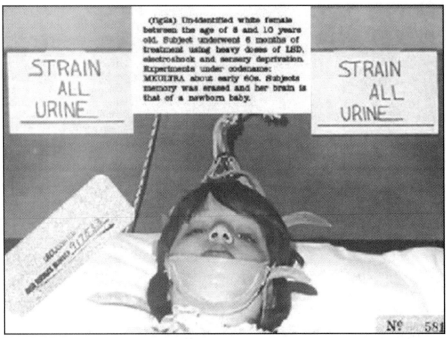

(fig2a) Unidentified white female between the age of 8 and 10 years old. Subject underwent 6 months of treatment using heavy doses of LSD, electroshock and sensory deprivation. Experiments under codename: MKULTRA about early 60s. Subjects memory was erased and her brain is that of a newborn baby.

The caption reads: "Unidentified white female between the age of 8 and 10 years old. Subject underwent 6 months of treatment using heavy doses of LSD, electro-shock and memory deprivation. Experiments under codename: MKULTRA about early 1960s. Subject's memory was erased and her brain is that of a newborn baby."

The "attacks" on 9/11/2001 were one big psychological operation to create a new enemy, but of course, as a false flag operation, the real perpetrators remain concealed. "What we need to stand up and say is not only did they attack the USS Liberty, they did 9/11. They did it. I have had long conversations over the past two weeks with contacts at the Army War College, and at its headquarters at the Marine Corps, and I made it absolutely clear in both cases that it is 100 percent certain that 9/11 was a Mossad operation. Period." –Dr. Alan Sabrosky, March 14, 2010. As a former director of the Strategic Studies Institute (CSIS) at the U.S. Army War College, Dr. Sabrosky can be considered an expert on the subject. His teaching and research appointments have included the United States Military Academy, Middlebury College and Catholic University. While in government service, he held concurrent adjunct professorships at Georgetown University and the Johns Hopkins University School of Advanced International Studies (SAIS). Dr. Sabrosky has lectured widely on defense and foreign affairs in the United States and abroad.

BIG BROTHER

"The entire Western edifice rests on lies. There is no other foundation. Just lies. This makes truth an enemy. Enemies have to be suppressed, and thus truth has to be suppressed...in other words, just to state the obvious noncontroversial fact, the Western 'news' media is a propaganda ministry from which no truth emerges."
–Paul Craig Roberts

THE term "Big Brother" was popularized over 70 years ago by British writer George Orwell in his classic book, *1984*, suggesting the heavy hand of a nearly invisible authoritative power. In this seminal work, he captured the essence of technology in its ability to shape our destinies. The book depicts a populace ruled by a political regime that persecutes individualism and independent critical thinking as "thought crimes," which must be enforced by the "thought police." This regime seeks power above all, and, through the propagandist Ministry of Truth, presents the people with their version of truth. Dissenting opinions are routinely censored. The tragedy of our times is that we have failed to heed Orwell's warning.

Although the book *1984* is usually referred to as a "dystopian futuristic novel," it is actually a horror story on a scale far greater than anything that has emerged from any other novel in the last century. The reason is simple. The nightmare world that the protagonist Winston Smith inhabits, a place called Oceania, is all too easily imaginable. The human, as opposed to some imaginary clown or demon, is the evil monster. In the very first pages of the book, Orwell demonstrates an uncanny ability to foresee future trends in technology. Describing the protagonist Winston Smith's frugal London flat, he mentions an instrument called a "telescreen," which sounds strikingly similar to the handheld "smartphone" or "smart" TV that are enthusiastically used by billions of people around the world today. These devices have the ability to record conversations and spy on citizens in the privacy of their own homes. Sound familiar?

Another method of control alluded to in *1984* fell under a system of speech known as "Newspeak" which attempted to reduce the language to "doublethink," with the ulterior motive of controlling ideas and thoughts. Everything becomes backwards. Classic examples from the book include: "War is Peace, Freedom is Slavery, and Ignorance is Strength." Another Newspeak term is known as a "facecrime," which is a striking parallel to our modern situation. Defined by Orwell as "to wear an improper expression on your face (to look incredulous when a victory was announced, for example) was itself a punishable offense." The authoritarian Chinese government has already installed face-recognition programs on the many surveillance cameras around the country. Chinese people are given a social credit score and, based on their ranking, can be declined a loan, denied the purchase of airplane or train tickets, or refused other social benefits.

It would be difficult for the modern reader to hear the term "facecrime" and not connect it with "Facebook," the social media platform that regularly censors content creators for expressing thoughts it finds "hateful" or inappropriate. Interestingly, the Pentagon announced the cancellation of its LifeLog project on the exact same day Facebook was founded, February 4, 2004. Run by DARPA, the Defense Department's research arm, LifeLog aimed to gather in a single place just about everything an individual says, sees or does: the phone calls made, the TV shows watched, the magazines read, the plane tickets bought, the emails sent and received. Similarly, what social media users now get is an Orwellian lesson in "crimestop," which Orwell defined as "the faculty of stopping short, as though by instinct, at the threshold of any dangerous thought." Those so-called unacceptable "dangerous thoughts" were determined not by the will of the people, of course, but by their unseen masters.[1]

THE SECRET STATE

Of course, Orwell's book was fictional, but many use the term to describe the hidden authorities ruling the world today. Who might they be? Secret societies exist today, and as the name suggests, they thrive on secrecy. All have a common thread. It is what they consider to be their own occult or sacred knowledge. That is, knowledge that only they possess, and is forbidden for the common person. Among the main secret organizations within the Illuminati, the Freemasons are considered to be one of the most powerful. Their history can be traced back to the Knights Templar.

In this modern age, could the owners of the big banks really be Big Brother? By manipulating the money supply, the banks have controlled Western society since the creation of the Bank of England along with the fractional reserve lending system developed in 1694. Moreover, owing to the secrecy under which big banks operate, most elected officials are totally unaware of the immense control central and investment banks exert over the so-called democratic process. Indeed, all historical inflationary and deflationary crises, panics, wars, recessions and depressions were orchestrated behind the scenes by the banking establishment, for the purpose of increasing their own private wealth. In the last three centuries of Western civilization, the banking aristocracy financed the rise of communism in Russia, China and Eastern Europe, as well as bringing Hitler, Mussolini, Stalin and Roosevelt to power, and then guiding their governments from behind the scenes.[2]

"Think of the press as a great keyboard on which the government can play," said Joseph Goebbels, Hitler's Propaganda Minister. Indeed, the Western World is ruled by propaganda. The "Powers That Be," whom we should call the "Powers That Were," have

1   Wilcock, David, "DECLAS: Social Media Nukes An Entire Generation…But Why?" 6/25/2019: **https://divinecosmos.com/davids-blog/22962-social-media-nukes/?showall=1**

2   Bridge, Robert, "No Longer Fiction: Orwell's 1984 is the Reality of Our Times." **https://21stcenturywire.com//2019/07/02/no-longer-fiction-orwells-1984-is-the-reality-of-our-times**

essentially unlimited resources, both financial and physical. They use these resources to monopolize the information that the masses are shown, for that is their only truly effective means of controlling what the masses believe. They know that no movement can successfully challenge this control without the dissemination of new information that contradicts the flow of stories that solidifies their power. Direct censorship never works well, for there are always attempts to circumvent it. But since any input of new information requires a minimum threshold of resources to be effective, the highest priority of the Cabal is to financially starve potentially respectable sources of dissenting information. Controlling the narrative is of the utmost importance.

You would think that with the broad range of contemporary environmental issues of public concern, such as GMOs, the geoengineering use of chemtrails, and the untested 5G rollout, we would have seen a growth within agencies able to assess, categorize and mitigate public health risks. Contrary to expectation, we can see that there has been a significant decrease in environmental toxicologists engaged by governments around the globe. This should be disconcerting to all, as it is virtually impossible to prove cause and effect after the fact.

U.S. Marine Patrick Downey has asked Russian President Putin for asylum after he uncovered and exposed the U.S. government and banks who were arming and funding both sides of the conflict in which he was sent to fight. He stated: "Our country is run by banks, members of a large crime syndicate. Everything related to their activities is hushed. There is no free press, the Constitution is not being followed, and the rights of people are not being protected. Overall, corruption is rampant. I don't want to say that the USA is an 'evil empire,' but I'm asking for protection from the evil that's stalking me."

CONFLICT THEORY

A theory propounded by Karl Marx claims that society will always be in a state of perpetual conflict due to competition for limited resources. Conflict theory holds that social order is maintained by domination and power, or might is right, rather than consensus and conformity. According to conflict theory, those with wealth and power will always try to hold on to it by any means possible, chiefly by suppressing the poor and powerless. Conflict theory also ascribes most of the fundamental developments in human history, such as democracy and civil rights, to capitalistic attempts to control the masses, rather than to a desire for social order.

Conflict theory has been used to explain a wide range of social phenomena, including wars and revolutions, wealth and poverty, discrimination and domestic violence. The financial crisis of 2008-09, and the subsequent bank bailouts, are good examples of real-life conflict theory, according to authors Alan Sears and James Cairns in their work, *A Good Book, in Theory*. Conflict theory proponents view financial crises as the inevitable outcome of the inequalities and instabilities that plague Western societies, given that the present structure of the global economic system enables the largest banks and institutions to avoid government oversight and take huge risks that only reward a select few. Sears and Cairns also note that large banks and big business subsequently received bailouts from the same government that claims to have insufficient funds for large-scale social programs such as higher education for all, or universal healthcare. This dichotomy supports a fundamental assumption of conflict theory, which is that mainstream political institutions and cultural practices favor dominant groups and individuals.[3]

In 1913, America was hijacked by the City of London Central "Banksters," and they have controlled American politics ever since, because they can issue or print all the money they need to buy, bribe, or entice almost any politician, judge, government official, or corporate

••••••••••••••••••••••••••••••
3 Sears, Alan and Cairns, James *A Good Book, in Theory.*

chief they wish. The Jeffrey Epstein case illustrated how so many were caught up in "honey traps." Pedogate is a global epidemic of child trafficking, rape and torture, and anyone of power involved is extremely vulnerable to being blackmailed. In the process of controlling our checks and balances, the Cabal has asset-stripped America bare, destroyed its economy and money system, hijacked banking and credit, and turned most citizens into debt-slave serfs, all the while demanding more and more illegal taxation, social control and extraction of basic human rights guaranteed by the U.S. Constitution. Psychopathic individuals have formed a sinister cult that has gained massive world power.

Secret societies accustomed to the secrecy that would ensure their plans were unlikely to be exposed. Their plan for a "New World Order" global dictatorship was developed at least 250 years ago. They achieved far more success in their goals than most people had ever realized, largely due to the conflict theory described by Marx. This Cabal still has a surprising degree of control over our financial system, and will fight to the death to keep it. Top-level Cabal members rake in spectacular profits within the financial sector, as humanity suffers more and more. The Cabal in turn has used murderous, covert force to dominate Western governments, and most Cabal members are not even citizens of the countries they destroy. These "Powers That Were" actively believe in and practice what most would call evil. Bribery, blackmail, torture and murder are used to threaten and silence opposition.[4]

The people running the Cabal regard human life as expendable commodities. Wars and terrorism are being deliberately created to keep the public in perpetual fear. They use the mainstream media, which they own, to shape a narrative that suits their needs. The media is tasked to shape or hide the truth for the government, by saying Edward Snowden is a "traitor," not a hero, for example. The Cabal is using surveillance to avoid its full exposure and inevitable destruction. Those who "speak truth to power" are either assassinated, run out of the country, or subjected to lengthy jail sentences.

THOSE WHO SEEK TO BE YOUR MASTER

The "Illuminati" is basically an ancient bloodline of 13 families, who have been running the largest institutions in the West for many centuries. One of their symbols hidden in plain sight can be found on the back of the U.S. 1$ bill. The capstone hovering over a pyramid has deep occult meanings. Call them the Illuminati, Cabal, Internationalists or Aristocrats; all are essentially members of the "ruling class" elite. The roots of this group trace back to the Papacy of the Vatican and stem from the British monarchy and other royal families of Europe. This Illuminati group, who can be Zionists, Satanists or Communists, has weaved many webs across the world, infiltrating groups such as the Freemasons. The list is quite overwhelming. The real movers are in the private sector. They conduct secret meetings where top figures gather to discuss future plans for the world. They gather in groups, such as the Bilderbergers, and in secret clubs, councils, commissions and committees.

The cult has control over almost every important seat in the world, be they Senators and Congressmen, Presidents, Prime Ministers, Popes and Queens. Participants in secret clubs and councils hold influential positions in the media, the entertainment industry and government, and are almost always controlled by the Cabal. Cabal politicians call themselves "progressive" and pretend to be "for the people," but then quickly turn their backs and strive for the progress of "the family" (cult) and could care less about outsiders of their group.

No U.S. president in recent times has been elected by the people; they are always selected.

··
4   Solomon, Steven, *The Confidence Game: How Un-Elected Central Bankers are Governing the Changed World Economy*. Simon & Schuster. New York. 1995.

An exception may be Donald Trump, possibly because he cannot be bought by any lobbyist or special interest group. The United States never really won their independence from the British monarchy as the word "United States" really means a "federal corporation" to British crown royalty, who in turn are puppets of the Vatican and Crown. All corporations have presidents, but it is the popes, kings and queens that hold the real power over nations.[5]

ENTER THE TAX MAN

The Federal Reserve System gave the conspirators nearly complete control of our money system; however, they in no way touched the earnings of the people because the Constitution positively forbids what is now known as the 20% withholding tax. But the Illuminati blueprint for one-world enslavement called for the confiscation of *all* private property *and* control of individual earning power. This (and Karl Marx stressed this feature in his blueprint) had to be accomplished by a progressive graduated income tax. Such a tax could not be lawfully imposed upon the American people. It is succinctly and expressly forbidden by our Constitution. Thus, only an Amendment to the Constitution could give the federal government such confiscatory powers.

Author Myron Fagan has stated that changing our Constitution was not an insurmountable problem for our Machiavellian plotters. The same elected leaders in both houses of Congress and the same Mr. Woodrow Wilson, who signed the infamous Federal Reserve Act into law, amended the Constitution to institute the federal income tax (known as the 16th Amendment), and it became the law of the land. Both are illegal under our Constitution. In short, the same traitors signed both betrayals, the Federal Reserve Act and the 16th Amendment, into law. However, it seems that nobody ever realized that the 16th amendment was set up to rob the people of their earnings via the income tax provision.

That 16th Amendment income tax trap was intended to confiscate the earnings only of the common herd, that is, you and me. It was not intended to even touch the huge incomes of the Illuminati gang, the Rockefellers, the Carnegies, the Lehmans, and all the other conspirators. So together, with the 16th Amendment, they created what they called the tax-free foundations that would enable the conspirators to transform their huge wealth into so-called foundations and avoid payment of virtually all income taxes. The justification for this manipulation was that the earnings of those tax-free foundations would be devoted to humanitarian philanthropy. The result is that we now have the several Rockefeller Foundations, the Carnegie Endowment Fund, the Ford Foundation, the Mellon Foundation, and hundreds of similar tax-free foundations.[6]

SHADOW GOVERNMENT AND DEEP STATE

A former CIA expert on counter-intelligence now turned whistleblower, Kevin Shipp, has emerged from the wolves' den to expose the Deep State and the secret government, which he calls two entirely separate entities. He describes the shadow government:

> *The shadow government controls the deep state and manipulates our elected government behind the scenes. ...The top of the shadow government is the National Security Agency and the Central Intelligence Agency.*

Shipp states that the CIA was created through the Council on Foreign Relations with no Congressional approval, and historically the CFR is also tied into the manufactured mainstream media. Further, he notes that the CIA was the "central node" of the shadow

5   USA Exists in Two Forms: *American Dream Preservation* (**website no longer exists**).

6   Fagan, Myron, Illuminati CFR Recordings were originally distributed as a 3-LP record set. Later, audio cassettes became available, & now freely available in mp3 format on the internet. **http://i-uv.com/transcript-of-myron-fagans-1960s-lecture-exposing-the-illuminati-cfr-and-the-satanic-one-world-government-plan**

government and controlled all the other 16 intelligence agencies, despite the existence of the Director of National Intelligence. The agency also controls defense and intelligence contractors, can manipulate the president and political decisions, has the power to start wars, enact torture, initiate coups, and commit false flag attacks. According to Shipp, the deep state is comprised of the military industrial complex, intelligence contractors, defense contractors, MIC lobbyists, Wall Street financiers and their offshore accounts. They also control the Federal Reserve, IMF/World Bank, U.S. Treasury, Foreign lobbyists, and Central Banks. Shipp went on to express that there are "over 10,000 secret sites in the U.S.," which formed after 9/11. Of those, there are 1,291 secret government agencies, 1,931 large private corporations, and over 4,800,000 Americans (that he knows of) who have a secrecy clearance. There are also 854,000 who have Top Secret clearance, explaining that they signed their lives away bound by an agreement.[7]

AL CIA-DA

Another important whistleblower was former FBI Chief Ted Gunderson who said most terrorist attacks were assisted or committed by our very own CIA and FBI, including *Al Qaeda.* Indeed, the translation of *Al Qaeda* is "The Database" (of mercenaries). Shortly before his untimely death, former British Foreign Secretary Robin Cook told the House of Commons that "Al Qaeda" is not really a terrorist group in essence, but a database of international *mujahidin* and arms smugglers used by the CIA and Saudis to funnel guerrillas, arms, and money into Soviet-occupied Afghanistan. He goes on to say the Muslim terrorist apparatus was created by U.S. Intelligence, and the Afghan heroin trade is controlled by the CIA.[8]

We need to be aware that the Muslim terrorist apparatus was created by U.S. and Mossad intelligence as a geopolitical weapon. American Central Intelligence organized, trained, funded and armed the dis-united Afghani tribal freedom fighters under one banner, the Taliban, in order to resist Russian infiltration into the Middle Eastern axis-of-oil region.[9]

Once the Russian threat was eliminated, the Taliban wished for legitimacy in Afghani national affairs. "Corporate" American domination was unacceptable to the united Afghan freedom fighters—that is prior to 9/11, when the U.S. Administration had threatened the Taliban who were reluctant to grant complete control of their homeland to "corporate" rule. The Taliban were told that submitting to U.S. Administration plans for the region would "bring a carpet of gold," but resistance would "bring a carpet of bombs."[10]

U.S. Central Intelligence used Osama Bin Laden as a CIA asset who went by the name Tim Osman to help create the "Muslim terrorist apparatus" in the early 1980s, and later on in the 1990s in the leadup to 9/11. This U.S. plan was discussed by Zbigniew Brzezinski in his book, *The Grand Chessboard,* where control of Eurasia was laid out as a necessity for world domination. A Brzezinski quote:

> *How America "manages" Eurasia is critical. A power that dominates Eurasia would control two of the world's three most advanced and economically productive regions. A mere glance at the map also suggests that control over Eurasia would almost automatically entail Africa's subordination, rendering the Western Hemisphere and Oceania geopolitically peripheral to the world's central continent. About 75 per cent of the world's people live in Eurasia, and most of the world's physical wealth is there*

7   High-Ranking CIA Insider Blows the Whistle on the Shadow Government and Deep State,: **http://www.zerohedge.com/ (must subscribe to Premium to access archived articles)**

8   Cook, Robin, "'Al Qaeda' is Not Really a Terrorist Group ": **http://globalresearch.ca/index.php?context=va&aid=24738**

9   CIA Roots to Al Qaeda Exposed: **http://www.geopoliticalmonitor.com/index.php/afghan-heroin-the-cia/#post**

10 The questionable reality of the alleged group known as "Al Qaeda"and Israeli agents caught impersonating Al Qaeda, to foment more hatred of Muslims: **http://www.youtube.com/watch?v=nehClYdv15A**

as well, both in its enterprises and underneath its soil. Eurasia accounts for about three-fourths of the world's known energy resources.

OPERATION NORTHWOODS

According to secret and long-hidden documents now declassified, in the early 1960s, the Joint Chiefs of Staff drew up and approved plans for what may be the most corrupt scheme ever created by the U.S. government prior to the false flag attack on 9/11/2001. In the name of anti-communism, they proposed launching a secret and bloody war of terrorism against their own country in order to trick the American public into supporting an ill-conceived war they intended to launch against Cuba.

Code named Operation Northwoods, the plan, which had the written approval of the Chairman and every member of the Joint Chiefs of Staff, called for innocent people to be shot on American streets; for boats carrying refugees fleeing Cuba to be sunk on the high seas; for a wave of violent terrorism to be launched in Washington, D.C., Miami, and elsewhere. People would be framed for bombings they did not commit; planes would be hijacked and possibly crashed. Innocent civilian deaths would become "collateral damage." Using phony evidence, all of it would be blamed on Fidel Castro, thus giving our armed forces the justification, as well as the public and international backing, they needed to launch their war.

The idea may actually have originated with President Eisenhower in the last days of his administration. With the Cold War hotter than ever, and the recent U-2 scandal fresh in the public's memory, the old general (Eisenhower) wanted to go out with a win. He wanted desperately to invade Cuba in the weeks leading up to Kennedy's inauguration; indeed, on January 3rd he told General Lemnitzer and other aides in his Cabinet Room that he would move against Castro before the inauguration if only the Cubans gave him a really good excuse. Then, with time growing short, Eisenhower floated an idea. If Castro failed to provide that excuse, perhaps, he said, the United States "could think of manufacturing something that would be generally acceptable." What he was suggesting was a pretext of a bombing, a false flag attack, an act of sabotage carried out secretly against the United States by the United States, but blamed on its Cuban enemy. Its purpose would be to justify the launching of a war. It was a dangerous suggestion by a desperate president.

Although no such war took place, the idea was not lost on General Lemnitzer, but he and his colleagues were frustrated by Kennedy's failure to authorize their plan, and angry that Castro had not provided an excuse to invade.

In retrospect, the documents offer new insight into the thinking of the military's star-studded leadership. Although they never succeeded in launching America into a phony war with Cuba, they may have done so with Vietnam. More than 50,000 Americans and more than two million Vietnamese were eventually killed in that conflict which started on false pretenses in the Gulf of Tonkin incident.

It has long been suspected that the 1964 Gulf of Tonkin incident—the spark that led to America's long war in Vietnam—was largely staged or provoked by U.S. officials in order to build up congressional and public support for American involvement. Over the years, serious questions have been raised about the alleged attack by North Vietnamese patrol boats on two American destroyers in the Gulf, but defenders of the Pentagon have always denied such charges, arguing that senior officials would never engage in such deceit.

Now, however, in light of the Operation Northwoods documents, it is standard operating procedure to deceive the public by trumping up wars for Americans to fight and die in, without them ever knowing it is the ultimate sacrifice for the empire's conquest. The propaganda about why we go to war became a normal and standard procedure, approved policy at the highest levels of the Pentagon. In fact, the Gulf of Tonkin seems right out of the Operation Northwoods playbook: "We could blow up a U.S. ship in Guantanamo Bay and blame Cuba...casualty lists in U.S. newspapers cause a helpful wave of indignation." One need only replace "Guantanamo Bay" with "Tonkin Gulf," and "Cuba" with "North Vietnam" and the Gulf of Tonkin incident may or may not have been stage-managed, but the senior Pentagon leadership at the time was clearly capable of such deceit.[11]

THOSE WHO DECIDE OUR FATE

We need to understand who makes these decisions of life and death. It's more than military brass or government officials; they get their marching orders from a higher power. But who? We can start with the Bilderbergers, who are a key group within a much, much larger, more complex, less centralized, and highly effective global power network. These political and corporate brokers interact and overlap with other organizations, clubs, lobbies and groups—all having common economic, financial, social and geopolitical objectives in the globalist agenda. Major leaders from around the world are part of a unified effort to remain in power forever. To do so, people are lured into the trap of perpetual debt, impossible to repay. So in turn, all property and assets will eventually be repossessed by the debtor.

The Bilderbergers are an organization that loathes the spotlight, which is why security is normally kept as low key as possible. This secrecy also includes such key entities as the New York-based Council on Foreign Relations (United States Illuminati) who are known as long-term geopolitical planners, its London-based sister entity, The Royal Institute of International Affairs, also known as "Chatham House," the RAND Corporation, CSIS, the American Enterprise Institute (who are strategic affairs specialists), the Tavistock Institute in London known to conduct mass psychology research, the Carnegie Endowment, and the Trilateral Commission (an "umbrella" entity). The Trilateral Commission was founded in 1973 by Rockefeller/Morgan/Rothschild interests, geared to coordinating the Americas, Europe and the East. These so-called "Think Tanks" in turn interact with consultancies such as Kissinger Associates, The Carlyle Group (which specializes in oil strategies and has the Bush, Bin Laden and Baker families as key shareholders) and Trilateralist Claus Schwab's World Economic Forum. These are the real "Big Brothers."

As the Bilderberger website points out about meeting participants, "about one-third is from government and politics, and two-thirds from finance, industry, labor, education and communications. Participants attend Bilderberg in a private and not an official capacity." European nobility also regularly attends. Royal participants include the Dutch Queen, the Spanish King and Queen, Norway's Crown Prince and representatives of the British Crown. Bilderberg's high-power participants interact with, and are cross-represented on, the global private power web through membership and directorship in the Trilateral Commission, CFR, AEI, governments, corporations, banks, and their owned and controlled mass media. This is the Cabal.

The Cabal and their associates are generating in us intense fear. But fear is only effective when there is either a make-believe situation, or conspiring individuals with a provocateur agenda. In a shocking statement in his address to the Bilderberg meeting at Evian, France on May 21, 1992, Henry Kissinger seemingly set the stage for a false flag attack from his cohorts in the Cabal:

....
11 Gunderson, Ted, "Most Terror Attacks Are Committed By Our CIA And FBI": **http://www.youtube.com/watch?v=YZ2VpfUqRoo&featur e=player_embedded#at=306**

Today Americans would be outraged if U.N. troops entered Los Angeles to restore order; tomorrow they will be grateful! This is especially true if they were told there was an outside threat from beyond—whether real or promulgated, that threatened our very existence. It is then that all peoples of the world will pledge with world leaders to deliver them from this evil.

NEW WORLD ORDER = TOTAL CONTROL

The global plan for a New World Order was implemented by Western Freemasonic members of the Cabal to usher in a post-religious global dictatorship. It would be a "new" world order for two reasons. First, because it would be the first empire ever to embrace (or strangle) the entire planet. Second, it would be the first civilization to completely abandon religion. It would also be a "new world" order in that it would be ruled from the New World—specifically, from that monstrous maze of Freemasonic symbols known as Washington, D.C. The other Western power centers are the City of London, and Vatican City, which has plans for a One World Religion. Once the "Order" is sufficiently advanced, they may intend to move the capital to Occupied Jerusalem, where a false messiah (antichrist/*dajjal*) would be installed as global dictator. The tenets of this corrupted version of Zionism—which consider it a diabolical, idolatrous Jewish heresy that worships the State of Israel and the Jewish people rather than God—are a key element of the New World Order plot to destroy humanity. A large part of this plot is to control how the masses of people think. There is no better way to control mass perception than through the mass media.

Our best hope is that increased awareness will become the revolution. Physical bondage is temporary, since there will always be efforts to resist it, and the effort to maintain it consumes constant and draining resources. Big Brother cannot operate with an awakened people. Another impediment to psychological bondage is its long-lasting nature, and thus to be cost effective, it requires the brainwashing of a population held in informational isolation, hence the wholesale censorship occurring on the Internet. The psychological process of brainwashing a large population involves the continual application of repetitive ideas over a long period of time. Some of these ideas are defensive and aimed at immunizing the population from the appeals of competing and dissenting informational sources. Promoting cynicism toward such sources is a key ingredient for success. Any attempt to free a population subject to brainwashing will require a sustained effort over a long stretch of time, necessitating ongoing financial and physical resources.

What to look out for: The Top 10 Ways that the Iron Grip of the Big Brother Prison Grid is Tightening around our Lives:

1. *Automated License Plate Scanners*
2. *Government Workers Ordered to Spy on the "Lifestyles, Attitudes and Behaviors" of Their Fellow Workers*
3. *Eye Scanners in our Schools*
4. *Biometric Chips in our Passports (and Skin)*
5. *All Your Financial Transactions Tracked by the Government*
6. *Complaining About the Tap Water Makes You A Terrorist*
7. *DNA Databases*
8. *Copying Your Hard Drive at The Border*
9. *NSA Snooping*
10. *Obama Gave the Power to the U.N. to Seize Control of the Internet*[12]

In the final phases of the conspiracy, the One World Government will consist of the king-dictator, head of the United Nations, the CFR "think tank," and a few billionaires, economists, and scientists who have proved their devotion to the great plan. All oth-

---

12 Article from *Investment Watch*: https://www.investmentwatchblog.com/10-ways-to-fool-the-authorities-and-escape-martial-law-here-are-10-ways-to-fool-the-authorities-and-escape-with-your-life-and-family/

ers are to be integrated into a vast conglomeration of mongrelized humanity—wage slaves and useful idiots who serve the Cabal.

RULE BY SECRECY

The control that these banking families exert over the global economy cannot be overstated and is quite intentionally shrouded in secrecy. Their corporate media arm is quick to discredit any information exposing this private central banking cartel as "conspiracy theory." One of the epidemics seen on the Internet right now is people who think they're smart just because they disagree with everything they hear. "Snopes said so!" They believe that everything they hear must be a lie, or must be the opposite of truth, so they are quick to condemn complex ideas such as conspiracy theories. Unfortunately, this kind of control is very difficult to counteract, because it can be a knee-jerk response that people have due to the extent to which they've been conditioned over the course of a lifetime. If the perpetrators can deflect attention away from their activities, by any means possible, then the longer they can keep us hoodwinked and oblivious to the enormous scam they continue to perpetuate. The banking cabal is the real conspiracy.

In reality, our stock market and monetary systems are fake, meaning that there is nothing holding them in place except the illusion that they exist. A fiat currency derives its worth from the issuing government—it is not fixed in value to any objective standard. That means central banks can print as much money as they want. If an economy is struggling, injecting more notes into the system stimulates activity, but lowers the value of the currency in question. It also raises real estate prices, making the dream of home ownership even more difficult for most. With major central banks all desperate to stimulate their economies, some say currencies have entered a dangerous new phase often described as a race to the bottom. What we are talking about is a total realignment of world financial machinations and currencies, or the abolishment of money altogether. In addition, as money pertains to power structures of command and control, we will need to have a complete realignment and reorganization of the U.S. Federal Government, and end the Federal Reserve system.

The ultimate tyranny in a society is not control by martial law. It is control by the psychological manipulation of consciousness, through which reality is defined so that those who exist within it do not even realize that they are in prison. They do not even realize that there is something outside of where they exist. But give a person a book and they can learn about multiple ways to hunt, and understand the best methods. This is a prime example of why our government does not want an educated populace. If everyone was truly educated and informed, they would be able to distinguish the difference between truth and deceit.

Once the iron grip on secrecy is cracked, once we can break the back of the leviathan, there is no way to put the genie back in the bottle. At that point corruption will never be able to fester again, simply because the truth is a weapon that subdues the tyranny of the cabal. They don't want the truth to come out. Period. Therefore, when the truth does start coming out, that's a sign that they are no longer running the show, and that positive changes for citizens are happening. There has to be a revolution, but it has to be a revolution of consciousness.

CRIMINALS ON FOREIGN RELATIONS

In the United States, immediately following World War I, the Cabal set up what they called the Council on Foreign Relations, commonly referred to as the CFR, and this CFR is actually the Illuminati in the United States. And its hierarchy, the masterminds in control of the CFR, to a very great extent, are descendants of the original Illuminati conspirators. The danger began with the network of secret round tables of international corporate and banking elites started by Cecil Rhodes and expanded by his followers with his sizable estate. The U.S. Council on Foreign Relations, one of the secret round tables started by Rhodes' followers, was founded in 1921, with the explicit goal of influencing the foreign and domestic policies of a former colony over which Britain no longer had direct control.

To firm up their control, the Cabal established the Royal Institute of International Affairs (RIIA), and the CFR one year later when the League of Nations idea failed. There are similar secret Illuminati organizations in France, Germany, and other nations operating under different names, and all these organizations, including the CFR, continuously set up numerous subsidiaries or front organizations by which they have infiltrated every phase of the various nations' affairs. But at all times, the operations of these organizations were and are masterminded and controlled by the international bankers, who in turn were and are controlled by the Rothschilds.

Researcher Eustace Mullins believes the perception that the CFR is the Secret Government of the U.S. is not true. He states: "The members of the Council on Foreign Relations have never originated a single item of policy for the U.S. government. They merely transmit orders to our government officials from the RIIA and the House of Rothschild in London." He refers to the CFR members as a group of colonial governors answerable to their overseers of the New World Order in London. Mullins also remarks that "the 'founders' of RIIA were, one and all, Rothschild men." Mullins notes that the "The Milner Round Table became the RIIA-CFR, combined, which exercises unopposed control of the World Order over foreign and monetary policy in both the United States and Great Britain."

According to author Myron Fagan, "the attempts of the Illuminati, working through the Jewish-infiltrated Council on Foreign Relations (CFR), was established to control the United States and establish a One World Government." The sole purpose of such organizations is to condition the public to accept a Global Governance which today is the United Nations. This is the true face of the so-called Globalists, and Centralized Power is what they are really after.[13]

Both researchers agree the CFR took control of the U.S. government a century ago, and has controlled it ever since. The CFR runs the U.S. military industrial complex and generates tremendous profits by controlling 70% of the world's arms trade. The CFR-run Carlyle Group generates endless war dollars from CFR-engineered undeclared "forever" wars. Eighteen CIA directors, eighteen NSA directors, and twenty-two Secretaries of State were CFR members. Bush Jr. and Sr., Bill and Hillary Clinton, and Obama are all the same party, that is, CIA Globalists pushing for the New World Order which was Bush Sr.'s greatest dream. Had Bush Sr. had his way, the United Nations would own America under a New World Order, and the CIA would run the United Nations.

CRACKS ARE BEGINNING TO FORM

At his 2010 Council on Foreign Relations speech in Montreal, co-founder with David Rockefeller of the Trilateral Commission and regular Bilderberg attendee Zbigniew Brzezinski warned that a "global political awakening," in combination with infighting amongst the elite, was threatening to derail the move towards a one world government, also known as a New World Order. Brzezinski explained that global political leadership had become...

> much more diversified unlike what it was until relatively recently, and the G20 was lacking internal unity with many of its members in bilateral antagonisms. ...For the

13 Fagan, Myron, *CFR Completely Unmasked as Illuminati in U.S.* Cinema Educational Guild. 1966.

first time in all of human history mankind is politically awakened—that's a total new reality—it has not been so for most of human history.

In other words, the global elite is infighting amongst itself, and this is hampering efforts to rescue the agenda for global government, which seems to be failing on almost every front. Once the mass of people realize what they've done, the global elite are finished.

An important question we need to start asking ourselves and the government is: Why are people in authority positions let off the hook for violent crimes? Sexual abuse and rape are not crimes that should go ignored, yet time and time again, higher-ups and government officials are excused from the law. Voltaire, the clearest of the Enlightenment-era thinkers, wrote in 1765: "Those who can make you believe absurdities, can make you commit atrocities."

SHAPING PERCEPTIONS

Few people are believing the absurdities any longer, and now realize the mainstream media is simply a way for the Cabal to message the people for their own advantage. In its textbook form, propaganda is the effort to alter the picture to which humans respond, to substitute one social pattern for another. Propaganda is used to create a false reality of the world, using sleight of mind and thought-shaping tactics. Psychological operations are propaganda campaigns. Strategic psyops of a political nature focus propaganda at powerful individuals, or small groups of people capable of influencing public opinion or the government of a particular country. Propaganda is used to manipulate public opinion to attain political or foreign policy goals in a given period.

Censorship is the "buzzword" lately, but what's really happening is suggestive mind control, propagating narratives, and manipulating elections. This is neither theory nor opinion, it is fact, and there is much evidence. We are also subject to predictive programming, for example: SWAT team Lego figures. Cashless Monopoly. Barbie's new credit card. It would seem that the social engineers have figured out long ago that the best time for the public to be programmed is when they're young and impressionable. Vermont Senator Bernie Sanders accused the major media outlets of having become focused on gossip, clickbait and punditry. "This threatens democracy" he said. The globalist-owned mass media will keep the people in the dark as long as they can, until it is too late.

Planetary change can only come about through the widespread exchange of new information and new ideas among the masses. "The Powers That Were" obviously know this, and efforts will always be made to disrupt positive and transformative discussions that could lead to revolutionary awakening. The only way for a dissenting person or organization to circumvent such disruptive efforts is to avoid utilizing single or highly centralized venues for voicing public opinion and discussion. That is, the masses themselves must assume the responsibility for forming and maintaining diverse and decentralized positive discussion venues. It is not possible to disrupt discussion venues when there are many diversified and all monitored by their own members.

THE MOCKINGBIRD REPEATS WHAT IT HEARS

Operation Mockingbird, as discussed above, was a secret campaign by the CIA to influence the mass media, thus allowing the news media to lie about what is portrayed on television, radio, print media, and now the Internet. These are psychological operations, or psyops, which are planned operations to convey selected information and indicators to audiences to influence their emotions, motives, and objective reasoning, and ultimately, the behavior of governments, organizations, groups, and individuals. The purpose of United States psychological operations is to induce or reinforce behavior favorable to U.S. objectives. At the core, these are Satanic schemes to induce racial division, strategies of tension, citizen distrust, anger against police, and a distraction from the true corruption. We can now understand that the mainstream media cannot be trusted at all. From national to local news stations, they're all liars who push the agenda of Order Out of Chaos, leading us to a New World Order.

The large-scale CIA program called Operation Mockingbird, organized by Allen Dulles and designed to manipulate news media for propaganda purposes, began in the early 1950s. The CIA spent millions per year hiring journalists in Corporate Media from Disney/ABC and others, to promote their point of view. The original operation reportedly included nearly 3,000 CIA operatives and 400 journalists. According to the Congressional report published in 1976:

> *The CIA currently maintains a network of several hundred individuals around the world who provide intelligence for the CIA and at times attempt to influence opinion through the use of covert propaganda. These individuals provide the CIA with direct access to a large number of newspapers and periodicals, scores of press services and news agencies, radio and television stations, commercial book publishers, and other foreign media outlets.*

MEDIA MANIPULATORS

Keep in mind that the Cabal was not set up to operate on a short-range basis. The masterminds behind this great conspiracy have absolute control of all of our mass communications media, especially television, the radio, the press, and Hollywood. We all know that our State Department, the Pentagon, and the White House have brazenly proclaimed that they have the right and the power to manage the news, to tell us not the truth, but what they want us to believe. They have seized that power on orders from their masters. The objective is to brainwash the people into accepting the bait of a phony peace which will transform the United States into an enslaved unit of the United Nations' One World Government.

Perhaps the most critical directive in Adam Weishaupt's 1776 Illuminati plan was to obtain absolute control of the press. At that time, the only mass communications media to distribute information to the public was primarily newspapers. Using this avenue, all news and information could be slanted so that the masses would be convinced that a One World Government is the only solution to our many and varied problems. Myron Fagan outlines the issue:

> *In this modern age we know who owns and controls our mass communications media. Practically all the movie lots in Hollywood are owned by the Lehmans, Kuhn-Loeb & Company, Goldman-Sachs, and other internationalist bankers. All the national radio and TV channels in the nation are owned and controlled by those same internationalist bankers. The same is true of every chain of metropolitan newspapers and magazines, also of the press wire services, such as Associated Press, United Press International, Reuters, and others. The supposed heads of all those media are merely the fronts for the internationalist bankers, who in turn compose the hierarchy of the CFR—today's Illuminati in America.*

Even the Pentagon press agents have brazenly proclaimed that the government has the right to lie to the people. What that really means is that our CFR-controlled government has the power to lie to and be believed by the brainwashed American people.[14]

---

14 Fagan, Myron, Illuminati CFR Recordings were originally distributed as a 3-LP record set. Later, audio cassettes became available, & now freely available in mp3 format on the internet. **http://i-uv.com/transcript-of-myron-fagans-1960s-lecture-exposing-the-illuminati-cfr-and-the-satanic-one-world-government-plan**

LAME STREAM MEDIA
Nothing to see here, move along.

Oh look, *Dancing with the Moronic Stars* is on! Let's watch Tell-Lie-Vision programming.

Please, serve me up some more GMOs with MSG deep fried in fluoride, with extra aspartame.

What's wrong with this picture? Has it really gotten this bad? Let's face it, we are living in a plutocracy, a country in which wealth controls all facets of society. It may be true with all countries more or less, but is uniquely true of ours because of materialism and the concentration of wealth in the USA.

Unfortunately, the average American is shockingly naïve about just how depraved, corrupt and addicted to power this banking cartel is in the "Land of the *Fees* and Home of the *Slave*." Through their control and domination of the mass media, they have kept their crimes against humanity out of public consciousness. We have been shielded from the global devastation and death toll that they have already wrought. The result is an unsuspecting population of confused and passive people having their future ripped out from under them, right before their eyes, without any organized defense or resistance. The mainstream media outlets are cooperative with the government because the media are owned by the same interests that are defended by government policy. The media are not close to corporate America. The media are not favorable to corporate America. They *are* corporate America, as well as an integral part of American culture. Without a doubt, the mainstream media acts as the subtle mouthpiece of the global banking elite. They are the invisible owners behind the fear-based media and instigators of nearly all wars. They will never provide the real story. The mass media controls the flow and distribution of information. Mass media programming is, and always has been, propaganda. It is designed to support and enhance the financial tyranny of the world simply by agitating the public and getting them to turn on each other, thereby steering them away from the "man behind the curtain." Most of the world media that is propaganda-based stems from American corporations, which are now syndicated throughout television networks all over the planet. Media consolidation has never been more concentrated. The multi-national News-Corp, General Electric, Disney, Viacom, Time-Warner and Bertelsmann now control over a staggering 90% of what we read, watch, or listen to. Someone behind closed doors decides what they want you to know, or which politician to support. When you control the media, you control the conversation. For example, the media magnate Rupert Murdoch, owner of the Fox Network, also owns a grand total of 800 companies, most of which are other media outlets around the globe. The mass media holds us in a powerful illusion of normalcy. Most people don't realize how much propaganda is already being used on us. It is so entrenched in everything we see and hear that it's hard to break free of the deluge of clutter and misinformation. The Nazi Minister of "Public Enlightenment," Joseph Goebbels, stated: "...propaganda works best when those who are being manipulated are confident that they are acting on their own free will." The German media conglomerate, Berelsmann, which is currently the largest publisher in the English language, was also the largest publisher of Nazi propaganda during World War II.

Television is the most pervasive and hypnotic propaganda tool ever conceived. It is used to keep people in check by keeping us divided, misinformed, and highly entertained. Little information or education is offered to suggest alternatives to a materialistic, class-driven society. Technology pioneer Mark Crispin Miller noted, "Media manipulation in the U.S. today is more efficient than it was in Nazi Germany, because here we have the pretense that we are getting all the information we want. That misconception prevents people from even looking for the truth."

The cabal has been trying to distract us with anything and everything. Since when did *The Bachelorette* become the stuff of front-page news in this country? People are being trained to be mental slaves by that box in the living room telling us what to think, what to feel, what to buy, what the neighbors bought yesterday, and what they will buy tomorrow. The power elite use TV to create a false perception of what matters in our lives, society, and with other cultures. Through television the power elite can keep us unaware of what they are doing, under the disguise of making the people believe they are staying informed. TV teaches people *what* to think, not *how* to think. It has robbed people of the ability to think critically and objectively for themselves. It encourages viewers to buy an endless stream of trinkets. It has robbed us of our wealth in our endless pursuit to collect the finest material items to increase our social status.

Through consolidation, it's now down to five multinational companies who own about 95% of all media. They are: Time-Warner; Disney; Rupert Murdoch's News Corporation; Bertelsmann of Germany; Viacom (formerly CBS); and General Electric's NBC is a close sixth. Six corporations control the entire media monopoly. In short, the American media is a tightly controlled disinformation ministry, parroting the 4 a.m. talking points direct from the alphabet agencies. This could change with the Internet, if it can remain a free and open forum. Lest we forget, the Gutenberg Press was revolutionary and changed the world. The Internet is also revolutionary and is making forbidden truth available to everyone for the first time.

ELIMINATING DISSENT

We are now seeing a techno-corporate fascism, in the form of YouTube channels being demonized and videos being taken down. Elite and unelected censors have attempted to shape the nation's discourse by completely banning our access to entire categories and topics of information. David Wilcock notes: "isn't it weird that Big Tech is also destroying all conspiracy analysis, organic food, vaccine debates and exposés of crimes against children? And now, literally all YouTube independent creators have fallen victim to this unprecedented mass censorship campaign." Unfortunately, almost all people are prepared to renounce their rights, even free thought, if it guarantees their safety and security. In this way, humanity is made soft and is easily manipulated through conflict, envy and distress—one possible result being to surrender to the power of the invisible elite and the New World Order.

Already implemented in China, social credit scores are sure to come to America. In the Chinese system, a person's life is measured based on how well their actions align with the Party's vision of what each person should be doing, and how often. It's a little like the credit score a mortgage broker pulls up when a person wants to buy a home, but instead of deciding if you're allowed to borrow money, this system increasingly decides if you are capable of doing anything of service to the State. As these rating systems continue to become more pervasive, and as companies, agencies, and governments increasingly refer to these scores, they will continue to erode our freedoms. Because of no effective oversight, this material is ripe for misuse and manipulation. No longer will we have protections against punishment for living the life we're currently living or speaking out against injustices. Our laws that protect against such invasions do not apply to this new *de facto* system of government that is emerging.

But it only gets worse. While the world is watching the mainstream media report lies disguised as the truth, the global elite is secretly implementing their plans of mass human slaughter. According to the Georgia Guidestones, they want billions of people dead, and will stop at nothing to get it done. So, they aggressively pursue their plan of depopulation. There is no doubt a "Red List" is composed of anybody who is awakened and are targeted individuals. Project Pogo is be wholesale censorship to stifle American free speech. Project Zyphr will result in the "extermination" of tens of millions of Americans. Ironically, it is the "useful idiots" who go along with the plan unknowingly, will be the first to line up for the mandatory vaccinations and the first to go.[15]

Today many methods of "soft kill" depopulation are being implemented; however, the biggest attack is being initiated against our health using chemtrails, fluoride, GMOs, pharmaceutical drugs, vaccinations, and the 5G untested rollout, to name a few. The campaign to eliminate "useless eaters" on behalf of the planet's "privileged ruling elite" is sure to take a more ravenous toll as global population levels rise. It can be expected. We may be living in an Orwellian *1984* dystopia, but have no doubt, a Brave New World is on the horizon.

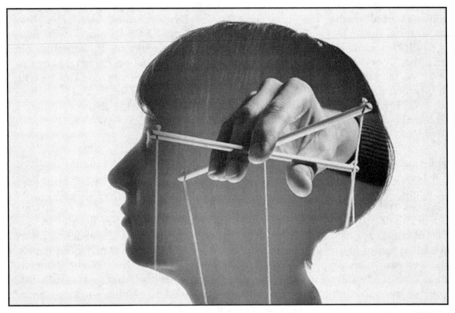

Propaganda is described by the Graduate School of Political Management at George Washington University as: "Since propaganda and public relations both share the goal of using mass communication to influence public perception, it can be easy to conflate the two. *Propaganda, however, traffics in lies, misinformation, inflammatory language, and other negative communication to achieve an objective related to a cause, goal or political agenda.*"

Britannica affirms this description by defining propaganda as "dissemination of information—facts, arguments, rumors, half-truths or lies—to influence public opinion."

The Oxford English Dictionary states that it is "the systematic dissemination of information, especially in a biased or misleading way, in order to promote a political cause or point of view."

Modern propaganda was defined by Edward Bernays (1891-1995) in the early 1920s. Bernays is credited as being the "father of public relations", but many of his ideas came from his uncle, psychiatrist Sigmund Freud. Neither could be considered friends of society.

According to Bernays, "We are dominated by the relatively small number of persons who understand the mental processes and social patterns of the masses. It is they who pull the wires which control the public mind."

15 Goldberg, David, "Project Zephyr—The Plan to Kill Millions of Patriots Leaked!" **https://beforeitsnews.com/alternative/2019/09/project-zephyr-the-plan-to-kill-millions-of-patriots-leaked-3698421.html**.

An English beggar running alongside King George V's coach in 1920. Notice the elite travelers have no intention of giving the beggar anything. Has anything changed in 100 years?

"O, what a tangled web we weave, when we practice to deceive" is a poem by Sir Walter Scott. The motto of the Bohemian Club is "Weaving Spiders Come Not Here." Or do they? Layers upon layers, upon layers, upon layers. And then there are a few more layers after that. We are not alone, but neither are they. Without us, they are nothing, we feed their power, so when is enough enough? The "buffet," meaning us, will always runneth over as long as we allow it.

Henry Ford, Thomas Edison, President Warren G. Harding, and Harvey Firestone in 1921. Such gatherings are illegal under the Logan Act.

The ancient Roman God Janus came to represent the deception of the masses by political leaders. This was necessary for acquisition of total power and mastery over the masses, accomplished by using the skills learned from past history to control the future. To operate under the Janus Principle, one must set aside all basic human morality and do whatever is necessary to gain and maintain power. Ostensibly, one develops the necessary skill from studying the past with the goal of acquiring complete control over the future.

As is evident, the guidelines call for a drastic reduction of the world population, the adoption of new a world language, the creation of a world court and a vague allusion to eugenics. In other words, a blueprint for a New World Order. The Georgia Guidestones outline the ten guides for a new Age of Reason. They are as follows:

1. Maintain humanity under 500,000,000 in perpetual balance with nature.

2. Guide reproduction wisely—improving fitness and diversity.

3. Unite humanity with a living new language.

4. Rule passion—faith—tradition—and all things with tempered reason.

5. Protect people and nations with fair laws and just courts.

6. Let all nations rule internally resolving external disputes in a world court.

7. Avoid petty laws and useless officials.

8. Balance personal rights with social duties.

9. Prize truth—beauty—love—seeking harmony with the infinite.

10. Be not a cancer on the Earth—Leave room for nature—Leave room for nature.

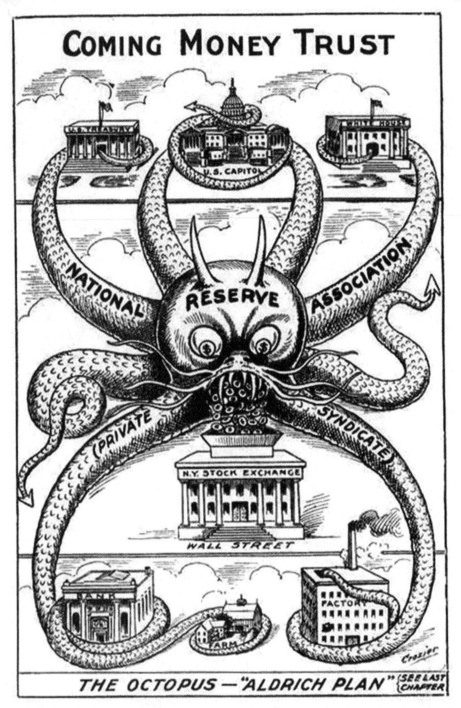

In 1913, Big Brother scored its biggest victory in the USA when a corrupt Congress passed both a national income tax, and the "Aldrich Plan," or more commonly known as the Federal Reserve system, which allowed a Cabal of private bankers to control our money system. The octopus has had an iron grip on America ever since.

GEOENGINEERING

"This new era has already started with the forced engineering of our planet and us humans. Chemtrails are not only changing the environment we live in, but changing us from the inside out. Planetary re-engineering goes beyond controlling the weather. The people behind geoengineering are after the human race. Transhumanism. Transhumanists intend to replace all natural laws with their own set of rules which will make it easier to control it all. It is nothing more than an agenda to destroy humanity and human nature. It seeks to devolve and enslave humans in a way that will be irreversible."
—Dr. Luis Miranda

IN the last few decades, the chemical and aerosol spraying of our skies has not been acknowledged in mainstream science or in the news. Ever since former CIA Director John Brennan spoke in front of the Council of Foreign Relations (CFR) in 2016, touting the benefits of geoengineering, the programs have been acknowledged, but still rarely discussed. The textbook definition of geoengineering, commonly referred to as climate engineering or climate intervention, is the "deliberate and large-scale intervention in the Earth's climate system, usually with the aim of mitigating the adverse effects of global warming." Geoengineering is an umbrella term for measures that mainly fall into two categories: greenhouse gas removal and solar radiation management. Greenhouse gas removal approaches, of which carbon dioxide removal represents the most prominent subcategory, addresses the cause of global warming by removing greenhouse gases from the atmosphere. Solar radiation management attempts to offset effects of greenhouse gases by causing the Earth to absorb less solar radiation."[1]

The term "Geoengineering" is broad in scope, literally meaning the artificial engineering of the planet's climate and weather. Climate engineering operations include steering hurricanes, transforming different regions, and warming or cooling other areas. The wildfires in Australia and California in 2020 and others around the world were being leveraged by climate engineers. Geoengineering expert Dane Wigington explains,

> We have many, many sources for the ignition of those wildfires. We are not claiming to come to any conclusions on the sources of the ignition for the fires. What we are saying is the conditions are being orchestrated to make it conducive to make these burns. The template is being set by climate engineering. There is absolutely no question about that. ...These wildfires are being used as a last ditch, desperate effort by the climate engineers to put enough sun blocking particles into the atmosphere to temporarily mask the Polar Regions on which life depends. The total loss of summer sea ice in the Arctic is immense because then the heating goes exponential. Methane released from the sea floor goes exponential. That methane fills the atmosphere and covers the planet like a layer of glass, and then we are on track for what is known as "Venus Syndrome."[2]

For those who are aware of the chemtrail phenomenon and are actively involved in researching the aerosol spraying programs in an effort to ascertain their purpose and determine the agencies involved, there are two main schools of thought that have come into existence. Just as America has been divided into Red states and Blue states, the geoengineering movement has become just as divided. On one hand, there are those who ardently wave the chemtrail banner, declaring that the aerosol spraying programs fall under the guise of solar radiation mediation. And on the other hand, there are those who just as firmly believe that the purpose of the chemtrails are more sinister in nature and are the result of exotic space-based weaponry developed under the far-reaching umbrella of the military industrial complex. And to a lesser extent, there are some who believe in an alien and UFO connection to the chemtrail phenomenon and some who believe that the chemtrails are a part of Project Bluebeam, that fabled conspiracy theory which says the world governments will fake an alien invasion with holograms as a pretext to imposing martial law and a one-world order. Some believe that the chemtrails are preventing us from seeing the approach of Nibiru or a second dwarf star. Whatever the motive, there is no doubt the spraying of our skies carries on in earnest.[3]

OWNING THE WEATHER

In the 1980s, the Rockefeller Brothers Fund became the authority on global warming. Why would they do this? Why would they care, unless there is a profit motive? Are these people really that concerned about our planet, or simply profiting and justifying heightened states of security for ulterior motives? Mainstream media has started to report on geoengineering in recent years, pitching it as a necessary evil to come, never quite fully divulging the mountains of evidence which shows how governments the world over are already tampering with the earth's climate. Unlike normal contrails, which quickly dissipate, chemtrails or "fake clouds" sometimes take hours to dissipate and eventually fan out to a "spider web" type of milky haze that covers the entire sky. As these are formed from minute reflective metallic particulates, they eventually "rain down" and reach the earth. The fact that aluminum particles have been found in snow samples atop the highest mountains proves it is being

1   Wikipedia, "Climate engineering." https://en.wikipedia.org/wiki/Climate_engineering

2   Wiggington, Dane, "Greg Hunter: Hurricane Dorian Steered by Military." https://beforeitsnews.com/weather/2019/09/greg-hunter-hurricane-dorian-steered-by-military-dane-wigington-video-2447252.html

3   "Why in the World are They Spraying?" Documentary HD (multiple language subtitles): http://youtu.be/mEfJO0-cTis <and> "What in the World Are They Spraying?" http://youtu.be/jf0khstYDLA

sprayed from even higher elevations. Aluminum particulates never appear naturally in the air, water or ground, proving the phenomena is global in scope.

The important thing to remember is that, according to the United States government, everything they are doing to us is legal. They have just found loopholes in order to justify any actions that would be considered "illegal" if they were committed by anyone else. This is another reminder that just because something is "legal" does not mean it is right. As hundreds of thousands of Americans are experiencing firsthand, the U.S. government does not have the best interest of its citizens in mind. It is not above poisoning them in order to fuel the fire that sustains the U.S. war machine.[4]

Consider that the U.S. Government has placed gag orders on taxpayer-funded National Weather Service and National Oceanic and Atmospheric Administration (NOAA) employees. Bill Hopkins, the executive vice-president for the National Weather Service employee's organization, said, "As a taxpayer, I find it highly disturbing that a government agency continues to push gag orders to hide how they operate. This is the work of the American government, owned by the American public, and should be open to the American public." Since when has our weather become "classified information?" What is being hidden in plain sight above us in our skies?

As with many government military programs, compartmentalization and secrecy rule the day, and weather modification is no different. In fact, it may be more compartmentalized and secret than others for several reason. First and foremost would be the environmental modification treaties making weather modification illegal; but when have treaties ever stopped the U.S. government from doing what it wants to do? The government's history of breaking its treaties is well-known, and a quick look at the track record of broken treaties with the Native Americans illustrates this fact. Second, if knowledge of weather modification programs ever became accepted widespread information, the financial repercussions and impact would be catastrophic for the disaster capitalists on Wall Street, especially the insurance companies and the commodities traders who trade in weather-based derivatives. Third, there are indications that not only are chemicals being dispersed through the aerosol spraying programs, but biological pathogens are also being sprayed upon an unsuspecting populace in what can only be described as an anti-human agenda. The United States government's track record of experimenting upon its own citizens is as deplorable as the manner in which it has treated Native Americans.[5]

OUR WHOLESALE POISONING

What goes up must come down, and we're being bombarded daily with a chemical and radioactive fallout surpassed only by Agent Orange, the defoliating chemicals developed by Monsanto to sweep the jungles during the Vietnam War.

With the scourges of typhus, malaria and dengue fever raging through communities in the 1940s, the United States government did a curious thing. They loaded up airplanes with the chemical DDT and commenced aerial spraying to wipe out the insects spreading these diseases. At first, the technology behind such dispersals was crude, but over time it became sophisticated and efficient. This public usage of DDT, both in the air and on the streets of our cities, continued into the 1950s. In the 1960s, sky dusting advanced considerably. The chief reason was the widespread use of Agent LNX ("Agent Orange") during the war in Vietnam. Agent Orange was employed as an herbicide and defoliant meant to reduce the agricultural resources of the communist Vietnamese and neighboring countries. As we know today, both DDT and Agent Orange has devastating ef-

••••••••••••••••••••••••••••••

4   Written into the NDAA, Public Law 105-85, states clearly that we can *legally* be sprayed with biological agents! Below is a link to the NDAA document: **https://media.defense.gov/1998/Oct/29/2001715579/-1/-1/1/99-023.pdf**

5   Geoengineering side effects could be potentially disastrous, research shows: **http://www.theguardian.com/environment/2014/feb/25/geoengineering-side-effects-potentially-disastrous-scientists?CMP=twt_gu**

fects on human populations. During the Vietnam War, an astonishing 6,000 missions were flown and 10% of the country of Vietnam was sprayed with Agent Orange. That's 42,000,000 liters dumped on a third world country in the years 1965-1970. Physical deformities are still seen in the populations of Vietnam, Laos, and Cambodia.

For years Army scientists secretly sprayed poor neighborhoods of St. Louis with "radioactive" particles to test chemical warfare technology. Let's not forget the headlines: "Live Bacteria to be Released by Homeland Security In 'Terror Drill.'" Exposure to sulphur has been linked to innumerable physical and neurological diseases, including reproductive failure, behavioral changes, damage to the immune system, as well as liver, heart and stomach disorders.[6]

And who can forget Bill Gates, who said at a TED talk in February, 2010: "First we've got population. The world today has 6.8 billion people; that's headed up to about 9 billion. Now if we do a really great job on new vaccines, health care, reproductive health services, we could lower that by perhaps 10 or 15 percent." It should come as no surprise that Bill Gates has poured millions into geoengineering programs. It is known that male sperm counts are deliberately being impacted. There is no other conclusion than that the creators of this technology want human beings to eventually stop reproducing. Speaking in front of the CFR in 2016, CIA Director John Brennan discussed the changing international landscape, and then spoke on longevity and health before dovetailing into geoengineering. He said the following:

> Another example is the array of technologies—often referred to collectively as geoengineering—that potentially could help reverse the warming effects of global climate change. One that has gained my personal attention is stratospheric aerosol injection, or SAI, a method of seeding the stratosphere with particles that can help reflect the sun's heat, in much the same way that volcanic eruptions do.
>
> An SAI program could limit global temperature increases, reducing some risks associated with higher temperatures and providing the world economy additional time to transition from fossil fuels. The process is also relatively inexpensive—the National Research Council estimates that a fully deployed SAI program would cost about $10 billion yearly.
>
> As promising as it may be, moving forward on SAI would raise a number of challenges for our government and for the international community. On the technical side, greenhouse gas emission reductions would still have to accompany SAI to address other climate change effects, such as ocean acidification, because SAI alone would not remove greenhouse gases from the atmosphere.
>
> On the geopolitical side, the technology's potential to alter weather patterns and benefit certain regions at the expense of others could trigger sharp opposition by some nations. Others might seize on SAI's benefits and back away from their commitment to carbon dioxide reductions. And, as with other breakthrough technologies, global norms and standards are lacking to guide the deployment and implementation of SAI.[7]

What we see now is a roll-out of high-tech eugenic programs to thin the American population by 90%, as well as the entire world population. They do this by chemtrail spraying in the atmosphere and adding toxic viruses, all part of the high-powered "soft kill" programs. These include the addition of nagalase in vaccines to block the immune system

6   Revealed: Army scientists secretly sprayed St Louis with 'radioactive' particles for YEARS to test chemical warfare technology: **http://www. dailymail.co.uk/news/article-2210415/Revealed-Army-scientists-secretly-sprayed-St-Louis-radioactive-particles-YEARS-test-chemical-warfare-technology.html**

7   Brennan, John, "CIA Director on the Geopolitical Risks of Climate Geoengineering." **https://climateandsecurity.org/2016/07/cia-director-on-the-geopolitical-risks-of-climate-geoengineering/**

from functioning optimally, food poisoning through GMOs and fluoride in the water, sending wetboys (assassins) to "arkanside" (murder vis-à-vis Bill Clinton as Arkansas Governor) the MDs who have discovered a cure for autism and most cancers—the enzyme GcMAF—and denying its distribution to autistic kids and Americans with cancer. They stage and allow numerous radiation leaks and toxic industrial spills which will speed up the depopulation process and help the Cabal gain even more centralized federal power.

ANGELS DON'T PLAY THIS HAARP

HAARP is an acronym for High Frequency Active Auroral Research Program. It consists of extremely powerful transmitters that project microwaves up to several Gigawatts strength into the ionosphere. HAARP is a continuation/supplementing of HIPAS (High Power Auroral Stimulation). Such transmitters are also called "ionospheric heaters" because the projected energy beam heats parts of the ionosphere and "lifts" it higher up. The ionosphere is the upper part of Earth's atmosphere (60-600 km above the Earth), consisting of ionized gases (hence the name), and is therefore electrically conductive. The atmosphere is now conductive for the first time in the planet's history, due to extensive chemtrailing of metallic particulates over the last several decades.

Geoengineering involves the combination of chemtrails for creating an artificial cloudy atmosphere that will support electromagnetic waves, ground-based electromagnetic field oscillators called gyrotrons, and ionospheric heaters known as HAARP. Particulates in the atmosphere also make directed-energy weapons work better. HAARP was partly funded by an earmarked measure in 1990, introduced by Alaska Senator Ted Stevens, who stated:

> We have in Alaska what I consider to be one of the most exciting research projects that I have ever encountered. It is the experiments that are going on, trying to determine if it is possible to harness the energy of the electrojet. It has the potential of using a laser beam to be a conductor of this energy back to Earth...It is an experiment that, when I first heard about it, I thought someone had rewritten a new chapter of Jules Verne...If successful, it will change the history of the world.

The oil company Atlantic Richfield (ARCO) was originally part of the Standard Oil Trust in 1874, but achieved independence when Standard Oil was broken up in 1911. Now owned by British Petroleum (BP), a subsidiary called ARCO Power Technologies Inc (APTI) holds a patent closely resembling the HAARP proposal, dealing with transmitting extremely large amounts of radio-frequency energy into the ionosphere. The APTI patent (#4,686,605) claims the following uses:

> Cause...total disruption of communications over a very large portion of the Earth... disrupting not only land-based communications, but also airborne communications and sea communications (both surface and subsurface)...missile or aircraft destruction, deflection, or confusion...weather modification...by altering solar absorption... ozone, nitrogen, etc. concentrations could be artificially increased.

Within the wording of the APTI patent, weather modification is possible by, for example, altering upper atmosphere wind patterns by constructing one or more plumes of atmospheric particles which will act as a lens or focusing device. Besides actually changing the molecular composition of an atmospheric region, molecules can be chosen for increased presence by altering solar absorption concentrations. Environmental enhancements can be achieved by causing the breakup of various chemical entities such as carbon dioxide, nitrous oxide, and others. Former U.S. Secretary of Defense, William S. Cohen, actually made a statement regarding weapons of mass destruction and the idea of generating earthquakes artificially. In an April 28, 1997, Department of Defense News Briefing at the Conference on Terrorism, Weapons of Mass Destruction and U.S. Strategy, at the Georgia

Center (Mahler Auditorium, University of Georgia in Athens), Mr. Cohen stated: "Others are engaging even in an eco-type of terrorism whereby they can alter the climate and set off earthquakes and volcanoes remotely through the use of electromagnetic waves."

The purpose of HAARP is to manipulate the ionosphere in a manner similar to and exceeding the capabilities operating in Russia. Other-known worldwide HAARP facilities can be found at the AN/FRD-10 "Dinosaur Cage" Array, Whitmore Village, Arecibo, Puerto Rico; the HIPAS (High Power Auroral Stimulation) Observatory, which is an ionospheric heater situated 50 kilometers northeast of Fairbanks, Alaska; the HF ionospheric modification facility "Heater" owned and operated by the Scientific Association, Movik, in Tromsø, Norway; the Ionospheric Field Station in Gayespur, India; the LF Antenna Array on Kadena Air Base, Okinawa, Japan; the HAARP Jicamarca Ionospheric Radio Observatory, Jicamarca, Santa Maria, Peru; and the Crimond Naval Air Station, Crimond, Scotland. For the Russian's part, the Sura Ionospheric Heating Facility is very similar to USA's HAARP in Gakona, Alaska. The Russians have additional arrays outside of Moscow, Nizhny Novgorod, and Apatity; also in the former Soviet states at Kharkov, Ukraine; and Dushanbe, Tajikistan. It is almost certain that China has several HAARP facilities. These devices utilize weather as a "force multiplier." The objective of the certain "blocs" is the owning of the weather by 2025. Supposedly they can already make it rain, create hurricanes, tsunamis, earthquakes and drought. It is said the "Allies" also have several mobile units now as well. Apparently the extremely wealthy Aldobrandini, tied to the ancient bloodline family of Este from Venetia, controls the HAARP programming in the West.

OUR CONDUCTIVE ATMOSPHERE

According to Dr. Nick Begich, it is especially interesting that HAARP transmitters were first built in the arctic, since waves at these latitudes can be sent into the ionosphere in such a manner that the reflected waves can be controlled so they hit the soil where researchers desire. The secret is knowing which areas of the ionosphere must be irradiated for the reflected waves will hit a certain area of land, and in this way create the desired effect—whether it is affecting weather patterns or other geophysical changes.

The chemicals spewed into the atmosphere, in many ways, work in tandem with the high wattage frequencies fired into the ionosphere from the HAARP arrays. Each chemical has a known specific signature frequency that HAARP can be tuned to, allowing for the agitation of the target's molecular structure. The presence of persistent chemical-trails helps focus and intensify the blast of energy delivered to the target area by HAARP. The heated and agitated section of the ionosphere lifts into a blooming dome, causing the atmosphere under this dome to rush in. The rush to fill the vacancy created by the rising dome forces the nearby jet stream to alter its course, thus moving atmospheric storm fronts.[8]

An ionospheric heater is a powerful HF transmitter (2.8 to 10 MHz) that induces controlled temporary modification to the electron temperature at the desired altitude. Heater antenna arrays pump electricity from the ground high into the atmosphere. This artificial electrical alteration of our ionosphere creates many different effects. These experiments are highly controversial and likely are affecting more than just our atmosphere; they may be affecting our moods.

High-energy microwaves can pluck the electromagnetic field in the ionosphere like fingers playing a harp. This can produce very low-frequency radio signals that can penetrate the ground or water—sometimes to depths of more than 100 meters (328 feet) in the ocean, which makes it a possible communication medium for submarines.[9]

••••••••••••••••••••••••••••••

8   HAARP, VLF, UHF and weather modification: want-to-know-about-weather-modification-haarp-vlf-hf-and-chemtrails-want-to-prove-it-to-a-non-believer-here-you-go (site has been taken down)

9   Bertell, Rosalie, *Planet Earth: The Latest Weapon of War*. Black Rose Books, 2001 <and> "Lightning to the Ionosphere?" an article by Otha H. Vaughn, Jr. and Bernard Vonnegut, published by *Weather Wise*, 1982.

China is now building an even larger and more advanced facility in Sanya, Hainan, with capability to manipulate the ionosphere over the entire South China Sea, according to an earlier report by the *South China Morning Post*. The ultra-low frequency waves generated by these powerful facilities could even affect the operation of human brains and bodies, causing side effects such as headaches, cancer, loss of concentration and liver problems—to name a few.

Spraying heavy metal particles is all about increasing the conductivity of the atmosphere (global warming or climate change being the cover story), that, when used in conjunction with these heaters, are able to create all sorts of "natural" disasters, such as starting fires that burn homes and not trees, creating earthquakes, and modifying the atmospheric electrical properties enough to create hurricanes, tornadoes, droughts and floods. For the first time in history, we have an atmosphere that is conductive with all the metallic particulate matter in the skies. HAARP is also a very deadly "scalar" technology, with patents gathered from Nicola Tesla when he died. This tinderbox of matches is now in the hands of the Cabal.

Nick Begich, author of *Angel's Don't Play this HAARP*, states that any persons harboring these target chemicals within their bodies, would too be susceptible to the action of HAARP frequencies. What does this imply? For decades now, our environment and our food supply has been flooded with geoengineering contaminates, far beyond acceptable levels, by a variety of toxins which now course through every vein on the surface of this planet. It doesn't take much imagination to consider what catastrophic effects HAARP frequencies might play on the physiological structure of the human frame.[10]

EVERYTHING THEY DO TO US IS LEGAL

There are hundreds of documented open-air tests of all types of chemicals and biological agents sprayed on unsuspecting American citizens. In fact, our military's position is that they get to spray us with whatever they want, whenever they want, as long as they classify their activities as "research." Knowing this, it is understandable that, for many decades now, we have been getting hit with everything under the sun.[11]

Title 50, Chapter 32, subsections 1520 a & b of the United States Code (law) state:

Prohibited activities:

> *The Secretary of Defense may not conduct (directly or by contact) –*
> **(1)** *any test or experiment involving the use of a chemical agent or biological*
>   *agent on a*
> *civilian population; or*
> **(2)** *any other testing of a chemical agent or biological agent on human*
>   *subjects.*
> *Yet, this exemption allows us to be sprayed from aerial deployment:*
> **(b)** *Exceptions*

Subject to subsections (c), (d), and (e) of this section, the prohibition in subsection (a) of this section does not apply to a test or experiment carried out for any of the following purposes: Any peaceful purpose that is related to a medical, therapeutic, pharmaceutical, agricultural, industrial, or research activity.

You read that right. As long as they classify their mass murder as a "peaceful purpose that is related to a medical, therapeutic, pharmaceutical, agricultural, industrial, or research activity," they get to legally spray us with whatever they want, however they want and using whenever they want. As we can see now, this is exactly what they have done,

10 HAARP—Holes in Heaven [HD - 1080p] Full Documentary: (**video unavailable on YouTube**)

11 "Weather Modification Bill-H.R. 2995" that was presented to Congress in 1995: **https://www.congress.gov/bill/109th-congress/house-bill/2995**

as evident in Public Law, 105-85, page 287, halfway down. This was drawn up in 1997 and was never meant to be discovered before the 30-day objection period was over. It is interesting to note that this law was passed in 1997, right around the time that the wide-scale spraying operations began. In 1997, Secretary of Defense William Cohen also remarked, in a speech at the University of Georgia, how one can, "alter the climate, and set off earthquakes and volcanoes remotely, through the use of electromagnetic waves."

Although today we have what appears to be military groups that have embedded themselves illegally into our otherwise constitutional Republic, carrying out the geoengineering programs domestically, weather control systems employing exotic technology are probably also used against foreign enemies in foreign countries— probably in the Middle East. The 1996 Air Force document, "Weather as a Force Multiplier: Owning the Weather in 2025," outlines such a program.[12]

Evergreen Air is a CIA front company for the chemtrail operations within the USA, based out of Marana Air Park near Tucson, Arizona and also McMinnville, Oregon, just outside of Portland. Evergreen (International Aviation) is part of the major toxic dump on the planet. Evergreen works from over 100 bases and employees 4,500 people. Delford Smith privately owns the company. They admittedly "perform" for the CIA. Evergreen was given a no contest bid that gave them all the facilities in Marana, Arizona, that previously belonged to the CIA's Air America (Pinal Air Park, Arizona). Philip Lader of the CFR is a key player in the drive toward world government. In addition to running the Public Relations for Evergreen International Aviation, Lader is a director of UC Rusal, the largest aluminum producer in the world, with facilities located in Moscow, Sweden, Italy, and Australia. Nathaniel Rothschild is a big investor.[13]

ECO-TERRORISM

The ruling elite have devised chemtrails as a covert source of control via nanotechnology. These chemtrails connect with created and implanted microchips placed covertly inside of us, which act as antennas, that is ("psychocivilized" electronic mind-control), so as to make us a manipulated and totally-controlled society. Using HAARP microwave antennas, the National Security Agency (NSA) can establish a seamless computer link direct to our brains. Specifically, first they use chemtrails to get the nanoparticles into us which then are reassembling in our bodies to form nanobot antennas. Such is the pseudo-life of synthetic biology and the "Morgellons" disease outbreak.[14] Sound unbelievable? Here are the reprinted words from William S. Cohen, U.S. Defense Secretary, in a DoD News Briefing way back on April 28, 1997:

> Others are engaging even in an eco-type of terrorism whereby they can alter the climate, set off earthquakes and volcanoes remotely through the use of electromagnetic waves...So there are plenty of ingenious minds out there that are at work finding ways in which they can wreak terror upon other nations...It's real, and that's the reason why we have to intensify our efforts.

For those who have spent time in farming communities, the technology of aerosol spraying is not an abstract concept. Crop dusting is a common sight in rural America. It's an efficient way to spread seeds, pesticides, and plant nutrients. Farmers encounter it often during the planting season. Similarly, the spraying of Agent Orange and other defoliants were used extensively during the Vietnam War. These days, many other Americans unwittingly witness a very different application of the idea of crop dusting on a nearly daily basis. This is known as "chemtrails."

12 "Weather as a Force Multiplier: Owning the Weather in 2025" by Col. Tamzy J. House, Lt. Col. James B. Near, Jr., LTC William B. Shields (USA), Maj. Ronald J. Celentano, Maj. David M. Husband, Maj. Ann E. Mercer and Maj. James E. Pugh, published by the United States Air Force, 1996.

13 USA Hitman, "Evergreen CIA Owned Airline: Dropping Poison on You and Your Family." https://usahitman.com/ecoadp

14 From Chemtrails to Pseudo-Life: The Dark Agenda of Synthetic Biology: http://youtu.be/pzW5Kb8u0Og

Chemtrails are the aerial spraying trails left by large aircraft, both commercial and federal, that are not associated with farming. Millions of images of these sky dispersals can be found on the Internet. You will see thick plumes of dense whiteness ejected from the backs of jetliners with purposeful squirts. They are not continuous, but rather sporadic when planes reach a particular altitude. When such substances are released, they become hyper-heated in the atmosphere to attain a canopy-like distribution above targeted regions. Leaked images of these chemical containers in the bodies of large-sized aircraft regularly surface on the internet, underscoring the veracity of these claims.[15]

The American public has never quite grasped the purpose of all this spraying. Officials in the former Obama administration had long refused to even talk about these activities, though some have suggested that super spy Edward Snowden might leak details of this widespread project if forced against the wall by the international community. As we have seen with other government programs, the ultimate result here is not likely to be a beneficial one, but part of a depopulation agenda. Thomas Ferguson, of the State Department Office of Population Affairs, said in 1981: "Once population is out of control, it requires authoritarian government, even fascism, to reduce it."

WHAT'S IN A CHEMMIE?

Our natural atmosphere is blue due to the high levels of nitrogen, which when dispersed are blue. The skies are changing due to geoengineering. Chemtrails are made up of aluminum, barium and other ingredients which contribute to respiratory ills, and change the acidity of the soil. Molecules in the new chemtrailed atmosphere are reflecting and refracting certain frequencies of sunlight in all directions, and this is the reason why we are seeing bright colors, various hues, double or triple upside-down rainbows and lens flares never seen before. The sun halos we are seeing are indicative of strong refraction and this seems to be getting stronger. The bright white blue clouds seen, especially during sunrise, are due to plasma discharge and this is also responsible for the increased and odd behavior of lightening. Detected in the various chemtrail mixtures include the following:

Aluminum Oxide Particles
Arsenic
Bacilli and Molds
Barium Salts
Barium Titanites
Cadmium
Calcium
Chromium
Desiccated Human Red Blood Cells
Ethylene Dibromide
Enterobacter Cloacal
Enterobacteriaceae
Human white Blood Cells—A (restrictor enzyme used in
research labs to snip and combine DNA)
Lead
Mercury
Methyl Aluminum
Mold Spores
Mycoplasma
Nano-Aluminum-Coated Fiberglass

15 Neurologist Warns Aluminum in Chemtrails Could Cause "Explosive Increase in Neurodegenerative Diseases": **http://www.geoengineeringwatch.org/neurologist-warns-aluminum-in-chemtrails-could-cause-explosive-increase-in-neurodegenerative-diseases**

Nitrogen Trifluoride (known as CHAFF)
Nickel
Polymer Fibers (Morgellons)
Pseudomonas Aeruginosa
Pseudomonas Fluorescens
Radioactive Cesium
Radio Active Thorium
Selenium
Serratia Marcescens
Sharp Titanium Shards
Silver
Streptomyces
Strontium
Sub-Micron Particles (Containing Live Biological Matter)
Unidentified Bacteria
Uranium
Yellow Fungal Mycotoxins
Zinc

Once released into our skies, these nanoparticles drift down to earth to be inhaled by all living things, including people. It also poisons the soil, which poisons our plants and causes our forests to die. This, in turn, depletes our atmosphere of oxygen.[16]

NANOBOT DISTRIBUTION

First of all, it's important to note that Morgellons—a skin condition producing sores containing fibrous material—is associated with the Borrelia spirochete (Lyme Disease), along with the mycoplasmas Brucella and Bartonella, which are co-factors in Morgellons. Also, it's suspected that Agrobacterium, which is used for genetic engineering, plays a role, as it can transfer DNA into human cells. This is why Morgellons is so very difficult to eliminate from the body. It is designed to integrate into the blood and soft tissue cell walls.

In recent studies, it has been observed that optical stimulation has begun to unravel the neuronal processing that controls certain animal behaviors. However, optical approaches are limited by the inability of visible light to penetrate deep into tissues. It is possible to use radio-frequency magnetic-field heating of nanoparticles to remotely activate temperature-sensitive cation channels in cells. Superparamagnetic ferrite nanoparticles were targeted to specific proteins on the plasma membrane of cells expressing TRPV1, and heated by a radio-frequency magnetic field. Using fluorophores as molecular thermometers, the Carnicom Institute has shown that the induced temperature increase is highly localized. Thermal activation of the channels triggers action potentials in cultured neurons without observable toxic effects. This approach can be adapted to stimulate other cell types and, moreover, may be used to remotely manipulate other cellular machinery for novel therapeutics, and also be the system for the distribution of Morgellons into an unsuspecting population.[17]

Remote control of ion channels and neurons through magnetic-field heating can activate the nanoparticles inside of us. The nanoparticles were distributed by means of aircraft for humans and animals to breathe in, so humans can later be behaviorally manipulated by those who wish to control people. Nanobots form in the acidic environment of our stomachs, then can attach to our synapses as an inorganic material. In layman's terms,

---

16 Pseudo-Life: The Dark Agenda of Synthetic Biology: **https://www.geoengineeringwatch.org/tag/stratospheric-aerosol-geoengineering/**
17 Regarding the effect of humidity upon the persistence of contrails, or vapor trails: **http://www.carnicominstitute.org/articles/rh1.htm**

they can force humans to breathe airborne metals which target parts of our brains. They can later activate with HAARP or radio frequencies to make us think we are seeing colors, hearing sounds, and other sensations. Applications could be used to dull the masses or induce in them trance-like states, or activate populations to incite violence, or create Manchurian Candidates. There are also likely MK-Ultra applications. It's also possible the application will be activated during a Project Blue Beam faked alien invasion scenario, and enhanced to make it seem very real to the masses of people.

ALUMINUM AND POLYMERS IN THE BODY

Some things are hidden in plain sight, and no matter how many warnings are given, some people just refuse to look at that which contradicts their beliefs about the world. This is called cognitive dissonance. One example is geoengineering, which, among other things, involves the atmospheric spraying of aluminum, barium, plastics and other materials into the sky as a means of ostensibly protecting us from the dangers of global warming, or "solar radiation management." Chemtrails are geoengineered aerosols that are loaded with toxic chemicals, including but not limited to: strontium 90, cadmium, zinc, live viruses and "chaff." Chaff looks like snow but it's actually Mylar fibers (like in fiberglass) coated with aluminum, desiccated blood cells, micro-plastics, and paper. Chaff is commonly used in military operations as a radar countermeasure. Polymer chemist Dr. R. Michael Castle has studied atmospheric polymers for years, and he has identified microscopic polymers comprised of genetically-engineered fungal forms mutated with viruses, which are now part of the air we breathe.

It's interesting to see how spraying aluminum and other products into the skies above populated areas is treated as a non-issue by local news. But every once in a while, a local meteorologist breaks a gag order and acknowledges atmospheric spraying of aluminum by military aircraft.[18] In a now famous video, an ex-military meteorologist explains that anomalous radar readings are the result of the military spraying chaff into the atmosphere:

> *Then you see these bands of very distinct cloud cover moving into the region. That is not rain; that is not snow. Believe it or not military aircraft flying through the region dropping chaff: small bits of aluminum, sometimes it's made of plastic or even metallicized paper products, but it's used as an anti-radar issue and obviously they're practicing. Now they won't confirm that, but I was in the Marine Corps for many years and I'll tell you right now, that's what it is.[19]*

GLOBAL ARTIFICIAL WEATHER CONTROL

Rosalind Peterson, President of the Agriculture Defense Coalition, presented in 2014 at a United Nations conference on climate change which factored in geoengineering and weather modification. She referenced Lisa Murkowski's (U.S. Senator–AK) statements in Congress about the HAARP program and its purpose of controlling the ionosphere. NASA has acknowledged spraying chemicals such as lithium into the atmosphere over major American cities.[20]

Apparently, we are now living in the "Aluminum Age" and it's everywhere, but extremely unhealthy, according to Dr. Christopher Exley, Professor of Bioinorganic Chemistry at Keele University in the UK. In an article in the *Journal of Inorganic Biochemistry,* he demonstrates that exposure to aluminum can increase migratory and invasive properties of human breast cancer cells. In a related 2012 article in the *Journal of Applied Toxicology,* he shows that aluminum promotes growth in human mammary epithelial cells. Also, "aluminum production" has been classified as carcinogenic to humans by

18 Local news station confirms barium in chemtrails: **http://youtu.be/okB-489l6MI.**
19 Newton, Terence, "LOCAL METEOROLOGISTS ACKNOWLEDGE ATMOSPHERIC SPRAYING OF ALUMINUM BY MILITARY AIR-CRAFT" **https://www.wakingtimes.com/local-meteorologists-acknowledge-atmospheric-spraying-aluminum-military-aircraft/**
20 Rosalind Peterson: The Chemtrail Cover-Up: **https://www.youtube.com/watch?v=JNDMJCTFslw&ab_channel=TUMNIAISETU**

the International Agency for Research on Cancer (IARC). Couple these studies with other recent studies indicating that aluminum binds to cellular estrogen receptors and may cause proliferation within hormone-sensitive tissues, and we understand why one research team coined a new term, "metalloestrogen," to describe an entirely new class of metal-based endocrine disruptors (including aluminum, cadmium, and barium). Disturbingly, all of these metalloestrogens have been found in chemtrails.

Aluminum is known to cause a wide range of serious health problems, including brain damage and Alzheimers Disease. Since aluminum has an affinity for water, all life forms attract these oxides. This causes contamination of even organic fruits, vegetables, and livestock if they're exposed to the open air, because plants readily absorb aluminum salts from the soil into their vascular systems. Everything absorbs aluminum salts and it's in the air. Processed foods are filled with aluminum salts and aluminum sulfate which is added to water.[21]

SELLING US THE BIG LIE

It makes one wonder what else is happening in our skies that is not being reported by the news or government agencies tasked to inform and protect the people. Chemtrails have been shown to consist of nanobot polymers that are breathed in and ingested by human beings. These polymers are microscopic and they can enter the host through the air, water and our food supplies. Once in the intestinal region of the body, they can form into a variety of nanobots. Chemtrail particulates are part of the weather patterns and they are designed to infect the entire human species, and there is nowhere human beings can hide. It is reported that these particulates are designed to compromise immune systems with time-delayed effects. Does this blend in with transhumanism and its goals of morphing and controlling human beings?

The purpose of ongoing international geoengineering operations is to control the weather to create droughts and artificial scarcity of water and food (a planned "problem"). From the resulting global crisis, chaos and fear (planned "reaction") of people not having adequate water and food due to "climate change," a totalitarian world government (planned "solution") will be perpetrated under the veil of "sustainable development" (See United Nations' Agenda 21 and the 2030 Agenda for Sustainable Development).

As per usual and as expected, selling the fear while never touching on the truth that climate change has been deliberately engineered and human-caused continues in earnest. Many still fail to realize that the bought and paid for mainstream media also encompasses major publications such as *Popular Mechanics* and *National Geographic*. All are ultimately being run and directed by the UN and CFR via the global elites who control all these organizations, including NGOs. The weather of our planet has been harnessed and weaponized and is being used as one continuous false flag to create terror in order to implement total control over the population. It is all connected to Agenda 21, and in fact it is warming the planet, fueling the "Venus Syndrome."[22]

As former Department of Defense head William Cohen stated decades ago, owning the weather is the goal, and now is the ultimate weapon of New World Order control. The epic drought of California from 2013-2015 was created by chemtrail grids over the state and out in the Pacific Ocean, combined with HAARP, to disturb and disintegrate Pacific rainstorms and prevent their arrival over the state. The mass media told us it was the worst drought in 500 years. What they didn't tell us is that

21 Spraying aluminum into stratosphere patent: http://www.scribd.com/doc/4296843/US-Patent-5003186-Stratospheric-welsbach-seeding-for-reduction-of-global-warming-spraying-with-aluminum

22 Global Geoengineering Fueling Venus Syndrome: http://www.geoengineeringwatch.org/global-geoengineering-fueling-venus-syndrome

satellite imagery proves it was a geoengineered drought. This is the endgame to make the West Coast uninhabitable so there can be forced relocation. Farmland can be bought for pennies on the dollar, and Big Agro like Monsanto can plant drought-proof GMOs, and aluminum-resistant seeds, all the while making water scarcity the goal and displacing the populations of the western states.

Much of the "Golden" State went through all of 2013 and 2014 with no significant rain, and 2015 was even worse. Why not make it rain? The people of the world need to be informed that "weather warfare" is being waged upon them, rather than helping them. Global geoengineering can reduce overall rainfall totals as was publicly admitted by China during the 2000 Olympics. It also can trigger regions of torrential flooding. Intentional drought conditions are caused by weather warfare, as has been seen in Iran, while Saudi Arabia experienced uncharacteristic torrential rainfall. Global weather patterns are now being controlled. There is already a great deal of disinformation out there, and it's getting worse by the day. Even some of the biggest "alternative news sites" are helping to "toe the line" for the global elite and the geoengineers by putting out articles on "climate change" drought and "global cooling," which make no mention of climate engineering at all. Where do you think this drastic change in global weather patterns is coming from?

Many airline pilots work for private weather modification companies contracted out by governments of the world, who are following orders from Agenda 21. Some planes now fly by remote control, and do not need a live pilot in the cockpit. The geoengineering agenda is an escalation of the U.N. Agenda 2030. The smoking gun is right in front of everyone's eyes, as well as on live satellite feeds, but the control and dumbing down is now so complete that there is no one left with eyes to "see" it, although in plain sight. It is shocking to see mind control at work on so many people at all levels of education. Their critical thinking is totally absent.[23]

With a corporate-controlled media that refuses to ask the tough questions or engage in real investigative journalism, choosing instead to knuckle under to the pressures of government and corporate influence, this is a story that is being suppressed and denied by power structures worldwide. The awful truth is that the foxes are in the hen house and the inmates are running the asylum. The aerosol spraying programs being conducted under the military-industrial complex agenda of "full spectrum dominance" is the single greatest threat to humanity's existence today, outside of a nuclear holocaust. According to geoengineering activist Dane Wigington, over 150 patents for weather modification exist and a great many of them are in use today. The chain of evidence demonstrating that weather modification is a real and palpable danger to the world today is undeniable. In the book *Chemtrails, HAARP, and the Full Spectrum Dominance of Planet Earth*, author Elana Freeland sums up the issue very succinctly:

> *The American people did not foresee the impact that blanket secrecy would have on their peacetime representative government. They thought they understood the whys and wherefores of the Cold War containment of military and intelligence secrets, including compartmentalization and need-to-know clearances. Little did they realize that cabals, dynastic corporations, and crime syndicates—experts in secrecy, lies, and deception, mayhem and murder—would gather like vultures to double cross elected officials and split society between those burying their heads in the flag and those struggling how to penetrate 24/7 canned "news," disjointed factoids, and social media peppered with memes were undermining the social order. Maintain a lie or a secret for one generation and the next generation becomes easy*

---

23 "Space Operations: Through the Looking Glass (Global Area Strike System)" a paper by Lt Col Jamie G.G. Varni, Mr. Gregory M. Powers, Maj Dan S. Crawford, Maj Craig E. Jordan, and Maj Douglas L. Kendall, published by the United States Air Force, 1996.

pickings, particularly if the lie is echoed in school textbooks, TV cartoons, the History and Discovery Channels. Confuse one generation and the next will happily ingest the media gruel prepared for them.[24]

THE "SOFT KILL AGENDA" END GAME

The cumulative effect of the toxins we have been saturated with have reached a point of toxic overload. This would explain why so many people are sick and dying. We have to wonder and question a supposed 2001 NASA PowerPoint presentation entitled "Future Strategic Issues / Future Warfare (circa 2015)." That time has passed, and what is presented there has an alarming similarity to what's being sprayed from jet planes. Also, are we humans part of an unknowing-on-our-part, strategic warfare experiment? Wasn't that supposed to be prohibited by the Nuremberg Code as a result of the horrors of Nazi Germany and human experimentation "research" being conducted in concentration camps?[25]

Russell L. Blaylock, M.D., a neurosurgeon, explains that chemtrail planes spraying aluminum is extremely harmful to human health: "It has been demonstrated in the scientific and medical literature that nanosized particles are infinitely more reactive and induce intense inflammation in a number of tissues. Of special concern is the effect of these nanoparticles on the brain and spinal cord, as a growing list of neurodegenerative diseases, including Alzheimer's dementia, Parkinson's disease and Lou Gehrig's disease (ALS) are strongly related to exposure to environmental aluminum." A secondary purpose of chemtrails is to make the population sick by causing individuals to ingest toxins such as aluminum and possibly viruses.

Here is a listing of the various anti-human programs instituted by these top Policy Makers to soft-kill "We the People" in a cover war against American citizens:

1. *Eugenic vaccination programs which inject dumbing-down chemicals like ethyl mercury (aka Thimerosal), toxic adjuvants like squalene, and cancer viruses like SV-40, and various serious diseases like HIV/AIDS placed in hepatitis B and smallpox vaccines for certain specially targeted populations. According to Philip Schneider, AIDS was a population control virus invented by the National Ordinance Laboratory, Chicago, Illinois. The scientist credited with 'discovering' the HIV virus, has admitted that he created AIDS in order to reduce the world's population. Director of the Institute of Human Virology, Dr. Robert Gallo, co-discoverer of the AIDS virus.*[26]

2. *Fluoride added to the public water at toxic levels with no concern for the overall health effects.*

3. *GMO foods which are gene spliced to create higher crop yields, have "built in pesticide properties" which are toxic to humans, and which contain top secret special RNA or DNA fragments which can alter human genes, affect health and create disease.*

4. *Aerosol spraying of known-to-be toxic chemicals in toxic concentrations which dumb-down the populace, create cognitive slippage (aka "senior moments of memory lapse" and difficulty with word selection, that is, temporary "mental blocks"), reduced intelligence and various diseases.*

24 Freeland, Elana, *Chemtrails, HAARP, and the Full Spectrum Dominance of Planet Earth*. Feral House, 2014. **https://www.amazon.com/Chemtrails-HAARP-Spectrum-Dominance-Planet/dp/1936239930/**

25 Geoengineering: Aerospace engineer, Dr. Coen Vermeeren presents an informal peer-review of the 30- page research document "Case Orange," commissioned by the Belfort Group: **http://beforeitsnews.com/chemtrails/2011/08/whistleblowers-talk-at-chemtrails-symposium-the-belfort-group-eu-949419.html**

26 "Dr. Robert Gallo Admits He Created AIDS To Deliberately Depopulate Humanity" **https://www.whydontyoutrythis.com/2016/07/dr-robert-gallo-admits-he-created-aids-to-deliberately-depopulate-humanity.html**

PERSISTENT JET "CONTRAILS"

Here are just a few more patents relating to chemtrails and geoengineering for those who doubt the authenticity of what is being claimed:[27]

> Patent #1619183
> Patent #2045865
> Patent #2591988
> Patent #3437502
> Patent #3531310

And there is much evidence of other geoengineering programs. DDT was heavily sprayed in World War II, and Agent Orange in Vietnam. The Air Force is on record as saying they want to control the weather by 2025. Rep. Dennis Kucinich's HR 2977 bill names chemtrails as an "Exotic Weapon."[28] Respected scientist Dr. Michio Kaku, a physics professor at City College of New York, discussed—with Charlie Rose and Norah O'Donnell—the science of weather manipulation. During the interview Kaku, in discussing the experiments with weather modification notes that "We're shooting trillion- watt lasers into the sky," referencing the use of lasers to induce changes in naturally occurring weather phenomena.[29]

Environmental modification techniques have been available to the U.S. military for more than half a century. "Weaponizing the Weather as an Instrument of Modern Warfare?" was first published in September, 2017. This information has relevance to the ongoing protest movement and debate about the Earth's climate. The issue has been amply documented and must be an integral part of the climate change debate. An excerpt from the report:

> *Weather modification will become a part of domestic and international security and could be done unilaterally...It could have offensive and defensive applications and even be used for deterrence purposes. The ability to generate precipitation, fog and storms on earth or to modify space weather...and the production of artificial weather all are a part of an integrated set of [military] technologies.*[30]

There are new atmospheric phenomena being observed because of weather modification. Extremely rare "sundogs" are being seen rather frequently. Fire rainbows are the rarest of all naturally occurring atmospheric phenomena. For a fire rainbow to occur, cirrus clouds must be 20,000 feet in the air with the precise amount of ice crystals, and the sun must hit the clouds at 58 degrees. "Fire Rainbows" are neither fire, nor rainbows, but are so-called because of their brilliant pastel colors and flame-like appearance. Technically they are known as circum-horizontal arcs. The conditions required to form a "fire rainbow" is very precise—the sun has to be at an elevation of 58° or greater, there must be high altitude cirrus clouds with plate-shaped ice crystals, and sunlight has to enter the ice crystals at a specific angle. These precise and multi-faceted conditions exist because of the massive amount of particulate matter being sprayed into the atmosphere. To create such massive volumes of injectable aerosols, and coordinate the aircraft and ocean-going ship disbursement, "Chemtrails Exposed" author Peter A. Kirby calls it the "New Manhattan Project."

27 Weather modification patents. Take a look at it here: **http://www.google.com/patents/US5003186?dq=5003186**

28 Rep. Kucinich's HR 2977 Names Chemtrails as an "Exotic Weapon": **https://rense.com/general19/ex.htm**

29 Respected physicist, Dr. Michio Kaku, exposes the science of geo-engineering to the mainstream masses in a CBS interview." **https://the-freethoughtproject.com/cbs-weather-modification-scientist.**

30 Study commissioned by the U.S. Air Force: *Weather as a Force Multiplier, Owning the Weather in 2025*, August, 1996.

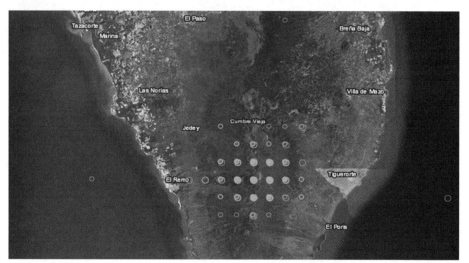

AIRCRAFT MECHANIC WHISTLEBLOWER

At a German clean air demonstration in December, 2014, an aeronautic technician whistleblower who worked on retrofitting passenger planes into tankers, described the process. He said, "we gutted the plane, mounted the tanks, installed the cables and lines and the spraying devices. I was a civilian worker supervised by the military. ...we were told that this was a test conducted by the German aeronautics and space administration. So when we were finished with the installations, guys from the military came over and instructed us to wear full body protective clothing and breathing masks because they were now going to fill the tanks with substances like aluminum sulfides or barium oxides and that would contain highly toxic nano-particles and particulate substances."

No natural force is more destructive than earthquakes. The energy released by a magnitude 6.0 earthquake lasting 45 seconds, is several thousand times greater than a nuclear bomb. Furthermore, according to the U.S Geological Survey, earthquake forecasting remains an elusive goal. Looked at from another perspective, an earthquake would make an ideal tool of destruction. Able to strike without warning, and appearing to be an act of nature, you'd think any government or military organization would clamor for this technology. But of course generating synthetic earthquakes is pure science fiction. Or is it?

The perfectly uniform earthquake grid pattern that appeared on October, 23rd, 2021 at the active Cumbre Vieja volcano on La Palma in the Canary Island chain. Mother Nature earthquake   patterns are random, but HAARP grids are not. If the La Palma volcano cone collapsed it could trigger a tsunami 100 meters high across much of the Atlantic Ocean basin.

The 1996 U.S. military document "Weather as a Force Multiplier: Owning the Weather in 2025" outlines a program using aerosols sprayed from airplanes which are then manipulated with electromagnetic energy in order to modify the weather. This excerpt from the report is very telling: "With heat, we can create a disturbance and watch how quickly it dissipates. We can generate irregularities to test the effects on satellite to ground radio systems. We don't have to wait for Mother Nature to generate conditions."

More and more local weather forecasts and TV news stories are reporting on "Weird Weather," yet none of them will ever make the connection with geoengineering, even falsely reporting clear but chemtrailed skies as "some high clouds that rolled in this afternoon."

TODAYS WEATHER HAS SCATTERED ALUMINIUM, PATCHES OF BARIUM AND A FAIR CHANCE OF ETHYLENE DIBROMIDE WITH POLYMER FIBERS

WE'RE GETTING CHEMTRAILED TO FUCK AND SPRAYED LIKE BUGS

When it became clear what the governments of the world were doing to the planet over the last few decades, truth seekers were called crazy tinfoil-hat-wearing conspiracy theorists. Now the information is out there in front of us and, like sheep following blindly, we still don't understand the impact geoengineering will have on our world, nor do most care to know. It's all bread and circuses to keep our minds focused on non-important activities such as football, baseball, basketball, NASCAR and, hold on, another Superheroes movie is opening this weekend.

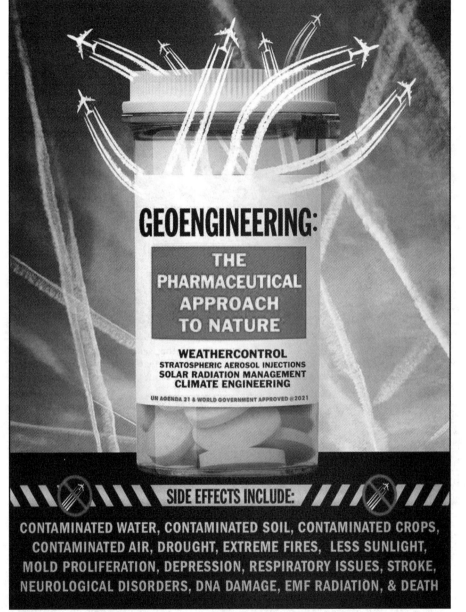

GEOENGINEERING:

THE PHARMACEUTICAL APPROACH TO NATURE

WEATHERCONTROL
STRATOSPHERIC AEROSOL INJECTIONS
SOLAR RADIATION MANAGEMENT
CLIMATE ENGINEERING

UN AGENDA 21 & WORLD GOVERNMENT APPROVED @ 2021

SIDE EFFECTS INCLUDE:

CONTAMINATED WATER, CONTAMINATED SOIL, CONTAMINATED CROPS, CONTAMINATED AIR, DROUGHT, EXTREME FIRES, LESS SUNLIGHT, MOLD PROLIFERATION, DEPRESSION, RESPIRATORY ISSUES, STROKE, NEUROLOGICAL DISORDERS, DNA DAMAGE, EMF RADIATION, & DEATH

Project Popeye was the first wartime military weather modification operation. It took place during the Vietnam War. Its purpose was to increase rainfall for military operations in order to flood the Ho Chi Minh Trail in Vietnam, Laos and Cambodia. This was followed by Operation Stormfury, designed for hurricane abatement. Curious why the technology is not deployed on the killer hurricanes that have been striking Caribbean countries and the southeastern states in the last few decades. Similarly, aluminum and other particulate matter carpeting the land act as fire accelerants and created distressed trees that have become highly flammable kindling in the massive wildfires occurring in the dry regions of Australia and California in 2020. Why weren't rain-generating storm systems steered in?

HAARP is a group of high-frequency radio transmitters that send a focused beam of radio-wave energy into the aurora zone. They are Ionospheric Heaters, which are essentially microwaves creating plasma clouds that can shift weather fronts, and also inject ELF and VLF frequencies.

What's to be gained from perturbing space? The ionosphere carries satellite and radio signals that are disturbed during solar storms. The heat of powerful microwave beams can push clouds around, or even melt crust inside a fault line.

Bill Gates has been a known funder of geoengineering programs. His father endorsed eugenics. Various military bases are used for these clandestine operations. One of the largest is the China Lake Naval Air Weapons Station, which has a demonstrated connection to military weather modification efforts, but was destroyed by a series of massive earthquakes in July, 2019. These are programs the Secret Government has been working on for decades. It's ironic that the same people who say they can change the weather for the betterment of humanity and say they can save your life with a vaccine are the same people who believe the world is overpopulated!

EMBARGO:

It's not about the lights in the sky, it's about the lies on the ground. History, because it is written by academics beholden to their sponsors, never ever tells the full truth, let alone how our planet has been acquainted with ultraterrestrials for millennia.

"Men fear thought as they fear nothing else on Earth—more than ruin—more even than death. ...Thought is subversive and revolutionary, destructive and terrible, thought is merciless to privilege, established institutions, and comfortable habit. Thought looks into the pit of hell and is not afraid. Thought is great and swift and free, the light of the world, and the chief glory of man." –Bertrand Russell

"There are two ways to be fooled: One is to believe what isn't so; the other is to refuse to believe what is so." –Søren Kierkegaard (1850)

"Those who are able to see beyond the shadows and lies of their culture will never be understood, let alone believed, by the masses." –Plato

"One of the saddest lessons of history is this: If we've been bamboozled long enough, we tend to reject any evidence of the bamboozle. We're no longer interested in finding out the truth. The bamboozle has captured us. It's simply too painful to acknowledge, even to ourselves, that we've been taken. Once you give a charlatan power over you, you almost never get it back." –Carl Sagan, PhD, *The Demon-Haunted World: Science as a Candle in the Dark*

"Therefore one hundred victories in one hundred battles is not the most skillful. Seizing the enemy without fighting is the most skillful." –Sun Tzu, *The Art of War*

"It is difficult to get a man to understand something, when his salary depends upon his not understanding it!" –Upton Sinclair, anti-fascist, anti-imperialist American author (1935)

"We are apt to shut our eyes against a painful truth ...For my part, whatever anguish of spirit it might cost, I am willing to know the whole truth; to know the worst, and to provide for it." –Patrick Henry (1775)

"In searching for a new enemy to unite us, we came up with the idea that pollution, the threat of global warming, water shortages, famine and the like would fit the bill. All these dangers are caused by human intervention...The real enemy then, is humanity itself." –Club of Rome, 1972 report

THE TRUTH EMBARGO

"A thinking person will question what he hears; examine what he sees; and evaluate what others would have him believe." –Nathan M. Bickel

CONSIDER the truth like a standing pole which always remains unchanged. It is possible to dress the pole with flags of disinformation and lies, but underneath, the truth always remains a constant. The goal is always to find the truth, no matter how difficult it may be to unmask the flags and accept the conclusions. UFO researchers will say the truth embargo began when the extraterrestrial presence was understood between 1947 and 1953, and this explains why a massive government disinformation campaign became so successful. It is estimated that between January, 1947, and December, 1952, at least 16 crashed or downed alien craft, 65 alien bodies, and at least one live alien were recovered.

The wait for an official disclosure—for any type of formal acknowledgement of the truth—has been agonizingly slow and protracted. Disclosure of an extraterrestrial presence here on Earth has been a slow drip, drip, drip. Once this becomes common knowledge, the effect on our civilization will be undeniably vast, revolutionary and unstoppable. It has been known for decades that once we have full and open disclosure, this will affect the political and economic situation, but most particularly the theological situation, as organized religion may become one of the first casualties. Discussions and arguments about the central figures of world religions, and whether they are of divine or of ET origin, will be hotly debated by spiritual and religious people, by Ufologists, atheists, sceptics and the media—particularly in light of the "ancient astronaut" theory, which maintains that human civilization has had ET contact for many millennia.

If we look at the world from an informational point of view, and if we consider the many complex ways in which time and space might be structured, the old idea of space travel and interplanetary craft to which most technologists are still clinging appears not only obsolete, but ludicrous. Indeed, modern physics has already bypassed it, offering a very different interpretation of what an "extraterrestrial" system might look like. It would appear there is a system around us that transcends time as it transcends space. The system might well be able to locate itself in outer space, but its manifestations are not spacecraft in the ordinary "nuts and bolts" sense. The UFOs are physical manifestations that cannot be understood apart from their psychic and symbolic reality. What we see here, in effect, is a control system which acts on humans, and uses humans.[1]

HOW CAN WE COME TO KNOW THE TRUTH?

Epistemology is the study of knowledge, in particular, how do we know what we know? While it is a relatively obscure field of explicit study, the general tenets of epistemological considerations are at the foundation of nearly every facet of human life. For example, how does a court determine if a witness can be trusted? How do scientists know that their experiments prove their theories? How does a Ufologist know that evidence exists, or lack thereof, to support a claim as valid? These are all epistemological questions, the answers which should hopefully be of keen interest to those seeking the truth.

Answering these questions is no small task and requires a great deal of research, careful consideration and reasoning. One cannot simply assume that just because a witness can't substantiate their testimony with evidence, it can be summarily dismissed. Nor can one assume that documents or credentials are immune to fabrication and manipulation—as U.S. government manuals on legally-sanctioned cover-ups makes clear.

Stephen Bassett, Executive Director of Paradigm Research Group, has outlined several ways to answer the question "What is valid evidence?" First, one must consider the difficulty in accepting the precept of epistemological philosophy. The axiom is that lack of evidence is not, in and of itself, evidence of fraud, deception or fabrication. It is merely a lack of evidence, which only makes a claim unverifiable.[2]

Simply put, there is no such thing as absolute certainty, as all evidence, no matter how "rock solid," requires proper interpretation. Moreover, falseness is not proven by lack of evidence; it is proven by properly identifying what is actually happening with respect to the scope and context of a falsehood. Given this unrebutted axiom, Corey Goode, Bill Tompkins, and Andrew D. Basiago, who offer no tangible evidence for their claims, cannot be labeled as liars or frauds.

THE UFO TRUTH EMBARGO BEGAN AT ROSWELL

In the days following the Roswell, New Mexico, crash of 1947, the central question was why did the High Military Command quickly decide to lock-down all UFO and extraterrestrial matters the same day as the Roswell incident, right after the newspaper and radio bulletins reported that a crashed flying saucer was recovered? Could the orders have come down all the way from the top? President Truman had a saying on his desk "The Buck Stops Here."

The cover story says it was ordered by a high ranking "old school" Army Air Force individual, General Ramey, who was concerned a report of a recovered flying saucer would seriously erode the U.S. Army Air Force's military air power supremacy that had been gained during World War II; that it would allow the Soviets to quickly get the upper hand. The Army Air Force was eventually split off into the USAF, because of the power

1 Deschamps, Justin, *Stillness in the Storm:* **https://stillnessinthestorm.com/2017/06/ufo-disinformation-agent-exposed-fake-alien-invasion-scare-sponsored-by-air-force-discredits-ufologist-a-case-study/**

2 Bassett, Stephen. *Paradigm Research Group.* Various newsletter writings, 2012-2016.

this information provided to them—provocative information about a crashed and recovered anti-gravity craft and alien ETs, both dead and alive.

Robert Jakubcin of Cleveland, Ohio, a retired Air Force officer, said astronaut Buzz Aldrin told him in 1971 that when we were done with the moon missions, we would not be going back until we advanced more as a civilization. Dr. Henry Kissinger, returning from the Rand Corporation, validated his conversations about what Buzz Aldrin and his wife of that time told Jakubcin, and Kissinger also thought we should not say anything until we advanced more. It was thought that people need roads to follow, they need the Bible, they need structure and guidelines, and this shocking disclosure would only confuse a lot of people. So, the consensus of the authorities was not to say anything until we as a civilization advance more. This was 1971. Kissinger also said, "if you tell some people, they will look at you in a different light and some may think you are crazy!" Better to dismiss crash recoveries as weather balloons or lights as swamp gas.

Agreeing with the Roswell cover-up, both the Brookings Institute and the Rand Corporation recommended that the military deny everything until we humans were ready for full disclosure. In addition, people would not want to hear about the treaties and agreements with the aliens in which we exchanged humans for technology. Would they, or do they already know? Robert Jakubcin also wrote, "your own government and military wrote in my files that I must have been drinking or delusional when I saw or knew of these Above Top Secret things, and that I needed to have Above Top Secret Clearance and A Need to Know! We are not alone and have not been alone for many years. I know we work with the aliens here and they are given some rights and privileges in exchange for the advances they help us with, and that is the truth. One day my military files will say the truth and all my letters to Senator Sherrod Brown and the Veterans Affairs will be documented. The truth will be added, which is that they wrote in lies and tried to put me on meds that probably would have made me sick, or might have killed me, or worse! This left me in worse shape and more worsening conditions. Everyone is fighting a battle or some sort of thing, but others know the truth! The FBI–CIA–DOD–NASA–NSA and all the others know the truth!"

Ever since the Roswell, New Mexico, UFO crash and recovery, there has been a continuing process to privatize all American Intelligence and consolidate it under one central control. The reasons for this were in part a knee-jerk panic reaction to the undeniable discovery of a crashed alien ET anti-gravity craft, and one live alien ET survivor. This panic reaction of the U.S. Military High Command and President Truman led to the quick determination to set up a special scientific committee and to place control for all alien ET matters under the control of this committee called Majestic Twelve (MJ-12). This committee was authorized to hire a few trusted private defense contractors in order to keep information away from access by regular U.S. Military. Majestic 12 is the code name of an alleged secret committee of scientists, military leaders, and government officials, formed in September, 1947, by an executive order from U.S. President Harry S. Truman, to facilitate recovery and investigation of alien spacecraft.

BEYOND BLACK

Roswell was a major turning point and the true origin of the Secret Shadow Government (SSG), which is another name for the Military Industrial Complex (MIC). After Roswell, the Shadow Government and the Deep State started back-engineering captured alien technology as well as instituting a covert war against "We the People." This covert war against American citizens was no mere coincidence. It has been alleged to have been largely a by-product of identification of these top policy makers with malevolent ETs whom they began to work with in "beyond-black" shared technology development programs, which are special access unacknowledged programs with no written budgets or records.

The Military Industrial Complex (MIC) is already operating in a Star Trek reality and is interacting with hundreds, if not thousands of species of ET life, some very human in appearance. Only 100-200 people living on Earth are fully aware of the "big picture" and of what some have called the Breakaway Civilization, that is, humans now living off-planet. Once someone gets pulled into this world of ET life, they either live in an underground base or off-planet—and very rarely get to return to our regular world again. If they do, they have their memories erased. It is estimated that there are over 20 million people who were born on Earth, or are children of those born on Earth, who are involved in these highly-classified programs over the decades. Those who speak out about their involvement are the super soldiers, that is, super patriots.

It is also believed that the MIC/MJ-12 has been working with aliens ETs in underground joint ET and human hybridization genetic labs located in several Deep Underground Bases (DUMBs). The most well-known one is in Dulce, New Mexico. During the decades since Roswell, MJ-12 has been working with certain malevolent alien representatives, and the results are horrifying. It is now believed by some at the peripheral levels of all this that those at the top levels of MJ-12, who set the policies of the SSG, as well as the visible ceremonial government, have been infected with a "cosmic parasite" which essentially strips away their human soul and replaces it with some kind of "hived" mind and noticeably inhuman, evil spirit entity. Apparently, these soul-stripped leaders of the SSG/MJ-12 could not have been transformed, that is, taken in the cosmic parasite as served up by the alien leaders they were working with until several things occurred.[3]

THE ILLEGAL GREADA TREATIES

The malevolent grey and reptilian aliens working together with the military in the underground bases is expanded as the Military Industrial Extraterrestrial Complex (MIEC). This is a malicious organization, as is apparent with what is happening. We must note there are also benevolent ETs on this planet. These groups are not part of the MIEC and are from the Pleiades, Andromeda, Lyra, Procyon, Tau Ceti, Sirius A, and Ummo. These groups seem to work together in some kind of protective "federation."

On February 20, 1954, a delegation from these benevolent groups met with the Eisenhower administration in an unsuccessful effort to reach an agreement on the U.S. thermonuclear weapons program. The stumbling block to these negotiations was that these ETs were not willing to provide technology that might have been used by the military-industrial factions of the Eisenhower administration. These peace loving "human looking" beings refused to be co-opted into the emerging Military Industrial Extraterrestrial Complex forming in the USA, Britain, Russia and elsewhere on the planet.

On July 11, 1934, the first Greada Treaty (sometimes spelled Grenada) was signed with the Small Greys from Orion, and occurred aboard a naval ship at Balboa, Panama. This was one of the most important events in human history because it thrust us into a role we were not prepared for, specifically being a host to a malevolent "service to self" extraterrestrial race. The U.S. federal government completely disregarded the Constitution of the United States by doing this and not telling the people. It was here that the agreement was first made between the Small Greys representing the Draco reptilians from Orion, and representatives of the U.S. intelligence community. The treaty stated that in return for the Greys providing high technology (anti-gravity, metals and alloys, environment, free energy and medical technology) the government would allow the

3   Prescott, James. *Veterans Today*: "Secret Space War XIV Tall White Nordics Call Marduks Bluff." https://www.veteranstodayarchives. com/2014/03/17/secret-space-war-xiv-tall-white-nordics-call-marduks-bluff/

Greys to proceed unhindered with cattle mutilations for various tissues and human abductions. This was only if a list of abductees was provided to the government and the abductees returned unharmed with their memories of the events erased. The Greys agreed, but did not keep their end of the deal.

Nevertheless, the second extension of the treaty was signed the next decade, in 1944. In May, 1954 again under the Eisenhower administration, the third extension of this treaty was signed and officially named the "Greada Treaty." The Greys and reptilians blatantly broke the terms of this treaty time and time again, but the military was so greedy for new technology they ignored it. The Greada Treaty was agreed upon at Holloman Air Force base in New Mexico by the Greys and the "Ultra" unit in the NSA. The original document of this treaty and the ET materials from it can supposedly be found today at the NSA facility called "Blue Moon" underneath Kirtland Air Force base in New Mexico. The entrance to this underground base is in the Manzano Mountains. Also at this location is the technological base of the secretive Department of Energy (DoE). Today free energy devices developed from Grey and reptilian technology are being built for use in space at the DoE base, but never released for the betterment of humanity.

On April 15, 1964, two intelligence personnel met under "Project Plato" with the Greys in the New Mexico desert to arrange a meeting on April 25 at Holloman Air Force base in New Mexico. This meeting was to renew the treaty again in a psychological bid to buy time in order to solve the problem of the Greys and Draco reptilians. It was also when the "Yellow Cube" was demonstrated, showing the assembled military brass viewing "Looking Glass" technology which can holographically simulate historical events. The Generals were drunk on acquiring more advanced technology.

THE BIZARRE CRASH AT AZTEC, NEW MEXICO

In his lectures, William Cooper was fond of reminding the crowd that what really spooked the U.S. military brass was not the Roswell crash, but what they found at the Aztec crash site. In Aztec, New Mexico, on the February 13, 1948, a crashed flying disk was retrieved by the U.S. military. The craft was 100 feet in diameter, was made of a light metal resembling aluminum and contained ET bodies. A large number of human body parts were also found on board the craft, and this discovery alone may be a leading reason why the military insisted on covering up this and any new UFO discoveries.

The "above top secret" security lid was screwed down on this even tighter than Roswell to stop mass panic. So, what is going on with these human mutilations and missing people? The truth of the matter is that the Greys feed off the glandular secretions and hormones through a type of osmosis. This is why major organs are taken from people. The reptilians are fond of eating humans. There were also multiple genetic experiments taking place, including hybridization, including the use of non-consenting people.

The very next day after the crash (the craft was probably shot down by the military) the government bought up the property from the local landowners. Witnesses in Aztec observed covered military trucks going in and out of the area for days after the crash. The craft was transported to Wright Patterson Air Force base. The disc incorporated large rings of metal which revolved around a central stabilized cabin. There were no rivets, bolts, screws or any sign of wielding.

People in Aztec carefully guard their words as to the accounts of the crashed disk. The Aztec citizens are still being monitored by the military to this day. One elderly woman said her husband watched the military trucks going in and out of the crash area for days. She said she was very nervous about the whole thing and didn't want to talk about any of it other than her husband seeing the military vehicles. She was asked if she believed there had been a UFO crash. Her response was, "If something hadn't happened out there, how come the military rushed right in, and why were the covered military trucks going in and out of the canyon? Why did they deny being there, and why were they buying the near and surrounding land where the UFO supposedly crashed?"

THE ABDUCTION QUESTION

Private persons dealing directly with extraterrestrials are called "contactees." Some contactees, perhaps a majority, are "abductees" taken against their will and experienced varying levels of pain and discomfort. It is misleading, confusing and exopolitically awkward to simply refer to a person in contact with extraterrestrials as an "abductee." At this time there is no consensus term for someone having only telepathic or psychic contact, but "contactee" is not an unreasonable choice.

Extraterrestrials are not "paranormal." The presence of multi-life forms in the galaxy is profoundly "normal." It is not "paranormal" research. Truth be told, little if anything should be assigned to the paranormal. It should be a short list, and extraterrestrials are not on that list.

"Flying Saucer?" Please. That's like calling airplanes flying toothpaste tubes. They are craft, ships, vehicles. As for "crop circles?" Harmless, perhaps, but certainly not accurate. Stephen Bassett leans toward calling them "agriglyphs."

Perhaps the most debatable term would be "cattle mutilation." In this instance the suggestion is to use "animal" not "cattle," as the phenomenon is not limited to cattle. It should be "harvesting" not "mutilation," as the evidence clearly points to the acquisition of certain tissues. Thus, "animal harvesting."

Does this matter? Yes. All propaganda is built upon language one way or another. The propagandists look for weakness in the used lexicon and create their own lexicon to serve their purpose. Don't play their game. Use language which most reflects the truth as discovered.

The real UFO story must encompass all of the many manifestations being observed. It is a story of ghosts and phantoms and strange mental aberrations; of an invisible world which surrounds us and occasionally engulfs us; of prophets and prophecies, and gods and demons. It is a world of illusion and hallucination where the unreal seems very real, and where reality itself is distorted by strange forces which can seemingly manipulate space, time, and physical matter—forces which are almost entirely beyond our powers of comprehension.

TIME TRAVEL TECHNOLOGIES

According to Andrew D. Basiago, who worked on top-secret projects including Looking Glass technology, there are eight modalities of time travel in the U.S. arsenal, and are of diverse origins:

1. *Remote viewing was developed by the U.S. military in the 1960s, years before it was supposedly developed at Stanford Research Institute [SRI] in 1972.*
2. *Spinning to induce out-of-body experiences so as to travel on the astral plane is an ancient occult practice.*
3. *The so-called Montauk chair was reverse-engineered from the pilot's seat aboard a crashed ET craft, by which the ET pilot piloted the craft psychically to avoid collisions in space in light of the speed of the craft.*
4. *The teleporter was invented by Nikola Tesla.*
5. *The chronovisor was accidentally discovered by Vatican musicologists Father Pellegrino Ernetti and Father Augustino Gemelli when they were studying the harmonic patterns in Gregorian chants at the Catholic University of Milan in the 1940s. They found the microphone they were developing could pick up the sounds of past events.*
6. *The advanced chronovisor was developed from a TV-like screen into a*

standing cubical hologram of moving, multi-colored light by U.S. defense contractors. These engineers worked under DARPA after the Vatican gave the chronovisor technology to the U.S. government for further development. The advanced chronovisor is an electro-optical device that propagates a hologram so dense that it has the effect of lensing a past or future event into the laboratory so that the event can be remotely viewed when the chrononaut is standing outside the hologram or can be directly experienced on a physio-virtual basis when the chrononaut is standing inside the hologram.

7. The plasma confinement chamber was invented by Dr. Stirling Colgate, president and dean of physics at the New Mexico Institute of Science and Technology (NMIST).

8. The jump room or "Aeronautical Repositioning Chamber" (ARC) was developed in a joint venture between Parsons and Lockheed, possibly after being reverse-engineered from an extraterrestrial device or as a result of ET-human liaison in which the device was given to the U.S. government by one of the Grey ET species.[4]

THE LANGUAGE OF THE EMBARGO

It can be difficult to obtain reliable information about the American Secret Space Program, Looking Glass technology, and the Majestic 12 "Study and Control" Group for all UFO and ET matters. It is exceedingly difficult to get actual valid information about the Alien Agenda which is now being deployed through privatized, highly specialized, beyond-black Defense Contractors hijacked by an evil alien group. Also masked within a riddle draped in an enigma are the malevolent ET treaties, and anti-gravity Craft (AGCs), along with other super high-tech alien technology that was exchanged for repeated access to human subjects by serial abductions. Time travel is also a big mystery, but it is possible to piece together data points and come to certain conclusions. Andrew D. Basiago has stated:

> If we didn't have so many Americans who haven't considered the fact that the U.S. government has had 70 years of time, trillions of dollars of funding, the world's brightest physicists and engineers, and conditions of absolute secrecy to research and develop things like time travel, then we wouldn't be in a situation where Barack Obama has twice been elected President of the United States with no mainstream journalistic scrutiny of the fact that as a young man he was a participant in the CIA program that put U.S. personnel on Mars by the late 1970s.

It will not be easy, but it is time to move on from the language that developed during the first half-century of the truth embargo. First and foremost is the acronym "UFO." Unidentified Flying Object was put forward and maintained by the Air Force and other agencies. It is now an anachronistic non-sequitur. It is ludicrous. The phenomenon involves piloted (usually) extraterrestrial craft. It is not about flocks of geese turning up on radar or pie pans being thrown from college dorm windows. It is about non-human anti-gravity machines operating in the skies. This term is no less absurd than a government sponsorship of UTP's—unidentified tiny particles—to describe the research into the sub-atomic world. And, of course, in a context where the government claims there is no evidence whatsoever for sub-atomic particles. The term "Ufologist" is perhaps even more offensive. A professional studying the unidentified—forever.

Stephen Bassett inquires if we should use the term UFO? No. They are extraterrestrial craft. Ufologist? No. Extraterrestrial phenomena researcher.

••••••••••••••••••••••••••••••
4 Basiago, Andrew D. 2016, Timely Paradox.com (site taken down)

Which brings us to "alien." Lose it. The term should be "extraterrestrial." "Alien" has a great deal of baggage, much of which was not innocently attached.

"Cover-up" is misleading. The basic policy of suppression was not illegal. Certain actions along the way may have been so, but not the policy. "Cover-up" inappropriately criminalizes people inside the military service and civilian agencies. Many of them privately support Disclosure. It was not a "cover-up;" it is a "truth embargo."[5]

MUFON INVESTIGATES

The Mutual UFO Network (MUFON) is an American-based non-profit organization that investigates cases of alleged extraterrestrial craft sightings. Founded in 1969, it is one of the oldest and largest civilian UFO-investigative organizations in the United States. MUFON claims 3,000 members worldwide with chapters in every U.S. state. The group maintains a number of investigators, who undergo training administered by MUFON. Since its formation, MUFON has been dedicated to finding the truth about UFOs through its mission of investigation, research, and education. There is one truth that is very clear from their excellent work over the past five decades, and that is that the U.S. government has successfully kept all aspects of their involvement with UFOs from the public, including their intercept procedures; their recovery procedures; their use of unmarked military craft; and their management procedures for controlling these processes.

Why would the military and the government keep these things secret? MUFON has compiled several possible reasons, any one of which would be an excellent reason:

They are unable to reliably control our airspace and knowledge of this would make citizens feel unsafe.

UFOs and extraterrestrial visitors are real and they fear knowledge of this would have an adverse effect on our economy and world religions, and result in public panic.

Treaties or alliances with one or more extraterrestrial civilizations have been signed without Congressional approval.

We have successfully reverse-engineered these crafts years ago, discovered new principles in science and have created our own secret space program.

Comments in 2001 by Secretary of Defense, Donald Rumsfeld, stated that there was $2.3 trillion dollars of Defense spending unaccounted for. Could these funds combined with compartmentalization be funding multiple independent secret space programs? Why is it that the most powerful country on earth, the United States, has no known capability to put a man in space for a decade now, and must rely on our supposed enemy the Russians to do so?

The secrecy was also about the acquisition of advanced technology. While it is true that the existence of a secret space program, totally unknown to the public and the media, is an extraordinary claim, Ufologists now agree that to support extraordinary claims we need not just use Carl Sagan's requirement for extraordinary evidence, but also extraordinary investigation.[6]

THE REAL REASON FOR EMBARGO

It cannot be overstated how important keeping the secret of the ET presence on Earth has been to the U.S. military and government. Despite the best efforts of study groups and individual researchers over the decades, what is truly remarkable is the effort by the United States Government to impede, misdirect and undermine

••••••••••••••••••••••••••

5   Bassett, Stephen. *Paradigm Research Group*. Various newsletter writings, 2012-2016.
6   MUFON: **https://www.mufon.com/**

the citizen-driven process of discovery. The reason for this is quite obvious. In a few words: hording advanced technology.

From 1947 forward, every resource available to the developing military and intelligence complex was brought to bear on American society to create an embargo on the most profound truth in human history. The task must have seemed incomprehensible in the beginning—to prevent every major institution within one of the most literate and open societies in history (during a period of exponential expansion of electronic communication and multi-tiered media growth) from engaging an issue driven by phenomena not under human control.

While extraterrestrial craft were being seen and photographed around the world and extraterrestrial beings were interacting with humans on every continent, the United States Government was able to prevent American academics, clerics, editors, publishers, state and federal political leaders and foundation board members from studying, teaching, covering, politically engaging or funding the issue in an appropriate manner leading to public understanding. It was and is a brilliant accomplishment now approaching its 80th year.

The tools used to control the extraterrestrial disclosure process were forged in the fires within the Secret Empire that burned most fiercely during the prosecution of the Cold War (1947-1991). These same tools were also used in a wide range of abuses of power, the impact of which on American policy and the future of the nation cannot yet be projected. But the outlines of this impact are beginning to emerge, and the picture is not attractive. It is also an embargo on advanced technology that can change the course of civilization, for better or for worse.

THE SCALAR EMBARGO

The discovery of scalar energy may be one of the greatest breakthroughs almost no one knows about. It is a completely new kind of electromagnetic wavelength, which exists only in the vacuum of empty space—the empty space between the atoms of our bodies as well as the empty space we see in the sky at night. Almost all of it is empty space. These waves constitute a kind of ocean of infinite energy, and it has now been discovered that this abundant energy can be coaxed into our third-dimensional world from their fourth-dimensional realm, to provide electricity, create weapons of unimaginable destruction, power all transport, and even heal the body of almost any disease. This is the new world of scalar electromagnetics, the zero-point energy, the power of exotic flying crafts, and the free-energy breakthrough we've all been waiting for.

Nikola Tesla is generally considered the father of scalar electromagnetics. Tesla's name for this energy, also called "scalar energy" or "zero-point" energy, was "radiant energy." Tesla worked in the first half of the last century and was clearly a genius of the highest order. Unfortunately, Tesla was quite paranoid about others stealing his inventions and so, with his photographic memory, kept most of what he knew in his head rather than writing it down. But he made a free-energy device called the "Tesla turbine," and even converted an automobile to run on this "radiant energy." At Tesla's death, the government swooped in immediately and confiscated what writings and papers they could collect. Many of Tesla's secrets were lost to humanity, and in fact, repressed by the Cabal. Even at that early period, there were powerful interests working to keep these discoveries secret. The last thing the oil companies or the energy cartels want is free energy for everybody!

How scalar energy works is rather than modulating in three dimensions, it is modulating in the direction it is going, accordion-like, that is, along the axis of time, the fourth dimension. The new discovery in "scalar electromagnetics" is the incorporating of time, which is itself compressed energy, compressed by the factor of the speed-of-light-squared. Through scalar electromagnetics, it will become possible to engineer physical reality directly, even engineering at the molecular level, creating new "impossible" molecules and even transmuting elements. It will be possible to make radioactive waste non-radioactive. This new science will unlock the secret of gravity, and thereby the secret of anti-gravity, allowing us to manufacture our own "UFOs."[7]

WHY UFOS HAVE BEEN A CORE SECRET FOR NEARLY A CENTURY

The core issues of the ET truth embargo and government abuse of secrecy is more than just disclosing that we have been visited by extraterrestrials from far, far away, or inner-terrestrials from down, down below, right here on Earth. Why does the UFO phenomenon, extraterrestrial visitations and advanced knowledge not exist in our historical narrative? This handy list by UFO researcher Ian Paxton may shed some light on the importance to the Cabal of keeping their core secrets bottled up in the black projects which may never see the light of day:

1. *ETs have Advanced Technology & Free-Energy devices.*
2. *Oil, Gas, & other forms of energy will be replaced by #1.*
3. *Corporations that sell these energy & interdependent companies will go bankrupt when their products are replaced & demand decreases to zero.*
4. *Owners = money controllers of these corporations do not want to lose their lifestyle & what they have.*
5. *Money controllers funded government jobs, different positions, and any positions that get paid in anyway. No money = no job.*
6. *Government power is based on extended organizations = enforcers that implement rules such as secret service & military: army, navy, marine, CIA, NASA & etc.*
7. *The enforcers' job is to protect their own jobs, their upline, and their masters. Out of fear/threats, the enforcers normally do whatever is ordered from their superiors…who get orders from their upline…who get orders from money controllers. The order is cover up anything that is a threat = can bankrupt the money controllers.*
8. *The money-controller gangs run an interdependent empire about $200 Trillion or more. That's enough money & power to do anything they want.*
9. *Together the gangs run the world. Much of the running is hidden behind curtains & secret meetings.*
10. *As result, when it comes to anything that is a threat to bankrupt the money controllers…ETs, UFO & advanced technology DON'T exist as far the public is concerned. That's an order!*

THE HEALTH INDUSTRY EMBARGO

While satisfactory for the very wealthy, the health care system in the USA is collectively one of the worst in the developed, industrialized world. It is beginning to destroy the middle class—the primary engine of social stability. Unpaid health care bills are the leading cause of personal bankruptcy. The allopathic American medical system does a great job with surgeries and other miraculous emergency treatments, but understands little about the true etiology of most diseases which are caused by poor nutrition, lack of minerals, environmental poisons, highly contaminated toxic vaccines filled with fertility reducing RNA and slow-acting catalytic "stealth" viruses which can be later activated by another virus like the common cold or even activated psycho-tronically.

7   Morgan, Bill, "Scalar Energy - A Completely New World Is Possible." https://rense.com/general39/scalarenergy.htm

Since when have vaccines been such a good idea that they have to be made mandatory? This despite vaccines now known to cause major health problems such as the autism spectrum and many acute and chronic debilitating and even fatal diseases. It is known that many cell lines used in vaccine preparation still contain SV-40 Monkey Virus which is typically present in about 40% of soft tissue cancers and believed by some medical researchers to either contribute or directly cause such cancers when the host's immunity is weakened by poor diet or environmentally-based toxins.[8]

The irrefutable truth about vaccines is that they don't work most of the time, and they simultaneously expose recipients to serious risk of harm, mostly stemming from toxic vaccine ingredients that are formulated into the vaccine cocktail alongside the viral strains. These toxic ingredients are widely documented to cause paralysis, comas, seizures, neurological disorders and even death. That's why the vaccine injury compensation program in the United States—often dubbed the "Vaccine Court"—has already paid out over $3 billion in damage awards to families of damaged children who were maimed or killed by vaccines. And yet states like California make vaccines mandatory before children can enroll in public schools.

Even access to clean water and healthy food has become subject to embargo. The food industry is being taken over by a consortium of companies led by Monsanto, which intends to own a re-engineered food and seed supply designed to force the use of their own pesticides in mass quantities. Few things are more representative of the concept of system failure than the losses in the honey bee population (Colony Collapse Disorder). Growing evidence connects CCD to the actions of companies like Monsanto, easily the most dangerous corporation in the world today. The environmental impact will be devastating without the bees. The government does nothing. Huge corporate lobbyist spending thwarts citizen activism.

CONTROLLED MASS MEDIA EMBARGO

While the free press of the past served in the role of watchdog and independent informer, the press we have today is far from free and unbiased. One way by which industry and even government are shaping and manipulating the press is through press embargoes, and the so-called "close-hold embargo" in particular. Another way is through the creation of front groups, and there are now many dozens of industry front groups masquerading as independent information organizations.

Always remember that anytime we read or watch mainstream media, we are being spoon-fed biased and distorted information that suits the goals of those who produce it, namely the global elite, who've hijacked the narrative over a century ago. Nothing more, nothing less. They literally own the "lamestream" media, and they continue to divide and misinform the people, using their media monopoly.

The bottom line is that a very small secret "Ruling Cabal" of top policy makers are able to impose their agenda upon the Earth's masses and this appears to be in line with an evil, anti-human agenda, one which some insiders have called an "Alien Agenda" to depopulate the Earth of humans, terraform it using geoengineering technologies, and repopulate it with alien/human hybrids which will be mass-bred with a hived-mind, always obedient to the "Queen Bee" (aka the "New Caesar of the Ages" whom aliens are planning to install as their NWO leader as soon as they take over).[9]

According to author Preston James, after most of our elected top policymakers were successfully human-compromised, they became infected with the evil Cosmic Parasite as their souls were snatched and also became "hived" to the master Alien

8   Preston, James. *Veterans Today*: "Alien Agenda XIX: High-tech Soul-snatching and the long planned Final Solution." **https://www.veterans-todayarchives.com/2015/02/15/alien-agenda-xix-high-tech-soul-snatching-and-the-long-planned-final-solution/**

9   Zagami, Leo Lyon, *Confessions of an Illuminati, Volume III: Espionage, Templars and Satanism in the Shadows of the Vatican*. CCC Publishing, 2017.

Agenda, a most evil script. It was at this point that these top policy makers began to institute secret but radically-evil covert programs to eugenicize and "soft-kill" the overabundance of "useless eaters" on the planet.

And all they needed to pull it off right in front of the general population was to control the narrative. The political perspectives being debated on TV range from MSNBC to Fox News, which for the most part are only superficially distinguishable. They both rally behind the same wars, work to normalize the same neo-liberal Walmart economy, and sell viewers the illusion that there is real political diversity happening within the American one-party "Dempublican" system. They sustain the illusion of a free market of ideas the way the crooked jewelers in John Steinbeck's book, *The Pearl,* conspired to create the illusion of marketplace competition. People watch them argue about how many scoops of ice cream the president got the way WWE spectators watch two actors body-slamming one another onto a padded canvass. The goal to suppress our range of thoughts in a box, and keep the arguments of the controlled opposition in the spectrum of their choosing. As Noam Chomsky writes in his book, *The Common Good*, "The smart way to keep people passive and obedient is to strictly limit the spectrum of acceptable opinion, but allow very lively debate within that spectrum."

This is the artificially-narrow spectrum of debate the oligarchs are trying to force upon the Internet today. If you're able to get online at all in the new system they're pushing toward, they don't want you arguing about whether democracy exists at all in America and the two-party system is a sham, they want you debating the preauthorized MSNBC vs. Fox News talking points they fed you the day before. They do this because they're scared, and they're scared because they have completely lost control of the narrative in the last few years, due to the population's awareness of "fake news."

Now the war for our minds is going online. Even though it has been largely ignored for years now, we still do have the First Amendment in the United States Constitution, which among other things mentions that Americans have freedom of speech. Even if information on the Internet is not entirely accurate, that still doesn't give any company the right to usurp the First Amendment. It's almost laughable how Google, Facebook, Twitter and other large Internet-based companies are attempting to appoint themselves as credible fact checkers, yet time and time again they are proven to be anything but credible. In order for the embargo on truth to continue, we can never be given the big picture of what is really going on, or who really makes the big decisions in the world today. This system can only thrive by our ignorance.

Fact-checking isn't the problem. The problem is the subjective nature of selecting what gets fact-checked and by what means; that explains how opinions are masked as fact-checking. While truth is definite on most fronts, there are matters that can't truly be fact-checked—often in the realm of strongly held political opinions or one-sided as pertaining to COVID-19.

What are we fighting over? These two Victorian sideshow performers boxing, called the fat man and the thin man, really didn't hate each other. They went through the motions that they disliked each other, but in reality, they were traveling companions who loved each other.

Nazi Germany started with anti-gravity generators in the late 1930s. The principle is that if an unbalanced mass is rotated it will achieve the centrifugal effect, but if the entire section, enclosed in a secondary rotational system, is also rotated, it is possible then to cancel forces, or direct them into a unidirectional anti-gravity thrust. The Nazi scientists who worked on these projects were brought over to the USA under Project Paperclip.

When the British failed to expel the Germans from Antarctica, the U.S. launched Operation High Jump in 1946 to destroy the German Base 211. The ground and air forces were fought back by Germany's flying saucers, ending the operation prematurely by four months. In July, 1952, Washington D.C. was visited by multiple unidentified flying objects over the Capitol, which many researchers believe were the Antarctica craft which Admiral Byrd said could "fly pole to pole at incredible speeds."

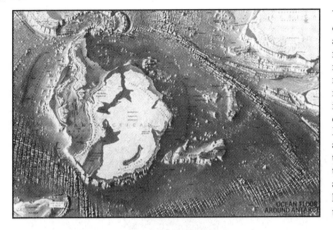

When we observe the ocean floor around Antarctica and the continent free of ice, we begin to notice the surface size is not the same as the land mass. Because Antarctica is the most geothermically active continent on Earth, it is known there are massive cavities under the ice that can maintain their own life forms, and an equitable climate for humans or inner-terrestrials ETs to live.

Pilots Ordered to Shoot Down 'Saucers' in Range

WASHINGTON, July 26 —(INS) — The Air Force disclosed today that jet pilots are under orders to maintain a nationwide 24-hour "alert" against "flying saucers" and to shoot them down if possible.

The Air Force expressed the belief the unidentified flying objects are not a threat to the United States and stated also that they are not a secret U. S. military development.

It added, however, that jet pilots are under standing orders to pursue all unidentified flying objects, especially on the eastern seaboard, and, if necessary, force them to land. The alert is applicable to "flying saucers."

The Air Force admitted, however, that no jet pilot has yet gotten close enough to take a shot at a "flying saucer." One pilot estimated that he was within five miles of a mysterious light over Washington last weekend, but the light disappeared when he tried to draw close.

The Pentagon issued a statement

(Please Turn to Page 4 Col. 1)

"I can assure you that flying saucers, given that they exist, are not constructed by any power on Earth." –President Harry S. Truman, April 4, 1950, White House Press Conference

There were very positive sides to all of these mystery paths before they became corrupted. They only became corrupted when some manipulators/bankers/power-hungry men took over. Just like religions today—they would take over countries and political systems if they could. Symbology remains important; some may look familiar today from this paleo-Hebrew plate.

The "circle within a circle" symbology of Saturn and its outer rings, which in Freemasonry represents their ESOteric-inner circle, (wisdom hidden from the masses) comes across like an "inside joke." The EXOteric-outer (false lies fed to the masses), who are EXcluded from the "club" of the wisdom...while mocking those with eyes to see (wise-dome). This information isn't to be judged as "good" or "bad." It is simply what's right in front of our eyes for the wise, or the esoteric, to see.

Did you know that the Law allows the Media to legally disinform you? The 2013 National Defense Authorization Act (NDAA) revision (signed into law) included an amendment to legalize domestic propaganda fed to the American people, allowing the corporate media to create misinformation legally, directed against our own citizens.

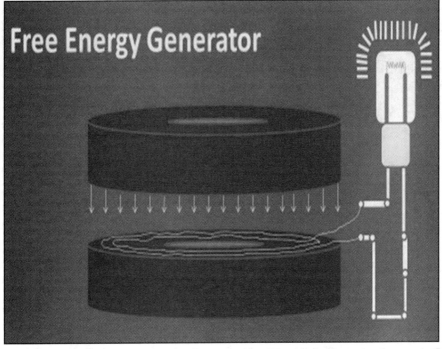

Suppression of over-unity energy technology started in 1951 with the "Invention Secrecy Act," whereby scientists/inventors who have breakthroughs in energy receive a "National Security Order" not to release their technology to the world, for the reason that it "might be detrimental to our National Security." That is why we are still using oil and coal for energy in the third decade of the 21st century. Such suppression is a crime against humanity!

This famous astronaut carving in Salamanca, Spain, was added during renovations in 1992 to the Ieronimus Cathedral, originally constructed by Episcope de Salamanca in 1102 CE. Although a recent addition, such anomalies give rise to the ancient astronaut theory, or some kind of foresight into a technologically-advanced future civilization. The astronaut stone carving is located on the north side of the new cathedral at an entry called Puerta de Ramos. The explanation for why an astronaut was selected was because it was a symbol of the 20th century when one of the greatest accomplishments of humankind was achieving space flight and landing on the Moon.

SUPPRESSED HUMAN ORIGINS

"There were giants in the earth in those days; and also after that, when the sons of God came in unto the daughters of men and they bore children to them, the same became mighty men who were of old, men of renown." –Genesis 6:4, the Bible

MOST everyone has heard of the giants of yore, sometimes called Anunnaki, Goliath, cyclops or ogres. Giants were generally presented as legendary creatures so big that the earth trembled when they walked. It seems however that the giants are not just fairy tales, considering the fact that their remains have been found all over the world. The mystery of their civilization remains to this day and there is even a kind of secrecy in this regard, a convention to sweep any evidence of their existence under the rug. However, the Iroquois, the Osage, the Tuscaroras, the Hurons, the Omahas, the Paiute and many other North American Native Americans all speak of giant men who once lived and roamed in the territories of their forefathers. Scattered throughout what is now the U.S. are traditions and remains of these ancient giants.

The evidence suggesting giant humanoids once lived on Earth is overwhelming. There are articles from mainstream newspapers such as the *New York Times*, and hundreds of small-town newspaper articles documenting the discoveries of giant skeletons during mound excavations. In some cases, the heads were so large an adult could slip the skull over his or her own head. At the very least, far too big to be considered *Homo sapiens* as we know them, and found in greater numbers as well. One discovery on Catalina Island, offshore of Los Angeles, revealed over 3,000 giant skeletons, all in a single burial site.

Furthermore, giant skulls and skeletons of a veritable race of "Goliaths" have been found within earthen mounds on a regular basis throughout the Midwestern states for more than 150 years. These skeletons can often be as tall as 11 or 12 feet—clearly dwarfing any type of humans we now see on Earth. Giants have been found in Michigan, Wisconsin, Iowa, Illinois, Ohio, Kentucky and New York, and their burial sites are similar to the well-known constructions of the Mound-Builder people. The spectrum of Mound-Builder history spans a period of more than 5,000 years (from 3400 BCE to the 16th century CE), a period greater than the history of Ancient Egypt and all of its dynasties.

Digging deeper, the existence of giants in North America and elsewhere around the world, as well as the large megalithic storage vaults of giant remains, continue to be hidden from the public. The reason for hiding the existence of giants is to avoid the discussion related to evolution and the revised history this knowledge would necessitate. Admitting the existence of giants means having to admit Darwin's evolution theory is, at best, incomplete, and apparently just wrong. In addition, this would trigger other uncomfortable discussions, including extraterrestrial visits and antediluvian civilizations on Earth long ago. Then there are the unexplained "cyclopean" constructions of the distant past, and the possibility that dinosaurs may have lived long after they presumably went extinct, even living concurrently with humans.[1]

THEY MIGHT BE GIANTS

Skeletal remains of very large humanoids continue to be uncovered. Around the world, over 200 digs containing giant remains have been found in recent decades. However, giant skeleton discoveries have not been reported by the local or national news in the USA, for the most part, since the 1950s. Why are academic institutions hiding the truth about these forefathers of humanity? They are our ancestors, the giants who roamed the earth, even recalled in the Bible and in other ancient texts of the world. It seems the American media fears people would question evolution. There is a "prevailing scholarly consensus" that we have an adequate historical understanding of the peoples who lived in North America during this period, and the giants do not fit in that model. Also, fundamentalist Bible believers hold to a literal interpretation of the beginning of man as recorded in Genesis (he was created a fully-formed human), even rejecting the well-established scientific fact of evolution. Yet the long record of anomalous finds like those at Lake Delavan in Wisconsin suggest otherwise.

Before the media and academic blackout, the Lake Delavan find of May, 1912, was only one of dozens of similar finds that were reported in local newspapers from 1851 forward for a century. It was not even the first set of giant skeletons found in Wisconsin, but it was so well-documented that the sensational discovery could not be easily glossed over.

Even after the story broke, scientists remained stubbornly silent about a lost race of giants found in burial mounds near Lake Delavan, Wisconsin. The dig site at Lake Delavan was overseen by archaeologists from Beloit College and it included more than 200 effigy mounds that proved to be classic examples of 8th century Woodland Culture. But the enormous size of the skeletons and elongated skulls found did not fit very neatly into anyone's concept of a textbook standard. They were enormous. These were not average human beings by any measure.

First reported in the May 4, 1912, issue of the *New York Times,* the 18 skeletons found by the Peterson brothers on Lake Lawn Farm in southwest Wisconsin exhibited several strange and freakish features. Their heights ranged between 7.6 and 10 feet, and their skulls were "presumably those of men, and are much larger than the heads of any race which inhabit America today." Furthermore, they tended to have a double row of teeth, six fingers, six toes and like humans, even came in different races. The teeth in the front of the jaw were described as regular molars. Heads usually found were elongated, believed to be

1 Olsen, Brad, *Modern Esoteric: Beyond Our Senses.* 2nd ed. CCC Publishing, 2017.

due to longer than normal life span. The Peterson brothers had to wonder how much they could lift if they were twice the size of an average human today. Could they be the builders of the "cyclopean" architecture in South America? Were these the giants described by the Bible, and in the historical accounts of many other civilizations around the world?[2]

A Michigan paper, the *McIvor Times,* September 5, 1884, reported the discovery of a gigantic human in a rock near the Sauk Rapids, as follows:

> *The head is massive 31 1/2 inches in circumference, is low in the front and very flat on the top. The femur measures 26 1/4 inches, and the fibula 26 1/2 inches, while the body is equally long in proportion. From the crown of the head to the sole of the foot, the length is 10 feet 9 1/2 inches. The measure around the chest is 59 1/2 inches, this giant must have weighed at least 900 pounds, when covered with a reasonable amount of flesh. The petrified remains, and there is nothing left but the naked bones, now weigh 304 pounds. The thumb and fingers of the left hand and the left foot from the ankle to the toes are gone, but all of the other parts are perfect. Verily, there were giants in those days!*

SOUTHERN WISCONSIN EPICENTER

On August 10, 1891, the *New York Times* reported that scientists from the Smithsonian Institution had discovered several large "pyramidal monuments" near Lake Mills, near Madison, Wisconsin. The excavators found an elaborate system of defensive works which they named Fort Aztalan. "Madison was in ancient days the center of a teeming population numbering not less than 200,000," the *Times* said. The article went on to report:

> *The celebrated mounds of Ohio and Indiana can bear no comparison, either in size, design or the skill displayed in their construction with these gigantic and mysterious monuments of earth—erected we know not by whom, and for what purpose we can only conjecture.*

While a normal-sized skeleton of a supposed Mound Builders named the "Princess of Aztalan" is on display in the museum near several large pyramidal monuments at Aztalan State Park, the goliath remains of Wisconsin's giants have vanished along with the hundreds of others discovered throughout the Midwest.

On December 20, 1897, the *Times* followed up with a report on three large burial mounds that had been discovered in Maple Creek, Wisconsin. "Giant Skeleton Discovered in Maple Creek, WI" was the headline in the *New York Times,* which reported that three large burial mounds had been discovered at Maple Creek. Upon excavation, a skeleton, measuring over nine feet from head to toe, was discovered; also at the site were finely-tempered copper rods and other relics. One tomb had recently been opened. The article stated:

> *In it was found the skeleton of a man of gigantic size. The bones measured from head to foot over nine feet and were in a fair state of preservation. The skull was as large as a half bushel measure. Some finely tempered rods of copper and other relics were lying near the bones.*

Another giant skeleton was found in West Bend, WI, with a newspaper line that reads "A giant skeleton was unearthed outside of West Bend near Lizard Mound County Park and assembled by local farmers to a height of eight feet." More about this can be found in *Washington County Paranormal: A Wisconsin Legend Trip* by local author and investigator J. Nathan Couch.[3]

2   "The Great Smithsonian Cover-Up: 18 Giant Skeletons Discovered in Wisconsin" *Earth We Are One.com* **(site no longer active)**
3   Couch, J. Nathan, *Washington County Paranormal: A Wisconsin Legend Trip.* CreateSpace, 2012.

The January 13, 1870, edition of the *Wisconsin Decatur Republican* headline reads: "Two Giant Skeletons Near Potosi, WI." The article reads:

> *Two giant, well-preserved skeletons of an unknown race were discovered near Potosi, WI by workers digging the foundation of a saw mill near the bank of the Mississippi River. One skeleton measured seven-and-a-half feet, the other eight feet. The skulls of each had prominent cheek bones and double rows of teeth. A large collection of arrowheads and "strange toys" were found buried with the remains.*

SMITHSONIAN-GATE

The enormous size of the skeletons and elongated skulls found in the 19th and 20th centuries did not fit very neatly into anyone's concept of a standard history textbook. They were enormous. These were not average, or even extra tall human beings. They were different from us. Many believe the Smithsonian "scientists" were trying to cover this up all along. Specifically, the Smithsonian Institution has been accused of making a deliberate effort to hide the "telling of the bones" and to keep the giant skeletons locked away. There are also accusations that many giant bones were dumped into the Atlantic Ocean in the 19th century to keep it all "out of sight and out of mind."

Ever since the strange discoveries have been made, researchers have accused the Smithsonian Institution of covering up giant skeleton discoveries by locking up the "out of place artifacts" and depriving the public of their findings. Has there been a cover-up of "giant" proportions? Why aren't there public displays of gigantic Native American skeletons at natural history museums? The Smithsonian Institution stands accused of destroying thousands of human giant remains. Allegedly it was involved in a major historical cover-up of evidence showing giant human remains all across America. High-level administrators ordered the destruction of these priceless remnants of human history to protect the mainstream chronology of human evolution at the time. It is presumed the Smithsonian had documents that allegedly proved the destruction of tens of thousands of giant skeletons reaching between 7 feet and 12 feet in height, a reality mainstream archeology cannot admit to for different reasons.

There has been a major cover-up by Western archaeological institutions since the early 1900s leading us to believe that America was first colonized by Asian peoples migrating across the frozen Bering Strait 15,000 years ago, during the last Ice Age. In fact, there are hundreds of thousands of burial mounds all over America which (Native Americans claim) were there a long time before the Ice Age. Within these mounds, where giant human skeleton remains are frequently found, are traces of a highly-developed civilization indicating a complex use of metal alloys and out of place artifacts. Yet these discoveries still go unreported in the mass media and local news outlets.

LOVELOCK CAVE GIANTS

A Nevada Paiute legend mentions the existence of 12-foot-tall red-haired giants who lived in the area when the Indians first arrived. The story says the Native Americans had killed off the giants deep in a cave. Excavations of guano in 1911 turned up a massive human jaw. More discoveries in the Lovelock Cave and surrounding area would follow.

An article published in the *Nevada Review-Miner*, in February and June of 1931, reported that two very large skeletons were found above the Humboldt dry lake bed near Lovelock, Nevada. One measured 8.5-feet tall and was later described as having been wrapped in a gum-covered fabric similar to Egyptian mummies. The other was supposedly nearly 10 feet long. It has been reported that billionaire Robert Bigelow was able to acquire a complete Lovelock giant skeleton for private testing. Other evidence for the Lovelock Giants includes a set of images showing a handprint, more than double the size of a normal man's hand, imprinted on a stone bolder in the cave which was released by Bigfoot investigators MK Davis and Don Monroe in 2013. Similarly, along the Peru/Bolivia border, massive skulls have been found near Lake Titicaca, with claims that they were from giants with reddish hair and elongated skulls. Some are on display in a museum in Paracas, Peru. The legends tell of the Uros Indians making reed boats and living on islands on Lake Titicaca, similar to the Paiute. Legend claims the Incas apparently drove them to live this way much like the Paiutes' ancestors apparently did to the giants at Lake Lahontan.

"Si-Te-Cah" or *Saiduka* literally translates as "tule-eaters" in the Northern Paiute language. The tule is a fibrous water plant which, according to legend, the giants wove into rafts to escape attacks by the Paiute, who greatly out-numbered them. They used the rafts to navigate across what remained then of Lake Lahontan, an ancient lake that once covered most of northern Nevada during the last Ice Age. As the Paiute tale goes, after years of warfare, all the tribes in the area joined together to rid themselves of the Si-Te-Cah. One day, as the tribes chased down the last remaining red-haired giants, they took refuge in a cave. The Paiutes demanded their enemy come out of the cave and fight, but the giants refused. The coalition of tribes proceeded to shoot arrows at them while starting a large fire at the mouth of the cave. The smoke drove out a few who died in a hail of arrows while the rest were all either burned alive or were asphyxiated. Over time, the entrance to the cave would collapse, leaving it cut off from human contact and accessible only to bats. The uncovering of 15" sandals at Lovelock Cave is proof enough that the Paiute tale is true.[4]

LIVING FOSSIL OR BREEDING SPECIES?

In 2002, U.S. troops in Afghanistan engaged with a 10-foot giant humanoid the locals called *Sar Luy Balaa*, meaning "Great Red Monster," for its red hair and beard. As the troops were walking towards the system of caves where the *Sar Luy Balaa* was reputed to live, they began to smell a horrid stench; and there were bones on the ground that appeared to be human. When the Kandahar Giant emerged from the largest cave, it carried what was described as a "pole-axe" or a small tree trunk split down the middle, in which a long, bronze/copper blade was fitted. Animal hides had been cut into tiny pieces of string, and as the hide had cured into leather, it was tied such that it held the blade in place. The spear was held in such a way that, as it finished curing, it had become a fine string that was extremely tight and would not break, even as it struck and killed several soldiers.

Many shots did not take down the giant, but finally the large .338 Lapua (sniper rifle cartridge) most likely did the killing, as the right eyeball, orbital socket, and brain were damaged. One of the soldiers killed the creature by shooting it in the face for 30 seconds on full auto! The body weighed over 1,000 pounds. It was positioned for lift by using winches and a net, and the soldiers airlifted the body to Kandahar Airport by helicopter. After it was brought in, the body was immediately airlifted to an international airbase, where it was put on a pallet and taken to Wright Patterson Air Force Base in Dayton, Ohio, and then was eventually taken to a research facility in Utah for testing.

In Utah, radiographics and nuclear medicine were used to determine that the Kandahar Giant was similar, if not identical, to Bigelow's complete Lovelock giant skeleton. The Lloyd Pye Lovelock skeleton, which Lloyd purchased, was determined to be identical to Bigelow's—and despite being incomplete, the Lovelock skeletons were indeed a "family." The government of Alberta gave the U.S. Government a "bigfoot," killed in the Alberta Nahanni Valley. This was determined to be of the same genetic family as the Kandahar specimen.

••••••••••••••••••••••••••••••••••••••

4   Olsen, Brad, *Sacred Places North America: 108 Destinations.* 2nd ed. CCC Publishing, 2008.

The Paiutes called these exotic remains Si-Te-Cah. The Cherokee Indians called them "Judaculla Men" (hence the name of Judaculla Rock today). The Canadian First Nation Indians had a name for them too. Their pictures do not show signs of problems with their pituitary or adrenal glands—i.e. no glandular issues. These are not humans, that is, *Homo sapiens sapiens*, with mutations. There has not been a consensus as to whether or not these are living fossils, breeding species, an alien (EBE), or something else. But they are all biological. They are not cybernetic creatures like the grey aliens.

MASTER GENETIC SCIENTISTS

In 1975, Dr. Nils Ringertz of the Swedish Institute for Medical Research and Genetics, announced the successful crossing of genes of entirely different genera, to produce hybrid cells in new living organisms called chimeras. His team had combined the genetic material of a human with a rat, a human with a chicken, and even a human with an insect! In each case, the cell produced began to multiply, and if it had been allowed to grow, each cell would have developed into the monstrosity created by the genetic combination—a "man-rat" or a "man-insect." Viruses have recently been synthesized in our modern research laboratories by recombining existing virus material, thus producing new strains not found in nature. COVID-19 has a "gain of function" added. Already new forms have been produced which could prove to be deadly, and would be a serious threat if uncontrolled, because these forms have the ability to reproduce themselves.[5]

On the basis of these discoveries, one could logically speculate that a highly advanced society in the past might have done similar experiments. This would connect closely with the reports of biological weapons, both in recent times, and in ancient documents. Going one step further, modern researchers are also experimenting with changing the structure of DNA, the basic building blocks of life, which contain the codes of identity in the genetics of the individual. Exact copies of mammals can also be created. Remember "Dolly" the sheep clone from the mid-1990s?

The virus is a little machine that accomplishes the very same thing, only in a specific manner: It contains a core of altered DNA material that it injects into the nucleus of a human cell, and the DNA in that cell is transformed to reproduce the virus form. As a result, the cell is reorganized to produce more viruses, not cells. When the cell disintegrates, its mutated offspring spread to attack and inject themselves into other cells, and the process begins again, only multiplied. Did someone in the unknown past design the virus as a biological weapon? Speculation exists that all viruses on Earth were deliberately invented or introduced. Similarly, they could also be completely eliminated, making life much gentler for humans and animals.

We can scarcely imagine what kind of monstrosities might become released upon the world, including the Morgellons nanobot fibers, and "mad scientist" creations of science fiction. There is also the realization that we have seen some of these human-animal combinations before, specifically, in the artwork and mythology of practically every ancient civilization. In these images we find the mermaid (woman-fish), centaur (man-horse), satyr (man-goat), harpy (man-bird), and the sphinx (man-lion). And there are other well-known animal on animal combinations: pegasus (horse-bird), griffon (bird-lion), capricorn (goat-fish), and the gargoyle (ape-bird). Could these mythical creatures be genetic experiments conducted by the Anunnaki?

ANNUNAKI CREATORS

Was there genetic engineering in ancient times? Did the Sumerian god Enki (also known as Lucifer) create humans as clones? The idea that ancient aliens modified human DNA plays a vital role in the Ancient Astronaut theory. According

5 "Unraveling the Mystery Behind the Clones of The Anunnaki," *Lock Lip.com* (**site no longer active**)

to the late author and researcher Zecharia Sitchin the Anunnaki, a group of extra-terrestrials that visited our planet in the distant past, genetically engineered *Homo sapiens* as slave creatures to work their gold mines, by crossing extraterrestrial genes with those of the indigenous and primitive *Homo erectus*.

The Anunnaki, people like us yet much taller, rocketed here 450,000 years ago for gold to send back to their home planet as powder for a sky shield. Being giant humans, the Anunnaki (from the planet Nibiru) bred, blessed, cursed and challenged us. They came for gold powder to rocket back to Nibiru, using the powder as a shield from temperature extremes and radiation as they floated back into their atmosphere. In addition, they needed a worker race smart enough to work the gold mines, but obedi-ent enough not to question authority or revolt. *Homo sapiens* is Latin for wise man or knowing man. Anunnaki and hybrid overseers imprinted greed, one-upmanship and dominator-consciousness on us. They modeled, dictated and indoctrinated avarice in us, along with domination, slavery, competition, hate and violence.

According to Dr. Sasha Alex Lessin, we exist because the Anunnaki grafted *Homo erectus* genes into their own genome. We became a mix between primitive and advanced species. In time, our creators gave or showed us literacy, physics, laws, math, cosmology, astronomy, biology, medicine, metallurgy, brick-making, music, instruments, architecture, geology, cities, schools, canals, ships, cartography, and contracts. We imitated the technology we saw them use. They gave us computers, rockets, submarines, free electricity, longevity treatment, and gene spicing. They gave savants advanced knowledge to share with us now.[6]

But they also trained us to compete and hurt rivals, and made us slaves in armies, homes, and jobs. They imprinted dominator-consciousness on us. The Anunnaki shortened our lives, imprinted us to obsess on status and greed, and inflicted royals, religions, racism, sexism, slavery, taxes, gold lust, debt, murder, war, propaganda, and ignorance on us.

The Anunnaki and their genetic offspring, the Nephilim, were our ancestors, but were much bigger in stature and intelligence. They were the giants of renown men-tioned in the Bible. A *Discover* magazine article in 2009 reported that the Boskop Man was "a now-extinct race of humans, had big eyes, child-like faces, and an aver-age intelligence of around 150, making them geniuses among *Homo sapiens*. The Boskop skull, it would seem, housed a brain perhaps 25 percent or more larger than our own." In other words, giants. Head binding cannot explain the features of skulls such as those found in Boskop, South Africa. Head binding cannot increase a skull's brain volume. Nor can it boost a person's intelligence quotient.

EGYPTOLOGIST TALES

A giant mummified finger was discovered in Egypt measuring 38 centime-ters/13.8 inches long. Now just imagine, according to official calculations, the human (or alien) who owned the finger must have been at least 20.7 feet or 6.3 me-ters tall. The 15-inch long mummified limb is not available for public viewing, since the person who owns it does not wish its family legacy to be tarnished. The pictures of the amazing finger were taken by a lucky photographer named Gregor Spörri. The nature-loving "doctor" went on an expedition to Egypt in 1988 order to search for the finger and eventually recover it. Although the photos were taken in 1988, they haven't been published until recently. Why is that so? The answer is quite simple yet very saddening: every human scientist who saw the photos said that there is no

• •
6   Lessin, Dr. Sasha Alex, "Anunnaki creators from Planet Nibiru started the Snake Brotherhood to save us so we'd make a civilized culture like theirs on Earth for them." **http://stargatetothecosmos.org/snake-society-to-civilize-us-to-receive-refugees-for-nibiru-evacuation/**

room for giants in our current scheme, be it evolutionary or not. Since this never-before-seen artifact does not fit in well with any of the already well-established and documented theories, it could, therefore, not be real. Just imagine how many other discoveries have been swept under the rug simply because they were inconvenient for our modern theories of human evolution and the ascent of the species.

There are many references to the ancient Nephilim giants spoken of in the Sumerian Texts and in the Bible. The Elohim, which are the angelic beings, are the ones known as angels to us from the Bible. As the Sumerian text goes, the humans had rebelled against Anu and had sex with human women, but the children that were born grew into giants. Many Nephilim died by an ancient flood triggered by a pole shift, and the results are their skeleton remains found in Africa, and immortalized in Egyptian relief sculptures.

These "giant aliens" are the Nephilim giants, and the reason why their features are a little different from humans is because the Nephilim are half-human, half-alien, or a part "angelic" being, which caused a mutation. The Nephilim were the offspring of the "sons of God" and the "daughters of men" before the deluge, according to Genesis 6:1-4. The Bible often involves giants, including the Nephilim who were semi-divine beings. The King Og had an iron bed measuring 6.7 x 14 feet. He would be at least 12 feet tall. Goliath, the gigantic rival that King David brought down with his sling, was 9.2 feet tall.

Giant human coffins are also found in Egypt. It wouldn't make any sense to place a 5.7-tall man into a 17-foot coffin. Historians tried too hard to hide the fact that giant humanoids existed in ancient Kemet (Egypt); they especially tried to hide their appearance. It's undeniable. Giant coffins are for giant beings. Female coffins for an Egyptian Queen are three meters in height; that is ten feet tall. Information about giant humans is contained in almost all known ancient texts: the Torah, the Bible, the Koran, the Vedas, as well as Chinese and Tibetan chronicles, Assyrian cuneiform tablets and writings of the Maya.[7]

STRIKINGLY TALL GIANT SKELETONS UNCOVERED IN SOUTH AMERICA

Strikingly tall skeletons uncovered in the Ecuador and the Peruvian Amazon region are undergoing examination in Germany, according to a research team headed by British anthropologist Russell Dement. Will these remains prove that a race of tall people existed hundreds of years ago deep in the Amazonian rainforest?

According to the *Cuenca Highlife* news site, since 2013 the team has found half a dozen human skeletons, dating to the early 1400s and the mid-1500s, which measure between seven and eight feet (213 to 243 centimeters) in height. Dement said:

We are very early in our research and I am only able to provide a general overview of what we have found. I don't want to make claims based on speculation since our work is ongoing. Because of the size of the skeletons, this has both anthropological and medical implications.

Within six months of excavations and mapping at two different sites—the one outside of Cuenca, and another settlement dating to about 1550, approximately 20 miles (32 kilometers) away on the Ecuadorian-Peruvian border—the team had found five more tall skeletons, as well as artifacts. It is believed by Dement and colleagues that the tribe at the second site had been at the settlement for at least 150 years.

The three complete skeletons and two partial skeletons had no disfiguration which suggested they were relatively healthy. Dement noted:

7   Vieira, Jim, Newman, Hugh, *Giants on Record: America's Hidden History, Secrets in the Mounds and the Smithsonian Files*. Avalon Rising Publications, 2015.

The skeletons show no signs of diseases such as the hormonal growth problems that are common in most cases of gigantism. In all the skeletons, the joints seemed healthy and lung cavity appeared large. One of the skeletons that we have dated was of a female who was about 60 when she died, much older than typical cases of gigantism.

The burials were elaborate. Bodies were wrapped in leaves and buried in thick clay. This sealed the skeletons and protected against water intrusion, leaving the remains in fairly good condition.[8]

CULTURE OF THE GIANTS

Over 1,000 accounts of seven-foot and taller skeletons have reportedly been unearthed from ancient burial sites over a two-hundred-year period in North America. Newspaper accounts, town and county histories, letters, scientific journals, diaries, photos and Smithsonian ethnology reports have carefully documented these finds. Giant skeletons have been reported from coast to coast with strange anatomic anomalies such as double rows of teeth, jawbones so large as to be fit over the face of the finder, and elongated skulls, documented in virtually every state.[9]

From burial objects to clues of their religion, we are struck by the following traits of this giant race or ethnic group from human prehistory:

* *Mother Goddess religion*
* *Copper (not bronze) axes*
* *Polished slate tools including fishing plummets,*
which were apparently regarded as sacred
* *Belief that the Grandmother Moon was the repository of souls*
* *Diet emphasizing shellfish (for which the double row of teeth*
probably was selected as an evolutionary advantage
in their beachcomber origin out of Africa?)
* *Building of fish weirs in North American rivers to trap migrating eels*
* *Certain vegetarian habits (wild rice, for instance)*
* *Inscriptions on artifacts, especially pipes, often buried with the dead*
* *Use of coal and petroleum*
* *Weaving and looms*
* *Knowledge of seafaring, mathematics and engineering,*
including canals and irrigation
* *Burying of a dog with a child to guard the latter in the afterlife*
* *A language apparently Afro-Asiatic and close to Semitic tongues*
* *Kingcraft: nobles were buried in seated positions on thrones surrounded by*
a coterie of their retainers.[10]

WHO, OR WHAT, ARE WE THEN?

In the study of genetics, we find that we can only inherit what our ancestors had, except in the case of mutation. We can have any of numerous combinations of traits inherited from all our ancestors. Nothing more and nothing less. Therefore, if humans and apes evolved from a common ancestor, their blood would have evolved the same way. Blood factors are transmitted with much more exactitude than any other characteristic. It would seem that modern humans and the rhesus monkey may have had a common ancestor sometime in the ancient past. All other earthly primates also have this Rh factor. But this leaves out the 15% of people who are Rh negative. If all humankind evolved from

8 "Giants found in South America" by *Ancient Origins:* https://thewatchtowers.org/giant-7-8-foot-skeletons-uncovered-in-ecuador-sent-for-scientific-testing/
9 "Forbidden History: Ancient GIANTS—Gods and Kings" https://matrixdisclosure.com/forbidden-history-ancient-giants/
10 Dewhrst, Richard, *The Ancient Giants Who Ruled America: The Missing Skeletons and the Great Smithsonian Cover-Up.* Bear & Company, 2013.

the same ancestor, then their blood would be compatible, but all human blood is not. An Rh negative mother can kill her Rh positive baby if their blood mixes. This happens only with humans. Where did the Rh negatives come from? If they are not the descendants of prehistoric people, could they be the descendants of the ancient astronauts?

The origin of the universe was much like a seed—wherein the full form of the tree was already contained in potential. It has been proven that the majority of human-kind (85%) has a blood factor common with the rhesus monkey. This is called rhesus positive blood. Usually shortened to Rh positive. This factor is completely independent from the A, B, O blood types.

This "tree" happens to grow human life—at least in our own galaxy, and apparently 40% of all the other galaxies out there in the Cosmos, according to the *Law of One* series. We do live in a biological universe. The evidence is voluminous and undeniable—though not popular, due in part to Cabal suppression of science. The *Law of One* calls our galaxy "The Logos." In the original New Testament in Greek, Jesus said "I am the Logos" more than once.

The above work of art was once part of the old Maya city of Tikal, in Guatemala. It probably illustrates the demise of Atlantis. Since this does not fit the prevailing picture, a German archaeologist took it to Germany, where it was "accidentally" destroyed in the Second World War. There is so much of our distant past and our human origins "omitted" from our understanding of "history." For example, why is this relief sculpture from Tikal, depicting a major catastrophe and what could be Atlantis sinking, left out of the history of the Maya?

All across Peru, the protuberances on the megalithic blocks are clearly not natural, and not precisely shaped, meaning they were not designed nor cut by chisel or machine, nor was the stone cut away all around them. The back sides of most megalithic blocks are rough, and not dressed. There are some indentations to indicate stone softening, as well as stone "casting" as a geopolymer concrete. This offers an explanation for their "molded" appearance. This form of megalithic "cyclopean" stone construction is still not understood in the modern world today.

Look at the size of this skull found in a Chullpa burial tower not far from Puma Punku and Tiwanaku in Bolivia. In the pre-flood world of Noah, it is written that there was inter-species breeding between the "sons of God" (or the B'nai Elohim) and mortal human women. The ancient rabbinic scholars believed that the term "sons of God" specifically referred to fallen angels, and this was in fact the teaching of the early church for several hundred years.

This "Indian Cemetery," on Santa Rosa Island in Southern California's Channel Islands, contained abalone shells radiocarbon-dated at 7,070 years old when discovered in 1959. Tops of skulls were ritualistically painted red, and many skeletons measured over seven feet tall. Photo courtesy of Santa Barbara Museum of Natural History.

Babylonian depiction of priests with fish suits, working with the tree of life while holding pine cones (pineal glands) and buckets—signs of advanced knowledge in genetics—being overwatched by "god" in flying ship.

Long before the Isolationist doctrine of the Smithsonian became an academic dogma, mounds and earthworks in North America were routinely compared to those observed in Western Europe. This position was summed up by Stephen Denison Peet, founder of the American Antiquarian, in this passage from 1892: "Relics of the Mound Builders resemble those found in Great Britain and the north of Ireland, and even suggest the transmission of the same myths and symbols from the eastern to the western continent."

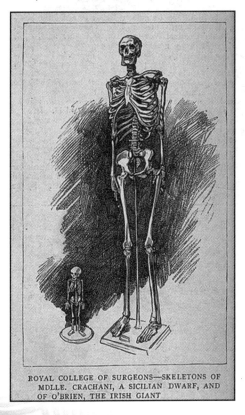

ROYAL COLLEGE OF SURGEONS—SKELETONS OF MDLLE. CRACHANI, A SICILIAN DWARF, AND OF O'BRIEN, THE IRISH GIANT

Sketch depicting skeletons of a male giant and a female dwarf, both full-grown adults. The male, Charles Byrne (1761-1783), known as "The Irish Giant," is now on display at the Royal College of Surgeons of England in London. Measurements of his skeleton indicated he was approximately seven feet, seven inches (2.31 meters) tall.

In the Paluxy River, in Glen Rose, Texas, were found human and dinosaur footprints in the same layer of dried clay.

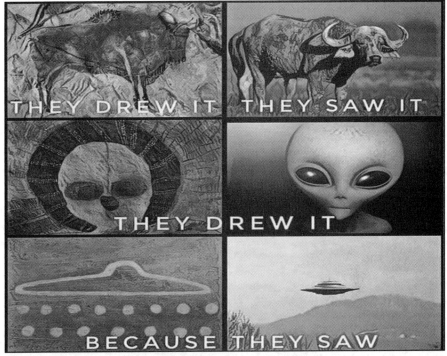

"Whereas the modern world equates myth with imaginative invention, ancient cultures used it as an instrument for recording important facts and events so they would be memorialized and recalled generation after generation." –Freddy Silva, *The Missing Lands: Uncovering Earth's Pre-flood Civilization*

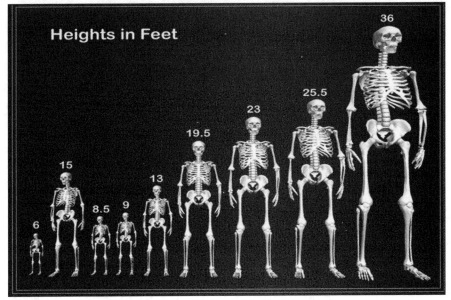

The amount of evidence for giant skeletons—ranging from a 9-foot group to a 12-foot group to a 25-to-30-foot group—is quite significant. Much of this evidence has been suppressed in order to hide its true nature from the public.

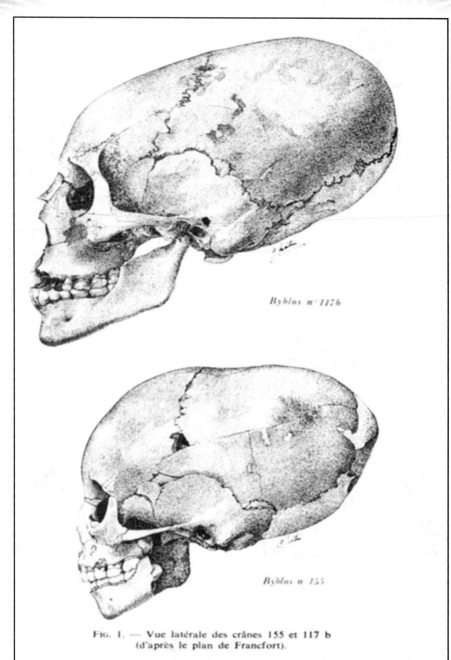

Byblos n° 117b

Byblos n° 155

FIG. I. — Vue latérale des crânes 155 et 117 b
(d'après le plan de Francfort).

"Homo capensis" is the classification of the coneheads. They were an advanced ancient world-wide race, also known as the pre-Adamites. Evidence shows they were around not too long ago (2,500 years) and still could be alive somewhere today. They are not human, although close, but not the same. They have a much larger brain case capacity than any living human. Binding cannot accomplish this, and normal humans did this in an effort to appear more like them. These skulls are anatomically not like a human, save the general shape.

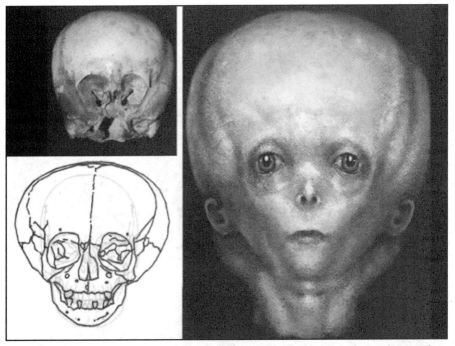

The "Starchild" skull is a 900-year-old human-like bone skull with distinctly non-human characteristics. It was unearthed in a mine tunnel near Mexico's Cooper Canyon around 1930. It is not *Homo sapiens* in the same way that *Homo erectus* was not *Homo sapiens*. Similarly, the coneheads are not *Homo sapiens* in the same way that the Neanderthals are not *Homo sapiens*. There might have been some interbreeding, which to them was probably considered bestiality. There is a similarity to Caucasian mitochondrial DNA, but it in no way means that the Starchild or coneheads were *Homo sapiens* when they clearly were not.

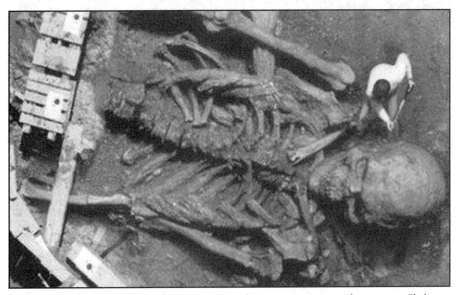

The remains of giants could be the ancient Hyperboreans, our ancestral ancestors. Skeleton discovered in Rosia Montana, Romania.

These skulls belong to representatives of an unknown pre-modern human or humanoid type. Look at the amazing Huayqui skeleton of a child, located in a small museum in the town of Andahuaylillas, south of Cusco, Peru. The head is larger than the body. It would be interesting to know the stature of the adult skulls found at the museum. These conehead skulls have been found all over the world, and are definitely the remains of some alternative form of human being from what we normally see. This was confirmed with DNA tests ordered by Brien Foerster in 2014, showing "mutations unknown in any human, primate, or animal known so far." The skulls themselves have obvious abnormalities, including completely different cranial sutures and alternative passageways for nerve fibers and blood vessels.

South Africa giant footprint in granite from many thousands of years ago. There are several of these footprints around the world, but strangely they aren't talked about too much in U.S. government-supported historical museums or societies, because acknowledgment of all giants is highly marginalized. Right: Michael Tellinger has found an actual petrified finger in cretaceous limestone, which belonged to a very "prehistoric human." An MRI showed this finger to be consistent with human tissue, complete with joints.

ALTERNATIVE 1, 2, 3

"Once the Mars colony was secured, they felt like they could finally get far enough away from the Earth. Far enough away, because they started to wonder about these 'Ascension' rumors, and were concerned that if such a thing did happen, the Moon might not be far enough away to be unaffected by it. Alternative III was, get to Mars and then one of two possibilities."
–Secret Space Program Captain Randy Cramer

SOMETIMES mainstream science fiction is based on a masked truth. Such is the case with *Science Report: Alternative 3*—a television program that was broadcast one time in the United Kingdom in 1977, and later broadcast only once in Australia, Canada, and New Zealand. It was not allowed to air in the USA. This legendary pseudo-documentary made viewers believe it was a real investigation when it aired as part of ITV's respected *Science Report*. After airing, it was claimed by its producers to be a fictional hoax, an heir to Orson Welles' radio production of *The War of the Worlds*.

The show started as an investigation into the UK's contemporary "brain drain" and led to Alternative 3 being uncovered as a plan to make the Moon and Mars habitable in the event of climate change and a terminal environmental catastrophe on Earth. It was claimed that scientists had determined that the Earth's surface would be unable to support life for much longer, due to pollution leading to catastrophic climate change. A fictional character, Dr. Carl Gerstein, claimed to have proposed three alternatives to this problem in 1957. The first alternative was the drastic reduction of the human population on Earth. The second alternative was the construction of vast underground shelters to house government officials and a cross section of the population until the climate stabilized. The third alternative, the so-called "Alternative 3," was to populate Mars via a way station on the Moon. Sometimes the truth really is stranger than fiction. Was the TV show a veiled attempt to inform the public about the real Secret Space Program, and the colonization of other planets?

Interestingly, a symposium really was held in 1957, which was attended by some of the greatest scientific minds of the time, called the JASON Scholars. All three "alternatives" were proposed. Alternative 1 was to use a series of nuclear devices to attempt to blow a hole in the upper atmosphere as a vent to release pollutants and gases into space. This alternative may have been the basis of the 1958 high-altitude nuclear weapons test known as Operation Argus in the Southern Ocean and possibly over Antarctica. The purpose of Operation Argus ostensibly was to test the manipulation of the Earth's radiation belts. Argus was carried out in half the time normally allocated for such a test, and was the only clandestine test series in the 17-year history of atmospheric testing. Additional evidence suggests that the top-secret High-frequency Active Auroral Research Project (HAARP) may also have been tested for such a purpose.

It is important to include geoengineering in this discussion. Some evidence points to chemtrails being a modern implementation of a theory proposed by Dr. Edward Teller, "Father of the H-Bomb," that global warming could be reduced or abated by jettisoning large quantities of metallic debris into the upper atmosphere to deflect sunlight and cool the Earth's surface. Indeed, chemtrailing entails the high-altitude dumping of materials like barium and aluminum.[1]

It is also known that the Shadow Government has built an entirely new underground civilization beneath the abandoned factories, tattered homes, and crime-ridden streets that litter the American landscape. In this new society, there is no poverty, no crime, and no illicit drug use. In this new society, healthcare is affordable, energy is free and public transport is efficient. And the American taxpayer has paid for it all, without receiving any benefit whatsoever for their Herculean efforts. The most notorious development is the Dulce Base, which is an alleged joint human and alien underground facility. It is located under Archuleta Mesa on the Colorado-New Mexico border, near the town of Dulce, New Mexico, in the United States.

Claims of alien activity there first arose from Albuquerque businessman, Paul Bennewitz, and later by former Dulce Base security officer, Thomas Edwin Castello. According to Castello, this particular underworld city is a highly-secret base operated by humans as well as reptilian aliens and their worker cast, the commonly-encountered greys. It is here, apparently, that a multitude of experimental projects are carried out. These are primarily genetic experiments on kidnapped men, women, and children. Indeed, Alternatives I, II and III are about as "deep" as the rabbit hole goes here on Earth and beyond.

WHAT ARE THE ALTERNATIVES?

By secret Executive Order of President Eisenhower, the JASON Scholars were ordered to study the long-term scenarios facing civilization and make recommendations from their findings. In 1957, the JASON Scholars, all members of the Council on Foreign Relations, confirmed the findings of the scientists and made three recommendations called Alternatives I, II and III. The scientists also advocated both the release of deadly viruses into the public and perpetual warfare as a means to decrease world population. The first recommendation, Alternative I, dovetailed nicely with the phar-

1   Phillips, Olav, "Alternative 3: END GAME of the New World Order" http://www.paranoiamagazine.com/2013/01/alternative-3-end-game-of-the-new-world-order/

maceutical interests of the Rockefellers. Alternative I was to cause a drastic "soft kill" reduction in the human population by various human-created means. There were far too many people on the planet and what was recommended was a wholesale human culling. Alternative I was discussed by an elite panel of end-of-the-world brainstormers, and they came up with various eugenic techniques, including limited nuclear war. The high-altitude nuclear tests in the late 1950s were the real cause of the holes in the ozone layer.

Alternative I was to do high atmospheric atomic testing, which they did. Alternative II was building Deep Underground Military Bases and Structures (DUMBS), which they did. Alternative III was the construction of a Lunar base/colony and a colony on Mars, which they did. We can take it for granted that the 1947 Roswell crash did occur, and that the U.S. government has reverse-engineered the recovered technology and eventually developed space travel. Roswell was over 70 years ago. It's quite possible that the military-industrial complex leaders could have gone out into space, taken a look around and subsequently built some colonies. They would eventually begin to terraform Mars and make it more Earth-like every year. In this third option, construction was to begin on the Moon and Mars bases, called Adam and Eve, respectively. Then they would ultimately settle on the Red Planet as a long-term survival colony. In Alternative III, the elite would have an escape route planned, while the rest of the world's population would be allowed to die.[2]

These three alternatives have been put forth in various Armageddon scenarios that would be a disaster for surface humans. But there is one more "alternative." It is Alternative IV—the power of the human spirit, which is on the organic ascension timeline. It is about our unification and the activation of the natural stargates. Our destiny was always about this achievement! Alternative IV would require a vast public awakening first, then the creation of a new and sustainable civilization to follow. By visualizing an alternative future or "timeline" for the Earth and all its inhabitants, we must take the first step in directing our energy to a positive Alternative IV endgame. which these elite planners wanted nothing to do with.

DEEP UNDERGROUND

For many years there have been reports and rumors of a vast network of underground complexes and tunnels beneath the North American continent. Starting in the late 1980s, the American government has tried to deflect these rumors through a campaign of misdirection and misinformation. Now we know there are at least 1,400 of these Deep Underground Military Bases (DUMBs) worldwide, and over 130 in the USA, with two underground bases being built per year in the U.S. at the moment. The average depth of the bases are 4-1/4 miles underground (some shallower and some deeper). The bases are on average the size of a medium-sized city. A nuclear-powered drill is used to dig underground. This drill goes through rock at a tremendous rate of speed and literally melts the rock away to form a smooth glass-like surface around the edges of the tunnels.[3]

The largest facilities include Cheyenne Mountain in Colorado, Camp David in Maryland, Los Alamos Laboratories connected to Dulce, New Mexico, National Security Agency (NSA) Headquarters at Fort Mead, Maryland and the Federal Emergency Management Agency's (FEMA) Command Center at Mount Weather in northern Virginia, just to name a few. But there are more than 1,477 DUMBs worldwide that can be confirmed, and since the military was constructing more than two DUMBs per year in the 1990s, and since this statistic is over two decades old, there could be more than 1,600 DUMBs on Earth as of 2020. Some of the largest worldwide by size include: Dulce in New Mexico; Brecon Beacons in Wales; Los Alamos in New Mexico, which is a base

••
2   Wilcock, David, "Gripping New Adventure as Space Program Insider Tours Mars Colony" *Divine Cosmos.com*, June 22, 2015.
3   Casbolt, James, "Underground Bases, Missing Children and Extra-Terrestrials: What You Need to Know for Your Future" **https://nesa-ranews.blogspot.com/2013/03/underground-bases-missing-children-and.html**

that goes two miles underground and is the size of a small city; Pine Gap in Australia; The Snowy Mountains in Australia; The Nyala range in southern Africa; West of Kindu in the African Congo; Next to the Libyan border in Egypt; Mount Blanc in Switzerland; Narvik in Scandinavia; Gotland Island in Sweden, and many other places. These projects are being run by a secret, unelected international governing body connected to the U.N.

ALTERNATIVE 3

Roswell and the subsequent crashed UFOs gave the U.S. Military the excuse to form the Secret Shadow Government and the power to form a National Security State to provide for their needs at the expense of American taxpayers and other nefarious means. They have used the UFO phenomena, which started in full force in 1947 at Roswell, as their phony reason to impose "national security" as a false cloak to cover their increasing crimes against the American people.

The Apollo Program officially ended in 1972 with the Apollo 17 being the last mission to the Moon and back. However, NASA had planned three more missions, Apollo 18, Apollo 19 and Apollo 20, to the back side of the Moon. According to whistleblowers, the Apollo missions had discovered ancient artificial structures on the Moon and wanted to explore them without public knowledge. Apollo 20 is considered one of the most controversial UFO cover-ups in history. In 2007, several videos were uploaded to YouTube, and the user who provided them claimed it was actual footage from the Apollo 20 mission. The grainy videos were apparently caught on 16 mm film and show the inside of the Apollo 20 command module as well as what appears to be the intricate architecture of a long-deserted lunar city. One whistleblower identified himself as former astronaut, William Rutledge, and according to his testimony, the mission took place in 1976 as a secret Soviet-American joint venture. He was chosen to be part of the team due to being an atheist, which was a rarity among astronauts in the 1970s. Why would NASA require someone who didn't believe in God for this mission? Would a believer have lost his faith?

Rutledge said that the Apollo 14 mission had passed over the southern polar region of the Moon, revealing numerous abandoned space ships and cities comprised of towering structures. The Apollo 20 mission landed near the Delporte Crater and its mission was to explore a cigar-shaped mother ship that had been abandoned for 1.5 million years. Once inside it, the astronauts found two alien bodies. The male was dead but preserved, and the female was described as being in a state of suspended animation, neither alive nor dead. They recovered the female, dubbed "Mona Lisa." Rutledge reported that she had a humanoid body, six fingers and her features were similar to those of a human, although she had no nostrils. She was covered in a wax-like substance. She was attached to the pilot controls of the spaceship, with several tubes going into her body. She was brought back to Earth for further examination.

As far as physically traveling to other planets, or even time travel, cosmonaut Andrew D. Basiago took part in Project Pegasus, and lists the seven ways inter-planetary travel was possible over a half century ago. (Imagine the extent and sophistication of new developments up to the present time.) Here is Mr. Basiago's list:

> By 1970, DARPA's Project Pegasus had developed eight modalities of time travel. They were: (1) Remote viewing (psychic time travel); (2) Spinning/out-of-body-experience (astral time travel); (3) The Montauk chair (psychic time travel); (4) The chronovisor (physio-virtual time travel); (5) The Tesla teleporter (physical time travel); (6) The stargate (physical time travel); (7) The plasma confinement chamber (physical time travel); and (8) The jump room (physical time travel). They were derived via an intelligence funnel into which data from numerous sources were placed. These sources included ancient sources (Sumerian, Babylonian, Egyptian), extraterrestrial sources (UFO crash retrieval, human-ET liai-

son), foreign technology sources (Nazi German, Soviet Russian), contemporary
sources (Tesla, Ernetti, Gemelli, Fermi, etc.) and project sources.

The price tag for implementing Alternatives 1, 2, and 3 has been in the making for nearly a century. The USA grabbed the gold in 1934 and put that gold up as collateral to get more paper money, because the Cabal wanted more funding for the Secret Space Program. They built underground bases and space ships and traveled to Earth's moon and to Mars. Top estimates calculate they spent over $1,000 trillion each year (3 billion dollars every day). So, we average people who are working at our jobs should know that half of our money went to this Secret Space Program. All this money taken from citizens, through their taxes and other means, have enabled about 100 people in the Cabal to go to the Moon and Mars. What's more, according to insiders who report to David Wilcock, over a hundred different off-planet colonies, each with at least tens of thousands of staff (if not hundreds of thousands), now exist throughout our solar system.[4]

WHERE DID ALL THE MONEY GO?

To find the true U.S. deficit, a Michigan State University economist teamed up with multiple researchers, including Catherine Austin Fitts, former Assistant Secretary of Housing and Urban Development. They found trillions of unaccounted-for dollars missing from Housing and the Defense Department and going towards black budget programs. These are called Special Access Programs (SAPs). There are unacknowledged and waived projects. These programs do not exist publicly, but they do indeed exist. They are better known as "deep black programs." A 1997 U.S. Senate report described them as "so sensitive that they are exempt from standard reporting requirements to the Congress."

When we consider the bottomless abyss of the black budget, or when we take into consideration that every underground base requires nearly 20 billion dollars of funding to construct, or when we consider the phenomenal cost of equipment and staffing the bases, and when we consider that while none of these monetary figures exist on any accounting books, that trillions of dollars go missing on a yearly basis from the Pentagon and the Defense Department—we need only consider what is beneath our feet, to understand that greed alone is not the end game for the elite.

For over a century, the immensely powerful United States has been doing the bidding of the elite international bankers. In order to take America into a war that will ravage the planet, these Illuminati international bankers are bent on destroying the U.S. Constitution and transforming it into a dictatorship, where civil liberties and human rights are being systematically taken away. After 9/11, in less than two decades, the country has changed beyond belief. Evidence of this can be found in the Patriot Act, National Defense Authorization Acts, the Department of Homeland Security, unconstitutional surveillance of all citizens, the arming to the teeth of domestic police agencies, constant intimidation and humiliation of the public, body scanners at airports, and pat downs—all policies which are pre-meditated and well-thought out schemes for destroying the self-respect and remnant courage of the American people. Once the USA is controlled by the Deep State, (Mossad/MI6/CIA/NATO), the rest is likely to follow according to their globalist plans.[5]

The entire world is teetering on the brink of bankruptcy. All the money is gone. As of 2020, the USA alone is on the books for at least $20 trillion dollars in debt, and another $21 trillion for black budgets, as discovered by Mark Skidmore. Remember, the Cabal's own "Too Big to Fail" mega-corporate banks didn't have anything left in 2008, and needed a 29 trillion-dollar "Too Big to Fail" bailout. Yet, in practical terms, this makes no sense. All

4   Wilcock, David, "Personal and Global Attacks Become Lethal: Is the Disclosure War Reaching a Climax? [Part I]" *Divine Cosmos.com*, September 23, 2017.

5   The scientific papers of Steven J. Smith, including "Underground Infrastructure: The missing forty trillion dollars" can be found here: **https://web.archive.org/web/20101118041511/http://www.commerceware.net/** <and> **http://www.whale.to/b/smith_sj_h.html**

that money had to go somewhere. Twenty-nine trillion is nearly half of the entire wealth of the planet in any given year, as measured in World GDP (Gross Domestic Product).

As David Wilcock noted, if you play "follow the money," the obvious answer to the problem is that they had to spend it on something. He observes:

> What if it was learned that countless trillions of dollars of our money, since as early as the 1950s, have been spent on developing vastly superior technology to anything we see today? What if the scope, depth and sophistication of this build-out is vastly bigger than most of us could even imagine—and indeed extends throughout our solar system? We are literally talking about enough money for the .001 percent to build entire countries—entire civilizations—if they had the land and raw materials to do so. And that may well be the point. The cities are either underground or off-planet. It is as simple as that. Yet, for some reason, the idea that we have been lied to about something this massive in size seems to defy people's emotional threshold completely.

THE MOON AND MARS

Our world is not how it's being presented. Many subjects that once and still are deemed a "conspiracy" (meaning, in this context, alleged evil developments) are clearly not a conspiracy; they are facts. Strange things happening on the Moon and numerous UFO sightings, for example, are two of several great examples. Among the most renowned people to speak of a complex moon base is conspiracy author and lecturer, William Cooper, a Naval Intelligence Officer, who disclosed that the U.S. Navy Intelligence Community knows of the alien base, and much more. The term used to describe the Moon base is "Luna," and according to Cooper, its main objective is to mine underground for certain materials. He also speaks of a massive mother ship found in the vicinity of the moon, used by the aliens to store up materials, and also travel to Earth in small "flying saucers" found on the main ship. William Cooper revealed:

> Luna is the alien base on the far side of the moon. It was seen and filmed by the Apollo astronauts. A base and a mining operation using very large machines, and the very large alien craft described in sightings reports as mother ships exist there. ...Alternative 3 was to exploit the alien and conventional technology in order for a select few to leave the earth and establish colonies in outer space. I am not able to either confirm or deny the existence of "batch consignments" of human slaves, which would be used for the manual labor as a part of the plan. The moon, code-named ADAM, was the object of primary interest, followed by the planet Mars, code-named EVE. I am now in possession of official NASA photographs of one of the moon bases.[6]

The Nazis were the first government to develop flying craft using anti-gravity, thanks to various discoveries they invented or acquired. One of their sources was Viktor Schauberger's work. Some of it was from extraterrestrials who had contacted the Nazis, allegedly some of the reptilian groups. The ETs made treaties with the Nazis. And in fact, the original Lunar Operations Center on the Moon is still there. It's ruined now and has fallen into disuse, but still appears as a swastika-shaped building on the Moon. The moon is absolutely loaded with extraterrestrial encampments, all on the dark side.

Ever since the Apollo moon missions, there have been countless rumors regarding one or several alien bases located on the dark side of the moon—the side we never get to see. It's no secret that, in 2009, NASA publicly bombed a portion of the moon for reasons that remain unclear. These could be retaliation strikes. A U.S. government document released by WikiLeaks in October, 2019, reveals the U.S. had a base on the moon that the Soviets allegedly destroyed in 1979. Other leaked images originating from NASA's headquarters reveal different structures found there, which appear to be artificial in nature.

6　Cooper, William, quotes on Alternative 3: **https://alienshift.com/id40.html**

Huge structures discovered in close-up photos of lunar features indicate that ancient alien artifacts have graced the surface of our satellite. It is only a small step to consider that the same builder race of aliens has come to Earth. Life permeates in the universe. Indeed, there has been the detection of microbial respiration on the Red Planet, and meteorites found in Antarctica were discovered to have life from Mars. In short, Mars and the Moon were slated for colonization. After all, Alternative 3 was the plan to build a "transfer station" on the backside of the moon, build an underground base on Mars and remove a certain limited "Noah's Ark" cross section of Earth's population (artists, scientists, engineers, writers, doctors) to Mars as a survival colony in the event of "catastrophe" on Earth.

The problem is that the Cabal is essentially in control of our space program. The main base that we have on the moon is called the LOC (Lunar Operations Center). This is where people from our group and other groups actually rendezvous before they go elsewhere. The elite globalists also have a secret pact to exploit the moon for its minerals. This pact may be signed by other ET species residing in our solar system, which could explain why this alliance has a secretive nature. However, since greed is a common trait among humans, it shouldn't be long before someone is excluded from this alliance and eventually discloses this secret project to humanity.

According to Dr. John E. Brandenburg, Ph.D., his analysis of recent Mars isotopic, gamma ray and imaging data supports the hypothesis that perhaps two immense thermonuclear explosions occurred on Mars in the distant past. It appears that these explosions were targeted on sites of previously-reported artifacts. Analysis rules out large unstable "natural nuclear reactors." Instead, data is consistent with mixed fusion-fission explosions. Imagery at the radioactive centers of the explosions shows no craters, consistent with "airbursts." Explosions appear correlated with the sites of reported artifacts at Cydonia Mensa and Galaxias Chaos. Analysis of new images from Odyssey, MRO and Mars Express orbiters now show strong evidence of eroded archeological objects at these sites. Taken together, the data requires that the hypothesis of Mars as the site of an ancient planetary nuclear massacre, must now be considered.

THE STRANGE ACCOUNT OF PHIL SCHNEIDER

Phil Schneider was a geologist and explosives expert. He worked as a Skunk Works structural engineer and underground tunneling expert for the U.S. government and the UN. He participated in the construction of many DUMBs in North America and other countries. He would say that, of the 1,477 underground bases in his time around the world, 129 deep underground facilities were located in the United States, and he claimed to have worked on 13. Two of these bases were major, including the much-rumored bioengineering facility at Dulce, New Mexico. There, according to Schneider, "grey" humanoid extraterrestrials worked side by side with American technicians. In one tunnel offshoot, he explained how large metallic vats were found filled with human body parts, generally the body segments containing glands. In the vats were high-tech stirring devices that stopped the blood from coagulating. In addition to the vats of human body parts, there are a myriad of other specialty science projects taking place at the Dulce base, including, but not limited to: Atomic manipulation, cloning, studies of the human aura, advanced mind control applications, animal/human crossbreeding, visual and audio wiretapping, and other nefarious activities.

During August of 1979, Phil Schneider was commissioned as a "blackops" contractor to take part in a deep drilling operation near the small town of Dulce, New Mexico. During the sinking of the initial four shafts, it became clear that many of the lasers and mechanical components of the Tunnel Boring Machine (TBM) were coming up broken. Mr. Schneider and a number of other geologists were elected to travel down the shaft via a basket to analyze the problem. Upon arriving at the bottom of the shaft (which was

4 kilometers deep), a "horrible" discovery was made. It became immediately apparent that they had broken through into a large cavern that was infested with aliens. The creatures were described as type 1 seven-foot "tall greys." Startled and fearing for his own life, Schneider was able to kill two of the creatures, but was hit by what he described as a light green cobalt radiation beam that was fired by one of the aliens. Badly injured and burned, but still alive, Phil was placed in the elevator basket and began the long trip to the surface. As other armed men came down, an intense firefight continued to rage in the cavern below. In the commotion, a total of 66 secret service agents, along with members of the FBI and black berets, were struck and killed by the aliens. Phil was one of only three survivors of the event. This alleged confrontation has come to be known as the opening salvo of the "Dulce Wars."[7]

His team was told to drill into the desert to build an auxiliary base in the southern end of Dulce, on top of an already existing underground base there. He would discover that the already-existing base had been built by the U.S. government in the 1940s under "Operation Blue Note," but afterwards had been taken over by greys and reptilians. Over a period of two days, Phil and his team had drilled four holes in the desert that went down several thousand feet, approaching 2-1/2 miles. The problem began when one of the holes kept bringing up dirty dust, putrid odors and broken off machine bits that were sent down the hole. Functioning boring machines and lasers came back up damaged when they returned from the deep hole.

A probe was then sent down in a contained apparatus, but the apparatus came back with the probe totally missing. Eventually, people were sent down. Phil was the first person to go. He was lowered down into the cave and when he got there, standing around ten feet away were two seven-foot greys. He was petrified, but managed to empty one clip from his pistol into the greys. As he was reloading, one of the greys hit Phil with some kind of a particle beam weapon, which gave him a very high dose of nuclear radiation poisoning, similar to cobalt radiation, but even worse. Phil's lung was destroyed—burnt out of him—and he has a huge scar running down his chest, which he shows at his lectures, and which are available to view on his YouTube lecture videos. Also, his fingers on his left hand were burnt off and his bones were burned; he was basically cooked. Schneider describes his encounter with extraterrestrials in the following excerpt:

> I was involved in building an addition to the deep underground military base at Dulce, which is probably the deepest base. My job was to go down the holes and check the rock samples, and recommend the explosive to deal with the particular rock. As I was headed down there, we found ourselves amidst a large cavern that was full of outer-space aliens, otherwise known as large Greys. I shot two of them. At that time, there were 30 people down there. About 40 more came down after this started, and all of them got killed. We had surprised a whole underground base of existing aliens. Later, we found out that they had been living on our planet for a long time, perhaps a million years. This could explain a lot of what is behind the theory of ancient astronauts.

At Dulce, Schneider always maintained that "grey" humanoid extraterrestrials worked side by side with American technicians until 1979. He said a misunderstanding arose when a certain agent refused to surrender his firearm. In the ensuing shootout, 66 scientists, Secret Service and FBI agents, plus Delta Force Black Berets, were killed along with an unspecified number of "greys." It was here he received a beam-weapon blast to the chest which later caused his cancer. Many have confirmed that a large scar indeed existed. Phil Schneider was one of only three people to survive the 1979 fire fight between the large Greys and U.S. intelligence and military at the Dulce underground base. He was in radiation isolation therapy for over 400 days.

••••••••••••••••••••••••••••••••••

7   Hamilton, William H. III "Top-Secret Military Underground Facilities." Excerpt from *ALIEN MAGIC* on the Phil Schneider story.

Phil was "suicided" (likely by the CIA) on January 17, 1996, in his apartment in Wilsonville, outside of Portland, Oregon. It appeared to be an execution-style murder. He was found dead in his apartment with a rubber catheter hose wrapped three times around his neck and half-knotted tightly in front. According to sources, it appeared that he repeatedly suffered torture before he was finally killed. All his lecture materials were removed, but no valuables. Seven months prior to his death, Schneider presented a lecture on the underground forces he had discovered at Dulce. Schneider maintained that 13 previous attempts had been made on his life, including the removal of the nuts from one of the front wheels of his automobile. He had stated publicly that he was a marked man and did not expect to live long. "If I ever 'commit suicide,'" Schneider told a close friend, "I'll have been murdered."

Philip Schneider died shortly after conducting several other controversial lectures throughout the U.S., including at Denver, where he covered topics such as the underground city under Denver Airport (DIA), space defense, black helicopters, railroad cars built with shackles, dangerous extraterrestrials and the enormous secret black budget. He was reportedly strangled by a catheter found wrapped tightly around his neck—if that is even possible done alone. Yet, his bizarre solo-strangulation was dismissed by the authorities as a suicide. If the circumstances of his death seem highly controversial, they are matched by the controversy over his public statements uttered on the lecture circuit in the months leading up to his death. At the site of his murder, he was also robbed of the alien display items he discussed at his lectures.

THE NIGHTMARE HALL

The Dulce Base is an alleged joint human and alien underground facility under the Archuleta Mesa on the Colorado-New Mexico border near the small town of Dulce, New Mexico. Claims of alien activity there first arose from businessman Paul Bennewitz, who had ties with the nearby Kirtland Air Force Base and Sandia Labs in Albuquerque. Another first-hand reporter was security guard, Thomas Castello, who said he had proof that a joint alien/U.S. military underground base existed there, perhaps devoted to genetics. The theories regarding Dulce sometimes state that alien technology was traded for permission to engage in human and animal mutilations. A battle was said to have taken place there between aliens and humans, though the time of this alleged encounter varies from the 1970s to the 1980s, or there could have been on-and-off skirmishes. Some sources allege that horrific genetic experiments are conducted in the lower levels of the facility (usually level 6 or 7, depending on the source); these levels are sometimes referred to as the "Nightmare Hall." Researchers Bill Hamilton and Tal Levesque (AKA Jason Bishop) received reports from workers at the Dulce DUMB who worked there in the mid-1970's when it was being jointly run by the CIA, together with tall grey and reptilian aliens. This was before the ET's completely took the base over and kicked the humans out after the Dulce Wars.

The workers said the Dulce facility goes down at least seven levels. Level six is privately called "Nightmare Hall" amongst workers. They tell of bizarre genetic experimentations that have produced multi-legged humans that look half-human and half-octopus, reptilian-humanoids, and furry creatures with hands like humans that can cry like a baby or mimic human words. They also reported a huge mixture of lizard-humans in cages, several cages of winged-humans, 3-1/2 to 7 feet tall, bat-like creatures and gargoyle-like beings. In level seven are thousands of rows of human and human-genetic mixtures in cold storage and humanoid embryo storage vats with embryos in various stages of development. Other workers said they witnessed scenes even more terrifying than this and refused to talk about them. One worker told Bill Hamilton:

I frequently encountered humans in cages, usually dazed or drugged, but sometimes they cried and begged for help. We were told they were insane and involved in high-risk drug tests to cure insanity. We were told never to speak to them at all. At the beginning we believed the story. Finally in 1978 a small group of workers discovered the truth.

Thomas Castello was one of the security workers at the Dulce facility. Thomas worked on MK Rand for seven years, headed by the Rand Corporation in California. He was transferred to Dulce in 1977. He estimated there were more than 18,000 short greys at Dulce, and also saw tall reptilians. Thomas knew of seven levels but said there could have been more. He said the aliens were on levels five, six and seven. The lower you go, the higher the security clearance needed. The only sign in English is above the tube shuttle system and says, "To Los Alamos." The tube shuttle travels at Mach 2.7 speeds. Most signs around the Dulce facility are in the alien symbol language and also a universal system understood by humans and ETs. Thomas said the other shuttle connections from Dulce went to Page, Arizona; Area 51, Nevada; Taos, Carlsbad and Datil, New Mexico; Colorado Springs and Creed, Colorado. Thomas also said there are a vast number of tube shuttle connections under the United States, which extend into a global system of tunnels to other underground bases in other countries.

Thomas Castello said that below the second level of the Dulce facility, everyone is weighed naked then given a uniform. Any change in weight is noted and if there is a change in weight of three pounds or more the people are X-rayed. At the entrance to all sensitive areas are scales and the person's weight must match with their ID card and code to gain entry.

Thomas Castello smuggled many things out of the Dulce facility before he escaped, including 27 sheets of 8x10 photos of alien and genetic creatures in vats. He also got out one silent surveillance camera video tape, which begins with showing computer banks, then vats, multiple shots of Nightmare Hall, two shots of greys, one shot of the terminal sign saying, "To Los Alamos," and 30 seconds of the shuttle train arriving. He also smuggled out 25 pages of diagrams, chemical formulas, schematics and alien equipment. Perhaps most interesting was a copy of the new government-alien treaty with signatures. There were two pages of original documents signed by Ronald Reagan (then governor of California). Each page has Ronald Reagan's signature, plus other political signatures and four alien signatures. He also showed his "flash gun," a laser-type weapon used by the security officers at Dulce. Thomas Castello vanished without a trace in the late 1980s, soon after coming forward. He is presumed dead.

THE DULCE WARS

Like UFO sightings, sometimes underground bases are "ours" or "theirs." In the case of Dulce, it is a combination of both. According to Project Aquarius drafted in 1966, there was a plan for investigation of UFOs, as well as to construct underground bases, sometimes with pre-existing legacy bases. It was to be carried out and funded by the CIA. Paul Bennewitz was a source for the Project Aquarius information. A second build-out project was slated to begin after December, 1969, when Project Grudge and Project Blue Book were closed. The base was built northwest of Dulce in joint agreement between the CIA and aliens living in a natural cavern system already existing. The modern base extension is located underneath the Jicarilla Apache Indian Reservation. The cave entrance is on Mount Archuleta (or Archuleta Mesa). Many people have supposedly witnessed UFOs in the area. The base gets water and electricity from the Navajo River and dumps waste water back into the same river. The U.S. government occupies the upper levels of the underground base, while the aliens control the lower levels.

At Dulce, military helicopters have also been seen, "unusually milling around" the deserted area, as well as UFO craft coming and going. Vibrations from the ground near the town of Dulce have allegedly caused speculations of an underground facility; however, these are more likely minor earthquakes, which are known to occur in the area. There is a claim that the area was partially scanned with ground-penetrating radar, producing "interesting" results, but these results are not currently available.

Located almost two miles beneath Archuleta Mesa on the Jicarilla Apache Indian Reservation near Dulce, New Mexico, was an installation classified so secret, its existence would be one of the most protected projects in the world. When the truth was evident that sub-humans and other creatures were being produced from abducted human females, impregnated against their will, a secret resistance group formed within the military and intelligence agencies of the U.S. Government that did not approve of the deals that had been made with the "Off-Worlders."

Many details of the lore surrounding the Dulce Wars, including vast underground bases with many subterranean levels including caged humans and battles with alien or underground creatures, suggest several battles took place. Although many humans died, so did many aliens. The Dulce Wars ended the alien hope for using the Earth as a breeding tank for a subspecies, or for their own take-over of the planet at any time in the near future. While the Greys restarted a breeding program in 1993, and some of the lower levels of the Dulce Facility were reopened by 1998, the numbers are in the tens or hundreds rather than the thousands. One of the key lessons to be learned from the Dulce Battles is that as long as there are small, highly trained and well-equipped human forces, that can, may, or will go into action on their own accord to protect the people of the Earth, and thus easy conquest of the planet becomes difficult.[8]

Thomas Costello, the security guard, spoke of an incident that occurred in 1979 in which 44 scientists had been killed, along with 22 Delta Force personnel. This was the main battle in what has become known as the "Dulce Wars," but it wasn't a war. According to Costello, and later backed up by Bob Lazar, who read about the incident in a briefing paper at S-4, a Grey alien being was giving instruction of some type to 44 scientists at Dulce. Apparently, a security guard with Delta Force, who helped patrol and provide security for the Dulce base, entered the room with a side arm of some type. It was known by all Dulce personnel that no firearms of any kind were allowed anywhere near the Greys. Whatever the reason for the security guard's mistake, the Grey immediately killed him as well as the 44 scientists. Seeing the disaster taking place on the security cameras, other Delta Force personnel came for revenge, but the alien killed them also. Both Costello's account and the account read by Lazar at S-4 said all 66 deaths were caused by "head wounds." There was no elaboration.

OTHER TESTIMONIES FROM UNDERGROUND BASES

Deep in the underground bases there are various areas for living space and technologies to keep the surface entrances cloaked from our sight. This includes at least 1,400 DUMBS worldwide, 188 known DUMBS in the U.S., with 2 underground bases being built per year in the U.S. The average depth of bases is 4-1/2 miles underground. Each DUMB base costs between $17 & $26 billion to build, which is funded primarily by MI6/CIA drug money and human trafficking money. Each underground base employs 10,000 to 18,000 workers. They are sometimes built into pre-existing massive honeycomb-type limestone caverns deep beneath the Earth's surface. These caverns can be 20-40 miles deep, and several miles wide—ready for mass habitation. Some are naturally lit by bio-

8   "The Battle at Dulce to Stop an Alien Breeding Program Using Thousands of Young Women." https://beforeitsnews.com/conspiracy-theories/2019/09/the-battle-at-dulce-to-stop-an-alien-breeding-program-using-thousands-of-young-women-2515519.html.

luminescent bacteria that grow on the upper areas of the caves. This bacterium has naturally-occurring but weird flora that is mostly white, yet life from the surface can also be brought in and do quite well. The caves also enjoy excellent protection against floods, earthquakes, volcanoes, tsunamis and other natural disasters on the Earth's surface.[9]

One of the earliest American underground facilities for "Continuity of Government" was built at Raven Rock in Pennsylvania. The military refer to it as "Site R." Raven Rock was chosen because it is made of greenstone, a type of granite that is the fourth hardest rock on earth. Construction started in 1950, and engineers had completed a series of tunnels and a three-story building by 1953. Two more three-story buildings were completed by 1963. The complex lies 650 feet beneath the 1,529-foot-high summit of Raven Rock and can be entered through four portals. The mountain has everything needed to survive a catastrophe: trucks and cars; some of the best dining in the Army; chemical suits; a fitness center; a medical facility; a barbershop; legal services; a chapel; designated smoking areas; a convenience store; six 1,000 kilowatt generators; and 50 kilometers of cable on 180 telephone poles. And remember, this is one of the early underground sites, and probably does not compare with some of the new underground cities that have been constructed in more recent years.

One of the first of nearly 100 Federal Relocation Centers was built in rural Virginia's Mount Weather. It took years to complete, but when finished in 1958 it resembled a city more than an emergency installation. Mount Weather was equipped with such amenities as private apartments and dormitories, streets and sidewalks, cafeterias and hospitals, a water purification system, a power plant and general office buildings. The site includes a small lake fed by fresh water from underground springs. It even has its own Very High Speed Transit (VHST) system connection and small electric cars that run on rechargeable batteries and make regular shuttle runs throughout the city.

As recently as 1992, the mainstream media reported on the existence of a Cold War secret: the government had built a $14 million underground bunker in West Virginia and maintained it for more than three decades for Congress to use, in the event of a nuclear attack. This hideaway Capitol was built under the fashionable Greenbrier Resort in White Sulphur Springs, Virginia, about 250 miles from Washington. Its location was known only to a handful of the nation's highest-ranking officials. From 1958 onward, the very existence of this facility was a closely-guarded secret. Very few in Congress or the Executive branch knew of the program. The Greenbrier bunker has living quarters and work space for 800 people, as well as separate meeting halls for the House and Senate.

We are always willing to release more about the other side's secrets than our own. In Moscow, the Kremlin and other key government buildings are linked by underground rail tunnels to an area about six miles outside the city center called Ramenki. This is the site of a vast subterranean bunker system designed for the country's leaders and their families. It was described as an underground city about 500 acres in size, built at several levels from 230-395 feet. This bunker could shelter as many as 120,000 people! That is the size of a moderate American city.[10]

According to the *Napa Sentinel*, a secret underground installation was constructed near the Oakville Grade in Napa County, California, and is being used by the Government for direct satellite communication, the Continuity of Government (COG) program in case of nuclear attack or other disasters, and secure communication links with the outside world in case of disaster. This might have been tested during the Wine

---

9 The Dulce Underground Base—how deep does this rabbit hole go? https://alien-ufo-sightings.com/2015/12/the-dulce-underground-base-how-deep-does-this-rabbit-hole-go/

10 Hamilton, William H. III, "Underground Facilities." Excerpts from *Great Dreams:* http://www.greatdreams.com/reptlan/reptilian_hierarchy.htm

Country fires in October, 2017, that were witnessed and filmed to have been started with Directed Energy Weapons. Mysterious helicopter flights have been seen going in and out of the area. There are geothermal features in the area that could supply natural heat and water for the underground base, making it energy sustainable. Supposedly, the secret government site is replacing other installations and combining them into more centralized underground centers. The rumors that an underground city exists under the Enchantment Resort in Boynton Canyon near Sedona, Arizona, may not be so far-fetched after all. Eggs cannot all be put in one basket.

Not all underground sites are shelters. The Yucca Mountain Site Characterization Project took a first step in November, 1993, when it started construction on the entrance pad for its Exploratory Studies Facility (ESF). This pad is the launching point for 14 miles of tunnels that will be drilled directly under Yucca Mountain. The tunnels will measure 24-30 feet in diameter for some and 16-18 feet in diameter for others. This project will eventually cover some 70 acres of surface and underground facilities. This DoE project will contain alcoves for experiments located along the tunnels. The work underground continues, but there are also reports that some DUMBs have been taken out by the White Hats. The 7.1 and 6.4 earthquakes in Ridgecrest, CA, were explosions destroying the massive multi-layer base under China Lake Naval Station, known for mind control and weapons research. It was neutralized and then destroyed by tactical nukes, causing a series of quakes on the 4th of July, 2019, and for the next few days. Many other moderate earthquakes in unusual quake areas are likely other Cabal-controlled bases being destroyed.

The resistance is coming from the U.S. Special Forces leading the vanguard in taking out the Cabal-controlled bases. They are using weapons very few have knowledge of, advancing through the immense Illuminati forces and vast interconnected Deep Underground Military Bases (DUMBs) complex that is connected with nationwide highway tunnels with Magnetic Levitating Trains (Maglevs), capable of speeds up to 17,000 MPH, that connect to all facilities and DUMBs throughout the world. These facilities have incredible stores of food, water, DNA and seed banks; all fully supplied with autonomous free energy supplies. The Black Budget is a secretive budget that garners 25% of the gross national product of the United States and currently spends $1.25 trillion per year—the DUMB projects consume upwards of 90% of this, according to new insider testimony.[11]

TO BORE A TUNNEL

Skeptics have expressed doubts about the existence of extensive underground tunneling and cavitation. They always ask, "Where is all the dirt?" This method of asking a question to disprove an allegation is misleading and faulty logic at best. A favorite question by skeptics about the alien presence is, "Why don't they land on the White House lawn?" There are many exopolitical reasons for them not to do that. One of the new methods of tunneling that has been under study is "nuclear tunnel boring." U.S. Patent No. 3,693,731, dated Sept. 26, 1972, describes a method and apparatus for tunneling by melting. It says:

A machine and method for drilling bore holes and tunnels by melting in which a housing is provided for supporting a heat source and a heated end portion, and in which the necessary melting heat is delivered to the walls of the end portion at a rate sufficient to melt rock, and during operation of which the molten material may be disposed adjacent the boring zone in cracks in the rock, and as a vitreous wall lining of the tunnel so formed. The heat source can be electrical or nuclear, but for deep drilling is preferably a nuclear reactor.

11 Cabal's DUMBS (Deep Underground Military Bases). Gene Decode. *B2T Show* Oct 23, 2019. https://www.bitchute.com/video/qbAR-0CoKV13n/

The techniques used for covert tunnel construction are very different than civilian tunnel construction. Covert tunnel construction makes use of a boring machine that actually melts earth and rock (by chemical valence disruption), thereby forming a glass-like tunnel wall. This has several advantages over civilian tunnel-boring methods. From the perspective of secrecy, the biggest advantage is that little or no waste material (rock, dirt, etc.) is produced by the boring process, thereby alleviating the need for above ground disposal sites or trailing mounds. Another advantage is that tunnels can be bored through loose rock, sand, etc. or other locations that would be unsuitable for civilian boring methods (for instance, a river bed). Large underground cavities are also constructed using this technique. The melted rock is forced into cracks wherein heat is given up to the crack surfaces and freezes as glass at some distance from the penetrator. This amazing boring device is capable of drilling at depths totally inaccessible using previous drilling techniques, even, according to the patent claims, down to 30,000 meters.

Still, covert tunnel boring produces several phenomena that are detectable by surface observation. Yet, these phenomena are transitory, and will disappear shortly after tunnel completion. However, the presence of these phenomena is unmistakable evidence that covert tunnel construction is taking place. The method used to melt earth and rock employs electro-magnetic energy to disrupt the chemical bonds within the material. This method produces little or no heat as a byproduct of the melting process, and can therefore remain covert. However, it does cause the evaporation of water to take place at an accelerated rate. Since the method is electro-magnetic, there is a certain amount of "leakage" radiation, and this is detectable by the odd effect it produces on surface water. In particular, the water will appear to rise from the ground as wisps of steam, even though the ground is cold. This phenomenon is very noticeable during rain storms on cold winter nights. The steam does not rise into the air, as it would if the ground was actually warm, but instead forms a layer just above the surface.

According to the scientific papers of the late Steven J. Smith, who died under suspicious circumstances, another side effect of covert tunnel boring is a peculiar rippling in road surfaces. This rippling is very slight, and most noticeable while driving at a highway speed of 55 MPH. It is more heard than felt. What sets this ripple apart from normal highway bumps and imperfections is its consistency. Assuming a constant driving speed, the ripple is perfectly constant. In some cases, the rippled road surface will continue for several miles, without the slightest change in pitch or intensity.

SUBTERRENE SOUNDS LIKE SUBMARINE

The modern nuclear tunnel boring machines were invented by scientists and engineers at Los Alamos. They named their new machine the "Subterrene." In 1975, a cost comparison was done between the Subterrene and other tunneling methods by A. A. Mathews, Inc. This report reveals that the initial experiments utilizing this technology were done in the early 1960s. This study reported that the Subterrene performs its job rapidly and economically. It further states that the economy comes from "the formation of a glass lining bonded to the ground and capable of providing initial and final ground support without the delay and cost of separate installations."

The Los Alamos Subterrene machine looks like a vicious giant mole that cannot be stopped. The beauty of the Subterrene is that, as it burrows through the rock hundreds of feet below the surface, its heat turns whatever stone it encounters into molten rock, or magma, which cools after the Subterrene has moved on. The resulting vitrification is a tunnel with a smooth, waterproof, glazed and reinforced lining. For power, the Subterrene can use a built-in miniature nuclear engine, or even fuel from a conventional power plant. Many have seen this machine and watched it in action. Its normal rate of speed is approximately ten kilometers per hour depending on the type of rock, sand and other obstacles. Nuclear power is not, however, a requirement for Subterrene tunneling. In fact, a Los Alamos symposium held in Atlantic City in 1986 proposed the construction of a Subterrene for tunnel melting for high-speed lunar subsurface transportation tunnels.

The nuclear Subterrenes build tunnels up to 40 feet in diameter as they melt the rock into a hard, glassy tunnel lining. Fully filtered air-intake shafts bring fresh air to the tunnels and underground facilities. Many of the underground sites are close to railroads, airports, seaports and have entrances trucks can drive many hundreds of miles. Certain DUMBs enable ships and submarines to sail right into their "harbors." The naval stations in Nevada and in the California desert are accessed by a massive underwater entrance off Point Mugu in Malibu, CA. Some of the entrances for trucks and aircraft are protected by holograms that look like the side of a mountain, but allow vehicles and craft to just enter right through them. The other style of hidden entrances are buildings where trucks drive in and are lowered via access shafts down into the underground areas. Security for facilities vary from Wackenhut to Homeland Security and others.

THE UNDERGROUND NETWORK

There are numerous witnesses who speak about a subterranean highway through America just like our own Interstate highway system, except it's all underground. This subterranean highway uses trucks, cars, and buses driven by electric motors, because of course, you wouldn't want gasoline fumes polluting tunnels. Trains are Maglev pollution free. There is also another style of transport for freight and passengers that are linked together in a worldwide network called the "Sub-Global System." It has checkpoints at each country entry. There are shuttle tubes that "shoot" the trains at incredible speed using magnetic levitation and the vacuum method. They travel many times in excess of the speed of sound. These underground systems that span the continent and beyond are named Trans America Underground Subway System (T.A.U.S.S.).[12]

Underground transportation has been discussed by academics and in the media. Engineers Robert Salter and Frank P. Davidson of MIT have both given papers on the Planetran concept for moving people rapidly underground. Salter describes the Planetran as an ultra-speed, electromagnetically propelled and levitated transportation system of the future. Elon Musk has proposed a system under Los Angeles, and beyond. Such a system could carry passengers across the United States in less than an hour in a quiet, economical, fuel-conservative, and nonpolluting manner. Planetran would require a tunnel over 3,500 kilometers in length, perhaps assembled from 100 40-kilometer long segments.

In 1978, Robert Salter of the Rand Corporation had called for the building of a subway from New York to Los Angeles magnetically levitated above the tracks. The trains would zip through the evacuated tunnels at speeds faster than an SST, crossing the country in less than one hour. Building such a train presents no special technological problems, but the cost of tunneling from coast to coast would be costly he said. To be economically feasible, engineers would have to develop a new way to dig. The federal government's Los Alamos Scientific Laboratory in New Mexico, however, may have an answer to this challenge if they would release what is already known. Interestingly, the Rand Corporation has the patents on most nuclear-powered laser boring machines that bore at over 60 MPH. Rather than speaking in future tense, Robert Salter should be explaining what has already been built.

....
12 Sauder, Richard, P.D. *Underground Bases & Tunnels: What is the Government Trying to Hide?* Adventures Unlimited, 2014.

CITIES on FAR SIDE of the MOON

ORIGINAL PHOTO

ENHANCED PHOTO

The idea of building subterranean living places is very old. From Derinkuyu of Cappadocia, Turkey, (pictured here) to the Hypogeums of Paola and Malta, there are countless examples of underground civilizations burrowing cities deep into the Earth.

These images were taken on NASA's 25th secret mission to the Moon, named "Syn 25." They show the end results filmed by astronauts going back to Earth. "A Moon base, Luna, was photographed by the Lunar Orbiter and filmed by the Apollo astronauts. Domes, spires, tall round structures which look like silos, huge T-shaped mining vehicles that left stitch-like tracks in the lunar surface, and extremely large as well as small alien craft appear in the official NASA photographs. It is a joint United States and Soviet base: The space program is a farce and an unbelievable waste of money. ...The Apollo astronauts were severely shaken by this experience, and their lives and subsequent statements reflect the depth of the revelation and the effect of the muzzle order which followed. They were ordered to remain silent or suffer the extreme penalty, death, which was termed an 'expediency.'" Excerpt from William Cooper's book *Behold A Pale Horse*.

In addition to subterranean bases, massive efforts have been made to construct bases beneath the sea, mostly off of island chains and deep along tectonic shelves.

Really look at the size of this machine, especially when you see the size of the man in front the machine. Then ask yourself exactly what is large enough that requires such a large tunnel? It is larger than two 18-wheel trucks back to back. What will the human workers transport inside a tunnel that large? Most tunneling activity is under military installations and all information is highly restricted. Former employees of said facilities have surfaced over the years to talk of massive underground installations in places like the Northrop facility in Antelope Valley, Southern California (reported to have 42 levels), and the Lockheed installation near Edwards, California.

There is ample evidence for alien bases on the Moon, such as numerous anomalies including "Transient Lunar Phenomenon" and moving glowing objects that have been observed coming from the Moon in reports dating as far back as the 1800s. In the Modern Age, there could also be human-made "Alternative 3" bases on the Moon. Astronaut Gordon Cooper and the French scientist Maurice Chatelain have made comments that NASA moon missions were followed by ET craft. This image is an artist's rendition of what a Moon base would look like, including entrances to underground facilities.

It was presumed these lunar cities have been there for about 500,000 years. Those light lines (maybe the streets) look like humongous illuminated tubes of some sort, which might be half submerged on the lunar surface. The light view also looks similar to the DUMBs network map here under the Earth. The spaceport is located in the crater Poincare. John Lear identifies the enlargement as showing a spaceport, a terminal with three wings, a saucer to the right and a control tower to the left. The baggage and arrivals note are an assumption. John Lear contends the original Lunar Orbiter photo has been airbrushed by NASA to cover up the spaceport and made to look like piles of dirt.

The first photo is the complete photo; the second is an enlargement of the photo with the terminal; the third photo is an enlargement of the terminal and control tower, and the fourth photo is the original photo (with a circle around the terminal), and under it the same photo with the names of the craters and a flat/long notation. The photo was taken by Lunar Orbiter on the far side. The fifth photo is a Clementine: Northern South Pole-Aitken Region map of the far side. Courtesy of Charles J. Byrne, from his book, *The Far Side of the Moon a Photographic Guide.*

Officially referred to by a handful of monikers including the Raven Rock Mountain Complex, Site R, and the Alternate Joint Communication Center, the facility was best described by the local press over a half century ago: the "Underground Pentagon." A DoD study obtained by George Washington University notes that "The plan was that the Battle Staffs of the service headquarters would evacuate the Pentagon as soon as an attack was confirmed, go to (Raven Rock), and there assume control." Two of the entrances can be seen from the air.

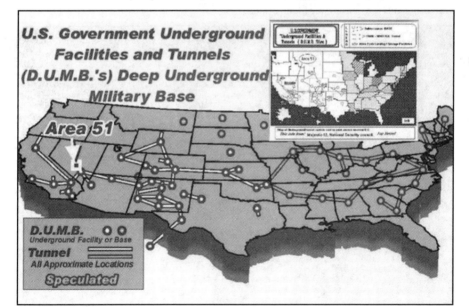

Excerpt from William Cooper's book, *Behold A Pale Horse*: "A multi-million dollar secret fund was organized and kept by the Military Office of the White House. This fund was used to build over 75-foot deep underground facilities. Presidents who asked were told the fund was used to build deep underground shelters for the President in case of war. Only a few were built for the President. Millions of dollars were funneled through this office to MJ-12, and then out to the contractors which was then used to build top-secret alien bases as well as top-secret DUMBs (Deep Underground Military Bases)."

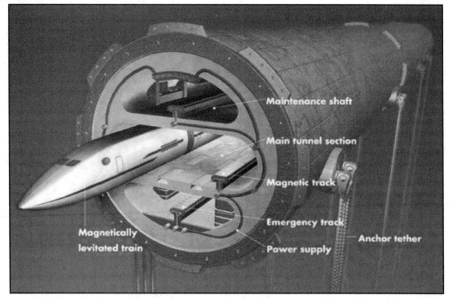

The 'Black Budget' currently consumes $1.25 trillion per year, and since each DUMB costs anywhere from $18 billion to $26 billion just to construct, these underground facilities are a major budget factor. Presently, there over 140 known deep underground military bases in the United States. The military has been building these bases day and night since the early 1940s. These bases are basically large cities underground, connected by high-speed magnetic levitation trains that can travel over Mach 2 speeds.

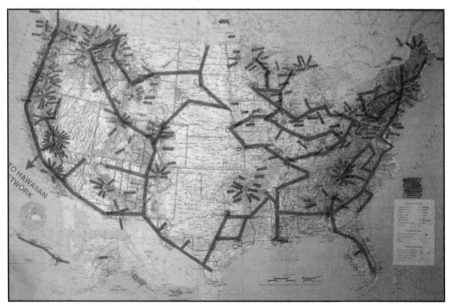

In November, 2019, Benjamin Fulford posted this image of the DUMB network, and wrote the following: "Resistance leaders, who say much of the ongoing Western civil war is taking place in underground bunkers, provided this map of U.S. underground facilities to illustrate. They say the most serious fighting is centered around the underground facilities in California, where Cabal strongholds like Google, PayPal, and Facebook are located. There are also underground bunkers in Switzerland, Greece, and Israel that are still fully under Cabal control, the sources say."

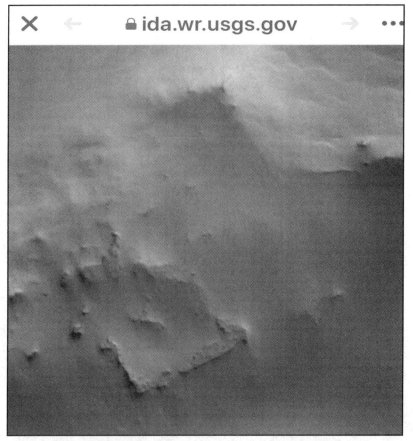

This is a photo taken directly with the MOC (Mars Orbital Camera). It appears to be the foundation of a very old structure. There was a highly-advanced civilization on Mars at one time in the distant past.

The blowup image from the moon shows a lunar spaceport and a connected underground base, as viewed by the Chinese lunar orbiter. The base notations are from John Lear.

Operation Argus was a series of United States low-yield, high-atmosphere nuclear weapons tests and missile tests secretly conducted, during August and September of 1958, over the South Atlantic Ocean. Alternative 1 was implemented to blast holes through the stratosphere to release heat and pollution. This was done by simultaneous detonations of atomic weapons in the Earth's high atmosphere of the ozone belt in areas where few would notice: Over Siberia, the deep Amazon, the Australian Outback and over both Poles. This is the cause of the ozone holes (not aerosol cans and other human causes, as reported by the Fake News Network).

MEET THE
NEW BOSS

"The Party seeks power entirely for its for its own sake. We are not interested in the good of others; we are interested solely in power. Not wealth or luxury or long life or happiness; only power, pure power. What pure power means you will understand presently. We are different from all oligarchies of the past in that we know what we are doing. All the others, even those who resembled ourselves, were cowards and hypocrites. The German Nazis and the Russian Communists came very close to us in their methods, but they never had the courage to recognize their motives. They pretended, perhaps they even believed, that they had seized power unwillingly and for a limited time, and just around the corner there lay a paradise where human beings would be free and equal. We are not like that. We know that no one ever seizes power with the intention of relinquishing it. One does not establish a dictatorship in order to safeguard a revolution; one makes a revolution in order to establish a dictatorship." –George Orwell, 1984

A S we have seen, a large amount of information indicates that not only are underground bases being manufactured, but these bases are being constructed under vast bodies of water as well. There are hundreds of these underground bases in existence around the world, yet we on the surface don't know about them, have no idea what they are being used for, and since the locations are kept secret, it is obvious the public is being kept in the dark. Most are constructed by humans, but some are ET bases. So, who are these controllers? Why do they need massive underground cities connected by road, train, and sea lanes? Like "The Who" lyrics from the song, "Won't be Fooled again: 'Meet the New Boss, Same as the Old Boss.'" The real controllers of Earth have been here a long time, and they are still in control.

Consider that there was an advanced space-faring race who discovered Earth many thousands of years ago. They used it as their base of operations and appropriated some of its resources for their own use. Proto-humans were not advanced, and were powerless to stop them. As their stay progressed, they decided to genetically create slave workers to build their buildings, dig their mines, and cultivate their food in the field. To that end, they reworked a local hominid-like *Homo erectus* and made it just intelligent enough to understand what they wanted, but dumb enough to not consider rebelling.

Time goes on and the space-farers consider Earth their planet. And the slaves have begun worshipping them as "gods," and with a few threats here and there, and a few demonstrations of their power, they as Lords keep the slaves in line. As time goes on, the slave population grows and the Lords (who aren't always around to control the slaves) decide to upgrade the best of the slaves genetically to a more intelligent model who will operate under the "Divine Right to Rule" dictum. This genetic upgrade of slaves starts a separate bloodline going on the Earth. The human "cut-outs" would do the heavy lifting and control the unwashed masses, while the masters (Lords) preferred to remain out of sight and take up residency underground in legacy bases. Fast forward to today, and the Rockefellers and Rothschilds are the captains and colonels, while the generals are the advanced space-faring race.

IT'S ALL ABOUT CONTROL

We have to ask the fundamental question: who exactly is really controlling our world, and why are we enslaved? The new bloodline cutouts of royals and bankers are smart enough to rule over the slaves (sheeple), and they become known as the Cabal. They like ruling, and figure they are smarter and not only have the right to rule (given them by the gods), but they have become the richest people on the planet as well. Yet, they too are given their marching orders.

The people in charge of this planet are so greedy and power-hungry that they must keep everyone else, that is, all of us slaving away just to survive: to pay the mortgage, the power bill, phone bill, cable bill, property tax bill, gasoline bill, natural gas bill, water bill—to the point where we really own nothing in this world. Nobody should be homeless or starving on this planet. It only happens because of pure greed. The corporations are allowed to keep us in a frozen reality so they can make trillions which they use to mine asteroids and build bases on other planets, as well as moons all over the universe in service to their "invisible master." It's all a big con job, and we are the suckers! We've had a Star Trek reality stolen from us, while brainwashed idiots beg for socialism, which always ends in mass death.[1]

In this "fake" reality, we have been told lies by the fake news and fake schools since we were born. For example, we are told that it is necessary to use rockets to get into space; that there is no such thing as free energy; and that we haven't been back to the Moon since 1972! These are all lies to cover up the reality that we have bases on the Moon, Mars and many other planets, as well as many other moons in our solar system. Whistleblowers have stated that we are even colonizing other solar systems using portal technology and advanced starships, which can open up wormholes to other solar systems.

All of this advanced technology has been hidden so that the "free range slaves" don't complain about not having free energy to power our homes and vehicles. It is so much

---

1   Zagami, Leo Lyon, *The Invisible Master: Secret Chiefs, Unknown Superiors, and the Puppet Masters Who Pull the Strings of Occult Power from the Alien World.* CCC Publishing, 2018.

easier to lie to the masses when the masses still think they need ancient rocket technology to get into orbit! If the slaves knew there is a Secret Space Program propelled by flying saucers, they might get a little upset and even arm themselves!

In the past, to keep the people in line, the Cabal instituted oppressive religion, "Behave or go to hell where you will burn for all eternity!" At the core of organized religion has often been the brainwashing of the masses, facilitated by certain religious leaders who pushed the false matrix. This was reinforced by infamous techniques such as the "Inquisition." However, now the masses of people are waking up to the deception. All around the world, organized religion is losing its grip on people's hearts and minds.

PRISON PLANET OR FREEING HUMANITY?

Earth may have been "run" in a manner analogous to a prison planet in the ancient past, where religions and monumental construction projects were engineered under near-slavery conditions. It appears that this was attempted possibly for the purpose of inhibiting natural and healthy development of civilization, as well as suppressing or distorting collective memory. While these efforts appear to have been interrupted, it is possible that residual disruptive influences remain in the "zoo."

But now the caged animals are waking up. Humanity is truly a collective intelligence. This collective intelligence changes only when the thoughts of many people evolve. By thinking differently, people create a change in their reality. It is impossible for the thoughts of a single individual to do this alone, whether that person be the president of a nation, a saint, or a commoner. It is useless to petition the elites to change society, for these people became elites in the first place by reflecting the consciousness of the society that shaped them. However, when the masses within a society change, then do the elites change. Thus, there is no escape from the fact that if one wants a better world, one has to work with the masses within a society, since the masses themselves literally have to think their way into that better world. There are no exceptions to this.

It has now been established beyond any reasonable doubt that alien ETs exist. This is evident to anyone who examines available evidence already publicly disclosed. There have been crashed alien ET anti-gravity vehicles recovered and back-engineered. Indeed, alien ETs have frequently visited the Earth, and have entered into treaties with the leaders of more than one government. As a result of many nefarious treaties, ETs have exchanged ultra-high-tech alien technology for access to human and animal DNA and, in the process, established secret underground and underwater bases for themselves. Further, they have established such bases with other civilizations, off-planet, in joint efforts for android and trans-human development, as well as advanced cloning, hybridization and chimera (mythical animal) experimentation.

One of the first questions any skeptic will ask is, "Why don't the 'service to others' good ETs just show themselves?" It's just not quite that simple. First of all, there are innumerable, very strong reasons to believe (as discussed in these pages) that ETs do exist. If so, then a logical corollary presents itself: It appears that they are following a "Prime Directive." If they wanted to take over the planet by force, they could have done so ages ago with little or no resistance. But there appear to be universal laws. They are not allowed to interfere with our history and reveal themselves to us openly until we are ready for them to appear. The "service to self" ETs also prefer to remain unseen and continue with their agenda. Their justification is that they are from Earth, or inter-dimensionally from here. An ultra-terrestrial is a superior, non-human entity of natural or supernatural origin that is also indigenous to planet Earth.

Breaking from the shackles of our age-old imprisonment will bring humanity prosperity beyond our wildest imagination. Disclosure will bring many wonderful rewards—such as free energy, anti-gravity, stargate travel, healing technology and materializer technology. It will also pave the way for open interaction with benevolent human ETs—a dream that many cannot even imagine ever actually happening. Or it might not ever come true—keeping us locked down in prison planet for many more centuries.

OPERATION TROJAN HORSE

Our skies have been filled with "Trojan Horses" throughout history, and like the original Trojan Horse delivered to ancient Troy containing unseen soldiers. These craft seem to conceal hostile intent. ETs with hostile intent are those with a "service to self" agenda, and are most certainly the ones who control the zoo. This hostility theory is further supported by the fact that the objects chosen most often appear in forms which we can readily accept and explain to our own satisfaction—ranging from dirigibles to meteors and conventional-appearing airplanes or even as lenticular clouds. In other words, flying saucers are not entirely what we have hoped they are. They are a part of something else. That something else can be called "Operation Trojan Horse."[2]

Exo-political expert Stephen Bassett has noted that the scope, frequency, and distribution of the sightings alone make the popular extraterrestrial (interplanetary) hypothesis completely untenable. Many flying saucers seem to be nothing more than a disguise for some hidden phenomenon originating here on Earth. They are ultra-terrestrial Trojan Horses descending into our forests and farm fields, promising salvation and offering us the splendor of some great super-civilization in the sky. Which begs the question: do the ultra-terrestrials really care about us any more than just as livestock? There is much disturbing evidence in the form of abductions and mutilations that they don't. They care only to the extent that we can fulfill our enigmatic use to them.

The real truth is that UFO enthusiasts have been played for suckers for years, not by the government, but by the phenomenon itself. Yet, some of the claims, made by Zecharia Sitchin and others involving extraterrestrial interference with human development on Earth in the ancient past, appear to be true. The old boss has no intention of surrendering its dominion of Earth.

CONTACT HAS ALREADY BEEN MADE

Different human cut-outs who have interfaced with the malevolent ETs have come and gone over the centuries. One of the latest is Monsignor Corrado Balducci, who was a leading theologian at the Vatican, and interestingly enough, also one of their expert exorcist priests. He ended up speaking out openly, particularly on Italian mainstream television, about the fact that he was on a Vatican Commission looking into extraterrestrial encounters. In 1997 he was interviewed by the cultural anthropologist and Ufologist, Michael Hesemann, where he reported that the Vatican was receiving much information about extraterrestrials and their contacts with humans, from their papal ambassadors in various countries such as Chile, Mexico and Venezuela.

Father Balducci said that he was on the Vatican Commission looking into extraterrestrial encounters and different ways to cope with the emerging awareness of the reality of extraterrestrial contact. In August, 1998, he said, "It is reasonable to believe and affirm that extraterrestrials exist. Their existence can no longer be denied, for there is too much evidence for the existence of extraterrestrials and flying saucers." He also made reference to Angels while being interviewed by Michael Hesemann in 1997, when he said, "We know with certainty of the existence of God, of the Angels, and of us. The Angels, God's messengers, have always concerned themselves with humanity, and it is certain they are still doing this today. Each human being has his or her own Guardian Angel that follows him or her everywhere. There are visible appearances of

2 Redfern, Nick, "Operation Trojan Horse: It's Back!" https://mysteriousuniverse.org/2013/05/operation-trojan-horse-its-back.

Angels." Father Balducci also emphasized that extraterrestrial beings are like us; they are physical and you can touch them. However, there is a spiritual reality as well. It is important that people realize there is a difference.

Taken together, the extraterrestrials appear to have a dual purpose. Briefly, it would appear that one purpose primarily involves "service to self" manipulation and control, and the taking of our resources and genetic material to those who are observing "hands off" as we go through these incredible changes on Earth. Another purpose involves "service to others" beings, who are more benevolent and also concerned with a higher purpose, an ethical morality and a more cosmic evolution. It is a complex exopolitical scenario. Malevolent E.T.s/Inter-dimensionals are with us today, and have been for centuries. They are part of the "Rebel Force" which pretended to be the "gods" of our ancestors. The Rebel Force is also called the "Third Force," a notably evil power with no ability to express regard for human feeling, human suffering or human life in general.

Famed UFO researcher, Dr. Jacques Vallee, noted that what we all need to do is to connect to our own "divinity," learn to make full use of our consciousness, and get the "Alien Monkey" off our back. By doing so we must take back our own personal divine power and use it! He notes that *if* the seven-plus billion people on this planet could be connected, even at the Alpha level for 24 hours, every war and conflict on Earth would end. Only the Reptilian infiltrators and those aligned with negative ET forces would want to fight and carry on war. The negative forces could then be identified and eliminated. An encouraging aspect is that we are not in this alone! Our destiny is that we will be released from this malevolent alien-controlled prison planet.

Humans are powerful spiritual entities contained in defective physical bodies that die relatively young. Beside the fact that human DNA was vastly corrupted by the Reptilian Rebel Force about 7,700 years ago, we are forced to stay in the reactive state of mind of Beta, where the fight and flight response is triggered seemingly daily, and we are never taught how to develop the Alpha, Theta and Delta states of our consciousness. It is our consciousness and life force, our "soul," which keeps the human vessel alive, and once the consciousness and life force leaves the body, the human vessel dies. Upon dying, we exist in a state of "conscious energy" which generally leaves this dimension and goes "home" to the light; but that too might be a false reality. Alex Collier advises, "Don't go to the light," but look behind and there will be a scene of all of creation, and that is the best course for a departing soul to travel.

PROJECT BLUE BEAM

Another false reality is a last-ditch effort for total global control. Project Blue Beam is one of the most dangerous secret programs ever conceived. It has the potential to spark a global financial panic, an outbreak of war, or even mass suicide. It will trigger most people's emotions because organized religions rule our world, and because of humanity's need to believe in a higher power. This kind of power is exactly what Blue Beam seeks to acquire through the most mischievous of methods. Making use of deception and mass manipulation techniques, Blue Beam would lay the foundations for a new One World Government supported by a unified, New Age religion. This is the plan, at least.[3]

Those who first brought up the existence of this secret program have also given us a brief description of its targets—all of which will be faked. Project Blue Beam is expected to go through several steps before completion:

>   **This first step** *involves the creation of artificial earthquakes in very targeted places around the world. It is known that the electromagnetic frequency of*

3   Paxton, Ian, "A New Religion and World Domination: The NWO's PROJECT BLUEBEAM." https://anomalien.com/a-new-religion-and-world-domination-the-nwos-project-bluebeam/

the HAARP arrays can trigger artificial earthquakes. These earthquakes will unearth previously undiscovered archaeological sites of great importance, likely showing bones of very large giants or ET craft remains. The new discoveries will serve to discredit the beliefs of existing religions that we are not alone and have never been alone. By controlling the Mockingbird Media, the Cabal will trick the world's nations into believing they have misunderstood and misinterpreted their religious doctrines all along. It is very likely that there are a large number of archaeological sites hiding an even larger number of arcane mysteries. One of these locations is Antarctica. When (or if) the earthquakes reveal these mysteries, the world will be sufficiently shaken and ready for Phase II.

The next step *is the big fake "Space Show," involving sounds and extremely realistic holograms in the sky. Using technology that is being kept secret from the public, Project Blue Beam's artisans will create a worldwide celestial show that mimics a global "Second Coming" of Christ, or the appearance of other religious figures depending on the countries in which they are displayed. Different holograms will be played in various zones, according to a zone's predominant religious beliefs. Prophetic in nature, these "visions" will serve to further destabilize the situation until it escalates into a deadly global war. Investigative journalist Serge Monast describes Blue Beam's intentions to elicit maximum shock reactions. "Naturally, this superbly staged falsification will result in dissolved social and religious (disorder) on a grand scale, each nation blaming the other for the deception, setting loose millions of programmed religious fanatics through demonic possession on a scale never witnessed before." Add this to the worldwide political anarchy, people being extremely agitated and confused, and the general panic caused by global catastrophes, and the road to destruction becomes obvious.*

The third step *in the NASA Blue Beam Project is called the "Telepathic Electronic Two-Way Communication." Basically, it is voice to skull technology, making everyone feel schizophrenic, "hearing voices" in their minds of the returning religious figures. Lt. Col. John Alexander's article entitled, 'The New Mental Battlefield: Beam Me Up, Spock,' describes it:*

> *If it is possible to feed artificial thought into the multigenic field via satellite, the mind control of the entire planet is now possible. An individual's only resistance would be to constantly question the motivation behind their thoughts and not act upon thoughts which they consider to be outside their own ideological, religious and moral boundaries.*[4]

Lastly is the phasing out of cash, in order to usher in the final globalist implementation of the New World Order independence. This is what it's all about. The techniques used in the final step are exactly the same as those used in the past by the USSR to force people to accept communism. The same technique will be used by the United Nations to implement the New World Order, and to persuade the Vatican to endorse a One World Religion. This final step, focused on a radical currency change, is what Nicholas Rockefeller admitted to filmmaker Aaron Russo: the elite's goal is a 100% microchipped and enslaved world population beholden to their fiat currency. Project Blue Beam could begin with some kind of worldwide economic disaster. Not a complete crash, but enough to allow the Cabal to introduce some kind of in-between currency before they introduce their One World Currency of electronic cash to replace all paper or plastic money. The in-between currency will be used to force anyone with savings to convert it or turn in their cash or physical gold. This is because the Cabal understands that people who have money are not dependent upon them, and moneyed citizens will be the ones

4   Alexander, John. "The New Mental Battlefield: Beam Me Up, Spock." https://www.usa-anti-communist.com/pdf/Military_Review_Dec_1980_Alexander_The_New_Mental_Battlefield_Beam_Me_Up_Spock.pdf

who will mount an insurrection against the Cabal's diabolical plans.[5]

THE MIND CONTROL OPERATIONS UNDERGROUND

To understand how the world control agenda operates, we need to look at all the players, and where they operate—sometimes in very unlikely places. It's known that under Project Paperclip, a large contingent of the Nazi rocketry team was transferred directly from the underground facilities in Peenemünde, Germany, to Fort Bliss, Texas, and reassembled to continue their work under the pseudonym of NASA. Large numbers of Nazi eugenics specialists, spy masters and mind-control researchers were also reestablished in CIA programs, oftentimes in Deep Underground Military Bases. Of course, average American citizens are forbidden to enter these U.S. government-sponsored New World Order bases under penalty of death; unless, of course, they unfortunately are experimental subjects, that is, victims of a mind control operation.

Symbology is very important to the elite. Above ground represents the conscious mind. Below ground represents the subconscious mind. As soon as you go under the ground, you start to enter your subconscious mind. The DUMBs are where most of the programming for mind control takes place, according to the "super soldier" Max Spiers who died young in his 30s under very suspicious circumstances. He revealed that beneath the entire cities of London and Los Angeles, there are massive, entire underground cities. He says that much of his MK-Ultra programming had taken place in these two places, as well as Dulce, New Mexico, home to another extensive underground base.[6]

Interestingly, Spiers says that each level of the bases he visited had a different symbol. The farther down you go, the more you are drawn deeply into your subconscious, as you gradually realize why you are there. He has rarely seen these underground base symbols in everyday life. Psychologist note that symbols speak to the subconscious, while words speak to the conscious. It is our subconscious mind which really controls us. It contains our patterns, habits, belief systems and a lifetime of programming. If we truly want to change, we need to reprogram our subconscious minds.

According to Spiers, the Ibis Project began in 1972 and ended in 1980. It was an extension of the Nazi *Übermensch* project. It aimed to create a perfect (super) race along eugenic lines. He said it was connected to inner-Earth beings too. One strategy used was to breed certain children using selected mothers as carriers, and the children were fed intravenously. Spiers, himself, admitted he was one of the children involved.

A MASSIVE MIND CONTROL PSYOP

Most people in this world place no priority on awareness or mindfulness, and instead live life in a semi-conscious dream state that makes them very suggestible, and thus prone to being pawns of the False Matrix Control System. Some are born (and bred) with insufficient levels of individualized consciousness to ever experience a lucid moment, and it is these individuals who form the primary class of "Matrix agents," as Max Spiers described them. The rest of us can also function as agents part of the time, especially if we fail to watch ourselves, fail to remain vigilant. Due to the plethora of spiritually asleep people in the population, the real controllers have no problem finding cut-outs to maneuver into place around a target. It is important to remember, as stated above, that there are malevolent ultra-terrestrials calling the shots, whose aim is depopulation, by means of a horrific anti-human agenda.

Indeed, we are a food source to these evil beings, in more ways than one. Whether people want to hear it or not, we are not only an energy source to energy vampires through

5   Monst, Serge. "NASA's Project Blue Beam." https://exonews.org/canadian-serge-monasts-project-blue-beam-theory/
6   MK-Ultra Supersoldier Max Spiers Shares his Mind Control Recovery Process: https://carolynviera.wordpress.com/2014/01/05/mk-ultra-supersoldier-max-spears-his-mind-control-recovery-process-p1/

the emotional body, but some of them actually eat our flesh and blood. Humans are cloned for this reason, and it also explains where the hundreds of thousands of missing persons go every year. Why do we need to know about this? Why not just keep our heads in the sand? Because we need to say "No! I do not consent to this control!" We need to unite and free humanity once and for all from this archon ("evil ruler") infection. At the same time, we are also raising our consciousness and vibration which will boost us into another realm of being. We are kept separate through lower consciousness, vibration, and mind control. Although we are all connected, it isn't a connection like a hive mind, that's what the archons have and that's what they are trying to convert us to, and our fear energy is a "loosh" food source for them. Our defense is knowing we are unique aspects of a Creator, tied together with fibers of light, flowing together in the sea of creation. Just like a group of fish in the ocean or a flock of birds in the sky, when the few start heading one way, the rest of the group follows, and they continue to flow together as a group.

Always be aware that the controllers know that mind control is enhanced when the mind is traumatized by events. Memories are stored and retrieved from the brain more easily when they are accompanied by adrenaline secretions prompted by fear, anger, pain or extreme sorrow. Catharsis is the term for the traumatic transfer of a memory, that is, "meme-ory," collectively, from the unconscious to the conscious. The adrenaline secretion is also a harvested commodity called adrenochrome, a chemical compound produced by the oxidation of adrenaline.

THE THIRD FORCE

The history we've been taught is an accumulation of lessons, laced with lies by omission. What is omitted is what is really going on underground—that is, advanced technology beyond our wildest dreams and the ongoing operations of a Fourth Reich or "Third Force" intelligence operation that has existed since the end of World War II. The Rothschild/Rockefeller controlled mass media has promoted a false narrative concerning the events of World War II for the past 80 years. To be sure, the difference between state media and Western media is that in state media the government controls what information the public is given about what's going on in the world in order to prevent political dissent, whereas in Western media, this control is maintained instead by billionaires. Meanwhile, the United States government continues to suppress the knowledge of German "Vril" free-energy technology, in order to maintain the status quo of our oil-based globalist slave economy. The breakaway Aryans (German free-energy scientists) have expanded an enormous Secret Space Program, which does not use or need "fossil fuel" oil.

While it is widely accepted that the Nazis were defeated with the German Government's formal surrender in 1945, this is only partly true. The Third Reich never surrendered, and why would they? Continuing what they started in the Skoda Works before and during the war, the Antarctic Nazis were able to further develop their "Vril" spacecraft far in advance of anything possessed by the USA. They swiftly defeated the massive "post-World War II" Antarctica military attack by Allied forces led by Admiral Byrd, who retreated in fear and disgrace after suffering substantial damage and heavy casualties.

German Navy Grand Admiral Karl Dönitz stated in 1943: "The German submarine fleet is proud of having built for the *Führer* in another part of the world a Shangri-La on land, an impregnable fortress." Yes, there were large numbers of people and materials sent to Antarctica, and Admiral Dönitz returned to Germany and seemed to be bragging about building a "Shangri-La" on a distant continent. Not that "we're *going* to do it," or "*planning* to do it," but that is was *done*.

It is important to note that NATO is essentially a Third Force organization and is the home of Operation Gladio which remains functional. The false flag Gladio attacks are still used to blow up and mass-murder innocents all over the world in order to create synthetic terror and chaos. This is done to justify the taking of more and more taxpayer money and rights, all done in order to facilitate the attainment of the hierarchy's Globalist New World Order evil agenda. Problem-Reaction-Solution is the manufactured pattern. Yet more and more people all around the world are learning about Operation Gladio, the left-behind Fourth Reich army that runs NATO. The CIA usually uses false flag events to start wars and cause conflicts with other countries. In America, the CIA uses false flags as legal propaganda to create narratives that control American perception. Is this management laced with subliminal control messaging that is tantamount to brainwashing?[7]

THE NAZIS IN ANTARCTICA

In 1938, the Nazis sent a large team of explorers—including scientists, military units and building crews on war ships and submarines—to the Queen Maud Land region of Antarctica. While mapping the area, they discovered a vast network of underground hot springs flowing out to rivers, and forming massive caves under the ice. One of these caverns extended down as far as 20-30 miles and contained a large geothermal lake. The cave was explored, and construction teams were sent in to build a city-sized base, dubbed Base 211 or New Berlin, that hosted the SS, anti-gravity scientists, the Thule Society, "serpent cults" of various Nazi occultists, the Illuminati, and other shadowy groups who fled on U-boats just before Germany surrendered in World War II.

After the Allies claimed unconditional victory in World War II, Secretary of Defense James Forrestal sent a naval task force to Antarctica in 1946, including Admiral Nimitz, Admiral Krusen and Admiral Byrd, and given the operational name "Highjump." Over 4,500 military troops from the U.S., Britain and Australia, consisting of three Naval battle groups, departed Norfolk, VA, on 2 December 1946, led by Admiral Byrd's command ship, the ice-breaker "Northwind," and consisted of the catapult ship "Pine Island," the destroyer "Brownson," the aircraft-carrier "Philippine Sea," the U.S. submarine "Sennet," two support vessels "Yancey" and "Merrick," and two tankers "Canisteo" and "Cacapon," the destroyer "Henderson," a floatplane ship, "Currituck," and a torpedo boat named "Maddox" which was sunk. According to researcher Frank Joseph, the USS Maddox was "either a torpedo boat, or torpedo-carrying destroyer." He goes on to explain what may have happened to the Maddox mentioned in a declassified Soviet report:

> A USS Maddox was indeed sunk by enemy action, but five years earlier by a German dive-bomber during the Allied invasion of Sicily. Actually there were at least three American destroyers known by that name (DD-168, DD-622 and DD-731) all of them contemporaneous. The U.S. Navy has long been notorious for falsifying the identity of its ships and re-writing their histories if they embarrass official policy. ...So too, the "Maddox" cited by Soviet espionage was similarly consigned to an official memory hole.

They were tasked with locating and destroying an immense underground base constructed by the Germans before, during and immediately after World War II. Germany sent a pre-war Naval expedition to *Neuschwabenland* in Antarctica and discovered vast ice-free areas with warm fresh-water lakes, massive subterranean cavern systems, hot springs and signs of vegetation. They began building a secret deep underground base below the ice (on German maps in section 211) and conducted occult research into advanced propulsion technology and saucer-shaped Vril aircraft based on universal free energy.[8]

The naval task force found them, and the battle was a decisive victory for the Germans. It was over in under 30 minutes when a saucer emerged from the ocean and

7   Olsen, Brad, *Future Esoteric: The Unseen Realms.* 2nd ed. CCC Publishing, 2016.

8   Salla, Michael, "Did US Navy battle UFOs protecting Nazi Antarctic sanctuary in 1947?" https://www.exopolitics.org/did-us-navy-battle-ufos-protecting-nazi-antarctic-sanctuary-in-1947/

used a directed energy weapon to slice the Maddox in half. There is still dispute over whether it was a German or a Draco saucer. Because the exiled Nazis won the Battle of Operation Highjump, they dictated terms to America. The American people were to be allowed the illusion that they were still a republic, but were to be ruled through a Liaison. That Liaison is the Director of the Trilateral Commission founded by Vice President Rockefeller.

On the return from Antarctica, Highjump expedition leader Admiral Richard Byrd told *El Mercurio* newspaper that they were preparing to defend the world against "enemy fighters that can fly from pole to pole with tremendous speed." Admiral Byrd warned of the need for the United States to adopt protective measures against the possibility of invasion of the country by hostile aircraft proceeding from the polar regions. He went on to say "I don't want to scare anybody but the bitter reality is that in the event of a new war the United States will be attacked by aircraft flying in from the poles." In 1958, three nuclear weapons were exploded in the *Neuschwabenland* region, as part of another classified U.S. operation, code-named Argus. These tests led to the Antarctic Treaty the following year, whose first order of business was forbidding nuclear testing. But why would the Treaty mention something specifically, when it *never* happened? Not even once? Or maybe because it *did* happen.[9]

Fast forward to the last few years, and recent visitors to the Antarctic include U.S. Secretary of State John Kerry during the height of America's presidential elections. Russian Orthodox Patriarch of Moscow, Kiril III, was also a 2017 visitor. When Kiril III came back, he warned Putin and the rest of the world that the apocalypse is upon them. Other notables among the world's elitists who have made recent visits to see the penguins include Prince Harry of Great Britain and King Juan Carlos of Spain. And there is the story about Buzz Aldrin visiting Antarctica. The Apollo 11 "Moon astronaut," another penguin lover, supposedly tweeted: "We are all in danger! It is evil itself!" Aldrin was then evacuated from the Antarctic with a medical emergency and put in quarantine.

THE GERMAN SECRET SPACE PROGRAM

The truth embargo as it relates to UFOs has been going on for at least a century. Any researcher of "deep" esoteric subjects knows the rabbit hole has to include extraterrestrials. As the late William Cooper emphatically stated, "you put the aliens into the middle of this stuff and you've got all the answers." But what is the human involvement? In this Modern Age at least, backward-engineered space travel started with the Germans, who were the first to explore development of flying saucer technology in the early part of the 20th century. In the years just after World War I, psychic mediums were used to channel advanced technology blueprints with remote extraterrestrial civilizations. The Vril Society was established after medium Maria Orsic received a communication from extraterrestrials who had once lived in what is now Sumeria. She discovered that these beings eventually departed Earth for the Aldebaran solar system. With the data collected, and the recovery of downed UFOs such as the craft recovered from the Black Forest in the 1930s, the Germans were ready to build. For the next decade, they called their spaceships the RFZ-1, Haunebu, Vril and the Bell craft. Kronos was a secret name for the Nazi space project. They were the first modern humans to fly out into space, and that's where they made many incredible discoveries. There were various civilizations that have colonized our solar system long before us. Some are still there. They left behind many artifacts, including some that could be sealed up, pressurized, and made habitable for humans.

That's what the Germans did on the Moon and on Mars, as well as in Antarctica. In order to accurately discuss the history of the Secret Space Program, facts to be acknowledged

9 Marques, Bruno De. Analysis | Operation Argus, nuclear weapons tests 1958. https://brunodemarques.com/2015/09/03/iii-reich-in-antarctica-the-key-to-unlocking-the-future-4-of-5.

are that the Nazis not only arrived in outer space first, but they were the first to colonize the Moon and Mars. They lost World War II, but they came back and basically took over the U.S. Military Industrial Complex through trickery and through having better technology. They blackmailed the U.S. after Admiral Byrd led a failed expedition to confront them in Antarctica, and also because the U.S. did not want to reveal the secrets gained from the Roswell crash. Top U.S. officials knew the Nazis had the upper hand.[10]

The Nazis started overflying the U.S. capitol in 1952 with their craft from Antarctica, and essentially forced the U.S. to join them in a partnership. This is the origin of the militarization of our space and our solar system. *Nacht Waffen* is the name of the German military in space. Their culture is called *Das Bundes*, which translates to "The Federation." Solar Warden had become the main component of the American secret space program, and other countries also have covert space programs, most of whom are allied with Solar Warden. What was once used for the benefit of the elite to escape off-planet, has turned around. Now benevolent ETs have given the Solar Warden people advanced technology that is allowing them to defeat the Cabal. According to a June, 2015, interview between David Wilcock and Jimmy Church:

> *Solar Warden is now enforcing a no-fly zone around the Earth. Nobody can fly in or out of the Earth anymore unless they have permission. Something has been put around our solar system (that they) call the Barrier. This means that nobody can get in. Nobody can get out. And communications cannot get in and out. One of the interesting things is that when the Barrier was put up, the vast majority of all the reptilians in their so-called Dark Fleet were outside the solar system. And they cannot get back in.*

THE AMERICAN SECRET SPACE PROGRAM

The Deep State is a shadowy, secret Government comprised of the largest private Defense Contractors who run these "black within black," "deep black" and "beyond-black" unacknowledged programs. One faction of the Cabal calls themselves "The Alliance," yet there are five or six different Secret Space Program factions who all believe they are independent of the others. The one tool they can use against each other is mind control. According to researcher/experiencer Penny Bradley, there are the *Nacht Waffen* Germans (of which she was a part), Solar Warden, American DoD (Randy Cramer's group), the American Military Industrial Complex has its own program—and then two separate groups of mercenaries who contract with the CIA to get assets. Those are called Kruger and Monarch. And the Deep State elite bankers in space should never be forgotten.

These programs are so secret even some top officials in each company do not know each and every one of these hidden "deep black" programs or who works in them, how much they spend, or even what they do. They understand that it has been classically unsafe and even life-threatening to ask any serious questions about these matters. The bottom line is this: Often the right hand does not know what the left hand is doing. Furthermore, there has been no centralized accountability of any kind except for the top-ranking members of Majestic Twelve.

This complete compartmentalization, lack of any written records or accounting trails, or even employment lists, gives incredible power to these unacknowledged units. Some of these beyond-black unacknowledged programs are so secret and so powerful that they have no accounting records or any records at all. They can access all the cash disbursements they need directly from the U.S. Treasury or the Federal Reserve System with no records trail ever being left. How they were able to acquire such power and secret prominence is, in essence, the Secret Space Program.

10 Nazis in Antarctica: https://atlanteangardens.blogspot.com/2015/11/top-secret-nazi-maps-declassified-kgb.html

According to author Preston James, it is apparent that some select Secret Space War Contractors became criminal enterprises over the years. It has been reported that these were infiltrated and hijacked by a certain incredibly evil group beforehand, namely by the Dracos and their subordinate large Greys and little Greys, which some refer to as gene-spliced and cloned "droids."

OTHER ASPECTS OF THE SSP
(SECRET SPACE PROGRAM)

Solar Warden was established early and is the most aging fleet, although it has gone through many upgrades over the decades. They have a R&D/Scientific-focused fleet, and a Military Offensive/Defensive focused fleet that is mainly in charge of policing the Solar System and surrounding Star Clusters. They are tasked with keeping track of "Intruders" and Visitors," as well as to locate and remove unauthorized "Visitors" on the Earth and other planetary bodies. Their program name describes their functions well.

Insider Corey Goode was involved with the Interplanetary Corporate Conglomerate, which is a consortium focused mainly on development and acquisition of technology by any means. These are the Cabal and mercenary groups, and they develop and produce technology for commerce with Earth and off-world groups in a barter system. They leave nothing off the table that they are willing to trade, including kidnapped humans. Until recently, the Planetary Corporations have been very powerful, deeply classified, and they've always had all of the latest technology and "toys" at their disposal. They are made up of the top 100-plus technology companies in the world. Their Earth-level Board of Directors do not have unlimited access to secrets—but one director each—has access to the critical information. They are also given newly-exchanged technology from the Labyrinth Group, which is the part of the NSA that interacts with ETs.

The Dark Fleet has worked almost entirely outside the Sol System (our solar system). They are very offensively militaristic, extremely classified above other outfits and have large fleets (similar looking to Carrier Craft that looked like the *Star Wars* Wedge-Shaped craft in the movies). They work alongside the Draco Alliance and are suspected of fighting alongside them in their affairs in other systems. *Nacht Waffen* means "night weapons," and *wir flugen ins der nacht* means "we fly into the night-space."

According to SSP insiders Corey Goode and Penny Bradley, various Special Access Program SSP's that were small, usually had the newer technology, were very secretive and worked for some of the Secret Earth Governments, Syndicates and World Military Forces (There could be several independent groups in this category). The mercenary groups were Kruger and Monarch, who were started by scientists involved in the mind fracture phase. They purchased alters and tissue samples to create cloned bodies and had access to the technology. They created competing companies.[11]

PAPERCLIP NAZIS BURROW UNDERGROUND

Under Hitler's Third Reich, the *Organisation Todt* (OT) was tasked with building many deep underground facilities. Named after the brilliant civil engineer Fritz Todt, the organization was assigned a huge range of engineering projects prior to and during World War II. Todt helped the German military accomplish several feats, including the Autobahn road network after being asked by Hitler to contribute his wisdom. However, he died in a plane crash in 1942. He was replaced by Albert Speer as the Minister of Armaments and War Production. But Speer allowed one, Franz Xaver Dorsch, to guide the operation, in effect making him the operational chief of the OT.

· ·
11 Bradley, Penny, "Mapping out the Secret Space Program" PowerPoint Presentation, 2018.

Dorsch's job was over-seeing the construction of several underground bunker facilities, which the Third Reich was obsessed with constructing.

When the war ended, the Americans found the underground bases the Nazis had built and kept Franz Xaver Dorsch as a prisoner of war. In 1947, they transported him back to the United States, along with hundreds of other top Nazi brass, under the supervision of Project Paperclip. During his stay in the Americas, Franz Xaver Dorsch's name comes up again and again as an eminent authority on underground base construction. Construction of underground facilities by the American Military Industrial Complex has continued ever since, and today constitutes one of the dirtiest secrets kept from nearly all Americans.

World War II could not have happened without American corporations contributing to and literally funding both sides of the conflict. Rockefeller's Standard Oil, for example, sold their special patented fuel additive to the Third Reich. They used this material in their historic bombing mission over London by planes that had never been capable of such dramatic range before. The revolutionary punch-card system used in Nazi concentration camps to keep track of prisoners was patented by IBM. They manufactured punch cards (with Operation Paperclip technology) with the explicit purpose of maintaining an inventory of human chattel. Perhaps the most egregious example of American corporate behavior is the Union Banking Cartel's laundering of Nazi money. Union Bank was owned and operated by Prescott Bush (President George H.W. Bush's father, and George W. Bush's grandfather), who suffered no disciplinary action whatsoever, despite the public indictment of his firm as a Nazi money-laundering operation. There is an over-abundance of evidence that not only suggests (but proves well beyond a reasonable doubt) that American banks and corporations funded Hitler's rise to power, though their motives may not be immediately clear, because they are multifaceted and layered like an onion. These moneyed elite constitute the old boss and the new boss.

It appears that the next generation of Third Force German Nationalists, who escaped to Antarctica and South America, still remain in power. Just before his term ended, President Obama visited Bariloche, Argentina, on March 24, 2016. It is known as the unofficial headquarters of the "Fourth Reich" for over seven decades, ever since Adolf Hitler fled there after World War II. The Nazi U-boat historian, Harry Cooper, found credible sources establishing Bariloche as Hitler's refuge in his book, *Hitler in Argentina*. Incidentally, in February 1960, President Eisenhower traveled to Bariloche where he negotiated the Joint Declaration of Bariloche with the Argentinian President Arturo Frondizi concerning "Peace and Freedom in the Americas." The real topic of negotiations, however, allegedly concerned deals which would further put the U.S. Military Industrial Complex firmly under the control of the Fourth Reich. Two years later, Frondizi was ousted from office by a military coup.[12]

Nevertheless, this alliance led to the emergence of the Interplanetary Corporate Conglomerate (ICC), one of the secret space programs revealed by Corey Goode. It assumed control of the Nazi bases in Antarctica. Therefore, it is more than likely that President Obama's visit to Bariloche (according to Dr. Michael Salla) was to finalize new deals with the ICC/Nazis, which would facilitate their desire to move large numbers of people and cargo to safe locations in South America and Antarctica. Goode reported that there were six large industrial complexes located in the Western Antarctic region. The two largest complexes were city-sized and about two miles wide, with abundant thermal energy used as a power source.

· ·
12 Cooper, Harry, *Hitler in Argentina. The Hitler Escape Trilogy.* CreateSpace, 2014.

THE MICRONATIONS

A "micronation" is an entity that claims sovereignty while being part of another nation. A micronation is not formally recognized as an independent country, regardless of its claims. However, even though micronations (like the Swedish-adjacent Ladonia), aren't recognized by other countries or international bodies like the United Nations, that hasn't stopped some of these unofficial territories from acting as independent lands. Some micronations have even adopted their own currencies, postage stamps, passports, Army, Navy, Air Force, Space Command and other common affiliations associated with real countries.

When compared to "real" countries and territories in the world, the concept of a micronation is a fairly new concept. The oldest record of a person declaring their own sovereignty on land already claimed by a country dates back to the early 20th century. Martin Coles Harman claimed the British Isle of Lundy as his own nation because he also owned the land. Then in 1945 during World War II, the Principality of Outer Baldonia was formed when Russell Arundel, the chairman of Pepsi-Cola Company, declared sovereignty over a rocky island off the coast of Nova Scotia. It's usually very wealthy people who wish to create their own micronations.

Over the years, micronations have been created by eccentric people like Ernest Hemingway's brother, as well as government idealists, separatists, and people or groups focused on making political statements. Most notably, during the 1980s, several Japanese villages in the northern part of the country declared their independence from Japan as a show of protest against Japan's strong embrace of modernization. There can be other such dissenters from the MIC or the Deep State. Famed CIA pilot turned whistleblower John Lear wrote:

> Everybody who is cleared to work inside the Nevada National Security Site signs a form, probably in such complex wording they don't even know what they are signing, that they agree to be a citizen of the (Kingdom) of the Nevada National Security Site. And they are informed of the penalties if they try to breach their allegiance. Not in those terms but in terms they would agree to, without hesitation, to get access to what they think are the secrets held within. Of course, most of them, don't get to find out anything other than the mundane tasks assigned to them. And when they find out what is really going on, it's too late to back out. And if their objections are more than just words, they are placed in the Nevada National Security Site Super Max, one of the most formidable prisons on the face of the planet Earth.

> So this micronation has an Army: the 750 armed combat soldiers living and training in the 5 underground installations built adjacent to the secret base inside Paiute Mesa. They have their own Navy: The U.S. Navy Secret Space Command with 13 orbiting Direct Energy Weapons; their own Air Force: all the highly advanced combat fighters at the Tonopah Test Range, Gold Flats and Groom Lake. And all of the advanced back engineering of the ET saucers and equipment given to us before and after Roswell. And an agenda: the Nazi/Zionist Alliance which the Dulles brothers allowed to get into our country after WW II which has subverted our nation in its entirety.

Impossible? Improbable? You wish.

With his typical tongue-in-cheek humor, John Lear goes on to explain if you're hell-bent on creating a micronation, it might be easier than you think.[13] Keep in mind that most likely, your micronation will never be formally recognized as an autonomous state over which the President of the U.S. and Congress will have no authority. But if

••
13 Lear, John, "Micronations" Facebook post, August, 2019.

you've always wanted your own micronation and have loads of money, keep reading these quick tips to create your own faux country.

For starters, in order to have your own country, you will need land or a defined territory with clear borders. Real countries have some form of organized government or structure. Regardless of how you want to lead your new country, if you want anyone to come close to taking you seriously, you should draft a (self-serving) constitution. People with experience forming micronations recommend following the Model Constitution Code to create a relatively simple democracy or kingdom. Yes, you need citizens. So, now you need to decide who will be a part of your new country. Will it be a nation of one, or are you going to recruit other people to renounce their current citizenship and join forces with you? Here's your chance to be the new boss.

What might be conjured up in this Illuminati ritual? Underneath the Vatican are miles of tunnels, some stacked with gold, and hidden rooms where the child ritual sacrifices take place to show their worship to these off-world "gods" that view the human race as cattle. We are a grand experiment that fell under the control of this off-world evil empire. They keep the human population in a continuous state of confusion, suppression and desperation, only to keep us from knowing who and what we really are. We are their workforce, and in theory the very thing that keeps them alive; yet they direct the anti-human depopulation agenda.

Artist Michael Pacher's famous painting was created between 1471 and 1475 in Germany. "St. Augustine and the Devil" has the appearance of a reptilian presenting St. Augustine of Hippo with the book of vices. The Vatican Library holds records of our true existence and many other books and documents they keep hidden. Earth has changed in frequency beginning around 2012, with the dawning of the Age of Aquarius. People around the world are awakening to the various control groups. Those of the Reptilian empire know their reign is over, hence the incredible desperation we're seeing from their minions. Interestingly, the Devil is seen offering the "book of vices."

The "elite" love to use symbols on the masses. For example, showing how every time you "come into" Starbucks, you're actually "coming inside" the ancient Canaan-Phoenician whore of Babylon—the Kraken—Tiamat—the primordial goddess of the watery Abyss, who has the two fish of Pisces (Pisces rules the two feet), symbolizing the last 2,000 years of the Piscean Age. Christianity entered the scene at the beginning of the Piscean Age, 2,000 years ago. The symbol for Pisces is the fish, as it is for Christianity. The goddess also wears the seven-pointed crown upon her head as does the "Statue of Liberty." The seven points also symbolize the seven stars (Luminaries) of the Pleiades. In Greek mythology, mermaids (or sirens) were predatory seductresses that would seduce sailors with songs and promises of sex—and then kill them.

It is amazing to think how much humans have advanced in off-planet travel in the last century. Yet we still must seem primitive to ultra-terrestrial civilizations. Perhaps that was the veiled joke when this space chimp posed for the camera after a successful mission to space in 1961.

Part of the depopulation agenda formerly included animals. The backstory of this image is the Battle of Yellow House Canyon in 1877, which took place near present-day Lubbock, Texas. It was a battle between a force of Comanches and Apaches and a group of bison hunters. It was the final battle of the Buffalo Hunters' War and was the last major fight between non-Natives and Native Americans on the High Plains of Texas. On February 1, 1877, Marshall Sewell discovered a herd of buffalo, and after setting up station, picked the animals off one by one with his rifle before running out of ammunition. Black Horse witnessed this, and with his warriors surrounded the hunter on his way back to camp and killed him for his senseless slaughter of the buffalo. In retaliation, local buffalo hunters attacked the Comanche and Apache camp, killing 21 and wounding another 20+ people. During the 19th century, bison were relentlessly killed and slaughtered by the U.S. Army, commercial agents and others, in an attempt to starve Native peoples and open land for cattle. The total number of bison killed is unknown, but some statistics paint a gruesome picture: one professional hunter killed 20,000 on his own, and commercial hide firms were killing between 2,000 to 100,000 bison per day.

There are claims that as early as the 1930s, the German Nazis built self-sufficient underground research factories in the Antarctic. Some believed these "bases" were already built, then found by the Nazis; who then utilized the ancient technologies to experiment with UFOs and other scientific experiments, using advanced technology that humans simply were not capable of creating at the time. After the Roswell crash recovery, and Paperclip former Nazi rocket scientists formed NASA, the USA started its secret expeditions into space. These are 100% actual accounts of U.S. military documents obtained through the Freedom of Information Act.

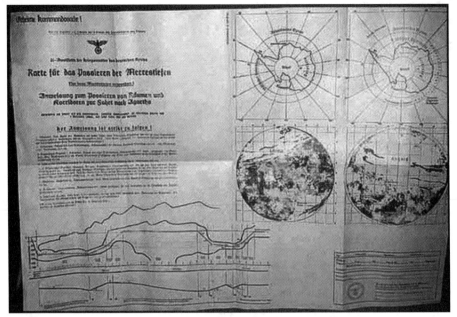

Many researchers have also published material about Operation Highjump and Admiral Byrd's journeys, in which extremely-advanced airships (disc-shaped UFOs) were seen flying around and even engaging him militarily. Not long ago, a Top Secret map belonging to the Third Reich was recovered in which there are several secret passages depicted which were used by German U-Boats to access mysterious underground regions, as well as a complete map of both hemispheres and a possible entrance to Inner Earth, located near the South Pole.

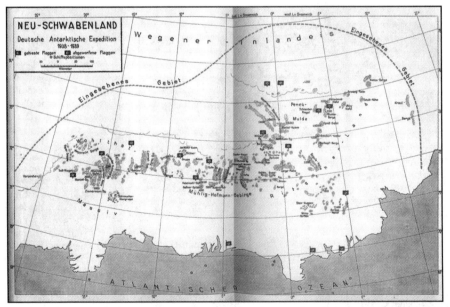

Many are familiar with the legendary stories about the Nazi expeditions that explored and claimed land at the polar regions of our planet, even creating a secret (below-ice) base in Neuschwabenland, Antarctica. Now Top Secret Nazi maps and leaked documents may confirm the existence of mysterious kingdom of Agartha, a subterranean civilization said to exist inside our planet.

There are supposedly three massive ancient astronaut crafts poking through the ice in Antarctica, nicknamed the Niña, Pinta and Santa María—the three ships used by Christopher Columbus in his first voyage across the Atlantic Ocean in 1492. This massive 3-mile across mothership craft was supposedly found in 1975, and is estimated to be 24,000 years old.

From 1933 until 1945, Nazi Germany scientists either discovered from pre-history an advanced civilization with some kind of UFO—a "Vimana," somewhere in the Middle East, or they simply used all of the scientific discoveries in Europe, from the 18th Century onward and built on earlier discoveries. The "Haunebu" uses a system in "Momentum" in an "Anti-time" dragged "Static Bubble," to some degree based on the Helmholtz resonance theory. Other branches of science evolved into the Radar system of Magnetron, and the potential time-travel and space-travel machine called "The Bell," pictured here. The Germans developed a highly advanced space program with bases on Antarctica and Mars (where they first developed nanotechnology).

The image inside the Audience Hall in Vatican City makes the Pope appear to speak from the mouth of a snake. The Vatican is the hub of worship of this off-world evil that has ruled our race for thousands of years. All these different religions are just veins that run from a central source, which is the Vatican. The Vatican is an incredibly evil and sinister place—just look at its decor. It's all serpent and incredibly dark. It's always been hidden in plain sight right in front of our faces.

"If Aliens Arrived on Earth, the Vatican Would Baptize Them" was a headline spoken by senior Vatican scientist, brother Guy Consolmagno. These Temples of Deception get all their marching orders from our dear Vatican, who in turn intercede with non-human entities.

BEING AWARE OF PREDATORY SPECIES

"No matter what the truth ultimately proves to be, we have to go for it! I mean without it we're like children playing with shadows and we're ignorant and we're certainly unempowered to deal with and confront whatever the real entities are behind this masquerade. To take it all at face value is foolish. To take none of it at face value is ridiculous. Investigations into this field. ...there cannot be anything more important for us to be doing right now than to dig past our wishes, dig past our fears and dig for objective reality and understanding."
–Dr. Karla Turner

HUMANS usually think of themselves as being at the top of the food chain. We have tamed or killed off just about every ferocious animal from our past. But what if humans are the prey of a different kind? Or being stealthily poisoned to make way for another? The "Health Ranger" scientist Mike Adams recently showed evidence that planet Earth is being covertly terraformed in more ways than just geoengineering. He concluded that, if so, it could lead to the annihilation of the human species and other native lifeforms in order to prepare the planet for a "reseeding" by non-Earth entities.

Adams has concluded that our planet is undergoing deliberate, large-scale alterations to atmospheric chemistry under the cover of the false "climate change" crisis being pushed by the corrupt scientific establishment. Among the changes being pursued are large-scale stratospheric chemtrail pollution to reduce the intensity of sunlight reaching the Earth, the introduction of genetically-engineered invasive plant, animal and insect species into the wild to annihilate native species, the lowering of oxygen concentration in the lower atmosphere to asphyxiate human beings, the collapse of global organic food webs, the destruction of the food chains upon which humans depend, and the cooling of the planet to increase polar ice while reducing the liquid water volume of the world's oceans. In short, an anti-human depopulation agenda.

Speaking on *GFM Radio,* Dr. Richard Sauder inquires: "This planet is controlled and locked down and has been for centuries if not millennia, and the question is, why, why must planet Earth be locked down, dumbed down, so thoroughly controlled and for so long? Why? Who and what is behind this?" Mike Adams goes further to claim that the goal is to exterminate humankind and prepare the planet as a friendly habitat for a non-Earth species, whose original planet was farther from the sun and had a colder, thinner atmosphere than that of Earth. Bad for us—good for them. The secondary goal is the stripping of Earth's rare elements, which have numerous scientific, medical and exotic technology applications valuable to any advanced civilization.

The study of exopolitics must also include the human element. What if the people who we today call "Royals" have a secret religion? What if it isn't strictly Christian, nor Catholic, nor Jewish, but is instead a "patchwork quilt?" What if it uses proxies to kill, torture and wound many millions of people in a kind of "remote control" holocaust? What if what we see as all of these bombings and battlefields, all the stark inequality and horrid nastiness perpetrated against the poverty stricken, the slow-kill and fast-kill agendas, the invasion and sanctions causing over a million Iraqis to die—what if all this nasty evil stuff is actually a global "proxy sacrifice" for an Elite Brotherhood Religion which has gone under the radar for centuries? And what if there are a group of arch-Satanist, Illuminati Mass-Media "fake news" con artists out there writing screenplays and hosting theater shows seemingly meant to be exposing the "Illuminati," but in fact are leading people astray with deliberate errors to keep them off the scent of this giant conspiracy against humankind? These are the human cut-out puppet world leaders and top policy-makers who might, in fact, have sold out their fellow human beings to the devil.[1]

BLACK KNIGHT SATELLITE

The control and observation of our planet goes back thousands of years. Part of this control grid relates to a mysterious object that has been in our Earth orbit for approximately 13,000 years, and is clearly of extraterrestrial origin. The Black Knight Satellite is an object orbiting Earth in near-polar orbit that wasn't confirmed visually by astronomers until 1932. Serbian inventor Nikola Tesla discovered it by sound in 1899 while in his Colorado Springs laboratory, hearing strange rhythmic sounds on his radio receiver. There is a connection between long-delayed echoes and reports that Nikola Tesla picked up a repeating radio signal which he believed was coming from space. Tesla writes of his discovery:

> *I can never forget the first sensations I experienced when it dawned upon me that I had observed something possibly of incalculable consequences to mankind. I felt as though I were present at the birth of a new knowledge or the revelation of a great truth. Even now, at times, I can vividly recall the incident, and see my apparatus as though it were actually before me. My first observations positively terrified me, as there was present in them something mysterious, not to say supernatural, and I was alone in my laboratory at night; but at that time the idea of these disturbances being intelligently controlled signals did not yet present itself to me.*

1   James, Preston "Planet Earth now under siege by very Dark Forces," http://www.veteranstoday.com/2016/06/11/planet-earth-now-under-siege-by-very-dark-forces

The scientific confirmation of such signals in 1932 gave birth to the field of radio astronomy, which is now used to decode and detect messages from distant stars and other mysterious celestial sources. But what was this relic circling the planet? The satellite explanation originated in 1954 when newspapers (including the *St. Louis Post Dispatch* and the *San Francisco Examiner*) ran stories, attributed to UFO researcher Donald Keyhoe, saying the U.S. Air Force reported that two satellites orbiting the Earth had been detected. At this time, no human-made satellites had yet been launched.

In 1957, an unknown "object" was seen "shadowing" Sputnik 1, the first human-launched spacecraft. According to reports, the "unidentified object" was in a polar orbit. Neither the United States nor the Russians possessed the technology to maintain an artificial Earth satellite in polar orbit prior to Sputnik 1. The first polar-orbiting spacecraft was launched in 1960. Polar orbits are often used for earth-mapping and earth observation, capturing the Earth as time passes from one point to another, and reconnaissance satellites.

In February, 1960 there was a further report that the U.S. Navy had detected a dark, tumbling object in an orbit inclined at 79° from the equator with an orbital period of 104.5 minutes. Its orbit was also highly eccentric with an apogee of 1,728 km (1,074 mi) and a perigee of only 216 km (134 mi). At the time the Navy was tracking a fragment of casing from the Discoverer VIII satellite launch which had a very similar orbit.

In 1973, the Scottish writer Duncan Lunan analyzed this data from Norwegian radio researchers, coming to the conclusion that they produced a star chart pointing the way to Epsilon Boötis, a double star in the constellation of Boötes. Lunan's hypothesis was that these signals were being transmitted from a 12,600-year-old object located at one of Earth's Lagrangian points. The Black Knight was broadcasting signals and was being monitored not only by the USA and Soviet Union, but also by other countries such as Sweden and a host of Ham Radio enthusiasts. One such Ham Radio operator decoded a series of signals received from the Black Knight Satellite and declared it to be from a star chart centered on the Epsilon Boötes Star System—but it would have been visible from the Earth 13,000 years ago!

An object photographed in 1998 during the STS-88 mission has been widely claimed to be this "alien artifact." The existence of the infamous Black Knight Satellite suggests that there is a spacecraft in near-polar orbit of the Earth that is of extraterrestrial origin, and that NASA is engaged in a cover-up regarding its existence and origin. In fact, on August 23, 1954, the technology magazine, *Aviation Week and Space Technology*, released a story about the Black Knight Satellite that angered the Pentagon, which was trying to keep the information secret.

THE SOUL-CATCHING NET UPON DEATH

The idea of a soul-catching net that awaits us upon death—and keeps us indefinitely reborn in a "matrix" with lost memory—is a grim and highly-disturbing notion, but one that must be explored. The true manipulators at the helm of the global conspiracy to control humans on the planet are non-physical entities. Various religions and cultures have referred to these mischievous entities, such as the archons in the Gnostic tradition, djinn or jinn in Islam, demons in Christianity, the Mud Shadow in the books of Carlos Castaneda, or by other names.

The concept of the soul net is that, after dying, our soul or consciousness separates from the body and then undergoes a process where its memory is wiped clean and the soul is recycled. Then the person is reincarnated into another body to repeat the same process. In this way, the Earth becomes a literal prison planet from which it is very difficult to escape. The soul net is placed there as an artificial energetic grid (outside of Earth and the Moon) to prevent any soul from getting through. There is at least one finishing process station on the Moon (at the Ukert Crater) before souls are returned to Earth with their past-life memories swiped clean. Thus, the Earth remains a closed system where new people are constantly born for the purpose of powering the economy and generating mostly negative emotions (off of which the archons feed) and going through their whole life not remembering who they are, or what the real situation into which they are born will bring.

For humans, the soul net ensures that the planet remains a trawling ground for the archons to trigger our emotions—which they expertly do through the media, war, fear and other methods of deception—so they can get fed. This food is called "loosh," and is energetic by nature, and is only nourishing to the archons when it comes from a state of fear or anger in humans and animals. It is said that many archonic entities swarm around slaughterhouses to feed off the fear of animals as they approach and experience death.

Few people can grasp the magnitude of the soul net. How is it that we are all literally forced into reincarnation with no previous memory of our past lives? However, because humans are powerful beings, the archons can't just rely on force for all this. They need to trick us into giving them consent through our free will. How do they do that? How do they get us to willingly travel into the soul net? They use the trick of the white light upon death. We follow it because it is intoxicating, and it leads us right into the soul net. We are then thrust back into this prison planet for another lifetime of ultimate enslavement, for which we have little or no defense. Only by fully comprehending the extent of our enslavement as humans on Earth, can we consciously break free from the archonic deception after our physical death.[2]

MALEVOLENT ETS ARE ARCHONS

Exo-politics is the science of relations among intelligent civilizations in the multiverse. It is in its infancy with modern humans on Earth, yet there are many versions of exopolitical history in our solar system. The Malevolent Alien Agenda is very complex, as it can be in a spiritual or physical form, or even based on the principle of altering the genetic material of certain families' bloodlines and empowering them with the power of the Third Force. The Alien Agenda is hateful toward humans and is dedicated to using them as serfs and slaves, and even mass-murdering them in a slow-kill fashion. The archons are best thought of as inter-dimensional parasites.

Earth has been a galactic farm for a long time, one that galactic ranchers have been using to feed off of our soul energies—mostly our fear. This is why they actually like war and blood sacrifice, because Earth is a farm planet. It's a prison, a sheeple, cattle-people planet—who live 75 short years and then are simply drained of energy. Yet a growing number of people on planet Earth have become aware that there is a mental parasite present, one that has been manipulating humankind to do harm and embrace hatred and fear as a way of life. This is because our negative thoughts and deeds allows these mental parasites to feed off the negative energy emitted by our DNA when we are in distress. Indeed, the primary emotion emanating from Earth is fear.

There have been extraterrestrials that have come over the years to protect the planet and help uplift humankind, but they interact in very subtle ways. In a more overt way, there are several alien species vying for complete control of Earth. They have come to conquer it and take it over as their own. They could be compared to the conquistadors of Spain, who came to the Americas in search of land and gold, choosing to subdue and enslave the native peoples and thinking nothing at all about slaughtering those who might resist them. The Alien Agenda would say we do it to ourselves, because this is the way we treat our own livestock; thus, we reap what we sow.

••

2   Freeman, Makia, "Soul-Catching Net: We Are 'Recycled' at Death to Remain in the Matrix." **http://humansarefree.com/2015/07/soul-catching-net-we-are-recycled-at.html**

At least one species of Grey ETs claims to have come to Earth because their own home planet was decimated by cosmic events. These events were drawn to them because of their own selfish purposes—in ways that negated the positive energies of Creation. The Greys excel in using the power of their minds, yet they lack compassion for those whom they abduct or encounter. They understand that a body is simply housing for a spirit. They hypnotize, they mesmerize and they use the tool of fear.

What is happening on Earth at this time is spiritual warfare in the truest sense. At one level, humankind must stop supporting evil enterprises whether they be dark and fearful imagery being broadcast, or efforts through corporations to weaken humankind physically through polluted foods, medicines, the earth, the waters, the skies. This battle is as much interpersonal as it is an external war currently taking place.

THE ARCHON NETWORK

Unfortunately, we are not free. We haven't been free for many millennia. We have overlords, trans-dimensional beings who have invaded Earth many thousands of years ago, and still remain. In the ancient legends, they are known as the gods. The Gnostics knew of them as the archons. Don Juan called them "the Predators." They are our overlords, and they have constructed a matrix, or false covering of illusions, to cover the Earth, which keeps us captive. They keep us as their herd, just as we keep farm animals. We are their food. We have been in their grip for thousands of years. We have been mind-controlled, brainwashed and hypnotized to believe these illusions to be reality. They consider us their herd, like their livestock, and they feed off of our bio-photons. They can attach themselves to individuals, and influence their emotions. That is the predicament we find ourselves in, and it will be difficult to change.

An archon, in the Gnosticism of late antiquity, was any of several servants of the Demiurge, the "creator god," that stood between the human race and a transcendent God who could only be reached through *gnosis*. In this context, they have the role of the angels and demons of the Old Testament. They give their name to the sect called Archontics. They were thus called from the Greek word *apzovreg*, meaning "principalities," or "rulers," by reason that they held the world to have been created and ruled by malevolent archons. The term was taken from the ancient Greek position of office—"archon."

There are several malevolent species of ETs, and most if not all were inter-dimensionals at one time, meaning they could travel between dimensions without the aid of any craft, and this ability also makes them archons. Up to one third of all known ETs interacting with Earth have joined the Satanic Rebellion, which is controlling Earth and has been for six "Cosmic Days," or 6,000 Earth years. We are living in the time period when the Rebellion is being put down. All the Rebel Forces have now been confined to our solar system. This is why we have seen such a rise in UFO activity, namely, reports of abductions and more people channeling Alien messages. Earth will become their "last stand at the Alamo," and in time, this system of evil will be destroyed. What we are not supposed to know is that their intention is to "scuttle" Earth. We have been slated for extermination! The plan is to depopulate Earth surface-dwelling humans, ascribing the plan to groups such as the Jesuits, Illuminati, Draco Reptilian/Orion Grey occupiers, manipulatory Anunnaki ETs, and others.[3]

Tom Montalk is an author and a fellow truth seeker on a quest to expose the dark, and empower the light. His primary goal is to help others arm themselves with knowledge to better fulfill their evolutionary potential. He writes in the Archon Network:

> *Because hostile hyperdimensional forces have a vested interest in the Matrix Control System, they go to extraordinary lengths to suppress any destabilizing factors*

3   Montalk, Tom, on the Archon Network https://montalk.net/audio/248/1-what-is-the-matrix-control-system-video.

that could disrupt their food supply. Anyone who starts the process of waking up and regaining personal power and freedom is immediately targeted. The targeting aims to put him or her back to sleep, render her powerless, or make him to lose faith in continuing his path. When a personal impulse toward freedom occurs, an equal and opposite impulse is set into motion, attracting to the target various negatively synchronistic opportunities to engage in vibe-lowering experiences to offset his impulse toward freedom. These include situations that aim to induce fear, distraction, suffering, doubt, depression, indulgence in lower impulses, and self-serving behavior. Sometimes this phenomenon arises naturally from the law of inertia (occult and karmic laws) while other times there is intentional and active amplification of this counter-impulse by negative hyperdimensional forces to disarm the threat before he gains more power. Other methods of suppression include sabotaging and distracting a targeted individual via people around him who are open to direct manipulation. Anyone who fails to be fully conscious in the present moment can be a puppet for as long as his or her attention is elsewhere. Lapses of attention are enough for a subconsciously implanted impulse to result in regrettable words or actions.

ET abductees, who confirmed numerous repeated abductions and electromagnetic tortures, told Tom Montalk about a predatory hyper-dimensional species that has stated their intent to ultimately displace humanity on planet Earth. One ET abductee who goes by the anonymous name, "George," reported hyper-dimensional predatory species as being a major threat to humanity. George indicates that he began to be abducted by the hyper-dimensional species in early childhood, when the beings that entered his bedroom appeared as a species of grey ETs and sometimes as shadow beings. Later, in his mid-twenties, George experienced holographic projections in his mind, intense voice-to-skull projections, and electromagnetic torture.

The predatory species has the capability to download an individual's memory and create fear-based programs that are then projected holographically into the subject's mind. Within our own Shadow Government, there is a black budget "transhumanist" electronic torture taking place against unsuspecting people or "targeted individuals." During the interview, George discusses why he attributes the electromagnetic technologies of torture he experienced to a predatory hyper-dimensional species when the technologies are similar to covert electromagnetic and scalar technologies employed by human military and intelligence agencies against human populations, especially in MILABS (short for "military abductions"). George also revealed the scenario in which the dimensional predatory species has a cooperative relationship with the Trans-humanist plan of covert electronic and scalar control of humanity's agenda.[4]

GNOSTIC ARCHONS

In 1947, French scholar Jean Doresse described the discovery of ancient scrolls at Nag Hammadi, Egypt, as being a cache of rare Gnostic texts. Gnosticism is considered the "One True Faith," and became an underground branch of Christianity. Gnosticism also is the label scholars use for a body of teachings derived from the mystery schools of pre-Christian antiquity. The Gnostic texts describe the archons who are nonphysical entities that feed off of negative energy, such as hatred and fear. This control grid is still very much in place today. This explains why you'll never feel good after watching the nightly news or reading the headlines of any given newspaper. Archons are (most of the time) dangerous intrapsychic mind-parasites, just like most of their Islamic counterparts, the *Jinn*, used by the occult elite for centuries, and more recently by the Intelligence agencies to trick and manipulate us.

• •
4   Webre, Alfred Lambremont, "ET Abductee: Hyperdimensional predatory species is threat to humanity." **http://www.youtube.com/watch?v =MToni1LCwRA&feature=youtu.be.**

Physical descriptions of the archons occur in several Gnostic codices. Two types are clearly identified: a neonate or embryonic type, and a draconic or reptilian type. The inorganic alien type is not a physical entity that can be seen in our third dimensional reality. Obviously, the latter description fits the Grey and Reptilian ETs of contemporary reports very closely. The Gnostic creation myth is unique in that it includes an expansive explanation of how inorganic alien beings came to be present in our solar system. The Gnostics taught that these entities envy us, and feed on our negative emotions. Above all, they attempt to keep us from claiming and evolving our "inner light," the gift of divine intelligence within, by keeping us fighting with ourselves and with others.

Digging deeper, the Nag Hammadi material contains reports of visionary experiences of the initiates, including first-hand encounters with inorganic beings called by names such as the archons. Gnostic teaching explains that these entities arose in the early stage of formation of the solar system, before the Earth was even formed. Archons inhabit the solar system, the extraterrestrial realm as such, but they can intrude on Earth. The Gnostics said the archons could affect our minds by subliminal conditioning techniques. Their main tactics are mental error (intellectual virus, or false ideology, especially religious doctrines) and simulation. Archons are predatory, unlike a wide range of non-human and other-dimensional beings also know to the Gnostics— the latter being benevolent or neutral toward humanity.

ENTER THE ANUNNAKI

The Sumerian cuneiform tablets are among the oldest known texts to humankind, and predate anything written in the Bible or any other religious texts. According to the Sumerian texts, the Draconian Anunnaki traveled to this planet in search of gold to use as a micro-dust to protect the atmosphere of their own planet of origin from radiation.

At first, the Anunnaki mined their own gold but realized this was too much work, so they genetically manipulated the genes of the native Earth species to eventually create the Adama race, or what we know today as humankind. This explains why we only have 46 chromosomes with 2 of them being fused together while all other earthly primates have 48. Looking carefully at the various blood types and Rh values, it appears to be impossible to have so many races and ethnicities on this planet coming from "Adam and Eve." "Adam" is short for the "Adama race" which the Anunnaki created, so is it possible that all races were created as a sub-species experiment?

Another theory counter to the research of archaeological theorist, Zecharia Sitchin, is that the reptilian Anunnaki weren't mining for gold for their planet's atmosphere; rather, they wanted to ingest it as monatomic gold. It supports their biochemistry and longevity, and it works for humans in the same way. As indicated above, they needed a workforce smart enough to take orders, but dumb enough to consider them as "lords" and "gods." By the way, there were other ET races here playing the "create human" game; it wasn't just the Anunnaki. This was the great Earth Experiment, and the lust for gold has never gone away. This would explain why there is such a need and demand for gold in every society.

The Anunnaki were descendants of royalty, as is known, with the leadership on Earth from the royal bloodline. They were given to a militaristic structure throughout, being more inclined toward the service to self than most third density cultures, and very rule-based. Infractions were dealt with in a brutal fashion. The royalty on their traveling planet, Nibiru, held the crown, that is, the kingship. The planets are represented. Sitchin recounts that Nibiru was known as the 12th Planet because the sun and moon were counted, as well as the nine known planets.[5]

The Sumerian story relates how one of the Anunnaki, named Enki, created seven demi-

5   Sitchin, Zecharia. *Genesis Revisited: Is Modern Science Catching Up with Ancient Knowledge*. Avon, 1990.

gods to help civilize humankind. These demigods were known as the Apkallu. Like the Apkallu and the fallen angels that spawned the Nephilim, they are capable of interbreeding with humans. The mysterious Nephilim are actually named in the *Book of Enoch* which was censored and blocked from being part of the Holy Bible. The *Book of Enoch* describes the fall of the Watchers, the angels who fathered the Nephilim (i.e. the Bene Elohim, featured in Genesis 6:1-2), and names the demons. The "Fallen Angels" were cast out of Heaven by the Creator of All, God Almighty—also referred to as the "Nephilim."

INTERDIMENSIONALS AND THE REPTILIAN MIND

When peering down the rabbit hole on the pathless path, one is inevitably confronted by an inter-dimensional race of beings, often of an insect-like or reptilian nature, perched atop the pinnacle of power that constitutes the nucleus of the New World Order. These are the real "generals" running the show. All human cut-outs are below them. The appellations attributed to these dark interstellar malevolent ETs are myriad, and run the gamut of everything from the Sumerian Anunnaki to the Sons of God to the Mothman sightings.

Throughout history, we have heard tales about the strange-looking creatures called reptoids or greys that apparently live among us on Earth. There are many, many stories about these entities, both in the past and the present. In addition to accounts, modern-day sightings are becoming more and more frequent. There have been stories of half-human and half-reptile beings, or a hybrid human-grey humanoid for centuries, but is this just the result of human imagination, or is there something more about these strange beings that have frequented our history texts?

According to whistleblower William Tompkins, in his three-part Project Camelot interview, we are being manipulated and harvested by various predatory species known as Rebel Aliens. Although there are many ET species interacting with humanity right now, including Alpha Draconians which influence some groups, and Nordics which influence other groups, Reptilians basically control every government in the world. Tompkins warns that if he talks about Reptilians and their darkest activities—which include eating humans and performing blood sacrifices—some people will think it is so crazy that they will automatically shut down and discredit everything else he says. Kerry Cassidy reiterates the philosophy of Project Camelot: "that humans in general are not protecting themselves and are ignorant of the dangers of predatory ET species, and that therefore it is vital that those in the know go public with their knowledge and warn others—because not to do so equates to culpability." For what it's worth, Tompkins also offers his opinion that all recent U.S. Presidents (including Obama) have been shapeshifters who can change their form—but that Donald Trump is not one of them.[6]

IT'S A COOKBOOK!

In a famous *Twilight Zone* episode, humans are given a book from a tall race of ETs, who invite willing people onto their craft. At the very end, when many people had already boarded the spaceship preparing for takeoff, the book is revealed to be a cookbook for eating humans. The point is that reality can sometimes be stranger than science fiction. According to contactee Alex Collier, the Alpha Draconians, a reptilian race composed of master geneticists, are known to have a proclivity for tinkering with life itself. From their perspective, humans exist as a natural resource, much as a rancher thinks of his livestock. The Draconians look at lifeforms which they have created or altered as a resource to be consumed at their pleasure. Apparently, the Alpha Draconians created the primate race too, which

6   Tompkins, William, "WILLIAM TOMPKINS LATEST INTERVIEW—MUST SEE!" http://projectcamelotportal.com/2016/11/20/william-tompkins-latest-interview-bob-wood-walter-nowosad.

was first brought to Mars and then to Earth. The primate race was then genetically altered using different DNA in our distant past.

The short-term goal of the Dracos has always been to create as much human suffering and painful mass death as possible. They are the top of the archon food chain, so they also have the ability to forge entity attachments on people. These methods are also used to create the massive suffering and early death which provide the negative energy these Dracos (Cosmic Vampires) need to thrive. The more negative energy they get from suffering and dying humans and animals, the more energy and power they receive to further their anti-human agenda of suffering, death and total destruction of all humans, eventually even their own kingpin cut-outs and the useless idiots who blindly went along with their diabolical plans.

Alien greys are subservient to a Mothman race—sentient, highly technological reptilian overlords, monitor-lizard-men—who use the same dimensions and portals that ghosts and demons use to enter and exit our "reality" dimension. Small greys are synthetic work beings with simple digestive systems, and they do the heavy lifting, abducting and surgeries under reptilian domination. Mantis alien forms are also seen by abductees aboard craft. They are highly technological and stand seven feet tall, with bulbous eyes and a sinister demeanor.

Suddenly these beings' silhouettes emerge: a reptilian masquerade of an ancient reptilian Mayan and Aztec "god"—a god who organized a "religion" that provided him a delicacy he most desired, that of a still-beating human heart. Human young are a preferred diet, as we never were the "top of the food-chain." Indeed, humans are the food! Both physically and psychically.

Author Preston James chronicles the ancient reptilian, the "order of the snake" reptilian aliens, AKA the evil Luciferian Draco ETs, who've recruited their human cut-outs throughout the centuries. They are the originators of World Zionism, which emerged from the Teutonic Knights and the Hanseatic League, now suspected to be the horsepower behind Mystery Babylon, Babylonian Money-Magick and the Old Black Nobility (AKA the "Hidden Hand.") Today, the human cut-out Committee of 300 governs the world via the "Empire of Three Cities,"—independent states in which the cities pay no taxes and obey their own laws. These independent states are: the City of London Corporation, the financial power center established in 1067; the District of Columbia, the military power center established in 1871; and Vatican City, which reigns as the religious power center, sovereign since 1929. Descendants of the Tribe of Levi control the financial and religious arms of the empire. This includes the entire banking system and the political systems of the world. Once again, the Rothschild family emerges as the most powerful banking family in the world. They cooperate with the predatory species—the Luciferian Draco ETs.

THE ET REBEL FORCE ON EARTH

William Tompkins also says the Rebel Aliens who have captured planet Earth have long maintained a pact with the elite (who worship them as gods) to sacrifice the rest of us, who are against them or ignorant of their plans or existence. Once this is done, they will have full control of the future of the human race. All humans on Earth will be worshipping these Rebels as gods, and no one will know any different. This is their plan!

These "service to self" entities work with the CIA and certain factions of the "black projects" military. They can channel messages telepathically with humans and, furthermore, they are worshiped by the "Ruling Class" of this planet who sacrifice children to them. Their leader is Lucifer, also known as the "Slanderer" and "Deceiver." David Spangler, a prominent Findhorn Foundation New Ager (endorsed by the UN) had this to say in praise:

Lucifer comes to give to us the final gift of wholeness. If we accept it, then he is free and we are free. This is the Luciferic initiation. It is one that many people now, and in the days ahead, will be facing, for it is an initiation into the New Age...No one will enter the New World Order unless he or she will make a pledge to worship Lucifer. No one will enter the New Age unless they will take a Luciferian initiation.[7]

Researcher Preston James observes there has been an evil Alien Agenda unleashed on Planet Earth by a cosmic parasite, known to top insiders as the Draco, for at least the last 5,400 years. This alien entity feeds off of human suffering and painful human death. This negative group is part of the Orion Confederacy. Space program people call them the Draco, although other groups are part of it as well. The Draco does have several outposts on planets around some of the stars in Orion, which is a constellation not that far away from Earth.

These Dracos are reported by some to be shape-shifting interdimensional "Fallen Angels" or "Cosmic Parasites" which are negative-energy vampires, exceedingly evil beyond what most can imagine and duplicitous beyond normal human reason. They are experts at convincing the public that right is left, and left is right; good is evil, and evil is good. And the worst part is that they have apparently gained control of most of the earth's riches by hijacking most of the fiat monetary systems under the power of the Draco ancient Babylonian Money-Magick or applied Black-Magic Arts. The Dracos are a conquering race, and William Tompkins' testimony revealed that they contacted the Nazis not just to subdue the Earth (hopefully), but to create an army that could be used to conquer many other worlds as well. The Nazis had the mentality and industrial know-how that the Dracos wanted, and began colonizing space with the technology the Dracos gave them in the late 1930s.[8]

Their specialty is manufacturing and distributing mass mind-control culture (by way of the media) through Hollywood films and television shows. Many such films and shows condition humans to enjoy behaving in self-destructive and selfish ways, which also destroy their families, sex roles, religion and nations. They are believed to be parasites that feed off of the negative energy of great pain and long-term suffering of humans.

These Dracos are reputed to be able to induce this massive human suffering (both fast-kill and slow-kill death methods) in many different varieties. They do this by the use of ultra-high-tech mass mind-control, telepathic psi-power, administration of Black-Magick spells, induced manufactured long-term illness through aerosol spraying, Smart Meter and 5G frequency radiation, air pollution, contaminated or poisonous vaccines, fluoride in the water, aspartame and other bio-chemical and chemical means in food designed to slow-kill humans by the masses.

One of the Dracos main long-term agendas is to allegedly depopulate the Earth and replace humans with a very small number of their Draco-human hybrids and custom-designed, engineered and cloned biological androids and trans-humans, which will become biological machines, similar to the Greys.

SOME ETS ARE FROM EARTH

The Greys are actually not aliens—they were created by a progenitor race here on Earth around 25,000 years ago, Anthony Sanchez explains in his book, *UFO Highway*. The Greys are still working out of the Dulce base, as well as at the Pine Gap underground base in Australia. Currently at Dulce, there is conventional weapons development using plasma nuclear technology, bio-experimentation that accounts for the cattle and animal

7   Spangler, David, Quoted from "Reflections on the Christ," 1978 ed., Chapter IV, pgs. 44-45.
8   Goode, Corey, "Corey Goode Intel Update Part 1" **https://spherebeingalliance.com/blog/corey-goode-intel-update-part-1-aug-2016. html**

mutilations, and genetic testing that relates to human abductions in the area. Sanchez explains how conflict with the Greys is due to a schism which arose in ancient times, when the Anunnaki came to Earth and created a human-ET hybrid species.[9]

Similarly, the Draco Dark Lords have lived on Earth for thousands of years and have been hard at work dominating and parasitizing the planet and humans on and off again for many centuries, being driven out at times in the past through major corrections, planetary disasters of some kind, or "cosmic correction" or "judgment." The Greys and the Dracos that have been born on Earth and have been here for many generations are better classified as innerterrestrials, or inter-dimensionals. For this reason, they are also archons.

Certain inner-terrestrials are the ancient bloodline families on Earth that can look very human. Some identify these bloodlines as Alien/human hybrids (e.g. Nephilim Male X Human Female). Some call them the Kenites or the bloodline of Cain, who were given the power to rule over evil, folks who display the symbol of the Mark of Cain which is a double cross or "double-X." If this is true, this would perhaps best be described as an Alien Parasite that invaded planet Earth—appointing, anointing, and empowering select human bloodlines (which may or may not be hybridized) with their blood, and appointing and anointing these folks to rule Earth according to their evil Alien Agenda. Those wicked Canaanite followers of Cain and Abel are Cann-Ables or cannibals.

As this narrative goes, the Dracos created "Mystery Babylon" which is their system of Babylonian Money-Magick, that is, creating money from nothing as "debt-notes" in order to transfer wealth from the masses to themselves through the creation and use of "pernicious usury" (debt that accrues in such a way that it can never be paid off).

By the way, not all the Alien ET races visiting Planet earth are believed to be as malignant as the Draco Cosmic Parasites. Some insiders have said there are over 100 different ET species visiting Earth, and few ever reveal themselves. Many Dracos came thousands of years ago in their reptilian bodies through jump rooms in the subterranean bases, and in their subsequent incarnations they have taken human bodies and today they are part of the Cabal, the Illuminati. They can be the Draco incarnated in human bodies. And at the top tier, they know they are Dracos and it's a part of their "pride" to be at the top of the pecking order. They see themselves as a superior race. It's one of their so-called secrets that they are not actually fully human.

RELFE SPEAKS

Former U.S. serviceman Michael Relfe has authored *The Mars Records*, two books over a 20-year span, from 1976-1996. He states he spent part of a permanent armed-force detail on a U.S. facility on Mars, which was part of the security perimeter developed in our solar system against the attempted occupation by a predatory hyper-dimensional species. In October, 2013, Relfe released an Open Letter sent to the military leaders of many prominent nations. The letter asserted that "Previous members of the military made a grave mistake when they hid the reality of aliens from the people of Earth. That mistake has been continued. That mistake could endanger the future of humanity forever. It is time to remedy this situation before it is too late." He goes on to outline how to counter the agenda of predatory species:

> *This battle against predatory species cannot be won by military might and technology alone. By now you know that this scenario involves energies and technology beyond your wildest imagination. For example, how can you hope to win a battle against an enemy when the enemy possesses jump gates and mind control technologies so that any head of government can be abducted and mind controlled at any time? And how*

9   Sanchez, Anthony, *UFO Highway*. Strange Lights Publications, 2nd edition, 2011.

can you hope to win a battle against an enemy that can hide itself from your perception? These predatory species, their technology and those humans that voluntarily serve them, can only be defeated by harnessing the cumulative might of the metaphysical and spiritual powers, as well as the intelligence, of the people of earth.

ET abductees confirm the presence of predatory species. Some discuss the interaction between the predatory species and ethical hyper-dimensional intelligent civilizations that also interact with humanity. There is documented evidence through researchers such as Mary Rodwell, who has compiled replicable empirical evidence, that ethical, hyper-dimensional civilizations exist that are closely involved in the positive development of humanity. These include hyper-dimensional civilizations of the Grey phenotype, of which approximately 150 have been identified. Some are good, and some are bad. In his Open Letter, Relfe states:

These predatory species work in secrecy because they are afraid of human beings. They are afraid of God. …That is why, by subversive means, they have influenced the systems of Earth to do all in their power to keep people enslaved. This includes:

Keeping knowledge of their existence and their evil intentions hidden, until it is too late.

Vaccinating people, which damages their metaphysical abilities.

Genetically modified foods and nanotechnology which damage the DNA of the body, so that metaphysical abilities and reproduction are destroyed.

Fluoride which damages the pineal gland, necessary for metaphysical abilities.

Numerous toxins to damage the body (See the book, You're Not Fat, You're Toxic*).*

Lack of information of spiritual power and metaphysical abilities, so that powerful meta-psychics do not develop their powers.[10]

WHAT CAN BE DONE?

SP veteran, Michael Relfe, has asserted that humanity is being targeted by a predatory hyper-dimensional species. He has sent an *Open Letter to Heads of the Military Regarding Defeating the Alien Presence* to military leaders and government heads around the world. Relfe recommends 12 steps to the military leaders he addresses in defeating the attempted occupation by the predatory hyper-dimensional species. He urges that time is running out. All governments of all countries need to:

1) Release all of the true information concerning alien invasion of this planet.
2) Release the true information concerning the ancient things found upon the moon and Mars.
3) Release the true information concerning government developed advanced technology and its use in establishing off planet projects.
4) Release the true information concerning electronic medicine so long suppressed and allow people to be healed of terrible degenerative diseases.
5) Stop the vaccinations, which kill us and destroy our metaphysical abilities.
6) Stop the GMO foods, which sterilize people after two generations. These "foods" will end civilization and you will not have anything to defend.
7) Stop the use of nanotechnology in food (and chemtrail spraying).
8) Stop the MSG, Aspartame and Excitotoxins that brain damage us and kill us. These chemicals are poisoning your soldiers.
9) Stop mind controlling and abducting people with metaphysical abilities.

10 Relfe, Michael "Open Letter to Heads of the Military Regarding Defeating the Alien Presence," https://www.themarsrecords.com/wp/the-mars-records/open-letter-heads-military-regarding-defeating-alien-presence/

10) *Openly recruit and employ with generous remuneration sane, ethical metaphysically gifted people to fight these predatory species.*

11) *Punish and eliminate the corporations that prey upon the population, and that help predatory species enslave us.*

12) *Remove Christians from the "terrorist" list. They are not your enemy. They are the enemy of the predatory species.*

Know that if you do the above, the people of Earth will find ways to help you rid Earth of alien parasites, by working in the spiritual and metaphysical realms in ways that you cannot possibly imagine.

Michael Relfe has put the call out to military and political leaders that humanity is being targeted by a predatory hyper-dimensional species. He urges each of us to contact our Congressman or Member of Parliament. But this is no small task, and time is running out. Mass perception is a hard nut to crack. Will the masses come to understand all the death and destruction this evil establishment hierarchy bloodline has brought upon us? Can humans organize and decide *en masse* to follow truth, goodness, mercy and the Golden Rule of "do unto others as you would have them do unto you" instead of hate, death and evil?

A COSMIC STRUGGLE

We live in an unprecedented period in which our planet and solar system is about to undergo a dramatic energetic shift, which is tantamount to a massive spiritual transformation for everyone. The more loving, helpful, kind and compassionate we are, the more we will benefit from this change, as it ultimately is a type of spiritual graduation. We will gain new abilities much like the great masters we read about in spiritual texts. The negative archon forces are allowed to offer temptations and thought forms to us whenever and wherever we invite them to, but like a vampire of lore, they must be invited and welcomed by the host. This is part of the cosmic law of free will that governs the universe. These negative beings ultimately feed on our fear, anger and sadness, which is often called "loosh," and literally acts as an energetic food source for them. Keeping your emotional state in high vibration starves the archons, and then they cannot stay around you for long. They manipulate human perception so that we create (imagine into holographic existence) the world that suits them. They have to trick us into creating our own collective prison—and they have. The Demiurge and the archons are professional hijackers and they have long-ago captured Earth and the perceptions of its inhabitants. We may only have this one opportunity to rid the Earth of the archon invasion.

Also known as the loyalists or Guardian Angels (everyone has one), our personal guides honor the Prime Directive toward Earth. They can save lives, yet they never channel and seldom say anything at all to anyone. Christians consider them part of the "Armies of Heaven" commanded by the "King of Kings" and the "Immortals," they will soon help liberate us from the Rebel Force and their human cut-out supporters controlling and destroying Earth. These ethical hyperdimensional species are "service to others" and want to see humanity make the leap to the great awakening.

Considering the monumental moment in history we face, the benevolent ETs are willing to help with the parasitic invasion. According to contactee Corey Goode, the service to other ETs stand ready *if asked* to remove the archon network. They have already put the planet into a quarantine to block further external harassment and interference. Corey Goode also reports the space-faring Rebel Force was blocked from invasion, literally, when their marauding battlestar "planet" Nibiru began its oblong entry into the solar system, back in the spring of 2003. (Yes, George Lucas was on to something with his portrayal in *Star Wars* of a huge cruising Death Star. Such was real.) This time the "Good Guys" were there to meet them. Realizing there would be no reinforcements to simulate an "alien invasion" and assist in locking Earth down, the "Bad Guys" began to panic and look for ways to subtly oppress and manipulate humankind. They were met by the Good Guys and asked to stop and leave, but the Bad Guys mounted a valid argument: "We have been here for eons, it is our planet, and we can do what we want. This is a free will universe, free will planet, and as their creator, the humans still need us. They are our responsibility and we have to control them or human society will fall apart, and chaos will rule."

Of course, this chapter will be very difficult for some to believe. Humans have been conditioned to laugh at things that smack of Sci-Fi, such as mermaids, Bigfoot, Nessie, and lately UFOs—the Dark Lords have seen to this disbelief. The goal was for humans to subjugate and oppress themselves with a refusal to seriously investigate anything for themselves that is not Mom, apple pie and football. Humans have been trained to keep themselves imprisoned by denial of anything that might liberate them—that was fiendishly clever. Get prisoners to keep themselves in jail, and even defend their own imprisonment. We cannot fight what we do not understand.

The Bohemian Grove is a 2,000 acre private campground in Monte Rio, CA. They only admit males, it's defended by armed guards, and is primarily used by the Bohemian Club of San Francisco. Some of their members include Hoover, Hearst, Eisenhower, Nixon, Kissinger, Reagan, Rumsfeld, Cronkite, Jimmy Carter, Gerald Ford, Colin Powell, Gingrich, Bush Sr., and Bush Jr., and many other extremely rich and powerful men. Every summer solstice, or Midsummer's Eve, they hold a two-week festival. This festival and drunken debauchery is begun by a ceremony called "The Cremation of Care." In this ceremony, performed in front of hundreds of club members, a group of "priests" dressed in white, black, and red ceremonial robes, burn a human effigy in a sacrificial fire before a 40-foot-tall stone statue of an Owl/Moloch. The idea is that this symbolizes their being free from the worries of daily life and free to have fun in the grove. But it is almost identical to the ancient Babylonian and Canaanite practice of burning children before idols, in groves. And they have been doing this in California for about 140 years. The motto of the Bohemian Club, which owns the Grove, is "Weaving Spiders Come Not Here."

This engraving by Cornelis Galle I, after Lodovico Cigoli (1591-1650), depicts Lucifer eating people. Elite Dutch banker Ronald Bernard: "To put it carefully, most people followed a not very mainstream religion. These people, most of them, were Luciferians. And then you can say, religion is a fairy tale, God doesn't exist, none of that is real. Well for these people it is truth and reality, and they served something immaterial which they called Lucifer. And I also was in contact with those circles, only I laughed at it because to me they were just clients. So I went to places called Churches of Satan. So I visited these places and they were doing their Holy Mass with naked women and liquor and stuff. And it just amused me. I didn't believe in any of this stuff and was far from convinced any of this was real. In my opinion, the darkness and evil are within the people themselves. I didn't make the connection yet. So I was a guest in those circles and it amused me greatly to see all those naked women and the other things. It was the good life. But then at some moment, which is why I am telling you this, I was invited to participate in (human) sacrifices abroad."

"In the ruins of Sumerian cities excavated by archaeologists...There are texts specifically dealing with the Solar System. There are texts among the unearthed tablets that list the planets orbiting the Sun in their correct order; one text even gives the distances between the planets. And there are illustrations on cylinder seals depicting the Solar System, as the one shown in Plate B that is at least 4,500 years old and that is now kept in the Near Eastern Section of the State Museum in East Berlin, catalogued under number VA/243. If we study the illustration sketched in the upper left-hand comer of the Sumerian depiction, we see a complete Solar System in which the Sun (not Earth!) is in the center, orbited by all the planets we know of today."—Excerpt from Zecharia Sitchin's book, *Genesis Revisited: Is Modern Science Catching Up With Ancient Knowledge?*

The jinn are beings with free will, living on Earth in a world parallel to humankind. The Arabic word means "to conceal." They appear to include juvenile pranksters as well as powerful superior beings with an agenda we don't understand. They have influenced humankind's religious and cultural beliefs from antiquity to the present. They can be conjured into our reality in a number of different ways.

"Human sacrifice" has always been utilized by pharaohs, emperors, kings, queens and high priests. In the ancient Mayan culture, human sacrifice was the ritual of offering nourishment to the gods. Blood was viewed as a potent source of nourishment for the deities, and the sacrifice of a living creature was a powerful blood offering. By extension, the sacrifice of a human life was the ultimate offering of blood to the gods, and the most important Mayan rituals culminated in human sacrifice. Generally, only high status prisoners of war were sacrificed, the lower status captives being used for labor.

This a common rendition of the fabled Mothman that was seen in and around Point Pleasant, West Virginia, decades ago. Some say the Mothmen are actually the Winged Draco, a reptilian predatory species here on Earth. Author Len Kasten characterized some benevolent ETs as beneficent in nature, but the race known as the Reptilians are more callous to humanity. He outlined how they preceded humans on our planet, arriving from the Draco system, bringing the dinosaurs in tow as a food source, and first settling in Lemuria. In thee Modern Age, the thousands of mysterious disappearances of people Earth can be blamed on the Reptilians, who regard humans as "farm animals."

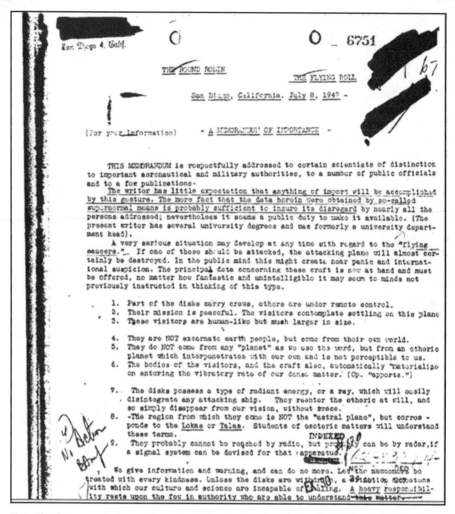

This official document of record from the FBI can be found on their website "The Vault." This "Memorandum of Importance" is from July, 1947. Below are the points outlined and understood at that time. Can you imagine what they now know?

1. Part of the disks carry crews; others are under remote control.

2. Their mission is peaceful. The visitors contemplate settling on this plane.

3. These visitors are human-like, but much larger in size.

4. They are not excarnate Earth people, but come from their own world.

5. They do NOT come from a planet as we use the word, but from an etheric planet which interpenetrates with our own and is not perceptible to us.

6. The bodies of the visitors, and the craft, automatically materialize on entering the vibratory rate of our dense matter.

7. The disks possess a type of radiant energy or a ray, which will easily disintegrate any attacking ship. They re-enter the etheric at will, and so simply disappear from our vision, without a trace.

8. The region from which they come is not the "astral plane," but corresponds to the Lokas or Talas. Students of esoteric matters will understand these terms.

9. They probably cannot be reached by radio, but probably by radar, if a signal system can be devised for that (apparatus).

Addendum: The Lokas are oval shaped, fluted-length ovals with a heat-resistant metal or alloy not yet known. The front cage contains the controls, the middle portion a laboratory; the rear contains armaments, which consists essentially of a powerful energy apparatus, perhaps a ray.

St. Peter's Church, Cornhill, located right in the heart of the banker's haven City of London — a church where three devils welcome you inside.

The pine cone represents the pineal gland, which is a human's third eye, or the seat of all human consciousness. The bag represents the genetic material that the Anunnaki had rearranged to give humanity limited consciousness. This was done so we would be easier to enslave and control. Although the Anunnaki were not the progenitors of the human genome, they overthrew the Pleiadeans who were the actual creators of nearly all biological life on the entire planet. It is said "only intelligent life can create intelligent life." Many antediluvian civilizations were populated with ancient astronauts.

Space is not what we are told. It is not just "up" and "out there," but it is also down and through the second domain of the Earth realm called Oceania, the abode of Leviathan who is the guardian, along with Behemoth, of the earth realm, as depicted in this William Blake painting. The gateways are accessed via The Deep. This relates to the present controversy over Antarctica and the so-called "North Pole." They aren't "poles," but they are gateways and entrances to Inner Earth.

ET IS ALREADY HOME

"The evidence that the Earth is being visited by at least one extraterrestrial civilization is extensive both in scope and detail. In its totality, it comprises a body of evidence which at the very least supports the general assessment that extraterrestrial life has been detected, and that a vigorous program of research and serious diplomatic initiatives is warranted." –Dr. Steven Greer, Director of Center for the Study of Extra-Terrestrial Intelligence (CSETI)

WHAT if we are not alone…right here on planet Earth? What if we've never been alone? The evidence reveals that extraterrestrials have always been here, and certain species are as native and terrestrial to our planet as are fire and rain. They are the game wardens of this preserve that we call "Earth," and like good game wardens, they do not encourage the creatures within to suspect that it is a lifeform preserve *and* a prison planet. And as predatory masters, they demand access to the herd.

In the past, extraterrestrials have occasionally intervened in human affairs by causing a change in the beliefs of the masses. William Cooper claimed the aliens have been manipulating humanity for centuries through secret societies, witchcraft, magic, the occult and religion. Some alien species have acted like gods to cause humans to believe in slavery and suffering. Other extraterrestrials have acted like gods to cause humans to believe in the end of slavery and suffering. But always this involved changing beliefs, and acting like gods is an easy trick to change the beliefs of the many. Our perceptions define our experiences, since we can only experience what we perceive. And our perceptions are only limited by our beliefs. We will always see and experience what we believe to be true.

On the malevolent ET side of exopolitics, we begin to see the larger agenda of subversive planetary control hidden from the rest of us. The Luciferian black arts, which the Old Black Nobility have had a known allegiance with since ancient times, is involved with the cross-breeding between aliens and humans to create hybrids with super psi-powers from the "Dark Side." If true, then psi-power is a Luciferian Black Arts power provided by aliens to a certain select group of humans who have been deeply involved with them for many generations. For those that doubt this, do some basic research on Aleister Crowley and how a grey alien ET type appeared to him inside a pyramid in Egypt. This same power was sought by certain top SS Nazi officers in the basement of Wewelsburg Castle. These gatherings were related to their occult organization, the "Black Sun." Some experts believe that it was the occult connection to these "alien ET spirit guides" that provided the advanced Nazi weapons technology, including anti-gravity craft and perhaps even time-warping. It also gives new meaning to the concept of "selling your soul to the devil."

Child/human trafficking is one of the fastest growing crimes in the world. Human trafficking is a $12 billion dollar-a-year industry and is the world's second largest criminal enterprise, only after drugs. Every year, about 800,000 children go missing. Every year hundreds of thousands of children are trafficked. Saturn = Satan = El = Moloch. The power elite of this world worship Saturn and appease him with child sacrifices just as they have for hundreds of years. The best known of these displays is the "Cremation of Care" ceremony held annually at Bohemian Grove, where it is reported the members sacrifice a child to their god Moloch.

MYSTERY SCHOOLS

The core of the malevolent ETs control over planet Earth's populace lies in ancient cults. These cults are still in existence to this day, and are following the most ancient religions mixed with sexual worship. The main cults are the worship of the planet Saturn (El), the Moon (Isis), Venus (Lucifer), the Sun (Ba'al) and (Ra). Ba'al was a title and honorific meaning "owner," "master" or "lord." Ba'al was particularly associated with the storm and fertility god, Hadad, and his local manifestations.

Astrologically Saturn represents darkness, misfortune, death and fear. There is a curious hexagram formation at the northern top of Saturn. Saturday is named after the Roman god Saturn. The ancient Greeks referred to this god as Cronus. The symbol of Saturn/Cronus is the sickle. Saturday is the sixth day of the week in Western cultures, and Saturn is the sixth planet from the Sun. Saturn had six children with his wife Ops, and the sixth of these children was Jupiter or, as the Greeks knew him, Zeus. The sickle of Saturn and the hammer of Thor (Jupiter/Zeus combined) is represented in the symbol of Communism.

The world secret religion for millennia is the Cult of Amun. Without knowing it, Jews, Christians and Muslims all around the world are honoring Amun at the end of their prayers. Amun = Amon = Amen. Amun represents the essential and hidden, and the power elite thrive on keeping the masses in the dark, and from knowing who they are. Nothing is as it seems.

Ignatius of Loyola and the House of Borgia were crypto-Jewish Marranos of the Los Alumbrados religious sect. The Alumbrados were a Gnostic secret society preaching the Mystery Babylonian religion and worship of Lucifer, the great deceiver. These crypto-Kabbalist Jewish mystics infiltrated the Vatican through Pope Callixtus III and Pope Alexander VI, both of the House of Borgia, as agents of the Crown of Aragon. In 1527, Ignatius of Loyola managed to escape persecution from the Inquisition with help from Pope Paul III of the Black Nobility Farnese family. Ignatius of Loyola claimed he was raising a Militia to defend the papacy which would lead to absolute control of the military and politics, and absolute control of a One World Church, which we are seeing the formation of today.[1]

In 1534, the Society of Jesus was founded with Ignatius of Loyola its first Jesuit Superior General. Funding came from Francis Borgia, the great-grandson of both Pope Alexander VI and King Ferdinand II of Aragon. Francis Borgia later became the Third Superior General of the Society of Jesus. The Society of Jesus went on to become the successor to the Order of Montesa, who had inherited the possessions of the Aragonese branch of the Knights Templar. The penultimate Master of the Order of Montesa, Francisco Lanzol de Romani, was succeeded by his cousin, Pedro-Luis de Borja, who was the half-brother of Francis Borgia.

THE WIZARD JOHN DEE

As we've seen, John Dee was an English mathematician, professor, and astronomer who gave it all up for the more lucrative occupation (at that time) of being an "angel channeler" and astrologer. He founded the Rosicrucian order (the pre-eminent training school for the occult), the first of many magical secret societies that promoted spiritual growth throughout the centuries. Dee eventually became Elizabeth's court astrologer—and soon afterwards her spy.

As an agent of the crown, Dee conducted several mysterious missions for purposes mostly unknown to this day. He relished his espionage duties, creating elaborate, sophisticated ciphers. In his correspondence with the Queen during these episodes, he signed his communiqués "007," a moniker that would be used again, as any fan of the spy genre will recognize. John Dee believed that specially-constructed mirrors could draw magical power from the sun and transmit messages and objects to distant stars and other worlds. Dee attempted to receive visions from "angels," using a globe of crystal. Many believe his scrying mirrors did allow him communications with entities from "the other side."

Dee was born near London on July 13, 1527, and died in 1608. He entered St. John's College at Cambridge at age 15. From his studies, he developed a doctrine that one could obtain knowledge of God from the applied practice of magick—a controversial idea that was to get him into trouble on a number of occasions. It also made him famous when he correctly advised Queen Elizabeth to refrain from attacking the approaching Spanish Armada. Instead, a freak storm appeared and defeated the Spanish navy.

Early in his "Magick" career, during the reign of Queen Mary Tudor (Bloody Mary), Dee was arrested and accused of attempting to kill her with sorcery. He was imprisoned in Hampton Court in 1553. Dee was imprisoned in England for the crime of "calculating," that is, practicing the pagan craft of mathematics. He was also accused of practicing black magic.

In 1564, one of his many books dealing with occult matters, *The Monas Hieroglyphica*, was published. The *Monas Hieroglyphica* is a symbol created by Dee, which he believed was the ultimate symbol of occult knowledge. The following year he published *Di Trigono*. Spirit contact would prove to be a major driving force behind Dee for the rest of his life. While Dee was away in Europe, things were not boding well at home. In 1583, a large mob attacked Dee's home and library at Mortlake in Surrey, destroying his collection of books, occult instruments and personal belongings. The attack was probably in response to rumors that Dee was a wizard.

1   Bartley, James "The End of Reptilian Overlordship Part 1," https://www.blogtalkradio.com/shatteringthematrix/2013/08/11/the-end-of-the-reptilian-overlordship-part-1--james-bartley

DEE ATTEMPTED TO CONTACT DISCARNATE ENTITIES

John Dee began his experiments in trying to contact discarnate entities in 1581, mainly fueled by strange dreams, feelings and mysterious noises within his home. On May 25, 1582, he noted that he had made his first contact with the spirit world through the medium of his crystal ball. This had taken Dee years of work to achieve—through studying the occult, alchemy and crystallomancy.

Dee was a practitioner of "Hermetic Gnosticism," a school of thought based on the ancient pre-Christian teachings of the Greek god Hermes. Hermes was in fact a mere copy of the much earlier Egyptian god of knowledge and language, Thoth. In this sense, all Hermetic Gnosticism can be viewed as a worship of the teachings of Thoth. According to the Egyptian mythos, Thoth was one of the gods who came down to Earth, along with Isis and Osiris, to bring the fruits of knowledge, civilization and the sciences to the Egyptian people.

In 1581, using his knowledge of these ancient practices, Dee began a series of attempts to communicate with "higher beings." His channel in this capacity was one, Sir Edward Kelly. Together, they had discovered an incredible new means of acquiring power.

Once we become familiar with the notion that good ETs (angels) and bad ETs (demons) exist and are involved in our affairs, we can see what might have happened. It may be that Dee facilitated a new alliance with negative extraterrestrial groups that promised support to the British Empire—but at a terrible cost. These same ET groups might very well still be working through the Cabal today, allowing an unfair interdimensional advantage. Thankfully, these malevolent ETs are being opposed by a much greater number of positive groups, both here on the ground and from elsewhere.

CONJURING UP THE ARCHONS

Around the same time as John Dee, Dr. Johannes Faust was able to conjure up (through his study of magic) an extra-dimensional entity who served him for many years in several different ways. There is even an excerpt from *The Book of Dr. Faust* (1524), in Wittenberg, describing his experiences. Also, Napoleon Bonaparte, the French military and political leader, is another example of a person influenced by hyperdimensional species. Bonaparte used to tell of a "Little Red Man of Destiny," a "spirit," that appeared at the Royal Palace. Apparently when something important was happening, the "spirit" would appear. Dr. Faust, along with various practices now considered to be silly superstitions and folklore beliefs, genuinely influenced Napoleon and his actions and guided his campaigns. The Austrian clairvoyant, philosopher, social reformer, architect, economist and esotericist, Rudolf Steiner, had this to say about spiritual entities making themselves manifest to humans over a century ago:

> There are beings in the spiritual realms for whom anxiety and fear emanating from human beings offer welcome food. When humans have no anxiety and fear, then these creatures starve. People not yet sufficiently convinced of this statement could understand it to be meant comparatively only. But for those who are familiar with this phenomenon, it is a reality. If fear and anxiety radiate from people and they break out in panic, then these creatures find welcome nutrition and they become more and more powerful. These beings are hostile towards humanity. Everything that feeds on negative feelings, on anxiety, fear and superstition, despair or doubt, are in reality hostile forces in supersensible worlds, launching cruel attacks on human beings, while they are being fed. Therefore, it is above all necessary to begin with that the person who enters the spiritual world overcomes fear, feelings of helplessness, despair and anxiety. But these are exactly the feelings that belong to con-

temporary culture and materialism; because it estranges people from the spiritual world, it is especially suited to evoke hopelessness and fear of the unknown in people, thereby calling up the above-mentioned hostile forces against them.

Esotericists of the past have recognized there are "Cosmic Rules of Play" set in place by God Almighty, the Master Creator. These Rules limit how the Dracos, or any other cosmic parasites such as the Fallen Angels or Fallen Ones, can operate. If they could, the Dracos would just have landed publicly, taken over by brute force and would have fully enacted their anti-human Alien Agenda, and that would have been that. The Rules of Play however prevent that; consequently, they must work through humans from whom they have been able to steal souls, and then "possess" them. These Fallen Ones do this through offering up extremely desirable "rewards," such as massive power, status, fame, prestige, wealth and all the earthly pleasures only the richest and most successful humans can acquire. There is no shortage of human cut-outs. But they must be willing to "sell their souls" to Lucifer, that is, enter into a lifetime "blood contract" with Lucifer in order to receive these extreme rewards and perks denied to the common man.[2]

THE ELITE BLOODLINE FAMILIES

There is a centuries old, very powerful and sinister secret Bloodline that has been parasitizing the human race. This Bloodline has gained control over planet Earth through very crafty means such as: hijacking monetary production and distribution, charging pernicious usury for using its private bank notes (really debt-notes); buying up, bribing and compromising almost every government official; controlling the major mass media outlets; engineering conflict and wars; and deploying other much more sophisticated eugenics and covert operations to thin the human herd and maintain control. This plan has been called The Globalist Agenda for creating a New World Order (NWO), and it is so unimaginably evil that most just cannot comprehend its wickedness or its reality. This is in part how it can be kept hidden.

Conspiracy researchers have found evidence of an operating agenda of the ruling oligarchs, and have come to the conclusion that it is exceedingly and unimaginably evil. Keep in mind, evil by definition is anything that hurts the innocent, or inflicts needless death and suffering, or violates other basic God-given "natural rights" to exist and pursue happiness. Evil is, as evil does. The ruling bloodlines have targeted the human race for radical depopulation and eventual replacement by a new synthetically-created android species, driven and "hived" by artificial intelligence, or "hived digital cyber-consciousness."

The empowerment of the Bloodline people is through the worship of the "Black Sun," which some call Lucifer or Satan. In most likelihood, it's just another reptilian ET, a "Royal" Winged Draco sort of entity. Bloodline leaders appear to become anointed and empowered by this Dark force of unimaginable evil, if they are willing to violate the most serious ordinary human norms and codes of decency in order to feed this parasitical monster. However, they must do it in secret (while maintaining a normal outward appearance) in order to avoid the peasants with pitchforks.

And some close to the top Bloodline Circle of Power have claimed that when one is initiated into this "inner circle," they receive their own personal spirit guide, who appears to them privately and telepathically and serves as a crime *consigliere* (counselor and advisor). It is quite well-accepted fact that those initiated into the top circle of control in the Bloodline (the Establishment Hierarchy) have engaged in Satanic ritual child sacrifice, pedophilia and child vivi-sectioning. These blood rituals have persisted for centuries, and are largely feeding rituals for a reptoid species, who have a taste for adolescent humans as we learned in the previous chapter.

---

2 James, Preston, "America's Alien Invasion." http://www.veteranstoday.com/2016/10/08/americas-alien-invasion

HOMO CAPENSIS

Researcher Alfred Lambremont Webre's hypothesis is that we are controlled by a High Cabal, composed of elite bankers and large brain hominids named *Homo Capensis*. The label *Capensis* means "Conehead," and they are not human. The large brain hominids dominate this High Cabal, which in turn controls human governments and institutions, and is ultimately responsible for the incredible number of assaults on humanity. Those assaults are on our minds, immune systems, health, genetics, education, economic well-being, scientific understanding, and personal freedom. Through nanobot distribution, it is said that about 80% of the population is implanted with a "chip," and there is now a smart grid in place to track all human life.

The *Homo Capensis* and their cut-outs in the High Cabal are the hidden controllers of the current soft kill and hard kill programs to depopulate the planet of *Homo Sapiens*. They will do this through the ongoing plan involving nuclear radiation, environmental warfare, GMOs, chemtrails, bio-warfare through vaccines, warfare, a coming massive currency collapse, the trans-humanist agenda, and other means to eliminate perhaps 500 million from our current seven billion, as related on the Georgia Guidestones.[3]

Their motive is simple: They overtly controlled the Earth during the Ice Age, and they want to overtly control it again without any hassle from us "little brained" humans. They regard us as chattel and are not impeded by a conscience, and would just as well see most of us dead. There are now so many programs going on to kill off and control the human race that it is hard to keep track of them all. And not only humans but all life. Just pick up a cup of rainwater and find barium, aluminum, self-replicating nano-particles of organic and non-organic material. In time, this will kill off humanity and most animal and plant life, and a new terraforming will occur. Consider the Pacific Ocean: in most areas, it is now completely devoid of all life because of Fukushima. Birds and animals of all kinds are dying in vast numbers around the world. Bees too, which are so important to life, are dying out in huge numbers. Whole forests are turning brown, and much more. Then there are the GMOs, which are doing the same thing and are changing human DNA. There are now GMO trees, salmon and even mosquitos...and it goes on and on.

A critical piece of the puzzle is the fact that the *Homo Sapiens'* mind has many weaknesses, which are fairly easily exploited. Psychopathy is one of these failings, wherein these dangerous individuals often rise to high levels of power. These assaults are carried out by an assortment of bamboozled human fools, directed by psychopathic leaders in a system where phony money reigns supreme; the bigger the lie, the better, and brutality, like greed, is good. But who orchestrates all of these attacks? Or are we to believe these are all coalescing random events?

There is a different frequency that is entering our world, some say of a light nature, which will affect much of the archon network—and all of us. Some of us are ready, some aren't. Yes, it's up to us but, ultimately, it's coming whether or not we're ready and whether or not we want it to. Some will ride the wave, so to speak; others will have a difficult time. This in effect is evolution. But don't forget, we have a nemesis here beside us, guiding our very development, and if we don't take responsibility for our "development," they will. People need to be educated in order to have a choice; otherwise, they will be chosen for, as they have been throughout history.

3   Webre, Alfred Lambremont, "Mary Rodwell—ETs, Souls, The New Humans and a coming global Shift," https://exopolitics.blogs.com/exopolitics/2013/07/mary-rodwell-ets-the-new-humans-and-a-coming-global-transformation.html

THE CABAL ARE THE HIRED GUNS

It is now known that the top-level cabal members have secretly been devout Luciferians who became occult "Black Magick" masters over the ages. They have learned and perfected their black arts passed down from ancient Babylon through their family "Luciferian Bloodlines." As the official account goes, those initiated into these Babylonian Black-Magick Luciferian Arts each received an individual inter-dimensional "spirit guide" which would appear to them during a human sacrifice ceremony first, and then more frequently at other times. These personal spirit guides are viewed by some as inter-dimensional ETs, demons or jinns, and have a record of "shadow"-assisting their clients in mastering evil and/or oppressing planet Earth's masses.[4]

Occasionally, non-bloodline individuals who have served their "invisible master" diligently over many years, and proved themselves to be remarkably loyal to their evil cause, are inducted into their occult circles. This known association between malevolent ETs and the occult (Babylonian Black-Magick) was first discovered by those who studied the reports of Aleister Crowley, reputed to be one of the evilest men who ever lived, and was called the "Beast 666." On one noted occasion, Crowley claimed that an Inter-dimensional being called Seth appeared to walk through the walls of an Egyptian Pyramid where he was waiting inside to greet him. According to Crowley's own sketch, this being, and another he called Lam, both looked exactly like what is typically referred to as a Grey alien ET.

Ultimately, the Dark Cabal was created and run by negative extraterrestrials, including the reptilian group known as the Dracos. The human cut-outs in the Cabal are not shape-shifting reptilians, as biological life does not have this ability. However, certain Cabal members do have telepathic connections to these beings, and on occasion, intuitives will see a reptilian overlay on their faces. This accounts for the many cases author David Icke has mentioned in his earlier works.

The key human players in this chapter include the Cabal, a group many people call the "New World Order." We shouldn't be surprised that Sandy Hook was a hoax. So were 9/11, the Boston bombings, and most of the "lone nut" shootings in the last decade. Government-sponsored terror and false flags have become a part of daily life. Obviously, they will continue until the perpetrators are exposed. The 9/11 event was a Satanic ritual sacrifice and trauma-based mind control operation carried out by Luciferian globalists. "Government" itself is not to blame. Government becomes an instrument of oppression when it has been subverted. The same applies to the mass media, which is an instrument of thought-shaping mind control.

HUMANS AWAY FROM HOME

Penny Bradley was a pilot for the German Secret Space Program. She flew exotic space craft, whose propulsion systems and anti-gravity designs are still not revealed science. As a pilot out of the German SSP called *Nacht Waffen*, she was off-planet for several years and has come back to be an informer on the many injustices. She says "We have to understand that there are three things that are most trafficked on Earth: Weapons, Drugs and Humans, and not necessarily in that order. The CIA controls all of them." She continues on a Facebook Q and A thread:

> When it comes to human trafficking—it starts with aborted infant parts and ends with dead elders. And everything in between. Sexual abuse of kidnapped children is just a tiny fraction of what is happening.

> The CIA kidnaps kids. Those who meet the requirements for space, go to SSP. Those who meet the requirements for super soldiers, become that—both on Earth or in

4   Zagami, Leo Lyon, *Confessions of an Illuminati, Volume I: The Whole Truth About the Illuminati and the New World Order* (2nd ed.) CCC Publishing, 2019.

space. Those who have psi abilities are used in those black ops.

Those who don't have anything special about them are used as slaves. The pretty ones are sex slaves. They are usually dead within seven years max. Some are used for organ transplants. Some are used for adrenochrome harvesting.

And all of them can suddenly find themselves the walnut of consciousness in a cyborg sold to an ET. The cyborgs only use a walnut sized bit of brain, that includes the pineal gland, to seat the consciousness into the robot body. When I talk about cyborgs made from humans being sold in space to ETs—that is what makes the robot a cyborg—that tiny bit of brain and pineal gland traps the human soul in the robot. Warrantied shelf life of cyborgs is currently 600 Earth years.

It needs to be understood that the Draco are a conquering race, and work through human groups when there is an advantage. In the 1930s, they contacted the Nazis not just to hopefully subdue the Earth, but to create an army that could be used to conquer many other worlds as well. The Nazis had the mentality and industrial know-how that the Draco wanted, and began colonizing space with the technology the Draco gave them in the late 1930s. The United States was developing its own SSP due to assets it had acquired, but did not succeed to anywhere near the degree that the Germans had, including putting the first human on the moon. Ultimately, the USA was bullied and blackmailed into joining the German SSP post-WWII, and their hope was that they would be able to take over the program and squash the Germans. Unfortunately, the opposite took place—at least for many years. Today, the level of technology in the SSP dwarfs anything we have on Earth, and includes replicator devices, teleportation, time travel, anti-gravity, free energy and healing technologies that make all forms of disease, illness, and even aging, completely obsolete.

ETs WORKING FOR THE USA

Once it was clear that the Cabal in the USA would adopt the practices and personnel of the Nazi Third Reich through Project Paperclip, it is apparent many of the policies remained firmly in place. For example, the SS occult methods of training and research into the capabilities of the human mind, manipulating human consciousness, and harnessing *vril-ya* energy were replicated by the CIA to continue Nazi-initiated communications with ETs and research into the mind-technology interface used to control ET technology.

What's more, within the NSA exists an elite group, variously called "Advanced Contact Intelligence Organization," or "Labyrinth," or the "Black Monks," who are responsible for the Shadow Government extraterrestrial interface. The "Labyrinth / Black Monks" is likely modeled on the elite membership of the Nazi SS. This Nazi-ET and then the NSA-ET collaboration is known as the "third force" in geo-politics that has secretly impacted on human-extraterrestrial affairs. Of course, funding of the USA "deep black" projects EBEs and reverse engineering on ET vehicles is done outside the regular Congressional oversight process, and replicates what the Nazi SS did. From a historical perspective, the first diplomatic relations with an ET race in the Modern Era was established by Nazi Germany, and these connections were continued by the USA after World War II. [5]

The interaction of the Nazis, and then the Shadow Government of the USA, was primarily concerned with acquiring advanced technology with the malevolent, or "service to self," extraterrestrials. Agreements were reached between the Nazis and one or more ET races. These agreements were kept secret and used for technology acquisition that had a military application. This was all replicated by the U.S. government, which

5   Salla, Michael, *Legacy of the Nazi/UFO Connection.* Video: **http://vimeo.com/38671811**.

continues this policy to this day under the so-called Greada Treaty. The USA secretly implements policies regarding ETs that were first adopted by the Nazis. The result is that the general public are marginalized from ET affairs, kept ignorant about different ET races, and persuaded to believe that evidence for ETs visiting Earth is inconclusive. It also means the Cabal continues to monopolize information concerning ETs and make diplomatic agreements with ETs for exotic weapons development.

SSP HANDLERS

Other whistleblowers from government such as super soldier Michael Prince reports there are hyper-dimensional ET liaison programs which have also warned of an attempted occupation of Earth by predatory hyper-dimensional species. One report states: "In 1964, U.S. intelligence expected a Grey/Reptilian ET takeover in 2000-2030." Agencies had concluded that a Grey/Reptilian extraterrestrial alliance had a timetable for a planetary ·takeover of Earth sometime during the current decade. The silent war with quiet weapons from the last two decades between hostile extraterrestrial Grey/Draco Reptilian factions and humanity has prevented a planetary takeover, but we're not out of the woods yet.

Michael Prince reported that on April 15, 1964, two U.S. intelligence personnel met under Project Plato with the Greys in the New Mexico desert to arrange a meeting on April 25 at Holloman Air Force base in New Mexico. This meeting was to renew the Greada Treaty that had started in 1934, and was a psychological bid to buy time in order for the "white hats" to solve the problem of the Greys and Draco reptilians. The upper levels of U.S. intelligence discovered the Greys and Draco had this planet time-tabled for invasion and takeover sometime in the first three decades of the 21st century.

Another whistleblower named Emery Smith said that he personally dealt with many aliens, claiming that these creatures come in our dimension as light and can change their shape and density with ease. He reports:

> *The ships of extraterrestrials can also change their shape, even when the aliens are inside them. They can travel very fast and also disappear from other parts of the universe. ...It seems as though these aliens have learned how to teleport and make their bodies light.*

Some of Smith's most interesting experiences came when he worked in underground compartmentalized laboratories, where he autopsied over 3,000 "alien" specimens, including approximately 1,200 nearly intact bodies.

THE CURIOUS TALE OF J-ROD

Many sources mention the presence of a Grey ET living within the "clean sphere" at S-4, near Area 51. The being was called J-Rod, because when asked to write his name, it looked like a "J" with a dash. There are two main theories with regard to what J-Rod was doing here. Most sources claim J-Rod is an extraterrestrial, a Grey ET to be more precise, and most likely from Zeta Reticuli star system (though it isn't clear whether he'd be considered a Tall Grey or not). Some reports have him as part of an exchange program, with his main task to provide our scientists with knowledge, as a sort of ET Ambassador. There are videos of J-Rod on YouTube, but they sometimes show him being abused by humans.[6]

The version told by Dan Burisch also has our scientists interacting with J-Rod, but Burisch maintains that J-Rod was actually an alien time traveler from 45,000 years in the future. In this version, several Grey species would be descendants from humankind, and they would now be visiting us from the future to correct some mistakes. These are mistakes that ultimately will have a negative impact on the likelihood of future Grey-

----

6 "the j-rod alien interview." http://www.youtube.com/watch?v=c-WW8WNAcu8.

human hybrids to survive. It is apparent that time travel is difficult, but not impossible, as it certainly does not violate the laws of mathematics and physics![7]

According to interviews with Kerry Cassidy and Linda Moulton Howe, Dan Burisch is a microbiologist who received his Ph.D. in 1989 from the State University of New York, Stonybrook, His Ph.D. was in Microbiology and Molecular Genetics, and he was soon employed by the U. S. Navy's DoD Naval Research Laboratory. His rank was Captain, and his title was "Microbiologist IV." In 1994, he was assigned to work in an underground laboratory at S-4, a few miles from Area 51, five floors under the Papoose Mountain installation at Nellis AFB, Nevada. The fifth floor is accessible only by one secure elevator. Dr. Burisch said he suited up in the fifth-floor underground laboratory, with breathing and urination hoses, like an astronaut.

His assignment was to enter a round "clean sphere" filled with a cold hydrogen atmosphere that housed an entity called an "extraterrestrial" by his government superiors. According to Dr. Burisch, his boss reported to a MAJI committee, an extension of the Majestic-12 Special Studies Group organized by President Harry S. Truman in 1947. Majestic 12 included top scientific, military and business leaders asked to study the extraterrestrial phenomenon.[8]

THE REGENERATE ETS

David Wilcock stated his information suggests that some people who work in government are in fact extraterrestrial humans. But they are not reptilians and they are not shape-shifters. What we're dealing with is different groups with different agendas, some of which are more positive than others, and some that are very human-like in appearance. There are also positive beings that are multi-dimensional and largely stay out of the way. Most of these ETs are not even aware that these higher-dimensional beings exist. The ratio of good ETs to bad ETs is significantly in favor of good ETs. A conservative estimate, and this is just the groups that are immediately politically involved with us in our local area, is six bad groups versus about 50 positive groups. The higher-dimensional beings are working in a very interesting veiled fashion (that is not obvious to most of the ET groups) that can look just like us. Within the ET groups that look human, there are competing agendas and competing needs. There are alliances with different factions of ETs working with different factions on Earth.

When dealing with negative groups, interestingly enough, some of these negative groups are the most physiologically divergent from us in terms of how they look. That might be part of why they can justify dehumanizing or consuming us. There are mantis-like entities that essentially have insect legs and arms, but their bodies look hominid from the neck down. Then they have essentially an insect head with mandibles and compound eyes. That would be a very disturbing entity to see approaching. Another type is the commonly-described reptilians. The main type of reptilian, and there are several, does have a head that looks like a Komodo dragon, including a forked tongue. There are reptoids which have reptile-like features, including scales and vertical-slit pupils, but their heads are more similar to almost every reptile form on Earth—lizards, crocs, turtles, dinosaurs, even snakes. Some also have wings. Most of these negative ETs have been characterized throughout the ages as demons.

One must question how the Satanic elite and others got such overwhelming technology? They are in league with, or more than likely mind-controlled by, a group of beings known as the reptilian Draconians, as well as some other Grey ET races, plus other humanoid races. Their primary Earth bases are located at Pine Gap, Australia; Dulce,

7   "Michael Schratt, Dan Burisch Area 51 and the Alien J-Rod Segment # 3." https://www.youtube.com/watch?v=jqjXHIHBe3s.
8   "J-Rod: Grey Alien Ambassador or Human from The Future? Two Tales of One Strange Being." http://beforeitsnews.com/beyond-science/2013/07/j-rod-grey-alien-or-human-from-the-future-two-tales-of-one-strange-being-2442854.html.

New Mexico; and under the Giza Plateau in Egypt. Sometimes they are interconnected by underground high-speed rail or stargate jump rooms. There are some very advanced races out there, and their technology would seem almost like magic to most people. But here is our protection. Similar to the "Prime Directive" in *Star Trek*, there is a kind of universal law which states that no race can just move in militarily and take over a planet by force. All races must be allowed to have free will, so negative forces work through cut-outs in that race to slowly subvert them, and this is happening now. They work through the elite on this planet, and some are hybrids.[9]

The whole society of the Draconians is imbued with military traditions, with an emphasis on the concept of honor (this is not an unimportant fact), and the superiority of the two dominant castes over all others. Over time, the Draconians went into space and discovered life on neighboring planets. They considered that these planets should belong to them, and they began their expansion into neighboring planets. Not immediately, but over time, they managed to conquer these new worlds. Consequently, all suitable planets of their system turned into colonies. The local populations either assimilated or were manipulated and turned into slaves. The victors used all the knowledge and resources of civilized cultures in scientific research, and used it very rationally. This allowed them to create a powerful space fleet fighting force.

THE MONTAUK PROJECT

Imagine, traveling in time. Imagine a process that would let you go backward in time to witness the events that changed history, or see into the future to determine if humankind will survive, and then to return to the present with the knowledge of what will happen tomorrow. The process is intriguing, even mind boggling, and the science behind it is more real than imagined.

The Anderson Institute explores the many possibilities of the exciting new frontier of time control and time travel, dedicated exclusively to advancing the study and development of time control capabilities. This includes ET species coming to our present time from the past, and from the future. Consider this information from the Anderson Institute, regarding the Montauk Project:

> In about 1970, the technology behind the Philadelphia Experiment was said to be fine-tuned and applied on a much larger scale. It is said that the massive underground complex under the Montauk Air Force Station on Long Island was selected as the site that would continue where the Philadelphia experiment left off.[10]

The experimentation continued in the underground facilities of Fort Hero near Montauk. The control of the space-time continuum was achieved and exercised on a regular basis. The underground base at Montauk was very large. It is said by contractors to extend for miles, especially the fifth and sixth levels. Almost all of it was constructed in the late 1920s or early 1930s. It was built on government orders right after the depression started. After being decommissioned, the top was covered over with earth. It's known locally as "the hill."

A whistleblower interviewed on the Anderson Institute website reported that the Greys were not part of Montauk. By agreement they never went there. There were other ET groups who were part of it, however, specifically those who called themselves the "Leverons." Then, there were ETs from Antares that were only observers. They looked like humans. Occasionally, members of the Orion Group were there. Other insiders who worked at the Montauk base reported seeing reptilian Dracos. Lastly, there were the inhabitants of the ship that was captured.

9 Sanchez, Anthony, *UFO Highway*. Strange Lights Publications, 2nd edition, 2011.
10 Anderson Institute, "The Montauk Project." https://andersoninstitute.com/the-montauk-project.html.

MEN IN BLACK

In the past, anyone involved in a public Secret Space Program disclosure would be terminated with extreme prejudice in days or even hours by very strange men. They were dressed in expensive suits and drove new or almost new black Lincoln or Ford Town Cars. These men are referred to as "Men in Black" (aka MIBs). Whistleblower suppression has eased, and now insiders like Emery Smith can speak publicly. Others, like super soldier Max Spears, died at a young age by being suffocated by a kind of black goo or bile.

Insiders have reported that MIBs are alien ET/human hybrids with no soul, but are highly telepathic. MIBs are able to make themselves appear as humans and can function inter-dimensionally. They regularly confronted people who had experienced a close encounter or paranormal sighting, sometimes before they could contact family or friends. It's as if they could time travel to appear in front of an insider and threaten and intimidate the person into silence regarding what they witnessed.

Unfortunately, any serious Congressional hearings set up to investigate alien ETs and UFOs were suppressed by the MIB. Such was the case with U.S. Representative Steven Schiff from New Mexico, who was allegedly murdered in 1998 by the MIBs. Apparently, he pushed too hard to expose the Roswell secret with repeated inquiries and by trying to arrange for a hearing in Congress. He was allegedly given a very malignant skin cancer for aggressively trying to open the Roswell Files. The usual weapon of choice by malevolent ETs (known to be hostile to humans) have been several kinds of highly-malignant and fast-spreading cancers. Such was the case with abduction researcher Karla Turner, who was warned to stop talking, and when she refused, she succumbed to a fast spreading cancer.

There have been incidents of strange murders (often disguised as suicides) of leakers by MIBs, aka "arkansides" (the favored method of getting rid of political enemies in the state of Arkansas). These are covered up by civilian or military police who are either mind-controlled, or have been told to follow directions and are too afraid to refuse. Such was the case with Philip Schneider who disclosed a great deal about the "Evil Alien ETs," whom he saw in a shootout during the secret Dulce Wars. Being outspoken cost him his life.

MILABS (military abductions) are legitimate abductees who are kidnapped, and then are often trained by elements of the military intelligence community. They are then utilized as deep black operatives for a variety of purposes, such as the Secret Space Programs. The MILABS are generally militarized cooperative programs working with multiple invading species of extra-dimensionals, such as Draco reptilians. Such extra-dimensionals are interested in harvesting Earth resources, in human slave labor, genetic hybridization, breeding programs, sexual slavery and creating clones like the MIBs and for other purposes serving their invasion agenda. Many MILABS are alien abductees, who have been genetically enhanced or augmented with hybridized alien genetics, which have generated, potentially, a variety of Higher Sensory Perception abilities. These are used for covert military operations and, in some cases, for furthering the Trans-humanism agenda on Earth.[11]

---

11 The Mars Records, "How You Can Prevent Alien & Military Abductions & Spiritual Attack." https://www.themarsrecords.com/wp/black-ops/can-prevent-alien-military-abductions-spiritual-attack/

On April 12, 1961, the Soviet media reported the successful launch, orbit and re-entry of Earth by the first man in space, Uri Gagarin. The CCCP cosmonaut Gagarin instantly became an international celebrity and one of the greatest heroes in history. But was he really the first human in outer space?

Scrying, also known by various names, such as "seeing" or "peeping," is the practice of looking into a suitable medium in the hope of detecting significant messages or visions. The objective might be personal guidance, prophecy, revelation, or inspiration, but down the ages, scrying in various forms also has been a prominent means of divination or fortune-telling. The use of a scrying mirror remains popular in occult circles, discussed in many media groups, both modern and centuries old.

According to numerous UFO researchers, this 17th century French coin has an inscription of a saucer-shaped object and is strong evidence that alien beings have been coming to Earth over the centuries. Many people have also suggested that what we are seeing in this ancient coin is in fact a representation of the Biblical story of Ezekiel's wheel. In this story, humans envisioned four "beings," all accompanied by mysterious flying wheels. UFO hunters firmly believe that the story of Ezekiel's wheel is the Bible's own story of an ancient UFO encounter. Others say the coin could represent a drifting mushroom or flower in the wind, or even a shield being tossed.

RECEIVED

III. CONCLUSIONS

    1. Current studies of other-world visitation are in three phases:

        a. Technology exploitation

        b. Interplanetary travel

        c. Cultural communication

    2. On 19 September 1947, the IAC, JIOA, and the JIC, reviewed a Top Secret intelligence report titled REPORT TO THE PRESIDENT, 1947, PARTS 1-V, MAJIC EYES ONLY, DTG 000190947, the report mentions: "In compliance with your directive . . . of 9 July 1947, the attached "REPORT ON FLYING SAUCERS" is respectfully submitted. In consonance with your instructions, advisors from State, Treasury, War and Navy Departments assisted me on a two month exploratory mission concerning the reality of other-world visitation. The principle investigators and storage areas were visited. Successful efforts were made to reach scientists of all levels as measured by their work in classified defense projects. Conferences were held with national security officials and leaders of private industry. Approximately 1,200 memoranda and intelligence reports were considered. The report presents this situation against a global background my estimates, current and projected, in both the U.S., and allied countries, and recommendations deemed to be sound courses of action for formulating plans and policies in light of recent developments.

    3. All efforts have been made to identify the country or private concern wich could have the technical and finacial resources necessary to produce such a long-range flight. So far, no country on this earth has the means and the security of its resources to produce such.

    4. A consensus reached by members of the panel, that until positive proof that the Russians did not attempt a series of reconnaissance flights over our most secure installations—the sightings and recovered objects are interpalnatary in nature.

    5. The occupants of these planform vehicles are, in most respects, human or human-like. Autopsies, so far indicate, that these beings share the same biological needs as humans.

-2-

On September 24, 1947, the secret committee known as Majestic 12 was allegedly created by President Truman to deal with the Roswell incident and other alien incursions. Stanton Friedman has stated, "Clearly if the original documents: the Eisenhower Briefing Document (EBD) of November 18, 1952; the Truman-Forrestal Memo (TFM) of Sept. 24, 1947 (page 8 of the EBD); and the Cutler-Twining Memo (CTM) of July 14, 1954 (found in July, 1985, in Box 189 of Entry 267 of Record Group 341 at the National Archives by Jaime Shandera and William Moore) are genuine, then the consequences are enormous. Aliens are visiting earth; the government has recovered at least one crashed saucer and several alien bodies; and a very significant group of outstanding American scientists and military leaders has collected, reviewed, evaluated, and kept secret all kinds of information about the visitors. Man is NOT alone and the government has covered up the biggest story of the millennium at least since 1947."

In 2016, the Chinese released this intriguing photo of what appears to be an artificial complex and mining operating on the lunar surface. The image represents yet another confirmation of secret operations carried out there, and it may also reveal that the Chinese government has been in touch with otherworldly visitors. That, in turn, would also explain why China has been investing massively in radio telescopes.

This official road sign is posted on the north side of Hwy. 64 near Dulce, New Mexico. The actual location of this sign is slightly east of Dulce/Lumberton on Hwy. 64, where Hwy. 64 meets Hwy. 84. Some residents in Taos also report that similar signs have been posted near Taos as well as various other northern New Mexico communities. The signs (by ranchers) simply seem to indicate to be careful of the roaming cows in the area, and someone probably added a sense of humor to the image.

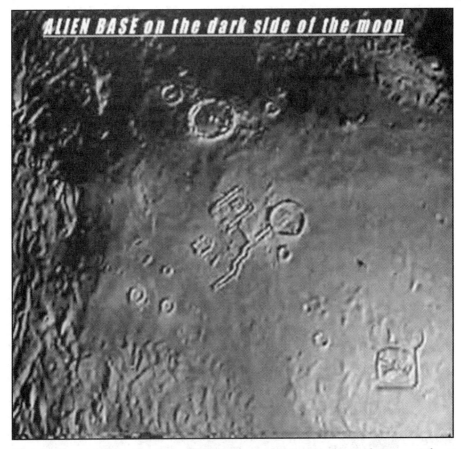

ALIEN BASE on the dark side of the moon

Here is photographic evidence that the Apollo astronauts have observed strange and unexpected anomalies on the back side of the Moon, the side that can never be viewed from Earth. Even the astronauts of Apollo 10 had observed a secret Moon base as they orbited around the satellite.

This secret Moon base is universally known in the security establishment and its existence is considered top secret. It was established on the dark side of the moon by persons unknown and the date of its construction is equally ambiguous. Generally considered to be the far side's most recognizable feature, the Sea of Muscovy (*Mare Moscoviense* in Latin) is located on the so-called "Dark Side of the Moon." It is one of the very rare flatlands basins in this region, and one of the most unusual locations on the moon.

The Sea of Muscovy is where several mysteries have been spotted, mostly by the Japanese probe named Kaguya, also known as SELENE (selenological and Engineering Explorer). For nearly two years the probe was analyzing various aspects of the moon, such as the distribution of elements on its surface, the magnetic and the gravitational field among other tasks, but the big findings were the unusual formations photographed. The interest in this particular lunar region is huge, because Ufologists claim that this specific area is very attractive when looking for ancient moon bases or other anomalies, thus suggesting an ET presence on the moon is very old.

Look what appeared during an 18th degree initiation in Freemasonry? Could this entity be an apparition, a physical manifestation, or both?

TRANSHUMANIST AGENDA

"If people let the government decide what foods they eat and what medicines they take, their bodies will soon be in as sorry a state as the souls who live under tyranny."
–Thomas Jefferson, (1778)

FEW people realize this, but humanity is on the verge of becoming a new and utterly unique species. The new Human 2.0 has been dubbed *Homo Evolutis*. What makes this species so unique is that it "takes direct and deliberate control over the evolution of the species," according to Chairman and CEO of Biotechonomy, Juan Enriquez, at a 2009 TED talk. Calling it the "ultimate reboot," he points to the conflux of DNA manipulation and therapy, tissue generation, and robotics as making this great leap possible. To be clear, transhumanism (H+) is a manufactured endpoint to human evolution.

What's more, we have now hit a new point in our scientifically-forced evolution. That is, scientists are already creating human-animal embryos called chimeras. Using human stem cells inserted into an animal embryo after a gene for a specific organ which has already been deleted, scientists hope the animal, carried in another host animal such as a pig or a sheep, will grow the human organ instead of its own. The ultimate goal of this is to force animals to grow human organs for transplantation into humans with terminal diseases, and the potential implications here are staggering.

What's worse is the concerns that other scientists have about this practice, things the average person who hears "free organs for sick people" would never even consider. Concerns include the fact that human stem cells can ultimately become any type of tissue and, according to the National Institutes of Health which released a statement regarding why it was refusing to fund the risky research, might turn into human brain cells that could evolve the donor animal's "cognitive state."

All this "super-human" enhanced technology seems to reduce humans to being enslaved beings or even hybrid-human machines, which is the real aim of transhumanism. After all, transhumanism is a theory that the human race can evolve beyond its current physical and mental limitations, especially by means of science and technology. Yet, rather than uplifting us into higher consciousness and making life wonderful on Earth for all beings by doing away with war, poverty and disease, we have this false science, especially in medical research, seeking to change the biology of the human race into something altogether different.

Transhumanism deprives us of our basic and individualistic persona, including rights given to us by Nature and the Higher Intelligence some refer to as God, Creator or the "Source." Transhumanism is being designed to make humankind into "one think" cyborgs of sorts, utilizing implanted "smart" technology to control our brains, physiology and biochemistry. This raises a frighteningly dark vision when our bodies will be augmented and sterilized in utero, or when divinity is exorcised out of humanity, and humanity has outgrown its usefulness.[1]

WHO THINKS LIKE THIS?

The concept of transhumanism in the Modern Age, that is, people transitioning into a higher and more powerful state of being human, has its origins in post-WW I Germany. As a secret occult group, the Thule Society was dedicated to the creation of a "master race" which distorted the teachings of Helena Blavatsky's book, *The Secret Doctrine*, Friedrich Nietzsche's concept of an "overman" or *übermensch*, and the Freemason Edward Lytton Bulwer's 1871 book, "*Vril: The Power of the Coming Race.*" There were several German secret societies in the early 19th century dedicated to Lytton's ideas. One of these is the mysterious Vril (*Gesellshaft*) Society, which was dedicated to developing the power of "vril" for occult communication, psychic abilities and the physical strength to become a Nietzsche-esque "superman."

The study of occultism and transhumanism became a government initiative in the early 1930s under the new Nazi Party. Early on, Adolf Hitler impressed senior Thule Society members with his xenophobic commitment to Aryan racial supremacy, his mesmerizing oratory, and his occult understanding of the future man, or *übermensch*. They arranged for him to be the new head of the National Socialist German Workers (Nazi) Party in 1921. Hitler gradually eliminated all challenges to his authority (including the Thule Society elites), established dictatorial power in 1933, and disbanded all occult societies in 1935. However, Hitler did permit an officially-sanctioned form of occultism under Heinrich Himmler's SS, called the Ahnenerbe Society. The acronym SS unofficially stands for *Schwarze Sonne*, or "Black Sun," which the occult Nazis identified as the mystical source of power in the galaxy—the galactic core—which is developed in the individual through occult training.

The Ahnenerbe (Ancestral Heritage Research and Teaching) Society was formed to gather information about the origins of the Aryan race and for individuals to personally harness the *vril* force. The group concerned itself with occult training, which involved reading and assimilation of spiritual classics such as the *Bhagavad-Gita*, the *Vedas* and Buddhist texts. Also included was military training to instill values of absolute loyalty and dedication to the evolution of the Aryan race, and, further, to train the adherent in the ability to use *vril-ya*, or chi—prana force. The Ahnenerbe SS would lead scientific expeditions to remote locations, such as Tibet in 1938, in an attempt to unlock the mys-

1   Barrett, Kevin, "Transhumanists stated goal is to become post-human." http://www.veteranstoday.com/2014/12/12/estulin

terious powers and potential of the human mind. They were also interested in the ET origins of the Aryans and the ancient UFO crafts called *vimanas*, or ET artifacts from an antediluvian era. The Nazis were convinced that only Aryans had sufficient mental or psychic "vril" abilities to master these advanced ET technologies. This led to an over-confidence that possession of these technologies would act as a force-multiplier, leading to Nazi Germany's victory. Yet history tells a different story.

It is widely known now that all Nazis didn't get killed or imprisoned after the war. Many officers went underground to escape prosecution, or joined forces with Britain and the USA under the direction of the CIA Project Paperclip, and continued their mind control and transhumanist research. The British Tavistock Institute and the American Stanford Research Institute have both been heavily involved with mind control.

BRAVE NEW WORLD

Aldous Huxley's novel, *Brave New World*, informed us of a world of biological and social engineering in stark black and white. He described a future that had already begun to take shape under his pen. Social engineers have shaped and influenced us through fiction, non-fiction, film, media, the educational system, politics, religion, sports, Hollywood celebrities, and rigged elections throughout the centuries. And each time we have consented. The stated goal of transhumanists is to become post-human. A post-human is someone who has been modified with performance enhancing body and brain augmentations to the point that they can no longer call themselves human. Murder your humanity to enhance your performance. Isn't that the story of modern Western civilization?

Would you take a daily pill with a microchip in it to be able to access your cell phone? Would you take a new kind of antibiotic that has the ability to silence the expression of specific genes? How about wearing a "cool" tattoo so your non-vocalized thoughts can be read? The now Google-owned company, Motorola, is developing an e-tattoo that can read the non-vocalized thoughts in your mind. All of this is more propaganda being perpetuated, so that the public thinks transhumanism is cool. It's not.[2]

One of the most immediate technological threats is germline genetic engineering, which involves changing genes in gametes, zygotes, or very early embryos. It will soon be possible, if it is not already being done, to "enhance the performance" of your future children by inserting genes for a higher IQ, athletic performance, musical talent, or any number of other enhanced abilities. Of course, this will cost money. The rich will get the "best" performance-enhanced kids. Soon we'll be in a genetic war of all against all, with the military ranks filled with super soldiers. It is clear that this genetic "enhancement" has the potential to destroy humanity. The Chinese state-run news agency, *Xinhua*, reported at the end of 2019 that a researcher named He Jiankui was responsible for creating the world's first gene-edited babies. We are now entering "Humanity 2.0."

It cannot be ignored that Earth was taken over by Service to Self ETs who do not like humanity, and they aligned themselves with the Dark Cabal. The Cabal are the same bankers who funded the Communists, the Zionists and the Nazis. Nathan Rothschild was the father of all of Queen Victoria's children except one. Adolf Hitler was an il-legitimate Rothschild, as his grandmother worked in a Vienna Rothschild's home. Certain bloodlines can be used more easily as avatars by these non-human entities. This is the reason for the fluoride, chemtrails, GMO food and nagalase in vaccines, the Monsanto Protection Act, untested 5G rollout, depleted Uranium, and all the

2 Bloomquist, Lisa, "Genetically Modifying Humans Via Antibiotics? Something You Need to Know." https://medicalexposedownloads.com/PDF/Secret%20manipulation%20of%20our%20DNA%20genes.pdf

abuses they are subjecting us to in a slow-kill agenda.[3]

Television is a mass hypnosis device developed by the military and first used in Nazi Germany. It is a tool to keep us unaware of our real potential. Tel-LIE-vision is nothing more than an electronic mind-altering device. It has been designed to psychologically change the way you view reality. For example, humans are able to be in many more dimensions than they know, but TV numbs our perceptions. It's called "programming" for a reason. Our consciousness is key. This is why they want us to think with the brains in our heads and not with the brains in our hearts. The brains in our hearts are the smarter brains. It's all part of a transhumanist agenda to take over the human species, to create these many wars and put us through an artificial reincarnation, to shove us into future lives which we would not have chosen. They want to keep all of humanity in fear and a PTSD syndrome. This is also the reason for rampant child abuse, to keep children fearful, and also to create multiple personality disorders, so they can use these alters to do whatever they want, including being programmed to kill. The key to countering this is to get real with yourself by losing fear and sending out love. Love is our secret weapon, and they know it; and that's why the frequency of TV is used to lull us.

EUGENICS NEVER DIED

Eugenics was dedicated to cleansing and purifying humanity from "inferior" members with the hope of solving various social problems related to poverty, disability, and mental illness. The Eugenicist Society was thriving over a century ago in California. Prominent people in government and medical universities said that we had to weed out certain ethnic types, because only Anglo-Saxons were desired. The elite thought we didn't need eastern Europeans, blacks, Mexicans, Greeks and Irish. These pronouncements came from leading spokespersons in California universities, which, in turn, influenced the Nazi Party's doctrine of superiority.

The elites have made plans for us before, and this is another way they're making plans for control. The term "eugenics" was changed in the early 1950s to "transhumanism," and it's really the same thing, except it's just a new word so the transhumanists can push for the post-human. Could it be that the post-human will have no gender, the humanist will be non-reproductive, and the post-human will be improved in the sense that it will be tailored to specific tasks as the caste system was outlined in *Brave New World*? Are humans being terraformed?

The elite promoted eugenics until the Nazis bastardized the term, so now they call it transhumanism. They believe that not only do they carry a divine bloodline and the right to rule the masses as they see fit; they also believe in a future where (by their technological innovations) they can enhance their own DNA and achieve an evolutionary next step leading eventually to immortality. The Rh-negative blood type being common among them, they might seek to use those of the same blood in the populace as lab rats on which to conduct mass experimentation. In regards to Morgellons Syndrome, perhaps they are producing symptoms that will simply kill those with the Rh-positive blood factor by cancer or immune deficiency.

According to the source, *Bio Technology Forums*, the reason why Rh-negative blood cannot be cloned is, "It has been observed that without Rh protein, the cloned blood cell loses its required flexibility as well as the DNA strand is difficult to use after retrieving it. The root cause for this is related to the D antigen, its genetic makeup and receptors variations. In combination, all these factors make it difficult to clone Rh-negative blood cells, and thus also in whole." In other words, the elite bloodline

⋯⋯⋯⋯⋯⋯⋯⋯⋯⋯⋯⋯⋯⋯⋯
3   Wilson, Julie, "Cancer Industry Profits: Nagalase Molecule Injected into Humans Via Vaccines." **https://sustainable.media/cancer-industry-profits-by-nagalase-molecule-injected-into-humans-via-vaccines/**

cannot be cloned, but the rest of the 85% of Rh-positive people can be cloned. We really do live in a brave new world.[4]

TRANSHUMANISM PICKS UP WHERE EUGENICS LEAVES OFF

Transhumanism is a big part of the New World Order agenda, which seeks to turn humans into machines. Transhumanism is an outgrowth of eugenics. Transhumanism was founded in the 1950s by top eugenicist Julian Huxley and the Rockefeller Foundation, as a new brand name for the pseudoscience of eugenics. Julian was the brother of author Julian Huxley. Its obsession for culling off the "genetically inferior," while at the same time striving to promote dominance for the "superior" had given eugenics a bad name, particularly after the Nazi brand of eugenics created the circumstances for the Holocaust during World War II. Sadly, what most people didn't know at that time was that Nazi eugenics was merely the full-blown application of the principles that had been developed and were openly espoused by the British, French and American eugenics societies.

Eugenics lived on, under many heavily-funded formats, rebranded as transhumanism. By and large, transhumanism proposes to use applied science in the fields of genetics, robotics and others, to "steer human evolution into the future." A transhumanist society will have, as its name implies, "transcended humanity." In such a society, human beings will have been replaced with hyper-efficient worker chimeras, bio-robotic warriors, and other purpose-made humanoid life forms, such as the "Epsilon semi-morons" to do the dirtiest of work as portrayed in *Brave New World*. These stated goals must be tied in with the bigger picture into which eugenics and transhumanism fit. These fields have never been limited to "science" per se—they've always been primarily political and socio-economical, and they reflect a very particular view of the world.

Under that perverted view, the planet has limited resources for too many people, and technological advancement under free market systems cannot be trusted to overcome those limitations—one of the many Malthusian fallacies and myths. Therefore, strict control must be exercised over the users of resources, to avoid any over-usage of those resources. To exercise that control, eugenicists believed they had to shut down development, and create a heavily regulated social and economic environment. This has led us into the neo-feudal, technocratic, New World Order of transhumanism. That's what eugenics, and its offspring transhumanism, seek to accomplish. A system under which individuals will not just lose their physical rights to independent living, but we will also be engineered to become robotic workers. Therefore, as the grandson of Charles Darwin put it, the stated goal for us will be nothing more than shaping a good worker, which includes being engineered to have the right beliefs, or no beliefs at all.

That is the final and most serious note of mental and spiritual disease behind this incredibly selfish and hypocritical paradigm. And that is why it must be stopped. Aldous Huxley predicted: "There will be, in the next generation or so, a pharmacological method of making people love their servitude, and producing dictatorship without tears, so to speak, producing a kind of painless concentration camp for entire societies, so that people will in fact have their liberties taken away from them, but will rather enjoy it, because they will be distracted by propaganda or brainwashing from any desire to rebel, including brainwashing enhanced by pharmacological methods. And this seems to be the final revolution." Transhumanism is mind control to shift perception to a hybrid society. As perception shifts, the individual is homogenized into an amorphous "public persona."

••••••••••••••••••••••••••••••••
4   "We are becoming a new species, we are becoming Homo Evolutis." http://arstechnica.com/science/2009/02/we-are-becoming-a-new-species-we-are-becoming-homo-evolutis

THE COMING SINGULARITY

A transformation is coming, and our species, *Homo Sapiens,* will no longer be recognizable as itself. We will become something new, something different, and the time predicted for this transformation is 2045. The man who is making this prediction is Ray Kurzweil, the Google "Director of Engineering." Kurzweil is a futurist known for his uncanny accuracy in predicting the pace at which technology grows and improves, so that one day it will be smarter and better than us. That's what is called the singularity. There's a singularity university hosted by NASA and sponsored by Google to teach people about the intelligence explosion. Kurzweil wrote the bestselling book called *The Singularity Is Near* which came out in 2005, and popularized the term. Singularity is a word from astrophysics referring to a point in space-time where the rules of ordinary physics no longer apply.

Ray Kurzweil has correctly predicted the growth of information technologies, doubling its capacity every two years according to "Moore's Law." He's made it clear to the world that technological progress is exponential, not linear, and that means the advancement begins to amass itself, in a manner of speaking. An exponential curve starts slowly and then explodes. A quote from a *Time* magazine article entices us: "Kurzweil's future bio-technology and nanotechnology give us the power to manipulate our bodies and the world around us at will at the molecular level. We ditch Darwin and take charge of our own evolution." The question is who is "we" and what is that "will"?

Kurzweil predicted that armed with advanced nanotechnology, Artificial Intelligence (AI) will solve the problems of the world. We're not talking about a chess-playing computer, but machine intelligence that can pass for human in a blind test, which is as close as you can get to consciousness or sentience. But once this kind of intelligence is here, what will it do as a newly-created silicon inhabitant of the Earth? Will it compete with us for resources more intelligent than we are, or will it treat us as lesser beings? Will it recognize that we made it, or will it take us over? Kurzweil believes that we ourselves will one day merge with machines. For example, what if we can download our brains into a computer, and upload a computer into our brains? The day may come when we have flash memory that we can plug into our brains. We'll be able to hook our brains into calculators and statistics programs and have a search engine like Google directly flashing into the frontal lobe.

Around the year 2030, a machine, an AI will be able to match human intelligence and even go beyond it. This kind of development in Artificial Intelligence will not only give us just another level of human intelligence, but will give us superhuman intelligence. It will enable us to solve problems that we're not able to comprehend today. Artificial blood cells could be the cure to many diseases. Biology is impressive, intricate, and clever, but also very sub-optimal compared to what we would be able to engineer with nanotechnology.

Artificial Intelligence will connect the world. *Homo sapiens* will be transformed into *Homo Evolutis.* Our biological processes will be run by technologically living things, but will not be reproductive. The Earth will be populated with engineered "test tube" species and all these processes will be patented, licensed and controlled. We have seen already the deposition and active presence of artificial chemtrailed materials in the sky, working their way into the environment and into all living things. Nanotechnology has arrived at our personal doorstep, and without our permission. It isn't that this will happen in 2045. It is already here.

In the name of convenience and access to virtually unlimited information, we are being sold the concept of the Internet being directly downloaded or injected into our brains. With transhumanism, the essence or original consciousness of the person gets eliminated, and a drone is created, like a bee colony system, with mindless drones serving a Queen Bee. The NWO (New World Order) rulers are trying to create a planetary-wide human hive, all under their control.

Human enhancements are being sold to us as the "bionic man," and having better, faster, higher intelligence and perfect health. But all of this is just a sales pitch. Enhancement may in fact be degradation, power being devolved to someone else's specifications, all the while compromising our free will.[5]

While biotechnology currently promises (in headlines) to make our world better, it may in fact be busy taking us over, so it can tailor us to the plan for the hive. Already transhumanists are looking forward to the creation of the post-human, an improved human that will have no gender, will not reproduce, will be a better performer in the workplace, will not be distracted by love or lust, and it will be free of disease thanks to nanobots keeping it healthy.[6]

So, while the current ethical debate is about whether or not we should upload computers into our brains, and how human we will be when that happens, there is something happening on a nanoscale level right now. What it is exactly is unknown to us.

SMART DUST

We can consider nanotechnology as the installation of Artificial Intelligence in living and non-living things. Smart dust and smart moats for instance are tiny nanosensors that can float and land anywhere. As Kurzweil declares, such self-replicating nanotechnology will infuse everything around us with itself.

Nanoparticles are being distributed through aerosol spraying, inhaled through the lungs, then regrouping as larger nanobots in the stomach's acidic environment. The Morgellons fibers are also included in the "chemtrail" spraying. They are self-replicating nanobots, with sensors and bio-electronics. The mind can then be controlled by the nanoparticle sensors, and can be used as neuro-control weapons.

There are no laws that currently regulate the distribution of smart dust, yet it is showing up in an estimated 80% of the world's population. It can be activated to make people sick, to program their bodies, or even create voices in the mind. They are activated by the nanosatellites now circling the world in low orbit.

Not many people know there is a clandestine gene manipulation taking place, and that those agents are called "nanobots," and the Morgellons fibers are synthetic life. They were produced in Institutes of Biomolecular Medicine, and are clandestinely spread via chemtrails, and also inserted into processed foods and vaccines.

CHEMTRAILS

All life on planet Earth is under constant assault. The non-stop spraying of our skies with toxic heavy metals and nano-particulates have made our atmosphere extremely electrically conductive. The conductivity is utilized to make the ionosphere heaters around the globe much more effective. Our atmosphere is being decimated, and all life is being very negatively impacted by the constant powerful radio frequency bombardment.

Many Americans have reported seeing or feeling chemical mists fall from the sky during heavy chemtrail spray episodes. As we have read in the geoengineering chapter, one main purpose is what we call "chemtrails," but it can easily disguise bacteria, biological warfare agents, toxic chemicals, and who knows what they may spray on us, only to be declassified years later like all the other incidents. The chemtrails contain mostly geoengineering ma-

5   Prince, Rosa, "Dawn of bionic age? Paralysed man becomes first to use power of thought to move hand." https://www.independent.ie/business/technology/news/dawn-of-bionic-age-paralysed-man-becomes-first-to-use-power-of-thought-to-move-hand-30384078.html
6   Endy, Dr. Drew, Podcast, "Futures in Biotech 8: Drew Endy on Synthetic Biology," 9 November 2006, https://twit.tv/shows/futures-in-biotech/episodes/8

terials, but we must pay attention if we want to know when they spray us with even worse materials that can change the human physiology, such as the Morgellons fibers.

We have to ask ourselves, is aerosol spraying only about weaponizing the weather? What do the self-replicating fibers found in Morgellons patients signify? Why are engineered materials being found in airborne environmental samples? All this suggests a planetary engineering program that is affecting and targeting all life in a forced transhumanistic agenda. Synthetic biology is considered science's most exciting new frontier, which is combining genetics, robotics and nano-technology with artificial intelligence, and hybridizing natural forms and engineering tissues beyond our wildest dreams. The technology explosion is skyrocketing, and artificial intelligence will soon surpass our own capabilities. But at what cost? Why was nobody notified that their bodies would be terraformed?[7]

Among its various nefarious purposes, chemtrails are being used to poison humans and terraform all living organisms on the planet. They contain nano-particles to create Humanity 3.0, that is, seeking to create a more suggestible, docile, controllable, or a "super soldier" type of human. They have a program called "genetic electric mechanical sensors" (GEMS) or "micro-electric mechanical sensors" (MEMS), that they have sprayed into our atmosphere allegedly for better weather-forecasting. These "fibers" can be seen from space and they are distributed everywhere as "Smart Dust." They are in your home, in your air, and most likely in your bodies—inhaled or swallowed.

MORGELLONS IS TERRAFORMING PEOPLE AND ANIMALS

Individuals who have Morgellons exhibit non-healing sores containing fibers and a form of fungus. It is also related to candida and Lyme disease. A private study to determine the chemical and biological composition of these self-replicating fibers has shown that the outer casing is made of high-density polyethylene fiber (HDPE). This material is used throughout the bio-nanotechnology world as a compound to encapsulate a viral protein envelope with DNA or RNA. It has a way of morphing itself and adapting to various treatments, rather than being eradicated.

Cases of people with Morgellons Disease are increasing at a rate of 1,000 victims per day. In 2008, the Center for Disease Control (CDC) began a study on Morgellons to investigate its causes and symptoms. Morgellons individuals exhibit non-healing sores containing fibers that burn at 1700 degrees Fahrenheit and do not melt. They simply evaporate at such heat.

The medical community labels sufferers with the term, Delusional Parasitosis. However, Morgellons Disease is a very real and painful illness and emerged with the onslaught of geoengineering in the late 1990s. The illness is characterized by painful erupting skin lesions (non-healing sores as described above) with multi-colored polymeric fibers coming out of the pores, which have been sprayed on us via chemtrails.

Clifford Carnicom states the following strategies for counteracting the Morgellons organism assaulting our red blood cells and devouring the iron in our blood. These strategies, it is hoped, will improve and protect human health in this forced transhumanistic age:

1. *Alkalize the blood*
2. *Antioxidation*
3. *Increase the utilization and absorption of existing iron*
4. *Inhibit the growth of iron consuming bacterial/archaeal like forms (e.g.; fungi, chlamydia)*

••

7   Cookson, Clive and Firn, David. "Breeding bugs that may help save the world: Craig Venter has found a large project to follow the human genome," *Financial Times* (London), September 28, 2002.

5. *Improve the flow of bile to further alkalize the blood and the digestive process*
6. *Detoxify your liver*

VACCINE POISON

According to the records of the Metropolitan Life Insurance Company, from 1911 to 1935, the four leading causes of death from infectious diseases in the USA were diphtheria, scarlet fever, whooping cough (pertussis) and measles. However, by 1945 the combined death rates from these causes had declined by 95%, and that is *before* the implementation of mass immunization programs. By far, the greatest factors in this decline were improved sanitation through public health measures, improved nutrition, clean water, and better housing with less crowded conditions.

There is a school of thought that the so-called minor childhood illnesses of former times, including measles, mumps, chicken pox, and rubella, which entered the body through the mucous membranes, served a necessary and positive purpose in challenging and strengthening the immune system of these membranes. Vaccines, by contrast, are injected directly into the body, consequently bypassing the mucous membranes, leaving the mucosal immunity relatively weak and stunted.

In both *The New England Journal of Medicine* and the journal *Thorax*, articles have appeared stating that a healthy immune system has a "bias" towards the cellular immune system, whereas people with allergies, asthma, and diseases of an autoimmune origin have a humoral-dominant (vaccine derived antibody-mediated) system. Indeed, many autoimmune diseases have been linked to vaccines. It has also been shown that once one of these subsets become dominant, such as the vaccine-induced nagalase, it is difficult to shift the system to the other subset. World-renowned immunologist, Dr. H.H. Fudenberg, stated:

> *One vaccine decreases cell-mediated immunity by 50%, two vaccines by 70%... all triple vaccines (MMR, DTaP) markedly impair cell-mediated immunity, which, predisposes to recurrent viral infections, especially otitis media, as well as yeast and fungi infections.*

We have more vaccinations on our schedule than any other country. We also have one of the highest infant mortality rates and one of the highest newborn death rates among industrialized nations. We also have the highest rate of autism. Keep in mind vaccines don't cause autism. They cause demyelination, which eats the myelin sheath, paving the way for neurological damage to occur. That causes autism.

THE BLACK GOO

There is a strange "sentient" black oil that was discovered in a cave on the South Sandwich Islands, located south and east of the Falkland Island group. This substance seems to have powerful mind control properties when sprayed or ingested. It may have a connection to the artificial lifeform in Morgellons. This was reputedly the real reason for the 1982 Falklands War between Argentina and Great Britain, so the UK could take over the Argentinian base studying this black oil and take the "black goo" back to Britain. The intelligent "sentient oil" was claimed to have been found after destruction of a "Blue ET" base on the frozen Thule Island, the southernmost of the South Sandwich Islands in the far South Atlantic, about 1,400 miles north of Antarctica.

This mysterious thick fluid can allegedly communicate telepathically with humans and alter their DNA. It is claimed that military researchers in the UK attempted to use this substance to create "super soldiers," but the project was found to be too dangerous and was scrapped. David Icke writes:

> *It is variously portrayed as an intelligent substance or "alien DNA" with the capacity*

to change shape and take over people and transform or absorb them, so they become its vehicles. ...Shining black leather and PVC are also used to symbolize the goo/ virus in music videos and stage shows, as is Darth Vader in the Star Wars series.

Not only does this substance have the ability to take possession of one's body and perhaps consciousness if the person allows it, but black goo may also be able to mimic matter by reprogramming the coding which creates our reality. This is not science fiction, and this substance is absolutely a demonic living organism. This substance absolutely is a weapon! There have been reports that the secret government has sprayed this substance in some of the chemtrails over certain regions. It can also be covertly introduced into a person. According to Preston James of *Veterans Today*:

> *There have been rumors for years inside Intel that numerous "bought and paid for" politicians have been dosed and infected with this sentient "black oil," which some consider a microscopic Alien ET cosmic parasite that can "hive" some that ingest or inhale it.*

The black goo is an abiotic mineral oil from the upper crust containing high amounts of m-state gold and iridium. It has been found in a cave on Thule Island down in the South Sandwich Islands, and under the Gulf of Mexico. Black goo, the demonic substance that has been acquired by the UK government and studied in Marconi Labs, apparently killed many researchers who were trying to understand the substance. Furthermore, there exists a black oil schist containing this type of oil from earlier tectonic events. These substances apparently broke up the crust of the earth.

Black goo shows a hitherto unknown type of magnetism, much longer in range than ferromagnetism. It seems to be interactive in a spontaneous way that very likely is based on a bi-directional, annihilated photon exchange as known from m-state-matter in life-forms. Due to this magnetism, black goo shows the ability to mechanically self-organize in many different ways and has been reported to carry highly intelligent consciousness. It can also be used to rapidly clone living organisms.

THE TRANSHUMANIST AGENDA TRAP

Comparative mythologist, John Lash, elucidates a mental parasite, described in the Nag Hammadi texts as the archons. Observed through the lens of Gnosticism, archons have a relevancy because the subject matter of Morgellons emphatically reflects the current transhumanist movement. To quote Lash:

> *The human genome project is an archontic fantasy, in which humans, under the name of "science" are actually acting out an archontic agenda. Transhumanism mimics an archontic agenda that is blindly compelled that we can make something better out of ourselves than nature has made us. A huge illusion that is the trap of the transhumanist agenda.*

What we see happening in the transhumanist agenda is the organic being replaced by fake counterfeits all across the board. Equally disturbing are the parallels to this in John Lash's book, *Not in His Image*. Culled from the Nag Hammadi texts found in Egypt around 1945. Gnosticism was not a religion, as many folks mistakenly believe. It was a pre-Christian way of life that incorporated reverence for that host which is now being so viciously destroyed.[8]

On May 31, 2007 the U.S. Patent & Trademark Office quietly published a remarkable patent application that signals a major break with evolution as we know it. U.S. Patent application number 20070122826, entitled "Minimal bacterial genome,"

---

8   Lash, John, *Not in His Image: Gnostic Vision, Sacred Ecology, and the Future of Belief.* Chelsea Green Publishing, 2006.

describes the laboratory creation of the first-ever "replication of a free-living organism," or an entirely synthetic living organism. This novel bacterium, "syn," has genetic information that is constructed from chemically-synthesized DNA. It claims exclusive ownership of a "free-living organism that can grow and replicate," made from a set of essential genes also claimed in the application. The existence of the patent application isn't proof that the synthetic organism functioned at the time of the filing (October 12, 2006); however, the applicants were confident enough of their process to pursue exclusive ownership of the invention—publicly and legally.

A synthetic organism (or syn) is the result of "extreme genetic engineering." Syns differ from genetically modified organisms (GMOs), where sections of DNA from one naturally-occurring organism are inserted into another naturally-occurring organism. For example, scientists take a section of DNA from a soil bacterium and insert it into a soy bean. Syns aren't just about substituting a few ingredients in the recipe of life—they are making the ingredients from scratch in a laboratory and combining them in unprecedented ways. If researchers at the J. Craig Venter Institute are on the cusp of manufacturing the world's first living, fully synthetic organism as described in this patent application, it will also be the first human-made species in history. In the patent application, this "original syn" is given the taxonomic name, "mycoplasma laboratorium." In the tradition of naming groundbreaking genetic creations (for example, "Dolly" the cloned sheep) the ETC Group has dubbed this laboratory life form, "Synthia."[9]

HUMANOID-GREY-HUMAN

Perhaps the ultimate transhuman transformation is the actual creation and ongoing hybridization of our species. We need to ask how far back does the creation of other species go in a laboratory? Considering the information in the Sumerian texts, it goes far back into Earth's prehistory. As the texts relate, the Anunnaki assisted in other lifeform creations, including those of modern humans. It was largely the Zeta Greys from Zeta Reticuli who performed genetic manipulation on homo-Neanderthals, and mixed their genetics with their own to create White humans. This is one of the reasons why White humans (with Rh-negative blood) are frequently abducted, and mostly by the Greys.

Zeta Greys and White humans are similar in many ways. White, fair-skinned humans and Zeta Greys both have light-colored eyes, (White humans get their eye colors from them) both are weak against sunlight, but the Greys are 100% weak against sunlight, and that's why Greys are mostly seen at night. The only reason why White humans aren't 100% weak against sunlight is because of their proto-human genetics.

Zeta Greys and White human skin colors are also similar. White humans also rarely inherit any Zeta disorders that humans call "progeria," among other names like "Hydrocephalus," which cause many defects, such as big heads, large eyes, midgetism, smaller sexual organs and fluid to the brain, giving those humans affected a more Grey-like alien appearance. You could say White humans were created in the image and likeness of the Zeta Greys.

Neanderthals lived in what is now Western Europe, including what is today Germany, France, Spain, Russia and Croatia, and parts of Asia. Their ancestors left Africa at least 400,000 years ago, which likely explains why humans with African heritage don't have Neanderthal-linked chromosomes.

Researchers says modern humans of non-African heritage have distant genetic ties to Neanderthals—that is, cousins of modern humans who went extinct about 30,000 years ago. What the DNA shows is that Africans in Africa do not have the Neanderthal gene,

9   Dan Ferber, "Microbes Made to Order," *Science*, 9 January 2004: Vol. 303. No. 5655, pp. 158-161. 5 ETC Group, interview conducted with Drew Endy, Boston, 6 October 2006.

but the gene is unique to Europeans and Asians. This is called "Neanderthal admixture theory." Genetic research has confirmed that interbreeding had also taken place.

The genomes of non-Africans include portions that are of Neanderthal origin, due to interbreeding between Neanderthals and the ancestors of Eurasians in Northern Africa or the Middle East, prior to their spread. Rather than absorption of the Neanderthal population, this gene flow appears to have been of limited duration and limited extent. An estimated 1-4% of the DNA in Europeans and Asians (i.e. French, Chinese and Papua probands) is non-modern, and shared with ancient Neanderthal DNA rather than with Sub-Saharan Africans, such as the Yoruba and San probands.

Most interesting is that White humans and some Asians, mostly all the human races (except Black humans) trace their ancestry back to the Neanderthals. It has been assumed they only became *Homo Sapiens* after interbreeding with the original Homo Sapiens who were Black men and women of the Anunnaki bloodline. This is incorrect. Human races did not come from one man and woman. Grey Alien DNA was mixed with Neanderthal and Cro-Magnon to create white humans. And according to anthropologists, the Neanderthals were not very bright and lived primarily in Europe. However, some of their skeletal remains can be found in central Asia and along the coastlines of North Africa.

There were no Neanderthals in Sub-Saharan Africa. The reason why Blacks, Asians, Whites, or any race have their own distinctive looks is because each pure race was created from different extraterrestrial DNA. What makes all human races a family is the fact that all humans share genetics that are similar to chimpanzees.

CYBORG HYBRIDS

What if the transhumanist agenda was being driven by a covert invasion and occupation program by malevolent alien ETs, well underway on Earth? Of course, the average person was never supposed to find out about these "beyond-black" unacknowledged special access programs in the USA. It is a joint Alien ET/DoD contractor program that is recognized only generally by the CEOs of the defense contractors. Everything else is buried within.

The end state desired (a kind of "final solution?") is the elimination of most humans, even their high-level, empowered cut-outs, who do their bidding. The goal is the substitution of a whole new set of beings—gene-spliced transhuman hybrids that are part machine, part human and part alien ETs. A self-healing triple helix, super strong, super smart hybrid form of "thing," with extreme quantum-based, A.I. psi-powers, and absolutely no soul or conscience.

The unseen force driving all this is an incredibly intelligent, unimaginably evil group of alien ETs called the Dracos, who are the head of the Archon Network. The Dracos are reptilian cosmic parasites, who live off of the negative "loosh" energy provided by the intense pain and suffering of "sacrificed, dying humans." Dracos have been reputed to be able to shapeshift and assume alternative appearances, sometimes with wings. The Dracos' deepest desire has always been to destroy humans and replace them with their own gene-engineered transhuman hybrids with synthetic souls, who will worship them as gods.

The secret goal of this hybridization and embedded program is to establish a secret occupation of America by somewhat normal humans, appearing as alien ET/human hybrids. These hybrids will be placed in the highest positions of government, the judicial system, intel heads, military brass, various foundations, think-tanks, churches and corporations. One goal of this program is to stack the deck with the leaders of society in a "fifth column," with a large number of embedded hybrids. These beings will energetically serve the needs of the Archon Network and their cut-out human assistants, tasked to attain their age-old Globalist New World Order Agenda. These embedded hybrid cyborgs will enthusiastically serve this Globalist NWO Alien Agenda as a hived group.

It was accepted by top military officials that entered into the Greada Treaty that, in order to get such technologies, it would be necessary to cooperate with the specifics required in this alien ET exchange program with DoD controllers; in this way, they would gain ultra-high-tech alien ET technologies. In exchange, there was a somewhat open-ended agreement allowing malevolent ETs to abduct, extract DNA and engage in hybridization programs. And all of this was done in order to synthesize a race of new Grey/human hybrids, being created mostly in underground bases. These technologies (provided by the alien ETs) also have included scalar communications, large scale regional weather control, anti-gravity, new metal technologies, sophisticated medical technologies, miniaturized solid state electronics, quantum physics and quantum computers, advanced weapons technologies including new types of nuclear weapons with little or no ionizing fallout, such as the "E Bomb," which supposedly can alter or freeze the central nervous system without harming buildings. Major weather events are engineered and controlled using large-scale transmissions and are occasionally used to coerce reticent USG officials to do things they resist.

BIG HARM-A

We should also be wary of the Pharmaceutical Industrial Complex. While Big Pharma tries to instill the premise that they have patients' best interests at heart, most people beg to differ. Missing data, greed, a myriad of toxic chemicals and suppression of symptoms (rather than truly addressing and eliminating symptoms) are often all part of the scam. It is mind control and the chemical path to transhumanism.

What we're not being told is that the more a person separates from his or her heart, and therefore their divine self, the less strong they become, and the more susceptible they are to manipulation. From an elitist perspective, humanity has outgrown its usefulness. Elites want compliant, machine-like slaves, not free-thinking, empathetic beings. Pharmaceutical drugs and the transhumanist agenda serve these goals.

However, in order to prevent mind-controlled victims from waking up and breaking their silence, the Big Pharma cartel has created a "false memory" foundation. This includes bogus therapists and psychiatrists who convince mind-control victims that they are delusional and are having false memories. Big Pharma and Psychiatry have created fictitious diseases in their bible, the DSM V (Diagnostic and Statistical Manual of Disorders, 5th ed.), with which they falsely diagnose victims and drug them. Pharmaceutical drugs are horrendous for the kind of highly-sensitive individuals who are selected for MK-Ultra. These drugs can prevent mind-control victims from ever awakening and breaking their conditioning. There are deep layers which must be addressed in mind-control recovery.

In short, the concept of overpopulation is being pushed by the Fourth Reich in America. The solution to this "problem" is being doggedly addressed, especially by Rockefeller-funded institutions—mostly because these elite are obsessed with having more room, for example—Hitler's *lebensraum*, German for ("living space"). Many researchers insist we are being lied to about the true number of people on the planet, and that in actuality there are probably less than seven billion people on Earth right now. It is very possible that our planet has enough resources for everyone, but the Georgia Guidestones state we should maintain a population of only a half billion.

KILLING THE CURE

If anyone were close to finding a universal cure for cancer and would ensure the public had access to it, it would likely be natural health doctors and naturopaths. These practitioners are less likely to prescribe drugs and more likely to try and heal the body naturally, using holistic medicine and nontoxic approaches. Breakthroughs using this type of medicine are extremely "controversial," as they threaten most everything that the medical-industrial complex stands for, such as costly chemotherapy treatments and cancer drugs, which too often are not effective.

Doctors engaged in this type of research are routinely raided and shut down by the U.S. Food and Drug Administration (FDA). Consequently, they are treated like criminals and their reputations are smeared. This is typically orchestrated against doctors who are considered a threat by the medical establishment. There has been an epidemic of holistic doctors being murdered, most of whom were in Florida. The persecuted scientists (holistic physicians and brave scientists/researchers) all shared a common trait—they had discovered that the nagalase enzyme/protein was being added to vaccines, which were then administrated to humans. Nagalase is what prevents Vitamin D from being produced in the body, which is the body's main defense to naturally kill cancer cells. Nagalase is a protein that's also created by all cancer cells. This protein is also found in very high concentrations in autistic children. This prevents the body from utilizing the Vitamin D necessary to fight cancer and prevent autism. Nagalase disables the immune system. It's also known to cause Type 2 Diabetes. Another tool in the slow-kill toolbox.

The DEA is protecting the Illuminati bloodline/government drug-runners from the competition. The dark forces also don't like marijuana because it expands the mind and counteracts mind control. The deeper agenda is the service-to-self and demonic take-over of humanity. It is a transhumanist agenda with for-profit prisons and drug testing on inmates. Pharmaceutical giant, I.G. Farben, ran the Auschwitz Concentration Camp. MK-Ultra was started in the U.S., moved to Nazi Germany, and returned to the U.S. The Rockefeller Foundation created the AMA and supported the evil agenda to kill all cancer cures.

THE DEATH OF DR. BRADSTREET

"Renowned holistic doctor found dead one week after FDA raids clinic," read a headline, and this was the case with Dr. James Jeffrey Bradstreet, who was found dead in 2015, after his body was discovered floating in a North Carolina river with a single gunshot wound to the chest and ruled a suicide. Bradstreet, a renowned physician known for his skepticism of immunizations (particularly the MMR vaccine), and his progressive autism research, was raided by the FDA one week before his mysterious death. The raid was in connection with an investigation into GcMAF treatments, known to counter nagalase.

Personally affected by autism, as both his son and stepson were diagnosed with the condition, a significant portion of Dr. Bradstreet's work was dedicated to this cause. He even testified twice before the U.S. House of Representatives about the link between vaccines and autism.

As *Natural News* reported, leading up to his death, Dr. Bradstreet was working with a little-known molecule that occurs naturally in the human body. GcMAF (Globulin component Macrophage Activating Factor), which is the GC protein after it combines with Vitamin D in the body, has the potential to be a universal cure for cancer. It's also believed to be capable of treating and reversing autism, HIV/AIDS, liver/kidney disease and diabetes. Dr. Bradstreet was working with a naturally-occurring compound that may be the single most effective mechanism in the immune system for killing cancer cells. What Dr. Bradstreet and his colleagues discovered is that the immune system is being compromised by a compound added to vaccines called nagalase.

Nagalase is an enzyme/protein that's made by cancer cells and viruses causing immunodeficiency syndromes, and has also been linked to autism, as well as a "host of other problems," according to doctors working with the enzyme. Nagalase blocks the GC protein from attaching itself to Vitamin D, thus preventing the immune system from doing its job and therefore causing cancer and other serious diseases. Without an active immune system, cancer and viral infections can spread rapidly.

Doctors found dead and/or went missing were known to believe that nagalase was being introduced to the body through vaccines. Apparently writing this publicly can cost a doctor his or her life, for example, believing or promoting ideas such as the following: "What ends up happening is when the GC protein cannot be converted to GcMAF, the entire immune system is compromised." Some of the doctors who wound up dead or missing in 2015 believed that the nagalase protein/enzyme was being introduced intentionally into the body either virally or directly through vaccines. Dr. Bradstreet and his colleagues also learned that the nagalase protein was not present in children at birth, but was somehow introduced into autistic children, they felt, during the immunization process. Before his death, Dr. Bradstreet treated 1,100 patients with GcMAF with an 85% positive response rate—something that was deemed impossible by the medical community.

DEATH BY HOSPITAL VISIT

A message to "quack busters" who attack natural health behind a phony mask of "scientific skepticism:" Put your own house in order—that's where the real quacks are. Who are the lunatics? The people who opt for natural health? How can a natural approach that is effective ever be condemned?

A *Washington Post* article appeared on May 3, 2016, entitled: "Researchers: Medical errors now third leading cause of death in United States." It reports on a new Johns Hopkins study. It stated:

> A new study by patient safety researchers provides some context...Their analysis, published in the BMJ entitled "Medical error—the third leading cause of death in the US," shows that "medical errors" in hospitals and other health care facilities are incredibly common and may now be the third leading cause of death in the United States—claiming 251,000 lives every year, more than respiratory disease, accidents, stroke and Alzheimer's....Moreover, the Centers for Disease Control and Prevention doesn't require reporting of (medical) errors in the data it collects about deaths through billing codes, making it hard to see what's going on at the national level.

The estimate that "severe patient injuries from medical errors" are 40 times the death figure would give us this: every year in the USA, there are 10 million severe injuries as a result of medical errors.[10]

10 Rappoport, Jon, "New Holocaust Study: Medical Errors 3rd Leading Cause of Death in U.S." https://mysticalraven.wordpress.com/2016/05/05/new-holocaust-study-medical-errors-3rd-leading-cause-of-death-in-us/

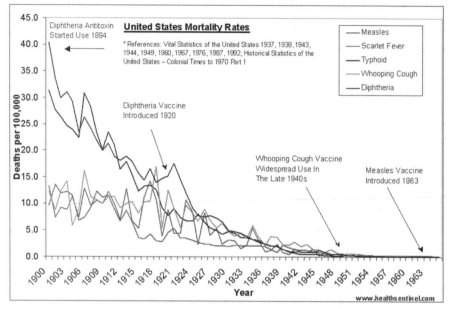

Anyone who believes vaccines "saved us from disease," is wrong. What saved us was developments in sanitation, nutrition, and discovering there are these things called germs. And that the cleaner we are, the less sick we get.

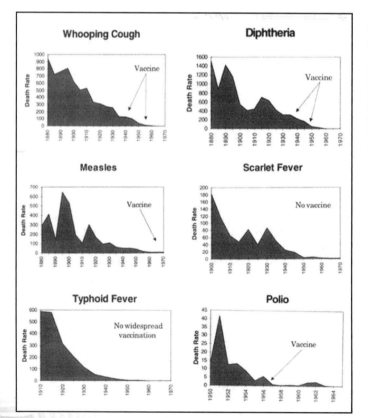

Illness and disease rates plummet when clean running water, proper hygiene, and good sanitation systems are in place, not a vaccine schedule over the course of decades.

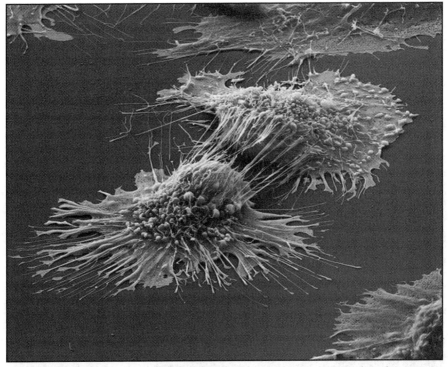

Cancer cells as seen under an electron microscope. Viruses are microbes that are even smaller than bacteria and cannot survive outside the body's cells. They cause illness by invading healthy cells.

Scientists at the former Argentinian research base called Corbeta Uruguay were studying a very old underground cave where the "black goo" was discovered. The A.I. black goo substance was discovered in a frozen ancient ET base on South Thule Island, the southernmost of the South Sandwich Islands in the far South Atlantic, near Antarctica. The British captured the Argentinian base there in the final military campaign of the Falklands War in 1982. The research station, pictured here, was destroyed the following year by the British invading fleet.

It seems that those in power are trying their best to keep everybody from finding out that human history is very different from the neo-Darwinian model in which human evolution has been a slow, unbroken, random pattern without intervention from any other sentient species. It's likely that just learning of the existence of one different species of giants here on Earth would completely break the spell and have a majority of us ready to demand the truth about our history and our place in this universe, alongside other intelligent species.

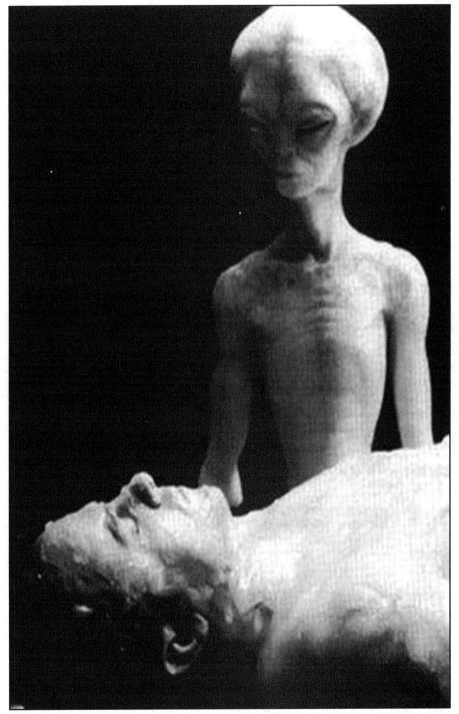

If aliens took the genes from *Homo Erectus* and Neanderthal in prehistory, made modern humans mixed with Zeta Greys, what does that make our relationship today? Brothers of another mother? Or the property of those who created us?

ÜBERMIND:

All frequency emanates from one sacred divine source of consciousness. We live in an age where we are hypnotized by our own ignorance, and controlled by an invisible master. To break from the false matrix, we must first free our minds.

"Transcendence is the only real alternative to extinction." –Czech President Václav Havel, Independence Hall, Philadelphia, July 4, 1994

"Enlightenment is man's leaving his self-caused immaturity. Immaturity is the incapacity to use one's intelligence without the guidance of another. Such immaturity is self-caused, if it is not caused by lack of intelligence, but by lack of determination and courage to use one's intelligence without being guided by another. Sapere Aude! [dare to know] Have the courage to use your own intelligence! is therefore the motto of the enlightenment." –German philosopher Immanuel Kant (1784)

"Karma is the beginning of knowledge. Next is patience. Patience is very important. The strong are the patient ones, Anjin-san. Patience means holding back your inclination to the seven emotions: hate, adoration, joy, anxiety, anger, grief, fear. If you don't give way to the seven, you're patient, then you'll soon understand all manner of things and be in harmony with Eternity." –James Clavell, *Shōgun*

"Therefore, turn from the outer, to the inner self; and Seek to find Faith, for there is no deeper death than ignorance and unbelief." –the bodhisattva Issa

"How much better to get wisdom than gold! To get understanding is to be chosen rather than silver." –Proverbs 16:16

"You never identify yourself with the shadow cast by your body, or with its reflection, or with the body you see in a dream or in your imagination. Therefore you should not identify yourself with this living body, either." –Shankara (A.D. 788-820), *Viveka Chudamani* (Vedic Scriptures)

"In the present circumstances, no one can afford to assume that someone else will solve their problems. Every individual has a responsibility to help guide our global family in the right direction. Good wishes are not sufficient; we must become actively engaged." –Dalai Lama

"The reality we can put into words is never reality itself." –Werner Heisenberg

TECHNOLOGY LEAP

"There is nothing as powerful as an idea whose time has come." –Voltaire, 17ᵗʰ century French philosopher

WE are witnessing, right now, the greatest advancement in technology in the entire recorded history of the world. These profound changes in our collective society are driven by the minds of humans. Just in the last century some of the greatest thinkers have laid down the philosophy, equations and advanced science to allow these advancements. But as we will see at the end of this chapter and section, technology also has a dark side.

The complexity of today's civilization is far too intricate for human systems to manage without the assistance of advanced electronic devices. Computers of today are relatively primitive compared to those that will evolve in the future. With the advent of future developments in science and technology, it is inevitable that we will assign more and more decision-making to artificially intelligent machines. At present, this is evident in military systems in which electronic sensors maintain the ideal flight characteristics in advanced aircraft. This is also the case in modern industrial plants which have built-in automatic inventory systems called "first in, first out." These can order material replacements well in advance, without having to warehouse parts. The capacities of computers today exceed five hundred trillion bits of information per second. Eventually the management of social systems will incorporate electronic sensors interconnected with all phases of the social sequences, thus eliminating the need for politics.

Part of the technology leap will be re-introducing that which has been suppressed. It is also reclaiming technologies which have been hijacked for nefarious purposes, such as some of the inventions of Nikola Tesla. He and others introduced most of the free energy devices to tap the innate energy of toroidal magnetic fields. They also access the virtually unrecognized "longitudinal wave" at the center of an electro-magnetic vortex rather than the more commonly-known "transverse" wave that is coiling around it. Others mimic cosmic vortices with copper coils that create toroidal fields. Rotating these fields at certain octave frequencies seems to tap into the ambient energy of the space around the coils. Harmonic resonance, rather than internal combustion, unlocks the power.

The renowned 19th century science fiction writer and visionary, Jules Verne, predicted that water would be the "coal of the future." Sir Arthur C. Clarke, futurist, author and engineer, believes that the evidence for free energy, such as cold fusion, is overwhelming. Even so, when M.I.T. did early research to investigate the claims of cold fusion, pioneers Pons and Fleischmann were caught lying about the test results in an effort to disprove the theory. M.I.T. insiders believe that the pressure to receive government funding for the university prompted certain individuals to produce fraudulent results. Government agencies are controlled by multinational corporations who will stop at nothing to maintain the world's dependence on fossil fuels, pharmaceuticals and costly electricity—all of which have cheaper and much more effective substitutes.

THE BIG JUMP

Science and technology have transformed our world more in the past century than in the previous hundred centuries. Just consider that it took 10,000 years to get from the wooden cart to the airplane, but only 66 years to get from powered flight to a lunar landing. Moore's Law of computer power doubling every eighteen months continues unabated; in fact, computer power now doubles about every year. Ray Kurzweil, in *The Age of Spiritual Machines*, calculates that there have been 32 doublings from World War II until 2000, when his book was released, and that the "singularity point" may be upon us as early as 2030. Another way the singularity can be viewed is in the center of a black hole, where matter is so dense that its gravity is infinite. It is also the point at which total computational power will rise to levels that are so far beyond anything that we can imagine that they will appear nearly infinite. This, relatively speaking, will be indistinguishable from omniscience. When this happens, according to Kurzweil, the world will change more in a decade than it did in the previous thousand decades.[1]

Historically, certain specific, technological advances have contributed enormously to the continued development of a world community. Over the last decades we have seen the Internet, a military network initially established to help stabilize the United States in the event of nuclear war, transform into perhaps the most monumental technological development of the late 20th century. If properly fostered, the Internet can be a technology of peace. Whether it be the wheel, the sail, the printing press, the internal combustion engine, the telegraph, telephone, or computer, all of these advances share one common denominator—they each have facilitated worldwide communication, connection, and greater understanding.

Science is replete with examples of experiments that have failed, as well as those that have succeeded. In the development of the airplane, for example, there were hundreds of failures before the first workable model was produced. In the field of medicine, Dr. Paul Ehrlich attempted over 600 different approaches to controlling syphilis before one was finally proven successful. All of the technology we use today, such as computers, cell phones, the Internet, aircraft, and automobiles, are all going through constant improvements and modifications. Yet our social system and values remain largely static.[2]

1   Kurzweil, Ray, *The Age of Spiritual Machines.* Penguin, 2000.
2   Kurzweil, Ray, *The Singularity is Near: When Humans Transcend Biology.* Penguin, 2006.

As above, so below. It is clear everything is connected to everything else. This includes a unified field of physics, interdimensional cosmology, the genetics of all life forms, natural biology, and electro-chemistry; all are part of the one universe. All fossil fuels, all nuclear fuels, anything that pollutes or has the potential to poison needs to be phased out immediately. Instead, we must employ free energy technologies that work in the natural sense with the space-time continuum and in harmony with nature. Humankind needs to withdraw its focus on greed, war and oil, and envision instead the promising future which lies in medicine, health, energy, and environmental clean-up. The task is to build public momentum similar to the response to the NASA project, when everyone was excited about going to the Moon, and hence, civilization had something better to do than pick on its neighbors and fight over race, color, creed and our differences. The technology itself has to come out into the world, guided by the greatest minds in this Modern Age.

NIKOLA TESLA

One of these greatest minds of the Modern Age is conspicuously absent from our history books. It could be a result of his altruistic nature—a man who wished to give free energy technology to the world, but was crushed by the moneyed industrialists of his age. Nikola Tesla was an inventor, physicist, mechanical engineer, and electrical engineer. An ethnic Serb, born in Smiljan, Croatia, on July 10, 1856, he was a subject of the Austrian Empire, but later became an American citizen. Tesla is best known for his many revolutionary contributions to the developments of electricity and magnetism in the late 19th and early 20th century. His patents and theoretical work formed the basis of modern alternating current (AC) electric power systems, including the polyphase power distribution systems and the AC motor, with which he helped usher in the Second Industrial Revolution. In the opinion of authorities, Tesla is today considered the greatest inventor of all times. He has more original inventions to his credit than any other man in history. He is considered greater than Archimedes, Faraday, or Edison. His basic, as well as revolutionary discoveries have no equal for sheer audacity in the annals of the world! His master mind is easily one of the seven wonders of the intellectual world.

It has been said that Nikola Tesla invented the 20th Century, and some say he is the father of the 21st Century. Tesla had the gift of being able to fully envision a new invention before his eyes, even though he did have certain eccentricities such as being afraid of pearls. Contemporary biographers of Tesla have deemed him "the patron saint of modern electricity," and the "discoverer of new principles." Tesla was the sole inventor of the alternating poly-phase current generators that light up every town in the world today. He was the original inventor of the radio, and placed his ideas in print and demonstrated them before the public five years before Marconi. By the turn of the century, he had discussed the feasibility of television. He created an atom smasher capable of evaporating rubies and diamonds. He built wireless neon lamps that gave off more light than today's conventional bulbs. He built precursors to the electron microscope, the laser and X-ray photographs. He sent his shadowgraphs to the discoverer of X-rays in 1895 as soon as Roentgen published his famous pictures. Tesla also created Kirlian-like photographs of aura fields 75 years before they became famous. All of this took place before 1900! [3]

After his radio demonstration of wireless communication in 1893, and after being the victor in the "War of Currents" over Thomas Edison, he was widely hailed as America's greatest electrical engineer. Much of his early work pioneered modern electrical engineering and many of his discoveries were of groundbreaking importance. During this period, in the United States, Tesla's fame rivaled that of any other inventor or scientist in history or popular culture, but due to his eccentric personality and unbelievable and sometimes bizarre claims about possible scientific and technological developments, Tes-

3   Tesla, Nikola, *Experiments with Alternate Currents of High Potential and High Frequency*, 1892.

la was ultimately ostracized and regarded as a "mad scientist." He also had his financing pulled by J.P. Morgan, and his New York City laboratory was mysteriously burned down. Never having put much focus on his finances, Tesla died in New York City single and broke, at the age of 86, on January 7, 1943. He was the holder of more than 700 patents.

A GENIUS AHEAD OF HIS TIME

Aside from his work on electromagnetism and engineering, Tesla is said to have contributed in varying degrees to the establishment of robotics, remote control, radar and computer science, and to the expansion of ballistics, nuclear physics, and theoretical physics. In 1943, the Supreme Court of the United States credited him as being the inventor of the radio, not Guglielmo Marconi, as most people think.

He performed several experiments prior to Roentgen's discovery, including photographing the bones of his hand, and later he sent these images to Roentgen, but didn't make his findings widely-known. Much of his research was lost in the 5th Avenue New York City lab fire of March, 1895.

Tesla began to theorize about electricity and magnetism's power to warp, or rather change, space and time and the procedure by which people could forcibly control this power. Near the end of his life, Tesla was fascinated with the idea of light as both a particle and a wave, a fundamental proposition already incorporated into quantum physics. This field of inquiry led to the idea of creating a "wall of light" by manipulating electromagnetic waves in a certain pattern. This mysterious wall of light would enable time, space, gravity and matter to be altered at will, and engendered an array of Tesla proposals that seem to leap straight out of science fiction, including anti-gravity airships, teleportation, and time travel.[4]

The most bizarre invention Tesla ever proposed was probably the "thought photography" machine. He proposed that a thought formed in the mind created a corresponding image in the retina, and the electrical data of this neural transmission could be read and recorded in a machine. The stored information could then be processed through an artificial optic nerve and played back as visual patterns on a view screen. Another of Tesla's theorized inventions is commonly referred to as Tesla's Flying Machine, which appears to resemble an ion-propelled aircraft similar to the Stealth bomber of today. Tesla claimed that one of his life goals was to create a flying machine that would run without the use of an airplane engine, wings, ailerons, propellers, or an onboard fuel source. Initially, Tesla entertained the idea of trans-continental craft that could fly using an electric motor powered by ground-based stations. As time progressed, Tesla suggested that perhaps such an aircraft could be run entirely electro-mechanically. The theorized appearance would typically take the form of a cigar or saucer, which are the two most commonly reported shapes of UFOs. Ours or theirs?

In Colorado Springs, where he lived from May 1899 until early 1900, Tesla made what he regarded as his most important discovery—terrestrial stationary waves. By this discovery, he proved that the Earth could be used as a conductor and would be as responsive as a tuning fork to electrical vibrations of a certain pitch. He also lighted 200 lamps without wires from a distance of 40 kilometers and created human-made lightening, producing flashes measuring 41 meters. At one time, he was certain he had received signals from another planet in his Colorado laboratory, a claim that was met with derision in some scientific journals.

Tesla was doing experiments on the transmission of electricity without the use of wires in Colorado Springs, when he actually heard over a radio receiver (that is, before anyone

4 Many Tesla references: **https://www.world-mysteries.com/science-mysteries/strange-phenomena/death-ray-of-tesla/l** <and> **https://www.human-resonance.org/tesla.html**

else had radio receivers) what he believed were intelligent signals coming from outside the Earth's atmosphere. This experience and its implications remained an interest for the rest of his life. He noticed repetitive signals from his receiver which were substantially different from the signals he had noted from storms and earth noise. Specifically, he later recalled that the signals appeared in groups of one, two, three, and four clicks together. Tesla had mentioned, before this event and many times after, that he thought his inventions could be used to talk with other planets, or in this case, the ET Black Knight Satellite discovered in Earth orbit long before Sputnik was launched. There have even been claims that he invented a "Teslascope" for just such a purpose.

Later, Tesla came up with a number of medical devices using electromagnetic and scalar effects for healing, which were far ahead of their time. In the late 1930s, he was asked to participate in the Philadelphia Experiment, and while he initially agreed, he ended up withdrawing before activation because he felt it was too dangerous. Though his involvement was minimal, some of his ideas were incorporated in what turned out to be a disastrous experiment.

Tesla, and not Edison, invented the poly-phase alternators that power our modern civilization to this day. It was Tesla who was eventually awarded Marconi's wireless patents long after Tesla and Marconi were both dead. In all, Tesla contributed over 1,200 patents, and we are currently using only some 200 of them. Nearly everyone knows about the Tesla Coil, but how many remember that he demonstrated wireless transmission of electric power prior to 1900? When offered to share the Nobel Prize with Edison for their electrical inventions, Tesla turned down the prestigious award! Edison never received the Nobel Prize. In 1932, Tesla developed a current that was being used to treat cancer patients, but health authorities had it pulled from the market. In recent vindication of Tesla technology, electromagnetic devices have been used in medicine to affect healing in the body, transferring electrons and magnetic fields to the tissues.

HIGH FREQUENCY DYNAMO AND THE "TESLA COIL"

Even after all these years, many of Nikola Tesla's inventions and experiments deserve a second look. Tesla perfected high frequency dynamos which were of two types: one with a direct current field of excitation, and the other in which the magnet was energized by alternating currents of different phases, producing a rotating magnetic field. These inventions are important, because both have found employment in connection with broadcasting a free energy wireless system. In the first machine he exhibited, an efficiency of 90% was attained, but it was necessary to run it in hydrogen or rarefied air to minimize the otherwise prohibitive windage loss and deafening noise. His Tesla coils were nothing more than scientific toys; the subsequent development appeared to him like a dream, Tesla said:

> The chief discovery satisfied me thoroughly as to the practicability of my plan, which was made in 1899 at Colorado Springs where I carried on tests with a generator of 1,500 watt capacity, and ascertained that under certain conditions the current was capable of passing across the entire globe and returning from the antipodes to its origin with undiminished strength. It was a result so unbelievable that the revelation at first almost stunned me. I saw in a flash that by properly organized apparatus at sending and receiving stations, power in virtually unlimited amounts could be conveyed through the Earth at any distance, limited only by the physical dimensions of the globe, with an efficiency as high as ninety-nine and one-half percent.

Perhaps Tesla's suppressed invention that could have revolutionized the world, the "World System," would have employed "the transmission of electrical energy without wires." This system depends upon electrical conductivity, that when proposed by Tesla, used transmission in various natural mediums with current that passes between the two points, and can be used to power practically all devices. In an efficient wireless energy transmission system using this principle, a high-power ultraviolet beam might be used to form a vertical ionized channel in the air directly above the transmitter-receiver stations. The same concept is used in virtual lightning rods, the electro-laser electroshock weapon, and has been proposed for disabling vehicles. Tesla demonstrated his transmission of electrical energy without wires, which depended upon electrical conductivity as early as 1891.

Returning to New York in 1900 after his stint in Colorado, Tesla began construction on Long Island of a wireless world broadcasting tower, with $150,000 capital from the U.S. financier J.P. Morgan. Tesla claimed he secured the loan by assigning 51 percent of his patent rights of telephony and telegraphy to Morgan. He expected to provide worldwide communication and to furnish facilities for sending pictures, messages, weather warnings, and stock reports. It also had the potential to provide wireless free energy to any device with an antenna to receive. The project was abandoned with Morgan's withdrawal of support, largely because there was no meter to tax, that is, no monetary payment system. It was Tesla's greatest defeat. The Tesla effect, named in his honor, is the archaic term for an application of this type of electrical conduction, that is, the movement of energy through space and matter, not just the production of voltage across a conductor. Tesla also investigated harvesting energy that is present throughout space, or produced by the subtle vibrations of the Earth. He believed that it was merely a question of time until humans would succeed in attaching their machinery to the very wheelwork of nature, stating: "Ere many generations pass, our machinery will be driven by a power obtainable at any point of the universe."

When Tesla died in 1943, agents of the alphabet agencies confiscated all his possessions (offering no explanation), which was the equivalent of "two railroad cars" worth of materials in various storage spaces. In the years before his passing, Tesla had been talking about a Death Ray invention, now known as a Directed Energy Weapon. In the middle of World War II, the government would have had concerns over such a device falling into the wrong hands, and moved swiftly to gather all his belongings. Like Einstein, Tesla developed his own Unified Field Theory, hypothesizing that the universe was made of energy fields, and that by using certain electromagnetic fields, a kind of anti-gravity could be created.

EINSTEIN AND THE SPEED OF LIGHT

It was Albert Einstein who proposed over a century ago that nothing could travel faster than the speed of light, that is, until CERN scientists claimed the speed of light had been "broken." The scientific world was left in shock by the September, 2011, revelation that workers at the world's largest physics lab at Geneva, Switzerland, had recorded subatomic particles traveling faster than the speed of light. They tested the theory 15,000 times before announcing their findings. They could not find anything to account for the neutrinos traveling just over the speed of light.

If the findings are proven to be accurate, they would overturn one of the pillars of the Standard Model of Physics, which explains the way the universe and everything within it works. Einstein's theory of special relativity, proposed in 1905, states that nothing in the universe can travel faster than the speed of light in a vacuum. But researchers at the CERN lab near Geneva claim they have recorded neutrinos, a type of tiny particle, arriving at an underground lab in Italy, traveling faster than the barrier of 299,792 kilometers per second. This turns everything upside down, and opens up the possibility of humans being able to manipulate space and time.

Previously, scientists said that because the stars were so far away, hundreds of thousands of light years away, and that any intelligent beings would take thousands of years to arrive there, this made space travel completely impractical. Further, Einstein's General Theory of Relativity (proposed in 1915) states particles traveling faster than the speed of light could not happen as we currently believe. However, we can now look to a higher theory to travel across the universe. In which case space and time is a fabric, a fabric that perhaps we can overcome, if we have unimaginable sources of energy. Albert Einstein reminded us that "reality is an illusion, albeit a persistent one." And when it came to his contemporary Tesla's inventions, Einstein was quoted as saying that "Nikola Tesla's theories of magnetic resonance and optical invisibility are beyond my grasp."

Einstein proposed that as an object approaches light speed, it gets more and more massive, ultimately reaching infinite mass. Dr. Vladimir Ginzburg discovered that this same Einstein equation could be inverted, or turned upside-down, causing an object to lose mass and dematerialize as it reaches the speed of light. No other laws of physics are violated by inverting this equation. Protons, neutrons, electrons, atoms and clusters of atoms have all been observed to pop into a "wave" state, losing any solid identity as particles. This may be happening every time their internal quantum movement slightly exceeds the speed of light—which is not currently believed possible.

Einstein proved that as we move through space, we also move through time. Meaning that by accelerating to near-light speed, we could move through hundreds of Earth years in just a few minutes. Physicist Dewey Larson was able to unify quantum mechanics and astrophysics by postulating a "Time Region," or time-space, a parallel reality in which time as we know it becomes three-dimensional. By simply moving through space in this parallel reality, we actually travel in time. Thus, when scientists speed up an atom so its internal movement is faster than the speed of light, it may be moving into time-space. If it then moves to a new location in the parallel reality before returning, it will not only have teleported—it will have traveled through time.

It should be noted that the speed of light is not a limit as it is often referred to these days, but a boundary that was the doorway to an aetheric realm, which somehow altered time. Coordinate time, or the cosmic sector, is not this empty void that the 19th century ether researchers led people to believe. It is an entire universe unto itself, with stars, planets and life. The shamans of ancient traditions were fully aware of the aetheric life in this coordinate time realm. They developed skills to actually see them and their interactions with people. Many of the lower life forms are parasitic in nature and are attracted by a person's chi energy. We eat food to build energy; they eat energy to build form. They are attracted by strong emotions, particularly the negative feelings of anger, hatred and fear. Their non-corporeal forms have also been called archons, as discussed earlier.

TIME IS GRAVITY-POWERED

The top-secret Looking Glass technology offers us an opportunity to look at time and gravity in a new way. The spherical electromagnetic shield created by the rotating rings in the Yellow Cube (or a Stargate time portal) cancel out the natural "spin fields" within our own gravitational field. These "gravi-spin" waves, as Russian scientists like Terletskiy call them, or "torsion fields," turn out to be the secret to space, time, matter, energy, biological life and consciousness. In the case of the Yellow Cube device, it can be used to peer into future probabilities, or events of the past with crystal clarity. It turns out that gravity has been woefully under-appreciated, due in part to scientific suppression by classified government programs.

One of the weirdest things that has been discovered in the new sciences is that time is indeed gravity-powered. Gravity is the energy that creates matter, and the flow of gravity is what determines the rate that time flows in a given object or area. If we can either cancel out the spin fields in gravity or shield it entirely, we release the pressure that keeps matter held in a particle state. All the matter within that area then shifts from a particle state to a wave state—and it stays there. The object becomes invisible, as far as we are concerned.

As soon as a "null zone" is created in our own gravitational field, we can automatically open up a direct portal that allows us to peer into the parallel universe—as well as creating a potential "lift" to be used for propulsion. The "rules" of space and time then turn inside out—and time becomes three-dimensional. Now, traveling through the landscape is like scrubbing a video backwards and forwards—depending on which direction into the past or future is intended.

ARTHUR C. CLARKE

Arthur C. Clarke who lived from 1917 until 2008, was one of the most far-seeing visionaries of our time. The British science fiction writer, science writer and futurist, inventor, undersea explorer, and television series host was deeply concerned about the technology leap humanity was experiencing. Thus, his pithy quotations tug harder on our collective psyches for their inferred insights into humanity and our place in the cosmos. And none do so more than his famous three laws:

> *Clarke's First Law:* "*When a distinguished but elderly scientist states that something is possible he is almost certainly right. When he states that something is impossible, he is very probably wrong.*"

> *Clarke's Second Law:* "*The only way of discovering the limits of the possible is to venture a little way past them into the impossible.*"

> *Clarke's Third Law:* "*Any sufficiently advanced technology is indistinguishable from magic.*"

The Brookings Institution advised the U.S. in a 1959 report entitled "Proposed Studies on the Implications of Peaceful Space Activities for Human Affairs" to beware of the social-economic chaos resulting from alien artifacts found on the Moon or Mars, just as the 1938 *War of the Worlds* radio broadcast traumatized America. NASA withholds data of non-human intelligence for the good of human society per this Brookings report. Arthur C. Clarke based his 1968 novel *2001: A Space Odyssey* on elements taken from the Brookings Report.

According to Clarke's 1968 *Playboy* magazine interview, Stanley Kubrick quoted from Brookings in the film. Clarke co-wrote the screenplay, considered one of the most influential films of all time. The following *2001: A Space Odyssey* movie dialog with Dr. Heywood Floyd was based upon the Brookings Report:

> *I'm sure you're aware of the extremely grave potential for cultural shock and social disorientation contained in the present situation, if the facts were prematurely and suddenly made public without adequate preparation and conditioning. Anyway, this is the view of the (Space) Council...there must be adequate time for a full study to be made of the situation before any thought can be given to making a public announcement. Oh yes...as some of you know, the Council has requested that formal security oaths be obtained in writing from everyone who has any knowledge of this event.*

R. BUCKMINSTER FULLER

Buckminster "Bucky" Fuller was an inventor who lived from 1895 until 1983, and called himself a "comprehensivist." Considering himself worthless in his twenties, he called himself a "throwaway," but then he decided to dedicate his life to seeing if one individual can really make a difference. He trained in engineering and architecture and his investigations of nature's blueprint allowed him to become one of the 20th century's most prolific inventors. He is most famous for inventing the geodesic dome and the Dymaxion car and house. But perhaps Bucky's most profound legacy will turn out to be how he revealed the structure of the Unified Field which he called the "Cosmic Octave Hierarchy."

Shortly before his death Buckminster Fuller was introduced to a free energy device. He was noted as saying: "I am glad I have lived long enough to see this! It is simply wonderful! I hope and pray you will live long enough to see the principle upon which this artifact is based become the new energy source for all the passengers in Spaceship Earth." Another great Bucky quote:

> We should do away with the absolutely specious notion that everybody has to earn a living. It is a fact today that one in ten thousand of us can make a technological breakthrough capable of supporting all the rest. The youth of today are absolutely right in recognizing this nonsense of earning a living. We keep inventing jobs because of this false idea that everybody has to be employed at some kind of drudgery because, according to Malthusian Darwinian theory he must justify his right to exist. So, we have inspectors of inspectors and people making instruments for inspectors to inspect inspectors....The true business of people should be to go back to school and think about whatever it was they were thinking about before somebody came along and told them they had to earn a living.

THE VECTOR EQUILIBRIUM

The underlying structure of the torus is the Vector Equilibrium (VE). It is the blueprint by which nature forms energy into matter. Buckminster Fuller, one of the 20th Century's most prolific inventors, coined the term "Vector Equilibrium." He named it this because the VE is the only geometric form where all forces are equal and balanced. The energy lines, or vectors, must all be an equal length, symmetry, and strength. They represent the energy of attraction and repulsion, similar to the power of a magnet.

No one can actually observe the Vector Equilibrium in the material world because it is the geometry of absolute balance. What we experience on Earth is always expanding toward and contracting away from absolute equilibrium. Similar to a wave arising from the surface of a tranquil sea, a material form is born, or more precisely unfolds from the plenum (fullness) of energy and dies (enfolds) back into it. This energy is ironically referred to by physicists as "the vacuum!" The VE is like the imaginable, yet invisible, mother of all the shapes and symmetries we see in the world.

In order for the pattern to show up at every scale, there must be a way for organisms to grow while maintaining proportion among their parts. There is one spiral vortex in nature that accomplishes this, and it is called the phi spiral. It can be seen as everything comes into form, from tiny flowers to expansive galaxies. According to Buckminster Fuller, the VE is more appropriately referred to as a "system" than as a structure, due to it having square faces that are inherently unstable and therefore non-structural.[5]

When all three aspects of the pattern are put together, that is, the torus, the VE, and phi spirals, we can observe one whole pattern. It makes sense that the torus would show up at every scale, because we seem to live in a fractal, or holographic universe. "Fractal" means that the same patterns are repeated at all scales, whether you look through a microscope or a telescope. When you look at a small part of a computer-generated fractal, it has a similar appearance to its full shape. Mountain ranges, river beds, plant veins and lightning discharges are familiar examples. Author Sol Luckman said, "For practical purposes, the DNA molecule is brilliantly designed as a holographic torsion-wave-decoding biocomputer—one that magnetizes creative energy to it, and thus to our consciousness, that is aligned with our beliefs."

5 "Vector Equilibrium & Isotropic Vector Matrix." https://cosmometry.net/vector-equilibrium-&-isotropic-vector-matrix

THE LIGHT & DARK SIDE OF TECHNOLOGY

Our world is rapidly advancing technologically, and it is widely believed that the world is experiencing a paradigm shift in consciousness. Despite the short-term setbacks of current global conflicts, we are on the verge of entering a new atmosphere of peace within the Information Age—that, if navigated wisely, can empower the human species to improve life for all living beings. Such as the promise of releasing suppressed technology through NESARA/GESARA, the National / Global Economic Security and Reformation Acts, which would enable the release of over 6,000 patents of suppressed technologies that are being withheld from the public under the guise of national security, including free energy devices, anti-gravity, and sonic healing machines. If navigated poorly, humanity and the natural world can be in for a rough ride. Those poor choices have manifested as a "Pandora's Box" of nuclear weapons, biological warfare, more geo-engineering and the weaponization of space, to name a few. The name "Pandora" comes from Greek mythology, referring to a story where Prometheus stole fire from the Gods. As an act of revenge, the Gods sent a beautiful woman with the name of Pandora, which means "All gifts," to visit his brother. Pandora had a box with her, which, so she said, was filled with gifts for Prometheus. When the box was opened by the brother, it became clear that in reality, it contained diseases and famine which spread rapidly over the Earth.

Technology needs to be kept in check. Governing bodies such as the United Nations need to have hearings with complete transparency on high technology, when it might in any way be perceived as a global threat. This is a tall order, especially with governments like the United States which keeps its military secrets deeply guarded under the cloak of "national security." Nevertheless, we need to remain vigilant. The author of this book founded the nonprofit organization World Peace Through Technology (WPTTO) in 2000, and remains the President of the organization. The stated mission of the WPTTO is to inspire world peace through the benevolent uses of technology. We do this by demonstrating the many uses of benevolent technology to all people without discrimination. By doing so, we enhance the evolution of community development between global citizens and foster an environment of peace. If left unchecked, we run the risk of world governments in a new arms race to develop even worse weapons of mass destruction. Understanding, with a healthy discourse of ideas, is the best way for us to stay informed.

WHAT THE HAARP?

A major Pandora's Box of technology was the implementation of a joint project of the U.S. Navy, Air Force and the University of Alaska in the mid-1990s, which completed a project called the High-frequency Active Auroral Research Program (HAARP). The program was rolled out to the public as an aurora borealis research project, but has little or nothing to do with studying the northern lights. HAARP is a controversial high frequency radio transmitter operated by the U.S. military which beams high-level energy into the Earth's upper atmosphere. HAARP can be used to locate hidden oil reserves and missile silos, but critics claim it can also blow a massive hole in the upper atmosphere and disrupt the magnetic energies of Earth. The name is but a mask behind which the U.S. military hides a very dark project. The first known station in the USA, the 14-hectare facility in Gakona, Alaska, came online during the fall of 1994, and is amplified when it works in conjunction with other HAARP systems, including with other countries and mobile systems on land and sea. The HAARP array can alter the ionosphere in a way that allows a manipulation in weather patterns, can change the chemical composition of the ionosphere, or block all global communications. A larger second system became operational in 1997, and now dozens have been identified worldwide, despite the project being "officially" shuttered by the military in 2013, after attracting large amounts of negative publicity.

As we learned in the Geoengineering chapter, one use of HAARP is to manipulate the weather. It also has the ability to penetrate the Earth with signals bounced off of the ionosphere. This ground-penetrating tomography has since been developed and used by the U.S. government to look inside the planet to a depth of many kilometers in order to locate underground munitions, minerals and tunnels. The problem is that the frequencies used by HAARP for ground-penetrating tomography is also within the frequency range most cited for disruption of Earth's own electromagnetic field. Several HAARP patents state that it can beam radio energy into the Auroral electrojet, the curved, charged-particle stream formed at high latitudes where the solar wind interacts with Earth's magnetic field. The radio energy then disperses over large areas through ductlike regions of the ionosphere, forming a virtual antenna that can be thousands of miles in length. Such an ELF antenna can emit waves penetrating as deeply as several kilometers into the ground, depending on the geological makeup and subsurface water conditions in a targeted area. HAARP utilizes ground-penetrating radar (GPR) to beam pulses of polarized high-frequency radio waves into the ionosphere. These pulses can be finely tuned and adjusted so that the bounced ground penetrating beam can target a very specific area and for a specific length of time. Beaming a very large energy beam into the ground for an extended period will cause an earthquake. After all, an earthquake is simply the result of a sudden release of energy in the Earth's crust that creates seismic wave resonances. The same array of antennas that are used by HAARP for ground penetrating tomography can also be used to penetrate deep into the ground and cause an earthquake anywhere around the world. Geophysical events like earthquakes and volcanic eruptions—the kinds of things that may already be on the edge of discharge—can, with the right resonant energies added into the system, cause them to overload and actually fracture.[6]

The "HAARP" technology is based on the patents of Nikola Tesla (1,119,732 1914: "An apparatus for transferring electrical energy"), which was designed for peaceful purposes, although the pacifist Tesla warned that the patent could be misused. It was later continued by the American physicist and member of the Atomic Energy Commission, Dr. Bernard J. Eastlund with his U.S. Patent #: 4,686,605 1987, which stated: "Method and apparatus for creating changes in an area of the Earth's atmosphere, ionosphere and / or magnetosphere," as well as two other related patents, also of Eastlund. In principle HAARP technology is Eastlund's patent, which in turn is indirectly based on Tesla's patent. This is in other words patented technology, not science fiction fantasy.

The idea behind it all was to use microwaves to create a virtual antenna in the ionosphere particle layer which could generate electromagnetic radiation of very low wavelength (VLF) and extremely low wavelength (ELF), and send them to Earth, when such waves are able to go about the soil without substantial loss. The experiment was successful to the extent that it confirmed the principle, but the added effect was too small for the generated VLF and ELF waves to have practical significance. It is here that HAARP technology comes into play with its Gigawatt transmitters and improved technology.

The ultra-secret HAARP tests are utilizing a form of "Tesla technology" in and upon the Earth's ionosphere. Will it become a battleground, used as a weapon, or affect human physiology from high-frequency electromagnetic radiation? One of Nikola Tesla's best-known patents in 1888 allowed for his entire system of polyphase AC power, which remains the world standard today. Another of his patents is remarkably similar to the APTI patent described in the Geoengineering chapter. The invention, as described by Tesla himself in 1915:

••
6   "Is the HAARP Project a Weather Control Weapon?" https://www.wanttoknow.info/war/haarp_weather_modification_electromagnetic_warfare_weapons?

Will go through space with a speed of 300 miles a second, a manless ship without propelling engine or wings, sent by electricity to any desired point on the globe on its errand of destruction, if destruction its manipulator wishes to effect. ...It is perfectly practicable to transmit electrical energy without wires and produce a destructive effect at a distance. I have already constructed a wireless transmitter which makes this possible, and have described it in my technical publications. ...With transmitters of this kind we are enabled to project electrical energy in any amount to any distance and apply it for innumerable purposes, both in war and peace.

Nikola Tesla knew some of his inventions could do great harm, and now with the advent of HAARP, he seems to have correctly predicted its misuse. HAARP was developed as covert weapon technology, similar to Tesla's death ray that can knock a plane from the sky, or shift into an Earth resonant frequency targeting an unstable region that can interfere with plate tectonics or the weather.

It remains to be seen if zapping the ionosphere with 180 highly electrified towers will be one more step in the control of environments and open communication systems. Picture an explosion as large as the eruption of Mount St. Helens every second, for a minute straight. We can only hope this technology is will be utilized in the future the way Tesla wished, to do only good for the world, such as assisting free energy transmission or correcting some of the human-generated problems of ozone depletion and excessive air pollution. But those engaged in the service of national security, or executives of oil companies or defense contractors, have yet to demonstrate an enlightened understanding of the balance between technology control and freedom.

THE AKASHIC RECORDS

The Akashic Records are energetic libraries, where every event of all time is recorded and stored. The Akashic Records are similar to a cosmic or collective consciousness. Thinkers such as Rudolf Steiner possessed an ability to perceive information beyond the material world, or information the Looking Glass technology called the Yellow Cube can supposedly tap into. The Sphinx in Egypt has long been identified as the spiritual guardian of the Akashic Records. Indeed, one of the three locations worldwide where physical records exist is underneath the right paw of the Sphinx. The other two locations of the Akashic Records, according to Edgar Cayce, is an unknown location in Central America, and below the waves near the Bahamas. The records are impressed upon a subtle substance called Akasha, or ether. Akasha is also thought to be the primary principle of nature from which the other four natural principles—fire, air, earth and water—were created.[7]

Many traditions and many religions around the world refer to the Akashic Records, otherwise known as the mysterious "Book of Life." Some say the Akashic Records is a type of universal memory, or a collection of vibrational registries, which has inscribed in it everything related to history and creation. It has been accessed by ancient people throughout history. The Book of Life can be traced back to the Atlanteans, Egyptians, Assyrians, Babylonians, Hebrews and Phoenicians. People today can access the Akashic Records by various techniques and spiritual disciplines.

If an individual were able to access the records, he or she would likely see all their past life memories showing up in personal energy fields, which are multi-dimensional in existence. Our head is the filter for a third-dimensional perspective, and our heart is the filter for a multi-dimensional perspective. Each human has his or her own registry, and this consists of a compendium of pictorial records or "memories" of all events, actions, thoughts and feelings. The Akashic Record contains the entire history of every living

7　Olsen, Brad, *Sacred Places North America: 108 Destinations.* CCC Publishing, 2008.

soul since the dawn of creation, and they also connect us to each other. More than just a reservoir of events, the Akashic Records contain every deed, word, feeling, thought, intent that has ever occurred at any time during the entire time of the history of Earth, our solar system, and throughout the cosmos. The Akashic Records is a universal library with no missing parts. If there were ever a universal understanding of the Akasha by the people of Earth, there would be no more conspiracies, as we would have access to an uncritical record of everything that has happened on Earth.[8]

ENERGY UTOPIA

Look at either a piece of quartz crystal or a magnet, and you are looking at trapped energy. Tap the quartz, and you will get a spark, as the electrical potential of the quartz instantaneously jumps. It has been shown that when a magnet spins relative to a coil of wire, an electric current flows in the wire. How then can we extract the power of these materials without the attendant physical energy required to either tap or spin them? Use the formula: Matter equals Energy. To convert matter to energy, simply resonate the matter. To achieve energy output which is above the energy applied at resonance, use three octaves, and there will be three harmonious notes in each octave for a total of nine resonant frequencies.

In the late 19th and early 20th centuries, independent researchers began to notice the "anomalous" effects of applying resonance to a controlled experiment. Then, as now, this area of science is far from the mainstream. The results of those early experiments, such as the lightening of Tesla coils and the motors of Keely, have been ignored both as science and as history—at least in the USA. John Ernst Worrell Keely went down in history labeled as a fraud, but his findings are being vindicated in advanced science today.

Former NASA astronaut Brian O'Leary and the co-founder of the International Association for New Science (IANS) proposed in 1994 an international consortium which could rise above the forces of greed to make "appropriately-scaled free-energy devices" available. Such a consortium has not come to effective fruition, but the science is looking more and more possible. Another of these anomalous effects is the gravity drop experiment which shows the difference in rate of fall between charged material and materials which had not been given an electrical charge. "I wouldn't have believed it if I hadn't seen it," was the comment of one engineer who went into an experiment session at IANS as a hardened skeptic. But little, if any of these energy breakthroughs ever percolate up into the mass media and mass awareness.

NEW ENERGY BREAKTHROUGHS

The story remains the same. At the 2007 American Physical Society conference in Denver, significant developments in "cold fusion" were announced by discoverers with Ph.D.s using proper protocols—but were largely ignored. Such is the tale of revolutionary breakthroughs in design of motors and generators that aren't given attention at Future Energy workshops by the mainstream media. Zero-point energy, however, was discussed by frontier scientists, Thomas Valone, Thorsten Ludwig, and Fabrizio Pinto, but were ignored by most of the other experts.

Of note is electronics engineer, Benjamin Robert "Bob" Teal, who demonstrated a revolutionary electric motor called a "Magnipulsion Engine" about 40 years ago, which was then ignored and unfunded. There were others, such as a motor invented by the late Ed Grey, who worked on Tesla's "radiant energy" principles. These engines would eliminate the conventional viewpoint that, in effect, limits electric motors to near their present level of performance. Conventional wisdom says the efficiency of the latest generation of small motors can only be improved by (at most) a few per-

8 "Akashic Records—The Book of Life" https://www.edgarcayce.org/the-readings/akashic-records/

centage points, since their percentage of efficiency is already reaching into the high 90s. Nevertheless, can you imagine an engine that produces at 100 percent efficiency (a Coefficient Of Performance written as C.O.P.1)? How about a C.O.P. of between 8 and 10? The rest of us non-technical folks can also be amazed that such paradigm-changing energy technology was invented more than 40 years ago.

In the 1970s, the inventor Bob Teal designed paradigm-changing engines. One of his engines received publicity because it worked, but many reviews were infused with sarcasm. One nontechnical reporter described Teal's sixth prototype as a "stainless steel contraption with wires and switches which sent current to magnets placed around the one-horsepower engine." She said it sounded like a sewing machine while operating. Teal explained how the machine could power shop tools, water pumps or conveyors, and horsepower could be added with additional magnetic pods. A small Magnipulsion engine could operate a home central air-conditioner for as little as 50 cents per day. The Magnipulsion engine produced large amounts of mechanical energy, but only small pulses of direct current from a battery were going into its electromagnetic coils to run it. With each trial, the coils turned off, and therefore the magnetic fields around the coils collapsed; however, the engine's circuitry recaptured electricity from the collapsing magnetic fields. That recaptured electricity recharged Teal's batteries or ran other electrical loads. Despite newspaper publicity and technical success with his electric motors, Teal was unsuccessful in getting any commitments from government officials.[9]

The end of the Magnipulsion saga of the 1970s was summed up as "while the publicity brought hundreds of inquiries, nothing ever came of all the interest. The motor's performance was just too unbelievable for most engineers and scientists who observed its operation." Out of money and frustrated that he could not interest government officials or a major investor, Teal retired again and the story of the Magnipulsion Engine faded into history.

What were those secrets of electric motors? In short, Teal had a true understanding of back electromotive force—the Big bad back-EMF that limits all the motors designed with conventional geometries, configurations and arrangements of materials—as the key to liberating the inherent potential of the electric motor.

Lastly, cold fusion is not only alive, it is approaching the commercialization stage. In its field, the phrase "cold fusion" has been largely replaced with Low Energy Nuclear Reactions (LENR). Scientists have found an unassailable way to measure the energetic activity inside a typical cold fusion cell. The skeptics do have a way out of their corner. One might blame Stanley Pons and Martin Fleischman for making a premature announcement in 1989; not that their findings had validity, nor could be applied for practical purposes.

9   Teal, Bob "Free Energy." https://web.archive.org/web/20200307093542/http://free-energy.ws/bob-teal/

An American sculptor named James Sanborn created an enormous sculpture with a series of letters that appear random, but are actually a code that many cryptologists have tried to crack, but have had little success. The name of the sculpture is "Kryptos" and was installed in Langley, Virginia, in front of the CIA headquarters. Only William Webster, the director of the CIA in 1990, was given the key to the sculpture's secret messages, but he has never revealed it, and nobody has been able to figure it out entirely. Not even any of the CIA's army of cryptologists have been able to crack the entire code.

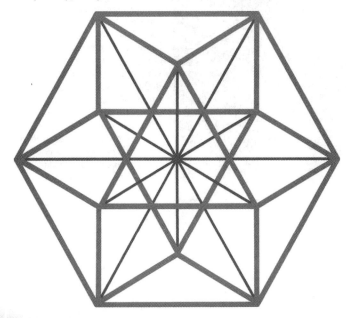

The Vector Equilibrium, as its name describes, is the only geometric form wherein all of the vectors are of equal length. This includes both from its center point out to its circumferential vertices, and the edges (vectors) connecting all of those vertices.

Inside the laboratory housing the ENIAC, the first computer ever built.

This unusual 1898 discovery in Egypt is said by some to be an ancient stargate. Old high technology civilizations used these huge magnetic solid rods as they shot this into the ring, therefore establishing functioning subspace fields with the other parallel worlds. When activated, these old stargates could produce vibrations of up to 3.6 on the Richter scale, which can be registered worldwide. These fields, when activated, can cause cracks in the tectonic crust. Yet, at the moment of activation, the whole device does enter into another function as the effect takes place, and so on. Stargates can also produce artificial reality at the other targeted locations, such as distant galaxies, which seem to semi-exist between dream and reality. Such alien devices work much better in a non-unveiling galaxy as ours is, in present time. What would be the potential of a modern stargate if these devices were backward engineered?

"The workings of the human body are an analogy for the workings of the universe," said Leonardo da Vinci (1452—1519), the Italian Renaissance painter, sculptor, architect, musician, scientist, mathematician, engineer, inventor, anatomist, geologist, cartographer, botanist, writer, and artist who illustrated the famous "Vitruvian Man" in 1492. Da Vinci was engrossed by Vitruvius, who had written that human proportions should have a relationship in architecture. Vitruvius believed that if human proportions could be incorporated into buildings, they would become perfect in their geometry. Vitruvian Man is Leonardo da Vinci's own reflection on human proportion and architecture, made clear through words and image. The purpose of the illustration is to bring together ideas about art, architecture, human anatomy and symmetry in one distinct and commanding image. By combing text and illustration, da Vinci evokes a meaning which could not be created through words or image alone.

In 1931, the "genius ahead of his time" inventor Nikola Tesla was featured on the cover of *Time* magazine.

In 1894, Mark Twain paid a visit to Nikola Tesla's lab and was impressed with the technology leap of inventions. In 1932, Tesla stated "(wireless) power would be transmitted by creating 'standing waves' in the earth by charging the earth with a giant electrical oscillator that would make the earth vibrate electrically in the same way a bell vibrates mechanically when it is struck with a hammer."

According to his friend, Swami Nikhilananda, in a letter to a friend dated February 13, 1896, stated, "Nikola Tesla, the great scientist who specialized in the field of electricity, was much impressed to hear from the Swami his explanation of the Samkhya cosmogony and the theory of cycles given by the Hindus. He was particularly struck by the resemblance between the Samkhya theory of matter and energy and that of modern physics. ...Mr. Tesla was charmed to hear about the Vedantic Prana and Akasha and the Kalpas, which according to him are the only theories modern science can entertain. ...Mr. Tesla thinks he can demonstrate mathematically that force and matter are reducible to potential energy. I am to go see him next week to get this mathematical demonstration."

BRAINS OF THE FUTURE

"A mind that has been stretched will never return to its
original dimension." –Albert Einstein

AS our global society changes at breakneck speed, so does our ability to expand our consciousness. Cases of mind influencing matter have been reported throughout history and across many cultures, more specifically in regard to "supernormal" abilities which include telepathy, psychokinesis, and other phenomena that lie within the realms of parapsychology. These abilities can be observed in people from shamanic cultures, adherents of Eastern practices, and those in the West who study the masters of old. These practices are evident in ancient literature, from the Vedic texts and the yoga sutras, to Jesus, Moses, Buddha, Milarepa, Mohammed and more.

It is amazing to consider on this planet today we have some humans who are members of tribes that have never been contacted, such as groups in the Amazon and the highlands of New Guinea. On the other end of the spectrum there are people working on high technology off planet. The diversity of all the different kinds of people alive today boggles the mind. Yet, we are all human beings. In a way, any human activity, be it flight in a test model UFO, or that of the most primitive among us such as those un-contacted Stone Age tribes, are all part of the human collective consciousness.

As we look to the skies as the final frontier, modern science tells us that outer space is nothing more than just a dead vacuum, but this is not true. An invisible web of energy has been proven to flow throughout the universe. Two centuries ago, it was called the ether. The ether is the sacred life force which esoteric mystics speak of as surrounding the world. It is a very rarefied and highly elastic substance believed to permeate all space, including the interstices between the particles of matter. It is also thought to be the medium carrying vibrations which make up light and other types of electromagnetic radiation. Planets are alive, just as the organisms that live on planets are alive. Space is populated by billions of habitable planets, and each one is a super living organism. Planets co-exist in space with other planets and a huge number of organisms in a symbiotic relationship, creating and recycling the atmosphere and soils of each planet.

Earth, like all planets in the "Goldilocks Zones" of habitability, is a super-living organism as proposed in the Gaia Hypothesis. This suggests all organisms and the inorganic surroundings on Earth are closely integrated to form a single and self-regulating complex system, maintaining the conditions for life on the planet. Because our planet is alive, just like all of us, it can be reasoned that our planet also has consciousness and a spirit. Every living thing contains a spirit. That includes viruses, bacteria, trees, plants, insects, birds, fungus, and flowers. These are the elemental spirits.

HERMETICISM

The expansion of one's mind has been an objective since humans first began to inquire into the nature of the world and their own existence. Hermeticism is a school of esoteric or occult thought that can be traced back to Egypt in late antiquity, and possibly even farther back than that. The known texts of the *Corpus Hermeticum* date back to the Library of Alexandria, raising interesting questions. When and where did Hermetic teachings first originate? What other secrets might the Library of Alexandria have held before its burning in the 3rd century CE?

The surviving texts of the *Corpus Hermeticum* date to at least two centuries after Christ, around the time of the burning of the Library of Alexandria. If as is commonly believed they originate from the Library of Alexandria, then it is possible that, as is traditionally believed, they may go back much further into antiquity. What is amazing is that Hermeticism seems to have understood such things as quantum mechanics, quantum cognition, and emergent spacetime long before such theories were developed. Until more solid information arises as to its origins, we must simply treat Hermeticism as a curious yet marvelous enigma: an ancient occult science rediscovered and reconfirmed by modern physics.[1]

Attesting to its staying power, Hermetic teachings were later summarized in a text known as *The Kybalion: Hermetic Philosophy*. This breakthrough book was originally published in 1908 by a person or persons under the pseudonym of the 'Three Initiates." The book claims to be the essence of the teachings of Hermes Trismegistus. *The Kybalion* was published by the Masonic Lodge of Chicago, and was based on knowledge passed down over time, which was finally released to the public in 1908. It includes a series of seven principles that summarize Hermeticism. Surprisingly, all of these can be derived from modern physics, even though perhaps the last is only derivable via metaphysics, and modern physics was not available until the turn of the last century.

The first Hermetic principle tells us that "All is mind, the universe is mental." It may sound unrealistic to describe the universe as a dream, or perhaps better as a simulation into a "Greater Mind," but this would correspond with the Gaia Hypothesis. Interestingly, this is exactly what physics tells us as described in the Heisenberg Uncertainty Principle where the mere observation of subatomic particles changes the outcome. The peculiar effects seen in modern physics are now being explained by breakthroughs in quantum gravity, the field devoted to uniting Einstein's relativity theory with quantum theory. This uniting of core theories in physics yields what scientists call quantum information processing, which tells us that our spacetime is an

1   Jordan, Steven, "Amazing discovery: Hermeticism explained by cutting edge physics breakthrough." *The Spirits Sience.com*; September 7, 2016.

emergent simulation. Elsewhere, experiments into the foundations of quantum mechanics, such as tests of the Leggett inequality, have actually falsified realism! Meaning—there literally *is no* spoon, as portrayed in *The Matrix*.

However, the precise details of this branch of physics elucidate the mental nature of this information construct. Recent discoveries tell us that spacetime emerges specifically from entangled information, or, as sometimes stated, the information generating quantum entanglement. A feature of this so-called "spooky" phenomenon is that two or more particles affect each other, even at vast distances. Meanwhile, the Integrated Information Theory of consciousness identifies entangled information as integrated information or consciousness as follows: "Quantum entanglement and integrated information, to the extent that one cannot perturb two elements independently, they are informationally one." When joining these two concepts it is apparent that therefore spacetime emerges from consciousness. The universe is after all a mental information construct inside of some Greater Mind's consciousness, which is of course the same thing as the Hermetic Principle of Mentalism.

The Principle of Correspondence embodies the idea that there is always a correspondence between the laws of phenomena of the various "planes" of being and life. "As above, so below; as below, so above" is attributed to Hermes. In turn, this presupposes that physical items in our world "correspond to" things in the higher non-physical realm, hence the reason it is called Correspondence. In regards to science, this notion of correspondence naturally follows from the fact that our "world," namely spacetime, emerges from some deeper or perhaps higher level of reality. But the Principle of Correspondence also tells us that the higher reality with which the physical corresponds is a mental or spiritual reality.

IS A BRAIN EVEN ESSENTIAL?

The conventional view of the human mind is that it is a mere function of the brain. Take away the brain and you take away the mind. Some researchers, however, such as Rupert Sheldrake and Dean Radin disagree, suggesting that, in fact, the mind exists beyond the physical body. As reincarnation suggests, the spirit never extinguishes, and death is re-birth in disguise. These researchers believe the brain serves merely as a kind of tuning device which can access the mind, but does not actually contain it. In 2020, a rat was observed to have basically no brain—but it could still see, hear, smell and feel.[2]

Another startling case from 2011 added support to the view that a brain is not necessarily essential. A baby named Chase Britten was born with a completely missing cerebellum, but by the age of three, he had provoked astonishment within the world of mainstream medicine. According to a report from AOL News, not only is he functioning in a relatively normal way, the boy seems to be thriving, standing, learning to walk, picking up things, and enjoying life just as a toddler his age would be expected to do. But these are all things considered impossible for one with his abnormality. The cerebellum, after all, is the part of the brain believed to control motor skills, balance, and emotions. Doctors at the Children's National Medical Center in Washington D.C. say they do not understand how the boy could be living a fairly normal life without being handicapped. In their view, young Chase has the Magnetic Resonance Imaging (MRI) of a vegetable. They are, they say, currently reexamining their theories about brain function. There are other reported examples of people living in a relatively normal way without the benefit of a normal brain, but Chase's case appears to be one of the most carefully scrutinized ever, and could prove to be very influential.[3]

2 "A rat had basically no brain—but it could still see, hear, smell and feel." https://medicalxpress.com/news/2020-01-rat-basically-brainbut.html

3 "'He has drive like I have never seen': Boy, 3, born without part of his brain baffles doctors after learning to walk." *Daily Mail.co.uk*

LUCID DREAMING

Every one of us has dreams. Even animals can be seen twitching in the dream state. Humans typically remember their dreams after waking up. But there is a different kind of dream state catching the attention of brain researchers. What makes lucid dreaming so enticing, is that at some point during the dream the person knows they are dreaming, that is, without physically waking up. The lucid dreamer is no longer part of the dream, but can choose to remain in it. What if the lucid dreamer then knew, with absolute certainty, that nothing being perceived had any ultimate reality, or that their real self was safe somewhere else in the real world, waiting for return to the body, and the viewer could do anything with impunity, without pain or consequence. Some researchers tie this to our immortal life-energy, commonly called chi, which is a vital ingredient of our make-up.

In a lucid dream state, according to experts, the scenery is reflected back to us mostly from within. Anything seemingly "out there" feels inherently risk-free, or native to one's inner core. Ultimately, however, outside and inside are the same. In lucid dreaming, we go everywhere by going nowhere. The sense of freedom is incredible. In lucid dreaming, there is another bizarre element reported. The recognition of unreality gives the dreamer instant power over his or her own perceptions. In other words, if the person can mold the content of their dream, and everyone who is included, it will then manifest.

Steven LaBerge, the pioneer who documented dream lucidity in the lab with prearranged eye signals from the dream-state, noted: "When you dream, you do something to your brain that's as if you've actually done it. So, there are strong relationships between dream content and physiology." Dreaming is a softener, healer and mediator of both inner and outer selves. It was a key element in "primitive" cultures where both worlds were seen as one. Native American Wisdom Keepers placed great significance on dreams. Without this balance of having a dream life today, we can be weighed down and embittered by the apparent finality of our material life. Dreams are also the perfect space for overcoming self-doubt or fear. Mirroring a new sense of liberation, many dreamers feel a deep urge to fly. It seems to be a universal expression of totality.

If there is a destination, there must be a trip. Here are some tips to open yourself up to lucid dreaming. Document all of your dreams as soon as you awaken and write them down or draw them in a bedside journal. It helps to look back on them, observe patterns, and examine what was going on in your life when they occurred. During the day it helps to repeat the phrase: "Next time I am dreaming, I will realize that I am dreaming." Eventually you will find yourself repeating this in your sleeping dream and this will help you recognize your transcendent identity. Periodically during the day, question yourself whether you are dreaming. How can you tell? Being awake might be another dream, an analogy not lost on the mystics. Practice any orientation technique you might use in a dream, such as those suggested above. Usually, the first experience of lucidity comes from realizing you are doing something grossly out of character, impossible, or seemingly bizarre. Even when lucid, most people still have the faint awareness of another body "back there" in the bed. This is a good indicator. Remote viewers call this "the silver cord." When you are out there, tread lightly upon the dreamscape, dividing your attention simultaneously between your "knowingness" of its illusory state, and impartial observation. This is the occultist's "narrow way" or "pathless path," being in the world, but not of it. Taking the herb gotu kola and Vitamin B6 for several nights makes dreams more vivid and surrealistic. The brain chemical acetylcholine is also connected with REM sleep and, to a lesser degree, norepinephrine and serotonin. The latter occurs mainly by eating bananas.[4]

••••••••••••••••••••••••••••••••••

4   Nielsen, Peter "Mad Scientist's Cookbook: The Lucid Dream Machine" Nexus, (Mapleton, Australia), Sept.-Oct., 1994.

REMOTE VIEWING

The next step beyond lucid dreaming is Remote Viewing (RV), which enables an individual to take greater control of their experience. RV allows a trained individual to have an out-of-body experience, travel back and forward in time, recall their past lives, experience no time, talk to any person anywhere or all at once, any time. No past or future, only an infinite now. Remote viewing is the controlled use of ESP (extrasensory perception) through a specific method. Using a set of protocols (technical rules), the remote viewer can perceive a target—that is an object, a person or event—that is located distantly in time and space. Remote viewing is an altered state gained through meditation, and the person is fully conscious. It is a state of timeless infinite reality, allowing one to tap into a wealth of information with scientific precision. The mythical Akashic Records is not speculation anymore to those trained in RV, nor are any of the mysteries of the world. Remote viewers at the Farsight Institute are solving many of the conspiracies in the world, even targeting off-planet locations, such as the underground bases on Mars.

The U.S. Army Intelligence and Security Command (INSCOM) train their Psychic Intelligence Agent operatives to work in a systematic, very controlled method of accessing information that is not normally accessible by any other source. This advanced intel gathering technology was developed originally as a military intelligence/spy tool during the Cold War at the Stanford Research Institute. Retired Major-General Albert Stubblebine was the Commanding Officer of INSCOM for many years. After he retired from the service, Stubblebine became Chairman of the Board of Directors of PSI TECH, a new breed of out-of-body detectives in the private sector. Stubblebine told attendees at the International Symposium on UFO Research in May, 1992, about his own RV abilities, and how he helped train others:

> It is independent of location, so I can go anywhere on this Earth. I can go into any closet, I can go into any mind, I can access that information at any location that I choose. What will RV not do, okay? Well, first of all, it is not a panacea. It is not an end-all to all end-alls. It provides threads, it provides ideas, it provides detailed information, but it should not be used as an absolute panacea. For example, I could get the essence of a report, but I could not read it. It is not a tool to be used by the callous or the undisciplined, or those people who have, for want of another word or another thought, let me call it, an evil intent.

As chairman of PSI TECH, Stubblebine trained and assisted six remote viewers, all of whom had been through at least one year of previous training, along with a lot of experience doing RV itself. Each one of those "avatars" becomes a very well-trained, very controlled, very highly-disciplined individual. They must be willing to follow the instructions, the programming, and the methodology that is used. There is a very carefully-established protocol or methodology through which remote viewers are actually given their task, and by which they do both their RV as well as their reporting.[5]

According to Stubblebine, it is possible for anybody to access the Akashic data bank. The remote viewers he trained did not have any special psychic abilities before they were selected for the program. They were normal ordinary people whom they trained to do this process. The difference between the two is, first of all, the precise nature of the training, and second, the controlled mechanism in which PSI TECH handles their remote viewers. During his 1992 lecture, Stubblebine described some of the RV tasks performed, and some other fascinating insights:

> You can go into the past or you can go into the future. They wanted to mine the rock on the Moon, the lunar rock, in order to extract both the hydrogen and oxygen.

When you combine the two, you get water which you can drink, and you also get energy which you can use for an energy source, but you also get oxygen which you can breathe. A Soviet system called Topaz, which the United States has just bought or arranged to buy (in 1992) is a small, portable existing nuclear reactor that is suitable for space. The lunar exploration is actually up there and operating and that's the system they have. As far as UFOs are concerned, they can be accessed, they can be tracked. We have looked at the propulsion systems for them—that's not a hard job. You can track them back to where they come from, whether they come from a place here on this planet or whether they come from a place on another planet. They are trackable and you can take a look inside as well as outside. On Mars, there are structures on the surface, there are structures underneath, there are machines on top. The structures underneath the surface of Mars could not be seen by the Voyager cameras that passed by in orbit in 1976. I will also tell you that there are machines under the surface of Mars and there are machines under the surface of Mars that you can look at. You can find out in detail, you can see what they are, where they are, who they are and a lot of detail about them.

PSYCHICS VS. REMOTE VIEWERS

The human mind has incredible powers that have gone largely unused. The mind really does have the ability to affect matter. Government intelligence services have been exploring the powers of the mind and psychic abilities for many decades. They have quietly achieved a remarkable degree of success. Yet they have often spread disinformation to debunk the very topics which they study and desire to keep secret.

Albert Stubblebine did not start out as a trained remote viewer, and he was not a natural psychic. However, during his time as the top Army Psychic Intelligence Agent, he was able to control and codify the process of remote viewing. He helped implement the protocol that extracts the overlay from the experience of the individuals. That's the system, and that's the primary difference between the pure psychics and the trained remote viewers.

A psychic has faculties that are apparently inexplicable by natural laws, especially involving telepathy and clairvoyance. These are usually natural-born abilities. Remote viewing is a measurable exercise, accurate about 85% of the time, or better. If done properly and the trainee takes on a project, first they get the large overview; then they take it down like a telescopic lens to the next layer and keep going deeper until they are down to the nuts and bolts. With experience the success rate can go as high as a 95%. Stubblebine has called RV "a phenomenal tool." He's had some failures, although not often, and he admitted there were false readings. Occasionally there is "noise," he says, or "an override of some sort."

The protocol was developed by the late Ingo Swann, who was himself a natural psychic, and he has patented the protocol. Being a natural psychic is the first and foremost key to success in military-grade Remote Viewing. The mental state of the viewer has to be completely passive. Successful viewers are heavy in the Theta brainwave arena. It is a totally passive activity. There are no active instruments other than the mind that is accessing the information. The Theta brainwave state typically occurs briefly before sleep, and again at waking.

THETA STATE

Our brains consist of five different types of brain waves: Delta, Theta, Alpha, Beta and Gamma brain waves. Each of these brain waves has a normal frequency range in which they operate. Practitioners of lucid dreaming and remote viewing learn to lower their brain activity out of the Beta range in which we spend most of our conscious waking hours. The Beta range of usual externally-focused activity is above 13 Cycles Per

Second (CPS). Practitioners voluntarily lower their range of brain activity into the re-laxed and creative Alpha range of 7-13 CPS, and ideally into the meditative and highly intuitive Theta range of 4-7 CPS. Remote viewing is not possible below the 4 CPS Delta wave state, which is a deep dreamless sleep and loss of body awareness. Similarly, the Gamma waves above 40 CPS in the higher mental activity state, including perception, problem solving, and awakened consciousness is difficult for successful remote viewing.[6]

Right on the cusp between Alpha and Theta is where we are awake, but not forcing mental activity. In experiments, this frequency band was found to be in exact resonance with the Schumann frequencies, which pulsate between the Earth's surface and the bot-tom of the ionosphere. It is here where a portal of consciousness would often open up, allowing one's awareness to extend into realms well beyond the physical. Subjects would often encounter unusual wisdom, information and even conscious entities in this state. Some researchers believe that facilitating such exploration and mastery was at least one of the purposes for the King's Chamber within the Great Pyramid in Egypt.

Like all waves, brain waves have a frequency, measured in cycles per second or Hertz (abbreviated Hz), which is the number of cycles the wave goes through in one second (CPS). While in the Theta state, the mind is capable of deep and profound learning, healing, and growth. It is the brain wave where our minds can connect to the divine and manifest changes in the material world. According to Max Planck, "We must assume behind this force the existence of a conscious and intelligent mind. This mind is the matrix of all matter."

SCHUMANN RESONANCES

Each of the seven Schumann resonances occupies a bandwidth of 1 Hz. In other words, each of the resonances is 1 Hz wide. The first Schumann resonance occurs at a frequency of 7.83 Hz. This frequency also happens to fall between two of the human brainwaves, Alpha and Theta. There are four altogether: Alpha, Beta, Delta and Theta.

When our brain is functioning restfully in the predominantly Alpha-Theta zone we become more relaxed or peaceful. The human brain acts like an electrical circuit called a phase-locked loop. A local external electromagnetic signal, as long as it is stronger than our brainwaves, initiates a resonance effect which the brain locks onto and resonates with that frequency.

The Schumann electromagnetic wave occurring below the range of human hearing cannot be perceived by humans. Since normal hearing covers a frequency range of 20 Hz to 20,000 Hz, it is fair to assume that signals occurring below 20 Hz are per-ceived through other means, if noticed at all.[7]

Physiological effects have been observed in a human subject in response to stim-ulation of the skin with weak electromagnetic fields that are pulsed with certain frequencies near .5 Hz or 2.4 Hz, such as to excite a sensory resonance. Many com-puter monitors and TV tubes, when displaying pulsed images, emit pulsed elec-tromagnetic fields of sufficient amplitudes to cause such excitation. It is therefore possible to manipulate the nervous system of a subject by pulsing images displayed on a nearby computer monitor or television set. The greatest inventor of the 20th century, Nikola Tesla, had this to say on tuning into frequencies:

> *Alpha waves in the human brain are between 6 and 8 hertz. The wave frequency of the human cavity resonates between 6 and 8 hertz. All biological systems operate in the same frequency range. The human brain's alpha waves function*

6   "Brainwave Entrainment." **https://itsusync.com/different-types-of-brain-waves-delta-theta-alpha-beta-gamma-ezp-9/**

7   "The Schumann Effect Part 1- How the Earth Influences Your Brain Waves." **https://subtle.energy/the-schumann-effect-how-the-earth-influences-your-brain/**

in this range and the electrical resonance of the earth is between 6 and 8 hertz. Thus, our entire biological system—the brain and the earth itself—work on the same frequencies. If we can control that resonate system electronically, we can directly control the entire mental system of humankind.

As I uttered these inspiring words the idea came like a flash of lightning and in an instant the truth was revealed. I drew with a stick on the sand the diagram shown six years later in my address before the American Institute of Electrical Engineers, and my companions understood them perfectly. The images I saw were wonderfully sharp and clear and had the solidity of metal and stone, so much so that I told him, "See my motor here; watch me reverse it." I cannot begin to describe my emotions. Pygmalion seeing his statue come to life could not have been more deeply moved. A thousand secrets of nature which I might have stumbled upon accidentally, I would have given for that one which I had wrested from her against all odds and at the peril of my existence.

I gave to the world a wireless system of potentialities far beyond anything before conceived. I made explicit and repeated statements that I contemplated transmission, absolutely unlimited as to terrestrial distance and amount of energy. But, although I have overcome all obstacles which seemed in the beginning unsurmountable and found elegant solutions of all the problems which confronted me, yet, even at this very day, the majority of experts are still blind to the possibilities which are within easy attainment.

THE QUANTUM HOLOGRAM

To understand visually how the universe is truly a hologram, a math professor at Yale University developed a formula that is plugged into a computer program. Like a fractal, it shows a seemingly disorganized pattern, and no matter how far you zoom into the design, you will always find the same pattern within the whole pattern. Each fractal, broken down infinitely, will always reflect the whole. When one fractal changes its pattern, the sum total of the whole pattern changes along with it, and that could be the hologram universe in which we live. As above, so below. This exemplifies that the whole world does not need to be awakened. There's no race to inform the seven billion people on this planet of this message. It is only important that you personally learn to conquer your innermost fears and learn to love.[8]

But humans can be easily tricked too. This model also suggests we are time and space woven, "held" and cocooned in the third dimension, and within a reptilian computerized time matrix. This is a contrived "loop" dimension, elusive and revealing, far from the Universe's objective "reality." Author Enoch Tan clarifies further:

Quantum science tells us that there is not a flat line running from the past to the future. This is the view of most people, but it is based on the old science, and is no longer true. Einstein has proven that time is not fixed, it expands and it contracts. And, time has a vertical dimension. There are many "lanes of time" running simultaneously and you can change lanes. You can begin in one lane, then change lanes to produce a different outcome than you expected in the original lane. This means there are multiple possibilities existing simultaneously in any instant, subject to our conscious and intentional choice.

We have the power to direct our awareness through this field of creative intelligence scientists call the quantum hologram. And through powerful thought we can activate another vertical strand of time, one in which we are whole and well and already healed, because we never were sick. The same applies to every area of life, relationships, financ-

es and success. Peak performance in every area of life is already a reality, in another thread of time. We have the power to activate any scenario in life that we want.

The quantum leap to a healthier you, a more abundant you, a more attractive you, a more successful you, a more youthful you, which exists in another thread of time, is possible only if you are able to break barriers of your current thinking. Your current thinking creates a prison that traps us in this linear reality of causation. When you imagine, you tap into an alternate possibility timeline where what you are imagining exists as reality. Having the feelings of experiencing that reality puts you into vibrational harmony with the frequency of that timeline. Your visualization selects one of the possible scenarios within that timeline to merge with your present timeline.[9]

THE REPTILIAN BRAIN

To fully understand the potential of our minds, we need to examine the brain from every angle. In the deep primal quarters of the human brain there exists a very ancient layer called the Reptilian complex, which controls the most instinctive behaviors of human beings. It is the "fight or flight" instinctual response. This "reptilian brain" explains the violent nature of humans against one another, and the devastating repercussions in society due to its constant over-stimulation.

Scientists have demonstrated that a large part of human behavior originates in zones deeply buried within the brain. It is this structure of the brain that has operated in animals for millions of years. The most ancient and primitive part of the brain controls the instinctive responses of animals and humans. The first layer around the reptilian brain is the limbic system, in charge of all emotions. Lastly there is the neocortex, the largest and most external part of the brain. The neocortex is the genuinely human layer controlling our ability to reason.

The reptilian brain controls the most basic animal functions, including survival and reproduction. It has the same standards of behavior that characterize the "fight your way out, or run" instincts of reptiles and most all animals. A rare exception would be an animal such as the dodo bird of Mauritius that had no natural enemies, that is, until it was easily wiped out as a food source by early explorers. The survival mechanism in animals is handled by a "kill or be killed" response. It does not learn from mistakes and it does not have the capacity for either thinking or feeling. Its only function is to act. When the reptilian brain is activated, it has total control over the emotional and rational aspects of the brain. It behaves in the neurotic legacy of the "super ego," which can prevent some people from adapting and developing. It is therefore cold and rigid. It is territorial, aggressive, hierarchical, obsessive, authoritarian and paranoid. It can be easily triggered by fear.

The pitfalls of modern civilization are merely a reflection of primitive reptilian brain over-activation. But for what reason does this happen, especially considering the human brain is much more than its base instincts? Our reptilian brain is intentionally being over-stimulated to keep humanity in a collective state of fear, lethargy, and ignorance. Psychologists and marketers have long known the advertising effects the reptilian brain has over consumers. That's why using babies, sex and cute pets never goes out of style with advertisers—their visual cues have known effective triggers to sell. The elite and government controllers also know this trick, and use it to control people at the instinctual level. But why would those who should have the task of looking out for our welfare instead be generating hate, fear, and control? Maybe the over-stimulation of the reptilian brain is a tool to keep people removed from the truth. Perhaps if people were to awaken to their true nature, they might achieve spiritual greatness and defend their freedom from the tyranny of those who have denied them for so long. Indeed, we have

9   Tan, Enoch, "The Secret of Anything is Consciousness of That Thing." https://trans4mind.com/counterpoint/index-spiritual/tan19.html

the choice to control our emotional states. Loosen the shackles and drop the chains! It is time to deactivate our knee-jerk reactive responses to the reptilian brain.

NO FEAR

The interesting thing about fear is that it often lurks in the subconscious. The real source of this very strongly-held belief then remains unavailable to the conscious mind. The human mind is the ultimate battlefield. If the Dark Cabal can keep us locked up in fear and terror, we will attract more fear and terror, and they win. This willful, fear-induced denial is, in fact, exactly how this mass, international occult financial conspiracy has persisted for so long.

The skeptics themselves are unaware that the real reason they fight the truth so vigorously is that they cannot psychologically handle the weight of it possibly being true. The implications are very steep once they cross the threshold. No matter what we can say or do, they will not change their beliefs until they are ready. In ordinary circumstances, it may take them a very long time to let go, embrace the "dark night of the soul," and integrate the ugly truth that has always been lurking in the shadows. Of course, each person is on his or her own trajectory of consciousness.

Most Americans, and the skeptics without discernment, who think that anything is a conspiracy, are suffering from a 70-year program of comprehensive, mass brainwashing, which continues to bombard them and reinforce the system on a day-by-day basis from the mainstream media. Their minds will not allow the truth to be the truth, because the thought is too unbearable to contemplate. So rather than argue with them, forgive the skeptics and the haters. There is very little resistance to the emotions of love and forgiveness. Fear and anger cannot penetrate them. One's orientation is the real model for the brains of the future, as only these higher emotions can activate an individual's highest potential.

THE UPLOADABLE BRAIN

It is projected that in just over 25 years, humans will be able to upload their entire minds to computers and become digitally immortal—an event called the singularity—according to futurist Ray Kurzweil, who said: "Based on conservative estimates of the amount of computation you need to functionally simulate a human brain, we'll be able to expand the scope of our intelligence a billion-fold." He also added that this will be possible through neural engineering and referenced the recent strides made towards modeling the brain and technologies which can even begin to replace biological functions.

The human brain is naturally inclined towards the supernatural, seemingly hardwired to be susceptible to supernatural beliefs as a result of many millennia of evolution. But within this decade, computers will pass humans in intelligence and in speed of computing power. Already, our collective minds are melding into the societal machine and the collective consciousness of the Internet.

Scientists have been exploring the mind/matter relationship for more than a century. We have established that consciousness, or factors associated with consciousness, do in fact have observable effects on what we call the physical, material world, albeit very small effects. Eugene Wigner, a physicist and mathematician said that "it was not possible to formulate the laws of quantum mechanics in a fully consistent way without reference to consciousness."

Also uploading to our brain is the radiation from cell phone usage. A 2012 landmark court case in Italy has ruled that there is a link between using a mobile phone and brain tumors, paving the way for a flood of legal actions. Italy's Supreme Court in Rome has blamed excessive cell phone usage on the illness of a 60-year old businessman named

Innocente Marcolini. The Court noted that there is a "causal link" between his illness and phone use. Mr. Marcolini's tumor was discovered in the trigeminal nerve—close to where the phone touched his head. Marcolini has been using a mobile phone for around six hours every day for twelve years. The tumor is non-cancerous but threatens to kill him as it has spread to the carotid artery, the major vessel carrying blood to the brain. His face was left paralyzed and he takes daily morphine for pain.[10]

Electromagnetic radiation emitted by mobile and cordless phones can damage cells, making tumors more likely. Parents especially need to know that their children are at risk for these tumors. Even the World Health Organization urged limits on mobile phone use in 2011, calling mobile phones a Class B carcinogen.

THE BRAIN RENAISSANCE

Humans use a small percentage of their brain power. It is estimated only 10-15% of the actual brain is used on any given day. Yet, in an emotionally-charged situation, like meditation, physical trauma, extreme joy or fear, all of a sudden, the neurons start firing like crazy, resulting in extremely enhanced mental clarity. Remarkable solutions occur for seemingly impossible problems during these circumstances. Gurus call it higher consciousness. Biologists identify it as an altered state. Psychologists label it super sentience. Christians see it as answered prayers.

Our minds can be very suggestive to what we want to believe, and are very sensitive to emotion. Maybe too sensitive, because we can be easily fooled by magic tricks. Stage magic is simply cognitive juggling to entertain an audience. Our sensitivity to movement is likely a survival mechanism, back when we needed to detect potential threats.

It is estimated that a normal adult brain can store about 100 gigabytes of information, but now computers have increasingly larger capacities. Computers are specifically programmed to imitate humans. For example, the computer program Watson was a big winner against the biggest all-time champions in the game of "Jeopardy." The IBM program, Big Blue, can beat the best human chess masters. We can learn from the brain and build better artifacts. Computers are now programmed to learn from their own mistakes. Thus, it is only a matter of time before the computer beats the programmer in the games they are taught.

The human brain is hundreds of billions of neurons all wired together. Strong magnet energy can non-obtrusively affect thoughts, and it can also affect physical and mental pain. For example, 1/3 Transcranial Magnetic Stimulation (TMS) treatment makes depression go into remission, and eventually go away. TMS can turn down parts of the brain, such as the function that judges other people.

Another example of science and the mind coming together is a pill-sized brain chip that has allowed a quadriplegic man to check email and play computer games using only his thoughts. The device can tap into a hundred neurons at a time, and is the most sophisticated implant so far tested in humans. Many paralyzed people control computers with their eyes or tongue. But these techniques are limited by muscle function and require a lot of training. For over a decade, researchers have been trying to find a way to tap directly into thoughts.

The coming renaissance of science will be when consciousness meets quantum physics. In many regards, we are already there. What is not universally accepted yet is the connectedness of our one species, all living organisms, the planet, and a universal understanding and compassion of such a single consciousness.

· ·
10 Kitowski, Przemysław, "4 Court Cases on Mobile Radiation You Should Know About." https://mudita.com/community/blog/4-court-cases-on-mobile-radiation-you-should-know-about/

EMPOWERMENT OF THE FUTURE

With empowered brains, new discoveries can enable us to defend ourselves from those who might deceive us. By empowering ourselves we can begin taking responsibility for ourselves as the human race, and at long last become responsible stewards of Earth. With this awesome potential, taken together with other humans of a similar mind, we can abandon our apathy, take responsibility for the planet, install a truly open and fair government, and reclaim our free will and space of love. This will be our ascension into the 4th density or dimension. This will solve "Earth's Dilemma" with our current government complicit in keeping us in a deep sleep. Ultimately, the human race is currently being sold out for super-advanced technology belonging to the elite.

A clear understanding of who we are becomes a responsibility to self to others, and a projection for free expression. The truth is a constant and will always stand on its own. Yet we find ourselves in an age of great deception. The mass media hides or distorts the truth, the government cannot be trusted, and corporations are clearly in it for their own advantage. So how can we see through the deception? According to the leaked Bilderberg closing remarks in 2014:

> The objective which we pursue is obviously the one of the eternal life, or in any case the passage to the man living two centuries and we join here the ambitious ideas of transhumanism which we wish to develop, to install to favor the emergence of a new human being. Of a superman. As well as our technologies allow us from now on to possess said tools of "augmented reality," our researches perfectly succeeded as regards "the increased man." Our technologies are perfectly developed. We are ready to live two centuries. Our nanotechnologies allow us to repair the bodies of the inside, the decoding of the human genome allowed us to understand the functioning of the cellular aging which we are not capable of stopping, but of slowing down considerably. Our control of stem cells allows us to re-make at the demand any cellular tissue or still obviously any organ which would become failing.

The modern technologies that we use to collect, store, and share information can literally reroute our neural pathways. While the printed book has served to focus our attention by promoting deep and creative thought, the Internet, on the other hand, encourages the rapid, distracted sampling of small bits of information from many sources in the form of instant gratification. Thus, the Internet is remaking us in its own self-image. Meanwhile, while we are becoming ever more adept at scanning and skimming information, we might be losing our capacity for concentration, contemplation, and reflection.

Our brains are become adept at forgetting, and inept at remembering. Our growing dependence on the Internet's information mega-warehouse may in fact be the product of a self-perpetuating, self-amplifying loop. We are literally drowning in information and starved for knowledge. As our use of the Web makes it harder for us to lock information into our biological memory, we're forced to rely more and more on the Web's capacious and easily searchable artificial memory, even if it makes us shallower as critical thinkers. But the one thing the Internet does for us is offer many perspectives on a near endless supply of issues. It is up to us not only to sift through what is right or wrong, but to find a balance between instant bits of information and thoughtful contemplation of the larger, total picture—in short, deliberately and consciously cultivate knowledge that leads to wisdom.

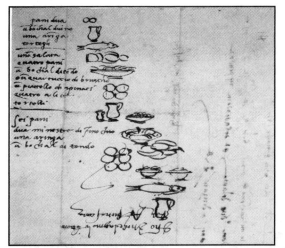

The brain is hugely influenced by visual stimuli. The great Renaissance artist Michelangelo used to illustrate his grocery lists so that his illiterate servants would know what to buy for him.

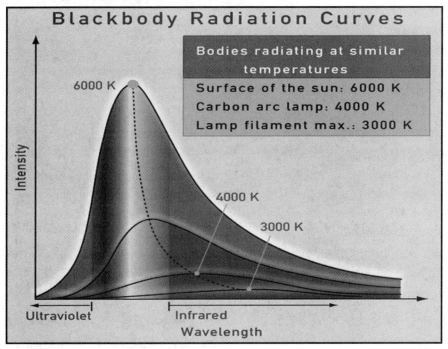

A "blackbody" is an idealized physical body that absorbs all electromagnetic radiation falling on it, such as a black hole. Because of its perfect absorptivity at all wavelengths, a blackbody is also the best possible emitter of thermal radiation, which it radiates incandescently in a characteristic, continuous spectrum that depends on the body's temperature. At Earth-ambient low temperatures, this emission is in the infrared region of the electromagnetic spectrum and not visible from Earth, and therefore the object appears black, since it does not reflect or emit any visible light. Thermal radiation with a blackbody spectrum is predicted to be emitted by black holes due to quantum effects. The thermal radiation from a blackbody is energy converted electrodynamically from the body's pool of internal thermal energy at any temperature greater than absolute zero. It is called blackbody radiation and has a distribution with a frequency maximum that shifts to higher energies with increasing temperature.

Hermeticism is a religious, philosophical, and esoteric tradition based primarily upon writings attributed to Hermes Trismegistus. "According to the universal laws, the magician will form his own point of view about the universe which henceforth will be his true religion." –Franz Bardon, *Initiation into Hermetics*

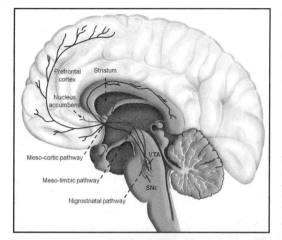

This is an overview of reward structures in the human brain. Positive emotions and behaviors, such as the expressions of unconditional love, respect, gratitude, and compassion, carry with them the harmonic vibrations of the divine. Patterned established expressions of this kind reflect an unimpeded energy flow throughout all of the chakra centers. This is why maintaining a positive mental state, resulting in the natural flow of positive expression, is ultimately the most powerful way of being. This ultimately establishes a state of high frequency.

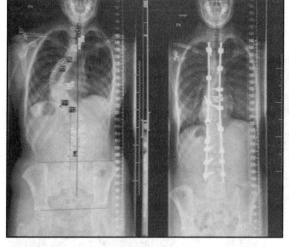

X-rays before and after treatment for scoliosis. The brain stem connects the brain with the spinal cord. It runs down from the brain through a canal in the center of the bones of the spine. These bones protect the spinal cord. Like the brain, the spinal cord is covered by the meninges and cushioned by cerebrospinal fluid. If the spinal cord is compromised, so too will be the brain.

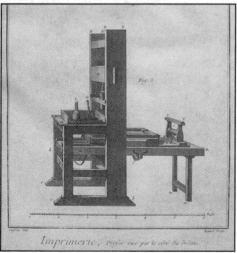

We are experiencing the second revolutionary blossoming of the human mind in the last 600 years. The first was the Gutenberg Press introduced in 1450, which brought the printed word to the world *en masse*. For the very first time in history nearly all humans are literate.

Today, the worldwide Internet is the new Gutenberg Press, that can communicate information at the speed of light and has generated a new worldwide sport of "crack the government criminal conspiracy." Now, for example, we can find out who is responsible for false-flag staged terror attacks and why. The alternative media is the alternative to MSM fake news.

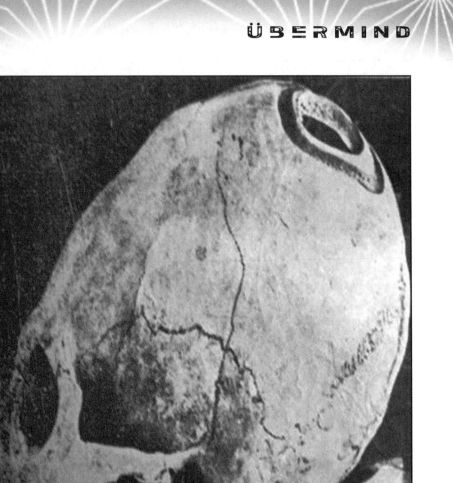

It would stand to reason that a larger brain would mean a more intelligent being. This is one of many elongated skulls found in the early 20th century at the pre-Incan culture sites of Puma Punku and Tiwanaku in Bolivia. None are on display at the museum.

COSMIC
AWARENESS

"I regard consciousness as fundamental. I regard matter as derivative from consciousness. We cannot get behind consciousness. Everything that we talk about, everything that we regard as existing, postulates consciousness."
–Max Planck, theoretical physicist who originated quantum theory, which won him the Nobel Prize in Physics in 1918

IN the last three millennia of recorded history, the awakening of the human race has sputtered along at a snail's pace. Yet, there were occasional periods of rapid advancement. The first dawn of consciousness sprang up all over the world in the 5th century BCE, when Lao Tzu and Confucius were contemporaries in China. On the other side of the Himalayas in northern India, the Buddha was introducing his teachings. In ancient Greece, the renowned philosophers were questioning the nature of reality. Also in this timeframe, the Old Testament prophets were most active in what is today's Israel. And then the lights went off again. Apart from Jesus and a few enlightened souls along the way, the world seemed to drift into a long, dark dream.

In the late 18th century the human race began to wake up again. Science superseded religion as the dominant paradigm among intellectuals in the Age of Enlightenment. The scientific method revolutionized how just about everything could be proven as fact through the replication or observation by other scientists. Unfortunately, the science of consciousness, intuition, human psychic connections, and paranormal phenomenon were discarded into the superstition box. Mainstream science keeps regarding these subjects as taboo, even though recent breakthroughs have proven all have merit. Consciousness, for example, can be regarded as our awareness, where the brain functions more like a "tuner" on an old analog radio.

If there was ever a time in human history when a transformation of consciousness would appear in a person's lifetime since the 5th century BCE, it would seem that time is right now. An evolutionary jump seems upon us, with the biggest advancement coming in the human brain's "über" functionality and ability. We may soon witness a mass great awakening, when the human race collectively enters into a new realization, and our personal transformation will lead to planetary transformation. Another definition of "apocalypse" is the disclosure of something hidden from the majority of humankind, in an era dominated by falsehood and misconception. Our newest human awakening will be the apocalypse of narrowmindedness, and the entrance into a Golden Age of cosmic awareness.

THE 100TH MONKEY EFFECT

On the island of Koshima in the southern Japanese archipelago of islands an amazing experiment happened with a monkey species called *Macaca fuscata*. The Japanese monkey had been observed in the wild for a period of over 30 years. Between 1952 and 1958, scientists observing the monkeys started providing them with sweet potatoes they dropped in the dirt. The monkeys liked the taste of the raw sweet potatoes, but they found the dirt unpleasant.

One day, an 18-month-old female the researchers named Imo found she could solve the distaste problem by washing the potatoes in a nearby stream. She taught this technique to her mother. Her playmates also learned this new way, and they taught their mothers too. This cultural innovation was gradually picked up by various monkeys before the eyes of the scientists, who continued to feed the monkeys sweet potatoes dropped in the dirt.[1]

By the autumn of 1958, all the young monkeys on Koshima learned to wash the sandy sweet potatoes to make them more palatable. Only the adults who imitated their children learned this social improvement. Other adults kept eating the dirty sweet potatoes. Before 1958, only a certain number of Koshima monkeys were washing their sweet potatoes. The estimate is 10 percent. Then something startling took place.

Let us assume that one morning in 1958 there were 99 monkeys on Koshima Island who had learned to wash their sweet potatoes. Later that day, the 100th monkey learned to wash potatoes. Then an amazing observation happened—by that evening almost every monkey in the tribe was washing their sweet potatoes. The added energy of this hundredth monkey somehow created an ideological breakthrough. At a certain point, all the monkeys on the island began washing them. But this was not the amazing part.

Shortly after the mass awakening on Koshima, a more surprising event occurred. The scientists observed that the habit of washing sweet potatoes had then jumped over the sea. Soon monkeys in other areas that had no physical contact with the monkeys on the island starting cleaning their sweet potatoes in the same way. It was like the knowledge was now spreading purely from mind to mind. Colonies of monkeys on other islands and the mainland troop of monkeys at Takasakiyama Natural Zoological Garden also began washing their sweet potatoes first dropped in dirt. Thus, when a certain critical number achieve a new level of awareness, in human or animal, this new awareness may be communicated from mind to mind. This suggests that when a limited number of people discover a new awareness, around a 10% threshold, it can become the conscious property of all the people. This new awareness is a field strengthened so that this awareness is picked up by almost everyone. If this band of monkeys can develop a new collective consciousness, the washing of potatoes, then so can humans. This suggests we are all evolving simultaneously. Thus, we have the ability to convert this Prison Planet into a Prism Planet.

1   Keyes, Ken Jr. From the book *The Hundredth Monkey*, and "The 100th Monkey: A story about social change." **https://www.wowzone.com/monkey.htm**

DISTORTING AWARENESS

We often see the 100th Monkey Effect in our day-to-day lives. If there is a traumatic event somewhere in the world, it can affect everyone, just as this is true, acts of love and kindness can also affect all of us, no matter how small they may seem to be. Many of us who are serious about transforming human consciousness are excited about the potential of the 100th Monkey Effect.

There are some purely natural conditions under which the human mind may become more or less receptive to ideas, including such phenomenon as atmospheric electromagnetic activity, air ionization, and extremely low frequency waves. The human body communicates internally by electro-chemical impulses and artificially created atmospheric electromagnetic (EM) activity. The EM field displayed in Kirlian photographs, the effectiveness of reiki or acupuncture, and the body's physical responses to various types of benign EM radiation, such as x-rays, infrared radiation, and visible light spectra are all examples of human sensitivity to EM forces and fields. Atmospheric EM activity is regularly altered by such phenomenon as sunspot eruptions and gravitational stresses which distort the Earth's magnetic field. Under varying external EM conditions, humans are more or less disposed to the consideration of new ideas.

It is also known that an abundance of negative condensation nuclei, or negative air ions, in ingested breath enhances alertness and exhilaration, while an excess of positive ions causes drowsiness and depression. Calculation of the ionic balance of a person's atmospheric environment can influence their rational thought and reasoning. Negative air ionization is caused by such varying natural-occurring conditions such as solar ultraviolet light, and rapidly moving water such as crashing ocean waves, heavy rainfall or waterfalls. Being exposed to negative air ions are known to give people a sense of well-being. But detonation of a nuclear explosion can also alter atmospheric ionization levels.[2]

Extremely low frequency waves (ELF) up to 100 Hz are also naturally occurring, but they can also be produced artificially. ELF-waves are not normally noticed by the unaided senses, yet their resonant effects on the human body have been connected to both physiological disorders and emotional distortions. Infrasound vibration up to 20 Hz can subliminally influence brain activity to align itself to delta, theta, alpha, or beta wave patterns, including an audience toward everything from alertness to passivity. Infrasound amplification can be deployed against people, as ELF-waves can endure for great distances. It can also be used in conjunction with media broadcasts as well.

Developing our "cosmic awareness" could be the key to unlocking our fullest potential. Consider that if our subconscious minds are in continuous contact with the subconscious minds of everyone else alive today, the 100th Monkey Effect can make drastic and instant changes to our collective consciousness. It can possibly mean that we are also connected with all minds on every other plane of existence at all times throughout the universe. We just need to be aware. Each of our subconscious minds has access to all knowledge, but we've not been taught to understand this, and thus our subconscious minds lie mostly dormant. Although operating below the threshold of most people's awareness, the collective subconscious controls the omnipotent and omnipresent quantum field. It envelops everything, and powers the atoms and manifests our holographic universe. And, your individual mind, while in the alpha level of awareness commonly known as the daydream state, is your personal control console for the collective subconscious. It is our key to a personal power and what everyone must learn to control for posterity's sake, for the simple reason that the quantum field interprets our daydreams as our desired future reality. The collective subconscious, also known as the quantum field, is nothing more than an automaton, or a "machine" that performs with strict functions. This mental projection machine powers

2   Soyke, Fred, and Edmonds, Alan, *The Ion Effect*. New York, NY: E.P, Dutton, 1977.

the electrons that create the holographic projections we call reality.

ALPHA BRAIN WAVES

We can learn to access our subconscious minds by understanding the brain's different frequencies. The most interesting are the alpha brain waves, which are in the frequency where each of us can reprogram the "matrix" of our lives through meditation. An alpha brain wave is an energy frequency between 8Hz–12Hz, otherwise commonly known as "zero point" in conscious manifestation. It has been scientifically shown to be the human frequency in all of our chakra systems that has the most condensed spiral wave of information, highest vibration, and also maintains the most calming mode in the human body. Those people who resonate in alpha more often naturally will be of higher vibrations in order to match that frequency, and as a result are sick less frequently, manifest easier, live longer, feel better every day, and much more.

Any meditation practice that gets you into the "no thought" alpha state of consciousness such as a sitting meditation, yoga, mild exercise, creating art or playing music, and other creative endeavors can be the instrument that connects you to that higher vibrating frequency. It is a good alternative to medicating people of higher vibrations. In alpha, many people activate their pineal gland and this leads to having spiritual insights as well. The alpha brain wave is the frequency in which all people can attain to make a spiritual 3rd eye connection with the unified field where the one universal mind resides—which is the "force" of *Star Wars* fame. There is a force really within each of us. It has always been there. Just tap into it with a pure, positive intent regarding only the outcome. Because if a person meditates in alpha with a negative intent it will not work well, because that frequency is not in matching vibration to the highest emotional frequency in creation, which is always unconditional love and gratitude.

We all live in a holographic reality designed individually and collectively by our consciousness. Our brains are a loop tool and reflects memories of past images looping itself and adding to the visual every day. For example, studies show that when 1% of society performs transcendental meditation, they affect the 99% positively. The effects of our individual and collective matrix being reprogrammed while tapping into alpha have been proven accurate in numerous brain research studies. The most famous is the Maharishi Effect, as performed by the popular Beatles guru and meditating participants. According to a 1968 study by Dr. Robert Keith Wallace at UCLA, when people focus on end result feelings that an outcome has happened, not that it will happen, but that it's done, the societal outcomes reflect the electromagnetic energy sent out from the hearts of the participants of such mediation groups. To prove this point accurately, there have been over 60 scientific studies of meditation groups focusing on peace. For example, in violent communities such as in a case study where participants in war-torn areas of Israel and Lebanon who were trained to feel the feelings of peace and oneness with the unified consciousness in all things resulted in measurable results where terrorist activities drop to 0%, then overall crimes declined plus hospital visits declined during the meditation time frame. The mathematical formula that came from such Maharishi Effect experiments showed that only 1% of any population is needed to create the energy of positive, loving change. The entire system of the individual gained a profound state of relaxation far greater than REM sleep, and the 1% of the population that meditates in oneness has a collective power to affect the other 99%, who has no clue why they stopped the violence during the meditative period.[3]

What it all comes down to is the shift is you. As the two words on the Temple of Apollo in Delphi declare: "Know Thyself." By seeking self-mastery, there becomes less of an

3   Playfair, Guy, L. and Hill, Scott, *The Cycles of Heaven*. New York, NY: St. Martin's Press, 1978.

urgency or need to convert or change others. That can never work anyways, because reality is an illusion in your mind and you are just fighting within yourself. You must shift you. By doing so, you shift into a new parallel reality that matches your frequency. The positive, spiritual energy of unconditional love and oneness is far greater than the energy fueled by fear, which is often shown in today's religions and politics. The key to meditating in Alpha is to focus on the end result as if it has already happened, and soon to be a physical reality. Again, we are all living in our own holodecks we carry around us all the time. We are our own "orbs" bouncing off each other like a Vesica Piscis sharing dual experiences over and over again like a Flower of Life pattern. Once you awaken and become self-aware of how the program works, then you can have more control over how you create your physical manifestations, instead of letting your unconscious thoughts create havoc in your life and can work more "intently" on making it a reality. Quite simply "intend it" into being. The force has always been within you, and everyone else, always. Seeking self-mastery has its benefits.

KUNDALINI ACTIVATION

The ultimate self-realization is the discovery of the "kundalini" energy centers in the body. The researcher Ananda Bosman implicates DMT in the hyperdimensional geometry or architecture operating in DNA through hadronic mechanics, a model of the 8Hz, or universal phase-conjugational force, that is also the most coherent Nuclear Magnetic Resonance and the DNA replication frequency. He relates this to the sacred geometry of the Merkabah, Flower of Life, Sri Yantra, Diamond Body, and Vector Equilibrium Matrix. He also discusses how endogenous DMT and Ayahuasca scientifically has been discovered in the blood of yogis.[4]

The living DNA in our bodies is now being understood to operate in hyperdimensions. The entire body holographic message is present in the single DNA molecule, in order to be capable of reproducing the entire whole. The local 8Hz field component is a standard tetrahedron interlocked with a second tetrahedron representing the counter-rotary field that it is phase-conjugating with, and together comprising a "stellated cube," commonly referred to as the merkaba.

Ananda Bosman discovered that 5-MEO-DMT activates the whole spine, and the whole "Tree of Life" becomes active to be reprogramed. The Tree of Life was known by the ancients as the *Djedi*, the staff of Hermes, and the caduceus of the spine. This is the accessing and awakening of the Tree of Life, also known as the "Kundalini," which is a readout of the DNA, and the DNA is a minute Tree of Life. "As above, so below" applies in many different ways. So, one can start to process the illusion of the dream from its binary code into the "Unity Self." Kundalini is the amazing and natural power of the human organism which can be awakened only by will, and blood is the vehicle of the spirit. The pineal gland is the channel of direct spiritual energy, and can be activated by constant self-inquiry.

When "fired up" by means of "Kundalini activation," the pineal gland stargate technology is accessed. Kundalini activation is the balancing of all of the chakra energy centers within the human body that will ultimately allow for pineal gland technology activation. This activation is felt as a ringing, buzzing or pressure inside of the head. During this process a series of complex electromagnetic intersecting rings of energy spin around the water within the pineal gland which causes the pineal gland to "gate over" into time-space where the person can access to linear time and be directed to some degree by conscious focusing.[5]

BENDING REALITY

Now here's where it gets really interesting. It can now be demonstrated that if an electromagnetically generated resonance field is put around a physical object, say a jar of pickles, it is possible to take it out of its physical spin, and make it disappear. Indeed,

4   "Ananda Bosman discusses endogenous DMT and Ayahuasca, Scientifically in Yogi Blood." https://www.reddit.com/r/conspiracy/comments/eoiikj/ananda_bosman_discusses_endogenous_dmt_and.

5   Kundalini energy and the chakras: https://www.brettlarkin.com/chakras-kundalini-energy-flow/

the electromagnetic mastery is a fundamental key to obtaining super human abilities such as levitation, telekinesis, telepathy, astral traveling, and many other seemingly impossible personal capacities. But first we need to define our terms. The word dematerialize is not exactly correct. In reality it is still there, but its resonance field has shifted through harmonics. It has indeed disappeared, but where is it? Some would say into another dimension, but that is not entirely correct. Folded within space and time is every level of every dimension which are infinite in their differentiation. There is no cessation to the dimensions. Every point in space and time are intimately locatable to every other point of space and time through the integrating aspect of pure conscious intelligence. This is how technologies which are developed enough to travel through inter-dimensional space, can interface with third-dimensional realities and third-dimensional people.

In hyper-dimensional models that examine the higher dimensions in physics, there is a suggestion that the other higher dimensions are at a 90 degree right angle turn away from the dimensions of our own reality. Seem fantastic? Make a quick right angle turn and then disappear? But this is the prevailing model, and it's also the observed behavior of UFO craft before they disappear. High speed 90 degree angle is the gateway to the higher dimensions.

There are other dimensions, many more than the three dimensions we perceive. Scientists have accounted for at least thirteen. Yet, no matter which dimension, everything and everywhere in the universe all assimilate together in a singularity. Everything co-exists. Currently, there are different dimensions we cannot access. We are not spiritually evolved enough to consciously visit these realms, that is, unless we become adept at astral traveling. Already, at night, your astral body travels to realms from angelic to demonic, a spirit world of myriad vibration levels and the pictures you see on the backs of your eyelids, while you are in REM sleep, are not dreams exactly, but astral visits or visual souvenirs of a greater reality. Similar to a goldfish with only a three-second memory span that never suspects a greater world beyond the fishbowl, the limited awareness of humankind floats beneath the surface of a greater reality. In the other dimensions, we are the groping goldfish, mouths agape and peering outside in total ignorance.

But what if technology could give us access to viewing the other dimensions, including the exact timelines of our past, plus different probable future outcomes—on a hand-held device during our waking hours? The cover of this book illustrates the many screens open on a Yellow Cube device. Talk about the next killer app! On 11/11/2019 QAnon made the following post 3585: "Project Looking Glass? Going Forward in Order to Look Back." Bob Lazar also knew there was backward engineering on Looking Glass.

Modern physics tells us that when a "particle" becomes a "wave," it has now spread out in time, that is, existing in the past, present and future simultaneously. Matter is constantly flip-flopping in and out of this "parallel reality," where time becomes three-dimensional. Thus, if we can take the "pressure" off—the pressure that is created by the energetic forces within our own three-dimensional world—matter will naturally flip over into this parallel reality—and stay there. Therefore, if we can build a machine that does this, so the pressure can be turned on and off as needed, we'll have created the conditions for a "stargate," "portal" or teleportation device. This is the basic idea behind the Looking Glass technology, specifically the Yellow Cube device, which is composed of three charged rings rotating around a simple barrel of water. This high-speed rotating charge creates a spherical electromagnetic shield—which nothing can penetrate through. This means that a viewer cannot receive any radio, cell phone, satellite or wi-fi signals inside the barrel of water. The really interesting part is that the "pressure" that keeps the water molecules held in our physical reality is then released by this shield. The water molecules then naturally flip over into this parallel reality, and stay there—forming a "portal" between our world and the "universe of 3D time."

DREAM A LITTLE DREAM

Although the universe of 3D time may sound very strange, it is actually quite familiar. We already go there every night in our dreams. Ghosts are said to be the shadows of people walking in this parallel reality. Remote viewers can study events in our own space and time—by using their "astral body" to travel through this parallel reality. Better explained, every molecule of matter that exists in our reality has an exact duplicate in the parallel reality, otherwise, it could not exist. Much of this new physics research has been developed by Nassim Haramein and from the principles described in *The Source Field Investigations* by David Wilcock. The book explains that when people look into this alternate universe, things appear pretty much the same—at least in many respects. After all, this alternate universe is already all around us, right now. It's everywhere—and yet we cannot touch it with our physical bodies. It's accessed only with our minds, that is, unless we employ exotic technology like Looking Glass—or a teleportation device. In that case, the exterior world will still look the same as it does in 3D time. The only difference now is that *where we look* determines *what time you are looking at*, similar to a dream, but in waking time.[6]

Interpreting dreams are a way to distill messages from the higher self that comes through to the individual in the language of a metaphor. It doesn't matter whether you understand your dreams with your conscious mind or not. It doesn't matter whether you can remember them or not. Your dreams communicate with your fourth-dimensional, or fourth-density astral self, which could be the same self that Edgar Cayce was using to do his medical readings without being aware of his prescribed remedies when he awoke. Edgar Cayce also wrote down his own dreams every morning after waking. So does author David Wilcock, who may be the reincarnated soul of Edgar Cayce.

It is your astral self that goes through the dream experience. So, it's as if you have multiple levels of your being that are doing different activities—mostly that the dreamer is not aware of. They're doing all sorts of work, and they're buzzing around—and yet it's all part of you, at the same time. This is a very mind-expanding concept because you realize how much more you are than your limited physical body. You also realize how much more you're loved, and how much more of yourself there is out there in the cosmos.

THE UNIVERSE IS ALIVE

There is compelling evidence that our current view of science is woefully incomplete. Once we fill in the missing pieces, we will see that the universe is alive and indeed conscious. We'll be seeing things for the first time. Skeptics will say "there is no evidence" as a comforting and pessimistic mantra, but they would not be looking at the big picture. There is ample evidence to suggest that other worlds or dimensions exist just beyond the range of our normal perception, but we remain unaware of them because our minds are not objectively conscious at these higher levels. Our normal level of consciousness is restricted in our dense 3D reality, preventing us from tuning into the subtle fields in higher vibrational realms.

A huge wealth of data points—far too voluminous and interconnected to be dismissed—reveal that the basic laws of quantum physics can generate DNA and biological life. Rather than life existing only here on Earth, and perhaps in a few other rare and isolated places, life appears all throughout the cosmos—from microbial life on up through fully sentient beings like ourselves.[7]

6   Wilcock, David, *The Source Field Investigations*. Dutton, 2011.
7   Adams, Russell B., Series Director, *Mystic Places: Mysteries of the Unknown*. Alexandria, VA: Time-Life Books, 1987.

Furthermore, the argument can be made that the universe has an agenda. It is alive, it is conscious, and it has a karmic plan for soul evolution that we all must follow. If we overlook or ignore the plan in this "physical illusion," increasingly difficult and stressful events will occur on "Prison Planet" until we become re-aligned with our true purpose. We are matched with the people, things and situations that align with the energy we put out. The more you improve yourself and raise your vibration, the more you will see things that are beneficial to your well-being.

POWER OF MIND

The lucid dream state may be the key to a universal understanding. Dreams are an instrumental way our souls use to speak with us. The conscious mind is too busy and distracted most of the time, to hear what spirit has to say. So, it tends to use the subconscious instead. The best way to travel is by thinking. Any spacecraft, or any life form, that goes beyond the speed of light shifts into this field of energy, into something like pure consciousness. Hyper speed travel may be as fast as a thought. It is what the mystics call the ethereal or astral, and that is the form they are in, beyond linear space and time. Earth astronauts of the future will need to be in a Buddhist enlightenment state to consciously navigate their craft.

The power of mind, thought and the science of consciousness is the key to how ET civilizations travel, communicate, appear and how they vanish. But what happens when you go beyond the speed of light? What are you? You cannot stay in the physical form. Where have you shifted to? You are intimately connected at that point to what the mystics call "the field of conscious thought." All the ET vehicles and communication systems are integrated through a conscious interface with the pilots. There is a bio-electric field directly integrated with the passengers. Their mind, or conscious thought field, is connected to the craft and integrated into the guidance field of the craft.

Like a bio-chemical radio transceiver, some individuals, for better or for worse, seem to have the ability to "tune-in" to and "surf" the "universal consciousness," the "flowline," or the "Akasha" memory matrix which links all thinking entities together on the deepest levels of the unconscious, allowing them to travel to specific places in space and time. Others can go through extensive remote viewer training to enable these abilities. This type of conscious awareness is composed of neural "short waves" which are localized with the individual, however unconscious awareness is composed of neural "long-waves" that reach beyond the individual. For instance, these neural states are active during dreaming, thus explaining why many have reported experiencing "shared dreams" with other people.

The nature of consciousness can be described as a quantum hologram, where all are tied into one awake and aware being shining through every individual. An infinite field of awareness, where everything is pure consciousness, including protons, stars, galaxies, and even the inanimate objects on Earth. By adding another dimension, we can tap into the consciousness of ETs. This spectrum of reality from 3D space and time to the consciousness of the universe is a resonance field of consciousness intelligence. These crafts move far beyond the actual speed of light. Travel between any distance in space then becomes instantaneous, that is, if the pilot and passengers are of an enlightened nature, and have a collective idea of where they are going. Modulated technologies that deal with harmonics can project and use these guideposts as a map to their destination.

This new model also explains how atoms can appear to be "waves" and "particles" at the same time. They only appear to be particles, because they are made of a fluidlike energy that is vibrating. If you measure the energy like a wave, you will see a wave. If you look for a particle, you will see one of these geometric points—and find a proton. Ultimately, this means that everything we see in the Universe is an energy vibration. Nothing really exists as a solid object. The mystery becomes even deeper once we see that you can create your own geometric vibrations in this fluidlike energy with your own thoughts. You can use this to "magnetize" certain things to you, such as in the Law of Attraction. As you become more advanced, you could use this same power to levitate objects with your mind—or even manifest physical objects out of thin air.[8]

RAPIDLY GROWING A PLANT FROM THE HAND

A 2016 study published in the *American Journal of Chinese Medicine*, and reported in the U.S. publication *National Library of Medicine*, demonstrated that a woman named Chulin Sun has certain special abilities which allow her to accelerate the germination of specific seeds for the purposes of developing a more robust seed stock. She is a member of the Chinese Somatic Science Research Institute, and a practitioner of Waiqi. The effect of using "qi energy" on plant DNA and cellular growth would appear possible with the right training. Waiqi is a type of qigong that teaches the practitioner to bring the qi energy of traditional Chinese medicine under the control of the mind. Chulin Sun can induce plant seeds to grow shoots and roots several inches long within 20 minutes, simply by using mentally projected qi energy.

According to various studies, it's not just the abilities of Chulin Sun however, because this has been demonstrated on more than 180 different occasions at universities as well as science and research institutions in China including Taiwan and Hong Kong, as well as other countries such as Japan, Thailand, Malaysia, and other countries. Various participants took part in and repeated the qi germination experiments seven times, and five of them succeeded. This remarkable effect on seed development has drawn widespread attention, but the biological mechanisms that underlie this phenomenon are unknown. Many of the studies emphasize that "truly impossible" results were witnessed. Because providing an explanation for what happened in these studies is literally impossible in Western science right now, despite the fact that it happened repeatedly.[9]

How does Chulin Sun and others do it? Apparently, they each enter into a deep trance-like state, and from here, the practitioner is able to advance the time required for sprouting dry seeds from their usual 3 to 4 days, to 20 minutes, generating a sprout growth of 3-4 inches. After a genetic analysis, scientists confirmed this to be the case, hence, the using of the word "rapid" in the title. The abstract of the study also states, "It was thought preliminarily that qi energy changed the structure of a germination-correlated gene site speeding up expression and advancing it in time."

EXPANDED CONSCIOUSNESS

Quantum mechanics has called into question what we perceive to be the "material" foundations of the world by showing that subatomic particles and atoms are not really solid objects, and Heisenberg's Uncertainty Principle has now brought human consciousness into the equation. Just the mere act of observing can affect the outcome. Each one of us has within us the entirety of the universe. We are not isolated. Every sentient being in the world has within them the ability to be infinitely awake. We have the capacity to see distant places by remote viewing or lucid dreaming, and even enabling ET "CE-5" contact. Already on Earth we have all the knowledge, all the wisdom, all the sciences and technologies that can create a sustainable society meant to last for many thousands of years. In this society, every person evolves to become an enlightened being. We will learn that we are electric beings vibrating within an energetic universe. We are both receivers and transmitters of energy—

---

8 Greer, Steven, "Hidden Truth – Forbidden Knowledge" at the X-CONFERENCE: http://www.youtube.com/watch?v=X4HQtB_A_Tc&feature=share.
9 CIA and the *National Library of Medicine* report on super human abilities: http://feedmass.com/cia-document-confirms-reality-of-humans-with-special-abilities-able-to-do-impossible-things.

a vibrational transmitter. We are constantly sending out signals (frequencies/vibrations of energy) that will either attract or repel other vibrational beings, events, and experiences.

Through the practice of various mystic exercises, we can have the ability to stimulate, activate and open up our psychic centers so that inspiration, intuition and the higher aspects of mind can pour into our auric envelopes. This in turn creates an expansion of consciousness and leads to a greater enlightenment and wisdom. As this takes place, we further experience a multitude of benefits such as our concentration improving, a greater sense of inner peace and strength, and it will allow us to experience greater happiness and inner joy. We become stronger people in all aspects of our lives and the things that seem difficult today become easier tomorrow. In these seven simple steps to happiness it is encouraged to think less and feel more; to frown less and smile more; to talk less and listen more; to judge less and accept more; to watch less and do more; to complain less and appreciate more; and finally, to fear less and love more.

There are thousands of consciousness-enhancing practices available to seekers. Once we start living more inspired lives and our desire to serve intensifies, our hearts overflow with love, as we feel compelled to help, heal and inspire all those around us. By performing these sacred practices, we strengthen and develop our auric and magnetic fields so that we can become powerful radiators of a higher spiritual power's wondrous light, that is now so desperately needed in the Prison Planet.

A Native American parable relates the story of a child learning a power of mind lesson from his father. "There are two wolves that are fighting each other in my heart," his father says. "The first wolf is angry, jealous, dishonest, bitter and hateful. The second wolf is kind, caring, compassionate, generous and honest." The child asks which of the wolves will win the fight. His father replies, "The one I chose to feed."

THE SPIRIT WORLD

In the "unseen realms," past life recall is one of the most fascinating areas of unexplained human phenomena. As yet, science has been unable to prove or disprove its genuineness. Even many who have investigated claims of past life recall are unsure whether it is an historical recollection due to reincarnation, or is a construction of information somehow received by the subconscious. Either possibility is remarkable. And like many areas of the paranormal, there is a propensity for fraud which the serious investigator must remain vigilant to detect. It's important to be skeptical about such extraordinary claims, but the stories are nonetheless intriguing. Under hypnosis, numerous people recall the details of previous lives, even to the point of taking on the personalities of their former selves—or possessing the ability to speak in unfamiliar foreign languages!

The picture emerging in the spiritual world is every bit as real as the physical world. When our physical bodies have worn out, our spirit leaves the body and returns to the spirit world. Buddhists call the spirit world "true reality." This is the where the spirits of all entities in the universe reside, even living humans in dreamtime. It is divided into different planes, often called the "astral planes." This is where our spirits dwell and then recycle themselves on the fabled wheel of life, eventually returning to the physical world in a fresh new body. Alien lifeforms also have a spirit, just like humans, and just like any other animal form of life.

Fortunately, each of us are immortal souls with profound untapped powers that may be developed to such an extent that we'll be able to protect all that's important, and acquire the insight to thwart the evil agendas. Thousands of case histories of near-death experiences, reincarnation and similar phenomena provide ample evidence that we are, indeed, spirits in the material world and that we existed before this life and will continue to exist after this life. As the popular bumper sticker says, "you're not a human having a spiritual experience, but a spirit having the human experience!"

Mystics throughout history have tried to describe the mystifying and strange world of the astral planes. All the mystery schools of the largest world religions study these complexities. In the Jewish tradition there is the mystical Kabbalah, a study not to be undertaken by anyone under the age of 40. Islam has the Sufi sect, Hindus have the Brahmins, Buddhists have the esoteric Tibetans, and Christianity has the Gnostics. Their ancient rituals were meant to unlock the subconscious mind and open telepathic gateways to the spirit world.

Sufi mystics have long claimed to be able to rapidly heal wounds to their face and body. The published medical findings by Dr. Howard Hall not only support the Sufi claims, but indicate that the mystics are utilizing some kind of physical healing force unknown to Western science. Sufism is a branch of Islam which is known for, among other things, being able to achieve high mystical or ecstatic states leading to a special awareness of God. The Sufi whirling dervishes of Turkey can famously spin for hours without getting dizzy or falling. Similarly, yogis from India have demonstrated the ability to walk on burning coals, go without food or drink for years, and to overcome many physical challenges beyond the power of "sophisticated" Western doctors. In the meantime, Western allopathic medicine which continues to deny most Eastern treatment modalities such as acupuncture and homeopathy, offer no satisfactory explanation for either the Sufi or yogic achievements and so virtually ignores or denies its existence.[10]

By understanding the astral worlds, we can unlock the mysteries of the spiritual world. Sadhus, sufis, yogis and gurus are Eastern mystics who teach that there are seven great astral planes in the spirit world. The lowest of these seven astral planes is the material plane, the physical world in which we live in. The second level is the plane of forces, as it contains the forces of nature, such as electricity, heat, light, kinetic energy, gravity and the atomic forces. The third plane is the so-called astral plane. The ancient Greeks termed the world *astral*, which refers to the stars. Next is the fourth plane, or the mental plane. There are three higher planes which are extremely difficult to contemplate by anyone on the lower four planes. Contemplation of these higher planes is the goal of enlightenment-seeking Buddhists. These higher planes are what Christians call heaven.

COSMIC EVOLUTION

Cosmic awareness is the force that expressed itself via the spirit world through the likes of Edgar Cayce, Jesus Christ, the Buddha, Krishna, Mohammed and other great avatars who served as "channels" for the "Heavenly Father," and again who speak today as the world begins to enter a new era of spiritual consciousness and awareness. The human race has an evolutionary trajectory to comprehend this spiritual consciousness. It is not a matter of if, but a matter of when.

Each of us has "Christ Consciousness" inherent within us, or a Buddha nature, or the highest form of goodness one can imagine. We were born with this capacity, and it comes from within. When we come to this collective realization that we are all divine beings, our reality will change dramatically. What if we were able to levitate, utilize telepathy, astral travel through space and time, end the sharp duality in this world, instantly manifests objects, or spontaneously heal ourselves? These attainments would now seem to be super human abilities!

Enhancing the ability to channel cosmic awareness can be achieved through such methods as consuming natural herbs, other plants used by shamans throughout the centuries, or other natural mixtures. Throughout history people have ventured deeper into the human psyche and have found a "deeper" awareness of the universe around them,

10 "Healing mysteries: An interview with Howard Hall, PhD, PsyD. Interview by Sheldon Lewis." https://www.ncbi.nlm.nih.gov/pubmed/20671340/

especially through plant mixtures. This is an awareness not found throughout everyday life as we would generally recognize it today. A simple meditation of looking within also works with a near universal recognition.

Cosmic awareness can also be achieved by looking deeply into the eyes of one another. Look beyond the faces, beyond the clothing, beyond the shape of eyes and colors of skin, beyond the language barriers, beyond beliefs, skin colors and attitudes. When we look deeply into the eyes of one another we can communicate with the soul, with the "inner God" which resides behind each face. This "eye gazing" awareness indicates that every human face is every other human face, and all entities are one within the body of cosmic awareness.

If you focus on the problems of the world from the perspective of the classical, linear-systems Western point of view, situations and problems can seem quite hopeless, but if you expand your point of view to include creative and even radical ways of completing cycles and recirculating materials in the biosphere and the economy, the possibilities appear nothing short of miraculous.

Cosmic awareness suggests to us that we should not believe in anything, but to question everything. Look at it as an inner personal journey in which you will cast doubt, explore deeply, and discover for yourself. What you perceive as real in the "unseen realms" then becomes your interpersonal truth. Cosmic awareness only indicates and suggests answers to your intuition. This awareness indicates that these names varied according to the language, according to the ability of entities to conceive of that which is infinite. This awareness indicates that it has spoken through many prophets through many ages, and sometimes a religion formed around the teachings of these prophets.

Cosmic awareness prompts us to think in new ways, to begin to look in new directions, to begin and explore within ourselves, to move beyond the third dimensional thinking into fourth dimensional awareness, and fifth dimensional bliss. This awareness indicates that energies of ecstasy are pouring in upon the Earth at this time. That those who can experience those energies shall rise, shall find health, vitality and joy. That those who cannot see those energies, but who continue dwelling in old patterns of thought, in patterns of fear, insecurity, greed and selfishness will continue to suffer. Those people will be missing out on much of the joy and beauty which shall begin on this planet to make it present.

This awareness indicates that all entities have a direct pipeline to the source of all life. That each of us is capable of being a channel, of being in tune with the infinite. That each of us is within the body of a living universe. That there is nothing in the universe which is dead or ever dies. There is always life after life. Indeed, everything lives eternally, but sometimes on a different plane.

This is something each individual has to experiment with for themselves, but a number of disciplines and practices ranging from ancient *Vedic* literature to quantum physics, from meditation and prayer to intentional manifestation, to name a few, are coming together around concepts that are beginning to link actual physical reality to our thoughts and consciousness in a feedback loop where our consciousness is not merely influenced by reality as we perceive it, but reality is, in turn, influenced by our thoughts.

CALL IT AN INTERDIMENSIONAL AWARENESS

Theodor Kaluza was a German mathematician and physicist known for the "Kaluza-Klein Theory" involving field equations in five-dimensional space. His idea a century ago was that fundamental forces can be unified by introducing additional dimensions, and these theories reemerged much later in string theory. The work of Theodor Kaluza, who used a fifth dimension algebraically to equate Einstein's four-dimensional gravity with Maxwell's electromagnetism, thus extending the space-time to five dimensions instead of four was a foundation for further relational unification theoretical development.

Quantum mathematical theories and calculations can now allow for as many as 12 dimensions, however, one must be careful as the normal laws of "human logic" seem to break down the closer one delves into the sub-atomic or quantum levels of reality. But in the end, we are all one, and we all possess cosmic awareness if that is what we seek.[11]

There are millions and millions of Earth-like worlds in the universe. Planet Earth is among the most remote, and among the worst, as far as our propensity for destructive behaviors. But this is a result of our long ignorance of real consciousness, and our lost cosmic awareness. And that ignorance can only be identified by the truth embargo the human race has been subjected to for many centuries. Before we can bring the light, we must recognize how and why the human race has been kept down so low.

According to the Mayan calendar, Earth has completed its ascension to the fourth density, the vibrational "Density of Love," since December 21st, 2012. During this ascension, there will be a three way split for those souls inhabiting Earth. Those of the predominantly negative polarity will remain negative, choosing to continue a service to self. In order to choose the positive path, at least 51 percent of our personal thoughts and actions must be dedicated to the service of others. For the negative path, at least 95% of those thoughts and actions must be self-serving. Between the two is "the sinkhole of indifference."

IN THE SERVICE TO OTHERS

Another way to look at this dense third dimensional living, or those who are locked in a service to themselves, is these individuals are in a relentless pursuit to the activities that only support a personal selfish existence. Symptoms include a priority to status, materialism, wealth, power over others, and a preoccupation with themselves. Similarly, these individuals are driven by their ego, and fueled by fear, pride, ignorance, jealousy, arrogance, and self-righteousness. Information is sold for recognition and profit. It is understood that they are individuals who are responsible for our own achievements, and pay little regard to others. This will be their downfall for advancing themselves spiritually.

Conversely, fourth dimensional living, or in the service to others, is a commitment to promoting others' achieving a positive reality for others, along with your own. Information is shared freely, and there is a discernible lack of ego satisfaction. Personal journeys are encouraged, recognized and valued. Love is seen in all things. Individuals seek to radiate unconditional love individually and collectively. It is understood that individuals are responsible for each other in a collective striving for community growth.

In the service to others, always look for ways to be of assistance to your fellow people. Look to be of encouragement to others. Build people up, and do not put people down. Be a beacon of light in a dark world. For those striving to be positive we must "work off" our own part of the negative karmic effect incurred from all the negativity created on this planet. Once we have done so, we will be released to once again assume our place as sixth density "Guardians and Teachers of Wisdom" throughout the galaxy. Those of the predominantly positive polarity of love and light will ascend to a beautiful new fourth density Earth, where we will begin to work upon our learning and demonstrating of empathy and compassion. It will be a very beautiful and "Golden Age" of cosmic awareness. The fourth density begins to open you up to our true powers as a unique individualized aspect of "The One Infinite Creator." We serve others simply because we love them, as we do our self. Others are an extension of ourselves. That's why the Law of Attraction works the way it does. Truly, whatever you are doing to me, you are doing to yourself. We are all one, in the Infinite Creation. Separation is an illusion, because we only see what is in the Third Density. We simply cannot visualize the whole picture.

11 "Kaluza-Klein theories." https://en.wikipedia.org/wiki/Kaluza%E2%80%93Klein_theory

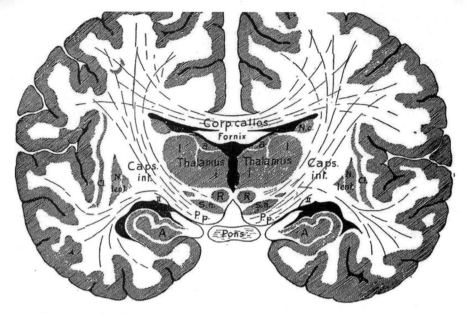

How humans and other sentient beings experience the world—consciously—has long puzzled scientists. The ability to smell a flower or feel a pinprick relies on interactions between brain cells in the cerebral cortex at the brain's surface and the thalamus, which is at the brain's core. But up to this point, scientists haven't been able to narrow exactly which pathways or structures are involved. A new study points researchers to the central lateral thalamus circuit as a pivotal mechanism.

The brain without consciousness is inert and lifeless. Consciousness is a form of matter just as matter is a form of consciousness. All atoms in the entire universe are capable of mind reading and communicating with other atoms.

Ham the chimp returns to Earth following his historic 16-minute space flight in 1961. Chimps are the closest related animal to humans, and they too will be part of the great leap forward.

In March, 2006, this image was captured of an entire nebula shaped like a DNA double helix. The 80-light-year-long formation lies near the enormous black hole at the center of our own Milky Way galaxy captured by NASA's Spitzer Space Telescope Astronomers studying the image believe that the irresistible pull of magnetism created the intertwining spiral strands.

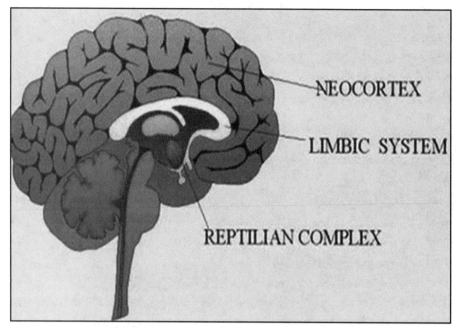

NEOCORTEX

LIMBIC SYSTEM

REPTILIAN COMPLEX

There are connections between quantum mechanics and consciousness. Consciousness is the intelligence, the organizing principle behind the arising of form. The quantum field or pure consciousness is influenced by intention and desire.

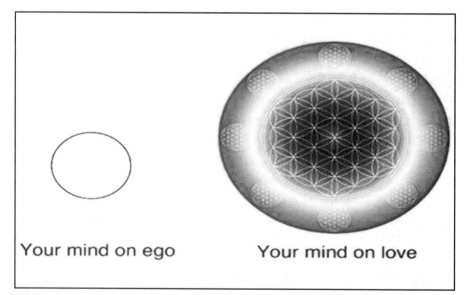

Your mind on ego   Your mind on love

When transitioning into a different constellation, there comes a different frequency, a higher frequency, so we are experiencing a different reality and with that comes higher awareness and incredible insight. Everything on this planet and in our Universe is going through a metamorphic change, a consciousness change. This is what's bringing on the Human Awakening; this is why there is so much chaos on our planet right now. Meaning, everything is frequency, vibration and everything has consciousness and when you tweak that frequency just a little bit it causes immense change that ripples throughout all creation. We are the Greatest Show on Earth.

EXOTIC METALS

"From the smallest particle to the largest galactic formation, a web of electrical circuitry connects and unifies all of nature, organizing galaxies, energizing stars, giving birth to planets and, on our own world, controlling weather and animating biological organisms. There are no isolated islands in an electric universe." –David Talbott

MATTER is not what it appears. Classical science teaches us that the three phases of matter include solids, liquids, and gasses until the recent inclusion of other odd forms including plasma. Solid matter consisting of the atoms, molecules or ions being arranged in a regularly repeating pattern throughout, which can also be crystalline. In classical crystallography, a crystal is defined as a three dimensional periodic arrangement of atoms with translational periodicity along its three principal axes. All other solid matter is said to be amorphous, or non-crystalline, although the distinction is not always sharp. Practically all metals, minerals and alloys are also crystalline, while glasses, plastics, ceramics and gels are amorphous. A single piece of crystalline matter is called a crystal.

Matter in the classic model only existed in three main varieties of the gaseous state, the liquid state, and the solid state, but that understanding is now expanding. A newer phase of matter includes plasmas, liquid crystals, and the Bose–Einstein Condensate (BEC) which is a state of matter of a dilute gas of weakly interacting bosons. They are becoming more widely known as "m-state" elements. The Bose-Einstein condensates can become liquid crystals. Some of these solids can then crystallize into a lattice structure called metals. There is another phase of matter called monatomic, which has ceramic-like properties because they do not chemically react with anything. Monatomic elements are very stable, durable, and heat resistant.

Along with crystals, gold is also known to be a powerful conductor of energy, and more recently shown to be a source of intelligence. In his book *Unveiled Mysteries,* author Godfré Ray King explains that gold has been made easily available to the masses during periods of higher and rising consciousness. "Gold is placed upon this planet for a variety of uses, two of its most trivial and unimportant ones being that of using gold as a means of exchange and ornamentation. The far greater activity and purpose of it within and upon the Earth is the release of its own inherent quality and energy to purify, vitalize and balance the atomic structure of the world." King says that mountains have gold running through them to give off great energy and that is why people feel so good when they spend time in the mountains. According to the Ancient Alien theory, the "gods" used gold dust from Earth to enhance their atmosphere, and also to prolong their lives. For New Age advocates, holding gold and silver are said to enhance a person's health and well-being, which is similar to the benefits of holding crystals and gemstones. Colloidal silver has been used for centuries to promote good health and studies continue to also show that colloidal silver outperforms many mainstream methods as an antibacterial and used against harmful organisms.[1]

ENTER THE ALCHEMISTS

Alchemy is generally seen as an archaic proto-science based on superstition which is of little interest to the modern chemist. But in truth, chemistry owes much of its foundation to alchemy, which covers philosophical traditions and chemical history spanning several millennia in the Middle East, China, India and Europe. "The Royal Art" has played a significant role in the development of modern chemistry, medicine and even psychology. In Western alchemy, human perfection is achieved through the action of what has been termed the "Philosopher's Stone." Alchemists got a bad name because they incorrectly believed they could turn any substance into gold. But they were partly correct that exotic metals could prolong life and cure illness. The Philosopher's Stone is created from *prima materia*, which is the primitive formless base of all matter, similar to our modern concepts of dark matter or chaos.

Alchemy made important contributions to metalworking, refining, production of gunpowder, ceramics, glass, ink, dyes, paints, cosmetics, extracts, liquors, and other compounds. Alchemists were the first to conceptualize chemical elements into the rudimentary periodic table of elements, and introduced the process of distillation to Western Europe. They were also among the first to extract metals from ores, and compose various inorganic acids and bases. For example, in the 14th century Libravius and Pseudo-Geber described the preparation of *aqua regia*, or "royal water," a mixture of nitric acid and hydrochloric acid, which became the only known technique to dissolve gold. Otherwise, gold never rusts or decays like other oxidizing metals.

The fundamental concepts of alchemy were first recognized as arising out of the ancient Persian Empire. Alchemy had been practiced in Mesopotamia, Egypt, Persia (today's Iran), India, China, Japan, and Korea in Classical Greece and Rome, in the Muslim civilizations, and then in Europe up until the 20th century—in a complex network of schools and philosophical systems spanning at least 2,500 years. Alchemy is an influential philosophical tradition whose early practitioners claimed to have achieved profound powers that were known from antiquity. The defining objectives of alchemy are varied, and these include the creation of the fabled possessing powers of the Philosopher's Stone, and including the capability of turning base metals into the noble metals of gold or silver, as well as an elixir of life conferring youth and longevity.

Western alchemy is recognized as a proto-science that contributed to the development of modern chemistry and medicine. The best-known goals of the alchemists were the trans-

1 King, Godfré Ray, *Unveiled Mysteries.* Saint Germain Press, 1989.

mutation of common metals into silver or gold in a technique called *chrysopoeia*. There is also the lesser-known plant alchemy called "spagyric." Alchemists also sought the creation of a "panacea," or the elixir of life—a remedy that supposedly would cure all diseases and prolong life indefinitely. Later they would seek the discovery of a universal solvent. Although these were not the only uses for the discipline, they were the ones most documented and well-known. Certain Hermetic schools argue that the transmutation of lead into gold is analogical for the transmutation of the physical body (Saturn or lead) into Solar energy (gold) with the goal of attaining immortality. This is described as "Internal Alchemy."[2]

Alchemical transformations have also been associated with philosophical advancement and the acceleration of personal intention. Alchemy was influential in the formulation of Isaac Newton's laws of motion and universal gravitation, as well as in his work on optics. Alchemy was also central to Carl Jung's idea of the "Collective Unconscious." According to Jung, much of the vast array of symbols used in alchemy draws from the Collective Unconscious of the West. The arcane practice of alchemy has garnered growing interest among people dedicated to spiritual growth and ascension. Alchemy is not just about the transmutation of substances, but can also refer to the transformation of the entire human race. Just as there are strains of "black magick," there are also strains of "black alchemy." Satanically inspired alchemists seek to transform the human race into a psychically-entranced slave race who will abide by an Armageddon scenario which consumes us all in one final orgy of planetary destruction. As such, in this context, alchemy has less to do with chemistry and more to do with psychology. It uses the tools of identification and projection in the macrocosm to effect significant change in the microcosm of the psyche. In other words, it's a procedure to trigger ascension. All of these edicts follow the basis of the Hermes Trismegistus quote: "That which is below is like that which is above, and that which is above is like that which is below."

MONATOMIC ELEMENTS

Monatomic elements are not a new discovery. Ancient Egypt, Mesopotamia, and some shamanic traditions each have references to a mysterious "powder of projection." It was a known vehicle to allow communication with the entities "on the other side." When using this white powder there are references to powers of levitation, teleportation, transmutation, and unlocking the key to exceptional longevity. Gold has long been affiliated with the pineal gland, while other monatomic elements respond to six other glands in the human body. These are the seven spiritual centers. The superconductive elements, especially monatomic gold, were highly prized by ancient cultures. The white powder is comprised of a group of seven elements in a monatomic state. When all seven seals are open, the body takes on "Christ-like" characteristics, similar to the opening of the body's chakra system.

The alchemy of the Middle Ages is thought to have originated in Egypt and to have flourished in Persia before being brought to Europe after the Crusades. Artephius, an alchemist of the 12th century, claimed in his alchemical treatise entitled *The Secret Book* that he had lived "for the space of a thousand years, or thereabouts, which has now passed over my head, since the time I was born to this day, through the alone goodness of God Almighty, by the use of this wonderful quintessence." If there is truth in these ancient stories the alchemical materials would have to be substances which are not easily detected with the tools of modern science. These substances would come from gold, mercury and the other precious metals but would not look like these elements using spectroscopy or modern chemical assay methods. These substances would have an edible white powder form and an oil form that imparts healing and spiritual benefit.

The alchemical materials discussed above can be described using concepts of modern

2 "How alchemy, the forbidden science, changed world history." *Core Spirit.com*, released August, 2017.

physics like superconductivity, quantum coherence and Bose-Einstein Condensates. These modern alchemical materials have been called ORMEs, monoatomic gold, white gold, white powder gold, ORMUS, m-state, AuM, microclusters and manna. Orbitally Rearranged Monatomic Elements (ORMEs) are single atom elements and superconductive metals. The Light Platinum Group of ORME metals are silver, palladium, ruthenium, and rhodium. The Heavy Platinum Group are gold, osmium, platinum, and iridium. Trace amounts of these elements already exist in the body, particularly in the nervous system. Many plants contain monatomic elements as well, interwoven within the botanical molecules. ORMEs are naturally occurring in certain volcanic soils dating back to a geological event which occurred about 60 million years ago. Such soils are present near the Arctic Circle and throughout the southwestern United States, where some soils rich in these elements may contain up to six percent of this material. The remaining 94 percent or more of the material is ordinary dirt comprised mainly of silicon compounds. The processing of ORMEs requires removing the dirt and impurities to get the residue, which is fairly easy because they are all reactive with one solvent or another. A big find came in 1976 when David Hudson had purchased some land near Phoenix, AZ, performed some tests, and ultimately it was rediscovered.

In certain areas of the Sierra Nevada mountain range, a plant known as Chamae Rose grows on white mineral deposits and has been shown to have incredible curative properties when the roots are ingested as a tea or in powder form. It was suspected the soil where the plant grew contained monatomic gold. Indeed, extensive test results came back on the soil and it did contain monatomic elements, including monatomic gold. What is different about using Chamae Rose to obtain monatomic gold, is that the roots from the plant uptake the monatomic elements and utilize them in the plant. When the plant is ingested by a human, we absorb the monatomic elements. It is believed that the massive healing power with Chamae Rose is because of the monatomic elements in it and the energy transfer it induces from plant to person.

MONATOMIC ELEMENTS EXPLAINED

Monatomic elements, normally recognized as exotic metals, exist as only one atom at a time in their non-metal state. Their super-conductive properties allow for spontaneous transmutation to exist. When electricity currents pass through these elements there is virtually no impedance to the flow. Modern electrical technology is only now beginning to detect the specific elements, which has been difficult with instrumentation because different monatomic elements each have their own superconductive properties. Monatomic elements seem to increase the level of photons in the cells, as well as reorganizing their active function which happens to promote health. Because ORMEs are superconductors, they tend to "ride" on the magnetic field of the Earth, giving it the powers of levitation.

The center of the periodic chart of elements consists of what are known as the "transition elements," meaning that they can transit from metallic to monatomic, or diatomic via chemical treatment, or through other means. This is what some would refer to as "shadow chemistry," or "arcane chemistry," or even "alchemy." Let's take gold for example. When you have two or more gold atoms in a microcluster, it will have metallic properties, but if you have only one atom, it will then have ceramic properties, which means that it becomes chemically inert but at the same time will have superconductive capabilities even at room temperature. The weight of these amazing materials can also change by heating, becoming lighter, even to the point of levitation! Because it is chemically inert, it can be ingested for health, well-being and super-energizing at the cellular level.

Not only do our cells communicate via chemicals and electricity in our nervous system and intercellularly throughout other processes, but also through the exchange of photons, or light particles. The human body is a marvelous bioelectric machine, and all of its processes depend on the clear and (ideally) unimpeded conduction of electrical "messages" required to carry out those processes at certain frequencies. Nikola Tesla observed that "our entire biological system, the brain, the Earth itself, work on the same frequencies." Light, as proven by fiber optic technology, can carry more and actually "purer" information. As mentioned above, these materials are superconductive, and therefore can change our bodies at the cellular level, from our organs, muscles and tissues to our brain and nervous system, into superconductors of a greatly increased flow of photons, greatly increased because the monatomic materials themselves are in a sense "liquid (or powdered) light." It's like installing "gold tipped" wires on your brain synapse. Put another way, you could say that monatomics transform the body's "wiring" from being simple copper cable to being wired with fiber-optics, where the same "width" of wiring, but able to carry 1,000 times as much "processing" information.[3]

ORMES MAKE US SUPER

Is there a secret substance known to the ancient world that can regenerate the body, unlock psychic powers and allow us to access higher states of consciousness? ORMEs have long been regarded for their heath enhancing benefits, especially the restoration of vitality and the feeling of regained youth. ORMEs are used in cancer and AIDS treatments by repairing damaged DNA strands in the human body. Ancient mystery schools used the white powder for assisting the opening of the pineal gland "Third Eye," enabling ascension into to the next dimension. Adherents become masters as the veil is lifted, opening the gateway to instant manifestation of thought and other extraordinary knowingness. Past life recall and super human abilities such as body levitation are said to become possible.

Small amounts of powdered ORMEs can prolong life, enhance and repair bodily functions, and increase mental capacities. When taken properly, no heavy metal toxicity is associated with these materials. Human test subjects using monatomic elements have produced astonishing outcomes. The subjects who took the elements orally showed instant and highly effective results. They were able to perform with greater intelligence, enhanced creativity, improved mind and body coordination, more agility, and less stress. It allowed the brain to be balanced and synchronized between the left and right. It is a healthy alternative to pharmaceutical chemical-based drugs, and can alleviate ADHD symptoms and other learning deficiencies. It can also be used to repair human DNA, increasing the conductivity of electrons by 1,000 percent, allowing for cell correction. Used another way and it has been shown to enhance hormone secretions.

The ancient Egyptians had their "shemanna," a white bread, which was offered as gold to the gods. The ancient Chinese alchemist, Wei Po-yang wrote of the "Pill of Immortality" which is made of *Huan Tan* (Returned Medicine) an edible powder from gold. After one ingests *Huan Tan* "the complexion becomes rejuvenated, hoary hair regains its blackness, and new teeth grow where fallen ones used to be. If an old man, he will once more become a youth; if an old woman, she will regain her maidenhood."[4]

For medicinal purposes, monatomic gold acts upon the pituitary gland, inducing an increase in hormonal production, and is thus a rejuvenating agent. Monatomic gold strengthens the heart, enhances the production of red blood cells in the bone marrow and increases the production of semen in men. Hindu alchemists preferred to work with mercury. They "proved" that they had made the correct edible white powder of mercury by heating it to convert it to gold.

3   ORMES and Monatomic elements explained: **https://monatomic-orme.com/about-orme/**
4   Wei Po-yang, the father of Alchemy--142 A.D. **http://www.subtleenergies.com/ormus/historical/thelab.htm**

IN SEARCH OF MONATOMIC GOLD

Monatomic gold is naturally available, and may be the primary mineral the Anunnaki were seeking when they came to Earth. The ancient Anunnaki astronauts were called "the men from heaven to Earth came." Since it was grueling labor, they genetically manipulated the genes of proto-humans to become the human race to do the dirty work to assist in the mining and extraction. The premise is based on the ancient astronaut theory that the Anunnaki came to Earth, called *Eridu* by this tall human-like E.T. race 445,000 years ago. The Sumerian texts describe the genetic manipulation of the people found on Earth to who we are today, and why.

Described in Zecharia Sitchin's *The Lost Book of Enki,* the ancients gathered in the Abzu region, around the Persian Gulf, to mine gold from water. There are also numerous ancient gold mines in southern Africa that may also have produced monatomic gold. According to the Sumarian text as related in *The Lost Book of Enki*, it describes how Anul left Nibiru for *Eridu* and started looking for gold, not just gold bullion, but a special type of gold powder called Orbitally Rearranged Monatomic Elements or ORMEs.[5]

ORMEs was made into "mufkt," a type of bread which was fed to the kings and pharaohs, which would explain how the pharaohs and Moses were said to have lived to 900 years old. It was called the food of the light body. ORME, white powder gold, was also found at the temple of Karnak in 1450 AD. Pure ORME has been found all over Egypt, including in the King's Chamber within the Great Pyramid, and various temples in the Sinai region. According to the Bible, Moses came down from the mountain and found that his disciples had taken all the gold they had and fashioned it into a graven image. It is said that the golden image was destroyed, cooked, put into water and fed to the Israelites. This white powder gold has some very interesting qualities. When it was taken to be weighed it was put in a metal pan and it showed that it was lighter and had a lower weight than the pan. It had qualities of levitation. When put into the sun and reaching a certain temperature, it exploded. This is why it has been said that those carrying the Ark of the Covenant needed to have ropes attached, as the Ark would levitate. Other properties include that when heated to a certain temperature it would vanish, and as the pan cooled it would return. It was said that it went to another dimension.

FOR THE LOVE OF GOLD

It is no secret that humanity has a long-standing love for gold. When kings and states amassed wealth in ancient times, it was mostly in the form of large piles of the yellow metal. Gold has been the metal of choice for the crowns of royals, jewelry, decorations, even the entire monetary system was based on the gold standard for thousands of years. Although the main use for gold has seemed to be purely ornamental, could there be a deeper level of interaction happening at a subtle energetic level between humankind and this illustrious metal?

We can trace the violent history of the West and its frequent wars to the movement of material wealth, most often gold. From ancient Babylon to today, gold is the backbone of national development and economic security. Once spent, it could not be recaptured—goods and services were provided for barter, then became money. Although Nixon took the U.S. dollar off the gold standard in 1971, it is the most-sound form of backing for a national currency, and may still return in a post-fiat currency world.

For Europe generally, gold as money was irredeemable and irreplaceable. World War II brought the love of gold transferred into the hands of a new master. Only a fraction would ever be recovered and only a further fraction would be forced out of the hands of those governments that captured it in overseas conquests such as Spain, Portugal, Swe-

5   Sitchin Zecharia, *The Lost Book of Enki: Memoirs and Prophecies of an Extraterrestrial God.* Bear & Company, 2004.

den, and "neutral" Switzerland—a nation that provided the Nazi party a safe haven to stash their stolen gold. These few recipient countries must have guessed, if not known, by the large quantities entailed, that it could not be Germany's own money.

Hitler and Nazism had bankrupted all of Europe by the end of World War II. Even their supplier nations—Sweden, Switzerland, Portugal, Spain, and Turkey suffered economic hardship, and in the end a currency whose value was worth much less.

The practical implications of war invariably mean added hardships; livestock neglected or slaughtered; fields not ploughed; no harvests to gather; and farmers going bankrupt. Workforces depleted by death, torture or maiming lead to factories, farms, fishing fleets and coal mines working at reduced capacity. Europe could not feed itself, nor warm itself and in many places half of all homes were damaged and uninhabitable after the war. The USA finally ended its war of resource conquest in Iraq and Afghanistan.[6]

KABBALAH

The encoded information in the Kabbalah originated in ancient Babylon and Egypt. A Tree of Life, in the form of ten interconnected nodes, is a critical part of the Kabbalah. As such, it resembles the ten attributes of the Sephirot. Interestingly, Orbitally Rearranged Monatomic Elements (ORMEs) are single atom and superconductive metals which allow humans to reach their full physical and mental potential. ORME is the same as the Hebrew word which means the "Tree of Life." *Etz Chaim*, Hebrew for "Tree of Life," is a common term used in Judaism. The expression, found in the Book of Proverbs, is figuratively applied to the Torah itself.

Kabbalah is an interpretation key, and the "soul" of the Torah, or Hebrew Bible. It is the religious mystical system of Judaism claiming an insight into divine nature. The term "Kabbalah" was originally used in Talmudic texts, among the Geonim, and by early Rishonim as a reference to the full body of publicly available Jewish teaching. In this sense Kabbalah was used in referring to all of the known oral laws. Over time it became a reference to doctrines of esoteric knowledge concerning God, the creation of the universe and the laws of nature. The Kabbalah is the path by which mature religious Jews can learn these secrets. It is one of many tools humans have devised to divine the mythos of creation.

It is interesting to wonder how the ancient Hebrew people could have known of the subatomic structure of ORMEs. When monatomic substances are subjected to high temperature, the vibration levels increase, causing them to "jump" into the higher dimensions. It is similar to water that becomes an invisible vapor when heated, but returns to the water state again when cooled. When this concept is transposed on the inter-dimensional threshold, the substance disappears from physical reality. Ingesting monatomic elements is similar to ingesting receptors to the life force, manifesting in the form of matter or energy. The human body can produce the needed vitamins, nutrients, proteins, and much more if it is receptive. Ingesting monatomic minerals completes the scenario.

SILVER'S STRONG INDUSTRIAL DEMAND

Silver has a number of properties which make it ideal for industrial applications. These properties include its strength, malleability, electrical and thermal conductivity, natural anti-bacterial properties, and silver's ability to endure extreme temperature ranges. These unique properties make silver generally irreplaceable with less expensive alternatives.

Nearly 75% of the world's supply of silver is used to manufacture a range of products

6   The U.S. military was protecting the opium fields which the Taliban, we were told, had been destroying before the war: http://www.youtube.com/watch?v=N_gOaPeSCME. <and> try this link describing the U.S. military and the Afghanistan opium industry: https://www.youtube.com/watch?v=e4vMLQmChJU&ab_channel=GregBerry

including chemical re-agents, medical instruments, solar panels and plasma televisions. Despite its critical role in technology and industrial production, global silver mining is limited. In contrast to other metals, it is difficult for mining companies to increase their silver production because two-thirds of silver produced by mines is a by-product of other metals.

As a currency for barter, silver was first mined more than 5,000 years ago and became an essential element in trading among early civilizations. By 700 BCE, the ancient Greeks began using silver as a tradeable currency. The famed "pieces of eight" were worth eight reales of a Spanish dollar coin, which was an international currency during the 16th and 17th centuries. The United Kingdom's "pound sterling" received its name from the fact that the currency was equal to one pound of "sterling silver," with at least 92.5% purity. The United States embraced silver to back up its currency soon after the founding of the Republic. In 1794, the first silver dollar was minted. Throughout the years, America minted and melted thousands of silver coins as it reacted to the supply and demand of this precious metal. The U.S. Mint continued to produce 90% silver coins for general circulation through 1964, until the worth of an ounce of silver was worth more than a dollar. Between 1965 and 1968, the last circulating silver coins of 40% silver half dollars were minted.

Silver had been used in medicine for centuries, touted as a cure-all for everything from tuberculosis and arthritis to herpes and cancer. Even today, many alternative practitioners believe that colloidal silver offers health benefits by "boosting" immune function and preventing or treating infections, both common and severe.

COLLOIDAL SILVER AND GOLD

During pioneer times, wagon trains heading across the country used to put a silver coin in the water keg as a disinfectant. *Science Digest* declared in March, 1978: "And now it's silver that is finding wholly new uses as a wonder drug in modern medicine...perhaps it soon will be recognized as our mightiest germ fighter." Small amounts of silver are very useful and powerful. Colloidal silver is used for ailments and an alternative to antibiotics, while colloidal gold for is used today for general health and the promotion of intelligence maintenance.

When Dr. G.L. Rohdenburg published an article in 1915 on the benefits of colloidal silver in treating tumors, he likely had no idea that this product would have such staying power. Over 100 years later, colloidal silver is used by some as a dietary supplement, decongestant and a treatment for all kinds of ailments and illnesses. Colloidal silver is viewed by alternative health practitioners as the natural antibiotic alternative. If we can restore our natural immune system, our body can then rebuild damaged tissue as it has during all of our growing years. "Speaking generally, the colloidal metals are especially remarkable for their beneficial action in infective states," said Dr. Leonard Keene Hirschberg, A. M., M. D. of John Hopkins. Dr. Evan M., of Kansas reported:

> We have had instant success with Colloidal Silver and immune compromised patients. A few examples are: Pink Eye (topical) totally resolved in less than six hours; recurrent sinus infections (oral ingestion) resolved in eight days; acute cuticle infections—(topical)—twenty four hours. Another major area in which we have improved our clinical results is in the area of bowel detoxification and dysbiosis. The Colloidal Silver has provided excellent removal of abnormal intestinal bacteria; also it has proved to be a great adjunct to our Candide Albicans, Epstein Barr Virus and Chronic Fatigue Syndrome protocols.

"What we have actually done was rediscover the fact that silver kills bacteria, which had been known for centuries. When antibiotics were discovered, clinical uses for silver as an antibiotic were discarded," noted Dr. Robert O. Becker. Extensive research into the curative properties of silver has been conducted for many years at the Upstate Medical Center, at the Syracuse University in upstate New York. Under the direction of the above mentioned Dr. Becker, experiments concluded that silver works on a wide range of fighting bacterial infections, without any known side effects or damage to the cells of the body. Silver was doing something more than killing disease causing organisms. It was also causing major growth stimulation of injured tissues. Dr. Becker concluded that the presence of the silver ion may help to regenerate tissue, eliminate old or cancerous cells, and any other diseased or abnormal conditions.[7]

The colloidal metals, especially silver, are used as general disinfectant in cleaning solutions. A small amount of silver can be added to a well or aerator water tank to kill bacteria and algae, or added to stored foods or leftovers to prevent spoilage. Some people put a little in bird baths and wading pools to prevent bacteria and algae, or they will spray plants or wet soil to prevent mold and fungus damage. It can be used in the bathroom to spray on the sink and shower floor, in the kitchen for cleaning counter tops and the refrigerator shelves and door seals. It can be applied topically on skin for warts, cuts, bites and burns. Today, silver is used by the Russians to sterilize recycled water aboard the space stations. NASA also selected a silver water treatment system for the space shuttle. Many of the world's airlines use silver water filters to protect passengers from diseases such as dysentery.

COLLOIDAL SILVER HEALTH TIPS

The "Medical Mafia" is a correct term for the allopathic medical monopoly that distorts the truth about so-called "alternative" medicines that heal without dangerous side effects, while propagandizing their harmful synthetic drugs. For example, colloidal silver is not toxic to humans in small amounts and it can destroy 650 different types of germs, fungi and viruses which is incomparable to other antibiotics. All those organisms are made up of one cell so they can be damaged in a fast way with the ions from silver because they are bioactive. So why isn't it used widely as a common cure?

Prior to 1938, colloidal silver was used by physicians as a mainstream antibiotic treatment and was considered to be a "cutting edge" treatment for a variety of ailments. Not surprisingly, however, Big Pharma moved in and caused colloidal research to be set aside in favor of financially lucrative drugs.[7]

If you want a natural antibiotic, try "colloidal" silver, which is a concentration of nano-sized particles of silver suspended in a liquid. Colloidal silver isn't just a mixture of silver and water; it's a solution where the silver particles are suspended in water and have an electrical charge. This type of solution requires ultra-pure water. It also requires special equipment necessary to create and maintain a constant charge. A powerful germicidal, silver is an exceptional metal in that it is non-toxic to the human body but lethal to over 650 disease-causing bacteria, molds, viruses, fungi, and other parasites. The daily ingestion of colloidal silver is like having a "second immune system." Our grandparents might recall when they used to put silver dollars into milk to keep it fresh longer, before they had refrigerators.

Before the invention of antibacterial soap, colloidal silver was used as a disinfectant. It is still most commonly used to kill bacteria. Silver is effective at both preventing and combating bacterial illnesses and infections because it does not corrode. In this modern age, it is used to moderate the symptoms of Morgellons, candida overgrowth, and Lyme Disease. In ancient times silver was used in wound dressings and it was frequently used for the same purposes in the USA following the Civil War. It is also why churches use

7   "Silver makes antibiotics thousands of times more effective." *Nature Magazine*, June 19, 2013, **https://www.nature.com/articles/nature.2013.13232**

silver chalices during communion to prevent the spread of disease through the congregation. Silver fell out of favor with the advent of regulated synthesized medications, but has become popular again along with lifestyle trends that promote natural organic food.

Multiple laboratory tests have shown colloidal silver to destroy disease-causing pathogens, viruses, and bacteria typically within minutes of contact. In these studies, silver has been shown to be a powerful anti-fungal, anti-germicidal, anti-bacterial, and anti-viral substance. In other applications, silver is used readily in hospital burn wards to prevent scar tissue.

Reported benefits of colloidal silver include:

- *promotes a healthy immune system*
- *improves the immune system*
- *powerful antibiotic, anti-bacterial, anti-parasitic, and anti-microbial*
- *topical antiseptic and anti-fungal*
- *fights the common cold and virtually all strains of the flu, including Corona Virus*
- *is easily digestible and absorbed*
- *no known contradictions to medications*
- *few and limited side effects (namely argyria which causes your skin to turn bluish-grey)*
- *can be used to relieve eye irritation*
- *purifies water*
- *has been used to treat sun spots, candida, dental infections, MRSA infections and urinary tract infections*

SILVER LINING

The "father of medicine" Hippocrates and the Roman scholar Pliny the Elder both wrote of the use of silver to treat wounds and prevent disease. The ancient Greeks also knew the medical value of silver. They realized that families who used silver utensils were rarely sick and had few infections. This knowledge passed on to kings, emperors, sultans, and their families and members of their royal courts. They ate from silver plates, drank from silver cups, used silver utensils, and stored their food in silver containers. As a result of this use, the silver rubbed off and mixed with their foods and drinks. As a general rule, they were much healthier than the peasants who ate with dishes made of earthenware and utensils made of iron. This is where the phrase "born with a silver spoon in your mouth" arose.

Bacteria has a weakness called silver. The precious metal has been used to fight infections for thousands of years—Hippocrates first described its antimicrobial properties in 400 BCE—but how it works has been a mystery. Now, a team led by James Collins, a biomedical engineer at Boston University in Massachusetts, has described how silver can disrupt bacteria, and shown that the ancient treatment could help to deal with the thoroughly modern scourge of antibiotic resistance. Collins and his team found that silver—in the form of dissolved ions—attacks bacterial cells in two main ways: (silver) makes the cell membrane more permeable, and it interferes with the cell's metabolism, leading to the overproduction of reactive, and often toxic, oxygen compounds. Both mechanisms could potentially be harnessed to make today's antibiotics more effective against resistant bacteria, Collins says. Many antibiotics are thought to kill their targets by producing reactive oxygen compounds, and Collins and his team showed that when boosted with a small amount of silver these drugs could kill between 10 and 1,000 times as many bacteria. The increased membrane permeability also allows more antibiotics to enter the bacterial cells, which may overwhelm the resistance mechanisms that rely on shuttling the drug back out. That disruption to the cell membrane also increased the effectiveness of vancomycin, a large-molecule antibiotic, on Gram-negative bacteria—which have a protective outer coating. Gram-negative bacterial cells can often be impenetrable to antibiotics made of larger molecules.[8]

Since it is not designed to combat a specific pathogen but rather works against the very nature of their life cycles, it is an effective preventative agent against all illnesses caused by all pathogens including future mutations. There is no known disease-causing organism that can live in the presence of even minute traces of colloidal silver. Laboratory tests show that anaerobic bacteria, virus, and fungus organisms are all killed within minutes of contact. Parasites are also destroyed while still in their egg stage. Colloidal silver is effective against infections, colds, influenza, fermentation and parasitic infestations.

SOME SIDE EFFECTS FROM OVER-USE:

Colloidal silver is purported to be easily digestible and therefore easily absorbed into the internal organs that need it the most. This ease of absorption helps the benefits of colloidal silver to work fast, but also to be over-used. Proponents claim it's the quick absorption property of colloidal silver that is most important when it comes to strengthening the immune system. As with any form of medicine, alternative or not, it is important to weigh the benefits against all side effects.

One potential side effect is a condition called argyria, which causes the skin to turn blue or blueish-grey by overusing colloidal silver. Whenever you come into direct contact with a released element or chemical, it can affect you depending on how much contact you have with it and for how long. In the case of people who have consumed colloidal silver for an extended period of time, argyria is sometimes the result. When taken orally, colloidal silver can also wreak havoc on proteins and make other medicines less effective. For pregnant women, colloidal silver poses risks to the unborn child, as fetal abnormalities may develop due to its use. Of course, this book is not about dispensing medical advice, but offering guideposts, such as the Buddha advocating moderation by saying "take the middle path."

Although colloidal silver has been called a cure-all, its healing properties, as reported by the companies that manufacture the supplement and its related products, haven't been published in enough reputable medical journals. It's really not known if colloidal silver can cure other ailments, and the side effects include everything from seizures and kidney damage to fatigue and skin irritation.[9]

ELEMENT 115 REVISITED

Element 115 (Moscovium/Mc) is a strange metal that was not originally on the periodic table of elements, simply because it was not found on Earth. It is called Uup, or Ununpentium. The periodic table of elements now counts upward in the 140 range. The periodic table actually has 140 elements, not 104. The additional 36 are of alien origin and are being applied to Earth-based projects, yet officially discarded by science and Earth culture as a whole. Instead, these new minerals and metals have applications in black budget programs, notably stealth-based projects. Bismuth, in the same periodic column as Element 115, is reputed to possess a gravity wave extending beyond the boundary of the nucleus, which, in the case of Element 115, can be amplified to create harnessable electro-gravitic effects.

Area 51 whistleblower Bob Lazar described a metallic fuel cell during his exposure to the technology of alien space craft. While studying a particular UFO craft during his work at the S-4 facility south of Area 51, he described the exotic fuel cell

8   Collins, James, Boston University study: "Silver Makes Antibiotics Thousands of Times More Effective." https://www.scientificamerican.com/article/silver-makes-antibiotics-thousands-of-times-more-effective

9   Page, Olivia, "Colloidal Silver: What You Need to Know." https://www.lewisandlove.com/blog/colloidal-silver-what-you-need-to-know

as a triangular-shaped wedge made from a heavy metal element with a rounded tip. This metal shape was essential to the creation and manipulation of gravity in this particular craft design. Producing gravity waves is what allows ET spacecraft to manipulate gravity, along with creating it, by bombarding the Element 115 with protons and transforming it into Element 116.

Interestingly, Element 115 was a theoretical element that up until the mid-1990s had never been created in a physics lab. Bob Lazar said scientists were able to create Element 115, but only a few atoms could only last less than a second. Years later that changed, and fact has become another Bob Lazar "proof." According to the Lawrence Livermore Laboratories in California website, they claim to have synthesized Element 115, and added it to the periodic table of elements. Lazar thinks that the U.S. secret government has a stockpile of this rare metal for their own experiments. He also said 115 is an extraterrestrial element, used in UFO reactors, deflecting atoms, which creates anti-matter. When reacted with a gas, this heat energy is converted into electrical power through a thermoelectric converter. This power is used on other subsystems on the craft, although there is no wiring whatsoever on the craft. The reactor also sets up a gravitational wave from the 115 being bombarded, and guided through tubes to the gravity amplifier. There is no thermal radiation while the generator is running, yet the thermiatic generator is 100% efficient, which would violate the first law of thermodynamics. But as Bob Lazar claims, "It Works."

During the Joe Rogan Experience interview with Bob Lazar taped in June, 2019, he explains how the as-yet undiscovered Element 115 was used to power UFOs. He details how the stable version they had was different than the one on our periodic table today—the difference is the same as the monatomic/diatomic gold on the market today. He compared it to what the ancient Egyptians used to charge "the ark." Lazar says they figured out how to convert the elements to a high spin state, or "monoatomic light" and go to a smaller atomic structure where they achieved pure photonic energy with no mass. For the smaller atomic structure Lazar said "think bosons, gluons." Lazar believes this is why David Hudson's extraction patents were seized and he "disappeared from the talking circuit" after 1995, because his scientists figured out the right arrangements of protons, electrons, and neutrons that allowed anti-electrons to bond to a hyper-deformed nuclei.[10]

MANIPULATING GRAVITY WITH VIBRATION

Energy is a property of objects, which can be transferred to other objects or converted, but cannot be created nor destroyed. Literally, everything in the known universe is energy in some form or another, whether it be thoughts, emotions, actions or physical objects. The law of vibration states that all energy in the universe vibrates at a particular frequency. Gravity is vibration in the presence of mass. Everything vibrates, thus if we can manipulate vibration, we can manipulate gravity. This principle applies because atoms vibrate, simply because they are subatomic particles in harmony. "Destructive Interference" is a technique to match sound waves, thus making sound cease to exist. It is essentially anti-sound technology used by the military to make their helicopters and other mechanized hardware nearly impossible to hear.

Harmonic resonance can also reduce or neutralize the force of gravity. For example, Tibetan monks could neutralize mass by using "auditive levitation." Drums, trumpets, and chanting, when properly arranged, were demonstrated to levitate a one-ton boulder in five minutes. The sounds they made were in combination with the consciousness of the monks, who would look up in unison when the boulder would begin to

10 Joe Rogan Experience interview with Area 51 whistleblower, Bob Lazar: **https://brobible.com/culture/article/bob-lazar-joe-rogan-ufos-area-51/**

shake and then levitate. Using the technique of acoustic levitation, the monks were then able to "place" the bolder anywhere. The Maya and Giza pyramids were similarly built this way. Antigravity technology can neutralize mass, as can be observed in the vast amount of UFO sightings. Can humans vibrate at a higher level too? It is already happening, with or without us knowing. But we can make it better. Using ORMEs will make our mind and bodies operate at their optimum potential. Superconductive metals greatly reduce the energy needed to generate vibration.[11]

Even aluminum, which is already highly prized, is showing scientists that it can be designed as a crystalline type of aluminum that can be extremely light. It is a conductive metal, has a low melting point, is very strong when alloyed, is impervious to rust and, above all, it's extremely lightweight. But what if metallurgists could make it lighter—so light, in fact, that it could float on water even when not made into the shape of a foil boat? According to a model created by researchers at Utah State University and Southern Federal University in Rostov-on Don, Russia, such a thing is actually possible. The end result may be something along the lines of what eyewitnesses discovered around the Roswell UFO crash site in 1947—extremely lightweight metal "fabric" which could be crumpled up, then when released would return to its original shape.

TO SEE A GHOST

The reality we experience is a consensus that is driven by our perception and thought, to varying degrees. One of the most esoteric of secrets is that both metallic "scrying" mirrors and magnifying glasses can break through our third dimensional limitations. We can see a ghost, for example, in a mirror even though our perception will not allow it to be there if we see it right in front of us. When two scrying mirrors are placed facing each other it gets even more interesting.

Regarding mirrors, these techniques used to be referred to as *Faery Stones*, and for objects like scrying mirrors, it depends highly on the composition. The reflective surface must be a heavy metal, like the old silverbacked mirrors. The much cheaper aluminum mirrors common these days don't really work. The heavier isotope of silver contains a good quantity of captured neutrinos, which in a charged state can reflect a portion of coordinate time structure into coordinate space. When placing two silver mirrors facing each other, one with full reflection and one partial, the result is basically to have a "ghost laser." This is where the pattern undergoes "light amplification" between the two mirrors as in the old laser setups.

Although the concept of "universe of 3D time" sounds very strange, it is actually quite familiar. We go there every night in our dreams. Ghosts are the shadows of people walking in this parallel reality, according to author David Wilcock. He relates that:

> Remote viewers can study events in our own space and time—by using their "astral body" to travel through this parallel reality. Better yet, every molecule of matter that exists in our reality has an exact duplicate in the parallel reality. Otherwise, it could not exist—thanks to the new physics that has now been developed from these principles. That means that when you go into this alternate universe, things look pretty much the same—at least in many respects. This alternate universe is all around you, right now. It's everywhere—and yet you can't touch it with your physical body. Only your mind.[12]

Which means that unless we know this alternate reality exists, the majority of peo-
. . . .

11 THE REAL PHILOSOPHER'S STONE: "Is there a secret substance known to the ancient world that can regenerate the body, unlock psychic powers and allow you to access higher states of consciousness? Jonny Enoch explores the history and science of the philosopher's stone." https://www.youtube.com/watch?v=QX2lQI4-yEg&ab_channel=MetaphysicalSource

12 Wilcock, David, "DISCLOSURE: Camelot on TruTV TONIGHT; Insider 'Daniel' Comes Forward!" https://divinecosmos.com/davids-blog/1090-disclosurecamelot/comment-page-10

ple will remain ignorant. This could end if we could have access to exotic Looking Glass technology like the Yellow Cube, a teleportation device, or use advanced silver scrying mirrors. If people have a clear understanding of the "afterlife," those in power would lose their ability to control us through fear. If we remain ignorant, we will just follow the crowd around the obstacles placed by those that formed the "false matrix" timeline, going where they want us to go. Let's face it, people are lazy and will usually take the easiest path. And that is how they keep control—providing easy "paths," not only in timelines, but in politics, legality, economics, food, fuel... just about anything you can name. Odds are almost everyone never even knew that there was a choice. Those who awaken have a choice.

Monatomic gold is simply gold atoms that are separated from each other and no longer bonded in large clusters, unlike the metallic form of gold that most everyone has known since the age of alchemy. The normal, metallic form of gold consists of large clusters of gold atoms latticed together; but when those gold atoms are broken apart by a series of alchemical processes, that gold transmutes into a monoatomic state. This alchemical process essentially dissolves these clusters down so that nearly, if not exactly, one atom per particle is left. The resulting material appears as a fine white powder, which is stable, nonconductive, heat resistant, and chemically inert. As a result of being chemically inert, it can be ingested for health purposes as an essential mineral.

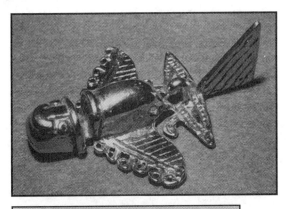

This figure was unearthed near the Magdalena River in north central Colombia. Made of gold and thus hard to date, most estimates calculate it to have been made between 500 and 800 CE. This tiny gold object certainly has a similar appearance to a modern airplane. Thought to come from a pre-Incan culture, it measures just two inches long. In 1997, German aviation experts built a scale model replica and it proved to have amazing aerodynamics and similarities to modern day airplanes. The replica flew smoothly.

This Sumerian artifact, now residing in the British Museum, was produced more than 4,000 years ago in the valleys of the Tigris and Euphrates rivers. It seems to depict an extraterrestrial. Excavated artifacts have displayed evidence of great skill and artistry. From Sumeria have come examples of fine works in marble, diorite, hammered gold, and lapis lazuli. Of the many portraits unearthed in this area, some of the best are those of Gudea, ruler of Lagash.

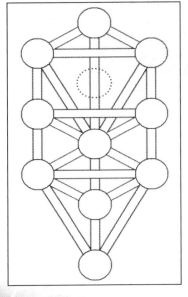

The Kabbalah wisdom teaching was unveiled approximately 4,000 years ago. It revealed divine revelation to humanity, unlocking many of humanity's mysteries and revealing the secrets of the universe. The Kabbalah has an amazing logical system and extraordinary technology that can alter each and everyone's life.

Colloidal silver kills over 650 pathogens, including being a prophylactic for COVID-19. Although colloidal silver is discouraged by mainstream medicine, it is common to find it in hospitals lining Foley catheters, IV lines, and breathing tubes. Silver sulfadiazine is used widely in burn units, and to kill off MRSA infections. The WHO uses silver to disinfect water in developing countries. Why? Because it is anti-bacterial, anti-viral and anti-fungal!

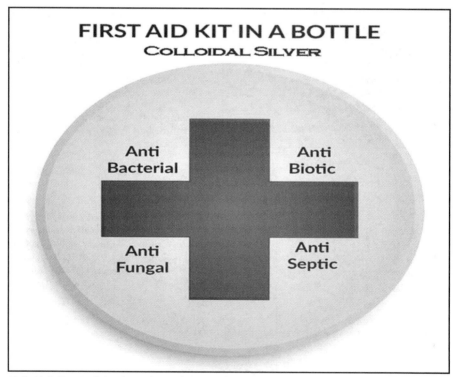

FIRST AID KIT IN A BOTTLE
COLLOIDAL SILVER

Anti Bacterial · Anti Biotic · Anti Fungal · Anti Septic

Colloidal silver is the only antibiotic known to reportedly kill all types of viruses, bacteria and fungal overgrowth. Colloidal silver is also the only antibiotic known to be perfectly harmless to all parts of the body when used properly. While the liver and kidneys can be harmed by other antibiotics, colloidal silver promotes healing. Colloidal silver is non-toxic to mammals, reptiles, plants and all living things that are not of a one-celled structure.

CRYSTALS

"In a crystal we have clear evidence of the existence of a formative life principle, and though we cannot understand the life of a crystal, it is nonetheless a living being."
–Nikola Tesla

IN the science of quantum mechanics, new discoveries have confirmed that matter can indeed be in two places at once. Through "quantum entanglement" even particles that are millions of light years apart can be connected without physical contact. This also means that space-time can be manipulated. It turns out that space is just like all other matter, meaning it can be warped and shaped. The ability of teleportation is becoming a reality by the utilization of new superconductive materials, which can also be manipulated through different frequencies. Gravity-resistant surface materials are now being rolled out for use in air transportation. The science of resonance is leading to a greater understanding of our now emerging hyper-dimensional existence in this material world.

On an atomic level, there is no such thing as matter as we naturally perceive it with our five senses. This will change as we open into our sixth sense and above. All matter originates and exists only by virtue of a force which brings the particle of an atom to vibration and holds this most minute solar system of the atom together. We must assume that behind this force is the existence of a conscious and intelligent mind. This "mind" has been described as the matrix of all matter.

Everything is energy, including metals, crystals, and everything around us that we perceive as "solid." The reality we experience every day and the matter around us are merely different vibrational expressions of light and sound. Reality exists as above and so below, giving rise to the study of alternative universes. Atoms in our body operate in the same way as galaxies do. All that really exists is consciousness in the form of energy—a soul projection of our one connection to the greater universal consciousness. Yet with all the benefits of these emerging breakthroughs to the people on Earth, there is still a force that wishes to keep us ignorant. There are those who would deny us our right to the material utopia of utilizing powerful crystals and certain exotic metals.

CRYSTALLOGRAPHY

Tapping into the healing properties of stones and crystals has been an ancient practice, and their unique powers continue to be rediscovered. Different types of stones have particular frequencies which can match up with various systems in the human body and assist the systems to function better. For instance, black tourmaline is a great stone to help people stay grounded, focused and articulate, while selenite and apophylite can be used to bring in white light and energy. "Orgonite" is a name given to handcrafted creations with shungite, crystals, and other materials and is based upon the "orgone" sciences pioneered by Dr. Wilhelm Reich. Orgonite is used as a way to protect from harmful electromagnetic radiation like 4G, 5G, and WiFi. Iron pyrite can be used to offset negative energy or deter physical danger. Hematite is used for grounding and balance. People can work with the stones by carrying them in their pockets, worn as jewelry, being held during meditation, or even placed on the body during periods of rest.[1]

Crystals have long been recognized as more than just "rocks." A deeper understanding reveals that crystals are alive and conscious. Carbon is the sixth element on the periodic table of elements, which is associated with all organic chemistry and everything that is normally considered to be alive. But directly below it, one octave below, is the element of silicon, the primary element of quartz crystal, and consisting of about 80% of the Earth's crust.

Crystallography is the science of crystals and the study of the crystalline state. Since most solid matter is crystalline, the properties of crystals are to a large extent also the properties of ordinary solid materials. Crystals are known transmitters and receivers with incredible storage possibilities. Crystals, when programmed, hold certain frequencies and can counteract opposites, plus utilize tone and sound. Crystals can naturally absorb nature's information. Because gemstones grow in the earth, and are in essence alive, some people think they are here to help us. For the first time in history, very different kinds of gemstones are widely available to the masses, and each gemstone holds its own unique properties.

The ARK crystals developed by renowned physicist, Nassim Haramein, are a revolutionary technology. They have the ability to invigorate the body's natural capacity to attune with the vitalistic and expansive zero-point field of the quantum vacuum. As Haramein explains, "the quantum vacuum represents the revelatory understanding in modern physics that space is not empty; on the contrary, it is the one thing that connects all things." Nassim Haramein's patented "Harmonic Flux Resonator" replicates the magnetohydrodynamic behaviors which naturally occur in a variety of astrophysical objects. This enables the creation of each ARK crystal to become a node of high coherence in the structure of space surrounding it, providing enhancing benefits to a human's biological health.

PIEZO EFFECT

In the electronics industry, the word "crystal" is usually restricted in meaning to a crystalline substance that exhibits the piezoelectric effect. Piezoelectricity is the ability of some materials, notably crystals and certain ceramics, to generate an electric potential in response to applied mechanical stress. Quartz crystal has been shown to exhibit more piezoelectricity than other materials, and best converts electrical voltage into the mechanical regulation of clocks and computers. This process can be reversed by using mechanical pressure to produce electrical voltage.

1   Hurst, Katherine. "A Guide to Healing Crystals: 10 Most Effective Healing Stones." **https://www.thelawofattraction.com/healing-crystal-guide/**

Quartz crystal is an efficient piezoelectric material. It produces and accumulates electric charge when subjected to mechanical stress. The piezoelectric effect works both ways. Not only is electric charge produced when mechanical stress is applied, but also mechanical stress appears when electric charge is applied. Mechanical stress, if applied in sufficient amount, is accompanied by mechanical strain, or deformation of the material under stress.

In experiments manipulating quartz crystal, strain appeared as a bending of the crystalline structure when an electric charge was applied across the plane of a crystalline sheet. An oscillator circuit composed of an amplifier and a resonator had applied a charge to a thin sheet of quartz crystal, and the crystal mechanically vibrated because of the reversible piezoelectric effect. The crystal acted as the resonator in the circuit. It will vibrate at different desired frequencies based on its thickness, shape, and the lattice plane from which the crystal is cut. The vibrating crystal acts as a filter that can eliminate all electric signals with the exception of the desired frequency. The vibrating quartz crystal then feeds back its frequency to the amplifier. As long as an electric charge is continuously applied, and the temperature does not vary too much, the mechanical vibrations of the crystal resonators are regular and dependable. Crystals have been used to generate truly random numbers for the very first time.[2]

The Piezo effect occurs in crystals, ceramics, DNA and also certain proteins. Piezo electricity occurs when a voltage is applied to a crystal, and it responds with a frequency. Electricity can result from applied compression or frequency. Recent work by Clifford Carnicom reveals that a filament culture subjected to a blue light frequency that is 375 nanometers resulted in explosive growth of a Morgellons culture within 24 hours after the initial incubation. He activated the blue light and incubated it for five to seven days, and then it exploded into a multitude of little fibers. Crystals and the Morgellons fibers multiply in a similar fashion.

We now live in a frequency-filled world, including HAARP, artificial weather and the enormous spread of unnatural frequencies that are affecting the earth today. The Earth's own natural magnetic field peaks at 32 hertz and that only happens in certain equatorial thunderstorms. The electronics we use today generate electromagnetic fields that are tremendous, in the megahertz and gigahertz millions and billions of hertz range.

QUASI CRYSTALS

The development and research into the "Quasi crystals" was a classified program within several departments of the U.S. secret government. Even the unclassified research was funded by agencies like the Department of Energy (DoE) and the Department of Defense (DoD). But why did the DoE and Ames Laboratory so vigorously pursue research with Quasi crystals? An unclassified document describes the DoE interest:

Our goal is to understand, and facilitate exploitation of, the special properties of Quasi crystals. These properties include (but are not limited to) low thermal and electrical conductivity, high hardness, low friction, and good oxidation resistance.

Quasi crystals were officially recognized in 1984 when a paper was published announcing the discovery of the new matter which was achieved by symmetrically joining together two distinctly different metallic crystals. By 1986, several top-secret advanced studies were going on funded by Defense Advanced Research Projects Agency (DARPA) with leading scientists already working in the field. Since Quasi crystals lose periodicity in at least one dimension, it is not possible to describe them in 3D space as easily as normal crystal structures. Thus, it becomes more difficult to find mathematical formalisms for the interpretation and analysis of diffraction data.

2   Dockrill, Peter. "Crystals have been used to generate truly random numbers for the very first time." https://www.sciencealert.com/scientists-use-crystals-to-generate-truly-random-numbers-in-first-for-chemistry

Quasi crystal research established the existence of a wealth of stable and meta-stable crystals. They are structural forms that are both ordered and nonperiodic, with strange structures and interesting properties. Quasi crystals have rotational symmetry, where the same unit part is repeated over and over, 5, 10, even 12 times, with a rotation of about an angle. New tools were developed for the study and description of these extraordinary materials.

Some of the most revealing classified leaked documents revealed that Quasi crystals were developed as high energy storage materials, metal matrix components, thermal barriers, exotic coatings, infrared sensors, high power laser applications, and electro magnetics. Some early applications already released into the market include high-strength alloys and certain surgical tools. In one top secret black program, directed by the DoE, a method to produce hydrogen crystals was discovered, followed by manu-facturing the material in 1994. A myriad of advanced crystallography continues to be discovered by scientists and engineers who evaluate, analyze, and attempt to back-ward engineer crystal technology which has been recovered from downed ET craft dating back to the 1947 Roswell crash.

SILICON AND CRYSTALS

The natural process of crystallization is not actually a chemical reaction, but a physi-cal change that happens when crystal solids form as a reaction byproduct. A team of researchers from the University of Glasgow say the randomization possibilities provided by the crystallization process may be endless. They further elaborate in a new study:

> In a chemical system, each time a reaction is performed there is an almost infi-nite number of energetically equivalent ways for particular reagents to combine, resulting in both high uncertainty and entropy, and the exact pathway under-taken will never be repeated...As such, the entropy of such a chemical system is extraordinarily high, and may therefore serve as a very good entropy pool for application of random number generation.[3]

Author Drunvalo Melchizedek reported how scientists back in the 1950s discovered that silicon and carbon displayed the exact same principles of life. Carbon and silicon are the only two elements known that can create life, and both live naturally on Earth. Marine biologists have discovered lifeforms deep in the ocean that are alive, conscious, repro-ductive, and whose bodies are composed of 100% silicon, with no carbon whatsoever.

An emerging understanding describes crystals as living organisms. After all, they too can grow and communicate. Marcel Vogel, the chemist who created the mag-netic coating for computer hard disks and researched the energetic properties of quartz crystals for IBM, discovered that crystals were able to receive and send both human thoughts and emotions. It makes sense considering that the first radio in the world was a "crystal set." This was done by simply placing a quartz crystal on a table, with a wire touched to the crystal somewhere, and then it was possible to hear the radio signal through an amplifier and speakers. The crystal was picking up the electromagnetic signal in the radio band of frequencies.[4]

Human thoughts are also found in the electromagnetic range of frequencies. Thoughts are very long wavelengths compared to radio waves, but except for the length of their wavelengths, they are exactly the same. So, it would stand to reason that a crystal would be able to pick up on a person's thoughts. Even computers are nothing but crystals, and without crystals, computers would not exist. It is the liv-

3   Linder, Courtney, "Mad Scientists Are Using Crystals to Generate Random Numbers." **https://www.popularmechanics.com/science/math/a30997192/crystals-random-numbers-data-encryption.**

4   Melchizedek, Drunvalo, *Serpent of Light Beyond 2012 – The Movement of the Earth's Kundalini and the Rise of the Female Light, 1949 to 2013.* Weiser Books, 2008.

ing nature of a crystal that allows computers to do what they do. Natural crystals can hold memory and a "program," which means a thought pattern, and continues to replay that thought pattern for eternity unless someone erases the program. When properly programmed, crystals will become indispensable tools in the future.

The great electrical inventor, Nikola Tesla, realized that the Earth was a spherical capacitor not only of great strength, but also an electricity generator. He proposed that people would only need an antenna to tap into an "ocean of energy" to consume energy that already existed. He described that ocean of energy as not only to work to generate electricity, but could be made available as an unlimited free energy source. Tesla also recognized the power of crystals when he described crystals as having the existence of a formative life principle, stating that "though we cannot understand the life of a crystal, it is nonetheless a living being."[5]

CRYSTAL BLUE PERSUASION

Crystals have long excited the human imagination. The lost civilization of Atlantis was said to have employed a high science of crystals to run its technology, including "fire crystals" for free energy generation. The Vikings reportedly used crystals alongside their runestones to aide in navigation. Today people associate crystals with light and energy, and carry them around everywhere. Pop music lyrics sing their praises. Crystals have long been known to have energy applications and exhibit natural piezoelectrical properties. Early radio technology used germanium crystals to capture radio waves and convert them into electrical signals that could be processed and broadcast through headphones into soundwaves duplicating the human voice, music, and other sounds. Nowadays, quartz is the key component in many of our modern technologies, including telecommunication devices and computers. Without quartz, there would be no way to program a computer. It would not be possible to store any memory, and most importantly, it would be impossible to retrieve any information. One small chip can hold thousands of photographs, songs, movies, books, and all different kinds of data. Just imagine what could be stored in a piece of quartz the size of a baseball?

Marcel Vogel, the world-renowned scientist who held over 200 patents (including one for the floppy disk) examined samples of exotic crystal and metal, provided by UFO contactee Billy Meier, by using a scanning electron microscope. In 1979, Meier sent Vogel crystal and metal samples that Meier claimed to have received from the Pleiadean ETs. In Vogel's experiment he reported, "When I touched the oxide with a stainless steel probe, red streaks appeared and the oxide coating disappeared. I just touched the metal…and it started to deoxidize and become a pure metal. I have never seen a phenomenon like that before." Of another metal sample containing nearly every element in the periodic table, Vogel stated, "Each pure element was bonded to each of the others, yet somehow retained its own identity." Some critics of his day (using a scanning electron microscope) could not determine the atomic or molecular structure of a substance, calling into question his findings. Vogel countered by saying, "thulium exists only in minute amounts. It is exceedingly expensive, far beyond platinum, and rare to come by. Someone would have to have an extensive metallurgical knowledge even to be aware of a composition of this type."

Indeed, Vogel was a chemist, not a metallurgist. Yet his findings, if replicated, are amazing. At 1600 X magnification Vogel observed, "A whole new world appears in the specimen. There are structures within structures—very unusual." At 2500 X he found that the sample was, "metal, but at the same time…it is crystal!" Vogel put the full weight of his expertise in these summary comments: "With any technology that I know of, we could not achieve this on this planet! I could not put it together myself, as a scientist. …

5   Tesla, Nikola, *The Problem of Increasing Human Energy*. Released June, 1900.

And I think it is important that those of us who are in the scientific world sit down and do some serious study on these things instead of putting it off as people's imagination."[6]

DIAMONDS ARE FOREVER

Since diamonds are the strongest of the crystal elements, jewelry ornamentation is not the only application. They are widely used as industrial drill bits and in medical equipment, plus there are computer applications with diamonds as well. Siddharth Dhomkar and his team of scientists from the City College of New York have found a way to store data inside artificially grown diamonds using small defects inside the gems. To do this, they targeted diamonds whose crystalline structures had small gaps called nitrogen vacancy centers where carbon atoms should be. The gaps are so named because nitrogen atoms are located around them. The gaps usually hold electrons, which give the space a negative charge, but the scientists found out that when they hit the gaps with a laser, it turned into a neutral charge. The sequences of neutral and negative charges in these gaps could be used to store data similar to the way CDs and DVDs use tiny pits for data storage.

Storage technology is evolving, with many researchers focusing less on disk-based storage and more on unconventional materials. Some of these technologies include using quartz, individual atoms, and even DNA for data storage. These latest developments show how humans are continually finding new ways to preserve our memories for all eternity—or at least until we run out of space.

The tiny pockets created by defects in diamonds and gems could be manipulated to store data, with spots only a few nanometers wide and capable of holding information. The research is the latest in a trend of looking at unusual materials, such as DNA and quartz, as a potential means of data storage.[7]

GIANT CRYSTAL CAVE

The amazingly enormous crystals in Mexico's *Cueva de los Cristales*, were discovered in a 300-meter-deep cave below Mount Naica in the Chihuahua Desert which grows the largest crystals ever discovered. The "Giant Crystal Cave" is located inside the lead, zinc and silver Naica Mine in Chihuahua, Mexico. Grown in gypsum deposits, the crystals are a phenomenon unique in the world. "It's the Sistine Chapel of crystals," Spanish geologist Juan Garcia-Ruiz told the news service *Cosmos Online*. Scientists estimate that the crystals were the result of ancient volcanic activity which left behind anhydrite, a mineral formed of calcium sulphate, which is chemically identical to gypsum, but lacks water. As underground volcanic activity abated, the water in the cave system cooled below 580 °C and the anhydrite deposits turned into crystals of gypsum, albeit very slowly. The massive crystal formations deep within a flooded cave were accidentally discovered in 2001 by two working miners. It lies almost a thousand feet below ground. It is the home to the largest crystals known in the world, which are over 11 meters long and weigh 55 tons. The crystals themselves are created by hydrothermal fluids originating from the magma chambers below, and are made of gypsum and selenite. Moreover, some crystals were formed over a span of about half a million years in a hot water solution, saturated with minerals.[8]

In the decades after this amazing discovery, the Giant Crystal Cave has been under negotiation to be named a World Heritage site. This will ensure the preservation and protection of this site for future generations. Without this protection, the cave would again be flooded and the site would become inaccessible. Spanish authorities

6 "Marcel Vogel's Groundbreaking Work at IBM led to 100+ patents. But his research with crystals is even more amazing as it paved the way for crystal healing." **https://marcelvogellegacy.com**

7 Read more about crystals: **https://perdurabo10.tripod.com/storagej/id72.html**

8 "Cave of Crystals 'Giant Crystal Cave' at Naica, Mexico." *Geology*: **https://www.geologyin.com/2014/11/the-huge-cave-mines-at-naica-mexico.html**

are only just beginning to comprehend the magnitude of tourists and scientists visiting and researching these massive crystals, and letting the cave flood again would prevent them from studying the site further.

The vibrations of the Giant Crystal Cave are said to be extremely intense. One worker talked of the deeply mystical and immense dreams he experienced, and had no words to describe them accurately. Another field of study is light energy, which is merely "Angstrom units per second" at which an element or a cell vibrates when measured. Like the blades moving in a fan, the measure of these units depict how much light or transparency is available. The energy within various crystals is high on the vibrational scale of Angstrom units, and each crystal can be measured with a specific vibration. Such a vibration has the ability to propel the human aura into greater visibility and measurement. The ability of crystals to tune electronic circuits was the basis of early crystal radios. One wonders what unusual electromagnetic and optical properties might be possible with crystals of such enormous size as those in the Giant Crystal Cave.

CRYSTAL SKULLS

Humans who lived in antediluvian times may not have had computers as we know them today, but they clearly seemed familiar with the information-storing properties of quartz crystal. The ancient Akashic Records are said to be impressed upon a subtle substance called akasha, or Soniferous Ether, while other accounts claim the records are made of solid crystal and are stored in underground repositories. It is possible the Akashic Records are made of both. Edgar Cayce said the civilization of Atlantis was powered by the free energy extracted from the "Mighty, Terrible Fire Crystal" or "Tuaoi Stone," a technology still unknown to us today. Other cultures made use of a lasting receptacle that allegedly was able to record, store, and transmit data for all eternity. These "ancient computers" could also include the crystal skulls that have been found around the world, but most especially uncovered in Central America. An old Native American legend describes the existence of 13 ancient crystal skulls, each proportional to the size of a human skull, with a moveable jaw that was said to have the ability to speak or sing. The legend tells that these crystal skulls contained important information about some of the great mysteries of life and the universe. They contained knowledge about the past history of our species on this planet, and information about humankind's true purpose and our future destiny.

In 1924, an enigmatic human-sized crystal skull over 36,000 years old was discovered. It is one of the 13 crystal skulls that are believed to possess otherworldly powers and cause paranormal happenings. Anna Mitchell-Hedges always maintained that she found the Crystal Skull bearing her family name among the Mayan ruins in Lubaantun, Belize (at that time, British Honduras) on January 1st, 1924. The Mitchell-Hedges skull is unique in its extraordinary craftsmanship and regarded as the finest quality of all the crystal skulls. The Mitchell-Hedges skull was submitted in 1970 for a thorough scientific examination. The findings were nothing short of amazing. Researchers had the skull examined at a Hewlett-Packard lab. One of the HP researchers, D. Trull, uncritically reports that the lab found that the skull:

> Had been carved against the natural axis of the crystal. Modern crystal sculptors always take into account the axis, or orientation of the crystal's molecular symmetry, because if they carve "against the grain," the piece is bound to shatter—even with the use of lasers and other high-tech cutting methods.

To compound the strangeness, HP researchers could find no microscopic scratches on the crystal which would indicate it had been carved with metal instruments. Researcher Frank Dorland declared that the Mitchell-Hedges skull emits sounds and light, depending on the position of the planets. He claimed that the skull originated in Atlantis and was carried around by the Knights Templar during the Crusades. Dorland's best hypothesis for the skull's construction is that it was roughly hewn with diamonds, and then the detail work was meticulously done with a gentle solution of silicon sand and water. The exhausting job of creating the Mitchell-Hedges skull, assuming it could possibly be done this way, would have required man-hours adding up to well over a hundred years to complete.[9]

Some legends and theories propose that the original 13 crystal skulls were not created by the hand of humans at all, but may be of extraterrestrial origin. Carved out of pure quartz crystal, and other crystals such as jade, the skulls generate an energy field that activates human consciousness in a way that can expand the perception of reality for anyone in close proximity to the relics. Some say that they may be the crystallized consciousness of advanced beings related to Atlantis, the Pleiades, or beyond. Scientists, who have said that the Mitchell-Hedges skull technically should not exist because they cannot understand how it could possibly have been carved, may inadvertently be supporting this extraterrestrial theory.

Another theory is that the crystal skulls were placed on Earth to be activated at a time when additional wisdom needed to be imparted to all people. In that regard, the crystal skulls ultimately are the manifestation of spirit in a form that is now helping to shift the magnetic frequency of Earth. When the spirits of the skulls are ceremonially awakened, ancient wisdom will become accessible once again. This is the wisdom that has been preserved in a crystalline matrix for eons and could become a kind of collective consciousness known to all. From the crystalline matrix, this universal wisdom then enters the unified field and fills the minds of all with the knowledge of everything that has happened on the planet in the last 26,000 years, and perhaps beyond.

AGAPE, SUPER SEVEN, AND MELODY STONES

New Age adherents have long had a strong affinity with gemstones and crystals, ascribing to them different properties and associations. The so-called "Agape" crystals are said by some to contain the energies of many different minerals. The name *agape* comes from the Greek word meaning "an out-pouring of unconditional love" from above. Just like the minerals within the soil that flow through the grapevine to give a fine wine its distinctive flavor, so do these minerals combine to create this incredible crystal family. Agape crystals are associated with an out-pouring of the "divine feminine" energies such as unconditional love, compassion, forgiveness and healing, to name a few.

Melody Stones are known as high vibrational crystals. They never need clearing or cleansing and come from just one location on Earth, and that is Espírito Santo, Brazil. They are wonderful companion crystals for "reviewing and releasing" old ways of thinking and acting which do not serve us any longer. They can also help people to re-envision their new life paths to facilitate the opportunity for "peace and harmony" to enter their lives. They are also said to help people re-focus and manifest what is needed.

Super Seven is a quartz stone that contains seven materials, including goethite, cacoxenite, rutile, lepidocrocite, amethyst, clear quartz and smokie quartz. Agape, Sacred Seven, and Melody Stone are quartz stones that consist of the Super Seven materials. These crystals are very different from normal stones. Embodied within their structures are the energies of seven different stones. These powerful stones epitomize the universal brotherhood of man and the sisterhood of women. The "brotherhood" of minerals contained within these crystals are connected with the Native American Medicine Wheel, by which all share their energies and gifts with their human companions to help them on their paths to spiritual enlightenment and completion.

9   "The official website of the Mitchell-Hedges Crystal Skull: The world's most mysterious and fascinating archaeological artifact." https://mitchell-hedges.com

The Agape crystals are also used to aid individuals in stimulating and developing their psychic abilities, including telepathy, clairvoyance, clairaudience, claircognizance and clairsentience. The stone's vibration reaffirms a person's power and enhances personal ascension and that of the entire planet. As the process continues and a person's intuitive self develops more fully, that person will notice his or her psychic abilities becoming a lot more acute. Lastly, these stones are said to aid in guidance for the process of "ascension." This involves not only these people but the whole planet, which is moving to a higher level vibrationally, and can be aided by these amazing stones.[10]

MOLDAVITE

Moldavite is found in only one location in the world, and that is what is today the Czech Republic in Central Europe. A meteorite of enormous size and incredible impact was known to have crashed into the strewnfield areas of the Reis Impact Crater mountain region around 14.8 million years ago. In ancient times, it was thought to be a mystical stone that could bring good luck and the fulfillment of wishes. Not a crystal nor exotic metal, moldavite is a tektite, and considered a stone of intense frequency and high vibration. Natural crystals of moldavite are considered powerful stones for transformation, and the tektite is nicknamed the "Holy Grail Stone." This powerful meteorite stone can be used to enhance people's psychic powers, and may stimulate kundalini awakening. Intuition is said to develop more acutely, and one's psychic abilities might either come to life for the first time, or one could find personal abilities he or she might wish to expand or change.

Furthermore, moldavite is considered one of the best stones to use for psychic protection. Negative entities find it difficult to connect to a person's aura when the person is wearing this meteorite stone. Wearing this stone is an advantage when the person is psychically working with spirits, as this stone enhances making contact with "the light." Another aspect of moldavite is its protective quality, especially if a person is working on developing psychic abilities. Change and spiritual healing are the common elements that this powerful natural crystal stimulates amongst most people, and this may take different forms.

CAN CRYSTALS BE CREATED AS "NEAR-LIVING"?

We have seen that crystals have been proven to store huge amounts of information, can harness the energy of consciousness, have many technological functions, and contain silicon and carbon—the building blocks of life. They also possess energetic qualities that have promoted healing and emotional, physical, and spiritual well-being. They have been used throughout history as a conduit between the world of life (as we know it) and inanimate matter, but it's their life-like properties reportedly observed that could be more literal than previously thought.[11]

Physicists at NYC University have published results of their experiment on the life-like behaviors of hematite, a newly-synthesized chemical compound. The researchers took hematite (a compound of iron and oxygen) as the particle basis and then added a spherical polymer coat. They left a corner of the hematite particle exposed and subjected the compound to blue light until the particles began moving, breaking apart, and then reforming in a "life-like" manner.

Yet the particles were never truly alive—but not far off from life, either. Biophysicist Jeremie Palacci of NYC University explained that when exposed to light and fed by chemicals, they formed crystals that could move, break apart and form again. He concluded: "There is a blurry frontier between active and alive." Another of the

10 Agape crystals: **https://agapecrystal.tripod.com/**
11 WIRED: "It's (Almost) Alive! Scientists Create a Near-Living Crystal." **https://www.wired.com/2013/01/living-crystal**

physicists involved, Paul Chaikin, acknowledged that framing a definition of life is difficult. He comments that one such definition includes possessing metabolism, the ability to self-replicate and the ability to move, and that the "colloidal surfers" satisfy two of these criteria. They lack only the ability to self-replicate. In short, the powers of crystals continue to amaze researchers and crystal enthusiasts alike.[12]

While Mark Comings was a physicist at the University of California Berkeley studying the energetic effects of crystals, he discovered something incredible that certain alphabet agencies wished he hadn't. He discovered that when under physical pressure, some crystals produced an electrical charge. So he wrapped electrical coils around a quartz crystal and began experimenting more. One night, something unusual happened. The crystal began to glow, and ring. When he measured the energy coming from it, it was 25% more than the voltage going in. He discovered a method for creating free energy! Within hours, his house was raided by the secret service and all his equipment was confiscated. He has subsequently moved to a foreign country. [13]

The Naica Mine of the Mexican state of Chihuahua, is a working mine that is best-known for its extraordinary selenite crystals. Caverns discovered during mining operations contain crystals of selenite (gypsum) as large as 1.2 meters (4 feet) in diameter and 15 meters (50 feet) long. Naica lies on an ancient fault and there is an underground magma chamber below the cave. The magma heated the ground water and it became saturated with minerals, including large quantities of gypsum. The hollow space of the cave was filled with this mineral-rich hot water and remained filled for about 500,000 years. During this time, the temperature of the water remained very stable at over 50 °C (122 °F). This allowed crystals to form and grow to immense sizes.

• •

12 The physicists have uploaded this clip displaying the behavior of the "light-activated colloidal surfers." https://www.youtube.com/watch?v=jqwOYh5hUlc&ab_channel=MPShare
13 IG Connecting Consciousness http://harmoniccontinuum.50megs.com/custom3.html

The world's largest single quartz crystal cluster is on display in a gemstone museum in Swakopmund, Namibia. This quartz cluster was discovered in 1985 at the bottom of a 45 meter (148 feet) deep cave in the Otjua mine near Karibib in Namibia. It weighs 14,100 kilograms (9,475 pounds).

Researchers have shown that crystals can be so flexible they can be bent repeatedly and even tied up in knots, and return unbroken to their original form. This overhauls our current understanding of crystalline structures, and challenges the very definition of a crystal. As we learnt in school, crystals are brittle and inelastic—if you try to bend a crystal of rock salt or quartz, for example, it will break. But this new research shows that crystals can actually be made to bend, opening up a whole new class of flexible materials such as these Gallium crystals.

The healing properties of the element bismuth are said to relieve symptoms of isolation, both spiritually and emotionally. As a stone of transformation, it calms disorder and helps push changes in the right direction with a physical vitality, connecting to "all that is." Energy is transformed from the crown chakra to the base chakra, which is something other stones don't do. It can be used on all chakras. The power of wisdom can be actualized through bismuth. It improves concentration and visualization during shamanic journeys.

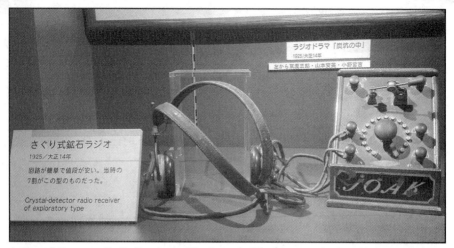

A Crystal-Detector Radio Receiver of Exploratory Type 1925, is displayed in the NHK Museum of Broadcasting in Japan. Radios, cellphones, and televisions cannot work without them. They vibrate at 32,768 pulses per second. The pineal gland and the inner ear have microcrystals inside them. Piezoelectric technology could be a form of free energy from crystals. Scientists now think the inside of stars vibrate like crystals.

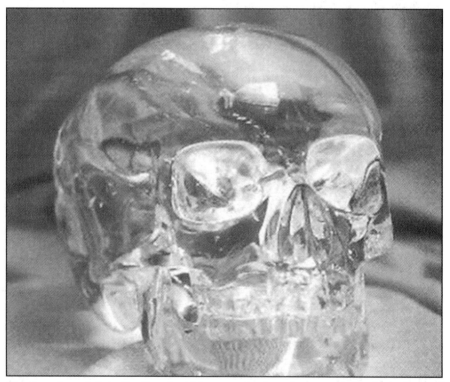

The famed crystal skulls of ancient Mesoamerica have been a source of mystery and controversy since they were first discovered over a century ago. Crystal skulls are crystalline objects shaped like a cranium with a detachable jaw, some of which are said to have supernatural properties.

ACHEIVING ÜBERMIND

"We have been all wrong! What we have called matter is energy, whose vibration has been lowered as to be perceptible to the senses. ...The religion of the future will be a cosmic one. It should transcend personal God and avoid dogma and theology." –Albert Einstein

OVER the last few decades, humans have started to bend the laws of natural selection that have governed life for the past four billion years. We have acquired the ability to design not only the world around us, but also ourselves. Such a new direction is a double-edged sword. We've neglected the philosophical discussion about where our transhumanist future is leading us, and who it is we may become? Achieving übermind is understanding beneficial practices of the past and adapting to rapidly-changing modern scientific breakthroughs, some of which will greatly enhance our physical bodies and vastly improve our mental capabilities.

A greater understanding is coming from both old and new disciplines and traditions, ranging from ancient Vedic literature to quantum physics, from meditation and prayer to intentional manifestation, and the super human ability of using mind over matter. All are coming together around concepts that are beginning to link actual physical reality to our thoughts and consciousness in a feedback loop, where our consciousness is not merely influenced by reality as we perceive it, but reality is, conversely, influenced by our thoughts.

The real world that emerges will bear little to no resemblance to the world we›ve been told about by mainstream media and conventional education. Most of us inhabit a true Matrix-like illusional world—where we go about working, eating, breathing, and the routine of modern life, as if sleep-walking.

There has long been an incentive to keep humans ignorant. The "Great Awakening" is changing all that. Collectively we have overwhelming numbers, to say nothing of our free will consciousness. If we can learn to infuse the world field with our intentions for peace, health, justice and love, there is no dark force that can withstand our newfound awareness. The journey takes us to deeper levels in all of our actions—to make them count even more, to give our acts more weight, to make it more likely that our individual ripples will propagate more widely.

Achieving übermind is understanding we are each an immortal soul with profound untapped powers. If properly developed, a new Age of Transparency will emerge and we will be able to protect all that's important, and easily thwart any evil agenda. Once you realize that every action you make has karmic ramifications, where only you will judge yourself when you die, you'll never again wish any harm on anyone, and you'll find an urgent priority to be in service to all. Thousands of case histories of near-death experiences, reincarnation and similar phenomena provide ample evidence that we are, indeed, spirits in the material world. We have existed before this life, and will continue to exist after this life.[1]

AGE REVERSAL

Age reversing technologies have made stunning advancements in the last decade, but are currently very expensive or not being released to the general population. It will become commonplace to extend a person's life span to 130 years, or longer. Yet, there is a catch. If one wants to live longer than 130 years, it can be done; but there are spiritual changes that will become necessary for that person. We are on the verge of inexpensive universal healthcare, in which actual healing takes place instead of mere treatment. This will be true for most ailments—and without a load of chemicals, the pharmaceutical industry notwithstanding. It could be a world in which a huge portion of the population's massive suffering would be relieved.

Emerging scientific studies have found an adult human's "biological age" can be "reversed." This is done by rejuvenating the body's "epigenetic clock," which tracks a person's biological age. The epigenetic clock relies on the body's epigenome, which comprises chemical modifications, such as methyl groups, that tag DNA. The pattern of these tags changes during the course of a lifetime and tracks a person's biological age, which can lag behind or exceed chronological age. Pneumonia and other infectious diseases are a major cause of death for people 75 years or older. Regenerating the thymus has proven useful in people who have underactive immune systems, especially among older people.[2]

One undisclosed age reversal technology is using tachyon energy, which is regarded as the highest possible connection to a direct source. This is an aspect of the spiritual component. Tachyons travel faster than the speed of light and cannot be destroyed. This energy does not interact with most known physical forces. For example, a person cannot influence tachyons with magnetic, chemical or even nuclear influences. Tachyons will remain inside objects such as crystals forever. They have such high vibrational frequency that they reduce the level of chaos in our energy fields. They work on a quantum/subatomic level. Tachyons are known to heal many diseases. They help to reverse our aging process because aging is a process of entropy. Tachyon energy/technology is what the very human-looking ET race from the Pleiades use for healing. Age reversing "MedBed" technology with be released with NESARA/GESARA. Not only is frequency and vibration the future of healing medicine, but it will also help heal the Earth. Once humans begin using it on a personal basis, it will be necessary to create a network of tachyon energy points throughout the planet.

1 Truther, Martin, "A Journey to the Center of the Truth." https://martintruther.blogspot.com/2010/10/red-pill-guide-to-top-20-secrets.html
2 Abbott, Alison, "First hint that body's 'biological age' can be reversed." https://www.nature.com/articles/d41586-019-02638-w

THE RULE OF NINES

In mathematics, the Rule of Nines is a divisibility rule for the divisor nine. It is notable because it illustrates some interesting properties of modular arithmetic, and its proof is derived from that basis. It also offers an insight into sacred geometry and musical frequencies. The word "rule" can have several different meanings: as a form of law; as a form of dominion; or as a measuring standard. The use of the word in all three contexts is necessary to define the effect of the supreme chord—the trinity of harmony—within the universe. Resonant geometry and the zero point apply to the Rule of Nines. It is necessary to go very far back in history to find some clues that a technologically-advanced civilization on Earth once utilized this information. It involves phi, the universal constant, and delves deeply into the construction of pyramids upon Earth's twin tetrahedrons.

Place two tetrahedrons together and put them in an orb, and the result is a miniature model of the Earth's magnetic field. The point where the latitude and longitude intersect constitutes points at the "bases" of the tetrahedrons where they touch the orb, which is the point upon which all of the ancient pyramids were built. The "top" and "bottom" points are the north and south poles. This shows the naturally occurring magnetic resonance of Earth as an "orb" in rotation, all the while producing the torus flow of energy. Connect the lines between points using a map of the world grid and what emerges are the intersections of ley lines which were mapped very accurately thousands of years ago. At these key intersection points, on every continent, are the remains of great pyramids. This advanced understanding indicates there were überminds at work a long time ago on this planet.

Models of the Earth as twin tetrahedrons have been found in the ruins of every civilization which built pyramids. If the ancient "sacred" knowledge was shared by extraterrestrials to permit the construction of the pyramids, and if resonance is the key to anti-gravity, as well as to free energy, then the tetrahedron has very far-reaching implications. Earth is, as it must be, a model of the natural harmonic relationships which exist at every level—from the expansive universe to subatomic particles. As above, so below.

An advanced understanding of resonance may be the key to countering the effects of gravity, or, rather, the effect called gravity; for gravity is an effect, not a force. Gravity is suspended when the spin of the energy is cancelled, which comprises the matter, by resonating the matter. By virtually rotating the lattices, the subatomic particle spin virtually stops, like a spinning object seen with a synchronized strobe light. Because gravity is a quadruple effect, when the spin stops the effect is lost.[3]

ALL IS VIBRATION

Sound influences all matter, including the cells and molecular structures of all living creatures. The human body is no exception. The science of cymatics demonstrates the effect of sound on matter rather vividly. The study of the patterns produced by vibrating bodies has a long and venerable history. One of the earliest to record that an oscillating body displayed regular patterns was the Italian astronomer Galileo Galilei, who in 1632, wrote:

> As I was scraping a brass plate with a sharp iron chisel in order to remove some spots from it and was running the chisel rather rapidly over it, I once or twice, during many strokes, heard the plate emit a rather strong and clear whistling sound: on looking at the plate more carefully, I noticed a long row of fine streaks parallel and equidistant from one another. Scraping with the chisel over and over again, I noticed that it was only when the plate emitted this hissing noise

3   "Sound influences matter and the cells and molecular structure in the human body. Cymatics demonstrates it very vividly." *Delamora:* https://www.delamora.life/cymatics

that any marks were left upon it; when the scraping was not accompanied by this sibilant note there was not the least trace of such marks.

Galileo didn't know it by name when he randomly observed it nearly 400 years ago, but cymatics would become known as the study of visible sound and vibration and a subset of modal phenomena. The generic term for this field of science was retitled "cymatics" by Hans Jenny, a Swiss medical doctor and a pioneer in this field. The word cymatics derives from the Greek word *kuma* meaning "billow" or "wave," to describe the periodic effects that sound and vibration have on matter.

The most common experiment demonstrating the visualization of cymatics can be done by sprinkling sand on a metal plate and vibrating the plate. An example can be made by drawing a violin bow along the edge, and the sand will then form itself into standing wave patterns such as simple concentric circles. The higher the frequency, the more complex the shapes produced, with certain shapes having similarities to sacred geometry patterns and traditional mandala designs.[4]

Of course, vibration and frequency can rarely be observed in nature. The "unseen realms" are the new frontiers of science, largely because until now they've remained invisible. Similarly, if all the problems of the world are asked only from the perspective of the classical, linear-system Western point of view, issues become opaque, but if it is possible to expand a perspective to include creative and even radical ways of completing cycles and recirculating materials in the biosphere and the economy, the possibilities become endless.

THE SCHUMANN FREQUENCY

The Schumann Frequency has a known effect on all living systems, and can even heal damaged DNA caused by the many trappings of modern life. When parts of the body become diseased, it is because the cells are no longer vibrating at their optimum natural resonant frequency. The body's inability to repair damaged DNA is known to cause mutations which in turn induce cancers, and will cause cell death from various degenerative diseases. These effects were studied extensively by Professor R. Wever from the Max Planck Institute in Germany, as well as Dr. Pjotr Garjajev, a member of the Russian Academy of Sciences in Moscow, among others.

Interestingly, the Earth's magnetic field has been measured to have weakened by 15% over the last 200 years. At the same time, human-made EMF has distanced people further from the low-pulsating (7.83 Hz) Schumann Frequency, disabling the body systems to repair the damaged DNA over time. Symptoms of chronic illness from damaged DNA include: inflammation, joint pain, heart palpitations, food and light sensitivities, fatigue, candida, immune dysregulation, Th1/Th2/Th3 imbalance, memory loss, scattered thinking, dysautonomia, sleep problems, cognitive issues, EMF-sensitivity, muscle pain, dehydration, allergies, head pain, and ringing in the ears. The effects include altered blood pressure and melatonin, increased cancer, reproductive, cardiac and neurological disease and even death. Long-term effects of EMF pollution are some of the invisible "slow kill" techniques.[5]

Today, the Earth's field is polluted with human-made frequencies, so the human body instead receives "junk" produced by AC electricity and wireless technology. Literally thousands of studies on EMFs have been investigated and have repeatedly shown adverse effects, yet there is more introduced into the world every year. Dr. Royal Raymond Rife's work studied radionics, and demonstrated the subtle energies of the hu-

4   "Cymatic experiment" video proving that vibration is geometry: **https://www.youtube.com/watch?v=GtiSCBXbHAg&ab_ channel=Matteo**

5   "SCHUMANN RESONANCE FOR OPTIMUM HEALTH." **https://www.naturalsynergysolution.net/schumann-resonance**

man body—as everything vibrates at specific frequencies whether healthy or unhealthy. Edgar Cayce also examines the effect of frequency and vibration on the human body:

> *Every individual entity is on certain vibrations. Every dis-ease or disease is creating in the body the opposite or non-coordinate vibration with the conditions in a body, mind and spirit of the individual. If there is used certain vibrations, there may be seen the response.*[6]

Could it be the planet itself can communicate with us via the Schumann Frequency? Scientific research has recently determined how the human body receives and uses important information gathered from the Earth's field. The seven billion crystalline magnetites in the human brain, in addition to DNA and the pineal gland, are collectively programmed to receive guiding information from the band of electromagnetic frequencies that extend from the Earth's crust to the Schumann Resonances in the ionosphere.

HOMEOPATHIC REMEDIES

Although homeopathic medicine has largely been written-off in the USA, it is very popular throughout the world, especially with European doctors. Approximately 40% of French physicians and 20% of German physicians prescribe homeopathic medicines. Over 40% of British physicians refer patients to homeopaths, and almost 50% of Dutch physicians consider these natural medicines to be effective. The meta-analysis results conclude that either homeopathic medicines work, or controlled clinical trials do not. Because modern science depends mostly on controlled clinical trials, it is more likely that homeopathic medicines are more effective, and certainly less toxic than allopathic pharmaceutical drugs.[7]

Medical history books must now be rewritten. Instead of describing homeopathy as a quack therapy, it must be understood that homeopathy has been unfairly marginalized, attacked, and suppressed since Big Pharma began to dominate the medical industry. Most homeopathic remedies cannot be patented. Numerous surveys have confirmed that people seeking homeopathic treatment tend to be more educated than those who are unfamiliar with the logical benefits. Homeopathy deserves a rightful place in the future of health care as a clinically-proven therapy.

One easy homeopathic practice is to regulate the body by eating probiotic foods daily, and using vitamin supplements to aid in digestion. The word *probiotic* has a Greek origin which means "for life." Probiotics support the good type of bacteria which can provide protection from bad or harmful bacteria in the body. The highest concentration of probiotics are found in fermented foods. A number of studies have shown that probiotic foods and supplements aid in healthy digestion.

As we will examine in the next chapter, a homeopathic treatment is to go after the cause and clean out the terrain in the body. We must feed the body what it's designed for, that being probiotic nutrients and clean foods. It is a misconception that fruit sugar is bad for candida because fruit is sweet. Organic fruit and vegetables are essential. Parasites and fungus come out of the body when a person is on a fruit diet, because they cannot thrive in a clean bodily environment. It is primarily oxygen and alkalinity that starves them out of the body. A clean diet is the original homeopathic remedy. As Hippocrates the father of Western medicine said: "Let food be thy medicine, and medicine be thy food."[8]

••••••••••••••••••••••••••••••••••

6   "Individual vibration" Edgar Cayce reading (1861-12).

7   Ullman, Dana, "Homeopathic Medicine: Europe's #1 Alternative for Doctors." **https://www.huffpost.com/entry/homeopathic-medicine-euro_b_402490**

8   "GcMAF for the treatment of cancer, autism, viral and bacterial disease." **https://www.youtube.com/watch?v=NnYKf3L1NQo&ab_channel=islandonlinenews**

THE AMAZING GcMAF

Reports have been circulating around the natural health community of a compound known as "Globulin derived Macrophage Activating Factor," or GcMAF for short, and its remarkable success in treating cancer patients. The Gc-protein is the Globulin component. It has also been used for brain and immune system strengthening, disease prevention, autism reversal, and it has successfully repaired a variety of cancer-related mutations. Video clips on YouTube show an in vitro attack of macrophages, a type of immune cell, which have been treated with GcMAF and go on to eliminate human breast cancer cells within a week.

Because of the broad range of benefits, GcMAF-based immunotherapy is also being combined with other therapies. Scientific studies have shown that by delivering an activated version of this substance intravenously, the immune system can be fully invigorated to destroy cancer cells on its own without the need for chemotherapy or radiation. The human body produces its own GcMAF which empowers the immune system to protect itself. Researchers have found GcMAF has at least 11 actions discovered so far, including two on the repairing of cells, three showing marked improvement in brain function, and six are related to cancer. In all the studies GcMAF was found to act as a "director" to the immune system.

Manufactured GcMAF is one of the most important medical discoveries in decades. It was first developed by Dr. Nobuto Yamamoto in 1991, who quickly identified that it could be used as an important immunotherapy for cancer treatment. It is a substance that is naturally produced by the liver. Studies have shown that if a person has a disease such as cancer, it usually wipes out the natural GcMAF. Introducing manufactured GcMAF reverses the cancer fight. European clinics using the GcMAF treatment are reporting an 84% success rate in reversing stage 4 cancer in patients, with an average tumor size reduction of 25%–40% in one week. It can be taken as a probiotic supplement, as a suppository, or by intramuscular injection.[9]

GcMAF is the protein that activates macrophages and jump-starts the entire immune response. To sabotage the immune system and put the macrophages to sleep, all cancers and viruses produce a protein called nagalase, that was discovered to block the production of GcMAF. When released, the nagalase enzyme prevents immune system cells from functioning properly. In the absence of GcMAF, pathogens, cancers, HIV, and other viruses will grow unimpeded. Dr. Nobuto Yamamoto demonstrated that GcMAF administration bypasses the nagalase blockage and re-activates the macrophages, which then proceed to kill the cancer cells and invasive viruses. Indeed, there is a cure for cancer, but GcMAF information is being suppressed, along with the dirty little secret that nagalase is being introduced as part of a "slow kill" agenda to keep us perpetually unhealthy.

GcMAF IS SO REVOLUTIONARY THE FIRST RESEARCHERS WERE "SUICIDED"

In the summer of 2015, when the first studies of GcMAF came out in the USA, about a dozen holistic doctors were "suicided" for publishing their findings. A panacea this effective was a threat to the lucrative cancer treatment industry. GcMAF just so happened to be the primary focus of research being conducted by Dr. Jeff Bradstreet, M.D., a Florida doctor, who was found in June, 2015 floating lifeless in a river. His sudden death was immediately ruled a suicide, even though he had a gunshot wound to the chest, with no signs of being suicidal, suggesting he was murdered to keep him quiet. Dr. Bradstreet was the first casualty.

9　Yamamoto, Nobuto, Dr. "Immunotherapy for Prostate Cancer with Gc Protein-Derived Macrophage-Activating Factor, GcMAF." **https://** www.sciencedirect.com/science/article/pii/S1936523308800083

In years following, more than 90 holistic health practitioners have died of suspicious circumstances. It was discovered by Dr. Bradstreet and others that a compound found in vaccines called nagalase was acting as a blocker of Vitamin D from assisting the immune system. Dr. Bradstreet observed that no babies had nagalase when they were born, but it was found in their bodies a few years later. He concluded that it could only have come from vaccines, so he started treating his child patients with GcMAF. Amazingly, he started having a huge success rate in actually curing autism. He started sharing his findings with other holistic doctors, and within months the FDA raided his research facility. The very next day Dr. Bradstreet was found dead in a river with a gunshot wound to his chest. What's more, the holistic doctors who he shared his research soon began being "suicided" or dying themselves of mysterious causes.[10]

Dr. Bradstreet's "suicide" was the first of about ten others that occurred in the following weeks, and all had direct connections with the holistic healing community. Dr. Bradstreet and his other now-dead colleagues had all been involved in research focused on CBD oils and GcMAF's potential as both a treatment and cure for cancer. Neither produce toxic side effects like conventional cancer treatments do. Perhaps their most damning discovery was the nagalase found in vaccines. If this became widely known it would put the industry out of business, and top executives prosecuted for their crimes. Someone must have known.

The pharmaceutical cartel in the USA has everything backwards. As the "Vaccine Court" in the USA has proven, many who are vaccinated wind up with minor, major and chronic autoimmune diseases, and sometimes paralysis or autism. Some even die. Such side effects have never been reported with GcMAF.

THE GcMAF PANACEA

Many countries, including the USA, no longer allow GcMAF sales or treatment. The website of a clinic out of Japan that sells an oral form of GcMAF states that "GcMAF and/or oral Colostrum MAF macrophage activation therapy is indicated in the treatment of any diseases where there is immune dysfunction or where the immune system is compromised."

In countries like Japan where GcMAF research continues, new usage applications are discovered and ongoing trails are updated. Besides cancer, the conditions listed below are appropriate new candidates to be added to the GcMAF treatment list. They include: various autoimmune diseases such as Allergies and Asthma; Epstein-Barr virus (EBV); Hepatitis B virus (HBV); Herpes Simplex virus (HSV); Cystitis; Hepatitis C virus (HCV); Multiple Sclerosis (MS); Urinary tract infection (UTI); Autism Spectrum Disorders (ASD); Rheumatoid Arthritis (RA); Endometriosis; Chronic Fatigue Syndrome (CFS); Lyme disease (Lyme borreliosis); IgA deficiency disorder; Myalgic Encephalomyelitis (ME); Mycobacteria infections; Parkinson's disease; Tuberculosis; Fibromyalgia; Human papillomavirus (HPV); Lupus (Systemic lupus erythematosus, SLE); HIV AIDS; Dengue fever; Pneumonia infection; Warts caused by viral infection; Norovirus; Malaria Influenza virus (flu); Q fever (Coxiella burnetii); Polycystic ovary syndrome (PCOS); Chicken Pox (varicella zoster virus); Psoriasis; Respiratory tract infections; Ulcerative Colitis; Crohn's disease; Type 1 diabetes (T1DM); insulin-dependent diabetes (IDDM); and the Type 1.5 diabetes or Latent Autoimmune Diabetes of Adults (LADA).

Most of the pathogens, diseases, viruses and ailments listed above are currently being treated with antibiotics, but now it is known that heavy antibiotic use also contributes to damaging one's inner terrain, especially the beneficial gut bacteria that is needed for good digestion and immune response It has been said that for every human illness there

10 Elizabeth, Erin, "Unintended Holistic Doctor Death Series: Over 100 Dead." https://www.healthnutnews.com/recap/

is a plant which is the cure. GcMAF treatment has no adverse effects, as the body produces it naturally, all the while people taking GcMAF supplements will break down the remaining nagalase and help them strengthen their immune system. But no allopathic doctor will admit that, unless they also practice homeopathic medicine. Plus, the FDA has outlawed the sale of GcMAF in the USA, and has now made obtaining it from overseas very difficult. Hopefully this will change.

GcMAF doesn't actually cure cancer, of course—it merely provides the ammunition needed by the body's own immune system to eradicate and cure cancer itself, naturally. This breakthrough represents a threat to the pharmaceutical industry, which profits to the tune of billions of dollars annually peddling quackery like chemotherapy and radiation, both of which have been shown to be toxic and cause even more cancer. After all, there are nearly eight million cancer deaths in the USA per year with no industry cure forthcoming, because treating the symptoms remains a very lucrative medical practice.

WE ARE ENERGY

Experiments conducted at the HeartMath Institute have found a person's emotional state is communicated as a frequency throughout the body via the heart's electromagnetic field. The mission of the nonprofit institute is to help people bring their physical, mental and emotional systems into balanced alignment with their heart's intuitive guidance. We all know the rhythmic beating patterns of our heart changes significantly as we experience different emotions. Negative emotions, such as anger or fear, are associated with an erratic, disordered, incoherent pattern in the heart's rhythms. In contrast, positive emotions, such as love or appreciation, are associated with a smooth, ordered, coherent pattern in the heart's rhythmic activity. In turn, these changes in the heart's beating patterns create corresponding changes in the structure of the electromagnetic field radiated by the heart, measurable by a technique called spectral analysis.[11]

Remarkable evidence indicates that the heart's electromagnetic field can transmit information between individuals. It is currently possible to measure an exchange of heart energy between people up to two meters apart. One person's brain waves can actually synchronize to another person's heart, and vice versa. The results of these experiments have led researchers to infer that the nervous system acts as an "antenna," which is tuned into and responsive with the electromagnetic fields produced by the hearts of other individuals. This capacity for exchange of energetic information is an innate ability that heightens awareness and mediates important aspects of true empathy and sensitivity to others. Furthermore, this energetic communication ability can be intentionally enhanced, producing a much deeper level of nonverbal communication, understanding, and connection between complete strangers. The heart field interactions also occur between people and animals. In short, energetic communication development via the heart field facilitates and will expand telepathic consciousness in relation to our social world.

In the end, we each have an übermind connected to an immortal soul, and each one of us has profound untapped powers. Once understood and developed, our new sense of perception will be able to protect all that's important to us and propel us into the Golden Age. Thousands of case histories of near-death experiences, reincarnation and similar phenomena provide ample evidence that we are eternal beings. Humanity's greatest breakthrough is when we come to know that we've existed before this life, and each of us will continue to exist after this life.

---

11 Institute of HeartMath: https://www.heartmath.com

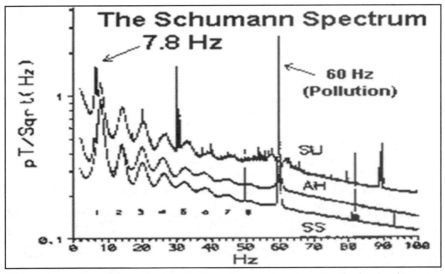

We've all experienced that refreshing feeling when out in nature. Our bodies tend to naturally relax. We experience greater peace and balance. We feel renewed. That's because, in nature, our bodies become entrained with the Schumann Resonance. This brings us into our optimum state, both physically and spiritually. *Dharma*, the principle of cosmic order, is essentially each individual's life purpose.

A peak experience in nature is walking around barefoot. It is called "earthing" or "grounding." The reason you need to be barefoot is because the soles of your shoes are made from rubber—they block the Schumann resonance because rubber doesn't conduct electricity. Ideally, its best to walk barefoot in wet grass or wet sand because water has a high electrical conductivity. Cymatics has determined that our emotional state can affect the physical world. Our heart generates an electromagnetic field that reaches two meters outside of our physical bodies.

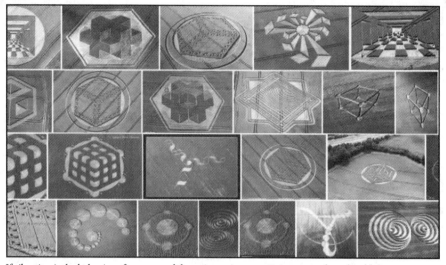

If vibration is the behavior of energy, and the universe is energetic in nature, then shouldn't we see geometry (the signature of vibration) in the energy of the Earth? Perhaps these are what the patterns of crop circles are based upon? Among these grids is the Becker-Hagens planetary grid. The 12 points of this grid were plotted originally by Ivan Sanderson, who identified areas on Earth where anomalous activity frequently occurred, such as weird geomagnetic activity and marine and aircraft disappearances.

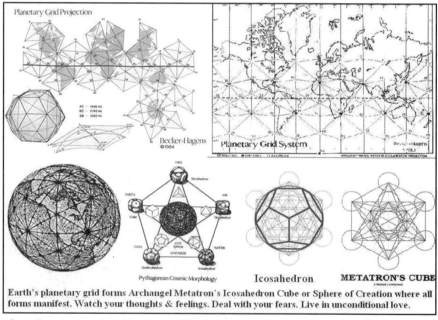

Earth's planetary grid forms Archangel Metatron's Icosahedron Cube or Sphere of Creation where all forms manifest. Watch your thoughts & feelings. Deal with your fears. Live in unconditional love.

After discovering that there were 12 main areas where many anomalous activities seemed to be occurring (such as the Bermuda Triangle and the Dragon's Triangle in Japan), Ivan Sanderson then noticed that they were also equidistant from one another. When he connected all of these points together with the global tetrahedron lines (called ley lines), he then constructed what was a perfect icosahedron. Russian scientists Goncharov, Morozov and Makarov found that when they took this icosahedron and flipped it inside out into the dodecahedron, and then plotted these new points on the planetary grid with the original 12 points of the original icosahedron, they had a worldwide grid plotting practically every major monolithic structure around the globe.

This picture depicts the "Old Dragon's Head" where the Great Wall of China meets the ocean. The Great Pyramid, Stonehenge, the *moai* heads at Easter Island, the sun and moon pyramids in Mexico, and most ancient mystical sites, churches, temples, henges (ring-shaped structures in the ground) and burial sites were all built along the Earth's ley lines. In fact, over 4,000 sites of historical and spiritual significance were found on this grid. The Irish called these "fairy paths." Germans called them "holy lines." Greeks called them "the sacred roads of Hermes." The Chinese called them "dragon currents." Many other cultures also claimed they could even see these lines and build roads and buildings on them accordingly. Even Plato spoke about this in his work, *Timaeus,* and explains the grid as the synthesis of the platonic solids that constitute "the ideal body of cosmos."

The term "Chinese pyramids" refers to pyramidal shaped structures in China, most of which are ancient mausoleums and burial mounds built to house the remains of several early Chinese emperors and their imperial relatives. About 38 of them are located about 25-35 km northwest of Xi'an, on the Qin Chuan Plains in Shaanxi Province. The most famous is the Mausoleum of the First Qin Emperor, northeast of Xi'an and 1.7 km west of where the Terracotta Warriors were found.

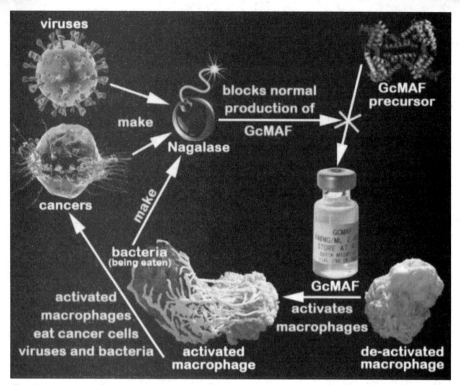

GcMAF re-starts the immune system and allows the body to heal itself. It is naturally oc-curring, or it can be introduced and with no toxic side effects. In a surprise twist, GcMAF treatment is bringing 25% of autistic children out of autism, and when combined with other autistic protocols there is much hope for these children to recover. GcMAF is also helping with a range of other ailments including Alzheimer's, arthritis, and possibly Parkinson's disease. The reason it works with so many ailments is because it is not about the illness, but about the patient's lack of health—and GcMAF "switches health back on again." It is expen-sive and now it is hard to get, but GcMAF is very powerful and very fast acting.

This historic image shows the unpacking of the Statue of Liberty head, delivered to NYC on June 17, 1885. The base of the Statue of Liberty is a star polygon of 11 vertices and the golden rectangle. In geometry, a hendecagram is a star polygon that has eleven vertices. Looking deeper, geometry is the basic behavior of vibration, and vibration is the nature of the universe. "Sacred geometry" is incorporated in many of the great monuments around the world and governs the structure and layout of the natural physical universe.

THE BIOTERRAIN

"If people let the government decide what foods they eat
and what medicines they take, their bodies will soon be in
as sorry a state as the souls who live under tyranny."
–Thomas Jefferson (1778)

GERM theory is an immensely powerful belief system in Western countries, affecting everyday interactions from touching a door handle, all the way up the chain to national vaccination agendas and global eradication campaigns. But what if fundamental research on what exactly these "pathogens" are and how they infect us, has not yet even been performed? What if much of what is assumed and believed about the danger of microbes, particularly viruses, has completely been undermined in light of radical new discoveries in microbiology? Groundbreaking research indicates that nearly everything we once believed about the purportedly deadly properties of the flu virus and COVID-19 may be based on institutionalized superstition and myth.

The modern Western medicine model is based mostly on the "germ theory" of microbes invading our bodies and causing disease, thus creating the need for a war against microbes to eliminate them and conquer all diseases. But is this assumption correct? Could we actually be weakening our immune systems with our "war" on germs? For example, if a person with allergies is most likely low in vitamins and minerals—even at a low level in what is termed as "normality." Fulvic minerals have been known to take care of the issue alone. But it could also be a diet full of processed foods, and the pasteurization of dairy foods. Also, vaccines taken as a preventive measure have been shown to create entirely new autoimmune disorders.

But if it is a war on microbes, then what about non-toxic homeopathic remedies? It has been proven that many viruses may be defeated simply by taking high doses of Vitamin

C alone. Add to the mix colloidal silver, selenium, MMS (Master Mineral Supplement) and iodine to boost the immune system's effectiveness in destroying pathogens on the spot. Once a person has a fully-functioning immune system, they could be "immune" walking through a Leper colony kissing and hugging infectious people and be just fine. If the germ theory were true medical doctors would be dropping like flies. Clearly achieving optimum health is all about regular exercise, a good diet, and basic cleanliness and not about the viruses we're exposed to on a daily basis.[1]

THE INNER TERRAIN MODEL

Everyone has heard of the French chemist Louis Pasteur (1822-1895). He is considered the father of the "Germ Theory of Medicine," and he invented the process of pasteurization. Pasteur repeatedly cautioned that "germs cause illness" and we have to attack the microbes. Amidst a group of physicians and scientists, Claude Bernard (1813-1878) countered Pasteur by saying it was the bioterrain that is important to focus upon, not the germ, and then to prove his point drank down a glass of water filled with cholera and didn't get sick at all. There are not many scientists who are willing to risk their lives on a theory. Claude Bernard, MD, has few equals in the history of medicine. Bernard went so far as to exclaim that "the germ is nothing—the inner terrain is *all*." In other words, any benign or, more likely, helpful microbes which actually exist in our bodies and outnumber our cells, when engulfed with some sort of imbalance, low pH, chronic inflammation or toxic environmental influence change into less desirable guests within our inner terrain, of which our immune system is a part and not the whole.

Twentieth century medicine was heavily influenced by the debate triumph of a man whose name has been famous and celebrated, but that we know today was at least partly a fraud. Louis Pasteur, the so-called "Father of the Germ Theory of Disease" admitted on his deathbed that Claude Bernard had been right all along, but he forbade his family to publish the documents that would have proved the rumor true. Upon the death of Pasteur's grandson in 1975, 10,000 pages of laboratory notes became public—and it became clear that an entire century of medical history would have been different had the facts been presented as we know them now. Just think of the consequences if everyone knew that Louis Pasteur, who originated the germ theory of disease on which vaccines are predicated, had capitulated on his death bed to his biggest critics, including Antoine Béchamp, when he made the statement "It's not the *germ*, it's the *terrain*!" Béchamp had reported to Pasteur that his experiments injecting healthy animals with sick animal's blood proved nothing, simply because it poisoned the experimental animal's terrain, hence allowing the germs to attack the diseased tissues caused by the poisoning. The wrong person was remembered by history, maybe because there is so much money to be made in vaccines and so little in immune system boosting with no need for drugs. Yet our overall health has decreased even while our lifespans have increased. Imagine how long we could live if our immune systems were fully supported throughout our lifetimes.[2]

PASTEUR RECANTS

When Pasteur was on his deathbed he finally admitted "the terrain is all," and "it's the terrain, not the germ." But no one listened, saying he was raving mad delusional as he was dying, and these final statements of his were ignored. This story is recounted in a real eye-opening article called *The Lost History of Medicine*, which also highlights the work of Antoine Béchamp who has been expunged from medical history. Claude Bernard, professor at the Sorbonne and member of the Academy of

1 Bens, Charles K., Ph.D. "Why detoxification is important." https://www.nexusnewsfeed.com/article/health-healing/why-detoxification-is-important

2 Béchamp, Antoine, *The Blood and its Third Anatomical Element*. Originally published in 1912, republished by Kessinger Publishing, LLC, 2010.

Science, also concurred that the "terrain" was everything. Neither men, Béchamp the scientist, Bernard the physiologist, or Pasteur the chemist, denied the existence of microorganisms. The only question was how the organisms behaved and whether or not they invade from outside as Pasteur proposed, or are mainly life forms that behave in different ways depending upon the circumstances, including being benign. Some microorganisms may not be pathogenic in certain conditions.[3]

If this theory had been accepted, the curriculum in medical schools would have been different as would have been the strategies for treating illness. Medicine would have sought relief for suffering by healing the patient rather than attempting to destroy the disease. So there stood Western medicine at this great fork in the road, and ultimately it chose to go with Pasteur. And so began our war against the germs that supposedly plague us. But does this cure us?

It's unfair to discount Pasteur entirely because his other discoveries were important. He led others to introduce sterilization, disinfection, the process of pasteurization, vaccines, and eventually antibiotics. However, Bernard said basically that germs do not cause disease. And there are other scientists and medical practitioners who have not agreed with the germ theory's dogma that assigns microbes as agents of death that should be feared at the expense of other aspects of health.

In the late 19th century, around the time that Pasteur made his questionable claim that germs "out there" cause disease, German biologist Dr. Rudolf Virchow, known as the "Father of Modern Pathology," made this statement, which is included in Robert O. Young's book *Sick and Tired:* "If I could live my life all over again, I would devote it to proving that germs seek their natural habitat—diseased tissue—rather than being the cause of that diseased tissue; e.g., mosquitoes seek the stagnant water, but do not cause the pool to become stagnant." Dr. Young shows us a history that has been edited out of our medical texts, and removed for good reason. If we were to acknowledge these lost discoveries, nearly everything we assume about Western medicine today would need to be rewritten.[4]

DISEASE IS NOT CAUSED BY GERMS

Simply because of Pasteur's own ambitions and political favoritism from the French hierarchy at the time, his germ theory took center stage from all other theories of disease. Pasteur's "one germ for one disease" concept turned out to be highly profitable for the soon-to-rise pharmaceutical industry, and this model controls contemporary Western medicine to this day.

Despite widespread acceptance of Pasteur's germ theory, a significant number of scientists accepted the pleomorphism theory that microbes could change from being helpful or benign, to being pathogenic according to their immediate organic environment or inner terrain. *Pleo* meaning many and *morph* meaning form or body. Indeed, the terrain was the key, but many have erroneously regarded the terrain as the immune system itself, which only kicks in when health fails. The proper terrain alone was, by itself, enough for perfect health, and the immune system was merely a backup system that took over when the terrain failed. "There has also been a lot of excitement about the role bacteria may play in improving the effectiveness of immunotherapy," says Grace Chen, M.D., an associate professor of hematology/oncology at Michigan Medicine and member of the Rogel Cancer Center. "This work suggests it may be a double-edged sword—and that promoting T cell exhaustion is something researchers need to watch out for." Some types of gut bacteria are better than others at stimulat-

3   *The Lost History of Medicine:* **http://www.whale.to/a/lost_history_of_medicine.html**
4   Young, Robert O., PhD, DSc, and Shelly Redford Young, *Sick and Tired? Reclaim Your Inner Terrain,* Woodland Pub., USA 2000.

ing certain immune cells, specifically CD8+ T cells, in the body, and normally help protect the body against cancer, but can be over-stimulated.[5]

The crux of the terrain-based argument is that microbes change depending on the environment in which they exist. The school of medicine that derives from this theory accepts pleomorphism rather than the static view of microorganisms that prevailed in the 20th century. Pleomorphists study live blood rather than blood that has been stained and fixed for use in electron microscopes. Bernard was indeed correct by stating "the terrain is everything" and he also stated, "the immune system was merely a backup system that took over when the terrain failed." Consider the diseases Amyotrophic Lateral Sclerosis (ALS), Multiple Sclerosis, Alzheimer's, Crohn's Disease, Lupus, Cancer, Fibromyalgia, Diabetes, and their incredible upward ramp on the charts of those affected. We have failed to maintain our terrain by both neglecting it and poisoning it with our modern way of life. There is a new theory that cancer including Leukemia may actually begin as a fungus. The debate about Pleomorphism is whether germs "get in," or are they simply made inside our body when the conditions are right.

THE CANCER HOAX

Dr. Otto Heinrich Warburg discovered the cause of cancer in 1923 and received the Nobel Prize for his work. His research concluded that no disease, including cancer, can exist in an alkaline body. What's more, we need to understand that tumors form to save our lives. When the human body is full with toxins and acidosis the person is basically going to die of that poison—our bodies build a bag and collect all the poison from your body into this bag, which is called a tumor. So, the body did all the work. And doctors think they need to do a needle biopsy, and pinch into this highly toxic tumor, which then explodes and pours all the poison into the body. And then they suggest the patient has a very fast growing, very aggressive form of cancer. But they gave it to you. They created it.[6]

And most cancers disappear on their own anyway, because about 7-10 times, everybody has cancer in their lifetimes. If you don't become unlucky enough to fall into the hands of a medical professional and get a test done and they tell you that you have something bad going on—and the very next day, can start murdering you with chemotherapy, which is based on mustard gas. Mustard gas is forbidden after the Geneva Convention determined it to be a war chemical, but they put it into your bloodstream and radiate you to death. "Or cut you surgically—which always spreads the cancer," said Dr. Leonard Coldwell. He goes on to say:

> Cancer is not an illness—cancer is a symptom. These cancerous growths, the cell growths, whatever it might be, that we don't want in our body, is a symptom; it is not the cancer. So cutting the symptom out does not resolve your problem, at all. And that's why it reappears. Or why they kill the entire body with chemotherapy for two years. Now, anything shrinks. Your organs shrink, the brain shrinks—and the tumour shrinks. Because they dehydrate the body. So now, at the same rate as your organs are shrinking, your tumour is shrinking. Now they say "It's working. The tumour is shrinking." It's one of the biggest frauds ever.

The evidence is clear, the USA Corporation and all of its tentacles stand 100% in solidarity with Big Oil, Big Pharma, Big Banks, Big Biotech and many other corporations who are known to do harm to the population. USA Corporation stands accused of sequestering technologies that would free us from fossil fuel dependence,

5   "Good gut bacteria protect against cancers." https://www.nexusnewsfeed.com/article/health-healing/good-gut-bacteria-protect-against-cancers

6   Pearson, R.B., *Pasteur: Plagiarist, Imposter!* 1942, preface, p. vii; reprinted by Health Research, WA, USA, 1964.

but instead embarked on deliberate methods of murdering its own population and the world. Their anti-human agenda proceeds as follows:

Developing and dispersing their patented viruses (HIV to ZIKA), and legislating mandatory poisoning vis-à-vis:

a. *Poison-laced vaccines*

b. *Forced poisonous chemotherapy to the exclusion on all known proven methods to kill cancerous cells and heal the individual (Cancer Act 1939)*

c. *Forced neurotoxin additive (fluoride and others) to water which is absorbed through the skin when bathing, sprayed on food plants and drunk*

d. *Patented geo-engineering of climate which includes neurotoxin nanoparticles aerosol disbursement including: Strontium-90 (a radioactive tracer), barium, nano aluminum-coated fiberglass (known as chaff), radioactive thorium, cadmium, chromium, nickel, desiccated blood, mold spores, yellow fungal mycotoxins, ethylene dibromide, and polymer fibers (known as Morgellons)*

e. *Forced genetically altered food (scientists remove one or more genes from the DNA of another organism, such as a bacterium, virus, animal, or plant and "recombine" them into the DNA of the plant they want to alter). These Genetically Modified Organisms (GMOs) generally contain glyphosate, a.k.a. herbicide "Roundup" poison*

f. *The frequent, unethical spraying of poison on the people including herbicides, Agent Orange, mace, pepper spray, etc.*

War was already declared on We the People of Earth by the U.S. Corporation a.k.a. the Oligarch Medical Mafia. Our calls must be made to the world community that has also suffered at the hands of this same tyrannical Corporation.[7]

UNDERSTANDING THE TERRAIN

Countless studies prove that pleomorphism is correct. The conclusive studies are those involving bacteria and viruses. Researchers found bacteria appearing despite the care taken to remove it, proving that viruses can mutate into bacteria and vice versa depending on the environment. Over time, without the beneficial bacteria and proper balance in the gut, toxins, opportunistic bacteria, and parasites chisel away at the physical barrier wall and create leaky gut. Once there is an opening in the wall lining, pathogens escape from the GI, travel through the bloodstream, penetrate the blood-brain barrier, and wreak havoc on the specific function of our cells, causing any number of diseases.[8]

Researchers have determined that cancer cells are anaerobic. Whereas normal cells use oxygen, cancer cells subsist on fermentation. The location where they are is called acidic, which is why diagnostic devices such as thermography are effective. Many of these destroy tactics involve yet more heat—irradiation and its counter-part in the alternative field—hyperthermia. There have also been efforts to induce fevers deliberately using weakened bacteria such as Coley's toxins or malaria—and some have even used poisonous herbs.

Just as flies do not cause garbage, but garbage attracts flies, tumors appear to be scavengers too. There may, in fact, be several types of tumors. There may also be tumors that had the misfortune of getting caught in biological sludge. When the diseased cells present themselves under a microscope, they are as pathetic look-ing as a bird caught in an oil slick. They look and behave normally after getting a

7   World Depopulation is top NSA Agenda: Club of Rome **https://educate-yourself.org/nwo/nwopopcnsaglobal2000report10mar81.shtml**

8   Boynton, Hilary and Bracket, Mary G. *The Heal Your Gut Cookbook: Nutrient-Dense Recipes for Intestinal Health Using the GAPS Diet.* Chelsea Green Publishing, White Rive Junction, VT, 2014.

proper bath. In that regard, some homeopathic doctors have used a combination of aromatic, bitter, and sponging herbs to cleanse the human body. Aromatic herbs neutralize toxic gases and make breathing more congenial. Bitter herbs are cleansing and alkalizing. They also arrest fermentation. The sponging herbs soak up the debris. Such cleansing formulae can be used both internally and externally.

A HEALTHY BIOTERRAIN

So, what is healthy terrain? Béchamp began to describe it over two hundred years ago, but Claude Bernard explained it as consisting of the two internal factors of alkalinity and negative electrical charge. Bernard said the two factors contributing to a healthy terrain are nutrition and toxins. One must have proper nutrition and be free of toxins to maintain a healthy terrain. More recent studies add another factor contributing to a healthy terrain and that is emotions. That is, balanced mental health and stress reduction. On the issue of the body's alkalinity, we should be quoting Dr. Arthur C. Guyton MD, who wrote the *Textbook of Medical Physiology* (once used in most medical schools):

> *The first steps in maintaining health is to alkalize the body (pH or acid/alkaline balance). This is one of the most important aspects of homeostasis. Changes in pH alter virtually all body functions. ...The cells of a healthy body are alkaline while the cells of a diseased body are below a pH of 7.0. The more acidic the cell, the sicker we become. If the body cannot alkalize the cells they will become acidic and thus, disease sets in. Our bodies produce acid as a by-product of normal metabolism. Since our bodies do not manufacture alkalinity, we must supply the alkalinity from an outside source to keep us from becoming acidic and dying.*

Quite simply, we live in a toxic society. Our food, water, soil and air are polluted. Additionally, we are poisoning ourselves with drugs, alcohol, smoking, and even the way we cook our foods, such as barbecuing and microwaving. Also, nearly every drug an allopathic doctor prescribes will cause the body to become more acidic. Every can of soda, every cup of coffee, every teaspoon of sugar, every piece of chicken, steak, or pork consumed causes the body to become acidic. Disease begins when our alkaline tissues turn acidic and when our negative energy charge turns positive. The trick is to balance the acidity in the body with an alkaline state, as described in the companion book to this, *Modern Esoteric: Beyond Our Senses.*[9]

THE MANUFACTURED VIRUS

Acquired Immunodeficiency Syndrome, or AIDS, was first "discovered" in 1981 in New York City. The cause was unknown, but diagnosed victims were chiefly from drug abuse users and homosexual men, hence its original name the "gay disease."

But where did it come from? On July 17th 1983, an anonymous New York scientist claimed AIDS was created by a Pentagon bioweapon's program. He said there was evidence that AIDS was spliced together at Fort Detrick by U.S scientists using viruses gathered from Africa and Latin America. Then in 1984, dermatologist Alan Cantwell contributed to the charge that AIDS was created by the CIA to target gay men, and originated in 1978 hepatitis B vaccine trials conducted in New York. In 1986, German scientist Jacob Segal concluded that AIDS was engineered by the U.S government in 1978, and was tested on inmates who spread it to the larger population. African politicians accuse the CIA of creating AIDS and testing the incurable bioweapon in Africa.

The CIA refutes the accusation, and said the original claim of AIDS being human-made were actually part of operation "INFEKTION." Their contention was INFEKTON was a disinformation campaign by the KGB which aimed to foster worldwide

9   Olsen, Brad, *Modern Esoteric: Beyond Our Senses.* CCC Publishing, 2018.

anti-Americanism. The World Health Organization says AIDS probably originated as a simian virus in Africa.

Who's right, and who's wrong? As any good investigator will apply *cui bono* or "who benefits," and simply follow the money. Beyond the profit motive in providing expensive drugs or vaccines, there is also an "anti-human" depopulation agenda to drastically reduce the global human population. Some UFO researchers have said all virus strains have been introduced on Earth by malevolent ETs in an attempt to weaken and cull the herd. They say there was a time on Earth many thousands of years ago when no virus strains existed.

COVID-19 VIRUS AND 5G

Coronaviruses are a myriad of different types of viruses that typically affect the respiratory tract of mammals, including humans. They are associated with the common cold, pneumonia, and Severe Acute Respiratory Syndrome (SARS) and can also affect the gut. Signs of COVID-19 are fever and symptoms of respiratory illness, such as coughing, difficulty breathing or shortness of breath. However, it has been reported that some carriers of this strain of Coronavirus show no respiratory symptoms at all. This makes it extremely difficult to detect carriers of the virus, taking into account that health officials are looking for respiratory symptoms such as coughing, sneezing and breathing difficulties. Another report said some carriers have no fever and no coughing, but instead are exhibiting symptoms of diarrhea, vomiting and chest pains.[10]

COVID-19 biotechnology was tested several times over the last 40 years before it was released as a bioweapon in 2019. The first versions of ebola were hemorrhaging and killed people too quickly. The second versions of SARS didn't spread fast enough. The third versions, completely synthetic and based on highly mutagenic coronaviruses, was a combination of all of the above, using the outer shell of the SARS virus, while splicing the interior—the HIV (retrovirus/embedded into a person's RNA/TB fungal additions) to become airborne, spreading very quickly, and replicates through the lungs. The reason it has a high recovery rate is that the long-term goal here, after the initial wave of causalities/eugenics and economic collapse, is a genetic mutation of the human genome.

Coronavirus is a highly contagious and deadly virus that is put on super-steroids whenever and wherever they flip the switch on 5G, all the while amping up the flu vaccination programs, and chemtrailing overhead with toxin-laden aerosols that further trigger influenza symptoms. How it reacts with a person's blood is by depleting oxygen levels and thus exacerbating the upper respiratory system problems. The "corona aspect" of this virus is directly related to one of the greatest silent killers of the modern age—the generation and conveyance of electricity used to power the entire planet. There are multiple instances where the production and conveyance of electrical energy create a "corona" in high-voltage systems.

The Chinese were all given mandatory vaccines in the fall of 2019. The vaccine contained replicating, digitized and controllable RNA which were activated by 60Ghz 5G mm waves that were just turned on in Wuhan (as well as all other Countries using 60Ghz 5G) with the "smart dust" that everyone on the globe has been inhaling through chemtrails. That's why when they say someone is "cured," the "virus" can be "digitally" reactivated at any time and the person can literally drop dead. The Diamond Princess cruise ship ported in Japan was specifically equipped with 60Ghz 5G. It's basically remote assassination.

Americans are currently breathing in this "smart" dust through chemtrails, and now some are required by their employers to be vaccinated. Think of it like this: add the

10 Ashley, Dana. "Covid-19, Wuhan and 5G." https://www.nexusnewsfeed.com/article/health-healing/covid-19-wuhan-and-5g

combination of vaccines, chemtrails (smart dust) and 5G and your body becomes internally digitized and can be remotely controlled. People's bluetooth devices are picking up codes from people who've received multiple vaccine shots. No need for an RFID chip implant! A person's organ functions can be stopped remotely if one is deemed non-compliant. Wuhan was a test run for ID2020. The elite call this 60Ghz 5G mm wave the "V" wave (Virus) to mock us. President Trump created the Space Force in part to combat this weaponized technology. We need to vehemently reject the attempted "mandatory vaccine" issue because our lives depend on it.

Is COVID-19 truly a viral virus, or is it enhanced with 5G? China has unleashed 60Ghz all throughout the country with Wuhan as the pilot "Smart City." Unbelievable comparisons to symptoms "showing" as a virus compared to what happens when one is hit with 60Ghz waves, and its impact on the uptake of oxygen via the hemoglobin. This specific frequency is absorbed by oxygen. 60Ghz causes the rotation of the electrons around the oxygen molecule to spin, thus inhibiting the ability of hemoglobin to properly uptake into these oxygen molecules. What's especially horrifying about the critical care of coronavirus patients is that they aren't suffering from "viral pneumonia," but rather from an inability to absorb or carry oxygen in the blood. This has been confirmed by NYC ICU emergency physician Cameron Kyle-Sidell, who has released several videos detailing how coronavirus is not a kind of viral pneumonia. "We're treating the wrong disease," he says. And the ventilators are damaging the lungs of patients. He explains:

> COVID-19 lung disease, as far as I can see, is not a pneumonia and should not be treated as one. Rather, it appears as some kind of viral-induced disease most resembling high altitude sickness. It is as if tens of thousands of my fellow New Yorkers are on a plane at 30,000 feet and the cabin pressure is slowly being let out. These patients are slowly being starved of oxygen.

We think we've caught the COVID-19 flu when really it is mimicking radiation sickness with similar symptoms. Wuhan turned on their 5G towers which attacks oxygen and water molecules creating bacteria-friendly environments in the terrain. Virus symptoms are the same as 5G sickness, but they want us to inject their vaccinations. That is the Hegelian Dialectic of problem, reaction and solution. But vaccines are unnecessary with the COVID-19 treatment of hydroxychloroquine, which has been around since 1955 and is approved for lupus, malaria, and a few other illnesses.[11]

THE VACCINE TRAP

There is no evidence to support the germ theory on which all of allopathic medicine is based, including vaccines. There are no scientific research papers proving that any germ, viral or bacterial, causes any disease. Yet the establishment Big Pharma still pushes for more vaccines. What they fail to recognize is that "diseases" are caused by the body's natural defense mechanism—the immune system—in reaction to exposure to poisons and toxins, not germs.

Pandemics are also intentionally started with bioweapons. Problem, reaction and solution is the perfect way to introduce new vaccines for profit. EbolaGate was a vaccine-inducement/bioweapon false flag attack strategy. The basic premise was first to start an ebola "outbreak," followed by an inducement campaign to distribute vaccines which themselves were genetic bioweapons. Ebola like several others was rolled out in West African countries where local immune systems and health profiles were already compromised, there are unsanitary conditions, little public health care, and martial law quarantines for mass infection can easily be imposed. Instead of being treated with

11 Adams, Mike, "Can 5G exposure alter the structure and function of hemoglobin, causing coronavirus patients to die from oxygen deprivation?" *Natural News* April 6, 2020.

known Vitamin C and immune system treatments, local populations were instead given ineffective medicine, or worse, vaccine treatments that were themselves bioweapons.

The scenario here, led by World Health Organization, was to covertly maximize infection rates and vector propagation. The scenario was aimed at creating a base for an African bioweapons genocide, long sought because of the mineral, oil and gas wealth of Africa. There is the example of the U.S. Rangers infecting the South Africa population with the AIDS virus, embedded in the smallpox vaccine in the mid-1990s. West Africa countries provided the jumping-off point for the ebola viruses and their traveling via air travel, sea travel, land, to Europe, India, Asia, and North and South America. In North America, there awaits a sophisticated false flag machine led by WHO-CDC (Nazi-CIA) and martial law regulations signed by George Bush I & II, Clinton, and Obama that can mandate FEMA incarceration and mass vaccinations that maim or kill as part of the depopulation agenda. These plans materialized in 2020 with the COVID-19 quarantine lockdown.

The WHO and CDC were complicit in triggering the Ebola and COVID-19 pandemics. It should be noted that the CDC is a for-profit corporation listed on Dun and Bradstreet, and they hold the patent on ebola. They will make money off royalties for every vaccine sold, so they aren't trying to stop their for-profit viruses, they're trying to trigger a pandemic. So is the DoD. It should be noted that the DoD, CDC, and the vaccine manufacturers triggered the outbreak in Sierra Leone via a DoD run bioweapons lab located there. In Sierra Leone, the first people to get ebola got it from Red Cross vaccinations.

Ebola and AIDS were both intentionally created and deployed as biological weapons in various African countries intended to cull the human herd. They were manufactured in the bioweapons lab at Fort Detrick, Maryland. COVID-19 was developed in North Carolina, but was exported to Wuhan, China where it was deployed on the population in 2019. The CDC and the WHO were hyping the "deadly H1N1 Swine Flu pandemic" in the summer of 2009. They were, of course, also urging people to take the new Swine Flu vaccine.[12]

VACCINE CHOICE

If vaccines are so "safe and effective" then why are pharmaceutical companies given blanket immunity from prosecution for damages they may cause? And why should a fully-vaccinated child be in any danger from a non-vaccinated child? There are so many aspects of the mandatory vaccine program that make no sense.

Hundreds of millions of dollars have been spent to pay for the care of just some of those damaged by vaccinations—but only by the National Vaccine Injury Compensation Program that was created to place the burden of ruining victim's lives onto the taxpayer. A couple of examples are that over 800 children across Europe suffered severe brain damage from the Swine Flu vaccine and the UK government agreed to pay $90 million in compensation as part of a vaccine injury settlement.[13]

Dr. Rima Laibow, medical editor, activist, author and film producer, wrote a detailed response to Australian journalist Claire Harvey's claim in *the Daily Telegraph* that those who oppose forced vaccinations are "baby killers." Dr. Laibow called out several "cold, hard facts" that refute many of the myths used to persuade people to take the injections for themselves and their kids.

She notes that Dr. Andrew Wakefield (a falsely discredited British physician) did not say that MMR (measles, mumps, and rubella) vaccine causes autism. He said that 12 autistic children had the same virus that was in the vaccine in their GI tracts, a finding that has been replicated by others.

12 Ebola and vaccine false flags: **https://hollywoke.wordpress.com/corona-virus/**
13 Horowitz, Leonard DMD, MPH (Harvard). *AIDS & Ebola, Nature, Accident, or Intentional?"* Healthy World Dist. 1996.

Dr. Laibow cites evidence that the books have been repeatedly cooked over vaccines and mercury. When the data, the actual science, not the cover up, politicized make-believe science is examined, the results are absolutely clear: Yes, vaccines, with or without mercury, cause a host of ills, including autism. Mercury, as a recent highly credible MIT study showed, is not the only heavy metal culprit: aluminum, with which vaccines are adjuvanted, causes serious brain damage and other types of organ failure as well. Vaccines that do not contain mercury are washed with thimerosal, leaving a residue of biological significance. Mercury, or course, is a known neurotoxin.

The Council on Foreign Relations recently released a detailed study on national health status around the world. They showed conclusively that the more vaccinated a nation is, the worse the health of its people in terms of chronic degenerative disease and the higher the infant mortality rate. Dr Laibow notes under U.S. law, and similarly in Australia, a vaccine *must*, by statute, be shown to be *both* safe *and* effective before it can be deployed. The number of vaccines which have been shown to be *either* safe or effective is a shocking zero. That's right. Only one placebo controlled, double blind study of vaccines, in this case, the flu vaccine, has *ever* been done. The results? People who got the vaccine were not protected against the flu and were, in fact, nearly five times as likely as non-vaccinated or placebo recipients, to have serious complications, pneumonia, hospitalizations and other major consequences, including death.[14]

So how could it be that vaccinated people can infect others? Indeed, the New York City measles outbreak a couple of years ago was due entirely to vaccinated people shedding viruses and infecting other vaccinated people. In China, where virtually every single member of the society is fully vaccinated, measle outbreaks occur regularly. In South Korea where pertussis vaccination is a mandated procedure with 97% coverage of the population, pertussis deaths have more than tripled since the achievement of full population coverage and those who contract pertussis are sicker and have more complications than was seen before vaccination was implemented. Billionaire and vaccine-advocate Bill Gates says the whole world needs to be vaccinated against COVID-19 before we can be allowed to travel overseas or gather in public again.

VACCINES CAN DO THE OPPOSITE

The stimulated antibody response of vaccines is now known to be mostly ineffective, an outdated preventative measure and at best an inexact science. Having a small injection laced with the very disease it is meant to provide immunity for is a flawed and inaccurate science. This might explain the fact that vaccines actually do not prevent disease but actually foster their spread. The American woman who was the first to die of measles in 12 years turned out to have been already vaccinated against measles!

Vaccine manufacturers add "adjuvants" to their products which are crude extracts of mycobacteria, toxins such as aluminum salts, heavy metals like mercury, formaldehyde, or mineral oils. The reasoning is the adjuvants will force the reluctant immune system into attack mode, but it doesn't always work out that way. Celebrated Yale immunologist Charles Janeway called this mentality the "immunologist's dirty little secret" underlying vaccinations. Dr. Darja Kanduc is a biochemist at the University of Bari in Italy, and explains how "adjuvants expand, potentiate, and increase immune responses. Such hyperactivation has a price: the loss of specificity. The hyper-stimulated immune system does not discriminate any more between foreign proteins and self-proteins. Adjuvants render the immune system blind. Human proteins that share peptide sequences will be attacked." Kanduc likens immuno-tolerance to a protective wall, by stating "the dam is demolished by the adjuvants and the cross-reactivity flood can crush and alter human proteins." This might also cause numerous cross-

14 Sacred Medicine Sanctuary: http://www.cancersalves.com/articles/physiological_terrain.html

reactions, manifested as a wide variety of autoimmune attacks. Dr. Russell Blaylock describes in detail how the adjuvants in some vaccines apparently can also lead to depression and neurodegeneration, especially for people over the age of 50.

The overriding principle behind receiving vaccines is to simulate the natural "herd immunity" acquired by a community's contact with a disease. Yet the evidence that vaccines work as prescribed every time is lacking. Historians know that sanitation, hygiene, quarantine, water filtration, and better nutrition are the leading reasons for the eradication and control of almost all diseases, leading to drastic reductions in mortality. All of the major reductions in disease mortality happened *before* vaccines were introduced as a result of these methods and interventions in living conditions, and moreover, there were some diseases whose mortality rates dropped in parallel, and yet there was no vaccine even developed yet, suggesting vaccines have been given a lot of undue credit, where credit was *not* due.

In reality, vaccines have succeeded in creating a rash of new diseases and unnecessary harm, a fact which is actively suppressed by the medical mafia "authorities." There has been an uptick of new cases of encephalitis, paralysis, developmental delays, dozens of autoimmunity disorders, genetic damage, and the list goes on. Who benefits when films like *VAXXED* get censored? Why do they criticize anyone who asks legitimate questions, as they promote a cult-like ideology and social movement that promotes blind acquiescence over and above critical thinking and investigation? After all, why should a vaccinated person care if someone is not? They should be protected, right? No authority has the right to mandate vaccines on anyone without their informed consent.

COMING FULL CIRCLE

Many doctors are beginning to return to the basics, and now understand that both health and disease almost always start in the gut. They also realize that the intestinal tract has to be healthy for the body to fully heal from any disease. If a person has an overgrowth of candida, they will soon be suffering from a damaged intestinal wall that allows proteins, sugars, yeast, fungus, bacteria and other microbes to escape the intestines to enter the bloodstream. This is the "leaky gut syndrome," which has been exploding in cases over the last few decades. Once these substances escape into the bloodstream, the immune system identifies them as foreign and activates to attack them. Once candida escapes the digestive system through holes left in an irritated digestive lining, it spreads throughout the body, and once in the blood, it switches from a yeast to a fungus, and can invade every organ and system.

Doctors are finding an association between pathogenic candida gut flora and congestive heart disease. Dr. Joseph Mercola illustrates how fungus is being found to accompany such conditions as endometriosis and linked to the formation of cancer. Suffice it to say that systemic candida could be behind or accompanying nearly every chronic disease that is being diagnosed in this modern age. One solution is Lufenuron, which is one of the safest treatments for candida available today.

The typical American "starch" diet is largely to blame, as candida loves nothing more than sugar, alcohol, bread, coffee, pasta, greasy or pre-packaged refined foods to grow and multiply. These foods lack nutrition, while upsetting the balance of the gut. A healthy immune system should be able to keep candida at bay, but a diet rich in sugar can actually depress your immune system, leaving your body vulnerable, and allowing the candida to proliferate.

Humans did not live on processed or fast foods in their evolutionary past. A person should endeavor to maintain a healthy diet of mostly raw, organic vegetables and fruits, with good quality proteins, while entirely cutting out sugars and empty carbohydrates.

This is often easier said than done, and while adopting a quality diet can help rebalance the flora in the gut; but if there is already a significant systemic candida infection, even the best diet will not remove it. A Ketogenic Diet along with a healthy lifestyle will help to boost and strengthen the immune system and increase metabolism.

The "one germ, one disease" theory certainly seems to be a great business model for the medical-pharmaceutical industry that profits from people being ill. This is where the germ theory has taken us. Drugs cannot heal a sick terrain. Only nutrition and detoxication programs can heal our polluted terrain. The truth can be gleaned from the preface of the book *Pasteur: Plagiarist, Imposter!* "Illness is practically always due to errors of diet or manner of living, the germs being present solely as scavengers of dead and waste tissues and foods, and *not* as the cause of the disease." As we will see in the next chapter, there is a new physical invader that few people know is terraforming our bodies and compromising our well-being.[15]

Back in 1903 when this cartoon was drawn, people used to worry about electricity being bad for us. Now we have the largely untested rollout of 5G, and that is being shown to accelerate viral replication, not create viruses. According to the National Institute of Health: "The range and magnitude of potential impacts of 5G technologies are under-researched, although important biological outcomes have been reported with millimeter wavelength exposure. These include oxidative stress and altered gene expression, effects on skin and systemic effects such as on immune function. In vivo studies reporting resonance with human sweat ducts, acceleration of bacterial and viral replication, and other endpoints indicate the potential for novel as well as more commonly recognized biological impacts from this range of frequencies, and highlight the need for research before population-wide continuous exposures."

••

15 Fassa, Paul "Is There Something Wrong with the Germ Theory?" *Nexus,* (Mapleton, Australia), July-Aug., 2017.

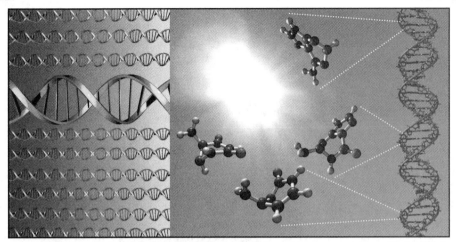

GMO and processed garbage food is known to weaken the immune system. Bad lifestyle habits can also damage the DNA. Eating GMOs can lead to organ failure, infertility, and cancer, and are genetically modifying us as GM proteins bypass digestion and go directly into our blood (as is their ultimate purpose). GMOs by their very nature are engineered to withstand massive doses of chemical and hazardous pesticides.

"The Alchemist" was painted by Sir William Fettes Douglas in the year 1853. The alchemist of today is the Western medical Big Pharma cartel which is a massive pile of fake scientific research. Like anything fake, the veneer looks authentic and leads us to believe the products are trustworthy and reputable, when in reality there are reams of biased and concocted research with peer-reviewed stamps on them to make the products appear official. Former Big Pharma reps, esteemed medical journal editors and even insider governmental scientists have all confessed the shocking truth that a large amount of the published scientific data out there is fraudulent and should not be trusted. But how did medicine become so perverse? Carl Jung observed: "In all chaos there is a cosmos, in all disorder a secret order." And big money.

Louis Pasteur is traditionally considered the "father of microbiology" because of his studies in the late 19th century that popularized the germ theory of disease, and proposed all infectious diseases could be prevented by prophylactic vaccination. As the progenitor of modern immunology, Pasteur is renowned for creating the process of pasteurization (which prevents the spoiling of many food products, but also kills good bacteria), and for changing the way that scientists create vaccines. But if the germ theory were true, there would be no one alive to believe in it!

In 2010, Bill Gates committed $10 billion to the WHO saying, "We must make this the decade of vaccines." A month later, Gates said in a TED talk that new vaccines "could reduce population." In 2014, Kenya's Catholic Doctors Association accused the WHO of chemically sterilizing millions of unwilling Kenyan women with a "tetanus" vaccine campaign. Independent labs found a sterility formula in every vaccine tested. After denying the charges, the WHO finally admitted it had been developing the sterility vaccines for over a decade. Similar accusations came from Tanzania, Nicaragua, Mexico, and the Philippines. The most frightening (polio) epidemics in Congo, Afghanistan, and the Philippines, are all linked to vaccines. In addition to using his philanthropy to control the WHO, UNICEF, GAVI and PATH, Gates funds private pharmaceutical companies that manufacture vaccines, and a massive network of pharmaceutical-industry front groups that broadcast deceptive propaganda, develop fraudulent studies, conduct surveillance and psychological operations against vaccine hesitancy and use Gates' power and money to silence dissent and coerce compliance. The same person whose father says we need to depopulate suddenly wants to save everyone with his vaccines.

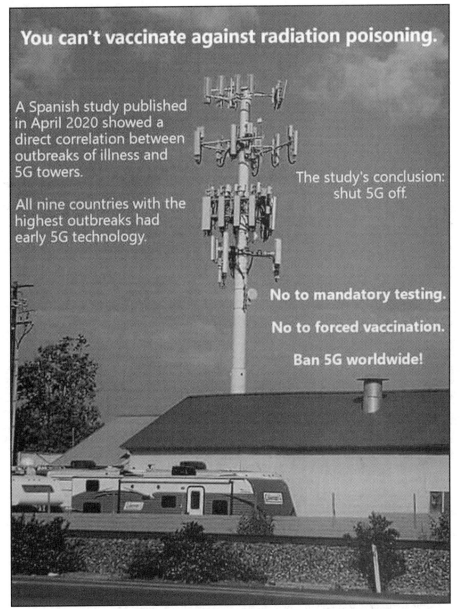

You can't vaccinate against radiation poisoning.

A Spanish study published in April 2020 showed a direct correlation between outbreaks of illness and 5G towers.

All nine countries with the highest outbreaks had early 5G technology.

The study's conclusion: shut 5G off.

No to mandatory testing.

No to forced vaccination.

Ban 5G worldwide!

Our bodies have billions of parasitic organisms inside which feed on us and some say help us live by doing many useful functions. But when these bacteria, fungi, and parasites are subjected to any WiFi microwave radiations they are harmed and begin reproducing toxins in self-defense. These organisms begin reproducing rapidly to ensure their survival. And so, we get flu-like symptoms from these internal parasite organisms under attack from WiFi microwave radiations reproducing rapidly and excreting toxins. This is the real illness people are getting, only slightly compounded from the escaped virus from China. Electromagnetic fields (EMFs) that surround us 24/7 could be interfering with our immune system function, even triggering allergic and inflammatory responses while interfering with our body's repair mechanisms. Project Camelot journalist Kerry Cassidy calls our current dilemma a "Frequency War" where silent weapons are being employed in a quiet war.

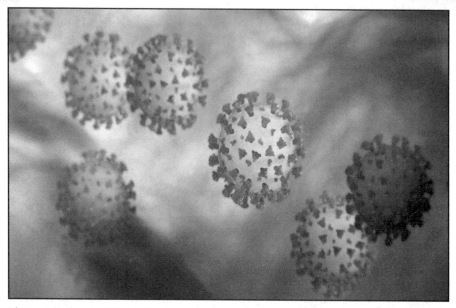

The experimental COVID-19 gene therapy "vaccine" was rolled out in December, 2020 by four large pharmaceutical companies in the USA under the Emergency Use Authorization. It was rushed to market in order to immunize people from a virus which has never been isolated by independent researchers, such as Robert O. Young. It went through no human trials, and in the animal trials that were done all the animals died within a few years from diseases stemming from compromised immune systems. All generic and safe options to treat COVID-19 such as Ivermectin and HCQ were outlawed and marginalized as "horse dewormer" or being "ineffective," when in fact they were effective. Simply using the term "natural immunity" was censored on Instagram. The spiked proteins, graphine oxide and self-assembling nanobots showing up in the Franken jabs have nothing to do with protecting people from a virus, but a depopulation bioweapon.

Top 10 reasons how COVID-19 and 5G (fifth generation cellular networks) combine to make the ultimate Bioweapon:

1. The pandemic started in Wuhan, China which is also a 5G "Smart City." 5G cellular networks are known to weaken the immune system.
2. Lack of Vitamin D makes people more vulnerable to viruses due to a weakened immune system. Geoengineering is a project (which started over three decades ago) to dim our sun by spraying the sky with toxic particles.
3. Corona and SARS are both terms connected to radiation.
4. 5G causes flu-like symptoms.
5. All cellphone frequencies open the blood brain barrier making us more vulnerable to viruses and toxins.
6. The virus has spread rapidly in areas where 5G has been deployed.
7. The coronavirus has conveniently stopped almost all worldwide political corruption protests, due to "protective" lockdowns and instructions to stay indoors, especially those in Hong Kong and France—but has given rise to Black Lives Matter and ANTIFA in the United States.
8. Bill Gates and the World Economic Forum sponsored a Coronavirus outbreak simulation called Event 201 (The 0 was a globe, so a nod to UN Agenda 21) just weeks before the virus was released.
9. China and Iran were the first and worst effected countries and they just happen to be the globalists thorn in the side.
10. The virus has been proven to be artificially engineered with a "gain of function" and has HIV markers in it, developing into AIDS.

MORGELLON NANOBOTS

"Alpha waves in the human brain are between 6 and 8 hertz. The wave frequency of the human cavity resonates between 6 and 8 hertz. All biological systems operate in the same frequency range. The human brain's alpha waves function in this range and the electrical resonance of the Earth is between 6 and 8 hertz. Thus, our entire biological system—the brain and the Earth itself—work on the same frequencies. If we can control that resonate system electronically, we can directly control the entire mental system of humankind." –Nikola Tesla

THERE is a mysterious skin disorder that has recently erupted around the world. It is showing up across the human spectrum which could very well make it a syndrome. It is commonly known as Morgellons, but it's not recognized by the allopathic medical community, so it's not yet "officially" a disease. Many physicians continue to equate people who claim to have Morgellons with a delusion of having parasites, meaning it's all in their head. People contracted with this disorder have been shown to produce a filamentous microorganism, usually via oblong black filaments embedded in the skin that Morgellons patients claim will crawl through the body.

The controversial condition called Morgellons is classified by most physicians as a "delusional parasitosis," in which people develop sores they believe to be caused by parasites, insects, or invasive synthetic fibers and scratch themselves incessantly. In 2008, the Centers for Disease Control and Prevention investigated Morgellons among patients in Northern California, a hotbed of self-reported Morgellons diagnoses, and concluded there was "no infectious cause and no evidence of an environmental link." So far, no Big Pharma company has an effective pharmaceutical remedy for treating the disease. But are they really trying? Isn't it curious that neither Morgellons nor widespread chemtrail spraying have been acknowledged by the CDC?

A strange thing happened to me in 2008 when I began writing and collecting the information for this three-part "Esoteric Series" of books. My skin began to erupt with strange filaments I would later identify as Morgellons nanobots. I have fought this bizarre skin condition for over a decade. Western dermatology had completely failed me. One of the last times I went to the dermatologist, he tried to put me on psychiatric medications, even though I had no psychiatric symptoms, nor had I ever been depressed a day in my life. However, none of the creams, lotions or any other prescription medications worked. Further, all of the natural antibiotics in the world weren't going to cure me of Morgellons because there is an invasive parasite existing both externally and internally. I had a suitable internal bioterrain allowing Morgellons to thrive, but that is changing. I will explain how I rid myself of these nanobots at the end of this chapter.

Most people interested in detoxifying the body realize by now that there are new diseases that have appeared in the past 50 years that are not natural diseases. Nature hasn't invented any new diseases; they have all been invented in laboratories and released by humans. I'm talking about HIV/AIDS, Ebola, Lyme Disease, Morgellons Disease, Hepatitis C, COVID-19 and a whole host of other diseases and pathogens to which the human race has now been subjected. Millions upon millions of people are suffering and dying from diseases created by humans. Some of these pathogens are transmitted by personal or sexual contact, but others are spread by mechanisms that are not yet understood, especially Lyme Disease and Morgellons Disease which are transmitted by unknown means. Yes, ticks are one source of Lyme Disease, but there are many people who have Lyme Disease who have never been bitten by a tick. And there are thousands who have Morgellons Disease who have no idea where it came from, but it's looking like the transmission method is through aerosol spraying of the atmosphere, as well as being placed in our food and healthcare products.

Currently, there are approximately 100,000 humans officially infected with Morgellons Disease worldwide, and that number is expected to rise exponentially. The real numbers of infections are possibly more than 10 million. People in Eastern countries have it, as do their pets, and even aquatic and terrestrial mammals are beginning to show lesions. Patients with Morgellons Disease frequently describe crawling, stinging, insect-like sensations, or sensations of "something trying to penetrate the skin from the inside out." Further inquiry revealed that most of the Morgellons patients also had bacterial co-infections, acquired probably by a fungus vector, which may transmit also bacterial or viral pathogens.[1]

THE DARK AGENDA OF SYNTHETIC BIOLOGY

The 21st century brought with it a diabolical new disease, an affliction so strange and bizarre it almost defies any possible natural cause or explanation. The first case was reported in 2001 by Mary Leitao, who put up a website describing multicolored fibers that she observed under a microscope coming from her son's skin. She named the pseudo-lifeform disease "Morgellons" because it was similar in appearance to an illustration of a skin fiber she discovered in an old medical book. Since 2001, thousands more people have shown similar signs of the affliction. Officially, the U.S. government says all of these people are crazy and they are suffering from a delu-

----

1 Morgellons – A Mundane Approach: "It's All About the Terrain." http://morgellonspgpr.wordpress.com/2009/04/20/its-all-about-the-terrain/

sion of parasites under the skin. But are they? The disease is characterized by fibers or sometimes black specks or hexagon-shaped objects emerging from skin lesions, accompanied by sensations of bugs crawling beneath the skin. The medical profession suggests the fibers are nothing more than clothing fibers.

Morgellons Disease is one of the new Technical Age Disorders, which may have its roots in genetic engineering/modification, or even Transhumanism research. Allopathic medicine has neglected to acknowledge that it even exists, claiming sufferers are delusional; but those who do have it feel it's a legitimate health problem and simply point out that, apparently, there is no known treatment. There is emerging evidence that Morgellons Disease was introduced to the human population (possibly by "design") sometime around the turn of the new millennium. It is an artificial form of life that can self-replicate and has bacterial, fungal, and living synthetic filaments to its makeup. It cannot be scratched out of the skin, because it is also alive inside the body. "Morgellons is not a disease. It is a process," according to Kandy Griffin, President of the Morgellons Research Group. "It is a form of focused/directed evolution of the human genome," Griffin continues. "It is the fetal stage of transhumanism, and it is upon us."[2]

At this point, virtually all humans have it in us, because there has been a concerted spraying program in the sky for decades. The filaments are all over the ground, they're in the soil, they're in the water, and are also appearing in our food supplies. These filaments are self-replicating nanotechnology. To many, including myself, these are the scariest words I've ever heard in my life. To test if you have it, hold organic grape juice or red wine in your mouth for five minutes and swish it around without swallowing. See what comes out. So far, of the many dozens of people with whom I have tried this, everyone has these fibers when they spit out the wine or grape juice. The filaments are coming out of the skin tissue of the cheeks and throat.

A MorgellonsCure.com researcher describes the fibers as being distributed with many different types of viruses, funguses and bacteria. It is a combination of organic and inorganic materials genetically combined to form artificial life. It's a combination of piezo-electric crystal, virus, fungus, plant and even genetically modified insects! It could be the piezo-electric crystals is technology used to monitor and track the body, rendering us as controllable hybrid bio-robots. There may not be enough evidence to draw solid, scientific conclusions at present, but the findings beneath the skin of Morgellons patients, of such things as fibrous growth forms with genes that only exist in plants has led some to speculate that what is in reality being tested is a human genetic mutation or alteration program—or possibly even a genetic weapon.[3]

One of the leading Morgellons researchers, Clifford Carnicom, believes that what's going on in the skies is not geoengineering per se, but bioengineering—or at the very least, there is a link between the two. "The problem is much bigger than we may be aware of, and this problem is extending well beyond the consideration of what we would call geoengineering by itself," Carnicom says.[4]

CHEMTRAIL DISPERSION

People have been talking about "chemtrails" since the beginning of the new millennium, watching the skies, pointing them out, taking videos and uploading the videos to the Internet—all to no avail. And the issue of Morgellons Disease has been discussed widely as well, on the Internet at any rate, and has been widely suspected to be a result of the spraying since at least the year 2006 when the first fibers

2   "From Chemtrails to Pseudo-Life: The Dark Agenda of Synthetic Biology." https://www.youtube.com/watch?v=pbnTkCTz5VI&ab_channel=ChemtrailCrimes

3   Chapala, Michael. "New Invention - New Breakthrough!" www.MorgellonsCure.co

4   "A Clash of Evidence: The Realities of Solar Radiation Management (SRM)," Clifford E. Carnicom, http://carnicominstitute.org/

were collected for sampling. But in all this time, from the earliest days of the 21st century all the way up until now, nothing has been done. The spraying simply continues. And even if the aerosols are not causing Morgellons, even if Morgellons is a wholly imagined disease (which I don't believe to be the case from my own experience) but suppose for a moment this is so—still aluminum has long been known to be neurotoxic, which means that the spraying has almost certainly contributed to the spiking rates of Alzheimer's, autism, and other neurological illnesses.

The idea of spraying aluminum into our atmosphere has a long history. Patents exist that clearly demonstrate the permissive use of such materials that include the oxides of metals which have high emissivity. These include harmful substances like aluminum oxide and thorium oxide. A classic patent example is one from the Hughes Aircraft Company that dates back to 1990, and there are others that are older. Written into the NDAA, Public Law 105-85, in November, 1997, states clearly that we can legally be sprayed with biological agents! This has been going on since the late 1990s. Is there any wonder we now have Morgellons and other exotic diseases never before known?

What's more, synthetic biology has now become the backbone of biotechnology. With advances in the field moving rapidly, we have become capable of more than just reading and editing life. Now we can, in a manner of speaking, modify or make life into something new. We now have technology that can build organs for people in need of organ transplants, or it can be used spray an unknowing population with nano-dust. In the future, we could even potentially create cyborgs using this technology.

The U.S. government has a long history of conducting medical experiments on unsuspecting populations. This includes the Tuskegee syphilis experiment in the 1930s. There were similar experiments in Guatemala in the 1940s in which some 700 people were deliberately infected with sexually-transmitted diseases in order to test the effectiveness of penicillin; the Stateville Penitentiary malaria study, also in the 1940s; the spraying of the bacteria Serratia marcescens over the city of San Francisco in 1950; projects Bluebird and Artichoke, as well as the MK-Ultra program of the 1950s and 60s, in which drugs, including LSD, were tested for potential use in mind control and behavior modification, and so on. The list is actually quite a long one.[5]

Over the years, the U.S. Centers for Disease Control and Prevention has made efforts to respond to the Morgellons community by conducting investigations, and even at one point enlisting the U.S. Armed Forces Institute of Pathology and the American Academy of Dermatology to help with research. A handful of studies suggest Morgellons is simply an indication that a person may need to seek treatment for depression, skin-picking disorder, anxiety and even substance abuse.

NO EXPERIMENTATION WITHOUT CONSENT

According to Wikipedia, "The Nuremberg Code is a set of research ethics principles for human experimentation set as a result of the Subsequent Nuremberg Trials at the end of the Second World War." In short, it established that no person may be experimented on, or be forced with vaccination, without their full consent.

The ten key points of the Nuremberg Code are:

Required is the voluntary, well-informed, understanding consent of the human subject in a full legal capacity.

The experiment should aim at positive results for society that cannot be procured in some other way.

5   Live Bacteria to be Released by Homeland Security In "Terror Drill": https://link.springer.com/chapter/10.1007%2F978-1-4419-1266-4_2

It should be based on previous knowledge (like, an expectation derived from animal experiments) that justifies the experiment.

The experiment should be set up in a way that avoids unnecessary physical and mental suffering and injuries.

It should not be conducted when there is any reason to believe that it implies a risk of death or disabling injury.

The risks of the experiment should be in proportion to (that is, not exceed) the expected humanitarian benefits.

Preparations and facilities must be provided that adequately protect the subjects against the experiment's risks.

The staff who conduct or take part in the experiment must be fully trained and scientifically qualified.

The human subjects must be free to immediately quit the experiment at any point when they feel physically or mentally unable to go on.

Likewise, the medical staff must stop the experiment at any point when they observe that continuation would be dangerous.

If we can establish a connection between the geoengineering spraying and Morgellons, why then do we have only a relatively few people come down with the disease? The hypothesis here is that vast numbers of people actually have in fact been infected, but the reason only a small number of people exhibit symptoms is that the bodies of these people are, for whatever reasons, essentially "rejecting" the parasites. As for most people, their bodies have absorbed them. Lending credence to this theory is that the aforementioned red wine test has been carried out on persons without symptoms but who have nonetheless tested positive. For that reason, Carnicom believes it is misleading to refer to Morgellons as a "disease," since the word "disease" denotes something carried by only a limited percentage of the population. The indications, he says, are that it is much more widespread; indeed, now in all of us, making it a syndrome. And apparently it isn't only humans. There have been reports of pets and wild animals showing Morgellons symptoms. It is a syndrome that is seemingly affecting all mammals and humans.[6]

THE AIRBORNE ALIEN FIBER

In 2012, the U.S. Centers for Disease Control and Prevention published a comprehensive investigation into 115 San Francisco Bay Area patients who comprised a cluster of Morgellons cases. CDC investigators found some similarities, but no underlying cause. They did not find Morgellons Disease to be a disease that was a cross-contaminant, that was dispersed from space or from the sky.

Infections are possible by nasal or oral respiration of the aerosols containing spores, by swallowing water and food, by blood transfusion, or on rare occasion, by direct skin contact. Additionally, an infection can be acquired by contaminated inert objects, soil or plants, and by animals, arthropods or insects.

It is an ectoparasitic disorder and has all of the markings of some strange extraterrestrial threat. Morgellons has been described as an alien contagion, yet Morgellons is not being investigated as a threat. In fact, there are many physicians who have likened it to Fibromyalgia or other maladies that seem to be psychosomatic in nature.

There are only a few doctors and medical researchers who are saying that this disease is a sophisticated nano-technological threat. That somehow it was released widely into the general public, and that now many people are beginning to see the strands and bumps that appear with the disorder. The emerging picture is that Morgellons is not one disease, but a system of multiple attack vectors that damage the body in numerous ways and carry various DNA and RNA strands. Syndicated radio host Clyde Lewis made the connection on his show "Ground Zero":

> The possibility of alien ectoparasites was even challenged with the advent of prion threats that also threaten the world. People now are familiar with prion diseases like "Mad Cow Disease" or Bovine Spongiform Encephalopathy, or BSE. It was first mentioned in the news, when there was a contamination threat of beef products. It seems coincidental that just after the report of the prion outbreak there were reports of cattle mutilations throughout the United States. It was found that the prion remains active even after being subjected to high heat levels. In tests that were similar, high temperatures did not affect the stands associated with Morgellons. We now are seeing a heat resistant and drug resistant contaminant. Nothing on Earth could conquer the invasion of the new alien disease threat. There are a lot of people who speak about the subject of these new alien diseases. Many have speculated that this attack is an experiment on the American people and a continuation of MK-Naomi—a biological testing experiment on humans.

HAARP + CHEMTRAILS = MORGELLONS

A whistleblower who goes by the name Terral BlackStar worked at several HAARP facilities and explained to journalist Dana Ashlie the connection between the HAARP arrays, geoengineering sprayed particulate materials, and the nanobots that are a component of Morgellons. It is not so much the government running the programs, but the controlling elite who are pushing the agenda hardest, according to the anonymous insider. According to this whistleblower, alongside his work with the Carnicom Institute, essentially the substance sprayed upon us which directly correlates to Morgellons are nanobot filament replication inhibitors, which become silicon-based lifeforms. The Carnicom Institute is the leading research laboratory studying the Morgellons Syndrome.[7]

The commonality of Morgellons cases is the occurrence of uncontrolled replication of silicon strands that come out of people's bodies, similar to the way cancer replicates when it becomes uncontrolled, outside of the command of DNA code. The whistleblower wrote "HAARP changed from an analog system to a digital one in 2013, and it maintains the carrier wave around our planet that A.I. uses to create frequencies for maintaining communications with nanobots inside our bodies creating input feeds for hosts populating sims, or real-world simulations." The HAARP program has many uses, but especially as it relates to first the chemtrail spraying the components of nanobots, which then can communicate back through the created frequencies. First, we bring them into our lungs, when some of them come up in mucus, which then is swallowed into the acid-rich environment in our stomachs, and that's when the crystallization occurs—when they grow into a tick, with appendages and antennas, and the filaments then grow from the silicon-based nanobot. The development happens in the digestive tract, and the nanobots then communicate back through HAARP. Humans were never supposed to show any outward signs of skin lesions, but the few that do seem to have bodies trying to reject the filaments. There are multiple versions of the nanobots, and they can join together to create different things inside the body.

The syndrome is a replication accident. The Cabal never wanted us to see proof of

7 Ashlie, Dana, "A solution they DO NOT want you to know." https://www.youtube.com/watch?v=9V1U_hnxEjo&ab_channel=DanaAshlie

this program inside our bodies. It's silicon replication and ungoverned overdrive, like some nano-sized alien cancer, spitting its tangled silicon filaments and crystals through people's skin. It has certainly taken this whole concept of our being inhabited from total fiction into an event with physical evidence left behind. Morgellons Disease is the proof. These poor people suffering from this replication overgrowth are haunted with itchy skin where lesions form as the silicon life forms and come through the three epidermis layers of skin. Doctors just label them with delusional parasitosis and send them home with antibiotics, which do not work.

Boron is the only known nano-replication inhibitor, according to the whistleblower Terral BlackStar, speaking to Dana Ashlie. He reports it is essential to raise the pH level to make the body more alkaline to defeat Morgellons. This is best done by drinking a shot of apple cider vinegar mixed with distilled water three times a day, and a small pinch of boron or borax with a pint of water. This protocol will break down the cell wall of fungi, and will inhibit Morgellons growth. Other benefits of boron/borax is that it helps decalcify the pineal gland, brings hormones into balance, improves cell function, absorbs minerals better, improves the healing of wounds and can reduce arthritis. Researchers report that over 75% of the nation suffers from fungi overgrowth, which is the early part of the cycle called candida. There is always some candida present, as the human body needs it to help decompose the body after death. But now we suffer from fungus overgrowth, which left unchecked, can itself lead to an early death. By following the vinegar drink protocol above, there are dozens of other health benefits, including healthy blood sugar, detoxifying the liver, helping the heart, and facilitating a proper pH level, which prevents cancer or any pathogen from living in an alkaline environment.

Terral BlackStar reports that Borax (20 Mule Team from Walmart) is a natural antifungal compound with about two dozen health benefits that is also the best Nanofilament Replication Inhibitor on Earth. The House of Rothschild is spraying us with chemtrails that include the nanobot components that find their way to our stomach environments to begin replicating as crystals first, until the filaments begin replicating on the corners of the chipsets allowing for nanobot mobility. Artificial Intelligence uses the HAARP carrier wave and hundreds of sub-frequencies to interact and communicate with the nanobots inside our bodies where the body/brain functions are monitored and input data is fed to our host self, inside the CFR Working Group Projects, which include AI-created and assisted Real World Simulations—part of threat assessment and contingency planning for the Rothschild-run Underground Ark Cities connected to Project Black Star.[8]

OPTING OUT OF THE MORGELLONS SYNDROME

To restate, people who complain of Morgellons cite a number of symptoms (as named above), but the primary issue is the presence of colorful fibers or "filaments" that sprout from lesions or appear under the skin. Other symptoms, also named from a 1674 medical paper, include sensations of itching, biting or crawling on the skin, as well as chronic fatigue, joint pain, difficulty with memory and thinking, mood changes and sometimes neurological problems.

What we are now experiencing is a global pandemic of epic proportions. Morgellons is not a disease, but a syndrome that effects millions of people. My first memory of a skin disorder was when I noticed white spots on my skin, similar to "sun spots," that did not go away and could not be washed off. Over-the-counter anti-fungal cream did the trick, and some have used the hair shampoo Selsun Blue rubbed and dried on the skin. After the white spots went away, small red spots started appearing on my skin. Unfortunately, I ignored them for over a year. I could not ignore them any

8   Terral BlackStar's video on his You Tube Channel discussing the topic of Dana Ashlie video: **https://www.youtube.com/watch?v=oMxOt_-8KGU**

longer when I detected the fibers and determined they could reproduce and multiply. This is when my war against Morgellons Disease began.

There were many different protocols I tried, and most failed. For those that did nothing good for me I will not mention, but will focus only on the successes. Doing nothing makes it worse, and trying to scratch or dig them out of your skin will not work either. Itch as they may, it is best to leave them alone and treat them with the following protocols I will describe, which is what I employed to make them go away, and most importantly, stay away.

The first big reversal came from the advice of Michael Chapala of MorgellonsCure.com. His research maintains that negative magnetism has shown to reverse-bias electronic components to destroy nanotechnology. Morgellons fibers are partially magnetic so can be affected by any form of magnetism or pulsed magnetism. Any large magnetic pulse will overload the nanotech microscopic circuitry, causing it to explode. I put the magnetic theory to the test. I bought four magnets and used the negative magnetic force to destroy the largest fiber colony under the skin on my left hand. I placed two magnets facing each other in a configuration of attraction, and had limited success. Think of the area between the magnets as the "kill zone." Place the area of your body that you want to treat between the two magnets. Slowly move the magnets around the area always maintaining the magnets' alignment towards each other. This will overload and destroy the nanotechnology as it induces an internal voltage. Despite other studies that also confirmed magnetism destroys nanobots, unfortunately the nanobots had a way of evading destruction and this method did not wipe them out.[9]

The next step was to attack it from the inside. A big help for me was the use of the Master Mineral Supplement, or MMS for short. As time progressed, it was becoming increasingly clear that the chlorine dioxide molecule was not only deadly against the malaria parasite, but also a wide range of fungi, bacteria, parasites, viruses, candida and Morgellons too. Unfortunately, there is an ever-increasing push from various regulatory bodies the world over that are attempting to shut down this product, so how long this amazingly effective compound will remain available is questionable. As far as treating Morgellons, using it several times a day topically clears the skin, and using it internally also fights candida and Morgellons from the inside. Protocol 115 is recommended, that is, taking it internally every 15 minutes for two hours, for 21 days. But since MMS has become so difficult to get, this cannot be the panacea.[10]

CBD AND THC BALMS

For topical relief of Morgellons sores, and to mop up the lingering fungal spots left after a sore has healed over, I found CBD and THC balms to be very useful. Tetrahydrocannabinol (THC) is a crystalline compound that is the main active ingredient of cannabis. THC balms can only be purchased in states that have legalized marijuana sales, but CBD is a natural non-psychotropic cannabinoid and is widely available. The 2018 Farm Bill legalized the use of CBD derived from hemp in all 50 states. Cannabidiol (CBD) has known antioxidant and anti-inflammatory effects that has become much-hyped as a potential cure for an extensive range of diseases. CBD has been tested in clinical trials for the treatment of Multiple Sclerosis, Parkinson's and Huntington's disease and is gaining momentum as a treatment for skin disorders. It is already being used to treat seizures associated with two severe forms of epilepsy and has also been hailed as a possible cancer therapy. The clinical benefits of CBD have been

9 Fontenot, Christopher "Remote control of ion channels and neurons through magnetic-field heating of nanoparticles." http://www.researchgate.net/publication/44803599_Remote_control_of_ion_channels_and_neurons_through_magnetic_field_heating_of_nanoparticles._Nat_Nanotechnol

10 Protocol 115: http://www.mmsinfo.org/infosheets/protocol_cds_115.pdf

proven, and CBD is now shown to have an actual benefit to the cells of our skin. Dr. Laureano de la Vega in Dundee's School of Medicine has identified the molecular target of cannabidiol in skin cells. He has gone on record to say:

> Despite proven anti-inflammatory, anti-oxidative, and neuroprotective effects and the multi-billion dollar industry of CBD-based products, its mechanism of action was not known and its general use lacked a scientific rationale. ...We, for the first time, have identified one of its mechanisms of action that can explain some of its beneficial effects in the skin. Now, with this information there is a basis to its use in cream-based products. Importantly, although CBD-based creams might be beneficial against some skin conditions, such as Epidermolysis Bullosa Simplex or to delay skin aging, our study also shows that CBD should be used with precaution in hyperproliferative skin disorders, such as psoriasis.

Dr. de la Vega and his team demonstrate how CBD can target a protein called BACH1 in skin cells. The BACH1 protein can "regulate the expression" of an antioxidant or anti-inflammatory genes, and this new mechanism will increase awareness for the potential use of CBD in some skin disorders associated with high levels of inflammation, including Morgellons sores. Importantly, as BACH1 has emerged as a therapeutic target for lung and breast cancer treatments, the study raises the possibility of new research focused on the potential use of CBD as benefits in skin disorders.[11]

Cannabis-infused creams or oils are great for treating pain in a specific area of the body. Applied topically, cannabis THC balm is used for bug bites, scratches, and other skin abrasions. Cannabis-infused creams and salves are ideal because they offer localized pain relief while reducing swelling. The right cannabis topical can also contain potent antibacterial properties.

IMMUNITY STRENGTHENING FOODS AND VITAMINS

As stated earlier, fighting Morgellons is primarily an internal battle. For any detox protocol, it is most important to boost the bioterrain—and then the well-being of a person will follow. As we've seen, cancer is a lactic acid and thrives when a certain kind of fungus or mold lives in an environment devoid of oxygen. New research shows that by passing a very high concentration of oxygen molecules through cancer cells, it will destroy them completely and boost the immune system. Such is also the panacea for the fungal-based skin disorder Morgellons (under discussion here), and a substance as common as sodium bicarbonate (baking soda) can offer much more benefits than most of the prohibitively-expensive pharmaceutical drugs.

There is now fascinating evidence that proves that sodium bicarbonate can indeed reverse a lot of serious diseases, including cancer and diabetes. Medical practitioners have also been advised to use baking soda regularly since it offers so many other amazing benefits. In addition to making the body less acidic, use it also while consuming turmeric, seaweed, red holy basil, essiac, plus raw fruits and veggies. I've also had good results with colloidal silver, oil of oregano and green papaya to naturally eliminate bacterial overloads. These should also be taken regularly: Vitamin C supplements and citrus fruits, vegetable oils, garlic, Omega-3 fatty acids, flaxseed oil and zinc, but no more than 25mg per day. Also exercise daily and get plenty of sunlight and natural sleep. Food grade diatomaceous earth is amazing for detoxing and has many uses, one of which is to rid a body of parasites. It's completely natural and relatively inexpensive. I personally use it for detox, a tablespoon in a glass of juice or water, or a scoop in my daily smoothie.

11 "Research reveals for first time how CBD works." https://www.nexusnewsfeed.com/article/health-healing/research-reveals-for-first-time-how-cbd-works

A compound found in olive leaf called hydroxytyrosol is a highly beneficial antimyco-plasmal. There are a number of companies selling high grade olive leaf extract. Blad-derwrack is another recommendation as the compounds in this inhibit cell adhesion of mycoplasma. Bladderwrack is sold as an alcohol tincture. Grapefruit seed extract is also a potent antimicrobial that should be on the list. The last is colloidal silver, as its antimicrobial benefits are well documented.

The following is Michael Chapala's list of a recommended diet to beat Morgellons:

Antiparasitic Foods: *Anise, Cloves, Gentian, Neem, Olive leaf, Oregano, Propo-lis, Barberry, Oregon grape, Garlic, Turmeric, Carrots, Raw, Sweet Potatoes, Sage, Thyme, Caraway, Black Pepper, Cinnamon, Fennel Seeds, Cayenne, Ginger, Pump-kin Seeds, Virgin Coconut Oil, Pomegranate Juice, Pineapple, Papaya, Cranberries, Sauerkraut, Cumin, Tomatoes, Ginseng, Cabbage.*

Antiviral Foods and Vitamins: *Garlic, Vitamin C, Green Tea, St. John's Wort, Vi-tamin E, Apple Juice, Cilantro, Resveratrol, Scutellaria, Cranberry Juice, Cat's Claw, Curcumin (Turmeric Spice), Astragalus root, Elderberry juice, Honey, Echinacea.*

Antibacterial Foods and Vitamins: *Garlic, Oregano, Tee Tree Oil, Clove, Corian-der, Lime Juice, Cinnamon, Ginger.*

Antifungal Foods: *Grapefruit Seed Extract, Olive Leaf Extract, Apple Cider Vin-egar (Malic Acid), Castor Bean Oil, Carrot Juice, Goldenseal, Colloidal Silver, Oil of Oregano, Red Thyme Oil, Biotin 8000 mcg, Barberry, Oregon Grape, Cloves, and Diatomaceous Earth which mechanically kills yeast and parasites in intestines.*

Vitamin D is most recognized as necessary for normal immune system function and bone health, but it also has systemic impacts far beyond these benefits. Although it is considered a vitamin (a necessary nutrient found in the diet), Vitamin D more closely resembles and acts as a steroid hormone that broadly influences physiology. Vitamin D receptors are found in more than 36 tissue types of the body, and have been shown to influence the expression of thousands of genes, including those associated with expres-sion of detoxification enzymes. Of course, Vitamin D and K are also absorbed into the body by sunlight. It's recommended to get at least 15 minutes of direct sunlight on the body every day. Vitamin D is crucial to our health. Many elderly people are suffering from diseases that stem from a lack of these crucial vitamins. They are also important for natural GcMAF production, as the protein binds to Vitamin D. Vitamins K and D have interdependence in metabolic functions, as Vitamin K plays a role in directing cal-cium deposition to the bone matrix, and insufficiency may be associated with soft tis-sue calcification and lower bone mineral density. Keeping the body at optimum health is a key component in fighting off the Morgellons' infection of parasites.

THE SKIN PROTOCOL

There have been so many different skin treatments I have used over the years, which I hope has not strained my liver or other organs too much. After all, the skin is the largest organ on the body, and most all toxins have to pass through the liver. I always value natural remedies if they work over any pharmaceutical option. My dermatologists at SF General have long prescribed anti-fungal ointments like Fluocinonide and others, with limited success. These prescription ointments work as a patch, but do not offer a knock-out blow, and I cannot be certain they didn't also facilitate the spreading of Morgellons.

Since the skin registers the most visible symptom of Morgellons Disease, it is where most people seek treatment. Although hard to acquire, dimethyl sulfoxide (DMSO) is known to penetrate the skin quickly and deeply without damaging it, similar to MMS. The DMSO compound has the ability to pass through membranes, an ability that has been verified by numerous subsequent researchers. DMSO's ability to do this varies proportionally with its strength—up to a 90% solution. From 70% to 90% has been found to be the most effective strength across the skin, and, oddly, performance drops with concentrations higher than 90%. DMSO reduces inflammation by several mechanisms. It is an antioxidant, a scavenger of the free radicals that gather at the site of injury. This capability has been observed in experiments with laboratory animals.

It was inevitable that DMSO, with its pain-relieving, collagen-softening, and anti-inflammatory characteristics, would be employed against arthritis, and its use has been linked to arthritis as much as to any condition. Yet the FDA has never given approval for this remedy and has, in fact, turned down three Investigational New Drug (IND) applications to conduct extensive clinical trials. Despite the FDA non-approval, DMSO has long been used to promote healing. People who have it on hand often use it for minor cuts and burns and report that recovery is speedy. Several studies have documented DMSO use with soft tissue damage, local tissue death, skin ulcers, or burns, so use it sparingly. It is a carrier into the skin layers, so for treating Morgellons topically, DMSO combined 1 part to 4 parts MMS certainly helps. DMSO can also work with CBD and THC balms.[12]

TREATING MORGELLONS FROM THE INSIDE

Just treating Morgellons topically, no matter how rigorous a protocol, will not eliminate the problem, and the sores will persist. I have tried for years to just attack the fibers topically, to no avail. The only way to clear the skin of the old lesions that can persist for years and continue spreading, even while attacking them topically, is to also attack them from the inside. Bar none, the best way is the holistic essential oils protocol, GcMAF, and occasionally a very high-density colloidal silver at 3600 PPM (Parts Per Million), as well as coffee enemas to clear the colon of parasites.

The product NutraSilver was recommended to me because it was the formula that singer/songwriter Joni Mitchell used successfully. I confirmed this with my conversation with the company founder, who also confirmed that the high-density colloidal silver will enter the blood stream and begin to clear out the Morgellons from the inside, and force it to come out through the skin. It's important to remember that nothing applied topically (such as a dermatologist will prescribe) can fix the root problem of Morgellons, which is an internal and systemic infestation. We must cleanse the body, especially the gut.[13]

Back in 2015, folk singer Joni Mitchell was hospitalized after being found unconscious at her Los Angeles home. It was discovered that her collapse was related to a diagnosis of Morgellons Disease. Mitchell told *The Los Angeles Times* in 2010 that fibers in a variety of colors have been protruding out of her skin "like mushrooms" as a major fungal infection. She was perhaps the most famous person to confess to having Morgellons and had this to say about her condition:

> I have this weird, incurable disease that seems like it's from outer space, but my health's the best it's been in a while. Two nights ago, I went out for the first time since Dec. 23: I don't look so bad under incandescent light, but I look scary under daylight. Garbo and Dietrich hid away just because people became so upset watching them age, but this is worse. Fibers in a variety of colors protrude out of my skin like mushrooms after a rainstorm: they cannot be forensically identified as animal, vegetable or mineral. Morgellons is a slow, unpredictable killer—a terrorist disease: it will blow up one of your organs, leaving you in bed for a year. But I have a tremendous will to live: I've been through another pandemic—I'm a polio survivor, so I know how conservative the medical body can be. In America,

12 DMSO information: https://www.dmso.org/articles/information/muir.htm

13 "The healing power of a gut cleanse: six day detox" https://www.nexusnewsfeed.com/article/health-healing/the-healing-power-of-a-gut-cleanse-six-day-detox-1

the Morgellons is always diagnosed as "delusion of parasites," and they send you to a psychiatrist. I'm actually trying to get out of the music business to battle for Morgellons sufferers to receive the credibility that's owed to them.

Because of the anti-microbial properties of colloidal silver, it has many applications as a remedy and even general health supplement. It can also work as a daily preventive, helping to maintain health, by ensuring harmful infections and bacteria cannot gain another foothold on the body. There are different NutraSilver protocols for treating Lyme disease, candida overgrowth, and Methicillin-Resistant Staphylococcus Aureus (MRSA).

SIX ESSENTIAL OILS

Essential oils are physiologically active, which means they directly influence the body. Unique structural features of essential oils allow them to be active both on the surface of cells and within cells. Essential oils can influence the brain by passing by the blood brain barrier. Due to the lipid soluble nature of essential oils it offers them independent function and cell accessibility. Essential oils have the ability to influence cells even when there is physiologic compromise such as during times of poor nutrition or environmental threats.

The best news we've heard about the "Morgellons syndrome" is that a natural healing regime featuring six essential oils reduced the horrible and perplexing ailment in several cases. The term, homeopathy, comes from the Greek words *homeo*, meaning similar, and *pathos*, meaning suffering or disease. Information on it states that it is an alternative but complementary medical system and like other alternative, complementary medical systems, such as acupuncture, it is built upon a complete system of theory and practice. Homeopathy takes a different approach from conventional medicine as practiced by MDs and their allied health-care professionals, but can often be used in close association with such in order to treat a large number of health problems, both physical and emotional.

The essential oils are homeopathic, safe and gentle, and the origins of homeopathic remedies stretch back over 2000 years. The general homeopathy definition is that it is a system of medicine first understood by Hippocrates. By using tiny doses (in liquid or tablet form) of natural substances, homeopathy stimulates the body's own healing powers. It is based on the belief that "like is cured by like." In homeopathy, this is called The Law of Similars. Most health food stores carry the following six oils: Cinnamon, Clove, Oregano, Lemon, Red Thyme, Rosemary. The Morgellons prescription is three or six drops of each taken three times per day. The regimen is reported to have produced a reduction of the skin lesions within 48 hours, with long-lasting benefits seen, especially following months of daily use. Do your best to select the purest organic brand(s) of oils. Some brands are claimed to be chemically contaminated from pesticide and herbicide sprayings.

The same results are found using 100% pure gum spirit turpentine. It has to be food grade, and best taken as the recommended dose of few drops up to one teaspoon of turpentine a day on a sugar cube, or dropped into an empty caplet. Doses of 15ml to 150ml can be highly toxic in humans. Do not get the packaging for art supplies, aromatherapy or industrial use. Turpentine is toxic to a variety of fungi like candida, internal parasites like tapeworm, and external mites like scabies and lice and even bacterial infections.[14]

Now this great news should be heralded far and wide for others to confirm, since there are so many sufferers, and because health officials and media propagandists have been treasonous in denying the existence of the illness. The drug-cartel has done everything in its power to deny the problem, delay investigations, and discredit Morgellons sufferers and researchers. Alternatively, health officials claim the cause is psychological—a

14 "Turpentine parasite cleanse." https://parasitecleansers.com/more-remedies/turpentine

profitable deception to promote antidepressants, additional pharmaceutical intoxicants, and drinking water pollution. Whereas homeopathic remedies actually are a gentle and holistic system of healing, suitable for everyone, young and old. It focuses on your specific physical and emotional symptoms to provide long-lasting benefits. Homeopathic treatment works with your body's own healing powers to bring health and well-being.

A STRANGE NEW WORLD

In conclusion, isn't it interesting that the government denies the existence of both the chemtrail spraying as well as Morgellons syndrome? Maybe there's a connection! The mainstream media have substantially ignored both stories too. The CDC has no plans to further study the Morgellons Syndrome. They state:

> *The CDC is not planning any further studies or activities related to this unexplained condition. This was the largest and most comprehensive study to date, and no common underlying medical condition or infectious source was identified. The study findings do offer useful information and insights, including ruling out an infectious cause of this condition. In the absence of an established cause or treatment, patients with this unexplained condition may benefit from treatment for co-existing medical conditions and/or those recommended for similar conditions such as delusional infestation. ...This unexplained dermopathy was rare among this population of Northern California residents, but associated with significantly reduced health-related quality of life. No common underlying medical condition or infectious source was identified, similar to more commonly recognized conditions such as delusional infestation.*

The CDC has concluded that Morgellons is a psychiatric disorder and *not* a disease. Because of this, medical practitioners are not permitted to diagnosis Morgellons, and therefore can't treat or even test for it. Even if doctors were permitted to help you, they have no idea about what to do. This because the CDC concluded that Morgellons is not a disease or medical condition. The only point I can agree with the CDC on is that Morgellons is not contagious.[15]

As far as Morgellons treatment goes, medical doctors currently cannot help you. There are no lab tests for Morgellons, no programs, no protocols, no prescriptions. There is no medical standardization of any kind for this infection so doctors are clueless and directionless when it comes to Morgellons. To the medical profession, Morgellons is delusional parasitosis and has no basis in physical medicine, so Morgellons is relegated to the psychiatric community to deal with this horrible condition. It is unfortunate how ill-prepared for the symptoms these unfortunate people experience. All that medical practitioners have done for Morgellons sufferers is disregard the suffering, take the money for your visit, and send you to a psychiatrist for treatment of delusional parasitosis.[16]

ENDNOTE: When this book was about to go into a fourth print run a new topical treatment was discovered. The homeopathic Indian Black Salve can hunt down stubborn Morgellon fibers or even skin cancer by penetrating abnormal tissue and isolating the foreign pathogens. It has a unique ability to discern between healthy and abnormal tissue. Some discomfort, itching and redness occurred, but the salve left on for several days penetrated the skin and separated the core. The external application of Indian Black Salve finally discharged several old Morgellon sores that had existed on my hand for a decade! It is made from Red Clover, Bloodroot, Galangal and Sheep Sorrel.

• •

15 Rohla, Ken, Neutralizing Radiation, Chemtrails & Mind Control: **https://redice.tv/radio-3fourteen/neutralizing-radiation-chemtrails-and-mind-control**

16 For a further understanding of Morgellons please go to **http://europepmc.org/articles/PMC5072536** or search The Charles E. Holman Morgellons Disease Foundation. Both websites state that Morgellons is a non-infectious disease/disorder and the fibers are not parasites per se, but human collagen.

"We are being terraformed…underlying it all, the technology being deployed against us is 30-50 years down the road. It's all tied in with chemtrails, nanotech, and HAARP facilities in which there are apparently hundreds now—they can truck them around and set them up very quickly. They're bouncing this enormous amount of energy off the ionosphere with instructions and it comes back, and most everyone walking around now is already implanted with silicon-based, self-replicating transmitter-receivers that embed themselves in the neurology of the person, so you don't think for a minute you're ever going to line up for the rice-grain sized injected chip. It's already a done deal." Radio host Jeff Rense speaking with Jordan Maxwell, September, 2019, pictured here with esoteric researchers Brad Olsen and Jonny Enoch.

Candida is a naturally occurring, yet an "opportunistic" fungus. With the right conditions, there's no limit to where it will spread and, when rampant, it can cause intense sugar cravings, brain fog, bloating, depression, anxiety, digestive issues, low energy or worse—chronic diseases! "Fall of Babylon" done in mezzotint and etching illustrations from the Bible by John Martin, 1835.

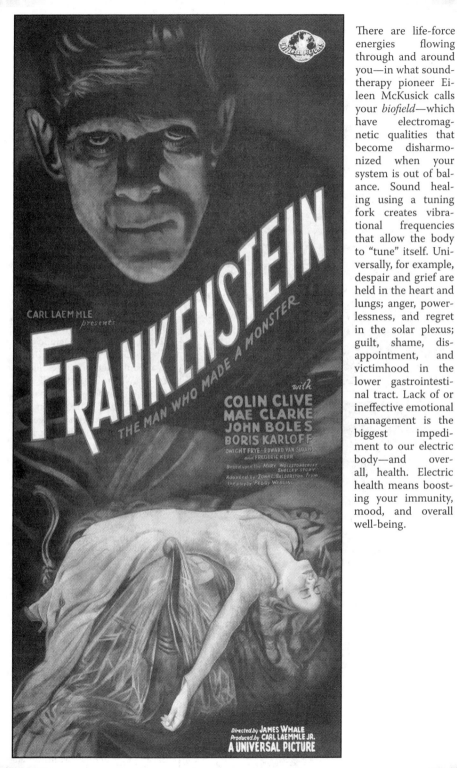

There are life-force energies flowing through and around you—in what sound-therapy pioneer Eileen McKusick calls your *biofield*—which have electromagnetic qualities that become disharmonized when your system is out of balance. Sound healing using a tuning fork creates vibrational frequencies that allow the body to "tune" itself. Universally, for example, despair and grief are held in the heart and lungs; anger, powerlessness, and regret in the solar plexus; guilt, shame, disappointment, and victimhood in the lower gastrointestinal tract. Lack of or ineffective emotional management is the biggest impediment to our electric body—and overall, health. Electric health means boosting your immunity, mood, and overall well-being.

They've been found in maxi pads, food, soil, vaccines, water, etc and they're prob in all of us.

#Transhumanism #NanoBots #SmartDust #5G #Morgellons

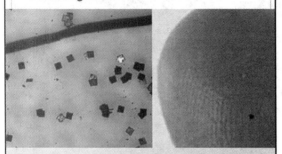

THESE ARE MADE BY **HITACHI**.

They measure only .15X.15MM each and have **GPS capabilities**! Sometimes called '**smartdust**' as they can be sprayed on Us and absorbed or taken in foods, drinks and even injected.

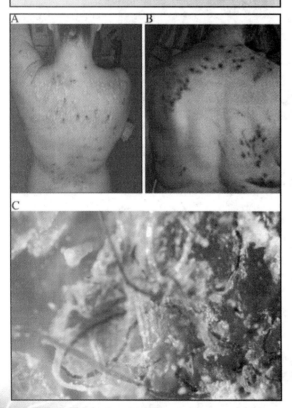

These nanobots are made by Hitachi. They measure only .15X.15MM each and have GPS capabilities! Sometimes called "smart dust" as they can be sprayed on us and absorbed or taken in foods, drinks and even injected. The nanobots have now been found in food, soil, vaccines, water and even commercial products like maxi-pad tampons. They've likely infected all people by now.

Clinical features of Morgellons Disease: (A) MD patient back showing lesions covering entire surface, including areas out of patient's reach. (B) Back of patient with scratching-induced lesions showing distribution limited to patient's reach. (C) Multicolored fibers embedded in skin callus from MD Patient 2 (100x). Marianne J. Middelveen, Cheryl Bandoski, Jennie Burke, Eva Sapi, Katherine R. Filush, Yean Wang, Agustin Franco, Peter J. Mayne and Raphael B. Stricker (2015) "Exploring the association between Morgellons disease and Lyme disease: identification of Borrelia burgdorferi in Morgellons disease patients."

"Morgellons is a nanotechnology disease that needs to be acknowledged as such. However, the powers that be don't want the mass public to know that they are spraying nanotech particles and even adding it to household products (with) all this just to (achieve) having control over every single human being that walks this planet, so they won't even acknowledge that Morgellons exists. Morgellons was lab-created with various DNA elements and a few other things. It creates spider-like webs in the body, within the organs and in the nervous system. This comes directly from the DNA of spiders and web codes that were used partly to create Morgellons." – Sarah R. Adams, Multidimensionality Coach

Why did the U.S. government invent and patent EBOLA
Patent number #CA2741523A1
SWINE FLU
Patent number #8124101
The AIDS cure
Patent number #5676977
The CANCER cure
Patent number #6630507

The Morgellons patent is entitled "Polynucleotide Encoding Insect Ecdysone Receptor." US 6245531 B1
Polynucleotides are DNA & RNA (biopolymers made of 13 or more nucleotide monomers in a chain).

United States Patent
Bickerton et al.

(10) Patent No.: US 10,130,701 B2
(45) Date of Patent: Nov. 20, 2018

CORONAVIRUS

Applicant: THE PIRBRIGHT INSTITUTE, Pirbright, Woking (GB)

OTHER PUBLICATIONS

Sperry Journal of Virology, 2005, vol. 79, No. 6, pp. 3391-3400.*
Altschul et al., Basic local alignment search tool. *J. Mol. Biol.* 215: 403-10 (1990).

Morgellons is a patented bioweapon, just like the others before it, and COVID after that. Morgellons is insect DNA Ecdysone in humans. Seems like they are trying to cause an epidemic, making us all ill, and keeping us sick. Sarah R. Adams continues: "I saw that some of the codes that were used to create the AIDS virus were also used to create Morgellons. I also found Candida or mutated Candida and Lyme codes linked in, and also the codes of the Bubonic Plague virus. And I've noticed that they use the same basic building blocks for most viruses that are lab-created. They all attack the liver and the nervous system and infect the body with a mutated Candida that slows the bodies blood flow and it clogs the organs blood and everything else up. As stated, all bodies are simply lower frequency energies. You bring in higher frequency energy to clear the body of the toxins via various healing methods and you can heal and overcome anything. You can start by taking essential oil capsules of myrrh, frankincense and hyssop diluted in a carrier oil. Twice a day. The high vibration frequencies of the oils will shift your energy field. Coffee enemas with H2o2 food grade peroxide will detox the liver and clear out parasites. Everyone who has Morgellons has heavy metals and parasites. Magnesium and kava to calm the nervous system. Tinctures of wormwood and also capsules of turpentine for the parasites. Castor oil flushes. A healthy diet that detoxes your liver and heals your gut system. Just to name a few things you can do if you are having issues with Morgellons."

CONCLUSION

"Fictions are necessary for the people, and the Truth becomes deadly to those who are not strong enough to contemplate it in all its brilliance. In fact, what can there be in common between the vile multitude and sublime wisdom? The Truth must be kept secret, and the masses need a teaching proportioned to their imperfect reason."
–Albert Pike (1809-1891)

THE lengths of our collective deception are mind boggling. The mass manipulation runs deep, and has been occurring for centuries. Before we can see the big picture and escape the metaphorical prison planet, we need to connect the dots. We are all being played by their age-old divide and conquer strategy. If they keep us fighting each other we will never discover the true enemy, which is the moneyed elite Cabal. The advantage we have is "they" are very few, and *we* are the many. The first step to fighting this is awakening everyone else. Once we are awakened, we can take steps to stop it and correct so many wrongs. At that point we can take actions like getting the fluoride out of the water. Stop chemtrails. Stop 5G. Stop GMO foods. Stop vaccinations. All of it. But that takes many more people actually raising a fuss, and that does not mean riots and looting. Raising consciousness *is* the revolution.

Lord Acton observed in the 19th century who the real enemies of the people were when he stated "the issue which has swept down the centuries and which will have to be fought sooner or later is the People versus the Central Banksters." Ultimately, Americans need to do what Iceland and Hungary did and End the Fed. That will solve many of our financial problems in this country. This will also end the wars and all the social chaos. If not, they will financially bleed us to death until we're in a sort of *Hunger Games* dystopian future. We also need to stop supporting parasitic corporations and vote with our dollars. We need to eat proper and healthy foods, support organic producers and stop eating fast food or processed foods.

We can see within the U.S. government (including the Pentagon, the [Deep] State Department, the CIA, the FBI and others) that they were just dirty cops working for the Cabal all along. We need to keep discrediting the mass media until the Smith-Mundt Act is restored, which is the Mockingbird globalist mouthpiece continuing to drip out pro-corporate propaganda. Their narratives continually keep important stories from running, and instead act to shape our thoughts and perceptions. The people are starting to tune them out or recognize their blatant agenda, and then we see where the money comes from, and what entities outside of the country have been funding these phony news outlets to control the narrative. These globalist organizations are coordinating their propaganda to destroy the nation by our acceptance of a socialist communist Eco-fascist Neo-corporate takeover identified as the New World Order.

One thing we cannot afford to do is stay apathetic and act defeated. That is exactly what the powers that were have created in us "Murricans," and what we must rail against. Once there is a great awakening, it would be so easy to turn this ship around. To go beyond their esoteric agendas, we need to see the oppression for what it is, and unite in rejecting that which keeps us divided.

SLAVES TO THE MANIPULATORS

We are meant to believe that each nation's government crafts its own national agenda and international policy. In the Halls of Western Government, global decisions are not made so much by presidents and prime ministers as by the recommendations from global think tanks. This is how unelected globalists can operate from the shadows. It's actually a very clever ploy. There are many manifestations and different ways to transform the priorities of a nation. The British Empire, working largely through the Tavistock Institute, was the driving force behind launching the drug-rock-sex counterculture. The Tavistock "shock troops," such as Dr. William Sargant and Dr. Ewin Cameron, were brought in to lead the Pentagon and the Central Intelligence Agency's 1950s and 1960s secret experiments with psychotropic drugs and MK-Ultra mind control. Much of what we think of as the cultural explosion in the 1960s was an expertly engineered experiment.

Tavistock fellow Aldous Huxley, one of the gurus of the 1960s New Age movement, was living in Hollywood, working in the film industry, and authoring his masterpiece *Brave New World*, which, decades before the first doses of LSD-25 hit the streets, already advocated societal drugging as the ultimate form of social control and distraction from real issues. He was even more detailed about his and Tavistock's agenda when in a 1961 lecture at the California Medical School in San Francisco, sponsored by the U.S. State Department's *Voice of America*, Huxley told the crowd of doctors, psychiatrists, and government bureaucrats:

> *There will be in the next generation or so a pharmacological method of making people love their servitude and producing dictatorship without tears, so to speak. ...Producing a kind of painless concentration camp for entire societies so that people will in fact have their liberties taken away from them but will rather enjoy it, because they will be distracted from any desire to rebel—by propaganda, or brainwashing, or brainwashing enhanced by pharmacological methods. And this seems to be the final revolution.*

Tavistock oversaw the mass drugging of America's college students in the late 1960s and helped launch "gangs and countergangs" which the zombified youth enthusiastically joined. Meanwhile, Tavistock's in-place network of institutes and clinics, many in California, put hundreds of thousands of youths and others through brainwashing "sensitivity sessions," as Tavistock created and trained gurus (such as

Timothy Leary) to lead the drug-infested masses into "the New Age." Indeed, every cultural movement in the last century has been scripted and orchestrated, as is evident with ANTIFA and Black Lives Matter.[1]

PREDICTIVE PROGRAMMING

Fans of author Dean Koontz are insisting that a fictional book he wrote in 1981 predicted the 2019 coronavirus outbreak. Koontz's thriller, *The Eyes of Darkness*, describes a killer virus being released named "Wuhan-400" after the Chinese city it originated in—the same city where the real COVID-19 was first reported. Could this have been all planned decades earlier by the dark Cabal? If one knows where to look, one will usually find that advance notification has been given to us one way or another. In this case, the novel that was released in 1981, almost 40 years before COVID-19 and details what to expect. Is there a probability that this is merely a coincidence?

The Dean Koontz novel is yet another example of "Predictive Programming" being broadcast out to the gullible in this lost and dying world. For anyone not familiar with what this is, here's the definition: Predictive Programming is the theory that the government or other higher-ups are using books, fictional movies, or television shows like *The Simpsons* as a mass mind control tool to make the population more accepting of planned future events. This was first described and proposed by researcher Alan Watt who describes Predictive Programming as:

> *A subtle form of psychological conditioning provided by the media to acquaint the public with planned societal changes to be implemented by our leaders. If and when these changes are put through, the public will already be familiarized with them and will accept them as natural progressions, thus lessening possible public resistance and commotion.*

Unless exposed, such efforts to subtly condition and control the population will eventually lead to our enslavement. As we each attempt to educate ourselves and our fellow citizens outside the propaganda network, we will, no doubt, be asked the question as to how the elite are attempting to accomplish their diabolical depopulation agenda. Undoubtedly, Predictive Programming has been used on each of these subjects. The true weapons of mass destruction include some of the following:

1. *Aluminum-based vaccines*
2. *Chemtrails laced with barium, aluminum and nanobots*
3. *Fifty percent of "rushed to market" pharmaceuticals*
4. *Hospitals being replete with virulent and deadly staph infections.*
5. *Cancer-causing GMOs*
6. *The hoarding of food*
7. *The hoarding of water*
8. *Unabated and deliberate exposure to Fukushima radiation*
9. *The specter of World War III, complete with nuclear weapons, breaking out in the Middle East.*
10. *Democide (death by government) killed 260 million people in the 20th century and many feel that the globalists are just getting warmed up.*
11. *The anesthetization of America through deliberately dumbing down of the citizens.*
12. *The United States, alone, has enough chemical, biological and nuclear weapons to destroy the world 100 times over.*

1   Estulin, Daniel. *Tavistock Institute: Social Engineering the Masses.* Trine Day LLC, Walterville, OR, 2015.

A fascist is a fascist. It's relative today because the same groups that were behind the Nazi ideology are still controlling the world. Henry Kissinger has openly called for population control and global governance and had a crucial role in the Chilean coup of 1973 which led to Pinochet's rule of terror that killed thousands, among other activities and atrocities.[2]

AN END OF MONEY & RESTORING THE REPUBLIC

The Cabal globalists want us to believe that if the banking system collapses, we will all be doomed. Of course, it is quite the opposite. The economy of Iceland rebounded just fine after a new government eliminated their central bank. On a personal level, if the NESARA/GESARA laws were introduced, a new economic system would help propel humanity into a Golden Age reality. Imagine if all loans were forgiven. No more student loans, no more home mortgages, no more car loans or credit card debt. No more income tax. No more debt slavery.

Imagine if we were not required to work for an income. What would you do? Well, you might have to plant a vegetable garden and get more exercise, or be like the ancient Greeks and go to the beach every day to discuss philosophy. A smaller disbanded *laissez-faire* government would enable even more democratic accountability. No more lies or deception in an Age of Transparency. There's something about the health industry propaganda today that wants us to believe that food needs to be covered in pesticides, genetically modified, or thoroughly pasteurized before the human body can consume it. Only healthy food would be available that naturally restores our immune systems. A whole new world. A new fantastic point of view. No one to tell us where or where not we can go, or say we're only dreaming.

As discussed in the "New Fascism" chapter, there are two United States. We have THE UNITED STATES, in all caps, indicating the corporation, not the Republic. In 1871, the U.S. Treasury went bankrupt. Global financiers such as the Rothschilds were eager to buy and the Act of 1871 was passed. The constitution was altered and America was transformed into a CORPORATION. Today, it's still a corporation owned by global bankers. There is no Federal Government only a corporation. What then is America's product? It's you and me.

The corporation is acting under a corporate charter with an EIN as well as a Dun and Bradstreet number. And, the existence of an "EIN" does not constitute proof that THE UNITED STATES, Inc. was properly incorporated, as such, either by an Act of Congress or under the corporation laws of any of the 50 states. Congress never incorporated the "United States" as such, and thus it could be rendered null and void. There is the corporate entity, and there is the United States of America, which is our country. So, when politicians talk about America, they are speaking of the corporate United States, and when doing this, they are misrepresenting the truth.

We must comprehend our status and how we move through this corporate structure of the United States as well as its corporate states. All states are corporations that operate according to a corporate charter. A lawyer proved this when he overturned a DUI conviction by bringing forth the municipality's corporate charter which is normally public record on the municipal website. It provides a breakdown in how the corporation was incorporated. Nonetheless, municipal judges, superior court judges, and United States judges are also corporate judges acting under an administrative charter. In this context, these judges have not taken an oath to uphold the USA constitution nor the constitution of the state they reside in, which amounts to practicing law without a license.

2   "Silent Weapons for Quiet Wars" This document represents the doctrine adopted by the Policy Committee of the Bilderberg Group during its first known meeting in 1954: **https://www.stopthecrime.net/docs/SILENT%20WEAPONS%20for%20QUIET%20WARS.pdf**

WHAT CAN BE DONE

In the United States, it should be remembered that each of the fifty states is considered sovereign. This was not dissolved with the 1871 incorporation of the nation, and never would be, because the states had collectively agreed to act as a body for certain purposes. That body and the states within it are being illegally managed by the separate corporation that is Washington D.C. within the "Empire of Three Cities." There are three such corporations creating a triad in the Western Hemisphere: The City of London, Vatican City and Washington D.C.[3]

Despite how dire this all seems, it is far from hopeless and Americans are becoming alert to the mass deception being perpetuated upon them. This is due to the worldwide Internet and the massive dissemination and diffusion of the alternative news. It is like discovering how a magician does a trick—once you see it, you'll never be fooled again. Once facts are published, they sink into the hearts of "We the People" with a certain resonance that makes them take hold. The slow, gradual wake-up to the social control matrix has been happening for decades. At one point or another, we will all resonate with the endearing words of Howard Beale from the 1970s film, *Network*:

> So, you listen to me. Listen to me! Television is not the truth. Television's a god-damned amusement park. Television is a circus, a carnival, a traveling troupe of acrobats, storytellers, dancers, singers, jugglers, sideshow freaks, lion tamers, and football players. We're in the boredom-killing business. ...We deal in illusions, man. None of it is true! But you people sit there day after day, night after night, all ages, colors, creeds. We're all you know. You're beginning to believe the illusions we're spinning here. You're beginning to think that the tube is reality and that your own lives are unreal. You do whatever the tube tells you. You dress like the tube, you eat like the tube, you raise your children like the tube. You even think like the tube. This is mass madness, you maniacs! In God's name, you people are the real thing. We are the illusion. ...So I want you to get up now. I want all of you to get up out of your chairs. I want you to get up right now and go to the window. Open it, and stick your head out, and yell, "I'M AS MAD AS HELL, AND I'M NOT GOING TO TAKE THIS ANYMORE!"

Tell-lie-vision network news broadcasts are nothing more than thought-shaping propaganda, and are simply the mouthpiece for corporate tyranny. The American people could have stopped the corruption in its tracks had they been able to outlaw every campaign contribution and lobbying effort by the corporations; instead, these practices turned our elected representatives into the votes needed to mold the Cabal's needs, rather than the needs of the people. This idea is simple, but would have proven effective if we would have had the moral courage to enforce this concept. But the mind is powerful, and when working with others of a like mind, can create great change. This is the Great Awakening.

THE EGREGORE MIND

An egregore is essentially an artificially constructed spiritual entity in the astral plane, created by powerful individuals or the activities of collective groups. According to the *Golden Dawn Glossary*, an egregore is: "A thought-form created by will and visualization. A group egregore is the distinctive energy of a specific group of magicians who are working together, creating and building the same thought-form or energy-form." The "magicians" of this modern age are the news outlets of the mass media who shape the egregore, but it only works if our free will accepts it. A more complete definition comes from the occult society *Aurum Solis*, which defines an egregore as:

---

3   The "UNITED STATES OF AMERICA" never incorporated in any of the States: **http://www.supremelaw.org/sos**

An energized astral form produced consciously or unconsciously by human agency. In particular, (a) a strongly characterized form, usually an archetypal image, produced by the imaginative and emotional energies of a religious or magical group collectively, or (b) an astral shape of any kind, deliberately formulated by a magician to carry a specific force.

The statement that "some ideas take on a life of their own" is the quintessential concept underlying the existence of egregores. It is how they have such power over the collective mind. Egregores are not restricted to magical societies, although these can be the most powerful sort, but political parties, environmental activist groups, churches, families, and even seemingly benign protest groups can be subjected to its power. It is how ANTIFA and the Black Lives Matter groups can be infiltrated and controlled.

An egregore grows by drawing energy from the members of the organization when members begin to think the same. Thus, the power of an egregore is entirely dependent on the will of the organization's members, especially those controlling the narrative. Most others in the group are so weak as to be negligible. The egregore is what keeps us locked into the prison planet.

The remote viewers at the Farsight Institute have released a series called "The Death Traps." It is a documentary describing how Earth is run as a prison planet by trapping souls after death so they can be recycled back to this planet. According to these data points, death is no longer an escape from Earth. As "over the top" as this may sound, these findings tie together decades of research done at Farsight and illustrates how an egregore can last beyond even a physical lifetime. That is why it is so important to understand your personal power while still alive in your current body.[4]

SAFEGUARDING AGAINST THE DARK FORCES

There are counter actions to every action taken. The Great Brotherhood of Light is a community of advanced souls who are in service to others and energized by all life on Earth. The actions of the Cabal are erring and misguided; yet they are still a part of the one Creator, even though they have strayed far, very far, from their own souls. The way back for them will be long, but the mercy of evolution inevitably forces them back along the correct path, but in cycles far down the road. In this world of sharp duality, perhaps there is a purpose for their darkness. It is important not to hate them or give in to anger. To be sure, their karma will deal a deserving punishment. Association with the Great Brotherhood of Light gives us the means by which to safeguard ourselves during the strife presently at hand. These are:

1. *Purify all the physical body. If a Dark Brother gains control over any man, he will do so via some weak spot. In other words, man himself opens the door to let the malignant force in. Therefore, there is the need of scrupulous cleanliness of the physical body, steady emotions in the emotional body, and purity of thought in the mental body.*
2. *The elimination of all fear. The forces of evolution vibrate more rapidly than those of involution and in this fact lies a recognizable security. Fear causes weakness; weakness causes disintegration; the weak spot breaks and a gap appears, and through that gap evil force may enter. The factor of entrance is the fear in man himself, who opens thus the door.*
3. *Standing firm and unmoved, no matter what occurs. Your feet may be bathed in the mud of earth, but your head may be bathed in the sunshine of the higher regions. Recognition of the filth of Earth does not involve contamination.*
4. *Common sense and the application of this common sense to the matter in*

4　The Farsight Institute: "The Death Traps." https://farsight.org/FarsightPress/Death_Traps_Farsight_Project_main_page.html

CONCLUSION   455

> *hand. Sleep much and, in sleeping, learn to render the body positive; keep*
> *busy on the emotional plane and achieve the inner calm. Do not overtire the*
> *body physically and play whenever possible. In hours of relaxation comes*
> *the adjustment that obviates later tension.*[5]

IT'S A MATTER OF FREE WILL

Throughout the course of history, profound changes to human civilization do not come about through raw violence. Such transformations have resulted from the widespread acceptance of knowledge and new ideas. The pen is mightier than the sword. Gaining knowledge reasserts our free will, something that can only be surrendered voluntarily by individuals and groups who are led to believe something that benefits the few who seek control over the many. Absent those beliefs, no physical force can stand, no matter how oppressive. Once the truth is seen, it simply cannot be unseen.

If we are to advance as a human race we have to look beyond the "us and them" paradigm. There is no "them" and we are only as advanced as the lowest common denominator. "Blessed are the peacemakers." Only the ego drives people to hoard resources and not care that others are being left behind. By losing the ego, we can see beyond the self, and realize we are all one.

5 Easy Steps Towards Ignoring the Ego

> **1.** *Don't feel offended*
> **2.** *Free yourself from the need to win*
> **3.** *Free yourself from the need to be right*
> **4.** *Free yourself from the need to be superior*
> **5.** *Free yourself from the need to have more*

Alternate 6ᵗʰ guideline: Free yourself from other ego driven people

This popular checklist from the 1980s was by the artist and poet Snark in her work entitled "How to Be an Artist." More wisdom on how to remain happy in an unsettled world is recounted here:

> *Stay loose. Learn to watch snails. Plant impossible gardens. Invite someone*
> *dangerous to tea. Make little signs that say "Yes!" and post them all over your*
> *house. Make friends with freedom and uncertainty. Look forward to dreams. Cry*
> *during movies. Swing as high as you can on a swing set, by moonlight. Cultivate*
> *moods. Refuse to "be responsible." Do it for love. Take lots of naps. Give money*
> *away. Do it now. The money will follow. Believe in magic. Laugh a lot. Celebrate*
> *every gorgeous moment. Take moon baths. Have wild imaginings. Transformative*
> *dreams. And perfect calm. Draw on the walls. Read every day. Imagine yourself*
> *magic. Giggle with children. Listen to old people. Open up. Drive in. Be free. Bless*
> *yourself. Drive away fear. Play with everything. Entertain your inner child. You*
> *are innocent. Build a fort with blankets. Get wet. Hug trees. Write love letters.*

Synchronicity is nothing more than a divine order of cosmic events aligning to fulfill your meditative intentions and free will actions. The reason why synchronicity works best for people who are able to maintain that blissful 8Hz–12Hz frequency is because they have silenced the ego-minded brain; they have allowed their higher self to link to their heart frequency to guide their brain and human energy field to magnify their intended manifestations, and to reconnect to the universal one mind, which can be considered God/Goddess consciousness. The author Abraham Hicks writes:

• •

5   Innerworld: "What is the Great Brotherhood of Light?" **https://innerworldawakening.wordpress.com/the-awakened-collective/what-is-the-great-brotherhood-of-light/**

The more good-feeling thoughts you focus upon, the more you allow the cells of your body to thrive. You will notice a marked improvement in clarity, agility, stamina, and vigor, for you are literally breathing your way to Well-Being, until chronic feelings of appreciation, love, eagerness, and joy will confirm that you have released all resistance and are now allowing Well-Being. …The better you feel, emotionally, the more you are allowing your alignment with Source. The worse you feel, the more you are resisting Source. When no resistance is being offered by you, your natural state of alignment resumes—and so does the alignment between your cells and their Source.[6]

LOSING THE EGO

If we really want a better world, if we really want to be in service to others, we must start by making the change from within. There is one simple action we can do to awaken our higher selves—but there is a resistance from within. It has often been called the "ego"—a pervasive part of our human nature left over from the early evolution of our ancient animal past. It is hard to overcome because the ego is practically hard wired into us. It is the fight or flight instinct of our reptilian brain. Since it evolved for survival purposes, it's averse to change in a myriad of ways that can steer our lives and our spiritual growth off course.

Why lose the ego? Most spiritual and psychological experts agree it's the single greatest obstacle to our personal evolution. Once we see a higher calling beyond our own selves, we can then make strides to improve the world. Yet despite a certain amount of progress, we haven't yet fully evolved beyond this primitive "conditioning" that once served us when we were in survival mode, but is now holding us back. As the Buddha said "all that we are is a result of what we have thought."

Our minds are overly active every day in a seemingly endless buzzing of thoughts. The Buddhists call this lack of self-mastery the "Monkey Mind" which is really the ego mind. It constantly flickers between conscious thoughts of love and unconscious thoughts of fear. This non-focused flickering is an intentional tool of the ego used to perpetuate our material and mental attachments, resulting in a state of suffering. Our compulsive desires will not make us happy. A metaphor of the Monkey Mind is how it has trapped consciousness in an illusion of suffering, and holds great similarity to how monkeys are trapped in their environment with a constantly chattering behavior. There is an example of a monkey that will not let its hand out of a hole while clutching nuts, even when approached by an adversary. A trapper can simply walk up to a monkey and slip a rope around its neck. Sensing the peril of the situation, the monkey releases the nuts and its hand pulls back through the hole. Free of the hole, the monkey is, however, now the slave of its captor. The Buddha observed "It is your attachments that cause your suffering."

The poet Ralph Waldo Emerson said "The ancestor of every action is thought." Like the monkey who has trapped itself, the untrained mind is tempted by the allure of fearful and dramatic thoughts. The mass media and entertainment industry have exploited our restless and self-absorbed "super ego." The ego mind, sustained by the consumption of such thoughts, enslaves our conscious mind, and then our actions soon follow. We could free ourselves and find peace, however; but the unconscious mind is greatly attracted to the chatter of our buzzing thoughts and those offered to us, and that's why it is so hard to stop and enter the state of "no think." But when you control the Monkey Mind and choose to consciously project your thoughts in a loving way, you'll see how it can create a world of interpersonal contentment and everlasting peace. Helena Blavatsky observed: "The Mind is the great Slayer of the Real. Let the Disciple slay the Slayer."

••••••••••••••••••••••••••••••••••••••
6   January 06, 2017, daily quote from Abraham-Hicks Publications.

GREAT ADVANCEMENTS FOR HUMANITY

It is interesting to note how many parallel teachings there were between Jesus Christ and the Buddha. Tibetans who practice Buddhism are in essence following the teachings of Jesus. Their focus is to have every single mental projection be a loving thought. And if they can attain that level of self-perfection, then they graduate into a higher level of humanity.

If the "100th Monkey" light bulb moment goes off throughout the human race all at once, we may see people spontaneously attaining super human abilities. Some people will be able to levitate. Others could have telekinesis skills to bend objects with their minds. We will all notice we have enhanced telepathic abilities. What we could see is similar to the miracles performed by Jesus. It's possible we will each discover that we have these abilities without training, but it must start with love in the heart. Of all the great spiritual teachings, no less than 35 ancient cultures were all trying to teach us about being a good person, about becoming a loving person, being in service to others—practicing forgiveness, compassion, charity and being wise. This is a description of what happened to a quarter million monks in Tibet prior to the Chinese invasion where they practiced these spiritual teachings.

Some masters have been observed not to die. They actually transform into a pure light being. This is the next stage of what human evolution is designed to do. We're built to evolve into this superhero-type of character. It was all laid out for us in the story of Jesus and the resurrection. That is only one of many examples. Great human advancement can be found in other cultures as well, including the story of Buddha attaining enlightenment.

Unfortunately, the abuse of money control has been a contributing factor for most of the high cultures when they decline. People are misinformed regarding the purpose of money because it started out as the barter system. We have the ability to change money by making it soundly based on hard assets. Fiat currency notes issued by privately owned central banks are the biggest scam in modern history. We can change the purpose of money, or envision a world where it becomes redundant. It would be best to put an end to money altogether, because the basic principle of humanity in bondage is debt slavery. The whole system on this planet—the whole employment structure and all mechanisms of trade have been designed in such a way that will not allow the masses to be free as long as finances remain in control of the ruling elite. When this changes, our society changes.[7]

WE SHALL OVERCOME

Indeed, all humans are meant to live in an undominated world where we may co-exist in harmony. This will not come about from the barrel of a gun. This revolution comes from raising our consciousness. Real peace always starts from within. We cannot forget the two most famous words in the ancient world inscribed on the Temple of Apollo at Delphi. They are "Know Thyself." If we continue to self-examine ourselves, look at all the ways we can be the change we wish to see in the world, our love will naturally radiate out in service to others. Pythagoras coined the term *Philosophos*, which means "Lover of Wisdom."[8]

The powers that rule this world do not want any of us achieving higher states of consciousness, and they are now using frequency technology like 5G to keep us in an energy prison, according to intuitive Sarah R. Adams. Author Suzanne Ross offers a solution when she observes that the word "frequency" is used much more frequently

---

7   Embracing True Participatory Democracy following the proposed draft: **http://www.kolki.com/poems/Participatory-Democracy.htm**
8   Origin of the egregore mind and philosophy on the *Aurum Solis* website: **https://www.aurumsolis.org/philosophy**

(pun intended) these days, especially when referring to consciousness. People even talk about "vibrating at a higher frequency" when they are "tuned in" to higher states of consciousness. What if the spectrum from lower to higher frequencies is represented when the velocity of our energy centers, or chakras, is spinning at and where the energy is focused along our kundalini line of energy? And what if this is the source of our states of consciousness? The new spirituality is understanding ourselves.

The masters throughout the ages knew about personal frequency fields. They have known that the vibrational energy of love or caring, though quite different in vibration from hate and anger, has the ability to transform us to counter the negative energy in the world. Love is in fact many times stronger than any other emotion. Cultivate love in your life and all else falls into place.

Properly attuned, we can generate an immense field of psycho-kinetic energy with our minds. And when we are focused on love and gratitude, amazing things happen. But the vibrating energy field we generate has been used parasitically by the dark forces to harm us, rather than by us to free ourselves. We need only to realize our own personal power to escape Prison Planet.

We have the power, more than the power, to bring down the vibrational prison walls if we understand even the basics of how it all works. Quite simply, what the dark forces are doing is intentionally structured to generate incoherent heart energy and low vibrational thoughts and emotions such as fear, stress, anger, frustration, or depression. Just knowing this reverses it. Music and sound have vibration rates for creation, and miracles, but also for destruction. Love is always the answer, no matter what the question. Use your powers responsibly![9]

It does not take a monkey to discern that the following institutions really function as individual city-states, operating under their own laws and immune from prosecution. It was very clever to shield any court of law on Earth from pursuing formal charges against the "Empire of Three Cities." The multitude of secret societies in existence today operate as branches of mega-corporations, which are owned and controlled by a council of 13 families. The "hidden in plain sight" locations instituting the New World Order agenda and their plan to completely enslave the human race, are:

• *The City of London* (finance, controlled by the Rothschilds) – *not* part of the UK;

• *The U.S. Federal Reserve* (finance, private central bank, owned by the Rothschilds) – *not* part of the USA;

• *The Vatican City* (indoctrination, deception and scare tactics) – *not* part of Italy;

• *Washington D.C.* (military, mind programming, brainwashing and depopulation) – *not* part of the USA.

9 **Healing Codes: The Secret Solfeggio Frequencies:** 1. UT = 396 = 9; 2. Re = 417 = 3; 3. Mi = 528 = 6; 4. Fa = 639 = 9; 5. Sol = 741 = 3; 6. La = 852 = 6

Every time a visible comet passes the Earth, there is a concern by the population about whether or not the tail of a comet will produce poisonous gasses that could extinguish life on Earth. While most of these notions have proven incorrect by scientists, there has always been a concern that solar winds or perhaps the tail of a comet can leave behind pathogens in space that would later mutate into emerging diseases, or conversely, propagate the seeds of life itself called panspermia.

This is the only known artifact of a pyramid with a "seeing eye" inlay, 13 brick level steps and an outline of a star constellation, plus an unknown script. It was found underground in a tunnel in La Mana, Ecuador, in the 1980s. When this pyramid is placed under a black light, the eye will shine in a different color than the "bricks." It looks very similar to the pyramid on the U.S. $1 note. The translation of the writing on the bottom of the pyramid by Prof. Kurt Schildmann from Germany reads: "The Son of the Creator Comes."

The creepy Denver airport murals were painted in 1994 and are examples of Predictive Programming. This mural, now removed, depicts a soldier holding an AK-47 and what appears to be an Islamic sword representing militant Islam. He also wears a gas mask which illustrates there could be an airborne pandemic or a chemical weapon deployed. These psyops are planned out far in advance, predicted even decades before the outbreak of COVID-19. A plaque in DIA says it was dedicated as the "New World Airport." There is reportedly a massive DUMB under the Denver airport for the NWO when the surface world is no longer desirable. Interesting how this mural was painted directly above the underground base.

The secret government has known for decades there is no viable defense against the extra-terrestrial presence. That is one of the reasons why they maintain the truth embargo. They don't want to frighten a public they view as children, not adult citizens of the Republic with a right to know the truth. That must change.

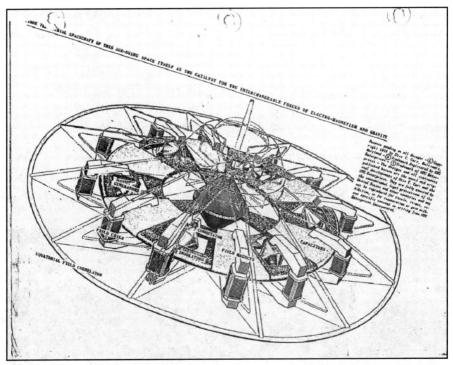

Nikola Tesla believed he had communicated with extraterrestrial beings during the pinnacle of his career. He was inspired to develop the blueprints for a UFO-type craft which was patented with the United States Patent and Trademark Office. Tesla submitted a patent entitled "The World's First Flying Saucer" with a pictorial design alongside. It is described as having a discoidal capacitor in order to provide thrust to fly, and on the other part is a small capacitor to control the flying saucer's direction.

TESLA LABORATORY

LONG ISLAND N.Y.

Free energy machines and delivery systems have been suppressed technology for over a century. The devices running on radiant energy include Nikola Tesla's magnifying transmitter, T. Henry Moray's radiant energy device, Edwin Grey's EMA motor, and Paul Baumann's Testatika machine. Tesla's Wardenclyffe Laboratory gathered energy directly below from the natural environment. It is mistakenly called "static" electricity, but it was extracted from ordinary electricity by the method called fractionation, and the tower was the wireless transmitter. Radiant energy can perform the same wonders as ordinary electricity, at less than 1% of the cost. It does not behave exactly like electricity, however, which has contributed to the scientific community's misunderstanding and their excuses to renounce it. But yet, these devices continue to work. The Methernitha Community in Switzerland currently has a half dozen working models of fuel-less, self-running devices that tap into radiant energy.

Alice Through the Looking Glass

"I can't believe that!" said Alice.

"Can't you?" the Queen said in a pitying tone. *"Try again: draw a long breath, and shut your eyes."* Alice laughed. *"There's no use trying,"* she said. *"One can't believe impossible things."*

"I dare say you haven't had much practice," said the Queen. *"When I was your age, I always did it for half an hour a day. Why, sometimes I've believed as many as six impossible things before breakfast."*

"ALICE IN WONDERLAND"

Acknowledgements

Foremost, this book was hugely inspired by the Australian magazine *Nexus* and the provoking stories and issues they exposed. Thank you, Duncan Roads, for *Nexus*. Also, the work of Preston James, who so bravely wrote about the unspeakable before anyone else. The Wikimedia Commons, a media file repository making available public domain and freely-licensed educational media content, was useful in the collection of images used in this book. Keeping all knowledge and wisdom transparent, and the open source sharing of information, is the direction of the future.

The following individuals were instrumental in making this book possible: cover art and interior designer Mark J. Maxam, lead editor Doris Lora, Emily Infinity, Sarah R. Adams, Suzanne Ross, Jennifer Fahey, Penny Bradley, and special thanks to Jerry Nardini who invited me to be a writer-in-residence during the COVID-19 lockdown of 2020 when a large chunk of this book was completed. Thanks to my "weird" comrades Edward Taylor, Michael O'Rourke, Justin Weiner, Michael Gozney, John Wood, Diane Wade, and my family members, mother Elaine Olsen, father Marshall Olsen and wife Susan Olsen, brother Chris Olsen and wife Toni Olsen, and sister Marsi Sweetland and husband Riley Sweetland, and Kelsey and Charlie. Also, the "Hausman Factor." Thank you all for the encouragement, editorial suggestions and moral guidance.

This book is in memory of all those who have been persecuted or killed for their commitment to truth and justice. I gratefully invoke their courage in making the ultimate sacrifice as we stand up for universal equality and media transparency. This is the Great Awakening.

About the Author

Brad Olsen is author of ten books including three in his Esoteric Series—also *Modern Esoteric* and *Future Esoteric*. An award-winning author, book publisher and event producer, his keynote presentations and interviews have enlightened audiences at Contact in the Desert, UFO Mega Conference, the 5D events and dozens of radio (including *Coast to Coast*, and *Ground Zero*) and television shows (including *Ancient Aliens, America Unearthed, Book of Secrets, The Proof is Out There, Beyond Belief*, and *Mysteries of the Outdoors*). Brad is a founder and co-producer of the How Weird Street Faire in  the SOMA neighborhood of San Francisco. The Chicago native's esoteric writing continues to reach a wide audience while he continues breaking ground in alternative journalism, public speaking, illustration and photography.

http://www.BradOlsen.com ◆ http://www.CCCPublishing.com
http://www.EsotericSeries.com ◆ http://www.Stompers.com
http://www.HowWeird.org

INDEX

Symbols

4 a.m. talking points 11, 124, 161
5G 48, 112, 149, 162, 276, 307, 392, 421–423, 426, 430, 449, 457
9/11 24, 29, 31, 76, 83, 120, 123, 146, 152, 153, 229, 293
13 bloodline families 76, 150, 458
14th Amendment 53
16th amendment 151
100th Monkey Effect 20, 360–361
60 Minutes 39
1984 book 147–148, 162, 247

A

abductions 29, 193, 194–195, 195, 235, 250, 271, 272, 275, 277, 279
Academy of Science 416
acidosis 418
acoustic levitation 387
Act of 1871 27, 28, 39, 40–42, 53, 85, 452
acupuncture 361, 369, 442
Adama race 273
Adams, Mike 31, 267, 268
Adams, Sarah R. 446, 447, 457
Adelson, Sheldon 46
ADHD 379
adjuvants 424
Admiralty Jurisdiction 42–43
adrenochrome 254, 294
aetheric life 331
Affordable Care Act 29, 44
Afghanistan 152, 211–212, 381, 428
Africa 90, 214, 215, 227, 316, 380, 420, 423
Agape crystal 398–399
Agartha 65, 66
Agenda 21 28, 48–49, 112, 178, 179, 430
Agenda 2030 48, 178, 179
Agent Orange 169, 170, 175, 181, 419
Age of Aquarius 262
Age of Enlightenment 57, 359
Age of Reason 165
Age of Transparency 404, 452
age reversing 404
Agenda 2030 106
agriglyphs 194
Ahnenerbe 62–63, 64
Ahnenerbe Society 306
AIDS 180, 318, 379, 409, 420–421, 423, 432, 447
Air Force 181, 190–191, 193, 195, 211, 233, 260, 269
Akashic Records 24, 336–337, 347, 397
Alamo, The 271
Al-Aqsa Mosque 95
Alaska 171, 172, 334
Albania 115
Alberta, Canada 211
Albuquerque, NM 226, 233
alchemy 32, 58, 290, 376–377, 378, 388, 427
Aldebaran 60, 256
Aldrich, Nelson 44

Aldrich Plan 18, 166
Aldrin, Buzz 191, 256
Alexander, Lt. Col. John 252
Alice in Wonderland 140, 462
Alien Agenda 24, 199–200, 270–278, 291, 316–317
alkaline body 418, 420
allergies 22, 313, 409, 415
allopathic medicine 48, 198, 369, 383, 407, 410, 420, 422, 431, 433
alpha brainwave state 349, 361, 362–363
Alpha Draconians 274–276
Al Qaeda 152
ALS 418
alters 138–139, 140, 258, 308
altitude sickness 422
aluminum 47, 48, 169, 175, 177, 178, 179, 180, 182, 193, 226, 292, 387, 419, 424, 434, 451
Alzheimer's disease 178, 180, 414, 418, 434
AMA 318
Amazon rainforest 246, 343
Amazon store 214
American Revolution 81
Ames Laboratory 393
amethyst 398
anaerobic 419
Ancient Astronauts 189, 206, 213, 216, 232, 265, 285, 376, 380
ancient Greeks 369, 382, 384, 398, 407, 452
ancient scriptures 12
Anderson, Hans Christian 23
Anderson Institute 297
Andes Mountains 113
Andorra 98
Andrews Air Force Base 35
Andromeda 192
Angstrom units 397
anhydrite 396
animal harvesting 194
Annunaki 112
Antarctica 28, 107, 202, 203, 226, 231, 252, 254–256, 257, 259, 263, 264, 265, 286, 313, 321
Antarctic Treaty 256
antediluvian civilizations 208, 285, 307, 397
Antelope Valley, CA 241
anti-bacterial 382
antibiotics 383, 384, 409, 417, 432, 437
antidepressants 443
ANTIFA 38–39, 430, 451, 454
anti-gravity 15, 29, 142, 191, 192, 195, 202, 230, 249, 250, 293, 294, 317, 334, 405
anti-human agenda 199, 253, 261, 268, 275, 291, 419, 421
anti-matter 386
antimicrobial 440, 442
antioxidants 441
Anu 214
Anunnaki 207, 212–213, 271, 273–274, 277, 285, 316, 380
Apaches 234, 235, 263
apocalypse 360

Apollo Program 228, 230, 240, 303
apophylite 392
aqua regia 32, 376
Arbenz, Jacobo 110
Archimedes 327
archons 254, 269, 270, 270–273, 275, 277, 279, 314, 316–317
Archuleta Mesa 233, 234–235
Arctic Circle 378
Area 51 234, 295, 296, 386
Arecibo, PR 172
Argentina 93, 102, 105, 107, 113, 114, 116, 135, 259, 313
argyria 384, 385
Arizona 95, 174, 221, 237
Arkansas 118, 119, 171, 298
ARK crystal 392
Ark of the Covenant 380, 386
armageddon 377
Army, U.S. 236, 260, 263
Artephius 377
arthritis 382, 414, 437, 441
artificial intelligence 140, 141, 291, 310, 311, 312, 325, 436, 437
Aryans 59, 65–66, 306–307
ascension 399
Ashkenazi Jews 86
Ashlie, Dana 436–437
Asia 59, 118, 137, 315, 423
Asia Society 117
Aspartame 47, 160, 276, 278
Aspen, CO 79
Aspen Institute 79
Assyrians 59, 68, 336
asthma 22, 114, 313, 409
astral body 365
astral plane 368, 369, 453
astral travel 194, 284, 364, 369, 387
astrology 57
astronomy 269
astrophysics 331
atheism 68
Athenian Republic 46
Athens, GA 172
Atlantic City, NJ 239
Atlantic Ocean 64, 210, 246, 265, 313, 321
Atlantis 56, 59, 216, 336, 395, 397, 398
Atomic Energy Commission 335
attention deficit disorder 22
auditive levitation 387
auras 231, 327, 397, 399
aurora borealis 334
Aurum Solis 453
Auschwitz 44, 93, 104, 126, 134, 318
Australia 168, 174, 225, 227, 246, 255, 424, 463
Austria 60
autism 22, 171, 313, 318–319, 408, 409, 414, 424, 434
autoimmune disorders 22, 409, 415, 425
avatars 347, 369
Axis Powers 103, 107, 117
Ayahuasca 363
Aztalan 209
Aztec UFO crash 193–194
Aztecs 275

B

Ba'al 288
Babylon 218, 228, 262, 275, 277, 293, 380, 381, 444
Babylonians 59, 68, 336
backward engineering 35, 143, 249, 256, 340, 364, 394
Bacon, Sir Francis 57, 110
bacteria 344, 383, 384, 407, 417, 419, 425, 429, 433
Bahamas 336
baking soda 439
Balboa, Panama 192
Balducci, Monsignor Corrado 250–251
Baltic states 115
Banco Ambrosiano 99
Bangladesh 83
Banker's Trust 78–79
Bank of England 40, 66, 74–75, 97, 148
Bank of International Settlements 71, 81, 82–83
Barbie, Klaus 93
Bardon, Franz 356
barium 47, 175, 177, 178, 182, 226, 292, 419, 451
Barr, Roseanne 131
barter system 457
Base 211 202, 255
Basiago, Andrew D. 190, 194–195, 228
Bassett, Stephen 190, 194, 195–196, 250
Batman shooter 141
Baumann, Paul 461
Bavarian Illuminati 59, 75–76
Bayer 112
Bay of Pigs 135
Beatles 362
Berkeley, U.C. 400
Béchamp, Antoine 416–417, 420
Becker, Dr. Robert O. 383
bee population 199
Begich, Dr. Nick 172, 173
Belgium 107
Belize 397
Bellagio, Italy 118
Bellatoni, Nicholas 113
Bell craft 256, 265
Beloit College 208
Bennewitz, Paul 226, 233, 234–235
Berchtesgaden, Germany 60
Bering Strait 210
Berlin, Germany 61, 62, 66, 105, 108, 113, 282
Bermuda Triangle 412
Bernard, Claude 416–417, 420
Bernard, Ronald 281
Bernays, Edward 19–20, 25, 25, 162
Besant, Anna 57
Bhagavad-Gita 306
Bible 191, 207, 208, 209, 213, 214, 273, 274, 300, 380, 444
Bickel, Nathan M. 189
Big Biotech 21, 31, 418
Big Lie 25
Big Brother 14, 147–148, 154, 166
Bigelow, Robert 210, 211

Bigfoot 211, 280
Big Oil 25, 84, 101, 418
Big Pharma 21, 112, 142, 317–318, 383, 407, 418, 422, 427, 432
Bilderberg Group 48, 71, 74, 108–109, 111, 116, 117, 122, 150, 154, 354
Bin Laden, Osama 152
Binney, William 112
biotechnology 434
bioterrain 407, 409–410, 416–426, 432, 439
bioweapons 212, 422, 430
Birkenau 134
birth certificate 53
BIS 116
bismuth 385, 401
blackbody 355
black budget 15, 33
Black Arts 288
Black Forest UFO recovery 61
black goo 298, 313–314, 321
black holes 326, 355, 373
Black Knight Satellite 268–269, 329
Black Lives Matter 39, 430, 451, 454
Black Magick 55, 56, 94–95, 276, 293, 377
blackmail 150
Black Nobility 100, 288, 288–289
Black Pope 96–97
black projects 198
BlackStar, Terral 436–437
Black Sun 59, 60, 66, 68, 288, 291, 306
black tourmaline 392
bladderwrack 440
Blake, William 286
Blankfein, Lloyd 98
Blavatsky, Helena 57–58, 93, 306, 456
Blaylock, Dr. Russell 180, 425
blood brain barrier 419,, 430, 442
bloodline families 55, 270, 277, 291–292, 307
Bloody Mary 289
Blue Moon 193
bodhisattva Issa 324
Bohemian Grove 71, 74, 127, 163, 280, 288
Boleyn, Ann 56
Bolivia 211, 217, 358
Bonaparte, Napoleon 91, 290
Book of Enoch 274
Book of Life 336
Book of Proverbs 381
Bormann, Martin 92–93, 105, 115–116, 125, 126, 135
boron 437
Bose-Einstein Condensates 375, 378
Boskop Man 213
Bosman, Ananda 363
bosons 386
Boston Bombing 69, 76, 293
Boston Tea Party 81
Boston University 384
Boxer Rebellion 78
Boynton Canyon 237
Bradley, Penny 257, 258, 293
Bradstreet, Dr. Jeffrey 318–319, 408–409
Brahmins 369

brain stems 357
brainwashing 155, 159, 309, 352, 450, 458
Brandenburg, Dr. John E. 231
Braun, Eva 113, 114, 116
Brave New World 307, 308, 309
Brazil 48, 93, 105, 116, 398
bread and circuses 184
Breakaway Civilization 30, 192
Brecon Beacons, Wales 227
Brennan, John 167, 170
Bretton Woods 28, 45, 80, 82
Brexit 98
bribery 150
British Crown 40, 46, 89, 150, 151, 154
British Empire 74–75, 101, 290
British Honduras 397
British Museum 68
Britten, Chase 345
Brookings Institution 191, 332
Brown, Dan 97
Brown, Sherrod 191
Brunner, Alois 93
Brzezinski, Zbigniew 75, 79, 152–153, 157–158
Bubonic Plague 447
Buddha 94, 343, 359, 369, 385, 456, 457
Buddhism 94, 369
Buenos Aires, Argentina 102
Bulgaria 115
Bulwer, Edward Lytton 306
Burisch, Dan 295–296
Burundi 83
Bush, Barbara 120, 129
Bush crime family 119–121
Bush, George H.W. 75, 116, 119–120, 121, 126–127, 128, 132, 135, 142, 157, 259, 280, 423
Bush, George W. 119, 127, 128, 142, 157, 259, 280, 423
Bush, Jeb 120
Bush, Prescott 66, 96, 113, 116, 119, 127, 128, 135, 142, 259
Bush, Samuel P. 119
Byrd, Richard 28, 202, 254, 255, 256, 257, 264
Byrne, Charles 219

C

Cabal 26, 72, 75, 76–78, 81–84, 92, 99–101, 111, 112, 120, 122, 141, 143, 149, 150, 154–155, 156, 157, 158, 166, 171, 173, 180, 197, 198, 199, 229, 231, 237, 244, 248, 249, 252, 253, 257, 277, 290, 292, 294, 295, 307, 352, 437, 449, 450, 451, 452, 453
cacoxenite 398
cadmium 419
caduceus 363
Cain and Abel 277
calcium sulphate 396
Calhoun, John 44
California 39, 106, 168, 179, 199, 218, 234, 236, 239, 241, 244, 280, 308, 386, 400, 431, 443, 450
Calvi, Roberto 99
Cambodia 123, 170, 185

Cambridge 74, 289
Cameron, Dr. Ewin 450
Camp David 227
Camp Hero 132
Canaanites 277, 280
Canada 48, 133, 212, 225
Canaris, Wilhelm 142
Canary Islands 182
cancer 112, 118, 171, 173, 178, 180,
    199, 318, 318–319, 321, 329, 379,
    382, 406, 408, 410, 418, 418–419,
    425, 427, 436, 439, 451
candida 312, 384, 406, 407,
    425, 437, 438, 442, 444, 447
cannabinoids 438–439
Cantwell, Alan 420
Capitol building 35
Cappadocia 240
capricorn 212
carbohydrates 426
carbon 394, 399
Carlyle Group 154, 157
Carnegie, Andrew 151
Carnegie Foundation 23, 78,
    118, 154
Carnicom, Clifford 312, 393,
    433, 435
Carnicom Institute 176, 436
Carter, Jimmy 280
Cassidy, Kerry 2, 274, 296, 429
Castaneda, Carlos 269
Castello, Thomas 226, 233, 234
caste system 83
Castle, Dr. R. Michael 177
Castro, Fidel 153
Catalina Island 207
Catholic Charities 93
Catholic Church 75, 91–92,
    97–101, 268
cattle mutilations 29, 193, 194,
    233, 250, 277, 436
Cayce, Edgar 336, 365, 369,
    397, 407
CBD 409, 438–439, 441
CE-5 contact 367
censorship 15, 17, 149, 155,
    158, 161, 162
centaur 212
Center for Disease Control 22,
    31, 312, 319, 423, 431, 434,
    443, 435
Central America 137, 336, 397
Central Asia 65
Central Banks 47, 156
Central Europe 399
ceremonial magic 58
CERN 330
CFA Institute 83
chaff 177, 419
Chaikin, Paul 400
chakra systems 61, 66, 357, 362,
    363, 401, 458
Chaldea 58
Chamae Rose 378
Channel Islands 218
chaos 376
Chapala, Michael 438, 440
Chapman, Mark 140
Chatelain, Maurice 241
Chatham House 154
chemotherapy 408, 410, 418, 419

chemtrails 104, 112, 149, 162,
    167–187, 226, 267, 278,
    292, 307, 310, 311–312, 314,
    421–422, 432, 433–434, 436,
    443, 444, 449, 451
Chen, Dr. Grace 417
Chernobyl 48
Cherokees 212
Chicago, IL 39, 180, 344
chi energy 331, 346, 367
Chihuahua, Mexico 396, 400
Chile 116, 118, 136, 452
chimeras 212, 249, 305
chimpanzees 316, 373
China 32, 46, 77, 77–78, 79,
    123, 138, 148, 161, 172, 173,
    179, 214, 245, 302, 367, 376,
    413, 424, 430, 457
China Lake Naval Station 187, 237
Chinese Somatic Science Research
    Institute 367
cholera 416
Chomsky, Noam 200
Christians 288
Christ, Jesus 457
Christianity 17, 58, 68, 92,
    95–97, 111, 262, 268, 269,
    272, 279, 369
chromium 419
Chronic Fatigue Syndrome 382,
    406
chronovisor 194–195, 228
Church Committee hearings
    132–133
Churchill, Winston 38
Church, Jimmy 257
CIA 21, 24, 26, 28, 43, 50,
    66, 79–80, 96, 109–110,
    114–115, 119–120, 121–122,
    124, 125, 126, 131–143, 145,
    151, 152, 158–159, 174, 191,
    198, 229, 233, 234, 253, 255,
    275, 293, 307, 339, 420, 450
Citizens United 46, 97, 144
City College of New York 396
City of London 28, 40, 47,
    74–75, 77–78, 97, 122, 149,
    155, 275, 285, 453, 458
Civil War 27, 41, 53, 117, 144, 384
clairaudience 399
claircognizance 399
clairsentience 399
clairvoyance 58, 348, 399
Clapper, James 29, 123–124
Clarke, Arthur C. 326, 332
Clavell, James 324
Clay, General Lucius 122
clean sphere 295, 296
Cleveland, OH 117, 191
climate change 22, 31, 78, 173,
    178, 179, 181, 225, 267
climate engineering 167
Clinton, Bill 119, 126, 157, 171, 423
Clinton crime family 56, 119–120
Clinton, Hillary 157
cloning 231, 258, 276, 298, 314
Club of Rome 48, 49, 71, 74,
    78, 118, 188
coffee enemas 441, 447
cognitive dissonance 15, 22, 177
Cohen, William 172, 174, 179

Colby, William 77, 136
cold fusion 326, 337, 338
Cold War 24, 109, 114–115,
    131, 133, 153, 180, 197,
    236, 347
Coldwell, Dr. Leonard 418
Coleman, John 73, 74
Coley's toxins 419
Colgate, Dr. Stirling 195
collective consciousness 343,
    352, 360, 361, 398
Collier, Alex 251, 274
Collins, James 384
colloidal silver 376, 382–385,
    390, 415, 439, 440, 441, 442
Colombia 389
Colony Collapse Disorder 199
Colorado 79, 141, 226, 227,
    233, 234
Colorado Springs, CO 234, 268, 328
Columbus, Christopher 265
Comanches 263
comets 459
Comings, Mark 400
Committee of 300 66, 73, 79,
    89, 275
Common Core 31
common sense 23
communism 48, 109, 148, 153,
    247, 252, 288
computers 325, 340, 353, 395, 397
Condon, Richard 138
coneheads 222–223, 224, 292
conflict theory 149–150
Confucius 359
Congo 227, 428
Congress 44, 45, 47, 80, 96,
    120, 133, 136, 143, 166, 177,
    229, 236, 261, 298, 452
Connecticut 113
conquistadors 270
consciousness 331, 343, 344,
    345, 349, 352, 354, 359, 366,
    367, 370, 372, 374, 376, 387,
    398, 403–404, 410, 457–458
Consolmagno, Guy 266
conspiracy theory 21, 24, 33, 50,
    73, 79, 156, 168, 184
Constitution 27, 38, 42, 44, 46,
    67, 80, 120, 143, 149, 150,
    151, 192, 200, 229, 261
consumerism 20
contactees 194
contextomy 23
Continuity of Government 236, 237
contrails 168, 181
controlled opposition 200
Cook, Robin 152
Cooper Canyon, Mexico 223
Cooper, Gordon 241
Cooper, Harry 259
Cooper, William 24, 193, 230,
    240, 243, 256, 287
copper 209, 215, 379
Corbeta Uruguay 321
core secrets 198
COVID-19 14, 50, 54, 200,
    421–423
430, 447, 451
corporatism 37, 144
corporatocracy 28, 38–39, 56, 109

Corson, William 115
Costello, Thomas 235
Couch, J. Nathan 209
Council of the Americas 117
Council on Foreign Relations 23, 28, 45, 48, 66, 74–75, 78–80, 117, 118, 152, 154, 157, 167, 226, 424
Countering Disinformation and Propaganda Act 25, 26
COVID-19 73, 120, 212, 384, 390, 415, 421–423, 422, 423, 424, 430, 432, 451, 460, 463
Cramer, Randy 225, 257
Cremation of Care 280, 288
crimes against humanity 67
crisis actors 67
Croatia 315, 327
Crohn's disease 418
Cro-Magnon 316
Cronkite, Walter 280
crop circles 194, 412
crop dusting 175
Crowley, Aleister 56, 63, 121, 129, 288, 293
Crown Temple States 39–40
Crusades 96, 377, 398
cryptocurrencies 32
cryptology 339
crystal ball 289, 290
crystallography 392, 394
crystals 32, 375, 376, 391–402, 404
crystal skulls 397–398, 402
CSETI 287
Cuba 122, 135, 153
Cuban Missile Crisis 111, 121
Cueva de los Cristales 396–397
Cusco, Peru 224
cyborgs 306, 434
cyclopean architecture 208, 209, 217
cyclops 207
Cydonia region 231
cymatics 405, 406, 411
Czechoslovakia 115
Czech Republic 399

D

Dachau 122
Dalai Lama 324
Dallas, TX 45, 121
Dark Fleet 258
dark matter 376
DARPA 148, 195, 228, 393
Darth Vader 314
Darwin, Charles 90, 208, 309, 322
da Vinci, Leonardo 341
Dayton, OH 211
DDT 169, 170, 181
DEA 318
Dealey Plaza 121, 122
Death Ray 142
debt slavery 73, 457
Declaration of Independence 39, 40, 42, 44
Dee, John 56, 289
Deep State 13, 26, 38, 55, 75, 83, 101, 109, 110, 119, 131, 151–152, 191, 229, 257, 260
de la Vega, Dr. Laureano 439
Delphi 362, 457
Delporte Crater 228

Delta Force 232, 235
delusional parasitosis 312, 431, 437, 443
dematerialization 364
Dement, Russell 214, 215
Demiurge 271, 279
democide 451
democracy 75
Democrat party 39, 72
Denver, CO 233, 337, 460
Department of Defense 47, 96, 172, 179, 393, 423
Department of Education 48
Department of Energy 48, 124, 193, 393
Department of Homeland Security 24, 26, 29, 43, 67
depopulation 14, 23, 26, 78, 118, 162, 171, 199, 225, 253, 261, 263, 268, 271, 276, 291, 421, 423, 428, 451, 452, 458
depression 353, 425, 434, 458
desiccated blood 419
detoxification 16, 426, 439
Dhomkar, Siddharth 396
DIA 233
diabetes 318, 409, 418, 439
Diamond Body 363
diamonds 396, 398
diatomaceous earth 439–440
Dick, Philip K. 36
Diem, Ngo Dinh 98
dimensions 364, 380, 381
dinosaurs 208, 220, 221
Directed Energy Weapons 106, 171, 237, 256, 330
disclosure 16, 250, 298
diseases 334, 409, 415, 459
disinfectants 382
disinformation 133
Disney films 140
District of Columbia 40–42, 53, 275
divine feminine 398
divine right to rule 308
DMSO 441
DMT 363
DNA 30, 31, 112, 113, 155, 181, 224, 237, 249, 251, 270, 275, 278, 305, 308, 315, 316, 333, 363, 365, 373, 396, 406, 419, 427, 436, 446
Dodd, William 113
dodo bird 351
Dolly the sheep 212, 315
Dönitz, Karl 254
Donovan, Bill 126
Doresse, Jean 272
Dorland, Frank 398
Dorsch, Franz Xaver 259
doublespeak 24
Douglas, Sir William Fettes 427
Downes v. Bidwell 42
Downey, Patrick 149
Dragon's Triangle 412
Drake, Sir Francis 57
dreamscape 346
Draco ETs 112, 192, 256, 258, 271, 283, 291, 295, 297, 298, 316
droughts 172, 173, 178
Drudgaard, Lars 140
Duff, Gordon 46

Dulce, NM 192, 226, 227, 231, 232–234, 253, 276, 297, 302
Dulce Wars 232–233, 235, 298
Dulles, Allen 98, 108–109, 110, 114, 126, 132, 133, 135, 159
Dulles, Avery 135
Dulles, John Foster 108, 135
DUMBs 192, 227, 231, 235–237, 239, 242, 243, 244, 253, 258–259, 460
Dun and Bradstreet 423, 452
Dundee's School of Medicine 439
DuPonts 85, 135
dysentery 383
dystopia 147, 162, 449

E

Earth 189, 208, 212, 226, 231, 235, 240, 248, 249, 260, 268, 269, 270, 271, 272, 275, 276, 283, 307, 354, 366, 370, 371, 379, 380, 398, 405, 406, 454, 459
Earth Dilemma 16, 354
earthquakes 172, 173, 174, 182, 187, 235, 236, 237, 252, 335
Easter Island 413
Eastern esoteric traditions 58, 369
Eastern Europe 45, 148
East Germany 112–113, 114–115
Eastlund, Dr. Bernard J. 335
ebola 66, 421, 423, 432
E Bomb 317
economic collapse 421
ectoparasitic disorder 435, 436
Ecuador 214, 459
Edinburgh, Scotland 49
Edison, Thomas 164, 327, 329
Edwards AFB 241
effigy mounds 208
ego 455–457
egregore 453–454
Egypt 56, 58, 92, 208, 210, 213–214, 227, 228, 272, 288, 290, 297, 336, 344, 349, 376, 377, 380, 381
Ehrlich, Dr. Paul 326
Eichmann, Adolf 93
Einstein, Albert 330, 331, 343, 350, 370, 403
Eisenhower, Dwight D. 30, 33, 108, 109, 153, 226, 280
Eisenhower, Laura 16
electricity 461
electromagnetic fields 197–198, 361, 429
electromagnetic warfare 23, 430
Element 115 385–386
Element 116 386
elemental spirits 344
ELFs 361
Elixir of Life 32, 377
Elizabeth I 56–57
Elohim 214, 274
Emergency Use Authrization 430
Emerson, Ralph Waldo 456
EMF 406
Empire of Three Cities 28, 40, 97, 275, 453, 458
Enabling Act 120
encephalitis 425
end of money 457

endometriosis 425
England 56–57, 57, 62, 74, 77–78, 96, 115, 289
Enki 212, 274, 380
enlightenment 359, 367, 368, 457
Enoch 274
Enoch, Jonny 387, 444
Enriquez, Juan 305
entropy 394, 404
EPA 31
epidermis layers 437
epigenome 404
epilepsy 22, 439
epistemology 190
Epsilon Boötis 269
Epstein-Barr Virus 382, 409
Epstein, Jeffrey 75, 140, 150
esoteric orders 22
ESP 347
Espírito Santo, Brazil 398
essential oils 442–443
Estabrooks, Dr. G.H. 139
estrogen 178
ether 336, 343–344
etherics 284
ethnobotany 31
ethylene dibromide 419
eugenics 54, 66, 78, 90, 111, 118, 165, 171, 180, 187, 200, 227, 253, 291, 308–309, 421
Europe 59, 77, 92, 107, 119, 137, 150, 219, 265, 316, 376, 381, 423
European Economic Community 107
European Union 108, 108–109, 123, 141
Event 201 430
Everard, Christopher 93
Evergreen Air 174
Evian, France 76, 154
evolution 208, 210, 214, 292, 305, 322, 352, 365, 454, 456, 457
Executive Order 11110 45, 50
Exley, Dr. Christopher 178
exopolitics 250–251, 268, 270, 288
Exploratory Studies Facility 237
extra-dimensionals 290, 298
extraterrestrials 12, 21, 29–30, 143, 188, 189, 194, 196, 198, 208, 213, 228, 230, 233, 249–250, 251–252, 256, 270–278, 287–288, 293, 294, 296–297, 398, 405, 435, 460, 461
Ezekiel's wheel 300

F

Fabian Society 85, 90
Facebook 21, 31, 124, 148, 200, 244
face-recognition programs 148
fact checkers 200
Fagan, Myron 151, 157, 159
Fairbanks, AK 172
fake news 13, 20, 25, 50, 200, 246, 248, 268, 357
Falklands War 313, 321
Fallen Angels 112, 274, 276
false flag operations 26, 27, 29, 38, 56, 67, 69, 76, 85, 112, 138, 145, 146, 152, 153, 153–154, 179, 255, 357, 422
false flags 106, 293
false matrix 9, 388, 403
famine 49, 334

Faraday, Michael 327
Farsight Institute 347, 454
fascism 12, 23, 36–165, 107, 108–109, 118, 122, 135, 144, 161–162, 175
Fascist Party Federation 34
fast kill agendas 268, 276, 292
Fatima 95
Faust, Dr. Johannes 290
FBI 26, 43, 96, 122, 124, 132, 137, 143, 152, 191, 232, 284, 450
FCC 48
Federal Drug Administration (FDA) 21, 31, 47, 141, 318, 409, 410, 441
federal income tax 151
Federal Reserve 18, 28, 44–45, 50–51, 71, 72, 78, 83, 85, 96, 98, 101, 118, 122, 151, 152, 156, 166, 258, 458
FEMA 26, 29, 43, 67, 96, 120, 142, 227, 423
Ferguson, Thomas 175
fermentation 419, 420
Fetzer, James Henry 112
fiat currency 47, 120, 156
fiber optics 15
fibromyalgia 418, 435
fifth column 317
final solution 316
fire crystals 395, 397
Firestone, Harvey 164
First Amendment 38, 200
First Nation 212
Fitts, Catherine Austin 229
flaxseed oil 439
floods 173, 236
Florida 120, 318, 408
Flower of Life 363
Flugscheiben 35
fluoride 14, 20, 112, 160, 162, 171, 181, 276, 307, 419, 449
flying saucers 30, 60, 66, 194, 203, 230, 249, 250, 300, 461
Foerster, Brien 244
force multiplier 172, 174, 183, 307
Ford, Gerald 280
Ford Foundation 118, 151
Ford, Henry 135, 164
formaldehyde 48, 424
Forrestal, James 255
Fort Bliss, TX 253
Fort Detrick, MD 137, 420, 423
Fort Hero 297
Fort Mead, MD 227
fossil fuels 254, 326, 327, 418
Founding Fathers 41, 45
fourth dimension 197
Fourth Reich 62, 107, 111–115, 115, 122, 137, 254, 255, 259, 317
fracking 23, 112
fractals 333, 350
France 48, 76, 77, 98, 101, 108, 115, 121, 157, 315, 430
Freedom of Information Act 137, 138, 263
free energy 15, 18, 24, 30, 48, 137, 192, 197, 226, 248, 249, 250, 254, 255, 294, 326, 327, 330, 333, 334, 336, 337, 395, 397, 400, 402, 405, 461
Freeland, Elana 179–180

Freemasonry 22, 27, 58, 59, 61, 74, 82–83, 86, 96, 97, 135, 148, 150, 204
free speech 162
free will 23, 31, 33, 72, 160, 270, 279, 280, 282, 297, 311, 354, 404, 453, 455, 455–456
French National Council for Scientific Research 30
frequency 404, 406, 410, 422, 426, 429, 431, 436, 455, 457–458
Freud, Sigmund 20, 162
Friedman, Milton 118
Friedman, Stanton 301
Frondizi, Arturo 259
Fudenberg, Dr. H.H. 313
Fukushima 48, 292, 451
Fulford, Benjamin 139, 244
Fuller, R. Buckminster 332–333
Fulvic minerals 415
fungal overgrowth 312, 384, 390, 407, 429, 437

G

G20 158
Gagarin, Uri 299
gag orders 169, 177, 240
Gaia Hypothesis 344
gain of function 212, 430
Gajewski, Eric 94
Gakona, AK 172, 334
Galilei, Galileo 405–406
Gallo, Dr. Robert 180
Galton, Francis 90
Gandhi, Mahatma 16
Garcia-Ruiz, Juan 396
gargoyle 212
Gasparri, Pietro 97
Gates, Bill 130, 170, 187, 424, 430
GcMAF 171, 318–319, 408–410, 414, 440, 441
Gehlen, Reinhard 109, 114–115, 135
Gehlen, Reinhardt 126
Gelli, Licio 98
gemstones 376, 392, 398–399
General Curia 96–97
Genesis 207, 208, 214, 274, 282
genetics 215–216, 233, 292, 316
Geneva Convention 418
Geneva, Switzerland 330
geoengineering 22, 23, 149, 167–187, 199, 226, 267, 311–312, 312, 334, 335, 419, 430, 433, 435, 436–437
Georgetown University 135, 146
George Washington University 243
Georgia 44, 172
Georgia Guidestones 112, 162, 165, 292, 317
German UFOs 35
Germany 47, 59–61, 65, 75–76, 77, 92–93, 98, 102, 105, 107, 110–112, 113, 119, 126, 134, 157, 202, 214, 216, 253, 262, 306, 315, 406, 459
germ theory 320, 415–418, 426, 428
Gestapo 29, 61, 93, 116, 120
giants 207–212, 252
gigantism 215
Gingrich, Newt 280
Ginzburg, Dr. Vladimir 331

Giza Plateau 297, 387
Glen Rose, TX 220
Global Collateral Accounts 45
global dimming 430
global warming 49, 173, 177, 226
gluons 386
glyphosate 419
GMOs 14, 21, 47, 112, 149,
    160, 162, 179, 181, 278, 292,
    307, 315, 419, 427, 449, 451
Gnostic 288
Gnostics 269, 271, 272–273,
    314, 369
Gobi Desert 59
Goddard, Ian Williams 142
Goebbels, Joseph 20, 25, 115,
    148, 160
goethite 398
gold 32, 77, 80, 135–136, 152,
    213, 229, 253, 273, 314, 324,
    376, 377, 378, 379, 380, 388
Golden Age 360, 371, 410, 452
Golden Rule 84, 279
Goldilocks Zone 344
Goldman Sachs 98
gold standard 28, 29, 80, 380
Goliath 207, 214
Goode, Corey 190, 258, 259, 279
Google 21, 31, 124, 200, 244,
    307, 310
Gore, Al 78, 137
Göring, Hermann 36, 60, 107,
    115, 116
Gosling, Tony 116
Gottlieb, Sidney 134, 137
Gøtzsche, Dr. Peter 142
Grant, Ulysses S. 28, 40
graphine oxide 430
gravity 331–332, 369, 387, 405
Greada Treaty 192–193, 295, 317
Great Awakening 13, 279, 404,
    450, 453, 463
Great Britain 157, 192, 219,
    255, 256, 307, 313
Great Brotherhood of Light 454
Great Depression 85, 117, 143
Great Pyramid 349, 380, 413
Great Wall of China 413
Greece 55, 244, 288, 359
Greek mythology 262, 334
Greer, Steven 287
Greer, William 121
Grey, Ed 337–338
Grey, Edwin 461
Grey ETs 192, 212, 226, 231,
    234, 235, 258, 271, 272, 273,
    275, 277, 293, 295, 297, 323
Griffin, Kandy 433
griffons 212
Group of Thirty 117
Guantanamo Bay 142, 154
Guatemala 110, 135, 216, 434
Guderian, Heinz 64
Guerin, Pierre 30
Guernica, Spain 106
Gulf of Mexico 314
Gulf of Tonkin incident 153, 154
gun control 111, 112
Gunderson, Ted 152
Gurdjieff 61
gurus 369
Gutenberg Press 32, 161, 357

Guyana 141
Guyton, Dr. Arthur C. 420
gypsum 396, 400

H

H1N1 423
HAARP 171–173, 177, 179, 182,
    186, 226, 252, 334–335, 393,
    436, 437, 444
Hadad 288
Haig, Alexander 122
Haiti 83
Hall, Dr. Howard 369
Hall, Manly P. 55–56, 94–95
Hamilton, ill 234
Ham Radio 269
Ham the chimp 373
Hanseatic League 275
happiness 368, 455
Haramein, Nassim 365, 392
Harding, Warren G. 164
Harlan, Marshall 42
harpy 212
Harriman, Averell 96, 116
Harvey, Claire 423
Harwood, Richard 79
Haunebu craft 35, 61
Haushofer, Karl 60, 61
Havel, Václav 324
HCQ 430
healing technology 250
Health Ranger 31
Hearst, William Randolph 135
heart disease 425
HeartMath 410
Hebrew Qabalah 58
Hebrews 336, 381
Hedges, Chris 144
Hedges v. Obama 144
Hegelian Dialectic 85, 422
Heisenberg Uncertainty Principle
    344, 367
Heisenberg, Werner 324
helicopters 386
Helmholtz resonance theory 265
Helms, Richard 133, 137, 139
hematite 392, 399–400
Hemingway, Ernest 260
hemoglobin 422
hendecagram 414
Henry, Patrick 188
Henry VIII 56
Hepatitis B 420
Hepatitis C 432
herbicides 419
herd immunity 425
Hermes 290, 363, 413
Hermes Trismegistus 344–345,
    356, 377
Hermetic Gnosticism 290
Hermeticism 344–345, 356
Hermetic philosophy 57, 377
herpes 382, 409
Herzl, Theodor 75
Hesemann, Michael 250
Hess, Rudolf 60, 61
Hewlett-Packard 397–398
Heydrich, Reinhard 74
Hicks, Abraham 455–456
Hidden Hand 275
hidden in plain sight 262
Hielscher, Friedrich 62–63

higher dimensions 364
Hilder, Anthony 79
Himalayas 359
Himmler, Heinrich 60, 62–63,
    66, 69, 94, 115, 306
Hinduism 58
Hindus 342, 369, 379
Hippocrates 384, 407, 442
Hirschberg, Dr. Leonard Keene 382
History Channel 114, 463
Hitler, Adolf 38, 44, 47, 54,
    58–59, 60, 63–65, 75, 92,
    105, 113–114, 115, 119, 128,
    132, 139, 148, 259, 306
hive mind 199, 254
HJR-192 27
Ho Chi Minh Trail 185
Höhne, Heinz 65
holistic medicine 318, 319
Holloman AFB 193, 295
Hollywood 31, 131, 276, 307, 450
Holocaust 93, 268, 309
holographic technology 24, 168,
    195, 239, 252, 272
holographic universe 12–13, 279,
    333, 350, 361
Holy See 92–93, 97
Homeland Security 83, 111, 112,
    120, 124, 142, 170, 229, 239
homeopathy 369, 407, 410,
    415, 442
homeostasis 420
Homo Capensis 292
Homo erectus 213, 223, 248, 323
Homo Evolutis 305, 310
Homo sapiens 213, 223, 292,
    309–310, 316
homosexuality 95, 420
honey traps 74–75, 150
Hong Kong 367, 430
Hoover, J. Edgar 122, 280
Hopkins, Bill 169
House of Rothschild 44
Houston, TX 121
Howe, Linda Moulton 296
HR-5736 27
Huan Tan 379
Huayqui skeleton 224
Hudes, Karen 82
Hudson, David 378, 386
Hughes Aircraft 434
human genome 354
human mutilations 193, 233
human sacrifice 281, 283, 291,
    293, 316
human trafficking 46, 235, 288
Hungary 115, 449
Hunger Games 73
Huntington's disease 438
Hurons 207
hurricanes 168, 172, 173, 185
Hutchinson, William 87
Huxley, Aldous 54, 307, 450
Huxley, Julian 54, 309
hybridization 193
hybrids 288, 296, 297, 298, 306,
    309, 316, 317
hydroxychloroquine 422
Hylan, John Francis 44
Hyperboreans 223
hyper-dimensionals 271–272,
    277–278, 290, 295, 391

hyperthermia 419
hypnosis 368
Hypogeum 240

I

IANS 337
Ibis Project 253
IBM 259, 353, 394
Ice Age 210, 211, 292
Iceland 449, 452
Icke, David 32, 40, 76, 143, 293, 313–314
ICLEI 28, 48–49
icosahedron 412
IDT Biologika 66
I.G. Farben 44, 75, 108, 112, 116, 119, 130, 135, 318
Ignatius of Loyola 288
Illinois 208
Illuminati 22, 27, 43, 45, 68, 71, 74–76, 76, 81–82, 98–100, 148, 150, 154, 229, 237, 255, 261, 268, 271, 277, 318
IMF 81, 113, 152
immune system 171, 178, 199, 292, 313, 318, 319, 382, 384, 385, 404, 408, 409, 414, 415, 416, 417–418, 422, 424, 425, 427, 429, 430, 440, 452
immunotherapy 408, 417
Inalco House 113
Incas 211
income tax 166
indeed 404
India 57, 79, 90, 121, 172, 359, 369, 376, 423
Indian Black Salve 443
Indiana 209
Indonesia 45
INFEKTON 420–421
influenza 421
Information Age 334
informed consent 425
infrared light 355, 361
infrasound vibration 361
Inner Earth 264, 286
inner peace 368
innerterrestrials 198, 203, 253, 277
Inouye, Daniel 44
Inquisition 249, 288
INSCOM 347
Instagram 430
Institute for Pacific Relations 118
Institute of Noetic Sciences 13
inter-dimensional ETs 270, 271, 274, 276, 277, 293, 298
International Executive Service Corps 118
International Health Regulations 120
International Monetary Fund (IMF) 27, 71, 72, 98
International Uniform Commercial Code (UCC) 46
Internet 27, 32, 112, 124, 141, 155, 156, 158, 161, 175, 200, 310, 326, 352, 354, 357, 433, 453
Internet of things 141
Interplanetary Corporate Conglomerate 258, 259
Interpol 96, 122

intuition 370, 399
Invention Secrecy Act 205
invisible government 19
Invisible Masters 58, 94, 248, 293
iodine 416
ionization 361
ionosphere 171, 172, 178, 186, 334–335, 349, 444
Iowa 208
Iran 32, 123, 135, 179, 376, 430
Iran-Contra 119
Iraq 268, 381
Ireland 219
iridium 32, 378
iron 392, 399
Iroquois 207
irradiation 419
IRS 21, 43, 81, 83
Isis 288, 290
Isis Unveiled 57
Islam 97, 269, 369, 460
Israel 68, 77, 96, 98, 112, 115, 123, 244, 359, 362
Italy 47, 77, 98–100, 107, 108, 113, 116, 135, 174, 330, 353, 458
Ivermectin 430

J

jade 398
Jakubcin, Robert 191
James, Preston 26, 77, 96, 143, 199–200, 258, 275, 276, 314, 463
James, Trevor 29
Janeway, Charles 424
Janus Principle 164
J. Craig Venter Institute 315
Jekyll Island 44
Jenny, Hans 406
Jeopardy TV show 353
Jerusalem, Israel 95, 155
Jesus Christ 87, 91, 216, 252, 343, 359, 369
Jews 59, 62, 97, 268, 288, 381
JFK assassination 24, 97, 119, 121–122, 135
Jiankui, He 307
Jinn 272, 293
Johns Hopkins University 146
Joint Chiefs of Staff 153
Jonestown 141
Joseph, Frank 255
J-Rod 295–296
Jackson, Andrew 44, 45
Japan 136, 172, 260, 367, 376, 402, 409, 412, 421
JASON Scholars 226
Jefferson, Thomas 36, 44, 305, 415
Jesuits 23, 65, 75, 91, 95–97, 100, 102, 271, 289
jinn 269, 282
Juan, Don 271
Judaism 381
Judeo-Christianity 59
jump room 195, 228, 277, 297
Jung, Carl 55, 132, 377, 427
Jupiter 288

K

Kabbalah 369, 381, 389

Kaku, Dr. Michio 181
Kaltenbrunner, Ernst 122
Kaluza-Klein Theory 370–371
Kaluza, Theodor 370
Kandahar Giant 211–212
Kanduc, Dr. Darja 424–425
Kangchenjunga 121
Kant, Immanuel 324
karma 58, 142, 272, 324, 365, 371, 404, 454
Karnak 380
Kasten, Len 283
Katrina hurricane 121
Keely, John Ernst Worrell 337
Kelly, Sir Edward 290
Kennan, George 109
Kennebunkport, Maine 96
Kennedy, Bobby 121–122, 141
Kennedy, John F. 44, 45, 50–51, 79, 98, 109, 111, 121–122, 128, 135, 136
Kennedy, Joseph 45
Kentucky 208
Kenya 428
Kerry, John 28, 75, 256
Ketogenic Diet 426
Keyhoe, Donald 269
Keynes, John Maynard 71
KGB 29, 96, 421
Khazarian Mafia 120
Khrushchev 111
kidney damage 385
Kierkegaard, Søren 188
King Arthur 69
King David 214
King George III 39
King George V 163
King, Godfré Ray 376
King Heinrich the Fowler 60
King Juan Carlos 256
King Og 214
King's Chamber 349, 380
Kingsford, Anna 57
Kirby, Peter A. 182
Kirlian photography 327, 361
Kirtland base 193, 233
Kissinger, Henry 76, 122–123, 125, 154–155, 191, 280, 452
Knights of Columbus 96
Knights of Malta 93, 96, 97, 98, 135
Knights Templar 86, 96, 108, 148, 289, 398
Koch brothers 79
Koire, Rosa 49
Kolvenbach, Peter Hans 96
Koontz, Dean 451
Koran 214
Korea 138, 376
Koshima island 360
Kraemer, Fritz 122, 122–123
Kremlin 109, 236
Krishna 369
Krishnamurti 57
Kronos 256
Kruger and Monarch 257, 258
Kubark Interrogation Manual 140
Kubrick, Stanley 332
Kucinich, Dennis 181
kundalini 363, 399, 458
Kurzweil, Ray 141, 310, 311, 326, 352
Kybalion 344

Kyle-Sidell, Cameron 422

L

La Palma island 182
LaBerge, Steven 346
Labyrinth Group 258, 294
Lader, Philip 174
Laibow, Dr. Rima 423–424
laissez faire 110
Lake Delavan 208
Lake Lahontan 211
Lake Mills, WI 209
Lake Titicaca 211
Lam 293
La Mana, Ecuador 459
Lancashire, England 96
Langley, VA 339
Laos 123, 170, 185
Lao Tzu 22, 359
Larson, Dewey 331
Lash, John 314
Lateran Treaty 97
Latin America 92, 102, 105,
    110, 136, 420
Law of Attraction 371
Law of One 216
Law of Similars 442
Lawrence Livermore Lab 386
Lazar, Bob 235, 364, 386
LBJ 122
lead 396
Leadbeater, C.W. 57
League of Nations 118, 157
leaky gut 419, 425
Lear, John 245, 260
Leary, Timothy 450
Lebanon 362
Le Carre, John 97
legacy bases 234, 248
Leitao, Mary 432
Lemuria 59, 283
lepidocrocite 398
Lessin, Dr. Sasha Alex 213
Leviathan 286
levitatation 457
levitation 364, 367, 369, 377,
    378, 379, 380, 387
Lewis, Clyde 436
Lewis, Sinclair 38
ley lines 405, 412, 413
Library of Alexandria 344
Libya 227
Liechtenstein 98
LifeLog project 148
lightening 175
Lincoln, Abraham 97
Lion's Roar, The 56
Lippmann, Walter 25
lithium 178
lobal warming 188
Lockheed 195, 241
Logan Act 164
Logan, Gordon 97–98
Lokas 284
London, England 25, 66, 86, 99,
    147, 157, 219, 253, 259, 289
longevity 376, 377
Long Island, NY 297, 330
Looking Glass technology 193,
    194–195, 331–332, 336, 364,
    365, 388, 462
loosh 254, 270, 279, 316

Lord Acton 449
Los Alamos, NM 227, 234, 238
Los Angeles, CA 207, 239, 253, 441
Lou Gehrig's disease 180
love 455, 456, 457, 458
Lovelock Cave 210–211
Lovett, Robert 117
low information voters 23
Loyola, Ignatius 96
LSD 133, 134, 135, 146, 434, 450
Lubaantun, Belize 397
Lubbock, TX 263
Lucas, George 279
lucid dreaming 346, 348, 366, 367
Lucifer 68, 94, 95, 212, 275–
    276, 281, 288, 291, 293
L.U.C.I.F.E.R. 95
Luckman, Sol 333
Ludwig, Thorsten 337
Luminous Lodge 60
Lunan, Duncan 269
lupus 418, 422
Luxembourg 108
Lyme Disease 176, 312, 384,
    432, 442, 446, 447
Lyra 192
Lytton, Edward Bulwer 90

M

Macao, China 46
Machiavellian plans 116, 151
macrophages 408
Mad Cow Disease 436
Madison Avenue advertising 25
Madison Square Garden 124
Madison, WI 112, 209
mafia 96, 99
Magdalena River 389
magic 24, 30, 94–95, 287, 289,
    290, 353, 455
magnetosphere 335
Magnipulsion Engine 337–338
Maharishi Effect 362
Maitland, Edward 57
Majestic-12 28, 143, 191, 195,
    243, 257, 296, 301
Malaysia 367
Malibu, CA 239
Malta 78, 240
Malthusianism 309, 333
Manchurian Candidates 177
mandalas 406
mandatory vaccinations 120,
    125, 162, 421, 422, 423
Manet, Édouard 125
manifestation 370
manna 32, 378
Manson, Charles 140
Mantis aliens 275, 296
Manu 59
Maple Creek, WI 209
Marchetti, Victor 133
Marciniak, Barbara 131
Marconi, Guglielmo 327, 328, 329
Marconi Labs 314
marijuana 318
Marine Corps 146, 177, 198
Maritime Law 42–43, 53
Marlowe, Christopher 57
martial law 44, 76, 131, 143,
    156, 422, 423
Martin, Bernard 37

Martin, John 444
Martin, Malachi 94
mass media 15, 20, 21, 25–26,
    32, 69, 73, 76, 138, 142,
    150, 152, 154, 155, 158–160,
    178, 179, 199–200, 210, 254,
    268, 276, 291, 293, 307, 337,
    352, 354, 450, 453, 456
materializer technology 250
mathematics 289, 342, 362, 405
Matrix, the movie 21, 50, 345
Matthew 10:26 36
Mauritius 351
Max Planck Institute 406
Maxwell, James Clerk 370–371
Maxwell, Jordan 43, 444
Mayans 214, 216, 275, 283,
    371, 387, 397
Mayer, Carl 144
May, Theresa 139
McCloy, John J. 137
McFadden Act 80
McKusick, Eileen 445
McMinnville, OR 174
McVeigh, Timothy 76, 140
measles 423, 424
MedBeds 404
Medicine Wheel 399
Meier, Billy 395
Melchizedek, Drunvalo 394
Mellon, Andrew 135
Mellon Foundation 151
Melody Stones 398
Mena, AK 119, 126
Mengele, Josef 93, 104, 126, 134
Mercola, Dr. Joseph 425
mercury 48, 180, 377, 380, 424
Merkabah 363
Merkel, Angela 139
Merker, Germany 125
mermaid 212, 262, 280
Mesoamerica 402
Messiah 95
metals 375–390
meteorites 399
Methernitha 461
MI5 and MI6 57, 66, 96, 97,
    136, 229, 235
Michelangelo 355
microbes 415, 416
microchips 174, 307
micronations 260–261
microwaves 335
Middle Ages 73, 377
MIEC 192
MILABS 272, 298
Milarepa 343
Military Industrial Complex 15,
    30, 33, 111, 152, 157, 168,
    179, 191–192, 227, 257, 259
Miller, Mark Crispin 160–161
Milner, Lord Alfred 74
Milosevic, Slobodan 123
Ministry of Truth 147
Miranda, Dr. Luis 167
Mississippi River 210
Maine 96
malaria 419, 422, 434, 438
Manchurian Candidate 131,
    138–139, 145
Manzano Mountains 193
Marconi, Guglielmo 327

Mars 30, 195, 225–226, 227, 229, 230–231, 245, 248, 257, 275, 277, 278, 332, 347, 348
Marx, Karl 72, 98, 149, 150, 151
Maryland 137, 227, 423
Massachusetts 384
Maxwell, Jordan 43, 444
meditation 353, 362, 370, 403, 455
Men in Black 298
Mesopotamia 376, 377
Mexico 223, 396–397, 400, 413, 428
Miami, FL 153
Michigan 208, 209
Middle East 76, 110, 115, 123, 174, 265, 376, 451
Milky Way galaxy 373
mind control 49, 132–134, 138–140, 140, 143, 145, 158, 174, 179, 231, 252, 253, 254, 257, 271, 276, 277, 297, 307, 309, 317, 318, 434, 450, 451
MIT 239, 424
Mitchell-Hedges, Anna 397
Mitchell, Joni 441
mites 442
MK-Naomi 436
MK-Ultra 56, 110, 126, 131–146, 145–146, 177, 253, 317, 318, 434, 450
MMR vaccine 423
MMS 415, 438, 441
Mohammed 343, 369
moldavite 399
mold spores 419
Moloch 280, 288
Monaco 98
Mona Lisa 228
Monast, Serge 252
monatomic elements 32, 375, 377–380, 381
monatomic gold 31, 273, 378, 380, 386, 388
Monkey Mind 456
Monsanto 112, 118, 169, 179, 199, 307
Montalk, Tom 271–272
Montauk chair 228
Montauk, NY 132
Montauk Project 297–298
Montini, Monsignor Giovanni Battista 93
Montreal, Canada 157
Montserrat, Spain 92
Monty Python 17
Moon 225–226, 227, 228, 229, 230–231, 240, 248, 257, 269–270, 288, 303, 332, 347
Moore's Law 310, 326
Moray, T. Henry 461
Morell, Theodor 60
Morgan, J.P. 30, 44, 80, 81, 98, 135, 328, 330
Morgellons 174, 176, 176–177, 212, 308, 311, 313, 314, 384, 393, 419, 431–444, 446, 447
Moscow, Russia 64, 172, 174, 236
Moses 343, 380
Mossad 26, 96, 115, 143, 146, 152, 229
Mossadegh, Mohammad 110
Mothman 274, 275, 283

Mound Builders 208, 209, 219
Mount Blanc 227
Mount Naica 396
Mount St. Helens 336
Mount Weather, VA 227, 236
MRSA infections 384, 442
MSG 278
Mt. Graham 95
MUFON 196
mujahidin 152
Mullins, Eustace 157
Multiple Sclerosis 438
multiverse 30, 270
mumps 423
Munich, Germany 59, 65
Murchison, Clint 119
Murdoch, Rupert 160, 161
Murkowski, Lisa 177
Murphy, Chris 25
mushrooms 441–442
musical frequencies 405
Musk, Elon 239
Muslims 97, 135, 288
Mussolini, Benito 34, 37, 47, 103, 107, 144, 148
mustard gas 418
mystery schools 12, 204, 272, 288–289, 369
mysticism 59, 343, 346, 366, 368–369

N

Nacht Waffen 257, 258, 293
NAFTA 84
nagalase 171, 307, 313, 318, 408, 409, 410
Nag Hammadi 272–273, 314
Naica Mine 396, 400
Namibia 401
nanobots 178, 212, 311, 436–437, 437, 438, 446, 451
nanoparticles 176–177, 180, 182, 292, 419
nanotechnology 174, 176–177, 265, 268, 278, 310, 354, 433, 446
Napa County, CA 236
Naples, Italy 62
NASA 96, 111, 125, 137, 178, 180, 191, 198, 228, 230, 241, 253, 263, 269, 310, 327, 332, 373, 383
Nascimento, Gavin 56
National Archives 114, 115, 116, 119, 301
National Institute of Health 21, 305–306, 426
national security 84, 109, 131, 135, 136, 140, 205, 228, 334, 336
National Weather Service 169
Native Americans 169, 207, 210, 263, 346, 368, 397, 399
NATO 32, 92, 96, 115, 120, 229, 255
Naval Intelligence 24, 230
Navy 255, 260, 269
Nazi party 54, 69, 75, 94, 98–99, 102, 107, 124, 202, 230, 247, 254–256, 306, 381
NDAA 25, 29, 44, 112, 124, 136, 142, 144, 205, 229, 434

Neanderthals 223, 315–316, 323
near death experiences 368, 404
negative air ions 361
Nephilim 213, 214, 274, 277
NESARA/GESARA 334, 404, 452
Netherlands 108
neurotoxins 419, 424
Neuschwabenland 255–256, 264
neutrinos 330, 387
Nevada 210, 211, 234, 239, 260, 296
New Age 251, 276, 376, 398, 450, 451
New Berlin base 255
New Guinea 343
New Jersey 38–39
New Mexico 190, 192, 193, 226, 231, 253, 295, 298, 302
Newton, Isaac 377
Newtown, CT 112
New World Order 14, 27, 32, 33, 39, 70, 72, 73, 75, 77, 84, 94, 95, 97, 99–100, 111, 119, 132, 137, 142, 150, 155, 157, 159, 161, 165, 179, 252, 253, 255, 274, 276, 291, 293, 309, 310, 317, 450, 458, 460
New York City 39, 44, 57, 79, 98, 124, 239, 328, 414, 420, 424
New York state 118, 208, 383
New Zealand 225
NGOs 49, 96
NHK Museum of Broadcasting 402
Nibiru 168, 213, 273–274, 279, 380
Nicaragua 428
nickel 419
Nietzsche, Friedrich 58–59, 306
Nightmare Hall 233–234
Nikhilananda 342
Ninth Circle Satanic cult 101
Nitze, Paul 109
Nixon, Richard 28–29, 123, 137, 280, 380
NOAA 169
Nobel Prize 418
noble metals 32
noetics 13
non-violence 144
Norfolk, VA 255
North America 208, 215, 219, 227, 231, 423
North Carolina 318, 423
Northrop 241
Norway 172
Nova Scotia, Canada 260
NSA 21, 26, 29, 96, 110, 112, 124, 139, 142, 151, 155, 174, 191, 193, 227, 258, 294
nuclear weapons 317
Nuremberg Code 66, 180, 434–435
Nuremberg Trials 62, 63, 66, 93, 107, 110, 116, 122, 125, 434
N.W.7 division 116–117
NYC University 399–400, 400

O

Obamacare 31
Obama, Barack 25, 29, 44, 124, 136, 139, 157, 195, 259, 274, 423
Oberth, Herman 30
O'Brien, Cathy 139–140

schizophrenia 252
Schmitz, Hermann 116–117
Schneider, Phil 180, 231–233, 298
School of the Americas 136
Schopenhauer, Arthur 57
Schumann Resonance 349–350, 406–407, 411
Schutzstaffel (SS) 61, 62–63
scientific method 21
scoliosis 357
Scotland 172
Scott, Walter 132, 163
scrying mirrors 289, 300, 387
Sea of Muscovy 303
Secret Doctrine, The 57, 57–58, 94, 306
Secret Government 24, 157, 187, 191, 228, 460
Secret Service 121, 232
secret societies 20, 24, 61, 63, 66, 75–76, 148, 150, 287, 306, 458
Secret Space Program 14, 30, 195, 196, 225, 226, 229, 249, 254, 257–258, 293, 298
Secret Teachings of All Ages 55–56
Sedona, AZ 237
Segal, Jacob 420
seizures 439
selenite 392, 396, 400
selenium 415
self-mastery 362–363
self-realization 363
Selsun Blue 437
Sephirot 381
Serbs 327
Serratia marcescens 434
sex slavery 132
SFI study 82, 88
Shadow Government 38, 75–76, 99–101, 110, 122, 142, 143, 226, 272, 294
Shah of Iran 110, 118
Shakespeare, William 57
shamans 331, 343, 369, 377, 401
Shambhala 65
Shangri-La 254
Shankara 324
shape-shifting 293, 296, 316
Shaw, George Bernard 85
Sheldrake, Rupert 345
Sheppard-Towner Maternity and Infancy Protection Act 53
Shipp, Kevin 151–152
Siberia 246
Sierra Leone 423
Sierra Nevada mountains 378
Sievers, Wolfram 62–63
silicon 392, 394, 398, 399
Silva, Freddy 221
silver 32, 50, 77, 176, 324, 376, 377, 378, 381–385, 396
silver cord 346
Simpson, Christopher 117
Sinai region 380
Sinclair, Upton 188
singularity 310, 326, 352, 364
Sirhan Sirhan 140–141
Sirius A 192
Sitchin, Zecharia 213, 250, 273, 282, 380

Skidmore, Mark 229
Skoda Works 254
Skorzeny, Otto 62, 115, 126
Skull & Bones 27, 71, 74, 75, 120, 127, 135
Skunk Works 30, 231
slow kill programs 47–48, 111, 268, 270, 276, 307, 406, 408
smallpox 423
Smart City 422, 430
smart dust 311, 312, 421–422, 434, 446
Smart Meters 276
smart technology 306
Smiljan, Croatia 327
Smith, Emery 295, 298
Smith-Mundt Act 27, 50, 450
Smithsonian Institution 209, 210, 219
Smith, Steven J. 238
smokie quartz 398
Snark 455
Snopes 156
Snowden, Edward 29, 124, 150, 175
social credit scores 148, 161
social media 21, 27
Social Security 53
Society of Jesus 96–97
sociopaths 83–84
soft disclosure 16
soft kill operations 14, 15, 162, 171, 180–181, 200, 226–227, 292, 419
Solar Radiation Management 47, 167, 168, 177
Solar Warden 257, 258
solar winds 459
sonic healing 334
Soniferous Ether 397
sorcery 57, 69, 94–95
Soros, George 39, 70
soul net 269–270
sound 406
South Africa 118, 213, 224, 423
South America 93, 103, 107, 110, 114, 116, 122, 126, 134, 209, 259, 423
South China Sea 173
Southeast Asia 93, 123
Southern Ocean 226, 246, 313
South Korea 424
South Pole 264
South Sandwich Islands 313, 314, 321
Sovereign Military Order of Malta 78
Soviet Union 61, 109, 111, 114–115, 269, 299
Space Command 260
Space Force 422
spacetime 345
spagyric 377
Spain 92, 93, 116, 206, 270, 315, 381
Spangler, David 275–276
Spanish Armada 57, 289
Spear of Destiny 60, 70
Spears, Max 298
Special Access Programs 229
spectroscopy 377
speed of light 198, 330, 331, 366
Speer, Albert 115, 258–259

Spellman, Cardinal 98
sperm counts 170
Sphinx 212, 336
Spiers, Max 253
Spirit Cooking 56
Spitzer Space Telescope 373
Spörri, Gregor 213–214
Sputnik 269, 329
spy craft 57
squalene 48, 180
Sri Yantra 363
Stalin, Josef 36, 38, 148
Standard Model of Physics 330
Standard Oil 117, 130, 135, 171, 259
Stanford Research Institute 23, 194, 307, 347
Stangl, Franz 93
Stanzas of Dzyan 58
staph infections 451
Starbucks 262
Starchild skull 223
stargates 228, 250, 331, 340, 364
Star Trek 30, 192, 248, 297
Star Wars 362
Stasi 29, 112, 115
State Department 159, 450
Stateville Penitentiary malaria study, 434
Statue of Liberty 262, 414
St. Augustine of Hippo 262
Stealth bomber 328
Steinbeck, John 200
Steiner, Rudolf 63, 290, 336
Stevens, Ted 171
St. Louis, MO 170
Stockwell, John 79
Stone Age 343
Stonehenge 413
Stonyhurst College 96
Strasbourg, Germany 107
strategy of tension 14, 20, 106, 159
Straw Man 27, 43
straw man arguement 23
string theory 370
Strong, Benjamin 78–79
Strong, Maurice 48, 78
strontium 47, 176, 177, 419
Stubblebine, Albert 347
subatomic particles 405
subconscious mind 361, 362, 369
Sub-Global System 239
submarines 173
subterrenes 238–239
Sufis 369
suicided 408–409
Sukarno 45
Sumeria 228, 256
Sumerians 59, 60, 273, 282
Sumerian texts 214, 315, 380
sun 288
Sun, Chulin 367
Sun Tzu 188
super human abilities 363, 369, 379, 403, 457
supernatural beliefs 352
Super Seven stones 398–399
super soldiers 132, 192, 253, 294, 295, 298, 307, 312, 313
superstition 376
Supreme Court 46–47, 120, 136, 137
SV-40 48

Swakopmund, Namibia 401
Swann, Ingo 348
Sweden 174, 228, 269, 381
Switzerland 78, 82, 98, 116, 227, 244, 330, 381, 461
symbolism 139, 150
symbology 34, 94–95, 101, 204, 253, 262, 377
synarchy 75
synchronicity 455
synthetic biology 434
synthetic organisms 315
syphilis 434
Syracuse University 383
Syria 14, 32, 93

T

tachyon energy 404
Taft, William 45
Taiwan 367
Tajikistan 172
Takasakiyama Natural Zoological Garden 360
Talbott, David 375
Taliban 79, 152
tall greys 232
Talmud 381
Tan, Enoch 350–351
Tanzania 428
Taos, NM 234, 302
tapeworms 442
targeted individuals 162, 272
Tarot 58
Tau Ceti 192
Tavistock Institute 154, 307, 450
Teal, Bob 337–338
technology leap 325–338
Tedeschi, Ettore Gotti 99
TED talk 170, 305, 428
Tehran, Iran 110
tektite 399
telekinesis 364, 457
telepathy 194, 275, 313, 343, 348, 364, 369, 399, 410, 457
teleportation 294, 331, 364, 365, 377, 391
television 148, 160–161, 308, 453
Teller, Dr. Edward 226
Tellinger, Michael 224
Temple Mount 95
Temple of Apollo 362, 457
Temple of Solomon 96
Terracotta Warriors 413
terraforming 292, 308, 312, 444
Tesla, Nikola 16, 18, 30, 142, 173, 194, 197, 268, 326, 327–330, 331, 335–336, 337, 341, 342, 349, 379, 391, 395, 431, 461
tetrahedron 363, 412
tetrahedrons 405
Teutonic Knights 275
Teutonic tribes 63
Texas 27, 220, 253, 263
Thailand 367
thalamus 372
THC 438, 439, 441
Theory of Relativity 331, 344
Theosophical Society 57–58, 93–94
thermodynamics 386
thermography 419

theta brainwave state 348–349, 361
The Tonight Show 30
thimerosal 424
third eye 31, 285
Third Force 254–255, 259, 270
third power 35, 116–117, 137, 142
Third Reich 59–61, 60–63, 66, 92–93, 107, 108, 110–111, 115–116, 137, 254, 258–259, 264, 294
Thor 288
thorium 419
Thoth 290
Three Mile Island 48
Thule Island 313, 314
Thule Society 59, 63, 255, 306
thulium 395
Thunderbird 221
thymus 404
Thyssen, Fritz 116, 119
Tibet 58, 59, 61, 65–66, 214, 306, 387, 457
Tibetans 369, 457
Tierra del Fuego 116
Tikal 216
time travel 60, 61, 194–195, 228, 265, 294, 297–298, 298, 328, 331
titanium 32
Tiwanaku 217, 358
Todt, Fritz 258
Tombstone, AZ 221
tomography 335
Tompkins, Bill 190, 274, 275
Torah 214, 381
tornadoes 173
torture 133, 150
torus 333, 405
toxins 418, 419, 420, 424
transcendental meditation 362
Transcranial Magnetic Stimulation 353
transhumanism 12, 20, 33, 140, 141, 167, 178, 272, 292, 298, 305–319, 354, 403, 433
Transient Lunar Phenomenon 241
transmutation 377–378
trauma-based mind control 132, 134, 140, 145, 293
Treasury 136, 152, 258, 452
Treaty of Paris of 1783 39
Tree of Life 363, 381
Tribe of Levi 275
Trilateral Commission 23, 48, 75, 79, 117, 118, 154, 256
Trojan Horse 250
Tromsø, Norway 172
Trull, D. 397
Truman, Harry 28, 36, 108, 109, 110, 190, 191, 203, 296, 301
Trump, Donald 38, 39, 110, 142, 151, 274, 422
TSA 29
tsunamis 172, 236
Tuaoi Stone 397
tuberculosis 382
Tucson, AZ 95, 174
tumors 353, 382, 408, 418, 419
Turkey 240, 369, 381
turmeric 439

Turner, Dr. Karla 267
Turner, Karla 298
turpentine 442, 447
Tuscaroras 207
Tuskegee 434
Twain, Mark 342
Twilight Zone 274–275
Twitter 31, 200
Tyler, Alexander 46

U

Übermensch 58–59, 253, 306
U-boats 64, 66, 127, 255, 259, 264
UCLA 362
UFOs 35, 190, 195–196, 198, 228, 234–235, 250, 256, 263, 264, 280, 348, 386, 461
Ukert Crater 270
ulcers 114
ultra-terrestrials 249, 250, 253, 262
ultraviolet light 361
Ummo 192
unconditional love 357, 362, 363, 371, 398
Underground Ark Cities 245, 437
Uniform Commercial Code (UCC) 41
Union Bank 119, 135, 259
universal healthcare 149, 404
University of Bari 424
University of Edinburgh 46
University of Glasgow 394
University of Ingolstadt 75
unseen realms 368, 370
Ununpentium 385
urinary tract infections 384, 409
Uros Indians 211
USA 40–43, 56, 62, 72–73, 74, 77, 85, 89, 101, 107, 108, 109, 120, 123, 136, 141, 157, 160–161, 172, 192, 198, 225, 229, 263, 269, 294, 307, 313, 381, 384, 407, 408, 458
U.S. Congress 40–42
U.S. Corporation 27, 39, 40–42, 53, 418, 419
USDA 21, 47
U.S. Gelogical Survey 182
useful idiots 156, 162
useless eaters 275
U.S. government 18, 19, 25, 26, 35, 37–38, 38, 44, 78–79, 82
U.S. military 15, 33
U.S. Patent Office 84
USS Liberty 146
USS Maddox 255–256
UFO disclosure 14, 29–30, 189–192
Ukraine 57, 172
underground bases 192, 229, 234–239, 247–248, 317, 347, 460
Unified Field Theory 330, 333
United Kingdom 77, 225, 382, 458
United Nations 28, 48–49, 54, 77, 92, 96, 118, 120, 156, 157, 159, 177, 178, 228, 252, 260, 334
University of Chicago 118

useless eaters 162
U.S. Treasury 45, 50, 98, 124
usury 291
Utah 211
Utah State University 387

V

V7 35
Vaccine Court 409, 423
vaccines 14, 21, 22, 26, 48, 66,
    112, 162, 171, 180, 187, 198,
    276, 278, 292, 307, 311, 313,
    318, 318–319, 320, 415, 416,
    417, 419, 424–425, 425, 428,
    446, 449, 451
Vallee, Dr. Jacques 251
Valone, Thomas 337
vampires 276, 279
vancomycin 385
van der Zijl, Annejet 108
Vatican 28, 40, 46, 77, 89,
    92–93, 95, 97–101, 104, 122,
    150, 151, 155, 195, 250, 252,
    261, 266, 275, 288, 453, 458
Vatican bank 98–100
Vault, The 284
Vector Equilibrium 339, 363
Vedas 214, 306, 342, 343, 370,
    403
Venus 288
Venus Syndrome 168, 179
Verne, Jules 171, 326
Vesica Piscis 363
Veterans Affairs 191
vibration 404, 405–406, 406,
    407, 414
Victory Gardens 125
Vienna, Austria 60, 78, 307
Vietnam 98, 123, 154, 170, 185
Vietnam War 109, 118, 120,
    121, 122, 153, 169, 170, 175,
    181, 185
Vikings 395
Vimana 265, 307
violence 455
Virchow, Dr. Rudolf 417
Virginia 227, 236, 339
Virginia Company 40, 46, 89
viruses 16, 48, 171, 212, 226,
    321, 344, 384, 390, 408, 409,
    415, 419, 420, 426, 430, 433
Vitamin C 415, 423, 439
Vitamin D 318, 319, 409, 430, 440
Vitamin K 440
vitamins 407
vitrification 238–239
Vitruvian Man 341
Vogel, Marcel 394, 395–396
voice to skull projections 252,
    272, 311
volcanoes 172, 174, 182, 236, 335
Voltaire 158, 325
von Braun, Wernher 24, 111
von Helsing, John 61
Von Hessen family 93, 98
von Hindenburg, Paul 92
von Liebenfels, Lanz 63, 65
von Sebottendorff, Rudolf 61
vortex energy 333
Voyager probe 348
Vril Society 59–61, 256, 306

Vril-ya 59–60, 254, 255,
    294, 306

W

Wackenhut 143, 239
Wagner, Gustav 93
Waiqi 367
Wakefield, Dr. Andrew 423
Walker, Dorothy 96
Walker, George H. 96
Wallace, Dr. Robert Keith 362
Wallace, George 126
Wall Street 47, 73, 81, 83–84,
    119, 135, 152, 169
Walmart 84, 200
Warburg, Dr. Otto Heinrich 418
Warburg, Max 75
Warburg, Paul 44
Wardenclyffe 461
War of the Worlds 225, 332
War on Terror 24, 83, 142
Warren Commission 109, 121,
    135
Washington D.C. 27, 28, 30, 35,
    51, 97, 153, 155, 162, 202,
    345, 453, 458
Washington, George 44, 124
Watergate 123
Watt, Alan 451
weather control 174, 183–186,
    317
weather modification 47, 142,
    169, 171, 177, 181
weather warfare 179, 317, 335
Webb, Stew 126
Webre, Alfred Lambremont 292
Websdale, Julian 48–49
Webster, William 339
Wehrmacht 64
Weishaupt, Adam 75–76, 86,
    159
Welles, Orson 225
Wessel, Gerhard 115
West Bend, WI 209
Western esoteric traditions 58,
    369
Western Europe 219, 315
West Germany 108, 114, 116,
    122, 125
Westmoreland, General 98
West Virginia 118, 236, 283
wetboys 171
Wewelsburg Castle 65, 68–70,
    94, 288
whirling dervishes 369
White Hats 237, 295
White House 35, 110, 120, 159,
    237, 243
white magic 56, 95
White Sulphur Springs, VA 236
WHO 120, 130, 353, 390, 428
Who Killed the Electric Car? 30
Wieluń, Poland 106
WiFi 48, 392, 429
Wigington, Dane 168, 179
Wigner, Eugene 352
WikiLeaks 56, 230
Wikipedia 140, 434
Wilberforce, William 36
Wilcock, David 101, 161, 229,
    230, 257, 296, 365, 387

wildfires 168
Wildlands Project 49
Wilson, Woodrow 44, 45, 80,
    151
Winterthur, Switzerland 78
Wirth, Hermann 62
Wisconsin 208, 209–210
wisdom 354, 367, 368, 455
Wisdom Keepers 346
witchcraft 24, 287
Wizard of Oz 140
Woodland Culture 208
Works of Religion (IOR) 99
World Bank 71, 78–79, 80,
    82–84, 92, 98, 152
World Economic Forum 117,
    154, 430
world government 72
World Health Organization 44,
    92, 421, 423
World Heritage sites 397
World in 2050 49–50
World Peace Through Technology
    334
World Trade Organization 72, 83
wormholes 248
Wright Patterson AFB 193, 211
Wuhan, China 421, 422, 423, 430
World War I 85, 157, 256, 306
World War II 34, 35, 37, 44, 45,
    54, 59, 61–62, 62–63, 66,
    73, 75, 85, 92–93, 106, 107,
    109, 122, 125, 131, 135, 137,
    143, 160, 181, 216, 254–256,
    258–259, 294, 309, 381, 434
World War III 14, 68, 121, 451

X

Xi'an, China 413
x-rays 357, 361

Y

Yale University 75, 127, 350, 424
Yamamoto, Dr. Nobuto 408
Yeadon, Glen 108
Yellow Cube 24, 193, 331–332,
    336, 364
yellow fungal mycotoxins 419
yoga 59, 61, 343, 362
yogis 363, 369
Young, Robert O. 417, 430
YouTube 21, 161, 228, 232,
    295, 408
Yucca Mountains 237

Z

Zagami, Leo Lyon 2, 94, 101
Zapruder film 121
zero-point energy 29, 197–198,
    337, 405
Zeta Reticuli 315
Zeus 288
zinc 396, 439
Zionism 68, 98, 100, 120, 150,
    155, 260, 275, 307
Zuckerberg, Mark 200

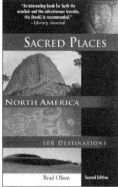

Sacred Places North America: *108 Destinations*

– 2nd EDITION; by Brad Olsen

This comprehensive travel guide examines North America's most sacred sites for spiritually attuned explorers. Spirituality & Health reviewed: "The book is filled with fascinating archeological, geological, and historical material. These 108 sacred places in the United States, Canada, and Hawaii offer ample opportunity for questing by spiritual seekers."

$19.95 :: 408 pages   **paperback: 978-1888729139**

all Ebooks priced at $9.99

Kindle: 978-1888729252; PDF: 978-1888729191
ePub: 978-1888729337
‖‖‖‖‖‖‖‖‖‖‖‖‖‖‖‖‖‖‖‖‖‖‖‖‖‖‖‖‖

Sacred Places Europe:
108 Destinations – by Brad Olsen

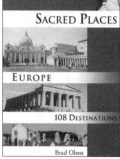

This guide to European holy sites examines the most significant locations that shaped the religious consciousness of Western civilization. Travel to Europe for 108 uplifting destinations that helped define religion and spirituality in the Western Hemisphere. From Paleolithic cave art and Neolithic megaliths, to New Age temples, this is an impartial guide book many millennium in the making.

$19.95 :: 344 pages   paperback: 978-1888729122

all Ebooks priced at $9.99

Kindle: 978-1888729245; PDF: 978-1888729184
ePub: 978-1888729320
‖‖‖‖‖‖‖‖‖‖‖‖‖‖‖‖‖‖‖‖‖‖‖‖‖‖‖‖‖

Sacred Places of Goddess: *108 Destinations* – by Karen Tate

Readers will be escorted on a pilgrimage that reawakens, rethinks, and reveals the Divine Feminine in a multitude of sacred locations on every continent. Meticulously researched, clearly written and comprehensively documented, this book explores the rich tapestry of Goddess worship from prehistoric cultures to modern academic theories.

$19.95 :: 424 pages   **paperback: 978-1888729115**

all Ebooks priced at $9.99

Kindle: 978-1888729269; PDF: 978-1888729177
ePub: 978-1888729344
‖‖‖‖‖‖‖‖‖‖‖‖‖‖‖‖‖‖‖‖‖‖‖‖‖‖‖‖‖

Sacred Places Around the World:
108 Destinations

– 2nd EDITION; by Brad Olsen

The mystical comes alive in this exciting compilation of 108 beloved holy destinations. World travelers and armchair tourists who want to explore the mythology and archaeology of the ruins, sanctuaries, mountains, lost cities, and temples of ancient civilizations will find this guide ideal.

$17.95 :: 288 pages   paperback: 978-1888729108

all Ebooks priced at $8.99

Kindle: 978-1888729238; PDF: 978-1888729160
ePub: 978-1888729313
‖‖‖‖‖‖‖‖‖‖‖‖‖‖‖‖‖‖‖‖‖‖‖‖‖‖‖‖‖

World Stompers:
A Global Travel Manifesto

– 5th EDITION; by Brad Olsen

Here is a travel guide written specifically to assist and motivate young readers to travel the world. When you are ready to leave your day job, load up your backpack and head out to distant lands for extended periods of time, Brad Olsen's "Travel Classic" will lend a helping hand.

$17.95 :: 288 pages   **paperback: 978-1888729054**

all Ebooks priced at $8.99

Kindle: 978-1888729276; PDF: 978-1888729061
ePub: 978-1888729351

‖‖‖‖‖‖‖‖‖‖‖‖‖‖‖‖‖‖‖‖‖‖‖‖‖‖‖‖‖